UPGRADE & MAINTAIN YOUR PC

Second Edition

JAMES KARNEY

MIS:
PRESS

A Subsidiary of
Henry Holt and Co., Inc.

Second Edition—1996

Printed in the United States of America.

Library of Congress Cataloging-in-Publication Data

Karney, James.
    Upgrade & Maintain Your PC / James Karney. —2nd ed.
        p.   cm.
    ISBN 1-55828-460-5
    1. Microcomputers—Maintenance and repair. 2. Microcomputers—
    Upgrading. I. Title.
    TK7887.K37   1996
    004.165—dc20   95-50552
                                                                               CIP

10 9 8 7 6 5 4 3 2 1

Associate Publisher: *Paul Farrell*   **Copy Edit Manager:** *Shari Chappell*
Managing Editor: *Cary Sullivan*   **Production Editor:** *Anne Incao*
Development Editor: *Judy Brief*   **Technical/Copy Editor:** *Bud Paulding*

ACKNOWLEDGMENTS

No book is the work of a single person. There are a host of people who, directly or indirectly, bring it to the reader. It is impossible to name all of them, but there are those worthy of special recognition. I wish to thank my Publisher, Paul Farrell, Editor, Judy Brief, Production Editor, Anne Incao, and the staff of MIS:Press. Gary Bouton did the wonderful cartoons that start each chapter, while Deborah and Gary Miller took care of the technical illustrations. My old and trusted friend, Bud Paulding, handled the technical edit, the copy edit, and did the lion's share of authoring the multimedia chapter. His combination of graduate work in English and love of multimedia and sound equipment made it a natural task assignment. My children, Shannon and Arwyn, kept me amused, and Janet, their mother, kept them entertained when deadlines drew near. A special note of thanks to my parents, and Aunt Anne and Uncle El. They instilled a love of books and curiosity about science that produced the knowledge to write this book. While they never lived to read it, they are a part of its production.

TABLE OF CONTENTS

CHAPTER 3 • Keeping Your PC Healthy   59

CHAPTER 4 • Becoming a Power User   113

CHAPTER 5 • Getting Under the Hood   165

CHAPTER 6 • Motherboards—Your System's Foundation   223

CHAPTER 7 • CPU—The Brains of the Operation   255

CHAPTER 8 • Working with Floppy Drives   283

CHAPTER 9 • The Big Closet—Hard Drives   303

CHAPTER 10 • The Fast Lane—SCSI, CD-ROM   341

CHAPTER 11 • The Multimedia PC   379

CHAPTER 12 • Selecting and Maintaining a Display System   439

CHAPTER 13 • Mice, Keyboards, and More—Input Devices   483

CHAPTER 14 • Connecting PCs—Modems, Faxes,and The Internet 539

CHAPTER 15 • Playing It Safe—Choosing and Adding a Backup System   579

CHAPTER 16 • Power Station   593

CHAPTER 17 • The Big Box   615

CHAPTER 18 • Selecting and Maintaining a Printer   633

CHAPTER 19 • A Bit About Laptops   665

CHAPTER 20 • Building Your Own PC   677

PREFACE TO THE FIRST EDITION

Have you ever brought a new piece of equipment home and searched out the manual only to find you couldn't quite understand it? There you were, thinking, "I need a manual for this manual."

One of the friendly things this book will do for you is provide sufficient information about computers, their components, and their care, so that you can grasp what that manual says—and gain the confidence to install a floppy disk drive, add a scanner, or upgrade your system with the pleasure that informed understanding brings.

Upgrade and Maintain Your PC seeks the solid, helpful, middle ground: no fractured English, no technobabble, no comic foolishness, and no reverent incantations. Instead, you'll find plenty of hard-won, real-world wisdom about computers, written in everyday English. Page after page of detailed step-by-step instructions and illustrations will ease you into accomplishing the task at hand—whether the task is to create an invaluable Rescue Disk, install a hard drive, troubleshoot a modem, or even assemble your own PC (having bought the components with the insight you'll gain after reading this book). If you are prepared to adopt a no-nonsense, non-technical approach to upgrading, trouble-shooting, maintaining, and even building your own PC, your book has arrived.

If you've just acquired your first PC and feel a mixture of excitement and anxiety, this book will make you feel comfortable with these wonderful information appliances. *Upgrade and Maintain Your PC* won't insult your intelligence or coddle your fears; it will give you the confidence to master your machine. The cheerful tone, helpful illustrations, and brief, clear explanations of how things work "under the hood" will serve you well. Read, learn, enjoy, and get out your screwdriver.

—Bud Paulding

Preface to the Second Edition

Since around 40,000 people bought the First Edition, we presume that the book was useful, and largely on target. This time around Jim has brought the book as up to the minute as is practical in an industry which renews half of itself, twice a year. Thus you will find Windows 95 information in every chapter where it is relevant, and updated information and advice on everything from Pentiums to 6x and 8x CD-ROM drives.

There are three new chapters: Chapter 2 discusses Operating Systems and gives advice on the best one to use, given your machine and your needs; Chapter 11 is an extensive treatment of Multimedia, including sound cards, CD-ROM drives, speakers, and how (as well as whether) to upgrade your present system; and Chapter 19 discusses Laptops and the things you can (and can't) do to upgrade them, as well as road-tested tips and advice for their use and care.

The entire book has been thoroughly gone over, to clarify, correct, and improve. Appendix H, the Glossary, has been considerably expanded to keep up with changes in the PC world. Appendix I gives you a lot of information about the programs on the CD-ROM disc at the back of the book (now ten times as many programs). Appendix A remains an extremely handy guide to the hands-on procedures in the book, and the troubleshooting flowcharts in Appendix G can be a huge help. As before, however, its main strength is its ability to explain computers and their workings so that the average person can enjoy both using and working on them.

— Bud Paulding

INTRODUCTION

FIRST THINGS FIRST

This book is a survival guide. Inside you will find easy-to-follow instructions on how to keep your PC running smoothly and how to achieve maximum performance. It provides help in deciding what kind of enhancements to add to an existing PC or how to figure out what features you need to include on a new one. It includes easy-to-understand explanations of how your computer works, and step-by-step instructions on how to install and remove components.

You don't have to be technically gifted or mathematically inclined to use this book. There are no complicated formulas (really, no formulas at all), and you can buy all the tools you need for under $20. In all likelihood you can pay for the cost of this book and the tools the first time you use it.

The concept for this book was fostered from my use of two other authors' work. More than a decade ago I owned a Volkswagen and relied on John Muir's books on how to keep your VW alive and running forever. In them he offered basic explanations of how things work and how to perform tasks ranging in simplicity from changing your oil to completely rebuilding your engine. My book is focused on doing the same thing for the PC.

Professor John Trimble's book, *Writing with Style, Conversations on the Art of Writing*, was my guide years ago as I journeyed from being a newspaper photographer into being a writer. This slender volume was fun to read and provided the facts needed to handle punctuation, and an understanding of how to weave a story. The book you are holding also focuses on providing facts—the information needed to buy, maintain, and upgrade a PC. It does not contain page after page of tables of numbers, instructions on how to write the ultimate program, or detailed instructions on how to use a soldering gun.

It doesn't contain any of those things just mentioned for one simple reason—you don't need them. The only tool required for 90% of PC maintenance and repair is a screwdriver—and a small one at that. All of those rows and rows of figures are very handy to someone in a repair facility, but all the numbers you need should be in the instructions which came with your computer or the part in question.

The problem most people have is not with the amount of information they have, but with making it understandable. A good example is the simple setting of a switch. The manual for your hot new video card says make sure jumper number six on DIPswitch one is off. You pick up the card, figure out what the DIPswitch is and find that it's marked open and closed. Most of the confusion in dealing with computers comes from dealing with two things: a fear of breaking something and confusing documentation. A DIP switch is just what it sounds like, a switch, just like a light switch. When a switch is closed, the contacts meet, allowing electricity to flow through it. That is an on condition. If you open the switch, you've turned it off because the line carrying the electrical current is interrupted.

I spend my working time, and much of my free time, in and around computers, As a writer for *PC Magazine*, MIS:Press book author, and college computer science instructor, I seem to constantly be taking a

PC apart, experimenting with new software, or answering someone else's questions about their machines. Often friends or students ask me, "Isn't there an easy-to-understand survival guide that will show me what I need to know and not go over my head?" It seems about mid-way through each term several students will ask why I don't write such a book. Well, now I have.

CHAPTER 1

THE ONCE
AND FUTURE PC

WHAT'S IN THIS CHAPTER

- ✔ The Shade-Tree Technician
- ✔ PC Basics
- ✔ How Computers Work
- ✔ You Can Maintain and Fix Your Own PC
- ✔ Your Computer's Sub-Systems
- ✔ The Operating System
- ✔ Applications Software

5

WHAT THIS CHAPTER IS ABOUT

It doesn't take long for personal computer users to find that the PC has become an integral part of their lives. They are wonderful machines that will speed our work, help us present our ideas, let us communicate with others, and even entertain us. The pace of PC development is amazing. It seems every day brings a new application or toy that makes us consider upgrading our machines. Many users feel that their PCs are magic boxes and have little idea of how to upgrade or maintain them. This chapter covers the basics of how a PC functions in fairly non-technical terms. It serves as a foundation for the four chapters that follow it. They contain the fundamentals of how to actually maintain your PC, and how to tell when you should upgrade your machine to take advantage of newer technology. You can keep your PC alive forever.

THE SHADE-TREE TECHNICIAN

I'll admit it, I like playing with computers. They are fun, do all kinds of neat things, and open a picture window to the world of information. The PC has revolutionized the way we do business and how we have fun. There are millions of them out there, and they keep improving and getting less expensive. Once you own one it becomes more important in your life. It can keep your tax records and store addresses of friends. It may dial your phone for you and plan the next addition to your house. In short, it becomes as important as your car.

In the old days many people could do most of the repairs on their own cars. The techniques required were fairly simple, and parts were easy to obtain. You just had to learn a few basics, get some tools, and know which parts did what. If you were lucky, there was a friend around who could show you how to do it and help you with the hard parts. Today cars have gotten more difficult to repair because, more and more, they are run by computers, computers that require specialized tools and training. On the other hand, your PC is actually very easy to repair. This book is the friend that can show you how to do it. People who fixed their own cars were known as *shade-tree mechanics*, as you could find them on Saturday afternoon under a tree doing something to their cars. This book will show you how to be a shade-tree technician, and have fun working in your computer's virtual front lawn.

WHY SHOULD YOU READ THIS BOOK?

Either you are standing in a bookstore (or maybe a friend's den), or you've just obtained a copy of this book as a gift. In any case, you're interested in computers. Maybe you just bought a new PC, or perhaps you're planning on upgrading an existing one. Maybe the one you have isn't working right. The first several chapters of this book contain all the information you need to keep most PCs happy and healthy throughout their normal lives. In addition, they offer tips on how to make your PC perform better and how to keep its most important part—your information—safe. The programs included on the CD-ROM are an electronic tool kit that will let you look inside your PC and see how it's doing. This first section of the book also helps you identify when a new component or *subsystem* can enhance your computer's operation, and helps you in deciding what to buy.

The chapters in the second section of the book focus on the subsystems of your computer. They offer explanations of how computers work, how to determine if they are working right, and how to fix them if they are not. If a component needs to be replaced, they offer suggestions on how to choose a new one and where to buy it, and then detail step-by-step how to perform repairs and replacements.

The third section of the book contains flow charts to help you diagnose problems—forms that can help you maintain an accurate inventory of your PC (which will save you time and trouble when you are upgrading or repairing your machine), the basic guides to common error conditions, and a resource directory of suppliers. That section of the book also contains documentation on using the CD-ROM included with the book.

HOW TO USE THIS BOOK

Read the First Four Chapters

What you need to know about using a personal computer safely is in Chapters 1 and 3. "Safely" means that if you use common sense, and follow the steps laid out in these chapters, you should be able to keep your data safe and your PC running smoothly. Sure, you may be confronted with a natural disaster of epic proportions, but the steps here will help minimize your risk. There is also information in Chapter 2 on choosing and using an operating system. These chapter will give you the basic skill needed to "talk" to your PC.

If you are not already familiar with how to keep your computer running properly, you should read the first four chapters. If you are already familiar with the basic parts of your PC and your operating system, you can just skim this chapter and then pick up again with Chapter 2. If you are a novice user, you should read this chapter before going on. It won't take long and it's not super-technical. It introduces you to the parts of your computer and the preventive maintenance required to keep it running properly. It also explains how to decide when to upgrade components.

The 90% Rule—You Can Fix It Yourself

The neat thing about the PC is the way it's designed. It's composed of readily-available, off-the-shelf parts. Even the big-name PC manufacturers assemble their machines from readily-available and relatively inexpensive components. With a Philips-head screwdriver and parts from either your local computer store or a mail order computer firm, plus about a half-hour's time, you can upgrade a hard disk, install a new video card, or add a scanner to your system.

It's even easier to add new memory or fine-tune your operating system. Chapter 5 provides step-by-step instructions on how to get inside your machine when you have to add or replace expansion cards. The following chapters provide detailed information on each of the different sub-systems of your computer, such as the motherboard, hard disk, or display system. When you are interested in possibly upgrading a component of your machine or need to troubleshoot its operation, you can go to that particular chapter for help.

Chapter 20 shows how you can assemble a complete PC from parts. With a freshly-charged electric screwdriver, and all the parts at hand, I've done that in under 20 minutes (of course, I've had some practice). Don't feel you have to be a techno-wizard to do that. If you want to try to assemble your own machine, the last chapter in this book shows you how to go about it. I know a grandmother with a background as a legal secretary who, with a little help, has recently upgraded her own machine and assembled a new one from spare parts. You can do it, too.

JUST WHAT IS A PC?

In the science-fiction movies of the 1950s and 60s, computers were large machines with rows of flashing lights, attended to by men in white lab coats, and full of mystery and power. Today computers are found everywhere; you can walk into K-Mart and buy a computer with the same power used by NASA to place John Glenn in orbit, for less than the price of taking a basketball team out for pizza. Computers have worked their way into everyday life; they work microwave ovens, VCRs, and cameras. These types of small computers found around your house and in your garage are very specialized, but the personal computer is a general-purpose tool. When most people think of a PC, they think of a box that can sit on a desktop with an accompanying monitor and keyboard (see Figure 1.1). The PC is the Swiss Army knife of the information age.

FIGURE 1.1 A typical personal computer.

A General-Purpose Tool

PCs perform a wide variety of tasks, depending on how they are configured. Almost all of them have a keyboard, most have a mouse, some are connected to bar-code readers, and a few are found in laboratories attached to elaborate sensing equipment. Large stores have PCs that control their temperature, lights, and alarm system. Some elaborate answering machines that accept calls through a switchboard are actually PC-based voice-mail systems. The text in your newspaper may not only have been typed in on a PC, but the entire publication—just like this book—may have been illustrated and typeset using one. In short, PCs are now used wherever people need to enter, search, use, and retrieve information.

By adding a CD-ROM drive (really just a specialized CD player similar to one used in hi-fi systems), you can access about 650 million characters of information, games, animation, and sound. A scanner can be used to give a PC eyes, allowing it to absorb photographs, artwork, and even read printed pages into editable form. Your PC can produce high-quality sound, and even be used to compose music.

You can edit video images, and talk to computers all the way across the planet, exchanging mail and even "chatting" with another person in real time. There are also CD-R, or CD-recordable drives, that can both create and read CD-ROM disks. You can use them to store vast amounts of data inexpensively, and you can even create your own music or multimedia CDs.

So how do you teach a PC to do all of these things? It's simple; in most cases it's nothing more than removing a few screws, snapping a new card into a slot inside the machine, and installing some new software in the system. If you do that by taking it into your local computer store, they may charge you $60 to $100 an hour to do the work, assuming you bought the new hardware there. You can save yourself time and money by ordering the components from a mail order house and installing them yourself.

If you need a bigger hard drive, or the one you have right now just died, you can save yourself the labor repair costs by doing the work at home. In many cases there really aren't any parts to replace. Ninety percent of repairs involve nothing more than restoring the system to the same condition it was in just before the problem occurred. In Chapter 3, I'll show you how simple care can reduce problems and help you keep your PC running properly. In Chapter 2 we cover the few simple tricks that can help you master any operating system quickly, and how to pick the right one for your needs. In Chapters 4 and 5, we'll cover the basics of system diagnostics and repairs (that almost anyone with the ability to read and use a screwdriver can perform) when parts of your computer do reach the end of their life cycle.

A BRIEF FORMAL INTRODUCTION

We've talked about how your PC is made up of parts—common, off-the-shelf parts. These parts are assembled into the particular sub-systems that make up your PC. When it comes time to repair or upgrade part of your PC, you'll find information and instructions in the chapter on that sub-system. So in order to use the rest of the book, you need to understand a little bit about what those sub-systems are and what they do.

If you want to see what the parts inside your computer look like while I discuss them, you might want to make your first exploratory mission inside the case. You'll need a Philips-head screwdriver. Turn the machine off and locate the four to six retaining screws that hold the cover of the case in place. On most machines they will be located in the back, opposite the side with the disk drives. On a few machines an access panel will be located on one side or the other. Make sure the power is off and remove the power cord (that's the line coming from the wall socket or power strip and into the back of the computer).

Now remove the screws, and slide the cover forward, off the case. As you do, make sure you don't dislodge any cables. The only other precautions are to not set liquids or messy foods in the work area, and if it's easy to collect static electricity, touch the side of the case to discharge any electrical charge before starting. The pictures in the following pages will help you identify components. If you are not feeling adventurous, we'll show you what they look like.

The Monitor

Let's start with the monitor, one component that you are probably already familiar with. The first computers used vacuum tubes, just like the first TV sets; today, the only vacuum tube in either a PC or a TV set is the big one that forms the screen. Everything else has gone to transistors, solid state electronics that have taken the place of all the tubes. In fact, a single chip can store the equivalent of more than a million transistors, which is one of the reasons that computers have gotten smaller, more powerful, and less expensive. The computer's monitor is basically just like your TV set, except that it receives its picture from a computer instead of from a distant broadcasting station. Monitors come in several varieties. A sample monitor is shown in Figure 1.2. For now, there are only three things to keep in mind with them: some can produce more colors than others, some offer more resolution (a better picture) than others, and some command premium prices by offering a variety of extras (such as the ability to automatically adjust to changes in resolution and color depth for a given program, or meet strict European environmental standards). The more color and the higher resolution, the better the image, the easier on your eyes, and the more money it costs. Fancy features are worth the money if you sit at your computer a lot and can afford them.

FIGURE 1.2 A sample monitor.

Input—Process—Output

The monitor is an example of an *output* device. When I teach computer literacy to freshman students, I tell them that you can understand everything about a computer by relating it to the "Input—Process—Output" model. That sounds pretty technical, but it's really pretty simple. If you make a cake you use the Input—Process—Output model: you put a bunch of ingredients in a bowl, you put them through the Process of being mixed together and baked, and out of the oven comes your dessert. The monitor is an Output device. It takes whatever is going on inside the computer and shows the results on the screen. Before you can process anything, it has to get inside the computer. The monitor is one of the ways a computer "talks" to us. The keyboard, which should also be a fairly familiar device, is one of the ways we can talk to the computer. When we press a key, a number representing that letter is sent to the computer—that's the *Input* (computer people often use the term I/O, which means input/output). There are other ways of getting information inside a computer, which we'll talk about in Chapter 13.

Cases

Most of the other components of the computer are contained inside the big box that sits on the desk or alongside it. The case is just that—a metal and plastic case. It is the shell that holds the different components of the PC. They come in several varieties, as seen in Figure 1.3. The "standard" case is designed to sit on a desktop, and has a reasonable amount of room both for repair access, and to hold optional components. "Baby" cases are designed to conserve space, and have less room for new toys. The "tower" case is designed to provide maximum room for accessories, and is a favorite for power users and as the hub of a *network* (where one machine is used to connect several machines together and provide common services).

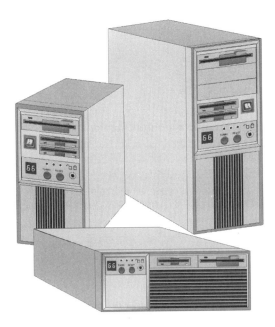

FIGURE 1.3 Different computer case types.

The Power Supply

The power supply converts electrical current from the wall socket into direct current at the proper voltage for your machine. It uses connectors that provide power to the different components inside the box. It usually contains a fan, which is used to cool the interior of the machine (see Figure 1.4). The parts inside all generate heat, and keeping a machine cool enough is very important; if it gets too hot you can damage or even destroy parts of your computer. Chapter 16 is dedicated to the power supply and keeping your machine cool. While the power supply is very easy to remove, you should never open the power supply itself; you can remove and replace it safely, however.

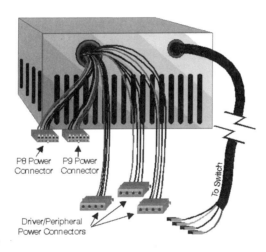

FIGURE 1.4 A typical computer power supply.

The Motherboard

The real work of the computer is done inside chips (a chip is a wafer of silicon that contains a series of switches). Each chip is designed to do specific tasks. The *motherboard*, as pictured in Figure 1.5, is the main collection of chips on the computer. It holds all the chips, and therefore provides all the functions, that are considered standard for a particular type of PC.

FIGURE 1.5 A Micronics 486 motherboard.

Expansion Cards

Mounted on the motherboard are several other major components, which we will cover in a minute. The motherboard itself is made of fiberglass and the wiring to connect all the chips together. Motherboards provide only basic services that the manufacturer knows will be needed by virtually everyone purchasing the product. The motherboard has *expansion slots* (fittings which allow other circuit cards to be inserted into it). *Expansion cards* (see Figure 1.6) allow users to buy exactly the extras or power they need for a given task: they are used to expand the function of the computer. Expansion cards are automatically wired into the motherboard. There is a host of different kinds of cards; some allow your machine to send and receive faxes, others allow you to attach external devices such as scanners or CD-ROM drives. There are cards that let you connect your machine to other computers, and some that can produce high-fidelity stereo sound. In reality, your PC is limited only by the imagination of engineers and the size of your budget.

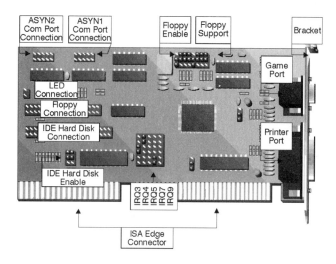

FIGURE 1.6 An expansion card.

The Central Processing Unit (CPU)

The CPU is the actual brain of the PC: the central processing unit does just what it says, the processing. Personal computer CPUs are undergoing constant evolution; they double in power about every 18 months. This means that they work faster and can do more, and as a result, PCs get more powerful and the machines in use today will become first less expensive, and then virtually obsolete. This is one of the reasons this book was written. Since PCs are made of components, you can upgrade parts of a machine without having to replace the entire computer. The CPU is often the largest chip in your computer, and is also known as a *microprocessor*. A typical CPU is shown in Figure 1.7. The most recent is the Pentium, and as this was written, it sells for from $350 to $600 wholesale—depending on speed. The 486, which it replaces, is now selling for about half of that, while it is now possible to buy a used 386 CPU for under $100. Details on the CPU, how to choose which one you need, diagnostics, and replacement are covered in Chapter 7.

FIGURE 1.7 An Intel 486 microprocessor.

Memory

In Chapters 3 and 4 we will be dealing with computer memory. The computer works like a giant switching station; switches are turned on and off to represent "yes" and "no" conditions. Memory chips are nothing more than microscopic banks of switches. When holding an electrical charge, they have a value of being *on*; if they have no current they are turned *off*. While this may seem just a little arcane at the moment, don't worry; it will become clearer as we move along. Memory is generally expressed in thousands of bytes or millions of bytes. Each byte allows a computer to store one of 256 numbers, ranging from zero to 255.

There are several different kinds of memory, which often confuse the novice with their names: ROM, RAM, DRAM, etc. Don't worry about how computers count, or about how the memory works right now. The only important things to keep in mind are that memory is stored in chips, and that it is based on electric current. When you turn the electric current off, the memory goes away. If you want to save the information, you must save it into a permanent form. On most PCs today, that means saving it onto magnetic media that work much like recording tape. To make access faster, the recording material is usually formed into disks.

Disk Drives

Disk drives work like filing cabinets and mailboxes. They can store large amounts of information permanently, and can be used to bring data into the system, to allow data to be removed from the system, and to take it to another machine. In effect, disk drives are both input and output devices. They require an expansion card so that they can communicate with your machine and the cables to connect it. The whole assembly is referred to as the *storage sub-system*. In the beginning, PCs didn't come with hard disks; most only had floppy drives. Floppy drives are slower and can store much less information. Their advantage is that the information they contain is stored on removable disks, which can be carried from one machine to another or stored outside the computer for safety. The name "floppy" came from the fact that the first floppy disks were flexible, compared to the hard metal platters used in *hard disk drives*). Today the average floppy drive can store a bit over one *megabyte* of information (a megabyte is roughly 1 million characters). Hard disks, on the other hand, can store large amounts of data. Figure 1.8 shows a cut-away of a hard disk drive. Today the average PC hard disk stores from 500 to 1,200 megabytes of data; large hard drives can store several *gigabytes* (a gigabyte is roughly one billion characters of data). This may seem like a phenomenal amount of information, but three things you learn quickly about PCs: they are never too fast, you can never have too much memory, and you never seem to have enough storage space. Chapters 8 and 9 deal with floppy and hard disks.

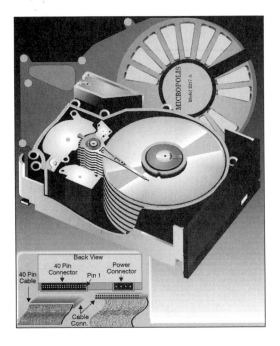

FIGURE 1.8 A hard disk drive.

Connections with the Outside World

Another of the standard components of the PC are its *I/O ports* or *connectors*. As I mentioned above, I/O stands for input/output. These ports are used to move data into and out of a computer. It might be to another PC, to a printer or to another accessory. *Serial ports* carry data in a steady stream (much like a one-lane highway) to devices like *modems* (which allow the computer to talk with other computers over the telephone lines and connect to the Internet), as well as communicate with other devices. These are also commonly referred to as *com* or *communications ports*, as that is what they are often used for. *Parallel* ports are like highways several lanes wide. Data can move at a faster rate. These are also commonly known as *printer ports* as they are commonly used to connect printers to a PC. Some motherboards provide connections directly to I/O ports, which are then connected by a cable to the outside of the case; this outside end of the cable usually has either a 9- or a 25-pin connector. Another cable, from an external device such as a modem or printer, is plugged into the connector.

Most systems require an expansion card to provide I/O services. These usually contain two serial and one parallel port; some also contain a second parallel port, or a joystick connection for playing games.

IT'S NOT JUST HARDWARE

So far we have focused on the hardware in your PC, but the hardware is only part of the story. Your PC is like a factory: it provides the place and the tools needed to make a product. A computer's product is information in the form of data that can be used by people to perform tasks. To manipulate the data we need *software* or *software programs*, which are lists of instructions to tell the CPU how to do the task, how to display images on the monitor, and how to interpret the input from the keyboard. The hardware and software are a bit like body and soul: the hardware is the physical part you can see, and the software brings the hardware to life to allow you to use it. Programs receive instructions from the keyboard or mouse and give you responses via the monitor or printer. They read and write files to and from your disks, and can even talk to you with the sound card if you have one. One of the things that differentiates the PC from other computers is the vast number of programs available at a reasonable cost. One of the reasons for this abundance is the sheer number of machines in use. These programs fall into several categories.

Operating Systems

All PCs require an *operating system.* Today there are several choices, but most PCs use either MS DOS, or a version of MS Windows. The *MS* stands for Microsoft, which has become a worldwide leader in software, and the dominant player in operating systems. The *DOS* (often used by itself) stands for Disk Operating System. Almost every PC until recently made use of MS DOS to handle its basic operations. IBM chose Microsoft to produce DOS for the original IBM PC. PC DOS 1.0 was followed by a succession of new editions, each offering additional features, such as the ability to use larger hard disks or floppy drives, or to handle files more efficiently. Today Microsoft Windows, once an add-on to DOS that made it easier to use, is taking over as a full-fledged operating system. MS Windows comes in several flavors. The current editions are Windows 95 and Windows NT. The first version is aimed at the general user, the second at power users and for advanced networking applications. You can still find systems that use the older Windows 3.1 and Windows for Workgroups editions along with MS DOS, but they lack the power and features of the newer 32-bit models. (More about that in Chapter 2.)

Before we go on, let me explain how the numbering system for most software packages works, using DOS as an example. MS DOS 6.0 is the sixth major release of the operating system. A full increase in number to the left of the decimal point generally means that the vendor has made major changes to the software. MS DOS 3.0 was succeeded by several minor variations—MS DOS 3.1, 3.2, and 3.3. These numbers to the first place right of the decimal indicate a significant enhancement to the existing software but not a total revision. MS-DOS 3.31 takes the numbering system one step further to the right. This indicates a minor change, possibly to add a specific enhancement or to correct a specific problem. Vendors will also sometimes place a letter behind the second decimal point to indicate a maintenance release (for example, WonderSoft 3.31a). These are usually to fix very specific problems and are generally not announced to the public.

What an Operating System Does

The modern PC is a very complex machine, and a software program, such as a spreadsheet or word processor, must be able to "talk to" the various parts of the computer. It has to open and close files, send output to the printer, and display material on the monitor. If a programmer had to worry about every little detail, the software would be very expensive and very tedious to produce. The operating system provides basic services like opening and closing files, managing their location on the disk, reporting information to the monitor, and routing output to your printer.

This standardization allows programmers to write their specifications to work with the operating system. This has two advantages: it reduces the time it takes to write programs, and it increases the chances that the software will work properly on a wide range of machines.

Many people feel that MS DOS is a very primitive operating system. It is primarily a *character-based environment*; that means that the communication is generally limited to the letters of the alphabet and numbers. As seen in Figure 1.9, graphical embellishments are very simple, limited to lines and things like blinking letters. In order to use the system effectively, you have to understand how to issue basic commands. Providing support for photographic or near-photographic images or fancy *user interfaces* (screen presentations) is very difficult. Often the commands are cryptic to the novice user. While there are many software packages that take advantage of MS DOS and improve on its basic functions, there are times when you have to understand some of the basic commands if you want to use it effectively.

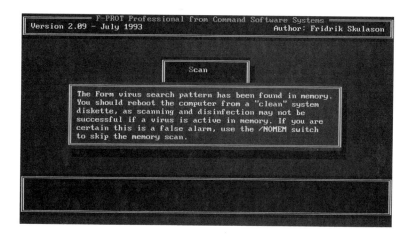

FIGURE 1.9 A typical MS DOS screen.

MS DOS was developed at a time when most computers were operated by trained technicians or computer scientists, and compared with other operating environments, it was actually considered quite *friendly* (that is, easy to use). Researchers at places like Xerox's Palo Alto Research Center developed better methods (graphical user interfaces or GUIs) that would allow users to operate computers in a more intuitive manner and with less training.

Graphical Environments

Today there are a number of easy- (or at least easier) to-use PC operating environments than MS DOS. The most popular of these is Microsoft Windows. The original versions up to Windows for Workgroups 3.11 were designed to work with DOS. Rather than being an entirely new operating system, Windows 3.1 is an operating environment. In effect, it sits on top of DOS and gives it a new face. Instead of issuing cryptic commands, the user can manipulate *program windows* (areas) on the screen and move files around without having to issue any typed commands. Windows offers some other advantages. Because of the way it controls your computer's environment, you can have more than one program running at the same time, and you can exchange information between those two programs. For example, you might have an accounting program that keeps track of your accounts receivables so that information can automatically be passed to another program to print out invoices or to send letters requesting overdue payment. Windows is also a much better environment for developers, since it provides a common *interface* (connection) for all the programs it uses. Figure 1.10 shows the new Windows 95 interface.

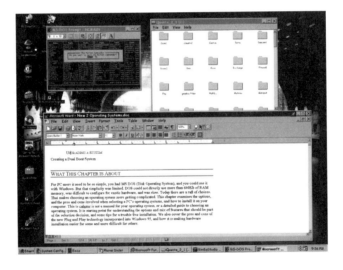

FIGURE 1.10 Windows 95 is the newest operating system for PCs.

The new versions of Windows (Windows 95 and Windows NT) are actually full-fledged operating systems, and there are other graphical environments like IBM's OS/2 and UNIX's X-Windows available. The next several years will see major advances in operating systems. MS DOS was actually a beginning, and never took full advantage the power of some of the newer microprocessors. These advanced operating systems make better use of your computer's resources, and can make installation of new accessories easier than before. The new Windows editions also provide built-in networking, and features to enhance software—making it easier to share both information between applications and users.

Utilities

There is no such thing as a perfect operating system or environment. As soon as one is released, programmers start working on refinements which they can offer for sale (or sometimes give away). Utilities (supplemental programs) extend the reach of the operating system or environment. Some provide easier ways to manage your files, some offer security enhancements, while some show you exactly what's going on inside the system. There are several excellent utilities included on the disk in the back of this book. We will cover their use in the appropriate chapters.

APPLICATIONS

Words and Numbers

More programs fit into the application category than the two just mentioned above (operating systems and utilities) because in reality it includes everything else in the way of software. The term *application* means basically that we are applying the computer's hardware and operating system to a specific task. The most common application in use today is word processors. Programs like Microsoft Word, Novell's WordPerfect, and Lotus' WordPro have not only replaced the dedicated word processor, but almost eliminated typewriters from the

American office. Figure 1.11 shows a typical screen containing a draft chapter from this book using Microsoft Word.

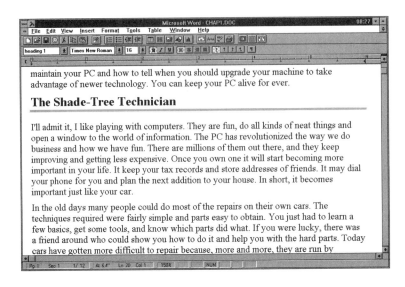

FIGURE 1.11 A Microsoft Word for Windows screen.

Computers, by their very nature, are known for their "number-crunching" ability. For example, spreadsheets are electronic ledgers; they allow you to very easily maintain financial data and mold financial scenarios. For example, what will happen if interest rates change or a tax rate goes up? Their use can range from simply keeping books for a household or small business, to creating complex statistical models. Another "number crunching" application is statistics. Dedicated statistical packages, such as SPSS for Windows (see Figure 1.12), offer all the functionality of mainframe programs (those that run on large, extremely expensive computers), and are in fact produced by the same vendors.

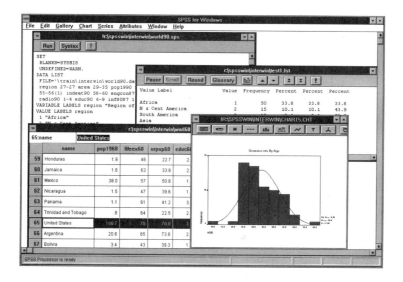

FIGURE 1.12 SPSS at work.

Computer Graphics

There are a variety of applications that can be used to turn your PC into an art studio, photographic darkroom, and small-press publishing house. Some applications, like Corel's CorelDRAW! or Adobe's Illustrator, are aimed at allowing you to draw complex illustrations, exploiting the computer's ability to draw precise, basic shapes such as circles and squares. Figure 1.13 shows a sample of the type of graphic that can be rendered with the use of a graphic application. Other programs are free-form. Fractal Design Painter is literally an art store on a disk, mimicking a wide range of traditional tools, while Adobe PhotoShop provides sophisticated photographic retouching and enhancement features.

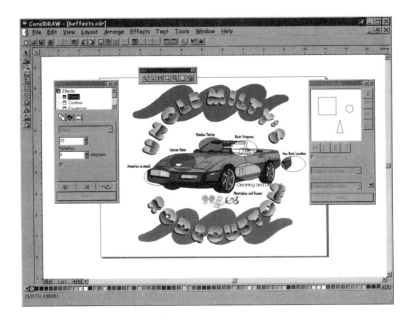

FIGURE 1.13 CorelDRAW at work.

Over the past few years, the PC has revolutionized the publishing industry. It started with the word processor, allowing us to electronically create and edit text. Today the PC is used to actually combine text and graphics into complex layouts, and automatically manage the complexities of a document such as footnotes, indexes, and tables of contents. Some programs are designed for short documents like brochures and flyers; others like FrameMaker for Windows, shown in Figure 1.14, have all the muscle needed to handle very complex publishing tasks.

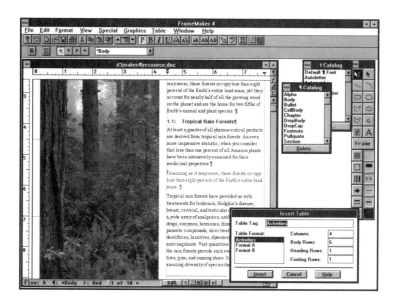

FIGURE 1.14 FrameMaker for Windows.

Other Applications

While the above list includes the major categories of software, there is a wide variety of other applications. The PC can be used to scan images and convert hard-copy letters and manuscripts into editable word-processing text. Electronic mail programs let you exchange letters and files easily with other users, either on *Local Area Networks* (a number of computers that have been cabled together so that they can share information), or via telephone lines. General communications programs allow computers to easily exchange files and to act as electronic bulletin boards.

Personal Information Managers can serve as electronic secretaries. They will dial your telephone, track your expenses, remind you of appointments and keep records of meetings and telephone conversations. Educational software includes electronic dictionaries, other reference materials, and tutorials on a wide range of subjects from ancient musical instruments to zoology. One example is Microsoft's multi-media Beethoven, shown in Figure 1.15.

FIGURE 1.15 Microsoft's Beethoven.

A complete listing of all the different types of applications and sketches of the available programs would require an encyclopedia. As your interest in computers grows, it's a good idea to subscribe to one or more of the popular periodicals, such as *PC Magazine* or *Windows Sources*, to keep up with new products that can make you more productive and enhance the time you spend at your computer. The resource guide in the back of the book includes a some short mentions of some of my favorite applications.

CHAPTER SUMMARY

Your PC is a general purpose tool. While it may be able to handle very complex tasks, and require significant engineering resources to design, it is actually very easy to maintain. This chapter has focused on an introduction to the different sub-systems of your PC and introduced some of its more common uses. The following chapters will take us deeper inside a PC and show you how to keep it running well.

CHAPTER 2

Choosing the Right Operating System

What's In This Chapter

- ✔ Operating System Options
- ✔ Choosing the Right Operating System
- ✔ Installation
- ✔ Upgrading a System
- ✔ Creating a Dual-Boot System

WHAT THIS CHAPTER IS ABOUT

For PC users it used to be so simple: you had MS-DOS (Disk Operating System), and you could use it with Windows. But that simplicity was limited. DOS could not directly use more than 640Kb of RAM (*Random Access Memory*), it was difficult to configure for exotic hardware, and it was slow. Today there are a raft of choices. That makes choosing an operating system more complicated. This chapter examines the options, and the pros and cons involved when selecting a PC's operating system, and how to install it on your computer. This chapter is not a manual for your operating system, or a technically-detailed guide to choosing an operating system. It is starting point for understanding your options and the mix of features that should be part of the decision, and some tips for a trouble-free installation. We also cover the pros and cons of the new Plug and Play technology incorporated into Windows 95, and how it is making hardware installation easier for some and more difficult for others.

If you are comfortable with the operating system on your computer, or you don't particularly care about other choices you may have, you may safely skip this chapter. On the other hand, if you are confused about the number of different operating systems out there, or if you are considering upgrading your current system, by all means read this chapter. It should help you make plans for the future or decide on an upgrade. You should note that, of necessity, this chapter is a bit more technical than the other early chapters (which we strongly urge you to read). If you need help with technical terms, consult the Glossary and the Index in the back of the book, as well as the particular chapters that deal with the matter at hand.

A DECISION THAT'S A BIT LIKE MARRIAGE

Marriage is a rite of passage that usually affects your entire life, even if it doesn't last forever. Choosing an operating system is a choice that effects every aspect of your computing life. It controls what software your machine can run, what hardware you can add, and how you interact with it.

NOTE

Usually a computer comes with an operating system, sometimes more than one (for example, both MS-DOS and Windows), so often the first choice has been made for you. But any PC with an 80386 or above CPU chip can run, at least minimally, most of the operating systems mentioned above. So there is the potential to upgrade your operating system as well as your hardware; and in fact, you may want to upgrade your hardware in order to run a newer, higher-powered operating system and the software applications it can run for you. This chapter can help you consider your choices and trade-offs, and avoid some of the problems which could otherwise arise.

There are two different markets for operating systems, the mass market (which includes most of us), and niche markets (which have special and often exotic needs). The mass market scenario goes like this: If an operating system is popular and well-designed, lots of developers will jump on the bandwagon and write programs, hardware vendors will write drivers for their products that support it, and prices will fall as users increase. If it is not well-planned and supported, the opposite fate lies in store: few programs come along, few vendors make hardware for the environment, and prices stay high. The niche-market client uses special, customized programs that usually came off a mainframe or mini-computer, and which can run on a high-powered PC. Such programs are often ported (moved to the PC platform) in some flavor of UNIX. Those applications are too limited and diverse to cover in this book, so we will stick to mainstream operating systems.

In the first edition of this book I didn't even have a chapter on operating systems. It wasn't needed—virtually everyone used DOS. Most power users ran Windows, and except for a few PC-based UNIX offerings, all were single-tasking, 16-bit operating systems. That means that the operating system uses a 16-bit "word" in its functions, twice as wide as an 8-bit word, and it can only work on one computing task at a time—even if it can have more than one file or program "open."

Today there are four main variations of Windows in common use: Windows 3.x (meaning Windows 3.0, 3.1, 3.11, or Windows for Workgroups); Windows 95; and two variations of Windows NT (New Technology). Then, there are IBM ís OS/2 (with a few flavors of its own), and a variety of UNIX versions. All but the first in the list are 32-bit systems (more about the ramifications of that in a minute). This chapter provides a basic insight into the changing world of operating systems, and provides general guidelines for choosing an operating system. As with marriage, you can look for the right features, but love and infatuation play a role as well. In the end it comes down to personal choice, and a system's ability to run the software you need on the computer you have. Then we turn to properly setting up an operating system on your PC. Since there are many variables, and since this is primarily a hardware book, a full treatment of any given operating system is beyond the scope of this volume.

A Bit of History

In the beginning of the PC era (before DOS) was CP/M, an operating system that looked much like the early versions of MS-DOS that replaced it. See Figure 2.1. IBM commissioned Microsoft to write a new operating system for their entry into the personal computer market. In so doing they created the cash cow that made Bill Gates the richest man in the country, and led to the dominance of his company in the industry. The actual IBM PC edition of the Microsoft operating system was (and still is) known as PC-DOS, and Microsoft made a variety of generic and customized editions that allowed IBM PC clones to run the same DOS-based software. Every PC made produced a royalty that was paid to Microsoft.

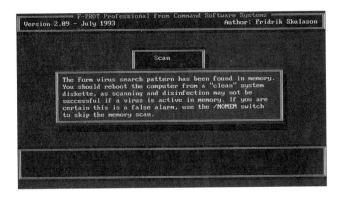

FIGURE 2.1 An MS-DOS screen.

DOS was/is a very limited operating system when compared to its newer 32-bit successors. During its heyday DOS went through a number of revisions to add support for hard drives, new types of floppy drives, and later, limited support for CD-ROM equipment. Through version 6.22, MS-DOS lacked direct support for a host of hardware devices, which had to be supported or provided by third-party companies. MS-DOS reached its prime with the 286-based AT computers, in a time when a megabyte of RAM and a 40Mb hard drive was a Power System. It had limited memory handling (only 640Kb of conventional RAM was available for application programs AND the operating system itself); as new applications made more demands, this restriction led to the development of a number of somewhat cumbersome schemes to increase its functionality, and IBM and Microsoft proposed a replacement called OS/2. This new operating system was to eliminate the 640 Kb memory limit, and allow long file names (DOS is limited to 8 letters, a period, and a three letter extension after the dot). In addition it would make adding new hardware much easier. The theory was that the new IBM environment would rule the PC world, combined with a new series of IBM hardware. That was the *theory*.

A funny thing happened to OS/2 on the way to market. The story differs, based on the teller, but IBM and Microsoft split the blanket. IBM continued to work on OS/2, while Microsoft put its efforts into Windows. The first versions of OS/2 suffered from a lack of application programs to run; the bad press over the breakup made developers nervous, and most took a wait and see approach. Lack of hardware support hindered OS/2 further, as did the (mistaken) perception that it was a system that would only run on the new IBM PS/2 line of PCs, equipped with IBM's proprietary MCA expansion bus. That combination all but doomed the new OS (Operating System). The first edition of Windows fared little better; it also suffered from a lack of applications, and from the inability of most PCs in those days to use a mouse or support the fancy graphics to really run Windows. Even the Windows 2.0 version was used mostly for graphics applications like CorelDRAW! These programs made use of the "What You See Is What You Get" interface, and required the mouse for drawing and manipulating on-screen objects. All of the old memory problems still existed, and with the advent of high-end graphics adapters and networking, things got even worse as more devices made increasing demands on limited resources.

A Window on the Future

The third full release, Windows 3.1, brought major changes. The new environment (it was not a full operating system, since it required DOS to run), was able to make use of more memory through some technical slight of hand, and was gaining in popularity with software developers, particularly in desktop publishing and graphics. Third-party programs came along that made it easier to mange memory and run lots of toys on a system (not easy, just easier). The momentum shifted among developers and users alike, and Windows 3.1 came to dominate the PC software and hardware worlds. See Figure 2.2.

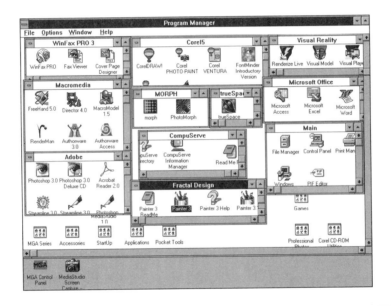

FIGURE 2.2 A Windows 3.1 screen showing Program Manager.

A new addition to the Microsoft line, Windows for Workgroups, offered easy networking. Users could share disks and printers with virtually no effort other than installing a network card and attaching the cable. At the same time, Microsoft was bringing out Windows NT, a super version that was to be a full-fledged operating system with very fancy network options. Meanwhile, an IBM team in Florida were working on a better version of OS/2, one that was not linked to the failed IBM PS/2 line, and which could run the majority of Windows 3.x applications—in some cases better than Windows itself—since it did not have the 640K memory limit. In short, the two major players in the arena were both focusing on new operating systems with easy-to-use and maintain graphical interfaces that made use of more powerful PCs.

THE FUTURE IS HERE (FOR NOW): THE 32-BIT MODERN WORLD

The newest offerings: Windows NT, Windows 95, and OS/2 Warp Connect are more than just pretty to look at. They promise more speed, and offer easier-to-use interfaces. There is built-in support for CD-ROM and SCSI technology, better multimedia operation, and they are less prone to crash.

The 640K limit is gone, adding hardware is (generally) easier, new software is already arriving with lots of enhanced features; you can run several programs at once—all actively; the new systems allow longer file names than you will ever need; and Plug and Play (PnP) hardware installation makes setting up most new systems a lot easier than ever before.

That all sounds wonderful, but there are several issues that make the new world of 32-bit operations a bit more complicated than that of DOS. Today our choices are a bit more difficult, with several options. The major player, Microsoft, has a range of 32-bit products—from single user (Windows 95) to enterprise server (Windows NT Server). IBM has its own OS/2, a bit older, and less popular—but with a dedicated following. The one that is right for you will depend on what you want to do with your computer. Windows 95 is the current mass-market option and a good choice for most of us, but a little comparison shopping is still a good idea.

A Case for Careful Consideration

Here are a few issues that you should consider when considering a new—or second—operating system. Keep in mind that these are general guidelines, and that your installation is unique in some ways—even if the hardware is similar. You, as user, are the final arbiter of quality and performance. After we look at the issues I'll go over the individual operating systems and cover them in relation to the following criteria.

Enhanced Features and Performance

There is a saying that goes "If it ain't broke, don't fix it." That is as true of operating systems as it is of cars and home appliances. The new 32-bit systems have to offer a feature set that is worth the money, effort, and time needed to get it working on your computer. For most people, that will be the case. The new operating systems take advantage of all the latest PCs have to offer: more power, better graphics, more features. The exceptions are folks with limited older 386 and early 486 systems, low memory (less than 8 to 12Mb), and aging display and storage systems. For them either an upgrade of CPU, RAM, and/or DOS and Windows 3.x is the best solution. If you have a 486 or a Pentium with at least 8Mb, Windows 95 or OS/2 Warp are worth considering. For those with a Pentium, P6 (Intel's next-generation successor to the Pentium line), or a RISC processor like the DEC Alpha or Power PC, and at least 16Mb of RAM, Windows NT is the primary contender. The exact choice will depend on a variety of factors we'll examine after converting the basics. There are several advantages to the new crop of operating environments that we can generalize about, and compare them to the older Windows and DOS products.

Full-fledged 32-bit Architecture

Unlike older operating systems designed for the original IBM PC and the 286, the newer versions make use of the 32-bit operations allowed by processors like the 486, Pentium, and P6. This not only makes for faster performance, but also overcomes the memory limitations that were imposed by the original PC—and carried into all past releases of DOS. Gone is the 640KB limit, and the hassles of memory managers that had to juggle conventional memory. This makes the newer OSes more stable, and less prone to memory and hardware conflicts (assuming good design on the part of the vendors).

Multi-Tasking/Multi-Threading Capability

The extra power in these operating systems grants a major advantage, the ability to tap your computer's power and do more than one thing at a time. The multitasking in Windows 3.x is not nearly as powerful as the type found in newer operating systems. These provide real preemptive multitasking. This means that the user can really allocate system resources to suit the needs of the task at hand. The older cooperative multitasking often resulted in very slow performance, and in some cases system crashes. Windows 95 and NT, as well as OS/2, are less likely to bring down your machine if a program causes a major problem. In most cases, only the program at fault is forced to close.

If you have at least 12 to 16Mb of RAM on your system with one of the three new operating systems, you can effectively run more than one program at a time, and perform tasks in the background like downloading files, printing, or compiling results of a calculation. The extra RAM also provides better speed in handling routine tasks like loading programs or moving files. The exact amount required will depend on the operating system, the applications, and the nature of your hardware. While there is no precise formula, it takes at least 8Mb to do any real multitasking, and at least 16Mb to see a boost. The adage is true, you can't have too much RAM.

An Object-Oriented User Interface

In DOS most programs used a character-based interface, i.e., they displayed letters and numbers on the screen, perhaps with menus. In Windows 3.1, the "desktop" (the appearance of the screen) was rather crude, with small simulated "pictures" (icons) representing directories on the hard disk. Today the rage is "objected-oriented" desktops, on which appear picture-objects that represent *Directories* (or *Folders*, as they are called in Windows 95 and NT), printers, programs, documents, etc., and which offer extensive use of the right mouse button (all but ignored in older environments). Figure 2.3 shows the Windows interface with the right mouse button in action. The Windows NT 3.5 and 3.51 interface is still in the basic Windows 3.1 form, but will be changed with the next release to look like Windows 95.

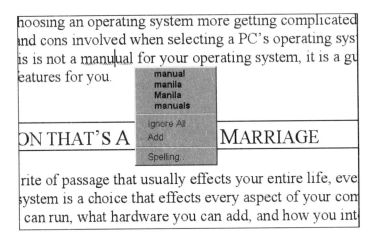

FIGURE 2.3 Using the right mouse button in Windows 95.

Hardware Support

Not all operating systems are created equal, and each has its own requirements to run properly. DOS will run in 1Mb of RAM, while Windows NT needs 16Mb, and wants 32Mb or more to run really well. Read the requirements carefully, and if there is a gap between what you have and what it needs, be willing to spend the money. I have often heard at users' groups that "Windows is slow." On questioning, the speakers confess that they are running a 386 with minimum RAM and an old VGA card.

Not all operating systems have *drivers* (special programs to enable use of a specific piece of hardware) for all add-on equipment. If you have an old video card, or a special scanner or CD-ROM drive, make sure it is supported. If the company that made the card is out of business, there may be no way to hook the device up with the new operating system. The vendors (both the operating system's and the hardware's) should have a list of supported products for reference.

The same is true for new hardware. If the new equipment is designed for the latest operating system, or a specific operating environment, there may not be drivers available for older operating systems. Is the new hardware compatible with your motherboard? Once again, it's a good idea to check compatibility lists.

N O T E Most major vendors of both hardware and software, including IBM and Microsoft, operate Forums on online services like CompuServe and America Online. They also have a presence on the Internet. These are good places to look for the latest compatibility lists and drivers, and to get technical support.

Legacy Software Compatibility

Will the new operating system run your existing software? Some applications are older 16-bit versions designed for DOS (older games are an example) that may run slowly, too fast, or not at all on some operating systems. Others are produced for a given operating system and will not run on others, even if they are both loaded on the same hardware. This is especially true of Windows software, which will not run on some versions of OS/2 or UNIX. If you have to buy all new software, will you be able to use the old files from major applications? How much will the migration cost?

Native Applications

The flip side of software compatibility is *native* software-programs, those that are designed from the ground up for the new operating system—and its 32-bit capability. These programs should be the ones that use all of its new features, provide improved performance, and gain in stability from its environment. There will be winners and losers in the operating systems wars that are sure to come. The losers are likely to fail from the lack of native applications.

Ease of Use and Maintenance

How easy is the operating system to use and keep up? The best are well-designed with the user in mind, offer features for keeping a hard disk well-organized, and have the ability to recover from problems without crashing.

Networking Features

Most of the newer operating systems (except for variations of OS/2) have some level of built-in networking, which can save money in fees and simplify installation if you want to connect machines. They may reduce the overall cost of setting up a local area network, making such a move or upgrade more attractive. The same is true for sharing printers, CD-ROMs and other devices. In addition, they can take advantage of, and in some cases simplify connecting to, the world-wide network known as the Internet.

Remote Access and the Internet

Remote access is the ability to log on to (access) a computer from a remote location, either via a modem or a network connection. UNIX has always had this feature, and a variety of third-party software has been developed for Windows that provides the same ability. Windows 95 and Windows NT have built-in remote access, and Windows NT Server can even act as an Internet or Wide Area Network hub.

Plus and Play (Or Plug and Play Around)

The major innovation, and sometimes major wrinkle, in 32-bit operating systems is *Plug and Play* (*PnP*). This is a combination hardware and software solution to the pains of adding new hardware to an operating system. The first major environment to include it is Windows 95. The idea is simple. The PC has a BIOS (*Basic Input-Output System*) that works with the operating system to distribute and set up flexible capabilities (such as memory address, DMA channels, and IRQs) for all the hardware components. The hardware vendors must also produce hardware that can be identified and configured on the fly. See Figure 2.4.

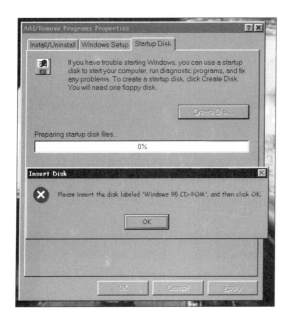

FIGURE 2.4 The Windows 95 Add New Hardware Wizard.

The theory is pretty good, and it works well when all the items in the system are fully compatible. The best examples of the technology are Windows 95 and new laptops with PCMCIA (PC-Card) adapters, which are generally painless to add to the machine (See Chapter 19). With older equipment it is often a bit more problematic. Here are some tips that can help make the transition easier. For more information on a given item check the appropriate chapter.

✔ **If you have an older BIOS on your motherboard, you should check with the maker for an update before adding a Plug and Play operating system.**

✔ **Make sure you have the latest drivers from the vendors of the cards you plan to have in the PC.**

✔ **Make a list of all known IRQ and memory assignments.** Consult Chapter 5 and use the Inventory Sheets at the back of the book, and the WinSleuth, ASQ, and Snooper programs on the CD-ROM to help get everything organized.

✔ **Start with a basic configuration: hard drive controller, video adapter, CD-ROM drive, Com and printer ports.** Then add more exotic items, like sound cards.

✔ **Sound cards can be the worst offenders, so add them last.** The one I like the best is the Creative Labs Sound Blaster AWE-32 PnP. This card has great sound and is fully PnP compatible.

✔ **If an object is causing problems, remove it, both from the machine and the operating system, and then reinstall it.** Make note of any drivers it uses and remark them out (see Chapter 3). In Windows 95, remove it from the Device Manager in Control Panel. If it still causes problems, try to force it or the other conflicting card to a separate address. The Windows 95 Device Manager has a Conflict Resolution Wizard that can help.

THE CONTENDERS

The following paragraphs are sort of thumbnail reviews of the current crop of operating systems. The opinions are my own, based on personal experience and trends in the industry. The are starting points for exploration, not gospel. Keep in mind that your needs and experience are the most important factors. Windows 95 is the dominant operating system, but not the only option.

Windows 95

This is 32-bit computing for the masses; inexpensive, fault-tolerant, and cute. It offers the best Plug and Play compatibility, a Macintosh-like, object-oriented interface, and lots of goodies—like built-in networking and Internet connectivity. You will need at least 8Mb of RAM to get things going well, and it likes 16 even better. There is excellent industry support, and a slew of good software. Its DOS (largely a streamlined Version 6.22) is better than plain DOS: I can get things to run in a DOS window that won't run on a basic DOS PC.

See Figure 2.5. It also has outstanding multimedia support—sound, animation, video, etc. Most older, DOS-based games appear to run very well, and new Windows 95-based games are appearing.

FIGURE 2.5 Windows 95 with a DOS session open.

There is no 640Kb conventional memory limit; it can use all the RAM you have on the system. The product is available as both an upgrade to existing versions of Windows, and as a stand-alone. While you can get an edition on floppy disks, the way to go is with a CD-ROM. I also recommend the Microsoft PLUS! Pack for an additional $40 or so. It adds a lot of neat features that should have been included in the original.

Windows 95 has a bit better networking support than the older Windows for Workgroups, and adds TCP/IP interfacing that allows single user direct access to the Internet via either SLIP- or PPP-style connections. See Figure 2.6.

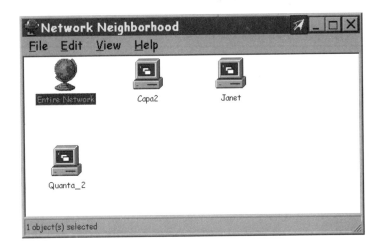

FIGURE 2.6 The Windows 95 Network Neighborhood Interface.

WINDOWS NT WORKSTATION

This is Windows on steroids. It wants at least 12Mb, and runs best on 24 or more. It can run several applications at once without slowing down, can manage up to two Intel or 4 DEC microprocessors, has full security, passwords, users accounts and outstanding network tools. The current interface is the same as the older 3.1 versions of plain Windows (see Figure 2.7), but it is not your father's Windows. It will run DOS, but not as well as Windows 95; it will run all true Windows 95 programs. This is a power user's system. You can configure super-size *RAIDs* (duplicate disks used for extra security), and its maximum file size could almost hold the entire Library of Congress in a single document (if you could get the data, and build a drive system big enough).

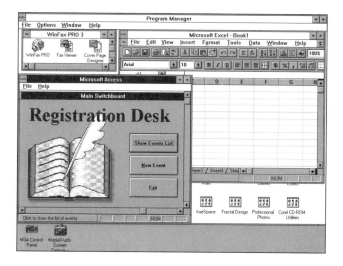

FIGURE 2.7 The Windows NT (and Windows 3.1x) Interface.

The *RAS* (Remote Access Service) makes it easy to dial out or dial into a Windows NT workstation, and can easily get you onto the Internet. That includes letting you log in via a laptop and access files, printers, fax hardware, and mail.

It is not for the novice; you need to understand systems to tune it and keep it running. I like it, and will like it better when they bring the multimedia and interface up to the level of Windows 95. It is a better operating environment; it is just not as easy to use, as DOS-friendly, or multimedia-ready as Windows 95.

TIP The Windows NT Resource Kit is the best general source of knowledge on networking, system performance and tuning, and network management available; it costs only $199 list price. If you are interested in any of the above topics, or have Windows NT, it is a must for your bookshelf.

Windows NT Server

This is the "Big Man on Campus at Microsoft," Super NT: all the good-ies in the base edition, and lots of power. You can run very large installations or a single workgroup with NT Server as the hub. It looks just like the Workstation version, but can support a lot of users. In fact, up to 255 people can dial into a server (or out to another network) including the Internet—over phone lines, if you have the connections and Com ports. It needs at least 16Mb and likes 48 or more. I like it even better than NT Workstation as a workstation—and am just waiting for the next release, with the Windows 95-style goodies, before I make it the weapon of choice in my lab.

OS/2 Warp

This was the first mass-market 32-bit operating system for Windows. Many of my fellow graduate students (and some professors) were members of the IBM design team that crafted this package. Its prob-lem was its perception and timing in the marketplace. It has many of the same features as Windows NT and Windows 95, but is not likely to survive. There is little third-party support—so software and native PnP support will be scarce. It has an object-oriented interface, limited networking, and few hardware drivers compared to the Windows platforms. As a result, I find it hard to recommend it except as an oddity for the collector.

Windows 3.x and DOS

The older versions of Windows are rapidly becoming obsolete. Other than Windows for Workgroups, they offer little networking support. As the months go by and Windows 95 takes more market share, these early editions will also lack the hardware support required to be viable. If you have an old machine that has less than 4Mb of RAM, Windows 3.x and DOS are your only options other than a major upgrade. Other than that, consider one of the newer 32-bit systems.

UNIX

The final operating system on our list is UNIX, the darling of university and college campuses. It was originally designed to play a space simulation, and became the first non-proprietary operating system. SCO makes a flavor of UNIX that runs on Intel-based PCs, and SUN Microsystems makes editions for a variety of microprocessors. The only reason to use UNIX on a PC is a need to link to other UNIX-based machines and run in a full-compatibility mode, or have software that requires it. For part of my studies there was a machine in the lab running SCO UNIX, and it saved quite a bit of money in commuter charges from the school. It is not for the timid, and is full of arcane commands. The character-based mode is difficult to learn, and the software for UNIX is expensive, up to ten or more times the same price as comparable software for Windows.

SETTING UP AN OPERATING SYSTEM

Placing an operating system on a PC is not a daunting task. In most cases the Setup installation will walk you through the steps with ease. Here is a brief check list to have at hand before setting it up. Keep in mind that each operating system varies, so these are generic tips.

✔ **Know Your Hardware:** you have to know the type of hard disk, controller, graphics (display) adapter and monitor, type of mouse, and any network card. Consult Chapter 3 and make a list using the System Inventory sheets in the back of this book.

✔ **Check the Hardware Compatibility List:** Most vendors provide lists of the operating systems their products are compatible with, and most operating systems have hardware lists as well. Double-check for special set-up requirements or drivers before starting to set up the system.

✔ **Have The Right Drivers:** Be sure to have the latest copies of any drivers for the devices mentioned above. If you use the wrong driver, or an outdated one, it could cause problems—or even crash the installation. Add the version and date of the drivers to the Inventory list.

✔ **Start With One Drive Partition:** Begin by setting up one partition, even if you plan to add more. Make it bootable, and load the system. It is easier to test that way, and you won't waste time on secondary formats if things don't go according to plan.

✔ **Install from CD-ROM or a Network if possible:** CD-ROM or Network setups are the best way to go. You don't have to stuff lots of disks and things go faster. With some systems, like Windows NT, you can specify a configuration from a network Setup directory to automatically configure machines to a standard set-up.

✔ **Run A Virus Check:** As soon as you have the system installed, run a virus check from a clean boot disk. It is a wise step to keep nasty minds away from your data. We provide two programs, S-Prot and Integrity Master on the CD-ROM at the back of the book.

THE BENEFITS OF DUAL BOOT SYSTEMS— OR, TWO MAY BE BETTER THAN ONE

You are not limited to a single operating system on a PC; it is possible to have two or even three available, and select which to use as the machine comes on line. I use a variety of boot and operating system combinations in my lab. Over the years I have had a variety of twin-operating systems, from CP/M and DOS to Windows and UNIX; the most common is a dual-boot configuration of DOS/Windows for Workgroups with either Windows 95 or Windows NT. One machine is even a triple-boot setup, with DOS, and all three versions of Windows. While that is overkill for the average user, for any power user I recommend a dual-boot system using DOS and your choice of a newer 32-bit OS. There are several reasons:

✔ **Compatibility:** Not all software or hardware is created equal. Some software or hardware will only run in a specific environment, but some programs want a real DOS. By having two operating systems on a machine you can use the one that supports the given device. The DOS shell in Windows 95 is pretty good, and it is the best of the lot at emulating the original DOS in 32-bit systems—but it is not perfect. There are a number of older programs that only work under DOS. While the newer operating systems have a DOS or Windows 3.x compatibility mode, it is not really DOS and not really Windows 3.x. For example, Lotus Screen Cam can capture a film clip of your actions as they appear, along with sound, but only under Windows 3.x. A new version may be in the works, but maybe not—and you have to pay for new software. With a dual-boot machine, just reboot into the proper environment when you have to run these "legacy" programs.

✔ **Redundant Access to Data:** A second operating system gives you two ways to access your disk and its data. If one operating system starts acting up, you may still get things running with the other, and be able to perform an overdue backup or access critical files.

✔ **Virus Protection:** One holiday season I spent the period between Christmas and New Year's Day fighting a strange collection of system crashes on our principal Windows NT Server. It looked like a problem with the SCSI system and hard drive. Since the operating system gave errors reporting a hardware fault, I focused on that line of recovery. All would be fine, then I would get a crash and be unable to load the operating system and its 2 gigabytes of data. But it would load MS-DOS. For more than a week I reloaded NT, only to have it crash a day or so later. I swapped out drives, controllers, drivers, and reinstalled. When I had to use a file on the system I booted into DOS and ran Windows for Workgroups. When my contacts at Microsoft came back from their holidays, I got an answer—the Form virus. This is a strain of boot-sector virus that is generally innocuous under DOS, but that keeps Windows NT and other 32-bit operating systems from loading. With tunnel vision and an error report that focused on SCSI hardware, I had been fighting relapses. A quick run of F-Prot and all was well. The dual-boot system makes it possible to switch and fix such situations.

✔ **Troubleshooting:** Just as a dual boot offers an extra approach when a virus strikes, it can provide a way to track down hardware or driver conflicts. It is not unusual to run into a problem the first time you reboot the system. With two operating systems it is often easier to bypass a driver conflict, since you only load the new drivers one at a time. Then you can go into the system and isolate the problem. You also have a way to edit or remove the offending file or command.

SETTING UP A DUAL BOOT ENVIRONMENT

How It Works

The majority of dual-boot installations use some form of loader that is invoked as the boot sector of the first hard disk is brought on line. Newer operating systems generally have an automatic boot into one system (if it detects a second system); either a hot-key over-ride or a menu of options will be available during the first few seconds.

WARNING

Of course, you must load the operating systems in a way that is compatible with dual-boot operation. If you just load a new operating environment over an existing one, the new system removes the older software.

You should carefully read the documentation for both operating systems before starting a dual-boot set-up. In some cases you must specifically load one system before the other. In most cases, a dual-boot configuration will include a copy of MS-DOS, and that should be the first system loaded. One system must be used to create an initial formatted partition.

The Installation

What You Will Need

Operating system disks, blank floppy disks, manuals, paper and pencil, a screwdriver—just in case you have to open the system to set a jumper.

The Process

Getting Ready

Assemble all the required disks, manuals, and some notepaper. Read the installation steps for both systems, and any documentation for creating a dual-boot system. Next plan the order of the installation: which system first, what drivers will be needed, and make sure you have all the required third-party software. If you already have one operating system on the disk, the next step may already be completed. In that case, just make sure it is the way you want it, and that it is compatible with your second system. If there is existing data on the disk, make a backup before proceeding.

Disk Structure

Figure out if you will be using just one type of disk partition. Some operating systems, like Windows NT, OS/2, and UNIX, offer high-performance disk structures that DOS or other operating systems can't read. Most do allow a DOS first partition, so you have to decide how much space to leave for DOS. If you only want a small DOS boot sector, leave some extra room for utilities and data—no less than 32 Mb. Keep in mind that when the system is booted into DOS, all those files on the other OS (Operating System) will be invisible, and inaccessible. I keep all critical data on a plain DOS partition, and leave the fancy formats for operating-system-specific files used by the newer OS.

NOTE Some operating systems vary in how (and even if) they handle larger (say, over 2Gb) hard drives. This may be a factor in how you configure your system and what drivers you will need. In most cases this problem is not insurmountable, but it will require an extra planning step.

Use the disk partition and formatting tools, like FDISK and FOR-MAT to set up the first partition, and any others that will use the structure of the first OS installed. Use a software label to denote the drive, partition, and operating system on that section of the disk. For example, the Quantum disk I have in this machine has two partitions: the first DOS partition is "quatm_dos_1," the second (NT area) is "quatm_NT_2." That helps both in figuring out what is what, and identifying the drive over a network. Write down the label, size, and OS information on your System Inventory notes.

Install the First Operating System

Go through the entire first Setup, including any special drivers, monitor setup, etc. Write down any settings, so you can match them during the second installation. Load any software that you want to operate under both operating systems, and check for proper function.

Load the Second Operating System

Follow the installation steps outlined by the publisher of the second operating system. Keep in mind that you are creating a dual-boot environment, and that the Setup routine defaults may not be the ones you want. For example: Windows 95 suggests that both another copy of Windows 3.x and the new Windows 95 reside in the same directory. If you do that, the older version of DOS will not be available. I make a habit of installing multiple Windows versions in totally separate directories. See Figure 2.8. Windows NT is an exception; it loads its stuff under an existing Windows 3.x installation in a separate subdirectory. Now create any additional disk partitions for the second operating system.

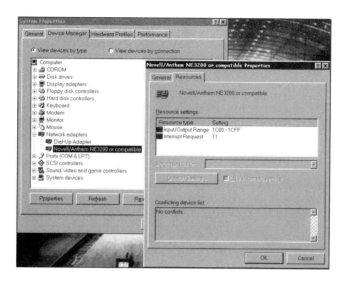

FIGURE 2.8 Windows 95 Setup Wizard.

Test the Installation

Use the proper procedures as given by the vendor to boot into both operating environments. Load any critical applications and drivers, then test by running your most commonly-used software. Access all drives, including CD-ROMs, and use multimedia and sound if you have them. Run a virus checker, and defragment the drives.

Make a Dark and Stormy Night Disk

Once everything is running, follow the procedures in Chapter 3 and in your operating system manual to create a rescue disk for the second operating system.

A Floppy-Based Alternative

If you don't want to create a permanent dual-boot system, you can still get some of the benefits. Long before hard drives for PCs we used floppies as both boot and storage drives. You can't boot NT from a floppy disk, but you can load DOS and the command prompt for Windows 95 from a single disk. This can be used to gain access to the system if it is configured to be bootable and has the required drivers for your hardware—basically a Dark and Stormy Night Disk.

The Triple-Header

For the really hard-core user, like a magazine reviewer, the triple-boot system can be a neat device. With a couple of commands you can run tests in three different operating environments with an identical hardware configuration. The trick is in figuring out how to access the third system, since most dual-boot systems are just that—planned for two environments. Here is my method for loading DOS/Windows for Workgroups, Windows 95, and Windows NT (or Windows NT Server).

The first step is to load DOS. If you want to add a non-DOS file system on a second or third disk partition, create it before moving on. Don't load any software until you have all three operating systems on the hard disk—just run the appropriate OS (operating system) setups. The second step is to set up Windows 3.11 or Windows for Workgroups if you want an older version of Windows on the system. Next I install Windows 95 in a separate directory and test the double boot. The F8 key is the one that invokes the operating system selection menu. Choose the last entry, which will bring up the old DOS, and make sure Windows 3.x works, then boot and test your Windows 95 operation.

Now load Windows NT or NT Server. You can install it into the original Windows 3.x directory. The NTLDR (NT Loader) program will be invoked each time the system boots, offering three choices; Windows NT, Windows NT in plain VGA mode, and Microsoft Windows (Windows 95). You can get into the old DOS by choosing the third option, then pressing **F8** and choosing the **Load Old Version of DOS**—the last option on the Windows 95 section menu.

Un-Installing a Multi-Boot Operating Environment

What happens if you want to (or have to) restore a multi-boot operating system to a single operating environment? The simplest way to get things in order is to have a Dark and Story Night Disk (DSND) that lets you use the DOS SYS command to restore the original single-system boot sector on the first or active partition of the primary hard drive. This replaces the multi-boot loader with a plain DOS master Boot Record. There are other options, depending on what you are trying to accomplish, so you should be familiar with your system's protocols. Both Windows NT and Windows 95 have repair options for a damaged set of systems files, if that is what you are really trying to repair. Windows 95 has an Un-install option on the Emergency Disk it offers to create during Setup. I have had mixed results with un-installers, so I always keep a plain DOS disk handy.

CHAPTER SUMMARY

The right choice for a PC's operating system depends on the power of a system, the type of applications you plan to use with it, any network it may be connected to, and personal preference. For most people, Windows 95 will work just fine, but there is no "one size fits all." Taking a little time at the beginning can make your computing experience more fun and more productive.

CHAPTER 3

KEEPING YOUR
PC HEALTHY

WHAT THIS CHAPTER IS ABOUT

The best way to fix problems is to keep them from happening. Proper care, a bit of common sense, and a little knowledge can go a long way towards keeping your computer running smoothly. This chapter covers steps every user should take in the way of preventive maintenance, whether you ever open your PC's case or not. Most of the tools we'll cover are software-related, with the possible exception of using a small screwdriver to make sure the cables are properly attached. The basic techniques discussed here, if properly followed, may not guarantee you'll never have a problem, but they can dramatically reduce its likelihood.

First we'll cover basic considerations in setting up a PC, such as surge protection and cabling. Then we'll go on to software configurations and maintaining proper backups.

To get the most benefit from this chapter, you should be seated at your computer and have a blank disk and your system manual at hand. It is assumed that you already have an operating system installed on your computer and have read the preceding chapters.

A MATTER OF ENVIRONMENT

Our PCs are a part of the world around them. They draw electricity from the local utility company, and that power can be disrupted by storms and heavy demands. People can spill things on them or detach their cables. Everyday usage modifies the structure of the file system on the hard disk and can slow operations. The installation of new software or addition of a new accessory can modify the start-up files, not always for the better. Strange and demented minds play games with computer viruses, wherein they try to infect other people's computers with damaging programs.

Forces of nature, like lightning storms, or hostile acts like a computer virus, may at first seem to be beyond our control, but there are steps we can take. The first step is to ensure that the basic environment your PC lives in is as risk-free as possible. Just as you would not let a small child play with a drawer full of sharp knives or dart across a busy highway, you should also make sure that your computer is as secure as possible.

Out of the Glass Castle

In the heyday of the mainframe, corporate computers were kept in sterile environments, working in air-conditioned comfort, breathing filtered air and using carefully-regulated power. While computers have become hardier, smaller, and less expensive, they still need a somewhat controlled environment. When setting up your PC you should try to avoid extremes of heat and cold, especially heat. I remember one winter seeing the image on the monitor of a Macintosh actually start to shimmer in an hourglass shape because the temperature in the room was high enough to overheat the machine's circuits.

Unlike your PC, the Macintosh did not have a fan to help cool the internal air. Most of the PCs in my laboratory actually have two fans. Today's microprocessors generate a lot of heat and the newer ones even have heat sinks built into them. You should place your PC so that none of its air intake or outlets are blocked, and so that there is a reasonable flow of air around the machine. A layer of dust inside it can act as an insulator, building up heat (not to mention that dust can get into floppy disks or into lubrication, literally gumming up the works). So you should also try to minimize how much dust is in the environment near your machine.

You can also help reduce the amount of heat inside your machine by not placing it in direct sunlight, or at least leaving it in a position that is shaded for most of the day. These same basic precautions also apply to your monitor and any other external components, such as a CD-ROM or printer.

A Healthy Diet

Your computer lives on electricity. While its 200- to 270-watt power supply may not consume that much more than a strong light bulb, it is a much more finicky eater than a reading lamp. Some communities have very good power supplies, with very few fluctuations in the strength of the current and very few power outages. Other users are less fortunate, living in areas where frequent storms or limited resources result in a loss of power.

You may think that you are getting 115-Volt Alternating Current from that plug in the wall, but that current may be alternating more than you are aware of. At its worst, your power may fail completely because of mechanical problems at a sub-station, a downed power line, or an electrical storm. There are three basic problems that can occur: over-voltage, under-voltage and line noise.

The Dangers of Over-Voltage

Severe over-voltage, as from a nearby lightning strike, can literally fry the internal components of your PC. Your PC's circuitry is designed to handle a reasonable fluctuation of the power coming into it. Lightning strikes can often produce a surge in power of over 20,000 volts. If your machine is the recipient of a surge like this, about all you can do is hope your insurance is paid up. If a severe thunderstorm is known to be in your area, it is probably a good idea to stop work and power down your machine.

WARNING

To be even safer, check your insurance policy. Most homeowners' policies will cover damage to your system, but... some may exclude (believe it or not!) devices with tubes or transistors in them (i.e., virtually everything on your computer system except its power switch). If you use your system for business, there may be limitations on the insurance company's liability so that truly disastrous damage would only be partially covered. Monitor your insurance, and upgrade it as needed.

But not all surges are quite so dramatic. Spikes and surges are often produced on local lines due to fluctuations in the amount of current provided by your local utility. *Spikes* are very short-lived jumps in the power supply, sometimes lasting only for about a billionth of a second. These can cause difficulties with your computer's RAM, producing erratic program behavior, or if you are writing to disk, may cause a problem with the file being written. *Surges* are much longer-lived, sometimes several milliseconds! Well, that may not seem like to a long time to you, but it extends the time that your computer is under stress.

Surge Protection

Surge protectors come in a variety of forms. See Figure 3.1. Most are inexpensive devices (running from $10 up) designed to stop over-voltage from reaching your PC. The most common type is the metal-oxide varistor (MOV). These short out the excess voltage, usually referred to as *clamping*. Of course the electricity has to go somewhere, and in this case it will be transferred into heat. A very large over-voltage can actually melt the MOV.

FIGURE 3.1 An assortment of surge protectors.

Even without something as flashy as a lighting strike, MOVs will wear out over time due to the smaller over-voltages that occur regularly in most power systems. Sometimes a MOV unit will just stop working, leaving your PC susceptible to damage. In other cases the unit can conceivably start a fire when it fails. As a rule it's a good idea to replace this type of surge protector every three or four years. Your local computer shop should carry an assortment of these devices and can help you in selecting one that is appropriate for your needs. The primary considerations are how fast they can work and how large an over-voltage they can dissipate. Faster clamping times and higher power absorption abilities are better. The better the abilities, as usual, the higher the cost.

Almost all PCs have some sort of built in surge protection, like a fuse or a circuit breaker. If too much power comes down the line, this component will fail, sacrificing itself rather than having the whole computer go down. That's a neat trick, but it's still going to mean a trip to the repair shop so that the circuit can be replaced. And who knows, it may not function quickly enough. For that reason, you should purchase an external surge protection device. These come in several varieties and range in cost from about $10 on up.

Some plug directly into the wall, offering 2 to 6 outlets. Curtis offers a series of Safe-Bloc units with different ratings. In general, the more expensive, the fancier the surge protection. As with most of these devices, an indicator light shows that the unit is functioning properly. If a surge is detected, the unit will clamp down in an attempt to keep the power from damaging the devices plugged into it.

QVS and a number of other vendors offer power strips with surge protection built into them. Some of these even provide connections for phone lines so that you can protect your modem from surges. Another form of surge protector is found in switch consoles that double as monitor stands, allowing you to selectively turn on and off different computer components connected by separate power cords.

WARNING

Surge protectors are safety devices, they are not a guarantee. If you have a lightning strike near your house on a nearby generator, the odds are very good that the current will blow out your average surge protector and keep right on going. And surge protectors don't fix all electrical line problems. They can't add extra power if there isn't enough there for proper function.

It's a good idea any time severe weather is in your area to save all critical data and power down your equipment. Then unplug the power leads from the wall socket.

NOTE There's another thing to consider when placing surge protectors; you may not have enough power on a given circuit to use all of the outlets that are provided on the surge protector. Keep in mind that just adding more outlets does not add more capacity. If the socket into which you plug your computer has had problems in the past with blown fuses or popped circuit breakers, you should consider another location, or possibly modifications to your wiring.

Under-Voltage and Power Failures—It's Not Always a Matter of Too Much

Brown-outs and black-outs can also cause problems with PCs. Under-voltage occurs when the power fed to the machine falls below the level it's designed for. Your PC can usually compensate for a 15-to-20% under- or over-voltage without any real problem. Voltage regulators are generally included with power-conditioning devices, which combine it with surge protection and, often, a standby power supply.

UPS Delivers

While surge protectors offer some measure of security against line problems, a good *Uninterruptible Power Supply (UPS)* offers surge protection as well as on-line battery back-up. In other words, in the event of an under-voltage or a complete failure of power, the UPS provides back-up power. Just how long the power will last depends on the unit you purchase. UPSs are based on battery power. When the power fails the UPS switches over to battery power, thus keeping your PC on line. In the past UPSs included a hefty measure of line-conditioning circuitry to protect equipment. Recent changes in UPS technology have reduced the cost of these units, but reduced their inherent noise-handling capabilities. Most newer units do, however, have some sort of surge suppression built in.

Choosing a Surge Protector or an UPS

All home systems should at least be on a surge suppressor and that surge suppressor should be changed at least every three or four years.

The $20 or $30 is cheap insurance. UPSs that provide 10 to 15 minutes of standby power can be had in the $200 to $300 range. While this may seem a bit high for some users, others will consider it cheap insurance if the information they are working with is valuable. Remember, when the power goes off, the information stored in your computer's RAM goes with it.

Many of the better UPS units and surge protectors now come with their own insurance. This is well worth having, but read the policy and understand what it *won't* cover.

T I P

Getting Wired

We have talked about the wires coming from the wall to the surge protector, and the power going into your computer. Now let's talk about that plate of spaghetti that comes out the back of your machine. If all you have attached to your computer is a monitor, a mouse, a keyboard and a printer, you can still have a fair number of cables dangling on the back of your desk. That's four power cords, and at least four cables. It's a good idea to minimize how intertwined the cables become, and it's an excellent idea to make sure all those cables and connectors are properly secured. I've gotten calls from more than one user convinced that they had a printer problem, when the difficulty was really with a loose cable. Make sure that your cables are long enough to provide some slack when the devices they are connecting are in their normal positions. Cables that are too short can be pulled loose or can be bent so that they weaken the wires inside. Extreme stress can also result in damage to the connectors themselves.

You may want to use some plastic twist-ties to hold the cables neatly together towards their middles.

T I P

AN ONGOING ARGUMENT

Every time you turn on your computer, or any other electronic device, you're sending a surge of electricity through the system. As the unit warms up, the heat causes some components to expand; when you turn it off, those components will contract as they cool. These changes place a stress on the system. How many times have you seen a light bulb fail just as you turned it on? The surge of power repeated over and over finally broke the filament. Every time you turn on your computer you are causing wear and tear on the chips, the motor in your hard disk, and the sensitive electronics inside your monitor.

For years a debate has raged over which causes more stress: leaving the machine on all the time, or turning it on and off. There is solid evidence that turning it on and off does wear out the components. I personally follow a middle ground in the debate. Given the pace of technology, most PCs will be replaced long before they'll die of natural causes. But there are some things you can do to minimize the risk of sudden death without running up your electric bill.

A Basic Rule of Thumb

My basic approach is to fire up the machine only once during the day. Then I leave it on until I'm finished with that day's work. Turning it on and off several times a day multiplies the amount of stress on its parts, and the unit draws a lot more power when it's first turned on than when it's fully up and running. It's a bit like the amount of energy it takes to get your car in motion from a standing stop, compared with the rate of consumption at normal operating speed.

NOTE   If you have a new "Green" PC, it has the ability to save energy and reduce power consumption by turning off components that have not been used for a set period of time. Consult your manual for specific details. Make sure that ALL the components—including the system BIOS—are Green compatible. If a device is not, it may hang if given a Green system command.

Be Patient

There are some cases, especially when you are installing new equipment, where you have to turn the machine off and on again several times. When you are doing this, be patient. Don't ever just flip your computer's switch on and then off again rapidly. When you shut the system down, give it at least 15 to 30 seconds to come to a complete rest. When you fire it up, let it attempt to go through the entire boot cycle before turning it off again if you find it is not behaving properly. Rapidly turning it on and off again is especially rough on your hard drive. The platters may have to go from standing still to spinning at 5400 rpm, and the heads are moving as they prepare to start reading data during the boot process. When you turn the machine on and off again quickly, you put a severe strain on those mechanical components.

Wait Until It Warms Up

Some people can jump out of bed, alive and alert and ready to go; others get moving a little more slowly in the morning. Your PC is one of these casual risers. Until the monitor is fully warmed up it doesn't show its true colors; as the platters of your hard disk expand, the physical data structure is altered just slightly. While this minute variance is usually not enough to make a difference, it's a good idea to wait until the unit's up to speed before reading and writing data.

It Was a Dark and Stormy Night

The subhead above sounds like the beginning of a mystery novel, and in most mystery novels it's not a matter of *if* tragedy will happen, but *when*. While hardware problems do occur and while all things mechanical will eventually fail, the majority of computer problems are software-related and, many times, easily avoided.

I make it a habit to keep a disk close at hand that contains all the files I need to get a somewhat confused computer back on line. I call this my *Dark and Stormy Night Disk*, and usually label it with the abbreviation, DSND, and also include the date I made it. I update this disk every time I add a new component or modify one of the basic start-up files. Before I can show you how to create such a disk, I need to explain the steps your PC takes in its warm-up cycle every time you turn it on. If you are already familiar with the *Power-On-Self-Test* (POST) and how to change your system's CMOS (a special chip that stores vital information which we will cover soon) start-up values, you may want to skim this material until you get to the sub-head titled: "Creating a Rescue Disk."

Each time the machine is powered up it goes through a self-test. This test makes sure that all the components are properly identified and in working order. Once this is completed, the operating system is loaded, and the configuration files are used to set up the machine for work. A problem detected in the test, or a mistake in one of the configuration files, can bring your machine to its knees. In most cases, knowing what's going on can help you to have everything back to normal in just a few minutes.

THE BOOT CYCLE

The term "booting a PC" is based on the phrase "pulling oneself up by one's own bootstraps." Every time you turn your PC off it loses all non-disk memory. It doesn't know anything about the outside world or its own components.

The Power On Self-Test may vary slightly from machine to machine, and any variations from the steps listed below for your computer should be listed in its operating manual. Most PCs will issue a single beep during the boot process and then provide access to the operating system. For Microsoft DOS, this means a C: prompt; for Windows NT or IBM's OS/2, you should see your workspace. If your system automatically loads a program such as Windows or WordPerfect, you will see that application's opening screen.

Here are the details of the standard Power-On-Self-Test:

✔ *Cleared for Takeoff:* Electrical current follows a permanent path and clears the CPU's (*Central Processing Unit*) internal memory. The machine then starts the boot sequence, which is locked in a Read-Only Memory (ROM) chip. This starts the actual POST (Power On Self-Test). If at this point, nothing seems to be happening, the power light doesn't come on, there is no sound from insider the computer and no series of beeps, you probably don't have power to the system. This could be due to several reasons: the surge protector isn't plugged into the wall (you did buy a surge protector, right?), the machine's power cord is not plugged into the surge protector; or there may be a malfunction with the computer's power supply unit.

If none of the above seems to be the problem, don't immediately panic and rush out to buy a new power supply. Check the circuit breaker and the fuse in your surge protector, if it has one. If this fails, check the circuit breaker or fuse that powers the wall plug. This may seem very obvious while you are reading this, but it may not be so obvious when your computer is not working. There is even a case on record of a user who called a technical support hotline to complain that her word processing program was not working. After several questions, the support technician learned that the power was out in the entire building.

✔ *Starting the Bus:* The CPU sends signals across the *system bus* (this is the major circuit which connects all the components to each other) to each component to make sure that it is functioning.

✔ *Video Check:* Now the POST focuses on your display system, testing the memory on your video card. At this point you should see some sort of message on your monitor. If you never get an image on your monitor, either this test or one of the preceding tests has failed. If you obviously have power to your computer and you still do not receive any image on your screen, there are several things you can check immediately. In some cases, everything may be going along fine, it's just that your monitor isn't turned on or plugged in. You can also check the cable that runs from the video card to the monitor. If this is loose or not plugged in, you may receive either no picture at all or one that is badly distorted.

Video problems are not limited to just the picture on your monitor. With the advent of souped-up and thus more complicated graphics adapters, as well as more complicated software to run them, it is not unusual to find conflicts that can lock up a system after installing a new display card or a software program that doesn't properly use it. Some of the software issues will be covered shortly in this chapter. For the hardware issues you will find troubleshooting help in Chapter 12.

✔ *Ram Test:* In the next step, your computer self tests all of its *RAM* (*Random Access Memory*). In most cases you'll see, on the display, a counter showing the memory as it tests. On some machines you can press either the **Space Bar** or the **Escape Key** to stop the memory test. If you have a lot of RAM on your system this test can take several seconds, so you may want to circumvent it. If there is a problem with RAM, you may get a message that a segment failed, in which case the machine may lock up. In some cases the machine may operate but it stops seeing memory above that location; for example, your 8Mb machine may become a 4Mb machine.

A memory failure does not always mean that one of your chips is bad. In the sections below we will discuss the system Setup or CMOS. If the Setup information is reading less memory than is actually there, the computer will not test it. Some systems will report an error in the Setup file but we'll cover that in a few minutes.

✔ *Checking the Keys:* At this point in the POST process, the computer checks to make sure that the keyboard is attached and that no keys are stuck. This is a very useful point in the POST, because the lights on the keyboard for the **Num Lock**, **Caps Lock**, and **Scroll Lock** should flash. If you are having trouble getting the machine to boot properly and the lights are flashing, you'll know that it passed the POST to this point, so in all likelihood your basic components—CPU, RAM, video display, and keyboard—are functioning properly, and you have power to the system.

✔ *Disk Drives Ready:* Once the keyboard test is complete the POST process moves on to your disk drives. You should hear each floppy drive as it is tested and its drive light should come on. If one of them does not light up during this phase it may be due to incorrect information in the Setup or the drive's data cable or power lead may have become detached. If you have a SCSI host adapter attached to your hard drive or CD-ROM, the SCSI bus will be activated. If your primary drive is a SCSI unit, you should see a message that the SCSI BIOS was installed.

✔ *Component Roll Call:* On all but the oldest PCs the machine now checks the CMOS chip to identify which components are on the system. *CMOS* stands for *Complimentary Metal Oxide Semi-conductor.* CMOS provides us with a very useful feature: it allows us to not only modify the date and time in the computer's internal clock, but lets us also tell it when we add new components to the system. The earliest machines did not have CMOS, making it much more difficult to add non-standard accessories. By running a Setup routine (which we'll discuss shortly) your computer can be updated easily to reflect the addition of a new floppy drive, hard drive, or even to change certain operating parameters of your CPU. Just how this program operates and what you are allowed to configure will vary, but we'll get back to that in a minute. This chip has its own battery supply so that it can store information even when the computer is turned off.

✔ *Calling All Cards:* The final step before loading the operating system is to check to see if there are any other components in the system that have their own BIOS. The BIOS (or *Basic Input/ Output System*) is a set of programs located in ROM that controls the communication between different parts of the computer system and accessory devices. Your computer has its own BIOS, which works with the CMOS mentioned above. If you've recently installed a new device such as a new video card or advanced hard disk controller that has its own BIOS, it is important that the card be installed properly. If the two sets of instructions (in the computer's BIOS and the new accessory BIOS) conflict, the offending instructions may halt the system. It would be just like being stopped at an intersection and being told to go in two directions at once, or not knowing which way to turn. The confusion can halt operation. In some cases such conflicts can be resolved without opening the case by making some software modifications; in others you may either have to adjust switches at the back of the computer, or open the case and remove the offending card. We'll cover those possibilities in Chapter 5.

✔ *System Ready:* Finally, if the POST and all the cards are loaded properly, you should see your operating system prompt and have full control of the system. If you get an error message that you do not understand during boot, refer to your manual or the lists contained in Appendix F of this book for more details.

SETUPS AND CMOS

Most of the Power-On-Self-Test activity is *hard-wired*, which means that it is contained in instructions that are literally burned into a chip, so that they don't go away when you turn off power to the computer. But since there is no such thing as a standard PC, it is impossible for a vendor to hard-wire how many floppy drives you might have, what kind of hard disk you have, or how much memory is on your system. The earliest PCs used switch settings to determine what kind of components were contained in the machine. Today we have a much better method.

The Power-On-Self-Test is stored permanently in a ROM chip; if you want to change the way the POST works, you have to remove the chip and put in another one. You certainly wouldn't want to do this every time you changed a disk drive in your system or added more memory. A CMOS chip is different. It can be modified by your computer's Setup program. Instead of being burned into the chip's silicon, these instructions are stored in electronic memory. To keep power to this chip when you turn your computer off, your system has a battery that is attached directly to the motherboard. Some systems even provide a back-up battery. If you look inside your case you may find a small blue barrel-shaped battery (or a container holding four AA-size batteries) connected to the motherboard by a pair of red and black wires. See Figure 3.2.

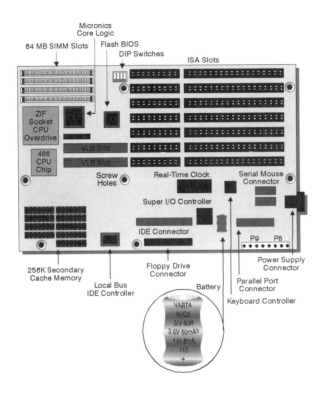

FIGURE 3.2   Battery pack on a motherboard.

Many of my friends have called to tell me that their computers aren't working because the battery powering their CMOS finally ran down. When this happens your computer won't know what type of floppy drives it has, the size of its hard disk, and it will forget the date and time. Every PC user should know, and preferably write down, the working settings of their CMOS setup. In fact, if you don't know the type of hard disk you have, and use the wrong number, your system will not boot and you may even damage your hard disk.

Running the Setup Program

The quickest way to find out exactly what your CMOS values are is to run the Setup program. Just how it works varies depending on the type of BIOS and CMOS instructions that are built into your computer.

Almost all computer manufacturers buy their components from three vendors, American MegaTrends (AMI), Award, or Phoenix Technologies. Usually if something is wrong with your CMOS the system will advise you during your Power-On-Self-Test and halt, asking your to press an appropriate key to enter the program.

Only the old 286 AT systems actually run a software program from a floppy disk or hard drive. 386 and later machines have them actually built into the system itself. If you have an old AT, you will need the Setup disk and you will have to run the program just like any other. For later machines the method of running the program will vary based on the BIOS manufacturer. In some cases you can only access Setup during the Power-On-Self-Test; with others you can access it any time the computer is at the DOS prompt, as well as by pressing a special key combination. Most current AMI based as systems require that you press the **Delete** key during the Power-On-Self-Test. Other key combinations to try are **Control+Alternate+S**, **Control+Alternate+Escape**, or the **F2** key. If you don't know the combination for your machine, you should identify the keystrokes by checking in your manual.

Running the Setup Routine

Let's run your Setup routine now and write down the information that is recorded for your configuration. You should store this where you can find it, for instance in the caddy where you keep your disks, or inside the front cover of your system manual.

WARNING

Do not change any Setup values that you do not understand. Doing so may adversely affect system performance and may damage your hard disk.

Follow the steps outlined in the manual to access your system configuration Setup. Award Systems often puts all the information on one screen; Phoenix Technologies frequently has their information spread across two screens, while AMI uses a menu to access several screens. While the information and features vary from vendor to vendor, there are some common features.

Figure 3.3 shows a standard configuration screen. The instructions at the bottom tell you how to change the values for a setting and how to move between options. The first two listings allow you to set the time and date. If you want to keep an accurate system clock you will probably be using CMOS at least twice a year to adjust for daylight savings time.

N O T E   Of course, you can do this indirectly through the Time and Date programs in DOS, or with the Control Panel in Windows; in Windows 95 your system should make the Daylight/Standard time correction automatically if you made the right choices when you installed it.

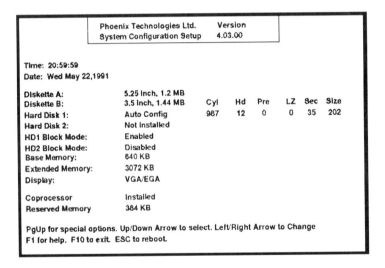

FIGURE 3.3 A typical CMOS Standard Configuration screen.

The next two listings let you tell the system the types of floppy disks that are installed on your system. If this information isn't present and correct, you will not be able to access the floppy drives and you will get an error message every time you boot the machine. The next entries do the same thing for your hard disk, but require more information. You must also tell the Setup routine a number of physical characteristics about your hard drive.

WARNING

Improper settings here can make it impossible to boot your system until they are set right, and may even physically damage your hard disk. Be sure that the numbers of values for your hard drive match the actual ones, as defined by *your* system's manufacturer. A Tech Support call is cheaper than a new hard drive!

This program is also where your system stores information about the amount and type of memory on your system. If this value is set incorrectly, your system may either hang or not make use of all the memory which is installed. There are also usually options to set the type of display system, keyboard, and if there is a coprocessor present. On Intel 80486-DX machines and later the coprocessor will always show as "installed," as it is built into the CPU.

SHORTCUT

At this time you should write down all the information included in your CMOS setup and store it in a safe place. I make it a practice to write the hard drive configuration on a label and attach it either to the hard drive itself, to the back of the PC itself, or to the first page of either the hard disk, controller, or system manual.

Later in this chapter, we'll use one of the software programs included on the disk in the back of this book, or your operating system Rescue Disk utility to automatically save the critical boot information onto our Dark and Stormy Night Disk. This nifty utility lets us automatically restore our Setup values if the battery runs low or something else wipes out this vital data. Since it *is* vital, I never rely on something as unreliable as a floppy disk as my only form of security. For this reason I also keep a hard-copy record of my CMOS setup.

Additional pages, or screens, in a Setup program usually provide access to advanced features. I'll explain some of the more common ones following, but you must either know what you are doing or check the following manual before changing any advanced features. Another good rule of thumb is to only change one feature at a time. Changing two features may cause conflicts that are very difficult to resolve. It is also very easy to get confused, and you can save yourself a lot of frustration by just doing it in a very organized and step-by-step manner.

Figure 3.4 shows the second page of the Phoenix setup for a Micronics motherboard. The first entry enables or disables the *BIOS Shadow RAM*; this is a common option which puts the system's BIOS, which is normally stored on a ROM chip, into RAM memory. This speeds up operations that must check with the BIOS, but can cause conflicts with some accessory cards.

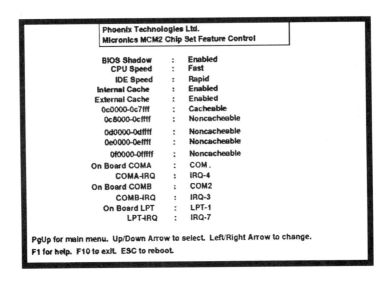

FIGURE 3.4 A typical CMOS Standard Configuration screen.

CPU Speed

The CPU setting allows you to adjust the speed of your central processor to either operate at its full capacity or to step down to a slower speed. The original PC and AT systems came out with a fixed CPU speed. Later versions of the 286 and all versions of later processors operate at a variety of speeds. There are a few programs, mostly older DOS-based games, that have difficulty with CPUs operating at the higher speeds. For this reason, many vendors have continued to offer both Setup and hot-key options that allow us to reduce the speed of the CPU. Today such incompatibilities are infrequent and unless you run into one, you should usually leave this option set at *Fast Speed Enabled* (sometimes also referred to as "Turbo"). Many systems also have a Turbo switch on the front of the case. When the Turbo switch is pressed in, the machine is usually operated at the faster speed, and the Turbo indicator light on front panel is lit.

This setting or switch is one to keep in mind if all of a sudden your machine seems to lose its get up and go. Some system BIOSes allow you to slow down or speed up the CPU speed by pressing the **Control+Alternate++** and **Control+Alternate+–** keys.

IDE Speed

Some newer hard drives can make use of accelerated modes unavailable on older drives, or operate in Enhanced IDE modes with features to improve performance. This Setup option allows you to enable some of these features. We'll cover all the intricacies of hard drive operation in Chapter 9.

Internal Cache

Intel 486 and later CPUs have a built-in *cache*. This is special memory that is set aside, sort of like a scratch pad. Using this memory is faster than going into the processor's hardware to find an instruction, and so speeds up basic operations of your computer. Generally speaking, if internal cache is available you should use it, unless it conflicts with some accessory you are using.

External Cache

Newer CPUs can also address *external cache*. This is a larger area of memory that can be used to hold instructions similar to the internal cache. Today it is common to find from 64K to 512K of external memory available on many motherboards. Unlike the internal cache, this is an option, not a built-in function of the system. You must have the internal cache turned on in the Setup program in a 486-based system to enable the external cache. If you set the preceding option off, you can't use the external cache at all. You'll notice in Figure 3.4 a series of numbers starting at 0C0000–0C7FFF. These are memory ranges (which I explain in Chapter 4). You'll notice that some of the ranges in the illustrations have been set to "cacheable" and others to "non-cacheable". Don't worry about the intricacies of these settings right now; I'll explain them in greater detail later. At present you should just make a note of what your current settings are. If you are reading this section because you are having difficulty, check Chapter 4, dealing with cache memory, or Chapter 5 for adding expansion cards.

Other Options

Some systems have on-board communication or printer ports, like the Micronics motherboard used in the example above. The final settings in the illustration are used to control the operation of these options.

As mentioned before, the AMI BIOS has a variety of additional settings. At the present time it is probably the most detailed of the CMOS setup routines. On most systems it is possible to change from one CMOS/BIOS system to another (for example, to replace Award with Phoenix or AMI). In some cases this will make no difference at all, in others it may offer access to additional features. Some board manufacturers simply buy BIOSes and Setup routines from the vendor who offers them the best deal. Others, like Micronics, work with BIOS vendors to fine-tune the Setup to their product. I have seen up to 20% improvement in performance as a result of such tweaking.

Exit Setup as indicated by your own program, without changing anything.

THE EISA CONFIGURATION UTILITY

If you have a system that makes use of EISA expansion slots, then you also have to set up your computer's expansion cards with the EISA *Configuration* (CF) program. This is supplied by your motherboard maker on a floppy disk. These utilities are upgraded on a regular basis when a board is new, so check for an enhanced edition of your **CF** file.

CREATING A RESCUE DISK

For this exercise we're going to use a either a program that is included in your operating system or a utility located on the disc in the back of the book, called WinSleuth Gold. If you have a dual boot system that runs either Windows NT or 95 and Windows for Workgroups, you can use both tools. Let's start with WinSleuth. Since the Windows 95 and NT software is automatic, it's easier to explain the related concepts of system care and the detailed steps with the older software. I advise most people to maintain a dual-boot system if they are running one of the new 32-bit operating environments like Windows NT or Windows 95.

As I mentioned in Chapter 2 on operating systems, it can be a good idea to have two operating systems. That way if a problem occurs with a boot sector virus, or you are unable to get to one operating system, you still have a reasonable chance of saving your data and rebuilding the drive with minimal effort using the other one. A well-maintained Rescue Disk is a key factor in safe computing. I keep both a DOS DSND and a Win 95 or Windows NT Rescue Disk for every system. Even if you don't run WinSleuth, please skim this section before going on so you understand the concepts.

To run WinSleuth Gold and create a rescue disk you will need both the disc that is contained in the sleeve at the back of this book, and a floppy that will work in the A: drive on your PC. This second disk should not contain any data you will want to keep. Format this second disk with the /s option so that you can use it as a bootable disk. If you are not familiar with DOS, this is done by typing **Format A: /s /v** with the disk inserted into the drive. If you get a message saying `bad command or file name` the Format file is either not situated in the directory in your Path statement or it isn't on your hard drive. In most cases, changing over to your DOS directory will solve the problem.

If you are unfamiliar with DOS or Windows, or are using another operating system, you should refer to your User's Manual for more information on formatting a disk. The Windows File Manager will also allow you to create a bootable floppy, using an option found under the Disk menu. If you need to exit Windows to get to a DOS prompt, choose the **Exit Windows** option located under the Program Manager File Menu (be sure to save any important work before exiting).

Complete instructions for the use of WinSleuth are contained on the CD-ROM disc in the back of the book. Installing the program located on the CD-ROM disc in the back of this book is quite simple. It is stored in a compressed file (Wins.exe) in its own directory (called Winslth). Create a matching directory on your hard drive and copy the file Wins.exe into it. If you need help copying files, consult your operating system's manual or Help files.

To uncompress the WinSleuth files, change to the appropriate directory and type **Wins** and hit **Return**, or use Windows **Run**. It is a self-extracting program that will decompress the files needed to set up and register each one. Make sure you've followed these instructions and have WinSleuth Gold ready to run before continuing.

This is a fully-functional version of the 3.05 edition of WinSleuth Gold. This software lets you examine and test your PC as well as optimize the way Microsoft Windows runs on your system. The newer versions of the program, which are currently available for sale in the stores, offer improved features, including the ability to automatically create a Dark and Stormy Night Disk. You can upgrade to the newer version of the software by calling the number that appears at the top of the program window.

Saving the CMOS Data

Within Windows, double-click on the **WinSleuth Gold** icon, which shows a computer being examined with a magnifying glass. Once the program is loaded, go to the File menu and choose the first option, which says **SAVE CMOS**. You will immediately see an information box. The program will ask you to insert a formatted disk in drive A:. Your screen will look similar to that shown in Figure 3.5.

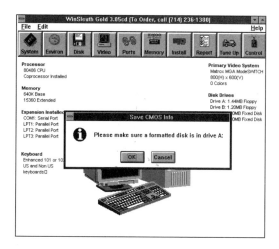

FIGURE 3.5 WinSleuth information box.

After the disk is in, click on **OK**. When you click **OK**, the program will read the information in your CMOS setup and save it in a special file, which will be copied to the floppy drive. For information on how to restore the data should your CMOS Setup become corrupted, or should the battery that maintains its power be exhausted, please refer to the WinSleuth instructions included on the disc.

N O T E

If you are not running Windows for Workgroups, you will be unable to store the CMOS on your Rescue Disk, but you still will be able to reset the CMOS values using the notes you took when you were using the Setup program. Floppy disks are fragile things, and even with fancy technology you may not be able to use the Rescue Disk. The same holds true for the startup files; I'll explain on the following pages. It's always a good idea to have backup hard copies of critical information.

WinSleuth Gold can also be used to examine your System Configuration, Inventory, and test its components. We will deal extensively with these features in Chapter 4. Right now, we'll use it to examine two of the most important files on your machine, and finish creating your Dark and Stormy Night Disk. For now, let's leave the program open on your screen and leave the disk with the CMOS Setup data in your A: drive.

Your PC's Critical Start-Up Files

Once your system completes the Power On Self-Test, it loads its operating system and then checks for the existence of startup files. These are special files that you can create to fine-tune your system's operation, and set desired Preferences and Configure options that aren't covered either in the BIOS or the system Setup. These vary from operating system to operating system. The DOS startup files, CONFIG.SYS and AUTOEXEC.BAT, are straight-forward examples of how these files work. CONFIG.SYS contains commands that can generally only be run by invoking this file during the boot process, and often contain commands that install drivers needed before the main operating environment can begin. The AUTOEXEC.BAT file, on the other hand, contains commands that can be entered at any time directly from the DOS prompt, but are automatically read by the system immediately after the CONFIG.SYS file has been dealt with.

All operating systems have some way to handle the tasks carried out by these two files. In Windows 95 most of the CONFIG.SYS functions are dealt with via the Control Panel; the same is generally true for Windows NT. It is beyond the scope of this book to cover all the options, so you should become familiar with the nuances of your own particular setup.

N O T E

CONFIG.SYS and AUTOEXEC.BAT are two very powerful files, as are the settings in the Windows Control Panel. Many new users don't pay enough attention to them, thus missing an opportunity to improve their system's performance. Any time you prepare to modify either one of these files you should first save a back-up copy, either in a different sub-directory or on a floppy disk. One common way to lock up a system temporarily is to improperly modify these two files. If you have backup copies on a bootable floppy disk, recovering from such an error is very simple; indeed, without such a backup copy, recovery can be frustrating, especially on a complicated system.

Configuring the System

The first of the two files that DOS (Disk Operating System) automatically looks at (if they are present) is CONFIG.SYS. If you have to use Real-Mode drivers for some devices on your system, Windows 95 will also use these files, even though they're not needed for the operating system itself. We're going to use WinSleuth Gold to examine the CONFIG.SYS file. Click on the button at the top right of the window that says **Tune Up** with the image of someone peering inside a car. The screen will change and directly underneath the button will be a listing of four files. Click on the little circle in front of the entry for CONFIG.SYS. Your screen should look similar to that shown in Figure 3.6.

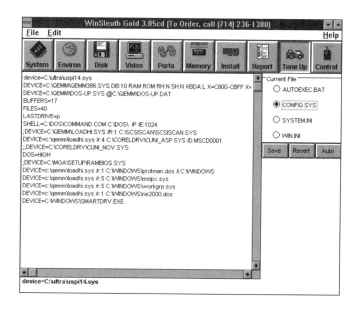

FIGURE 3.6 Editing a CONFIG.SYS file in WinSleuth Gold.

NOTE

If you are running a DOS-based system, and do not have a copy of Windows, have a strictly Windows 95 or Windows NT machine, or for some other reason cannot use WinSleuth Gold, another utility has been included on the CD-ROM disc called "ASQ." Installing it is similar to the process used above for WinSleuth Gold. Create a directory called ASQ on your hard disk, and copy the file ASQC.EXE into your new directory. This file is in the ASQ directory on the CD-ROM disc. From your own ASQ directory, type **ASQC** and press **Return**. This will expand the ASQ program and documentation files. You can now run the program by typing **ASQ** and then **Return**. This product is shareware, which should be licensed (i.e, paid for) if you intend to use it on a regular basis. Complete documentation is contained with the program. You can also use this same utility to view the AUTOEXEC.BAT file in the following section.

If you wish to view these files without using the utilities, use the following instructions to view the CONFIG.SYS file from DOS. Change to your boot directory, usually C:\. Now enter the following command at the keyboard: **DIR CON*.*** and then hit the **Return** or **Enter** key. The name of the file is **CONFIG.SYS**. We used the DOS wild card character (*) so that the **DIR** (Directory) command would show all files in the current directory which started with "con." If you don't have a CONFIG.SYS on your system, keep reading. We'll show you how to create one in a minute. If you do, please enter the following command: **TYPE CONFIG.SYS** and hit **Return** or **Enter**. Caution: You can also use the DOS command **Edit** to view these files, but beware: you can also change them using **Edit**; consult your DOS manual or Help facility, and be careful—be *sure* you have these critical files backed up onto a bootable floppy *before* you change them!

WARNING

WinSleuth Gold's **Tune Up** option not only displays the contents of your configuration file, but allows you to edit it. Unless you are already familiar with the operation of these files and know precisely what you want to change, you should not make modifications unless you understand *exactly* what you're doing.

Figure 3.7 shows the contents of a typical CONFIG.SYS file under DOS. As you can see, all the entries are similar in one respect: there is an item or name to the left of an equal sign, and the value for that entry is to the right of the equal sign.

```
device=C:\ultra\uspi14.sys
device=C:\windows\himem.sys
BUFFERS=17
FILES=40
LASTDRIVE=p
SHELL=C:\DOS\COMMAND.COM C:\DOS\ /P /E:512
DOS=HIGH
DEVICE=C:\WINDOWS\IFSHLP.SYS
STACKS=9,256
```

FIGURE 3.7 A typical CONFIG.SYS file.

The Two Functions of CONFIG.SYS

The CONFIG.SYS file allows us to do two things: it allows us to set certain *parameters* (limits) that DOS will observe while the machine is operating, and allows us to load *device drivers* (special programs to operate specific hardware) for things such as network cards, scanners, or fancy video adapters. In most cases, to change these parameters once such devices are installed, you will have to modify the CONFIG.SYS file and reboot the computer. This doesn't happen very often (unless you are an author and a magazine writer). These modifications are usually necessary when you install a new piece of hardware or software on your system. In many cases these modifications are done automatically by that program or device's installation procedure, but, especially under DOS, not always well: the changes a particular installation routine makes may adversely affect other parts of your system. This possibility, common with sound cards and under DOS games, for example, gives a couple of good reasons to (a) have these files previously backed up on a Rescue Disk or a DSND, and (b) get some insight into what these files do and how they work, so you can tinker when and if you have to. The advent of Windows 95 and Plug and Play technology will improve this situation. See Chapter 2 for more on PnP.

Setting System Parameters

The fourth line in Figure 3.7 shows the listing, FILES=40. This is an example of setting a *parameter*. A parameter is a value assigned to a setting that affects the way the command works. In this setting you are telling the system the maximum number of files that can be open at any one time is not to be greater than 40. This setting can be anywhere from 8 to 255. Some programs, such as advanced databases, may require very high file numbers. Any time you install a new program under DOS you should check to see what kind of file statement it requires. If you do not have enough files available, you may find that the program is not able to function and will give an "out of file" error message.

There are a variety of parameters that can be set using the CONFIG.SYS options. These vary based on the version of DOS that you are using, and the optimal setting will vary somewhat based upon your hardware configuration. For best results you should consult the documentation that came with your machine and the version of DOS you are using. You may also want to examine the section covering memory management in Chapter 4. Under Windows 95, all this should be handled automatically.

The Command Shell

Another very useful CONFIG.SYS command is the one that allows you to tell the operating system where to look for the command processor, no matter where it resides on your system. If this option is not set, DOS will look for the command processor (the COMMAND.COM program) in the root directory of the drive you booted from. The root directory is the highest level of a disk. The name comes from the fact that DOS uses a tree structure for files, with sub-directories branching off the root (nobody said the person who coined the term understood biology). A directory is an imaginary place on the drive that holds files. You can think of it as a file folder that holds individual files, and the drive as a file cabinet that holds directories. In fact, Window 95 calls directories "Folders."

It is very easy to copy files accidentally, and some old programs in their Install programs used to copy COMMAND.COM into the root directory of the primary hard disk. If the version of DOS you are using does not match the version of COMMAND.COM in that location, your system will either behave erratically or come to a screaming, screeching halt. I generally leave my COMMAND.COM in my DOS sub-directory. In order to make it accessible, even if there's another version in the root directory, I put a SHELL command in my CONFIG.SYS. Here's how it reads:

```
SHELL=C:\DOS\COMMAND.COM
```

There all all kinds of neat things you can do with your startup files that can make your life easier and your computer run better. Just which ones to use is a matter of personal taste and the way your PC is designed. Consult your manual for ideas, then experiment. Remember to make backup copies of the files and keep them safe before trying any adjustments. You might want to experiment using a separate, experimental floppy disk. This will make it even easier to recover from any failed experiments, by simply allowing your PC to boot normally.

Device Drivers

The CONFIG.SYS shown in Figure 3.7 also shows several DEVICE= Xx statements. These are device drivers. Some, like HIMEM.SYS, are software device drivers. HIMEM.SYS or the equivalent is required to run Microsoft Windows 3.1. Device drivers can look complicated, and some are. Most simply require making sure that you have spelled everything right. They won't cause any real problems if you are sure to have a rescue disk handy. For more information about HIMEM.SYS and other programs like Qualitas' 386 to the MAX or Quarterdeck's QEMM, see the section on memory management in Chapter 4. Other device drivers control physical devices; for example, DEVICE=C:\BOOT\USPI14.SYS is a device driver that is used to control my SCSI-based host adapter.

Buffers

Another common statement is BUFFERS=NN ("N" stands for a number). This is the number of one-sector (512 byte) buffers that DOS will set up. A buffer is an area in memory that DOS uses when information is being transferred to and from the disk. Generally speaking DOS will set a default of 15 buffers unless you set a `BUFFERS=NN` line in your CONFIG.SYS file. If you are using a disk-caching program such as SMARTDRV.EXE, or some other advanced buffering program that is found in other utilities such as PC Tools or 386 to the MAX, you might want to reduce the number to only 2 or 3. See that program's documentation for details. SMARTDRV is included with both DOS and Windows. If you used the regular Setup program provided to install Windows, it probably added a driver for SMARTDRV automatically.

Learning More About CONFIG.SYS

The above discussion covers some of the major options involved with CONFIG.SYS settings. Your DOS manual, or the documentation that comes with a third-party memory manager, offers detailed instructions for fine-tuning these settings. Such a discussion is beyond the scope of this book, given the wide number of possible options and configurations.

T I P There are many times that you may want to disable (make inactive) one or more lines in your CONFIG.SYS file. DOS and Windows 95 allow you to do this by placing a semicolon in front of the line. When you boot the machine that line is ignored. I sometimes use two semicolons in front of lines that are only used occasionally, as a reminder to myself when fine-tuning that these aren't normally loaded.

Kicking Back with AUTOEXEC.BAT

We're also going to use WinSleuth Gold to look at your system's AUTOEXEC.BAT file. Click on the radio button (the little circle) in front of the AUTOEXEC.BAT option just above the CONFIG.SYS button (already selected). Your screen should look similar to that shown in Figure 3.8. The last thing your system does before it gives control over to you is to read and execute the commands given in the AUTOEXEC.BAT file. Just like the CONFIG.SYS file, it must be located

in the root directory of your boot drive. In other words, if you normally boot from a hard disk (drive C:) then they both should be in
the C:\ directory.

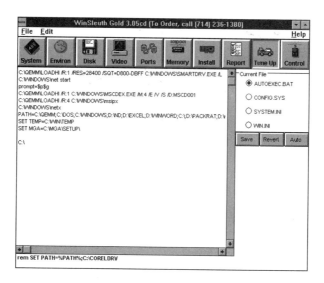

FIGURE 3.8 An AUTOEXEC.BAT file shown in WinSleuth Gold.

If you are not using WinSleuth Gold for some reason, you can see the contents
of your AUTOEXEC.BAT file just as you did CONFIG.SYS by using the DOS TYPE
command. See the note above Figure 3.7.

NOTE

There is a basic difference between AUTOEXEC.BAT and CONFIG.SYS.
CONFIG.SYS contains functions that are only adjustable as the system
is booted. If a device driver isn't loaded then, you'll have to enable the
request in the file and reboot the system. The name AUTOEXEC.BAT
comes from the fact that the contents of the file are really nothing more
than commands or programs that are automatically executed each
time the machine comes on. You can actually type any of these
names from the DOS prompt and have them operate the same way.
The extension .BAT in the filename is an abbreviation for "batch,"
indicating that these are just a batch of commands. Let's say that you

want to enter Windows every time you turn on your computer. If the last line in your AUTOEXEC.BAT file said WIN, on most systems it would automatically put you right into Windows.

Many people use this file to customize the way their machine operates. For example, one line in Figure 3.8 reads PROMPT=pg. This is DOS's code for setting up the prompt to include the current sub-directory, listed behind an angle bracket. Without this command, the machine would display nothing more than the current drive letter. You can change the prompt any time you want from the DOS command line by typing **PROMPT=** plus any specific options in your DOS manual.

Another useful function of AUTOEXEC.BAT is to set the Path. This is a listing of the drives and directories DOS will search when looking for a command file that you have requested be run, such as Windows or one of the DOS programs. If you have no Path statement, DOS will only look in the current directory or sub-directory and if it cannot find the file, will display BAD COMMAND OR FILE NAME. Keep in mind that DOS searches for programs in the order in which they are listed in the Path statement. Many programs like to include the name of their own personal sub-directory in your Path statement during their installation. This can slow down your system. It is not only that a long Path statement can tie up system resources (if only slightly), but it also results in a longer search before DOS finds the programs listed towards the end.

For more information on all possible options and commands that can be used in the AUTOEXEC.BAT file, you should consult your DOS manual. Keep in mind that many programs can modify the AUTO-EXEC.BAT during installation, not always with successful results—one of the reasons for making a Dark and Stormy Night Disk.

TURNING THE RESCUE DISK INTO A DARK AND STORMY NIGHT DISK

There's one major difference between the Rescue Disk you have already created and a Dark and Stormy Night Disk (DSND). The DSND contains all the other critical files needed to restore your system in the event that you are unable to boot it, which could happen because you accidentally erased a configuration file, there is a hardware conflict, or a less-than-perfect software installation routine. Generally speaking, you should update your DSND anytime your system configuration changes. Your rescue disk should still be in your A: drive. Use either the DOS **COPY** command or the Windows File Manager, whichever you are most comfortable with, to copy the CONFIG.SYS and the AUTOEXEC.BAT files over to the floppy.

Now create two sub-directories on the floppy disk: name one *BOOTFILE*, and the other *WIN_INI*. Into the BOOTFILE sub-directory, copy all of the device drivers or other programs referred to in your two startup files (this should just include device drivers, not any programs you load automatically from AUTOEXEC.BAT, like Windows itself). Copy to the WIN_INI sub-directory two files from your Windows directory, SYSTEM.INI and WIN.INI.

NOTE   WinSleuth Gold has an upgraded version of the software you used to create the rescue disk. Among its improved features is the ability to automatically create a Dark and Stormy Night Disk from a blank floppy diskette.

Once you have all the files copied, put a write-protect tab on the disk and store it in a safe place.

The Dark and Stormy Night Disk can help you restore files that may have been damaged as well as rehabilitate a corrupted Setup; but it won't quite have everything you need to carry out major restorations or rebuild a totally-failed hard drive. For this you should have a recovery disk available. This should include the following files, most of which can be found in the directory where you loaded DOS.

✔ **CHKDSK.EXE** This file lets you check the integrity of your disk and its file structure.

✔ **DEBUG.EXE** Needed to access the BIOS routine for your hard disk controller or your SCSI host adapter.

✔ **FDISK.EXE** Which is used to inspect and, if necessary, restore hard disk partitions. For more on this command and hard disk operations see Chapter 9.

✔ **FORMAT.COM** Which is used to place a format on a disk.

✔ **SYS.COM** Which is used to produce a bootable disk.

✔ **ASQ.EXE** Which is contained on the disk which came in the back of this book.

✔ **EDIT.COM** Or another simple DOS text editor that can be used to modify your configuration files.

WARNING

This disk should also be write-protected and kept in a safe place. Before you put the two of them away, try booting your system from the Dark and Stormy Night Disk and make sure that your system comes up properly. If not, make sure that the disk has the proper content and was properly formatted.

CREATING RESCUE DISKS UNDER WINDOWS 95 AND WINDOWS NT

The newer 32-bit versions of Windows come with built in tools for creating a rescue disk. The basic procedures are the same for both, but accessed a little differently—and the results are not equal. Let's start with Win95, then cover NT. You only need to read the part that deals with the operating system you use.

The Windows 95 Startup (Rescue) Disk

Windows 95 can automatically create a Startup Disk, which can be used to boot the system, make repairs, and in some cases uninstall a damaged installation of the operating system. Open the Control Panel, then choose the **Add/Remove Programs** option. (This was not one of the developers' better choices for placing this function— not very intuitive). Select the **Startup Disk** tab at the top of the window, as shown in Figure 3.9 below. Then insert a blank disk into your primary floppy drive and choose the option to create the disk.

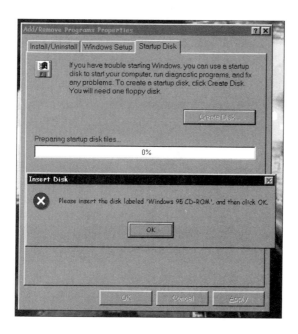

FIGURE 3.9 Telling Windows 95 to create a Startup disk.

While Windows is creating the disk, let's talk about its contents and short-comings. The good news: it will boot your system and let you make basic repairs. The preceding figure shows the files; along with those used to boot a PC are the CHKDSK and SCANDISK programs; (more about them next) for testing your hard drive, and the Win95 Registry Editor.

WARNING

Use care with the Registry Editor. This is a power tool that can be used—*WITH GREAT CARE*—to adjust the settings and drivers of your Windows installation in the event of trouble. If you do not know what a Registry Entry does, and how to change it, don't play with it. The Registry is critical to your system's operation. Some listings will modify how a program runs, others will keep your machine from working properly.

While the generated Startup Disk is a good beginning, I add a few files to mine. First is a basic text editor, like DOS Edit. Personally I use Norton Commander, which has not only an editor, but a file system utility as well. Then I add any DOS-level drivers to get on my network, and copies of any critical drivers that the operating system will need to function—especially those to recognize the CD-ROM drive. For EISA systems I add the CF configuration utility as well. These files can be a major help if the regular Windows installation won't boot.

You should update the rescue disk and the supplemental files you keep at hand any time you change the system components. It is also a good idea to keep a record of any network or Internet settings, IDs, and passwords in a safe place on paper. Be sure to place them in a secure location. If they are near the computer where anyone can find them, the safeguards they offer are wasted.

THE WINDOWS NT RESCUE DISK

The Windows NT rescue disk is designed simply to assist in the repair of a damaged existing installation of the operating system. Just like the Windows 95 routine, this utility will format the disk and copy files. Unlike it you can not use it to boot the system. Even so, it is a critical component of system care. I use this disk in conjunction with a DOS DSND, a DOS/NT dual-boot system, and a good set of backups (For more information on this see the preceding chapter). If your NT system is corrupted, the Rescue Disk can be used with the Windows NT Setup program to repair or replace the damaged files and restore the user accounts and most of your custom settings. For more information see your Windows NT manual.

For some reason the Microsoft team did not make the RDISK program a standard icon in the ADMIN group, but you can add it. Just open the group, then choose **Add** from the File menu. Browse into the System32 subdirectory of your NT directory. Then select the **RDISK.EXE** file. The icon looks like a doctor listening with his head cocked to one side. You should run this program when prompted during inital Setup, and rerun it any time you change the system configuration.

PERIODIC DISK MAINTENANCE

Your hard disk is a very busy piece of equipment which relies on a combination of magnetic, electronic, electrical, and mechanical parts to do its job. This component probably gets more wear and tear than any other piece of equipment in your machine. It also stores your most valuable computer asset: your data and the programs which access it. If you keep good backups as discussed in Chapter 15, you do have protection in case your hard disk fails totally (known as a *crash*) or if your data becomes corrupted.

Not all data loss is due to catastrophic events, such as the motor inside your hard disk failing. The way the data is organized on your hard disk and how well it is maintained has a lot to do with your system's performance and how trouble-free its operation is. Corrupted files can slowly eat away hard disk space, program files, and can cause erratic operation. Some filing systems are more elegant than others. MS-DOS's is a bit on the messy side. Over time, files become stored in a haphazard manner, reducing system performance. Keeping an eye on your file system and periodically tidying it up can go a long way towards making the computing part of your life more comfortable. A bit of preventive maintenance can go a long way towards keeping your hard disk healthy and running right.

The Scandisk and CHKDSK Commands— Undervalued and Often Overlooked

MS-DOS and most other operating systems provide some form of program to verify the integrity of your disks and their filing system. In DOS there are two such programs, SCANDISK and CHKDSK.EXE. Many uninformed users never run these programs. Well-informed, finicky users run at least CHKDSK every time the machine is turned on—and that isn't a bad habit to get into. This utility performs an inspection to make sure that all the directories are readable, the disk's File Allocation Table is valid, that there are no cross-linked files, and it also searches for any improperly—stored data on the drive. You should run CHKDSK frequently, and run it any time your machine locks up on you. If several files are open and the machine is shut down unexpectedly, those files can become damaged. While CHKD-SK can't fix everything on your hard disk, its regular use can minimize the risk of data loss. SCANDISK is more thorough, and you should run it at least once a week, more if you use your system a lot.

To run it under DOS, its file must be in your Path or you must be logged onto the directory where it is stored. Why don't you try it now? At the DOS prompt, type **CHKDSK** and hit **Return**. Under Windows 95 and Windows NT use SCANDISK on a regular basis. Figure 3.10, below, shows the dialog boxes for the Windows 95 version.

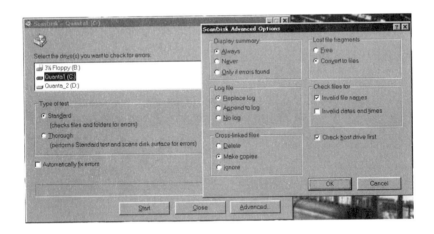

FIGURE 3.10 The Windows 95 Scandisk dialog boxes.

Do not run the CHKDSK program if you are in Windows 3.11! Doing so can result in loss of data! Exit Windows first and run it under plain DOS.

WARNING

These programs test the health of your current hard disk partition. If you want to check a different hard disk partition, you need to specify the drive you want to check. For SCANDISK under Windows use the dialog box. For CHKDSK specify the drive letter after the command itself. For example, CHKDSK D:.

You should see a report on your screen similar to the one shown in Figure 3.11 after running CHKDSK. The exact results will vary based on the size of your hard disk, the way it's organized, and what problems there might be with your file system. The first line shows the *volume label* (if there is one) that was given to the disk when it was formatted, followed by the time and date that the last format occurred. Beneath that is the *disk serial number*. This is the number assigned by DOS during the format. The next two lines in the report note that there were errors found and that the /F parameter was not specified. It is a warning that the program will not correct the errors it found.

```
Volume CONNER_1     created 05-14-1993 1:29p
Volume Serial Number is 1AC5-5BA5
Errors found, F parameter not specified
Corrections will not be written to disk

     1 lost allocation units found in 1 chains.
        8192 bytes disk space would be freed

 272457728 bytes total disk space
  63119360 bytes in 9 hidden files
   1597440 bytes in 195 directories
 121397248 bytes in 2766 user files
  86335488 bytes available on disk

      8192 bytes in each allocation unit
     33259 total allocation units on disk
     10539 available allocation units on disk

    655360 total bytes memory
    541888 bytes free
```

FIGURE 3.11 The CHKDSK report screen.

The reason I got this message is that I did not use the /F switch. If you do not enable the /F parameter (as it is called), CHKDSK only goes out and looks at the file system, it doesn't fix the errors it finds. Early versions of DOS did not issue this warning. If you forgot to put in the /F parameter, then DOS would blissfully appear as if it fixed problems when it hadn't. The next two lines show that there was an error found, and that there were fragments of a file left on the disk that were not reported as being a part of any specific file. If you specify the /F switch when you run CHKDSK, you will be asked if you want to fix errors like this. If you do, the data fragments will be stored in a file in your root directory which you can then examine and deal with. In the example up above, roughly eight kilobytes of space could be freed on the system by eliminating this file fragment.

CHKDSK also reports the total amount of storage space on the disk, how it is used, and how much is still available. Keep in mind that if you have broken up your disk into several *partitions* (divisions), CHKDSK is only reporting on one partition, not the total space located on the drive. The final part of the report gives a very simple run-down of the amount of RAM on the system and how much is available for program use. Computer scientists have funny ways of counting because their system is based on binary numbers. The 655360 bytes of memory reported above are equal to 640K because one kilobyte is equal to 1024 bytes. CHKDSK only reports the presence of memory in the first 640K; if you have memory above that, it is ignored.

Based on the version of DOS you are using, there are several other possible error messages or status reports, such as lost clusters, errors in the File Allocation Table, or problems with directories. For more information on CHKDSK and its possible messages, you should check your operating system User Guide. Keep in mind that the present book is a general guide. Be sure to study the manual for your own specific operating environment before using any command that will significantly alter your hard drive—like CHKDSK.

One handy way to run CHKDSK automatically is to add it as the last line in your AUTOEXEC.BAT file. If you do this, you should add the /F switch and make a separate entry with the appropriate drive letter for each hard disk partition on your system. Scandisk provides a similar report as shown in Figure 3.12, captured under Windows 95. The difference between the two programs is not in the reports they issue, but in the completeness of the tests and the amount of options you can set. CHKDSK is quick and easy, SCANDISK is a bit longer and more complete.

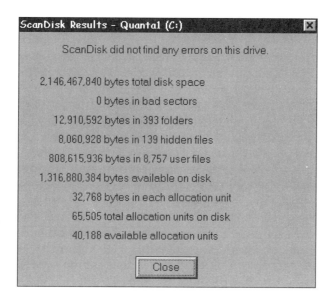

FIGURE 3.12 The Scandisk report.

File Management

A very subtle way you can improve your system's performance and reduce the risk of data loss is by practicing good housekeeping. In the everyday world, clutter leads to disorganization and the risk that something valuable will be lost or broken due to the untidy environment. Your hard disk is a virtual (i.e., electronic) warehouse that has the ability to store vast amounts of data. If that data isn't organized well, it will be more difficult for your operating system to retrieve and manage and easier for you to lose track of files or to accidentally erase them. Let's start with the lowest common denominator. The next few paragraphs focus on DOS file conventions. I'll get to the options with the longer 32-bit names next.

Keep It Consistent

DOS allows a maximum of eight letters for a file name and an optional three-letter extension, separated from the name by a period. While there are few absolute requirements as to how names must be given under DOS, the more consistent you are, the easier it will be to organize your data. In general, you should try to establish a regular system for naming files. With only eight letters for the name itself, you sometimes have to use creative abbreviations. If these are random choices, it can be almost impossible to know exactly what a file relates to; if you use someone's initials but sometimes leave out the middle initial and sometimes leave it in, you can't use a single search of the directory to pull up just those files. For example, my initials are JTK. If I sometimes named files JK and at other times JTK, plus the other available letters up to the maximum of eight, the search **JTK*.*** would not reveal the files that started with JK. If you use a combination that includes numbers to show revisions, it's a good habit to put a zero in front of numbers less than ten; otherwise, your second file will show up behind your 19th because of the way the operating system will sort them.

Be Conventional

The naming extension is one of the most powerful tools DOS has for naming files. The operating system recognizes several conventions: program files always carry one of two extensions, .EXE (executable) or .COM (command); batch files always carry the extension .BAT. Over time conventions have crept in for other file types as well; for instance, text files often carry a .TXT extension, or, optionally, .ASC for ASCII, indicating that it uses a standard text character set. Binary file names are usually followed by the extension .BIN. Many programs automatically assign an extension to their data files to make them easier to find. For example, Microsoft Word uses the .DOC extension for document; Ventura Publisher uses .CHP for chapter; and Excel uses .XLS for the spreadsheet.

You can take advantage of the extension's power by always using the same self-defined extension for a given class of files. I often use the .RPT extension for reports. The real key is not what you name the extension, but that you be consistent. If you have several revisions of a document, you can use the extension to indicate the revision number or the month it was created. For example, MRPT.MAY could be the monthly report for May.

Really Long Names: Win 95 and Windows NT

One of the advantages of the newer 32-bit operating systems is their ability to handle longer file names. In both Windows 95 and Windows NT, you can use up to 256 character—including spaces—for file names. That lets you use titles that have meaning, rather than just abbreviations. But there are some other considerations that might lead you to still practice some of the skills learned from the days of 8.3 naming conventions.

File Extensions

Keep in mind that many programs will continue to make use of the file extension to identify the type of file, and so should you. Is that file titled *My May Expense Report* a Word for Windows document or a spreadsheet? If you still use the .DOC or .XLS extension both you and the program will know.

Backwards Compatibility

If you plan to share files between 32-bit and older operating systems (like DOS and Windows for Workgroups) or programs designed for those environments, keep in mind that the longer names will not come across. They will be shortened, and if needed, the two last characters will be swapped out for a ~number combination. So all those names that start out with *My Letter to x* will become *mylett~1*. That can be a real pain when you want to locate a file. I still use a DOS-compatible start to a name, then add the other information after a space. That works better.

Organize Your Directories

Directories are much like folders in a filing cabinet; they let you divide up the system so that documents and programs are easy to find. If you set up your sub-directory system wisely, you can save yourself a lot of work, making it easier to find things and back up important files. DOS will let you nest sub-directories under sub-directories. Try to avoid nesting them too deeply; the further you have to go down the tree, the longer it takes to retrieve a file. This same advice holds true for Windows 95, which uses File Folders and sub-directories interchangeably—depending on the file viewer you use.

Keep The Root Directory Clean

One good habit is to minimize the number of files that are kept in your root directory. When I'm feeling very compulsive about this I often have nothing more in my root directory than my AUTO-EXEC.BAT and CONFIG.SYS files. COMMAND.COM is in the \DOS directory. I keep drivers in a sub-directory called *BOOTFILE* and all my own personal data in sub-directories off a main sub-directory titled *DATA*. Each program gets its own sub-directory with an appropriate title.

The advantage of this system is that it becomes very easy to locate a program, and any changes by a new program to the root directory. It also prevents a new program from overwriting existing drivers as it goes through its installation routine. For example, some graphics programs might load a scanner driver, overwriting an existing device driver just because they assume they need to do it. Some older DOS graphics programs come with their own mouse programs, which could overwrite the one you need to run Windows. By placing your boot files in their own sub-directory rather than the root directory, you prevent them from being overwritten. Then you can decide which one you want to keep.

Having a separate sub-directory for data files makes it easier to do regular backups. All you have to do to archive copies of your working files is back up that sub-directory. Since you have your program files on disk, you could even get by with only backing up the data directories, since your boot files and programs would already be available either in the boxes that contained the programs or on your Dark and Stormy Night Disk.

Protecting Files with the ATTRIBUTE Command

Most operating systems, including DOS and the newer versions of Windows, have some type of ATTRIBUTE command. This allows you to mark a file as *read-only*, which means that it can't be erased; as *hidden*, which means that it doesn't show up when a directory is scanned with the DIR command; and as *archive*, which indicates if it's been modified since the last time it was backed up. You can use the DOS ATTRIBUTE command, the Windows File Manager or some other utility to modify the ATTRIBUTE setting of your file. Setting a file to read-only makes it safe from accidental erasure. However, the drawback is that you can't go in and modify it unless you make a copy or reset the ATTRIBUTE.

Tidying Up

Depending on how much you use your system, you should periodically go through and tidy up your file system. You should start with a backup to make sure that you have copies of valuable files. I like to keep one total backup of the entire disk just in case something happens. By keeping regular backups, I can restore a totally erased disk in just a few minutes. Then I regularly back up files that have changed, and usually keep duplicate backups of very important files, like the manuscript of this book (backup options are discussed more fully in Chapter 15).

Once I've completed my backup, I go through and locate files that I won't be using regularly and search out copies of programs that I don't really need. Then I erase those files and their sub-directories. That frees up room on my hard disk. Once that's done, I can get down to the serious business of overcoming one of DOS's real performance-robbers.

Defragmenting Your Hard Disk

Imagine a very poorly-organized file system; one where parts of files, individual pages out of letters and parts of reports were scattered within different folders within a cabinet. Retrieving files in such an environment would not be nearly as efficient as in a well-organized system where everything was stored nicely and neatly in its proper place. DOS, unfortunately, is more disorganized than organized when placing files on a disk. Every time you Copy, Move or Rename a file, DOS moves it in pieces known as *clusters*. These clusters are managed by the *File Allocation Table* (FAT).

What happens is this: the FAT keeps a record of where space is available on the disk. When you manipulate a file, DOS searches for the first available space on the hard disk and starts storing the file. It doesn't look for an area large enough to contain the entire file; it just fills the first space and then looks on for another space. When you start with a newly-formatted disk and load programs on it, things stay fairly tidy. But over time, things get moved around more and more. As they do, it takes longer and longer to load files or run programs.

Early on in the PC game, several vendors such as Paul Mace (with Mace Utilities) and Peter Norton (the Norton Utilities), started marketing sets of programs aimed at maintaining a healthy PC. Many people bought these programs for the defragmenting program that was part of the package. A *defragmenter* is a routine that goes through your disk and reorganizes it. Most also go through and do a basic check of the hard disk, looking for bad clusters, and offering you several ways of relocating files for optimal performance. MS-DOS 6.0 includes a defragmenting routine licensed from Symantec, the people that sell Norton Utilities. This is not quite as full-featured as the stand-alone version, and if you are a power user or someone who does not have DOS 6.0, you'll probably want to pick up a copy of one of the third-party hard disk utilities, not only for the defragmenter, but for some of the other diagnostic tools they offer.

Running a defragmenter can take anywhere from a minute or two up to several hours, depending on the options you choose, the type of hard disk you are working with, and its size. Due to the variety in the types of programs available, I won't go into any great detail about their operation. If you have a very busy system, you should run a defragmenting routine at least once a week or any time you notice things starting to slow down a bit. The average home system can probably get by with running one every month or so.

WARNING

Defragmenters run some pretty exotic dance steps while waltzing your files around the floor of your disk drive. The first time you use a defragmenter on a given system, you should make sure that you have good backups of your data, and try working a small sample area first. While rare, there are cases when running one of these programs can muddle your data or corrupt the FAT (File Allocation Table). If this happens you may lose all the data on the disk. You should repeat such tests any time you replace any component of your hard disk system. You should also be careful when running such programs with advanced memory management software, such as Qualtas' 386 to the MAX or Quarterdeck's QEMM. Most of the modern disk defragmenters are very stable but there are a lot of variations in systems. Advanced caching controllers, software caches, and disk compression routines, such as Stacker or DOS's DoubleSpace, may not be totally compatible. Don't let this warning scare you from using a defragmenter. Such problems are rare; and once you know that a program works with your given configuration, you should be all right. The potential benefits well outweigh all of the risks.

Watch out for older versions of disk defragmenters (like the one that comes with older copies of DOS and Norton Utilities) and the new long file names available with 32-bit operating systems. They are not designed to work with them, and will truncate the names to 8 characters. Be sure to use only 32-bit versions that are compatible with the new names—like the Disk Defragmenter program that is bundled with Windows 95.

N O T E

I considered including a shareware defragmenter with this book. However, I felt that most shareware programmers did not have the resources to properly test all the different combinations of systems to ensure reasonably trouble-free operation given the wide variety of hard disks, controllers, memory management, and compression schemes available. For that reason, I feel safer sticking with well-known products from the big-name software houses when it comes to this class of software. My personal favorite is Norton's Speed Disk. PC Kwik has another good product. If there is a Users' Group in your area you might want to ask members to demonstrate their favorites before making a purchase.

HARD DISK DIAGNOSTICS

Along with defragmenters, most disk utility programs come with a variety of handy programs for keeping your system running smoothly. In this category are the disk diagnostics such as Norton's Disk Doctor. I run this program every month or so to make sure that my hard disk is performing properly (after first running CHKDSK). Make sure that the program you use is compatible with the operating system in use. Don't try to run a program that is not designed for the type of file system on your disk. Check out the manual for the software first.

The hard disk places data on magnetic media similar to that found on recording tape. Over time, this material starts to wear out. As it does, it becomes harder and harder for DOS to recover the files written on the weaker portions of the disk. Norton's Disk Doctor will go through and test the integrity of the recording surface, moving files out of areas that are becoming weak and marking them so that they can't be used in the future. Over a long period of time, the low-level format on your hard disk will drift. There are also programs available to restore the low-level format without removing data from your disk. Be careful when shopping however, because not all the low-level formatting utilities will work with all types of drives.

VIRUSES—THE PRODUCTS OF SICK MINDS

Some people have a strange sense of humor. They feel that they have to show everybody how smart they are by playing practical jokes. I've never understood the term "practical" joke. What can be practical about something that either embarrasses or harms another person in the name of humor? One day a sick mind came up with the idea of embedding programs within other programs that would do annoying or even damaging things to someone else's computer. A certain demented segment of our technical population decided that this would be a great challenge and jumped on the bandwagon.

This type of computer routine is commonly referred to as a *virus*, because it usually infects another program and then makes the computer behave as if it were sick. Some do nothing; others flash "happy birthday" messages or periodically post scatological lines on your monitor. The nastiest are the ones that actually go out and destroy data, often with some gleeful note proclaiming the intellectual prowess of the cretin that wrote it.

Computer viruses are usually embedded in another program, and passed from user to user either on infected floppy disks or through electronic bulletin boards. When they get onto a system, most attempt to replicate so that any floppy disk or transferred file carries the infection off to another site. A whole industry has sprung up providing software to search out and neutralize these viruses. One of the best of these programs is F-Prot from Command Software. A shareware edition of the search program S-Prot is included on the disc that is attached to the back of this book (if you use it on a regular basis you should register the program). It can identify almost 3,000 viruses. The company sells a full-featured combination program that will also eradicate viruses. I use two versions of their program: one that works on regular stand-alone PCs, and another that protects my network servers. I have also included another well-regarded anti-virus program called Integrity Master.

A virus can strike anyone. There have even been reports of viruses that made it all the way through quality control provided by some of the manufacturers of leading CD-ROMs. The people who create viruses are constantly searching for new ways to bypass security technology. If you only use shrink-wrapped software from major vendors, your risk of exposure is slight, but not non-existent. A few years ago, one of the major software houses in this country had a disgruntled employee who, on the way out, managed to plant a virus that got onto one of the production disks that shipped with their program.

Levels of Protection

If you work on a stand-alone PC, you can run virus software in the background that will constantly check all new files that are brought onto your hard disk or any floppies that are placed on your system, and warn you if it detects a virus. This requires some system overhead and usually lengthens the boot process because every time you turn on your computer, it will scan your system for the presence of a virus. This may be a bit annoying, but it does almost eliminate the risk of having a virus get on your system.

Another option is to periodically run a virus checker to see if your system is infected. A third method is to have some form of protection located on a network and store any important files on the network where they can be checked for viruses.

Once a virus has been detected, you have to eliminate or neutralize it. Most anti-virus programs contain both a "sniffer," the part that goes looking for viruses, and a set of inoculation routines targeted to eliminate specific viruses. At the present time there are about 3,000 known virus strains. The more advanced programs can neutralize almost all of these. There are some viruses with no known remedy.

NOTE

Virus protection programs have to be used before the virus does its real work. The majority of viruses do not cause instantaneous destruction but slowly work their way through your system and gain time to replicate and infect other computers. If you catch a virus during this period, and it can be corrected, no real harm is done. If it's a damaging virus and there is no remedy, you may have to just put yourself into the market for data recovery or a new hard disk. If you wait until the virus is done, i.e. it has destroyed your hard disk or whatever, it's usually too late to do anything but rebuild your file system. Every time you get a disk or file from an outside source, either a software vendor, a friend, or a remote service contacted by modem, it's a good idea to run an anti-virus scan. If you don't already have a virus checker on your system I suggest that you start using one. Try the S-Prot program included on the disk in the back of this book. It is a self-extracting file; just load it in its own directory and type the name **S-PROT**. The files will be unpacked and there is full documentation with it. The program is very easy to use, and created by one of the best people in the computer security business. This vendor, Command Software of Jupiter, FL make a line of such products—including ones that run over networks.

Every Once in a While Kick the Tires and Check the Gauges

Keeping a computer healthy is a bit like keeping a small child, or a horse, healthy; it's a matter of observation. As you become more familiar with your computer, you become aware of its idiosyncrasies and the way it should be operating. If it seems sluggish, or starts behaving erratically, something is wrong. In some cases, all you have to do is defragment your hard disk or run CHKDSK. I've seen people that complained that their system was far too slow but had accidentally stepped down the CPU, dramatically degrading system performance. It's also not uncommon to find a program slowing down after installing something new on your system, either hardware or software. Your PC is actually a collection of sub-systems which form a complicated environment. If a program changes your configuration files to its liking, it may shift them in a way that's harmful to some other application. When that happens, you have to find a compromise, or slightly modify your system, before running the programs.

The thing to keep in mind is that you must be aware of how your system operates and how it should be behaving. If it starts acting funny, or seems to be a "bit off," it's a good idea to take the time to try to find out what's wrong. It's a lot better to be observant and fix a problem early, than wait until you lose data or damage a component by failing to take appropriate corrective action.

CHAPTER SUMMARY

The personal computer is a marvelous device. Properly set up it will almost take care of itself; but you must provide it with an appropriate environment, keep good backups, and take the time to perform some minor preventive maintenance. Following the steps outlined in this chapter should go a long way towards keeping your PC running smoothly and keep you a happy user.

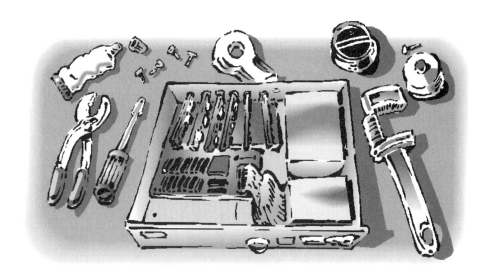

CHAPTER 4

BECOMING A POWER USER

WHAT'S IN THIS CHAPTER

- ✔ Using the IPO Model
- ✔ Boosting System Performance
- ✔ Reducing Bottlenecks
- ✔ Utilities and Diagnostic Software
- ✔ Memory Management
- ✔ Testing Your System
- ✔ Troubleshooting Techniques

WHAT THIS CHAPTER IS ABOUT

This chapter focuses on getting the most performance from your system and knowing how to optimize use of your computer's resources. Since the primary focus of this book is on hardware, this chapter serves only as an introduction to the different software tools and techniques used to improve system performance and reduce maintenance problems. When we start to work on a PC's performance, it's wise to know how to recover from problems. This chapter provides a basic education in memory management, software troubleshooting, and how to test your system's operation.

AS MUCH AN ART AS A SCIENCE

The Federal Government has a large book named the *Dictionary of Occupational Titles*. It defines the job descriptions, required training and range of pay for virtually every job you can think of. Search the pages and you will find all kinds of exotic occupations—including a large number relating to computers—but you won't find any description of the elusive *PC power user*.

Being a power user is not an occupation as much as a state of mind. The goal of the power user is to tweak as much performance out of his or her hardware and software as possible, until the machine is running the way he/she wants it to. But this is an elusive goal, in part because each user's needs are different. Some people need exceptional graphics performance, others need fast telecommunications, while others want to be able to find things in a hurry. As a result, there is no way to define the perfect PC because everyone's idea of it is different. Getting your machine tuned exactly right is more an art than a science.

Another problem with defining a power user is in the "skill set" needed. Some very obvious power users know absolutely nothing about programs, and know nothing about the intricacies of electronics, yet they are as able to keep their machines humming smoothly as any engineer or mathematician. My definition of a power user is "someone who can get their PC to do what they want it to do." The skills for that job involve being able to determine what part of your system needs to be adjusted or upgraded to meet your needs, and in knowing how to effect those changes.

One of the main goals of this book is to enable anyone to become a power user. The preceding chapters dealt with the fundamentals of how to keep your machine healthy. *This chapter is a preface for everything which comes after it.* If there was a doctor in the world who knew everything there was to know about therapeutics but knew nothing about diagnostics, that physician would be hard put to effect any form of cure. Physicians use a model for understanding how health and disease operate; power users have a similar model for assessing their needs and their PC's performance. The basis of this model revolves around the flow of data into the computer and the information they get out of it, along with the ability to recognize bottlenecks that hamper system performance.

The IPO Model

Everything related to your computer can be described in relation to three phrases: *input*, *process*, and *output* (*IPO*). These three functions are the core of all computer operations. Data has to go into the machine, be manipulated by it, and a result obtained. If you understand, even in the broadest terms how this works, you can apply it to anything involving your computer.

We can treat the computer as a black box. *Black box* is a term we use for something that carries on an operation but we don't have to know how. All we have to know is what goes in and what we expect to come out. For our PC to work properly, we have to give it good input, it has to have the capability of handling the request and processing the data, and it has to have the appropriate devices to produce the desired output.

If we have a program that requires a mouse for input and we don't have a mouse, we might be able to work around it some way but we certainly won't be as efficient. If we don't have enough memory or the right kind of software to perform the operations we want our computer to do, the machine won't be able to process our request. And if we're expecting color output from a black and white printer, we'll be disappointed. What this shows us is that the computer must have the proper combination of input, process, and output to perform a task. Keeping the IPO model running smoothly is the key to being a power user. Let's look at its most simple level, the system requirements.

UNDERSTANDING SYSTEM REQUIREMENTS AND SYSTEM RESOURCES

When you buy or build a machine, it's an open-ended affair; you can end up with a device that has the least amount of memory and the slowest CPU your motherboard will support, or you can go all the way and fill it with every imaginable extra. The only limiting factor seems to be money. When it comes to *using* a computer, however, we have to consider the needs of the software we're going to use. When a developer designs a program, she starts with a set of features that are to be included in the final product. In doing so, she must make assumptions about what kind of hardware and software *resources* or capabilities are needed to run that software effectively. A simple word processor may work well on a 286 with a megabyte of memory and a small hard disk; an AUTOCAD workstation may require 16Mb of memory, a 486 or a Pentium, and a large hard drive. Vendors post minimum (and sometimes recommended) system requirements on their literature and on the outside of the software's box. They usually read something like this:

System requirements: 486 or better PC, 8Mb of RAM (16Mb recommended), Windows 95 or Windows NT, mouse, PostScript printer.

What It All Means

The above requirements could be listed for one of several reasons; in many cases the minimum system requirements show the actual minimum hardware and software resources needed to run a program at all. The sample above shows a given version of Windows. These are almost always absolutes; the program needs certain capabilities of that operating environment to work at all. If you attempt to get by this and use an older version of Windows, the software may well not even load; or if it does come up on the screen, it will not behave properly.

The stated memory values are also often needed to get everything up and running. If there is a statement that something is recommended above the initial requirement, such as the added RAM stated above, it means that the vendor feels that although the program will run with less memory, it needs the extra resources to provide reasonable performance.

If you are planning on using your system for certain types of activity, it's a good idea to examine the types of software you plan on using to get an idea of the system resources you'll need, and to provide a platform to allow some extra room for growth.

Using the IPO Model to Get the Most from Your System

System requirements are only part of the picture. They provide the software developer's opinion of what you need to successfully use the program. The type and volume of work you do on an everyday basis also has a part to play in defining the right level of system resources for you.

For an example, let's look at scanning; scanners are neat tools that let us convert text and graphics on paper into a form that can be used inside the computer. We can scan the company logo or an official signature for use in documents. We can input pictures and incorporate them in newsletters and reports. Scanners allow us to manipulate images much as if we had a darkroom inside our computer; and *optical character recognition (OCR)* software will allow us to convert words on paper into editable text in a word processor. The minimum requirements for a scanner and its software might be something like: one free expansion slot, 4Mb of memory, Microsoft Windows, and 10Mb of free hard disk space.

If all we ever did with our scanner was bring in an occasional graphic, or convert three or four pages of text, those system resources might be adequate. But a full-page color photograph, scanned in so that most of its detail is preserved, can easily consume over 100Mb of hard disk space. On an ancient 386 or slow 486 computer with an average-performance hard drive, just scanning in the image can tax the system and leave the Windows hourglass on the screen long enough to go eat lunch, a leisurely lunch.

In other words, if you're planning on building a high performance graphics system, you'll need a fast CPU, a large capacity, high-performance hard disk, and a high-resolution monitor. If all you ever scan are small black and white images, you could handle the workload easily with a 486 and a 350Mb hard drive. The system could technically handle the process involved; but for high volume, the under-powered system would choke on the input. Scanning is a very intensive operation. It can produce bottlenecks in a couple of places; OCR can be very processor-intensive and the size of the files requires a lot of hard disk storage and disk activity. It's a good example of where system resources must be matched to the work.

If your computer isn't doing everything you want it to, the IPO model can be used to see where things are getting stuck, then see what has to be adjusted to get things moving smoothly. If you started out with small amounts of scanning and the scope of that kind of work started increasing, you might look at adding a fast hard disk and a more powerful CPU. While this might add $1,000 to the cost of your system, it would save a significant amount of time and the extra expense might be worth it. On the other hand, if scanning operations only occasionally taxed your system resources, you might very well want to spend the money on something else like more memory, a CD-ROM drive, or a backup system.

The perfect PC is the system that works best for you, one that performs the tasks you ask of it in a reasonable time. Evaluating your needs is not a one-time occurrence; it seems as soon as you get one part of your system running exactly the way you want it, some other component overloads. This is what keeps power users happily tinkering. It seems we're always looking for the elusive bottleneck.

The Once and Future Bottleneck

There's an old adage (old in PC terms anyway) that you can never have too much speed, too much memory, or too much hard disk space. While today's PC offers incredible increases in processing power, storage space, and graphics performance over the earliest personal computers, it never seems to be enough. The reason is very simple; as better resources become available, developers find ways to take advantage of them and offer more features. As better software becomes available, users start demanding more of their systems. As they do this, one or another subsystem soon becomes a performance bottleneck.

As our ability to handle graphics and on-screen colors got better, file sizes got bigger and the speed of the hard disk became a critical factor in how long it took to load a program or a large file. With the advent of Windows, and the increasing use of color on the desktop, the display system became the limiting factor and vendors brought to market high-performance adapters running ten to twenty times as fast as earlier models. The result: more people start working with color and they start filling up their hard disks.

This leapfrogging of one technology pushing the envelope on another is part of why vendors are constantly coming out with new products in an attempt to offer better performance and, of course, garner sales. The trick for the user is knowing where to spend his/her money. We're constantly presented with new toys that promise more productivity and better performance; which ones are worth buying? We want something that will really meet our needs, provide benefits, and not leave us in a situation where in six months our latest gadget will just have to be replaced with something else.

It is not always a matter of going out and buying new equipment; in some cases it's simply a matter of fine-tuning or adjusting the stuff we've already got. One of the skills in the art of power usage is paying attention to your system.

How Far Do You Have to Go?

A personal computer is an open-ended device. Improving performance or adding features can be as complicated as replacing the motherboard or as easy as changing a number in your Control Panel settings or on a line in your CONFIG.SYS file. In most cases, it lies somewhere in-between. When talking about upgrading a system, many people think about changing out a CPU or buying a whole new computer. But often this isn't necessary.

As with most topics dealing with computers, the trick is to handle things in an organized manner, taking things one step at a time. In fact, the technical term for this approach is called *stepwise procedures*. In some cases, the answer is obvious; you need more memory to run a program, or more space on your hard disk. But often, things are more subtle and several options, usually with different price tags, are available. The following list looks at the different sub-systems of your computer and offers possible areas of improvement. This should help give you an idea of the range of options available and serve as a starting point for your own research.

Hardware or Software

One of the first evaluations is to decide whether you have a hardware or a software problem (or opportunity, depending on how you look at it). Do you need more performance, or do you need additional features? In other words, do you want to add the ability to do desktop publishing or add fancy graphics? Do you want your database to sort faster, or do you want the ability to access more data? If it's straight features, sometimes the answer is in a new program. That program may demand extra resources or a peripheral, such as a CD-ROM drive, which may not currently be on your system. If that's the case, your solution may involve both hardware and software.

Look Around the Motherboard

Your system's motherboard, and the hardware located on it, comprise the majority of your system's hardware resources. If primary components, such as the CPU, are more than two years old, advancing technology is offering faster processors and expansion cards giving better performance. In that case, any one of a number of improvements may offer real productivity benefits.

The Microprocessor

Every 18 to 24 months, Intel and its competitors produce new Central Processing Units, offering anywhere from 50% to 100% more power than the previous model. Clock-doubling CPUs can often be inserted directly into your current processing socket in just a few minutes and require no other modifications to your system. Total cost of the swap-out will probably only be a few hundred dollars. That's quite a bit less than buying an entire new system. The latest and greatest hot microprocessor can sometimes amount to half of the price of a new system. Waiting six to eight months to upgrade to the latest and greatest is usually a wise approach. It gives time for any bugs in the design to be ferreted out and fixed, and for production levels to stabilize. At that point, prices usually drop significantly. If you are looking for a second system, you may want to consider an older processor with a somewhat more modern motherboard, which can often result in significant savings (see Chapter 6).

The Motherboard

New expansion-bus architectures, like the now-standard PCI local bus, can dramatically boost video display performance. A new motherboard may be necessary to take advantage of a faster microprocessor or to increase the amount of RAM available for software if you are running out of room. Generally speaking, you'll want to buy a motherboard and a processor together; in fact, with the newest processors, this is almost the only way to get one, matched with an appropriate motherboard. A well-tuned motherboard can add 20% or more to performance over a less well-engineered model (see Chapter 6).

Adding More Memory

If you are using Windows 95 or another advanced operating system, and have only the recommended amount of RAM, a couple of hundred dollars can quite often improve performance by adding a few more megabytes of memory. If you are still using DOS and not using an advanced memory manager such as the ones described later in this chapter, you're probably not getting full use of the RAM already on your system. In that case, a $70 investment may provide a significant performance boost (discussed later in this chapter).

Adding More Cache

Cache memory can be used to speed up CPU function. Most Pentium motherboards can seat between 8Kb to 512Kb of cache for less than $100. Most systems should have at least 128Kb of cache and if you are doing serious graphics or using the machine for networking, you should probably fill the machine up all the way, to either 256 or 512Kb. This is an easy upgrade which should only take a few minutes to perform (see Chapter 5).

Boosting Your Hard Disk

Storage memory is much slower than RAM. Over the past few years major strides have been made in hard disk design, offering faster and more reliable hard disks and better controller cards. The faster data moves from the hard disk into RAM, the faster programs come up. If your hard disk is already becoming crowded, you may want to consider the use of *software compression* to boost disk space. *RAM caches*, either through software at the operating system level, or through RAM memory actually contained on a controller card, can move frequently-used programs or data into a *virtual hard disk* that is actually on-line memory. This can make file access almost instantaneous. For details on using a software RAM disk you should consult your operating system manual. Periodicals such as *PC Magazine* have regular articles on hard disks and storage optimization issues which can be used to help make a purchase decision. For more information on storage systems see Chapter 9.

Getting the Picture

The popularity of Microsoft Windows has made display-adapter design one of the hottest areas in all of microcomputing. During peak periods over the past couple of years new video cards have been announced at the rate of about one a day. These new devices are much faster than their predecessors and offer resolution and features unheard of only a few years ago, at amazingly low prices. If you haven't upgraded your display system in the last year or so, you might be able to improve system performance three to ten times for a half hour's work and $200 to $400. Monitors have also improved in quality dramatically for the same reason. The newest units have their own microprocessors, along with enhanced ergonomics to reduce eyestrain and improve picture clarity. Most also incorporate new European standards to reduce possible risk from electromagnetic radiation, and have energy-saving features (see Chapter 12).

Adding a SCSI Bus

If you're considering joining the CD-ROM revolution, adding a hard disk, or a new backup system, you should consider adding a SCSI host adapter to your system. SCSI offers the most dramatic hard disk performance of any storage-related technology, and you can attach up to seven devices (and in some cases more) to any SCSI adapter card. For more information on SCSI alternatives, see Chapter 10.

Getting More Juice

If you are experiencing erratic system behavior, or your system is very prone to disruption during electrical disturbances or when the power flickers slightly, you may want to consider taming your household power supply by smoothing out your system's power source. Chapter 16 provides information on surge protectors, uninterruptible power supplies, cooling systems, and the power supply itself.

Tune Your Operating System

Make sure that you are using all the advantages that your operating system itself offers. Examining your owner's manual or a third-party book often uncovers modifications to your configuration that can enhance performance and provide better use of resources. The same is true for any operating environment that might run under your operating system, such as Microsoft Windows for Workgroups or another shell.

STEPWISE BEHAVIOR

Any time you approach a challenge with your computer, you should use a stepwise approach for two reasons: you're more likely to come up with the best possible solution, and you're less likely to get into serious trouble. Before moving on to a discussion of memory management and the later chapters that deal with specific upgrades, you should know how to use this technique, as described below. The keys are proceeding in an organized manner, and then analyzing your situation at the completion of each step. It's important to take whatever time is needed for each step and not to combine them unless you're absolutely sure of what you're doing.

Step 1: Analyze the Problem or Opportunity

This step is used to find exactly what you are trying to accomplish. It might be as simple as installing a new program or as complicated as replacing a motherboard.

Step 2: Identify Exactly What Resources You'll Need for a Successful Conclusion

Determine what tools, parts and documentation you'll need to perform whatever activity you're about to undertake. If you're going to install new software or add a part, make sure that the new component came with everything needed to install it, or that you have all the items that weren't included. While it doesn't happen often, vendors have been known to ship a product without all the disks, or minus a cable, or driver. Make sure that you have the right screwdriver needed to effect the installation or repairs.

Step 3: Be Prepared for Difficulty

Any time you start working inside your system, or installing a new piece of software, you should be prepared for a disruption of your system. The new device or program may overwrite a configuration file, making it impossible to boot from your hard disk. A new expansion card may conflict with another device already on the system. The Dark and Stormy Night Disk you should have prepared while reading the preceding chapter will let you get things going again if your configuration files or operating system become corrupt and require reinstallation. The diagnostic software included on the disk in the back of the book, along with the techniques presented later in this chapter and in the ones that follow, can show you how to avoid most common installation problems, and recover from them if they occur.

Step 4: Only Work on One Thing at a Time

Avoid the temptation to modify two settings at once—or to plug in two new expansion cards at the same time. You can do both during the same session, but get one up and running before you start on the second. As soon as you get one working, make an updated copy of your Dark and Stormy Night Disk, but keep a copy of your old one. If you're using new software that is supposed to help your hard disk run better, such as a defragmentation program (like the one that comes with both Windows 95 and later versions of DOS), be

sure that you have a good backup before you use it. If you are relying on new backup software, make certain that it can restore files
properly before you use it.

Step 5: Test, Test, Test

Once you have your new *whateveritis* installed, bring up your system
and run the software you use on a regular basis: make sure everything is working fine before you assume you're done. This is especially true if the procedures required that you open your case or modify
any of your primary configuration files, such as CONFIG.SYS,
AUTOEXEC.BAT, or your Windows SYSTEM files.

Step 6: Do the Paperwork

Once your installation is complete, fill out your registration card
(you might even want to do this while you're loading the software).
Part of your installation process is also to update your system's
Inventory. You can use the form in the back of the book to do this.
That way, you'll have a current record of the devices installed on
your system and their settings. This makes future installation, troubleshooting, and using technical support much easier.

Step 7: Know Your System

As you're working, keep a sense in the back of your head as to how
well the system is performing; this is the same thing we do intuitive-
ly when driving a car. We're aware of how it handles on the road,
if it's steering the same way, or if it's acceleration is behaving in its
usual way. If we ignore these things, we are at risk. The same thing
is true about a computer. And with our computers, we have an
added incentive to be aware of performance, because vendors are
always presenting us with new ways to enhance our system and
the way it helps us do our work. By being aware of what we want it
to do, we can know where we want to spend our resources and how
we want to improve it.

While memory managers offer sophisticated tools for analyzing and allocating memory resources, they're not the only tools you can use to boost your system's performance. A careful examination of your startup files, along with some third-party products, and tuning your operating system, can provide real benefits. There are a variety of techniques that can be used to speed up your system. Some involve nothing more than changing a line in a startup file; others may involve third-party products. Still others may require a major overhaul of your system. Let's examine some of the more common approaches towards reducing bottlenecks and increasing system performance.

DIAGNOSTIC SOFTWARE—SNOOPERS, BENCHMARKS, AND BOTTLENECKS

Diagnostic software can show even a novice how well his system's performing. It can help to identify problems, and in many cases, even correct them. We can divide diagnostic software into two broad classes; *snoopers* and *benchmarks*. *Snoopers* are programs that go inside our systems, look around, and come back with a report about what something is doing. They can tell us if a parallel port is active, test our memory and make sure that it is functioning properly, or examine our hard disk to see if it is storing data effectively. *Benchmarks*, on the other hand, test performance. They run the system through a series of operations and come back with a number that can be used to compare one system against another—or the same system against itself over time. Both sets of tools have their place.

As a computer journalist, I use benchmarks on a regular basis to evaluate one product against another. But I also use them on my own machine. Periodically I run a set of speed tests to make sure that everything on my system is healthy and performing up to par. I remember one incident a year or so ago when several people complained that one of the machines in the lab was behaving poorly. We ran a benchmark on the CPU and found that it was only performing at about 25% of its rated speed. It turned out that it had been forced into a slower mode, and resetting a switch brought things back to normal.

We also use a variety of snoopers to routinely check the integrity of hard disks, the operation of monitors, and the speed of traffic across our *local area network* (LAN). While part of the reason we do this is to make sure we have a level playing field for the products we test, it's also done to make sure that everything is working to its full ability. As new products become available, we then have known values and a good understanding of what our equipment is delivering. If a vendor promises that a new product will offer certain performance gains, we can use his projections along with our benchmarks and knowledge of how our system performs to decide if the new component will be worth its cost.

Having an idea of the IPO model helps in this regard. When Windows gained in popularity, the display system became a real bottleneck. The original PC had been designed to simply display characters on the screen, not all kinds of fancy graphics. Windows changed all that and created a strong demand for better video systems. Choosing the proper card can sometimes offer three to ten times better performance over a standard VGA display. Having an understanding of the kind of work you do, along with benchmarks of your current display system, helps you evaluate when it's time to upgrade.

BUILDING A DIAGNOSTIC & REPAIR LIBRARY

Most of us seem to settle on one word processor, one spreadsheet, or one telecommunications package; we get used to it and it meets all our needs. On the other hand, utilities don't fit into such a neat category and they are not constant companions like the applications mentioned above. So over time most users collect several sets of utilities, integrating different features into their everyday work habits. I'm going to mention a few of my favorite utilities and show you a bit of how they work. Talking about utilities is a favorite pastime of serious PC users, allowing us to exchange information about techniques and new tools at the same time.

Diagnostic software comes under the broad category known as *utilities*. They are not designed to perform regular, everyday tasks;

rather, utilities are designed to help you keep your system running smoothly and make regular program operation more efficient. Your PC is not a static environment. As you add new software, fill up your hard disk, or purchase new peripherals, the dynamic of your system changes. Utilities provide ways to both manage and evaluate your system.

Over the past decade, one of the most popular collections of such software has been the Norton Utilities, published by Symantec. This is now available for DOS and Windows 95. The Win95 software is a good model to use when developing a library of such tools. The current offering comes in three sets. The first is the general utilities, which has a variety of disk and system analysis and repair tools which can offer a range of information about how your system is performing, as shown in Figure 4.1. These utilities allow you to monitor the basic operation of your components and perform routine maintenance.

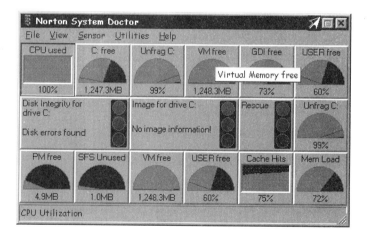

FIGURE 4.1 The Norton System Doctor for Windows 95.

The Norton Utilities come with a more robust disk examiner and defragmenation suite than that packaged with DOS or Windows 95. They offer easy configuration and a graphical readout of progress, as shown in Figure 4.2. Windows 95 offers a reasonable set of basic utilities, but the add-ons improve the scope of the bundled software. The Norton Utilities go far beyond the basics. With tools like Disk Editor you can (but should rarely attempt to) examine and modify the boot sector of your hard drives, In short, it offers a series of programs that can keep any system happier, and some that allow real power users the ability to recover from disaster.

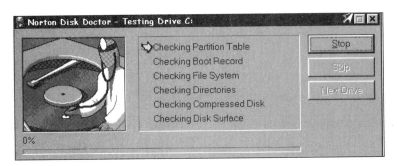

FIGURE 4.2 The Norton Disk Doctor at work.

There are bound to be a number of enhancements to the Windows 95 and Windows NT interfaces, just as there were for DOS and Windows 3.x. Norton is already marketing one, and so is Microsoft. The Microsoft product is called Plus!, and it contains a variety of utilities, screen savers, desktop themes, and an Internet Wizard that will help set up your system for surfing the Net—along with 20 free hours of Microsoft Network connect time. Norton Navigator is a file management program which seems to many an improvement over the Windows Explorer program that comes with Windows 95 (See Figure 4.3). It is especially useful if you use the Internet or compressed files in ZIP format, since it has built-in support for both zip and ftp operations, along with easy access to advanced file commands and searches. This set of utilities also includes fast find, archiving, and a program launcher task bar. Keep in mind that extra layers on the desktop add to your system overhead (the resources needed for efficient operation). So if you have a machine with no RAM to spare, this type of add-on can eat valuable system resources and slow your PC down. The third member of the new Symantec suite is Norton Antivirus, which is a well-known example of this type of system protector—a class of products I cover in another section.

FIGURE 4.3 The Norton Navigator in operation.

Several vendors have allowed us to provide diagnostic software, which you can use as the foundation of a utilities library (they are on the CD-ROM disc that accompanies this book). I am going to highlight some which should just show how this class of product can help you keep your system running. As this book was being printed, the first of the Windows 95 products were arriving. I'll cover those a bit later. If you are running a dual-boot system with DOS, the three programs I am about to mention will work when you boot to DOS. These tools can provide useful information about your system, even if your primary environment is Windows 95 or NT.

WARNING

Keep in mind that 16-bit (like DOS 6.22 or Windows for Workgroups) and 32-bit operating systems (like Windows 95 and Windows NT) are different kinds of beasts. If you use long file names under the 32-bit systems, the names will appear shortened under the older system. For example, a Windows 95 file named `MyComputerRecords` might be shown as `MtComp~1` under DOS. This is not a problem, just a work-around; the full name is still there and will show under Windows 95. BUT, if you use a 16-bit utility to defragment the drive, the file names may be shortened for real, and lose those long portions. Also, *NEVER* delete a hidden or system file unless you are sure of what you are doing. If it is a critical file, Windows or DOS may not load, or may stop working, if it is missing.

Qualitas has provided their ASQ utility, which we'll use a little while later to examine our computer's memory map. This program will work under DOS and Windows 95 in a DOS Window. Qualitas is one of two principal manufacturers of memory optimization software. Dariana Software has provided WinSleuth Gold. This is a Windows-based set of utilities that can be used to examine the different components of your system using a graphical interface. It will also display your memory map and aid in avoiding conflicts when installing new accessories in your machine. Dariana offers an enhanced version of WinSleuth, called Gold Plus, which I will use for some of the illustrations in this chapter when explaining the use of benchmarks. The third product is the shareware version (try-before-buy) of Command Software's SPROT, a virus-protection utility. In this chapter we'll deal with the first two of these products.

NOTE WinSleuth will work under Windows 95 and Windows for Workgroups. Keep in mind that it was designed for Windows 3.x. So some of the memory mapping features many produce some unusual results that don't exactly match reality, as in my copy's report that my 48MB RAM PC had -17408 K of extended memory that was not present. Everything else worked fine. Still, it offers an impressive collection of tools for examining and testing your system. See Figure 4.4.

FIGURE 4.4 WinSleuth Running Under Windows 95.

One of the most common ways to perform evaluation is through *benchmarks*. These are standardized tests designed to evaluate the performance of a component of your system. By keeping a record, you can gauge how your system performs over time; identify possible trouble spots; and locate areas for improvement. Knowledgeable users always keep their eyes open for new and useful utilities.

Some utilities are available as fancy, shrink-wrapped products (like Norton Utilities), some as shareware available on Bulletin Board Systems (or in the back of a book like this one) and through users' clubs. Computer magazines often offer utilities they have commissioned, either through commercial on-line services or as a bonus for a paid subscription. *PC Magazine* regularly offers a suite of utilities along with one of the most comprehensive sets of benchmarks available for testing both DOS and Windows operations. These can be obtained through a CompuServe gateway into Ziff-Davis Publishing Company's service known as ZIFFNET. Here are some examples of how benchmarks can be used to help you evaluate and tune your system.

Monitoring Your CPU Speed

There are a number of programs that test CPU performance. Some provide a raw number or a composite figure, based on certain calculations. Others index speed using well-known microprocessors, such as an Intel Pentium 90, as a guide. You can use this benchmark to compare the speed of your CPU and motherboard against known values.

When you are reading about new hardware, benchmarks can give you an idea of how much improvement might be expected if you upgrade your CPU. I use this test to compare the performance of motherboards that come into my lab. I have seen as much as a 35% variance between two motherboards configured the same way and using the same CPU. Many board vendors provide two or three well-known benchmarks so that potential buyers can gauge their speed. By comparing the same test from vendor to vendor, you can get an idea of the board's relative performance. Be careful though, and be sure that the boards were configured the same way when the tests were run. Periodically, I spot-check my CPU's performance using Norton Utilities' *System Information* program. A readout of the current version of SI for Win95 is shown below in Figure 4.5.

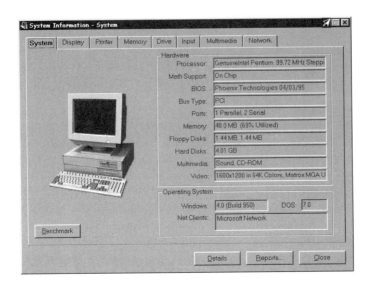

FIGURE 4.5 Norton System Information for Windows 95.

Some utilities allow you to monitor the CPU's performance while you are running your machine and doing everyday tasks. You can then see just how much of a load different applications put on the system. Some users find this a handy way to monitor system resources. If the system starts getting loaded and they are about to perform an intensive task, they will close some applications to speed the system up. There are similar utilities that measure other resources, such as memory.

If your machine is behaving erratically, you may want to use one of these utilities to keep an eye on things. It may be that one of your applications is using excessive resources and making the system unstable. If this is the case, you may be able to find ways to re-allocate system resources to avoid the problem (more about how to do this a little later).

USING WINSLEUTH GOLD TO EXAMINE YOUR HARD DISK

WinSleuth Gold is a general-purpose diagnostic tool and serves as a good introduction to using utilities and seeing what they can do for you. To get the most out of this portion of the chapter, you should read it at your computer with WinSleuth running under Windows. If you don't have a copy of Windows, I've included screenshots so you can get an idea of how these utilities work.

WinSleuth is stored on the disk as a compressed file. You should copy it into a temporary sub-directory on your hard disk. It is named WINS.EXE. Once the file is in the new location, type **WINS**. The different files will be unpacked. There is an Install program, which you can run under Windows and which will set the program up and move the files into their own directory. Once the installation is complete, you can remove all the files from the temporary directory. Figure 4.6 shows the WinSleuth Gold opening screen.

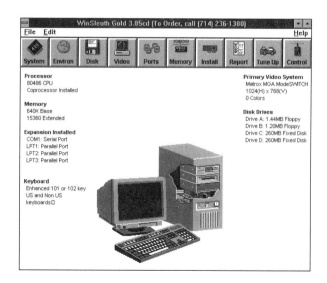

FIGURE 4.6 The WinSleuth Gold opening screen.

The buttons across the top, beneath the menu bar, provide access to the program's different operations. If you click on them with the mouse the report will change.

Taking Our Disk For a Drive

To get a hands-on sense of how diagnostic software can help you examine and assess your system, let's use WinSleuth Gold to assess and test our storage system. Open the program and click on the third button, marked **Disk**. Your screen should look similar to Figure 4.7. Follow along as I go through the features and describe them.

FIGURE 4.7 WinSleuth Gold's Storage Subsystem report.

The left-hand portion of the major area in the window should show a report giving the type and characteristics of the drives on your system. It shows the type and size of the drive, its organization, the type of *file allocation table* (*FAT*) and how the directory structure is organized. This is a much more complete report than that provided by your system's Setup.

To the right of the report is an animated drawing showing a hard disk with several buttons underneath it. If you click on the second button, which says **BIOS Disks**, it will provide you with a table showing the standard types and physical structure of the standard AT-class of hard disks. This table can be used for setting CMOS values if you have to install a drive, and if you are either not sure of the drive type number, or if you need to enter values manually into the drive table.

The **Disk Partition** button shows the starting and ending data for each partition on the drive. The fourth button allows you to prepare a graphic representation of your hard disk file structure, to see exactly which directories are consuming the most space. This can be very handy if you're trying to reorganize your drive or looking for older files that could easily be archived.

It's All In the Numbers

I talked about benchmarks a little earlier in this chapter. They are not an absolute, but a guide. Many utilities have some degree of benchmarking capabilities. WinSleuth is no exception. The last option in WinSleuth Gold allows you to run a standard set of benchmarks which measure the seek times for your drive and compare them to a well-known IDE drive, the Connor 34. Click on the **Benchmark** bar; you will be presented with a dialog box informing you that the test will take several minutes to run. Click on **OK**.

WinSleuth Gold will run a variety of tests to check out the functions of your hard disk. These tests exercise the disk and ascertain its average seek times as the machine acquires data. This is measured out on a bar graph similar to the one shown in Figure 4.8a. Your computer's disk is shown on the top bar and is compared to a Conner CP-3204 IDE disk drive as a reference.

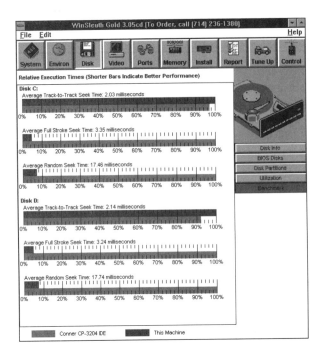

FIGURE 4.8a WinSleuth Gold benchmarks.

The advanced version of the program, WinSleuth Gold Plus, has a different interface and offers some advanced features, including comparisons of your drive against four other drives with different levels of performance. It can also test the surface of your disks (hard or floppy) to make sure that they can actually record and retrieve data. Tests like this should be run periodically, because a drive's capability deteriorates over time. Be aware that this kind of testing can also take a half-hour or more on a large hard disk. For comparison, its screen is shown in Figure 4.8b.

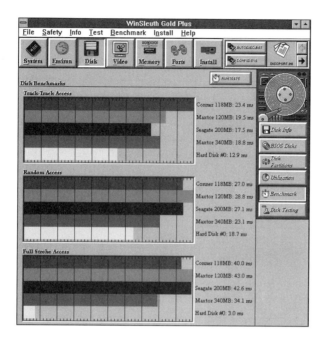

FIGURE 4.8b WinSleuth Gold Plus benchmarks.

The last entry in Figure 4.8b shows the Full Stroke Access time. My hard disk seems to perform very well against the reference disks, operating in less than a tenth of the time used by the others. But it does this in reality by means of caching performance, by holding recently-used information in RAM. If it's called for again, it can be acquired very quickly. This improves measured performance, but renders this test useless as a means of comparing the actual differences between several pieces of hardware, as one of the contestants has an unfair advantage.

GETTING THE PICTURE

Anyone who uses Microsoft Windows is probably aware of the importance of a high-performance and reliable display adapter. What you may not be aware of that not all *video drivers* (specialized programs to run a piece of hardware) are created equal. Many problems with Windows' instability are not a problem with Windows at all but with your display adapter or, in most cases, its driver. WinSleuth Gold provides several reports that help analyze your video card's capabilities and performance, performing both snooper and benchmark functions.

Click on the fourth button over, which chooses the **Video** report; and click on the button to the right that says **Device Capabilities**. This function shows the inner workings of your Windows device driver. Your graphics driver has a lot to do with how well and how reliably your system functions under Windows. Much of this information is too technical for a casual user; but it can help you in determining the nature of problems with some software. If you run into difficulty with a program, the information in this report may help you or a support technician determine if your video driver is at fault, or perhaps cannot even handle the requested operation.

The next button, **System Metrics**, under the Video Report, shows the different aspects of your Windows desktop based on the current display. Click on this button now. The first two lines, Screen Width and Screen Height, are both given in pixels and should exactly match those stated for your video card's driver. For example, if you are using standard VGA, the screen width would be 640 and the screen height 480.

If you change to a different resolution and re-run this test, you should get different results. If you are having trouble with your mouse cursor information and the like, this report may provide useful information. If you don't see a mouse cursor, yet the report shows that a mouse being present as "true," then Windows believes that there is a mouse but for some reason it is not being displayed on the screen. This may be a problem with the way your video driver is displaying the mouse cursor.

Pressing the **Hardware Info** button provides a report independent of the Windows device driver. This report, coupled with **Hardware Testing**, using the last button in the column, can provide a fairly complete report of your graphic adapter's capabilities. Hardware Testing directly tests the capabilities of your video adapter board and runs it through its various modes of operation. This tests several video operations not normally tested under Windows, since

Windows doesn't support those modes. If you need a more complete explanation of video technology, you can refer to Chapter 12, on the display sub-system, or use the video tutorial that comes with WinSleuth Gold.

Video Benchmarks

WinSleuth Gold also provides a basic benchmark comparison, using a standard graphics drawing of your video adapter, and compares it for reference to a Cirrus Logic Video Accelerator for Windows (See Figure 4.9). The Plus version of the software offers more advanced benchmarks and testing along comparisons of more advanced display adapters. *PC Magazine* offers benchmarks with extended testing of video adapters, including both device-specific testing and applications-based performance evaluations. Those benchmarks can be obtained from the magazine via the ZIFFNET area available through CompuServe.

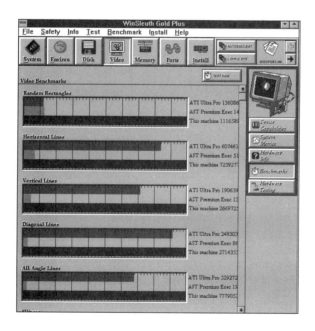

FIGURE 4.9 The Winsleuth Gold Video benchmarks.

REPORTING THE PORTS

This section of the program provides information on the parallel and serial ports of your machine. Clicking on the button which says **Ports** shows which ones are reported by the system BIOS, their memory addresses, and any installed devices that Windows is aware of. Clicking on the bottom button, **Port Testing**, will actually go out and see if something is attached. Be aware that a port attached to a mouse will not be tested because doing so might disrupt its activity.

The **Printer Capabilities** section reads the information Windows has on your printer, based on the printer driver, and can help in determining if your printer supports various features of your program.

The first button in the WinSleuth Gold button bar provides information about your system's basic Setups, including CMOS status, the BIOS, software Interrupts, and allows you to perform a sound test. There's also a brief tutorial that will explain different parts of your system.

The **Environment** menu provides detailed looks at how your system is using its resources, any network devices available, and what programs are using system resources.

KEEPING RECORDS

You can get hard copies of any of WinSleuth Gold's reports by clicking the third button from the right. The window then displays a list of available printouts. Clicking on them and then choosing the **Add** button moves them into a *print queue*, a list of requested jobs. If you place a selection in the queue that you don't want a copy of, just highlight it, then click on the **Remove** button to shift it back to the other side. Once you've finished making your selections, choose the **Print** button.

GETTING IT RIGHT THE FIRST TIME

So far, we've been exploring the ability of diagnostic routines, such as WinSleuth Gold, to examine our system and gauge its performance; but this class of programs can also be very useful when it comes to adding new products into our system or trying to get the best out of memory. Use your mouse to click on a button that shows an expansion card labeled **Install** on it. Your screen should look something similar to the one shown in Figure 4.10.

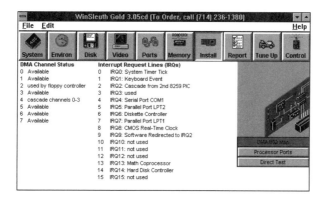

FIGURE 4.10 The WinSleuth IRQ and DMA report.

While we won't get into actually installing expansion cards until the next chapter, I want to show you how this program can make your life easier and reduce possible conflicts. You'll notice that there are two columns shown in this report. The first shows **DMA Channel** Status. DMA stands for *Direct Memory Access*. A device called the *DMA controller* provides special access to and from the system's memory. Devices using DMA can move data much faster than ones that don't. If two devices attempt to use the same DMA channel, your system may lock up; so it's important, when installing cards, to know which channels are available.

This report also shows what devices are currently using **Interrupt ReQuest** (IRQ) lines. IRQs are wires that connect devices on your system to the *Interrupt Controller*. Your PC is an Interrupt-driven machine; when a device needs attention from the CPU, it sends an

Interrupt signal on its line to the microprocessor asking for service. Your system only has a limited number of IRQ lines available. It is important not to have two devices sharing the same IRQ. This list lets you see which lines are in use. Be careful, though, because this list is not always totally accurate. A device may be using an IRQ in a way that the program can't pick up.

In the next chapter, I'll show you how to maintain an inventory for your PC to avoid such conflicts. To the right of the window, you will notice an animated drawing of an expansion card being inserted into a slot with three buttons underneath it. These buttons provide additional modes for this software. For more information on Interrupts, DMA and other functions of this program, you can consult WinSleuth help.

There are many more utilities on the market, far too many to go into any detail here. One of the original sets of utilities was developed by Peter Norton, with the inventive title of "The Norton Utilities." This suite of programs is still being marketed by Symantec. It includes routines for testing the speed of your CPU, your hard drive, and your memory. There are programs that will defragment your hard disk and rescue accidentally-erased files. I use the Norton set on a regular basis to inspect the health of my hard drive, defragment files, and occasionally to check the running speed of my CPU; see Figure 4.11.

FIGURE 4.11 The Norton Utilities for DOS.

Landmark Research International offers one of the most complete suites of diagnostic software. Some of their products are aimed at the average user; but they also provide very sophisticated diagnostic utilities for the professional. If you're getting very serious about building or repairing PCs, you may want to consider obtaining a set that matches the types of computers you are working on. They have released a Windows set.

A CRITICAL RESOURCE—YOUR SYSTEM'S MEMORY

Memory is one of your computer's most important resources. While most Windows 95 users give it little thought except if they run out of it, understanding how your PC uses it is fundamental to getting the most from your machine. The following discussion covers the topic well enough to let you control RAM properly. It is of benefit to those readers running Windows 95 and NT, and a necessity to DOS owners. If you don't know how memory is addressed and used, it is almost impossible to resolve device conflicts, and to tune your system for optimal performance. If you use DOS at all, there's one type of utility program that can play a serious role in helping your system run more efficiently every time you use it: *memory managers*. RAM is one of your personal computer's most precious resources, and proper use of that memory has been a problem right from the beginning. Windows 95 and Windows NT can map and use all the RAM memory in your system, but that was not always the case, and even today with the new operating systems, you can still experience memory conflicts.

The original PC was designed to use a maximum of 640Kb of memory. At the time this seemed like a lot. But today there are programs that won't even consider running with a paltry 640Kb of RAM. This memory limit is based on the fact that the original IBM-PC microprocessor, the Intel 8088, could only directly address 1Mb of RAM. The design engineers decided to allocate the upper 384Kb of that megabyte (a megabyte is actually 1024Kb of RAM, I'll explain that in a minute) for system resources rather than to be used for programs. The problem is that most PCs still use MS-DOS, and MS-DOS has that 640K limit built-in. Although there have been many workarounds (under both DOS and Windows), the 640Kb barrier is still a real problem.

Windows 3.11 and some other older operating environments perform slight-of-hand to get around the barrier. Memory managers are available for DOS and can do all kinds of fancy things to your system's memory to eke out every possible byte of space. Newer operating systems, such as Windows NT, Windows 95, and OS/2, can get past the 640Kb limit. They have their own memory management software built in. As is to be expected, improved third-party programs are appearing that offer additional memory-tuning features. No matter what operating system you use, understanding how memory works, and proper utilization of this resource will always be a critical factor in how well your PC performs and how well the software you use works.

Before we start our discussion of memory management itself, I need to define several terms and show how your system uses memory to perform its tasks. Since we'll actually be looking at the system configuration files, you should be sure that you have a working, bootable, Dark and Stormy Night Disk, or the appropriate recovery disk for your operating system. Have both if you use a dual-boot machine. While you can't do any permanent damage with the exercises in this chapter, if you inadvertently disrupt one of your system's startup files, you may need to boot from a floppy disk to set everything back to normal.

Your computer's memory comes in a number of different flavors, each with its own special purpose. Let's define a few terms before we get down to details:

ROM

ROM (read only memory) is what is used to boot your computer. This kind of memory never changes. It is usually burned into a chip with set values. An example of ROM is the instructions for performing your computer's *Power-On-Self-Test* (*POST*). Your system's ROM contains the options that are used by the operating system to manage its resources. Many of the add-in cards that are placed in your computer also contain their own ROM.

RAM

RAM, or *Random Access Memory*, can be both written to and read from. Unlike ROM, it is not permanent. When you turn off your computer, all the information stored in RAM is lost.

Storage Memory

Storage memory is memory that's stored outside of the RAM area that can be read and written to. Examples are data stored on floppy and hard disks. This is sort of semi-permanent memory; it's there as long as you want it to be. Some programs, including Microsoft Windows 3.1, can use available storage memory as if it were RAM (this technique is called *virtual memory*) by using that space to store parts of a program or file that are not actively being used. Storage memory is much slower than RAM.

We'll be focusing on RAM because that is where the actual work of running programs and manipulating data takes place. It's also used when the computer is turned on as an active storage area for instructions that explain how the system should interact with hardware devices and store files that we are actually working with. ROM is pretty much outside the user's control.

RAM can be divided into several categories based on the system's use of memory. Part of RAM is used to provide software *hooks* (connections) to the various hardware components. We usually use a technique known as a *memory map* to describe how RAM is organized, and where specific instructions or data are loaded into RAM. This map can be divided up into *regions*. For reasons important to engineers and computer scientists (but beyond the scope of our discussion), memory is traditionally broken up into *segments* of 64Kb each. *Conventional memory* occupies the first ten segments, yielding 640K. The remaining six segments, which complete up the first Mb of RAM on the system, are collectively referred to as *high DOS* memory.

Memory Is a Hexadecimal Matter

Before going on, I need to explain how *memory addresses* work. We're used to counting in decimal numbers using the digits zero through nine. Sometimes it's easier to count in multiples of fives: 5, 10, 15, 20, etc. That's one different way of counting. When dealing with memory addresses, computer professionals use another type of counting called *hexadecimal notation*, which is a numbering system using 16 digits. You don't have to learn to count in hexadecimals; you don't have to think in hexadecimals; but for memory management, you do have to understand how hexadecimal addresses work.

You'll be relieved to know that we start at zero when using hexadecimal notation. And we use the same ten digits, zero through nine. The change comes when we get to ten. When we are counting in decimals, each column can have a value from zero to nine; when we count from one and get to the number ten, the first column to the left gets the value of one, meaning there's one block of ten, and the original column (the ones column) shows that there are no ones at the present time, just 10 for our present count.

When counting in hex, each column can have up to sixteen rather than ten possible values. The way we do this is by using the letters A through F to represent the numbers ten through fifteen. The range zero through F accounts for sixteen total numbers; zero counts as a number. Just as with the example of the number 10 before, when we go one digit past the letter F, the rightmost column becomes zero and the column to the left becomes a one. The first megabyte of your system's memory occupies a memory range from 0000 to FFFF. The area of conventional memory, the first 640K in hexadecimal notation, would show as between 0000 to 9FFF. When the next digit rolls over, conventional memory ends, and we end up in high memory, which runs from A000 (commonly referred to as A-thousand, and C800 would be said as C-eight-hundred), to FFFF.

Reading the Memory Map

Now that I've explained briefly how hexadecimal notation works, we can see how it's used to describe memory locations within a PC's first Mb of RAM. By counting in hexadecimals, you can assign one number (zero through F) to a specific byte in memory. In hexadecimal, the first 640K of memory are represented by the hexadecimal numbers 0000 to 9FFF. This is the conventional memory referred to above.

When your system is booted, DOS normally loads the operating portions of itself, any device drivers, and then any programs you wish to be run, into this region. When this region's full, DOS is unable to allow you to load any further programs until one of the currently-running applications is terminated, even though there's another 384Kb of memory available within the first megabyte of RAM. At this point you might be wondering, "What about the memory above 1Mb of RAM, or how does the newer Windows use memory?" For right now we'll focus on conventional and high memory.

Because many people use software meant to run in the MS-DOS environment, and because PC operating systems have made great efforts to ensure the backward compatibility of software, operating system designers still have to contend with the 1Mb limit of the 8088 chip. The six segments of memory, ranging from 640Kb to 1024Kb, were reserved in 64Kb blocks by the original PC's designers for various functions. Furthermore, expansion cards such as video adapters, hard disk controllers, and SCSI host adapters often have ROM BIOSes on them. Those BIOSes must be loaded into RAM to allow the card and the computer to work together.

The following list describes how each of the segments is set aside. With efficiencies in operation of more modern personal computers, portions of these high memory areas can usually be used to relocate some of the stuff that normally resides in conventional memory, freeing up more space for programs. To use memory managers efficiently, it's wise to have a basic understanding of what is expected to be in those addresses. In the list below, each segment is identified by its hexadecimal address. The description then converts the address into Arabic numbers, explains what it is reserved for, and how you might take advantage of it. Refer also to Figure 4.12.

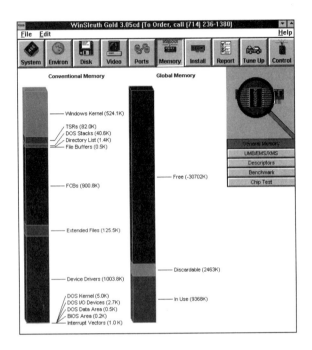

FIGURE 4.12 Basic memory map of the first Mb of system RAM.

Hexadecimal Address Range

✔ A000 to AFFF

This is the region immediately above conventional memory, from 640Kb to 704Kb. This is the range set aside for holding string data (structured sequence of characters) for EGA and VGA graphics cards. If you use a Windows accelerator, a monochrome video card or some other type of display adapter that doesn't use this range, you may be able to load device drivers or other conventional memory residents into this region.

✔ B000 to BFFF

Traditionally, this second segment, 704KB to 768KB was also reserved for video adapters. The first half of the block, B000 to

B7FF, was designed for the original monochrome graphics adapter. The back portion, B800 to BFFF, will be in use if you have a CGA, EGA, or VGA card. In other words, some portion of this area is also usually available for loading drivers that normally reside in conventional memory.

✔ C000 to CFFF

This range, from 768Kb to 832Kb, is traditionally used by video cards, as well as hard disk controllers and SCSI host adapters. The video areas normally occupy the first part of the segment from C000 to C7FFF, while disk controllers are often placed in the second half of the segment, from C800 to CFFF.

✔ D000 to DFFF

This region, from 832Kb to 896Kb, was set aside for optional expansion cards such as scanners, sound cards, and specialized graphics adapters. If you're not using these types of peripherals, this area is often available for reallocating a significant number of device drivers or supplemental programs known as *TSRs* (*Terminate and Stay Resident*).

✔ E000 to EFFF

The fifth block, ranging from 896Kb to 960Kb, is a good area for advanced peripherals, unless your system is using this area in upper memory for some specific purpose, such as shadowing the system's BIOS (for an explanation of *shadowing*, see the Note that follows). It's still a good area for doing it, but you may have to disable that function using the system's CMOS Setup. For more information on this see your system manual.

✔ F000 to FFFF

This final segment of the first 1Mb of RAM, which occupies the space from 960Kb to 1024Kb, is used on many systems to locate the ROM BIOS. Many designers have rigged their sequences so this area is only needed when the system is first coming on-line, and so it can be used to load device drivers and TSRs. You may want to test this, but keep in mind that if your system does not release the area, using it may lock up your computer, and you'll have to reconfigure your memory management.

You should check your system manual for information on shadow RAM, and also read the documentation of any expansion cards you plan on locating in the areas that might be used for shadow RAM on your system. The video card that I currently use requires some sort of shadowing to operate properly. Other cards will find this feature a problem. *Shadow RAM* is a way of loading part of the BIOS into RAM for faster operation. You might want to experiment with different settings and see which ones work and which ones don't. Then use some form of system benchmark test, such as Norton's System Information, or PC Magazine's Benchmark Utilities, to see which ones let your system run faster.

MEMORY MANAGERS, HIGH MEMORY, AND THE AREA ABOVE 1MB

Unless you have a very old system, you probably have more than 1MB of RAM on your computer. Even most entry-level systems today have 8Mb, and power users often have systems with 32Mb or more. Any machine that uses DOS, however, as its basic operating system, nevertheless has to squeak as much room out of that initial 640K as possible. Microsoft refers to any RAM on the system above the first megabyte as *extended memory*. The first 64K block of extended memory, running from 10000 to 11000 Hex is referred to as the *high memory area*, or *HMA*.

The HMA Region

Some programs, including Windows running under DOS, can make use of this first block for programs with proper memory management. The original 8088-based PCs have no way to make use of any memory above 1Mb, because the chip itself can only directly address that amount of memory. Its successor, the AT, was based on the 80286 chip, which can directly manage 16Mb of memory.

With this improvement in processing power, the first of the memory managers started to appear. Lotus, Intel, and Microsoft set a specification called *expanded memory*. This method allows storage of data in RAM by programs as a sort of swap area, allowing them to manipulate larger files than would be possible in the conventional 640Kb environment. It's commonly referred to as *LIM extended memory*, based on the initials of the firms that designed the standard.

An advanced version of this type of memory management is known as *EEMS*, meaning *Enhanced Extended Memory Specification*. This type of memory management allows you to run more than one program at the same time. Programs compliant with LIM 4.0 and later can use up to 32Mb of expanded memory, compared to the 8Mb allowed under earlier versions of the standard. In order to use this kind of memory management, the programs you plan on operating must be compatible, and you have to use special drivers to handle all the swapping that goes on behind the scenes.

386 and later computers can take advantage of even more sophisticated memory management methods, such as *VCPI* (which stands for *Virtual Control Program Interface*), XMS (which stands for *Extended Memory Specification*), and *DPMI* (which stands for *DOS Protected Mode Interface*). All these different acronyms may seem overwhelming; the point of mentioning them is to help you understand that there are a wide variety of methods in use for managing a PC's memory more effectively.

For Windows 95 and Windows NT users, most of the memory problems associated with the older DOS environment have gone away. On the down side, the newer operating systems require a lot more RAM and hard disk space to operate at peak performance.

MS-DOS comes with built-in memory management. DOS 6.x provides a utility, called *MemMaker*, which can be used to configure your machine even if you don't understand all the ins and outs of all the different types of alphabet soup you might be using. You can get even more sophisticated by using one of the leading third-party memory managers, such as 386 to the MAX from Qualitas or Quarterdeck Systems' QEMM. Which one will work best on your system is a complicated question.

All three will provide basic memory management. QEMM probably offers the most aggressive approach to tweaking every square byte of available memory, but I have found it a bit more complicated to use. 386 to the MAX and QEMM both do an admirable job under most conditions, and provide extra services not found in DOS' MemMaker, making them worthy additions to a DOS-based power user's library.

If you are using DOS 5.0 or earlier, you have to do your own memory management if you are not using a third-party memory manager. For information on memory management using DOS, you should consult your MS-DOS user's manual. The ins and outs of configuring specific hardware using DOS is far too involved a topic to be covered in this chapter.

USING THE ASQ UTILITY

Just talking about memory management and all the technical terms required can be very dry. To help you interactively examine your own system and see how memory management might help you operate it more effectively, we have included with this book part of a diagnostic utility, shipped with Qualitas 386 to the MAX. This can help you understand how your system uses memory, even if you normally use one of the newer 32-bit operating systems.

The ASQ program can be used to see just how your system is using memory, and even test the speed of the RAM chips installed on your system. It can also be used to scan where the ROM hooks are stored in the RAM, and to see what areas are free when you go to install a new accessory. To see how you can use this program and to help me to explain a bit more about how memory works, we'll use ASQ to examine our systems right now. To perform the following exercises you can either have your system booted into a version of DOS, or run them from Windows 95 in a DOS window. You may even want to try it both ways, and see the differences between the way the two environments use RAM. If you have a dual-boot system, as advocated in Chapter 2, you are all set. If not, then you can still use the software by booting from a floppy disk with the DOS system files to see how it operates under DOS.

The program included on the disc is a compressed file. To use it you will need to move it into its own sub-directory; then type **ASQC** and hit **Return**. Once the file has been unpacked and is in its own directory, you can run it by typing **ASQ** and hitting **Return**. You can run it under DOS or under Windows. As it loads, the program will scan your computer's environment and make a map of its memory usage.

If you wish, you can run the tutorial from the main menu. Simply use your cursor keys to move the highlight bar over the **Tutorial** option and press the **Return** key. There will be a sub-menu that offers lessons on **Memory**, **System Configuration**, and **Hardware**. Keep in mind that ASQ is shareware. If you decide to continue to use it after a short trial period, you should register it. Qualitas does not require payment for the shareware version, they only ask that if you use it, you register it. By doing so, you will obtain information on future upgrades of the program as well as information on their memory management software. You can use the **Registration** option from the **Introduction To ASQ** entry in the menu to print out a registration form, which you can fax to them at 301/678-6060. You can also receive a more powerful version of the software included with their memory manager 386 to the MAX by calling their toll-free telephone number, 800/733-1377, to reach their offices in Bethesda, MD.

Open up ASQ and choose the **System Analysis** option from the Main menu. To begin with, choose the **Memory Analysis** option by placing the light bar over it and pressing the **Return** key. You can move up and down in the menus if you need to by using the up and down cursor keys. The bottom of the ASQ screen details the controls for navigating in the product. The program offers context-sensitive help. Your screen should resemble the one shown in Figure 4.13.

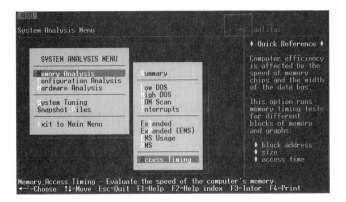

FIGURE 4.13 The ASQ System Analysis menu screen.

Make sure the light bar is over the entry called **Access Timing** and press the **Return** key. The main portion of your ASQ screen should look similar to Figure 4.14. Memory chip speed has an effect on overall system performance. This report shows the results of timing tests for different blocks of memory. It shows the block address, the size of the block and the access time in *nanoseconds* (a nanosecond is one billionth of a second). You can use the arrow keys to scroll up and down within the Report window. If you do, you will notice the hex addresses that we talked about earlier in the chapter. They run from 00000 through something like 0F800. Depending upon your system's memory configuration, your ending memory address might be somewhat different.

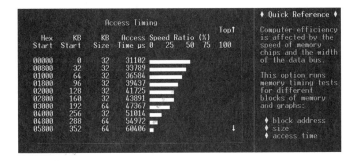

FIGURE 4.14 The ASQ Access Timing report.

RECOVERING VALUABLE REAL ESTATE AND AVOIDING CONFLICTS

If two device drivers or programs use the same address space at the same time, the system can either lock up or fail to boot at all. In low memory, where programs normally operate, the operating system manages ongoing memory resources. If the program is loaded, the operating system allocates a space; then when it is done (hopefully) the operating system makes the memory available for other operations. Device drivers and add-in cards get a little more difficult. They are usually pegged to operate at a specific address and if two or more things try to use the same space at the same time, your machine will get very confused. Either one of the devices will fail to operate at all, or the conflicting devices will get into an arm-wrestling contest and everything will come to a screaming, screeching halt.

Making the Best Use of Our Memory

When you install a memory manager, like 386 to the MAX, its Setup routine examines your system, usually requiring you to reboot your machine several times. As it does, it uses the same technology that ASQ uses to examine your system, to see how your operating system, device drivers, and any programs loaded during your AUTOEXEC.BAT routing, use memory. It then goes through a complicated analysis, checking the different possible memory configurations and identifying which one of them will provide the best performance.

Given that an average system may have between 5 to 15 different programs and drivers loaded during boot, and the ranges of possible memory addresses to be examined, it may very easily have to compare several million different options to arrive at an answer. Trying to accomplish this feat yourself would be an impossible task. Both Qualitas and Quarterdeck, however, have developed products that can accomplish this in mere minutes. They also offer reliable, if not fail-safe recovery routines that allow you to reset your system to its original parameters if they make a mistake.

During the writing of this book, I tested both products on several different computers with a wide range of peripherals attached. Both products allowed me to recover anywhere from 70Kb to 230Kb of conventional memory by using their memory management tools. Using a more trial and error approach with DOS 5.0, with its HIMEM.SYS and 386EMM.SYS software (and a good bit of trial and error), I was also able to recover a significant amount of conventional RAM. With DOS 6.0's MemMaker, I achieved similar results.

Avoiding Conflicts

Programs like the System Utility in Windows 95 and Windows NT's System Diagnostics, ASQ and Quarterdeck's Manifest allow you to examine the different devices loaded on your system so that you can see what memory areas, especially those in the high memory region, are being used by various devices on your system. This can be especially useful when you attempt to add new peripherals such as a SCSI host adapter or a scanner.

Figure 4.15 shows Manifest at work giving information on what areas of high memory are in use by what applications.

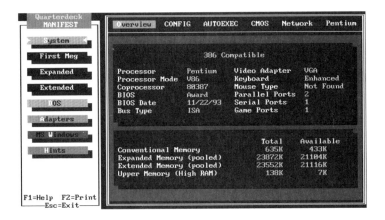

FIGURE 4.15 High memory usage from Quarterdeck's Manifest.

WinSleuth Gold, also located on the disc in the back of the book, can be used to graphically show your system's memory usage and resources. I've included Figure 4.16, taken using WinSleuth Gold Plus, which provides additional information beyond the program shipped with this book, to show how Windows is using memory resources. Both versions of the program allow you to see a graph depicting memory usage. To help in understanding the memory map produced by this tool, I've explained it in the following paragraphs.

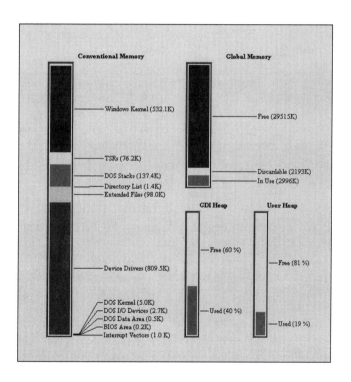

FIGURE 4.16 Memory usage and resources shown by WinSleuth Gold Plus.

Knowing how your conventional memory is used while you are running applications helps you decide when it is time to work on your memory management, and shows you how effectively your memory map is being used. As you add new accessories to your computer, your memory utilization changes. In most cases, if it affects the way your memory manager is working, you will usually get an error message during boot telling you that it was unable to re-allocate some program. If this happens, you should re-run the software used to set up your memory manager.

Global memory is the total amount of memory used by Windows and has two components: *discardable memory* is an area that can be released by an application for use by Windows or another application. *Free memory* is the area that is still available for use by Windows. *Global memory in use* is that which cannot be re-acquired until the application using it has released it.

The two bars in the lower right-hand corner of Figure 4.16 show the usage levels of the GDI and user heap. These are 128KB areas of RAM maintained by Windows. *GDI* stands for the *graphical device interface*; *user heap* deals with objects specific to the user interface such as control bars, menus and dialog boxes. If you open up Program Manager's help menu and choose **About Program Manager**, the bottom line of the dialog box usually will have a line showing the amount of free System Resources.

This figure is usually equal to the smaller of the two free areas shown on these bars. This report can be especially useful if you have problems with erratic system behavior, especially if Windows is locking up or telling you that you don't have enough free system resources. If you start tracking which programs are using and not releasing GDI and user heap resources, you've probably found the culprit. Several well-known applications don't always free up everything when they're done. When the heap gets too small, the system may start behaving erratically or even lock up. See Figure 4.17.

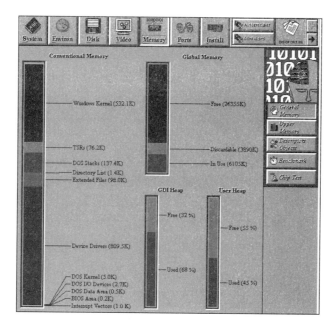

FIGURE 4.17 The WinSleuth Gold Plus memory map.

I have found that this problem is usually a combination of the software involved, along with your overall system memory management, and is quite likely involved with the video driver for your graphics card. You can try using a standard VGA driver, or reducing the number of device drivers loaded when you boot, and see if the problem persists. If it does, you should contact the manufacturer of your memory and various device drivers and request technical support.

USING THE MEM COMMAND TO CHECK RAM USAGE

MS-DOS 5.0 and later offers a utility that can be used to check memory any time you are at the DOS prompt. Typing **MEM** will yield a report showing basic conventional memory usage and how much RAM is currently free. Typing **MEM /c** (for complete) will include high memory area usage. If you are using Quarterdeck's QEMM, you will not see the high memory area even with the /c switch. A sample report is shown in Figure 4.18.

```
Conventional Memory :

   Name            Size in Decimal        Size in Hex
   --------------  -----------------      -------------
   MSDOS              9712    (  9.5K)        25F0
   USPI14             9104    (  8.9K)        2390
   QEMM386           13488    ( 13.2K)        34B0
   SMARTDRV           2464    (  2.4K)        9A0
   COMMAND            3392    (  3.3K)        D40
   SMARTDRV          28304    ( 27.6K)        6E90
   PROTMAN            2544    (  2.5K)        9F0
   NETX              43728    ( 42.7K)        AAD0
   FREE                 64    (  0.1K)        40
   FREE                 64    (  0.1K)        40
   FREE                 48    (  0.0K)        30
   FREE                 80    (  0.1K)        50
   FREE             542112    (529.4K)        845A0

   Total   FREE :   542368    (529.7K)

   Total bytes available to programs :       542368    (529.7K)
   Largest executable program size :     |   541904    (529.2K)

      15925248 bytes total EMS memory
      13123584 bytes free EMS memory

      15728640 bytes total contiguous extended memory
             0 bytes available contiguous extended memory
      13123584 bytes available XMS memory
               MS-DOS resident in High Memory Area
```

FIGURE 4.18 DOS memory report.

Anyone who is a serious PC user should be using some form of advanced memory management. It not only helps your system run more efficiently, but it makes it much easier to keep things running smoothly.

CHAPTER SUMMARY

This chapter has presented the basic techniques and skills needed to become a true PC power user. These include the ability to identify bottlenecks, use diagnostic software and utilities, manage a system's resources effectively, and use stepwise procedures when enhancing or repairing your system.

CHAPTER 5

GETTING UNDER THE HOOD

WHAT'S IN THIS CHAPTER

- ✔ Making Sense of Documentation
- ✔ Safe Work Habits
- ✔ Tool Kits
- ✔ Working with Hardware
- ✔ Expansion Bus Types

✔ Adding Expansion Cards

✔ Setting Jumpers and Switches

✔ Installing Memory

✔ Resolving Hardware Conflicts

✔ Using Tools

WHAT THIS CHAPTER IS ABOUT

Up until now we have focused on the things you can do without opening the case. This chapter introduces the basics of working inside your machine and shows you how to perform standard upgrades, such as adding an expansion card or installing a memory module. This chapter serves as a foundation for the repair and upgrade procedures explained in the rest of the book.

A RITE OF PASSAGE

If you've never ventured inside your computer's case before, you're about to become an initiate. While there is nothing very complicated in adding an expansion card, or hooking up a floppy drive, the mere act of opening the hood sets you apart from the casual user. It brings you face to face with the inner workings of your machine and gives you a better understanding of its design. Those who only interact with the computer via the keyboard or the mouse are relying on the PCs magic to get their work done, rather than forming a true relationship.

To properly proceed with the exercises in this chapter you will need a clear space, such as a desktop or workspace, and a few simple hand tools. You will have to open the case and observe a few simple cautions to avoid the minor possibility of damaging your machine. I mention this, not to frighten you off, for the risk is very slight; but so that you'll keep in mind that you do have to exercise reasonable care.

Adding new hardware generally means opening the case and installing expansion cards. While this can be intimidating to a new user and occasionally frustrating even to a veteran, the basics of installing new options inside your PC are very simple. You don't have to understand electronics, or know how to use a soldering gun to add or remove items from inside the case. All user-serviceable parts and add-ons will snap directly in or out much the same way you plug an electric appliance into a wall socket. This chapter explains what you need to know and what you'll usually need to work inside your computer.

GETTING READY

Being able to work inside your computer offers many advantages. It allows you to upgrade your system, so that you can be current with the latest advances of PC technology. It allows you to perform simple maintenance, saving both time and money, and it removes some of the mystery of the machine by giving you a better understanding of how it works. The PC may still seem like an almost magical device, yet you will have more control over it.

The physical act of installing a new expansion card, chip or memory module inside a PC is very straightforward and only requires a few seconds' effort. The skill comes in knowing where to place the new component and understanding how to integrate it into your system. There are a few concepts you will have to understand to be able use the information provided in the manuals that come with the new device or with your system.

Add-in products can be broken down into three main categories. First, there are some new products that your system will know how to recognize and use automatically, and second, you will on occasion need to replace existing products with upgraded versions. Performing these two operations is usually very simple: all you have to do is open the box, install the new part, and close it back up again. Third, expansion cards often involve adding hardware that was not part of your computer's original design. In order to work, the card must be properly introduced to your system so that it doesn't conflict with any other components, and software usually has to be placed onto your hard disk, allowing your computer to operate the new gadget.

Safety First

There are a few safety concerns when working with PCs; if you follow a few basic rules, there is no danger of hurting either yourself or damaging the machine. Before opening the case you should understand the concepts behind these safety rules that I list:

✔ *Electricity*

The PC uses electrical power. This is converted from alternating current (AC), the kind that comes from your wall socket, to direct current (DC) inside your PCs power supply. Touching the power supply (assuming it's properly grounded) or the other parts inside the case will not shock you; inside the power supply is the only place with enough current to do you any harm. All you have to do to avoid an electrical shock is to never open up the power supply. It is designed to be removed without you ever having to touch any of its internal components. This procedure is covered in Chapter 16. Of course, you do unplug the computer from the wall first. Keep in mind that, even if it is unplugged, the power supply may carry a significant electrical charge! Once again, don't open up the power supply.

✔ *Static Electricity*

You actually present more of an electrical threat to your computer than it does to you. The delicate electronic components contained inside the chips can be damaged by a discharge of static electricity. For this reason, you should always ground yourself by touching the case, or by wearing a grounding strap such as the one provided in many computer tool kits. It's nothing to be paranoid about; just exercise reasonable care.

✔ *Short Circuits*

PCs use a variety of small screws and other fasteners within and around their cases. Be sure to keep track of every screw as you work. I usually keep a small can or cup nearby whenever I open a case to hold screws as I remove them. If you drop a screw inside the case, recover it immediately. If you leave a screw inside the case and it's touching leads from two different components, it may short them out. In most cases this will just result in erratic behavior until you remove the offending piece of metal. But it is possible to permanently damage something. Once again, a little reasonable care should forestall any problem.

✔ *Food and Drinks*

It's not a good idea to eat or drink when working on a computer. The risk of spilling a Coke or coffee, or dripping hot-dog relish into your machine, is just not worth it. If you have to have refreshments nearby, put them on another table at a safe distance so that even if someone else knocks them over, they won't land on your prize possession.

The Right Tool For The Right Job

Almost all PC maintenance and upgrades can be performed with nothing more than a pair of screwdrivers, one Philips and one flat-head. There's no need for exotic electronic test equipment or a fancy tool kit. On the other hand, the simple tool kits available in most computer stores or through mail-order (about $15) can make life simpler. These usually include large and small screwdrivers, nut drivers, a pair of tweezers, a chip puller, and a plastic tube for holding spare screws and such. See Figure 5.1. My own personal kit also includes a pair of hemostats (for placing and removing jumpers), a set of needle-nosed pliers (handy for straightening out bent objects and setting jumpers), a small flashlight (peering in dark nooks and crannies), a magnifying glass or a pair of strong reading glasses (can be handy for reading print on circuit boards), a little "snake" (for locating dropped objects or holding screws while they are being installed), some very small screwdrivers, and a pen or pencil (for making notes. The screwdriver and pen can double for setting DIP switches). Since I do a lot of this kind of thing, I have an electric screwdriver. My total cost for this assemblage is probably about $45.

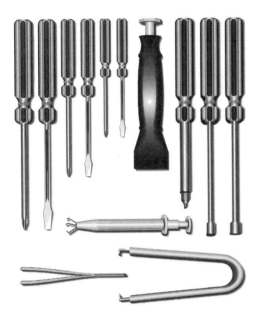

FIGURE 5.1 A typical PC tool kit.

Some folks like using magnetic screwdrivers or holders in a kit. That's OK, but keep in mind that a floppy disk can be corrupted and made unusable with exposure to a magnetic source. If you use one, keep it caged when not in use, and watch where you set it down—these things can bite.

NOTE

The Goodie Bag

As you work with PCs you will find yourself slowly accumulating a collection of miscellaneous parts—screws, jumpers, cables, expansion card plates, and the like. I have a couple of zip-lock bags to contain these odds and ends. Every time I get ready to start on a project, I set them off to one side of my work area. Invariably, it seems, a vendor won't include enough jumpers on his card, or I will somehow not be able to find just the right screw I need, and a quick rummage through the goodie bag lets me keep on working with a minimum of bother. I recommend never throwing away any of the loose parts or odds and ends that accumulate as you upgrade a machine. If a card dies and you have to replace it, strip off any connectors, jumpers and the like before sending it on to its final resting place. If you are just starting out, you might want to stop by your local computer repair shop, and as you are buying your tool kit ask the clerk if they happen to have a couple of spare jumpers and maybe a few extra case screws.

INSTALLATION BASICS

Let's start our exploration by opening your case and getting acquainted with the locations of the various major components. That will make it easier to understand the instructions below, and also give me a chance to explain the standard procedures in handling tools and components.

Turn off your machine and unplug it from your surge protector. Remove all the cables from your machine and orient it so that the back of the machine (where the power connector usually goes) is facing you. With most case designs, you should see a fan sitting behind a grill. This is the cooling fan contained inside your system's power supply.

There will be at least three and probably more cables coming from the back of your system. There will be a power cord leading to your surge protector or wall socket. You must be sure that the machine is turned off before removing this cable. Once the power is off the cables can be removed in any order.

One connection should go to the monitor, a round one should lead to the cord from the keyboard, and you may have other connections for a mouse, providing power to the monitor, an external hard drive, printer, etc. Most of these fittings should be fairly obvious and will only go into one socket. If you worry about being able to reconnect it properly, you might want to draw a little diagram, or use masking tape to attach labels to these cables until you are more familiar with them.

You may need to use a small screwdriver to remove some of the cable connections, possibly for your monitor, the serial port, and the printer.

Figure 5.2 shows the back of a standard case. While there are all kinds of variations in case design, almost all follow a similar pattern. A row of screws around the edge of the back of the case secures the cover, which is usually attached to the front of the case with sort of a sliding flange. To remove the cover, you have to unscrew the fasteners around the edge, and then use a combination of pulling and lifting up to unseat the cover from the front, then lift it free. See Figure 5.3.

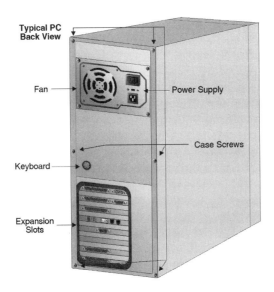

FIGURE 5.2 Back view of a standard mini tower style computer case.

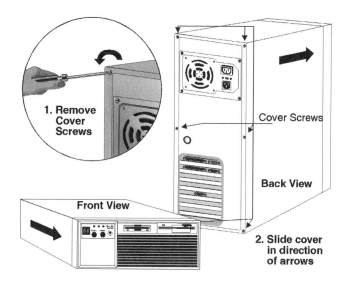

1. Remove Cover Screws

Cover Screws

Back View

Front View

2. Slide cover in direction of arrows

FIGURE 5.3 Lifting the cover off the chassis.

Because of the variations in motherboard and case design, it's impossible to describe all the potential combinations in a reasonable amount of space. There are a few common guidelines that can help you find your way around easily. The power supply is generally a shiny, silver box attached directly to the back of the case. It usually contains the system's cooling fan and it's attached using four screws.

A number of cables come out of the power supply. Two of these are attached directly to the motherboard and supply its power. The others are used to power disk drives and other internal components. For more information on power supplies, you can refer to Chapter 16.

You probably will also notice your floppy drives and hard drives nested in metal cages known as *bays*. The installation and care of both floppy and hard drives is covered in separate chapters (8 and 9) later in the book. Wires run from the drives to the power supply, and a set of ribbon cables runs from the drives either to an expansion card inside the system, or to the large (usually green) board full of chips located on the bottom of standard desktop cases (and on one wall of tower cases). This large board is known as the *motherboard*. Figure 5.4 shows the layout of the major components in a standard PC case. The exact placement on your machine may vary based on the type of motherboard and case.

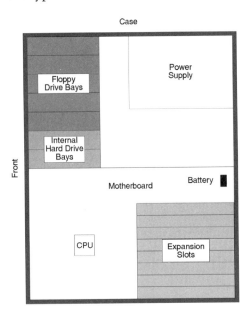

FIGURE 5.4 Layout of the major components in a standard PC case.

Along the back wall of your case are a series of raised slots. These are your expansion slots. Some of them may have cards seated in them that rise perpendicular to the motherboard. These are the expansion cards that provide specific functions for your computer and allow adding new features without having to upgrade the whole machine. One of these cards probably has cables running to your floppy drives and hard disk; these are used to pass data to and from the drives and the computer's microprocessor and memory banks. Some machines have this function built directly onto the motherboard. There are several different type of cards used to attach hard drives to a PC. They are explained in Chapter 9.

NOTE Some cases may have the expansion cards mounted into slots on another card, or the cards may be set at a 45-degree angle. Most will be way I describe them here.

Other cards manage your video display, and handle connections to modems, printers, and other external devices. There are a wide variety of expansion cards that can also be used to enable your machine to send and receive faxes, produce high fidelity sound, and even display regular TV programming in a window on your monitor.

As shown in Figure 5.4, there should also be a large square chip mounted on your motherboard. It may have a set of plastic cylinders rising up off it, which serve as a heat sink. This chip is your system's microprocessor, often (and not precisely) referred to as a *CPU* or *Central Processing Unit*. Most modern systems also have several banks of very small cards, each containing a row of chips. These are the machine's memory modules. The motherboard also contains a variety of other chips which provide various support functions. At first glance, the complexity of your PCs innards may seem daunting. In reality, you don't have to worry about what each of these chips do and the majority are permanently soldered into the motherboard. Most of your internal operations are nothing more than removing a screw, pulling out an expansion card, or placing in a new one. You might want to refer to your owner's manual and take a minute or two to familiarize yourself with the major components that I've just described.

A MODULAR DESIGN

To a novice user, the PC is the proverbial "black box:" you type on the keyboard or move the mouse and things happen on the screen. Those of us who have opened up the case understand that it is really a series of *modules*. Different functions are self-contained with the motherboard—the web that holds it all together. The motherboard provides basic services and is designed so that many components can be easily removed and replaced. This is similar to the design used in aviation. For example, in aircraft navigation equipment, radios and other electronic gadgets are fairly self-contained, with cables connecting them into the aircraft's power network. If a radio starts misbehaving, a mechanic can easily remove the radio and take it into a repair facility. A working unit can be snapped in as an immediate replacement. While the repair may take several days, the actual time spent working inside the aircraft is reduced to minutes.

That's one advantage of a modular design; another is the ease with which parts can be upgraded. As long as a new and improved component can be made compatible with the system as a whole and provided the resources to perform its function, upgrading a module is also only usually a matter of a few minutes' work.

An Open-Ended Design

This kind of construction is known as an open-system design. Many vendors compete to provide products that can be used inside our PCs, since as long as the new component is design-compatible, it can be incorporated into any existing system. Closed design does not allow for third-party vendors to provide products to expand the system's capability, and so requires the purchase of new products solely from the original manufacturer, which often involves purchasing a whole new unit. The PC, on the other hand, can often be made to perform tasks not envisioned by the original designers. The focus of this chapter is to concentrate on how you can use this open design, and the operation of its modular construction, to easily upgrade or repair your system.

EXPANSION CARDS

The Fundamentals

The engineers who designed the original PC included a very simple method of adding optional features directly to the motherboard. Located on the motherboard's surface are a series of long, narrow, rectangular slots. Inside the slots are connections. These grip the bottom of an expansion card, which has a matching series of connections. With the card fully seated, it becomes an integral part of the machine.

Expansion cards come in a number of different styles, but they all share the same basic design, as shown in Figure 5.5 and described in the following paragraph.

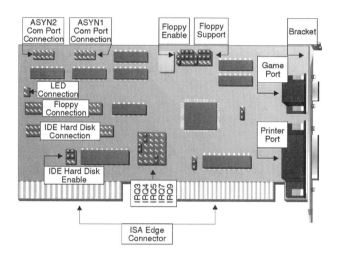

FIGURE 5.5 A PC expansion card.

Most cards are a rectangle made of fiberglass and in reality are printed circuit boards. The earliest PCs had a smaller size for a standard expansion card than do later models. With the exception of a few exotic case designs, cards sit perpendicular to the motherboard. A full-sized card refers to one that reaches all the way across the width of the case. The fiberglass of such a card is 13.25 inches long and 5.5 inches tall. An edge plate, or mounting bracket, is usually found at the back of the card; it is usually screwed into place at the back of the case to secure the card in its slot. This bracket often contains connectors that can be accessed from the rear of the case, as well as to expose configuration switches which can be adjusted without removing the case. There are different types of edge connectors depending on the type of card, as explained by what follows.

For the rest of this book, specific locations on an ISA or EISA card will be referred to as if the card were oriented with the mounting bracket on the right, and the edge connector (which fits into the slot on the motherboard) at the bottom. PCI cards will be discussed as if the mounting bracket were on the left. The difference is due to the fact that vendors make the ISA and EISA cards one way, the PCI facing the opposite way. The edge connectors are the parts that actually fit inside the expansion slot, and provide the electrical connections that carry data and power from the motherboard.

Not all cards occupy the full length of the slot. In fact, as the design for a given type of card matures, the cards tend to get smaller. While the size of the mounting bracket has been standardized, the actual dimensions of the board itself are often smaller than the maximum stated above, with a few even as short as six and a half inches or less. These are usually referred to as *half cards*.

In most cases, you will never have to worry about dealing with the chips on the motherboard; with some cards, there may be a removable chip to upgrade the BIOS or to add RAM on cards such as hard-disk controllers or video adapters. Expansion cards often contain various types of switches that can be used to adjust settings, and rows of pins that can be used for attaching cables or devices known as daughter cards. *Daughter cards* are expansion cards that attach directly to other cards and add functionality, such as memory, that would not be able to fit inside a normal full-slot, or which are an accessory module purchased as an option. Daughter cards can often pose a special challenge, since they can often take up more space than allowed for in a normal slot. Because of the limited area on the motherboard, expansion slots are normally spaced with no more than about 1.25 inches from slot center to slot center. If a daughter card pushes out beyond this range, it may overlap the adjacent slot. While this does not present a direct operating problem, it can reduce the actual number of available slots, because you'll be unable to fit a card in the neighboring position.

Some cards require nothing more than snapping into place and you can immediately use their features; these are standard components on most machines, and have predefined settings that work under most conditions. Adding some other cards may involve adjusting settings on the card, and possibly others on the motherboard, so that they do not conflict with other devices in the system, and to allow them to be properly recognized. In some cases, you may have to install special software to enable the card to operate properly and communicate with your operating system.

Slots and Buses

The expansion slot connects the card to your system's data bus. This is the pathway used to transfer data to and from the CPU and system memory. Over the years, as the PC has grown in power, there have been design changes so that the expansion bus could be improved to take advantage of more powerful CPUs and support the more elaborate features of modern expansion cards.

You can sort of think of the expansion slot as being much the same as the wall jack for a telephone. Most houses have a simple wall jack built to handle a single telephone line. If you add multi-line capabilities to your house, things get a little more complicated. Going to a two-line system requires a different kind of connection; going beyond two lines requires the use of special telephone switching equipment and a much more involved wiring structure. PC expansion slots also come with different levels of complexity as explained below.

There are two primary factors, width and speed, that affect the performance of an expansion bus, and performance is the primary reason why engineers have tried to improve on the original design. The wider the data bus and the faster the operating frequency, the more data can be moved per second.

Data Buses

The data bus is a bundle of wires used to transfer the data to and from the CPU. The wider the data bus, the more information can be moved at a time and (if the software is capable) the more complex the information can be. When discussing data buses, there are two numbers to keep in mind: one is the *external data path*; this is the number of bits that can be moved between the CPU and other components of the computer, such as RAM and expansion cards. The second is the *internal data path*, and refers to data that is moved only within the device itself. In some cases, the width of these two buses is the same; in others it's different.

It's Just a Matter of 1, 2, 3—Isn't It?

When we're counting, what happens when we want to count above the number nine? We add another place to the left. By doing this, we can go up to the number 99, because each number in the left column is equal to ten numbers in the right column. We use a similar system to increase the numbers we use inside a computer. Each wire carrying information can have a value of either zero or one. If two wires are linked together to carry a signal, we now have four combinations, since each wire can have two possible values. Go to four wires and we have 16 possible combinations. A *data bus* is a collection of wires used to transmit a number. It's sort of like a highway carrying information. Different components of your microprocessor get information off this bus.

Registers, Address, and Data Buses

Inside your CPU are two types of buses, the data bus just explained and the *address bus*. The address bus defines the location in memory in which data is to be placed, or from where it is to be sought. The total width of the address bus is very important, because it determines the total amount of memory the CPU, and therefore the entire system, can directly manipulate. Each position in memory has to have a specific location, just like you have the address for your house; there has to be one specific number for each and every position in memory. The width of the address bus determines the maximum number of available address combinations, and so determines the maximum amount of memory the computer can address. For example, a computer with 16 address lines can directly manipulate 65,536 different memory addresses.

The Original PC Bus

The first PC came with a series of 8-bit slots; that means that the number of bits that could be transferred across the bus in a single pass was eight. This matched the width of the data path of the original PCs 8088 CPU. You may still find one or two 8-bit expansion slots on a modern motherboard. These will support devices that still only need a simple 8-bit data path, such as a mouse adapter and many Com and parallel ports. Cards designed for the original PC and PC-XT were all 8-bit cards and were smaller in size than the ones used in later systems. See Figure 5.6.

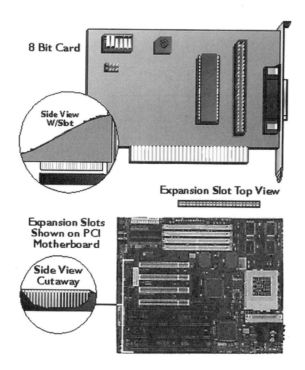

FIGURE 5.6 8-bit expansion card and slot.

The ISA Bus

With the arrival of the IBM AT-bus (Advanced Technology), widths changed to 16 bits and the design of the expansion slot was modified to provide a 16-bit connection. The AT-sized card is somewhat higher than the original 8-bit one used in the first PCs. To keep the system backward-compatible, the new slots were made with two parts; the longer back portion is identical to the original 8-bit connector, and a shorter segment was added in front to provide the additional width. See Figure 5.7.

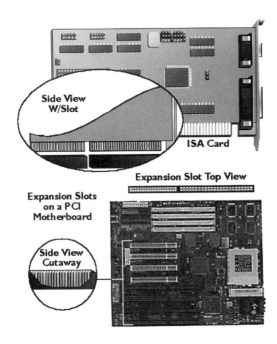

FIGURE 5.7 ISA expansion card and slot.

While some motherboards operate with an AT-style bus at different speeds, the convention is to operate at 8Mhz. That speed, coupled with a 16-bit data path, provides for a maximum transfer rate of about 6Mb per second. Of course, that's an ideal; most cards designed for this architecture don't come even close to that.

Originally this bus and card style were called *AT slots* because they showed up with the AT machines. When IBM introduced the PS/2, it decided to get fancy and modify the bus. IBM claimed the change to the Micro-Channel Architecture (MCA) bus would offer enhanced performance. Critics cried foul, claiming that the change was an effort by IBM to gain an advantage in the marketplace. Other manufacturers countered with a different advanced standard and the AT-bus design became known as *Industry Standard Architecture*, or *ISA* for short. The ISA bus is fairly simple, and although some newer expansion cards come with some degree of auto-configuration built into them, in most cases it's up to the user to make sure that the card settings do not conflict with some other part of the system. One of the reasons designers focused on improving the PCs expansion bus was to make it easier to install new cards.

Micro-Channel Architecture

As mentioned above, MCA is a special design produced by IBM to work with their PS/2 line. IBM offered to license use of this bus to other vendors, but only a few went along with the plan. MCA has never gained wide popularity and even IBM went back to making some machines with the old ISA-style connectors. The company still sells PS/2 machines with the MCA bus, but its lack of acceptance has limited the number of cards available, and made them more expensive than cards using other connectors. Due to the limited popularity of MCA, and the fact that you can't generally build your own MCA-based system, we won't explore this architecture any further. If you do for some reason have to install an expansion card in an MCA-based machine, the procedure is very similar to that involved for installing EISA-based cards, described below.

EISA and the Gang of Nine

EISA looks a lot like ISA and that's no accident. The acronym stands for *Enhanced Industry Standard Architecture*, and was developed by nine of IBM's competitors (which explains the use of the term "Gang of Nine" in relation to it). It was designed to compete with the technology designed into the MCA bus described above. It is a

32-bit architecture, designed to operate at 8Mhz per second. The EISA bus has several design characteristics that allow it to transfer data at up to 32Mb per second. 16- and 8-bit cards from the earlier ISA and XT designs can be used in EISA slots, but they won't perform any better than they did in the older system. Figure 5.8 shows the edge connector for an EISA slot. If you look straight down at an EISA slot, it looks just like the old ISA model, but it's actually a little deeper. The extra space is used to provide additional connection area for the EISA card, which increases the bandwidth (data transfer capability) and adds other features.

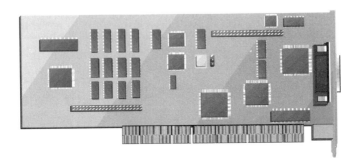

FIGURE 5.8 The edge connector for an EISA slot.

When you install a real EISA card, you must have a configuration file to go along with it. This software is installed using a special utility, which sets up the card. This makes it much easier to configure the system, since the unit can often automatically resolve potential conflicts.

Local Bus

The advent of Microsoft Windows pushed the demand for better display-adapter and hard-disk performance; one of the simplest ways to gain increased performance is to have a faster data bus. The designs mentioned above have a very limited bus speed. Local bus architecture provides a special bus access that connects directly to your system's CPU; this allows (at least in theory) for the local bus slot to operate as fast as the CPU.

VESA and VL-Bus

Local bus first appeared when several vendors first designed some proprietary slots for graphics adapters on their machines. Shortly thereafter, the Video Equipment Standards Association (VESA) produced a uniform local bus design (abbreviated as *VL-Bus*). It coupled a standard 16-bit expansion slot with part of an MCA expansion connector placed in front of it. This isn't an attempt to sneak MCA onto your motherboard; rather the designers just used a readily-available part to make it easy and cheap to implement on the motherboard. The standard allows local-bus transfer rates of up to 40Mb and local bus cards can easily perform 50% faster than their ISA counterparts. While a majority of products that use the bus are graphics adapters, you can also find hard disk controllers, SCSI host adapters, and other peripherals that make use of the extra speed.

PCI

If you want performance, make sure that your motherboard has PCI slots for your graphics adapter, SCSI host adapter, and network card. VESA rapidly became very popular, but on Pentium-based machines, Intel's newer *PCI* (Peripheral Component Interconnect) standard soon replaced it. Today almost all systems come with two or three PCI slots, and several ISA or EISA slots. Usually one position is shared. In other words, a PCI and a non-PCI slot are placed close together, so only one can be used, and both are aligned with the same opening. The older PC bus standards were designed around Intel's only family of microprocessors; but PCI is different. Like VESA, PCI is a local bus standard tying the expansion bus directly to the CPU; unlike VL-Bus, which peaks out at 40Mb, PCI can handle up to 133Mb per second. PCI is also very inexpensive for developers to integrate and the standard has wide industry support. You can get PCI buses on PCs, Macs, and even Unix workstations. See Figure 5.9.

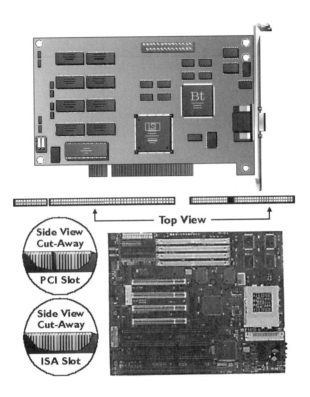

FIGURE 5.9 A PCI expansion card and slot.

CATCHING THE RIGHT BUS, WHAT DOES IT MEAN TO YOU?

The type of expansion bus a card should be designed for depends on its use. Generally speaking, a mouse card or other low-bandwidth device works fine as an 8-bit ISA design, while a good graphics adapter or hard drive interface needs the extra speed of PCI or EISA. See Figure 5.10.

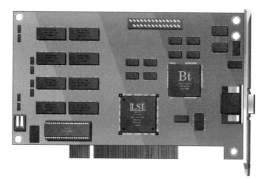

FIGURE 5.10 A PCI expansion card.

If you are planning on building a system that requires a lot of very intensive disk activity, such as a network file server, you may want to consider a PCI/EISA-based design. Otherwise, look for one with at least three PCI slots and the rest ISA-style.

FORMAL INTRODUCTIONS

When we add an expansion card into the system, it's a bit like performing a marriage. When the connection is made, two different families, the motherboard and the expansion card, are joined together into one unit. In society, a marriage is a contract that formally introduces the new family unit into the community; the act legalizes the connection and bestows certain privileges. When you add an expansion card, it also must be formally introduced. If it is not, conflicts may arise, and the new device may either not be seen by the system, or in a worst-case scenario, cause a conflict that keeps the system from operating at all.

Memory Addresses

One of the formal introductions must be to the BIOS. Earlier in the book we explained the memory addressing system that the PC uses to allocate resources. Many expansion cards must be given a specific memory address to work, based on settings made by using switches on the card itself. Some PCI buses can let cards share the same Interrupts, offering a real advantage. They also handle memory allocation in a way that overcomes a lot of the pain that used to be associated with card installation.

During the Power-On-Self-Test, your computer checks its memory to see if any additional BIOS routines should be loaded. In order to work, your new card must have a unique, absolute address range. Just how big a space is needed may vary from card to card. If two cards (or some other device on your system plus a card) share an address, there is a conflict and the system may hang up. This is why it is important to know what addresses are free before you start adding in new cards. Newer motherboards and operating systems like Windows 95 offer a feature known as *Plug and Play* or *PnP*. This is a method of automatically setting up cards and drivers so they do not conflict. Not all cards are PnP ready, and not all the ones that are work properly. The skills I cover here can overcome most of the installation hassles.

In most cases, the documentation that came with your new expansion card will recommend address settings for itself. If you don't have a whole lot of accessories installed on your system, it may be that the defaults (preset values) will work just fine and you don't have to set anything. If you have to keep several machines running, it's a handy trick to set standard devices at the same address. For example, most hard disk controllers are set to an address of either CC00 or C800; I try to set all of mine to C800, which makes figuring out where to put a new device nice and easy.

If you must set a specific memory address, this is usually done using a set of switches found on the card. We'll explain how these switches work shortly.

IRQs

Another potential area of conflict that may require adjusting a setting is the card's *Interrupt ReQuest* (IRQ), sometimes referred to as an Interrupt vector. Interrupts are a method used in your computer to allow a device to signal the CPU that it needs attention. This is a bit like the numbering system sometimes used in bakeries and ice cream shops. You take a number, and when your number comes up, it's your turn to be waited on. When a device needs service from the CPU, it generates an Interrupt request. A device must be assigned a unique IRQ to avoid a conflict. Once again, these are usually set by switches found on the surface of the expansion card. The only important thing to remember is that, as a rule, you shouldn't have two devices sharing the same IRQ. There are some standard assignments for certain IRQs. Generally speaking, IRQ 3 is used for your second Com port; IRQ 4 is assigned to the first Com port (don't ask me why they do it that way). IRQ 5 is for the second parallel printer port, and IRQ 7 for the first parallel printer port.

When setting IRQs for a new device, it's reasonably safe to use IRQ 5 if you don't have a second parallel printer port in your system and you haven't already assigned it to something else. If you have a Microsoft bus mouse, it may already be set to that Interrupt. If you already have a number of things installed and are running out of IRQs, you may have to remove or inactivate one of your devices. In several machines on my network I have removed or disabled the second serial port (Com2) so that my network interface card can use IRQ 3.

DMA

Some cards, especially sound cards and some hard disk controllers, may also make use of a DMA channel. DMA stands for *Direct Memory Access*, and this allows direct access to the system's RAM buffer (holding area) without having to go through the system's CPU. This has two benefits: one is that the device can address memory faster than would otherwise be possible; and the other is that the CPU is freed from that task so that it can do other things. DMA is provided through different channels known as (of course) *DMA channels*. If a card makes use of DMA, it must be assigned its own DMA channel. If two devices try to use the same DMA channel at the same time, either one device will not work or the system will hang up. The easiest way to avoid this conflict is to keep a good Inventory, as described later in this chapter.

Setting Switches

DIP Switches

DIP switches are a series of small switches, usually built into a small plastic block mounted on the surface of an expansion card. The acronym stands for *Dual In-line Package*. These work much like a row of light switches. When the circuit is *closed* or on, electricity can flow through the position, enabling a feature or setting a value. When the circuit is *open* or off, no current flows through and the feature is disabled or a different value is set. See Figure 5.11.

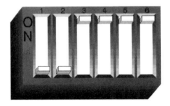

FIGURE 5.11 A bank of 4 DIP switches.

Jumpers

Jumpers are really a very simple form of switch. The pins coming out of the board are the poles and the small conducting sleeve, called a *jumper*, is used to close the circuit. If there is no jumper, the circuit is open or off. When you put the jumper on the pins, it's closed, making the connection. Just as with DIP switches, your manual may refer to jumper settings in a couple of different ways. Keep in mind that "closed" and "on" are synonymous terms, and so are "off" and "open." Sometimes jumper switches are found as just a pair of wires sticking up; sometimes there are three-wire jumpers, which allows setting two options, depending on which pair of pins are actually covered by the jumper. The pins will usually be labeled *1*, *2*, and *3*. Jumpering pins 1 and 2 selects one mode, while jumpering 2 and 3 chooses the other. Figure 5.12 shows an illustration of a three-pin jumper switch.

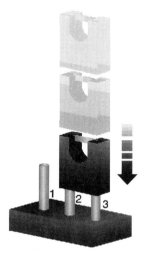

FIGURE 5.12 A three-pin jumper switch and jumper.

On some cards you will find a row of jumper pins. These are often used in combination, so that setting specific combinations allows for a wider range of options. For instance, an eight-bank set might be used to select a wide range of memory addresses.

The number of possible combinations of jumpers and DIP switches, and their uses with expansion cards are too involved for further instruction. Each expansion card is usually shipped with a manual which includes diagrams and tables showing how the switches and jumpers on that card are used. In the discussion that follows below on maintaining an Inventory and installing cards, I'll explain the basics of choosing an Interrupt and setting an address range, but you need to check with the manual that came with the card for the specifics on where switches are located, what they do, and how they should be set. The most important thing to remember is that if switches are set incorrectly, the device may not work properly, and may even lock up your system. Usually if this happens, it is not a real problem; you simply have to remove the card and adjust the settings until you find one that works.

Installing expansion cards is a basic computing skill and requires very little in the way of mechanical ability to accomplish. The above discussion may seem a bit daunting to the novice. Just keep in mind that your memory addresses and IRQs must not be in conflict with something else. Just so you can see how easy it actually is, I'm going to go through the basic procedure now. Then we can come back and discuss how to keep an Inventory of the cards in your system and avoid address and Interrupt conflicts.

Installing an Expansion Card

What You'll Need

- ✔ The expansion card itself
- ✔ The appropriate internal or external cable(s) to install your peripheral(s)
- ✔ Appropriate software drivers
- ✔ Screwdriver
- ✔ Hemostat
- ✔ Tweezers or pliers for placing jumpers
- ✔ The card's documentation
- ✔ Small flashlight and magnifying glass

Step 1

Turn off power to the system and remove the power cord. If you try to remove or install cards with the power turned on to the computer, you may seriously injure the cards and/or the motherboard.

Step 2

Remove the cover from your computer's case by removing the screws holding it along the back, outer edge of the machine.

Step 3

Touch the inside metal chassis to ground yourself.

Step 4

Now open the box that the expansion card came in and remove the card from its protective envelope. Depending on the type of card, you may have one or more jumpers which should be checked, and which may need to be reset before installing. You will need to refer to the expansion card's manual for additional instructions, and possibly a Readme file on an installation disk.

Step 5

Open the manual and identify any jumpers or DIP switches that have to be set. You will usually need to identify what the BIOS address and an I/O port are. Your manual should tell you what the combination of jumpers or DIP switches must be to select the proper range.

Step 6

Locate a free expansion slot of the correct type and remove its back cover plate.

T I P If this is a second PCI card in the same system, check to see which slot offers the best performance. Then place the most intensive card into the fastest slot; that is usually the hard drive controller or SCSI card, but you might want to place a network card in the position of honor in a network server.

Step 7

Once again, touch the edge of the case to make sure that you aren't carrying any static charge, then with gentle pressure, insert the card into the free slot. You may find it helps to hold the card at a slight angle while you line the edge connector up with the slot. Then straighten it to the perpendicular and gently push it into place. See Figure 5.13.

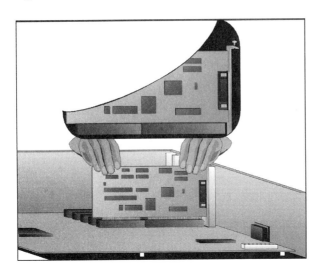

Figure 5.13 Installing a card into a slot.

WARNING

With PCI, EISA and VL-Bus expansion cards, be sure to only press straight down. Attempting to angle these cards in and out can jam the card in the expansion slot and possibly cause damage.

If you are installing an EISA card, be extra careful to be sure that the card is pushed completely to the bottom of the slot. Remember that EISA and slots are made with a deeper edge connector to enable the expanded capabilities.

Step 8

Use the screw that held the slot cover to fasten the card into place.

Step 9

If the card should be attached to another device, attach the appropriate cable to both the expansion card and the second device.

Installing Drivers and Testing the Installation

Step 1

Once you have verified that all the switches are set correctly, that the connections are properly made, and the cables properly attached, you are ready to turn the machine back on. Turn on any peripheral device that relates to the card's function as well.

Step 2

Install the driver software for your operating system and for any other applications you plan on running, following the instructions that came with the expansion card. Test all the software that you have installed drivers for, and make sure everything works. If you are installing the card on a Windows 95 machine, boot the PC and see if Windows will recognize it. You will need the Windows 95 disks or CD-ROM and the drivers that came with the new card.

If you are installing an EISA card, when you boot the computer you will have to use the Configuration utility to integrate the card into the system.

NOTE

Step 3

Replace the cover and place any spare screws, parts, etc. into your goodies bag for future use.

Step 4

Make a new Dark and Stormy Night Disk or Windows Rescue Disk as described in Chapter 2, so that you will have backup copies of all the new settings. For DOS users: you'll want to save copies of your CONFIG.SYS, AUTOEXEC.BAT, SYSTEM.INI, and WINDOWS.INI (the last two files are for Windows version 3.xx users only) off onto your bootable floppy.

REMOVING AN EXPANSION CARD

Step 1

Turn off power to the system and remove the power cord. If you try to remove or install cards with the power turned on in the computer, you may seriously injure the cards and/or the motherboard.

Step 2

Remove the cover from your computer's case by removing the screws holding it along the back, outer edge of the machine.

Step 3

Touch the inside metal chassis to ground yourself.

Step 4

Remove the screw that holds the mounting bracket to the case. Once again, touch the edge of the case to make sure that you aren't carrying any static charge, and remove the card by pulling gently but firmly straight up on it.

Step 5

Place the card into a static-resistant envelope.

Step 6

If you are not inserting another card into the slot, replace the cover plate and screw it down.

INSTALLING A DAUGHTER BOARD

If your expansion card comes with a daughter board that you wish to use, use the following procedure to install it. Daughter cards usually connect by using a series of pins similar to jumpers on one card, and a female fitting on the other to slide into. To install a daughter card, remove the card from the system, if necessary, using the procedure outlined above.

Be careful to avoid static electricity by grounding yourself before opening any protective envelopes or touching any of the electronic components inside the case. Follow the instructions that came with the card for setting any switches required to recognize the new hardware, and assemble the pieces as defined in the product's documentation. You may need to attach some form of cabling to the two cards. If so, be sure to follow any instructions for specific orientation of the cable. In most cases, this will involve making sure that the side of a ribbon cable with a red stripe on it is closest to Pin 1 on both cards. Once you've finished this assembly, place it into the machine, using the procedure for installing expansion cards.

TROUBLESHOOTING A NEW EXPANSION CARD INSTALLATION

Once everything is installed, turn on the machine and make sure everything boots correctly. Install any required drivers and test any software that's supposed to operate with the card. If everything works properly, put the cover back on and tighten everything down. If something isn't operating properly, you probably have an address or Interrupt conflict or have not installed the software correctly. To resolve possible conflicts, first make sure that you have installed everything properly, and that the card is securely seated in the slot.

Make sure that the software is properly installed and that all drivers are being loaded. To test this, keep an eye on the screen during the boot cycle to see that the drivers are being loaded properly. If the screen scrolls too fast to catch it, you can press the **Pause** button on your keyboard to halt the display. To get it moving again, press the **Spacebar**.

If you can't find a problem at this point, you'll have to make sure that there aren't any memory conflicts or hardware conflicts (IRQ or DMA). Try removing any non-essential cards and rebooting the machine. If it works now, reinstall the cards one at a time until you locate the card causing the problem. Then resolve any conflict between the two cards. Windows 95 users can use the System tool in the Control Panel to resolve the problem if the machine will load the operating system. If not, boot to DOS and try to get things running there by adjusting jumpers or other setting on the cards in the machine. If you are using a memory manager like Qualitas' 386 to the MAX, Quarterdeck's QEMM or DOS's HIMEM.SYS under DOS, disable them by *remarking them out* (use a semi-colon at the start of each line) in the CONFIG.SYS file and see if that resolves the problem. If so, use your memory manager's configuration utility to adjust the settings until everything is working properly.

MEMORY

One of the simplest and yet the most beneficial things most users can do to enhance their PC is to add more memory. Chapter 4 covered the basics of how memory works in your computer and how to manage it. I won't repeat that discussion here, except to note that it is hard to have too much memory in your system. The earliest PCs were often shipped with somewhere between 16 to 640Kb of RAM; this usually came in the form of a series of chips that had to be plugged onto the motherboard individually. Today adding memory is much easier, since most RAM (Random Access Memory) comes in the form of snap-in memory modules. These can take on several different forms based on the type of computer you have and its speed. Figure 5.14a shows a standard single *DRAM* (Dynamic Random Access Memory) chip, the kind formerly used. In Figure 5.14b is one of the newer *SIMM* (Single In-line Memory Module) cards.

FIGURE 5.14a A DRAM chip.

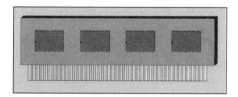

FIGURE 5.14b A SIMM module.

The older method required eight or nine chips to form one bank of memory, and in the early days, a bank of memory often only contained 4 or 16K of RAM. The early memory modules came with 256K of RAM per card, and these days 4Mb and 16Mb are commonplace, with higher-capacity cards on the way.

BUYING CONSIDERATIONS

Purchasing the Right Kind of Memory

If you have an older 286 or 386 system with DRAM on it, you should seriously consider upgrading the motherboard (and quite probably the CPU) if you need more memory. The cost of the older memory compared with the cost of upgrading the motherboard makes it more effective to just build a new system. Not only will the newer memory modules be cheaper than the old chips, but you'll end up with a system that is more flexible and has better performance. With that advice in mind, I'll limit the general discussion of standard RAM to SIMM-type modules. There are some variations with other types of RAM, but the basic rules apply to all forms of RAM technology.

Your motherboard is constructed to accept a certain type of memory module. Not all SIMMS are the same. Some operate at a faster speed than others, some have a different number of chips, and not all have exactly the same number of positions on their edge connectors. Your motherboard or system manual should list approved memory module types. There are a number of vendors who make SIMMs, and their products can generally be interchanged. It's a good idea to try to buy all of the memory from the same vendor. It reduces the chances of minor timing errors that can occur when mixing brands.

Memory operates at different speeds, which much be matched to your motherboard and your CPU. The faster the CPU, the faster the memory requirements are. The original IBM PC-XT had an 8088 processor which operated at a speed of 4.77 MHz. It used 150-*nanosecond* DRAM chips. Today many 386, 486, and Pentium machines use SIMMs that operate at 70 nanoseconds, roughly twice as fast as the memory used in the older computers. The faster memory is needed to match CPU speeds of 33MHz and faster.

How Much Memory Do You Need?

Before you get into the ins and outs of what type of memory you should buy (I'll explain all about that in a minute), you need to determine just how much memory you need. This depends in part upon the type of operating system and software you use and what kind of work you do. In general, for Windows 95 you should have at least 8Mb of RAM, and 16 is better. Double that for Windows NT, and triple it for Windows NT Server. If all you ever run is MS-DOS, 2 to 4Mb of RAM will probably meet your needs. If you're running Microsoft Windows (plain Windows, not the new stuff like 95 or NT), you should have at least 4Mb of total system RAM.

For a more detailed discussion on memory and memory management, you should refer to Chapter 4. This is really just intended to be a discussion of how to select and install memory, rather than its application.

NOTE

How to Purchase Memory Modules

Buying memory is a fairly straight-forward transaction, but there are a few things you must understand. The first thing is how memory is socketed into your motherboard. Memory is purchased in *banks* (rows), no matter whether you're using the older style DRAM chips or modern SIMMs. In the case of SIMMs, one module represents a certain amount of memory. For example, standard sizes are the now obsolete 256K, the fading 1Mb, the popular 4Mb and 16Mb modules. Coming on strong for power users are even larger SIMMS. As this book is written, 1Mb modules cost between $40 and $55 each from mail-order and wholesale suppliers, and slightly more from local computer stores. The larger-sized modules cost slightly less per Mb but you are paying more per card at a time.

You need to understand the different sizes of modules and how they interact before you order. SIMM modules are arranged in banks, usually of four cards each. In other words, you could put in four 256K modules and have 1Mb of RAM on the system. Most motherboards require adding four modules at a time. This is generally known as one *bank*. Depending on the way your motherboard is designed, you may have between one and four banks on your system on a special kind of carrier or bank, as shown in Figure 5.15. For example, if you want to add 8Mb to your system, you could add eight 1Mb modules, filling up one bank. A few motherboards will let you combine modules, but not within the same bank. So you could conceivably have 5Mb on a system by placing four 1Mb modules on one bank and four 265K modules on another.

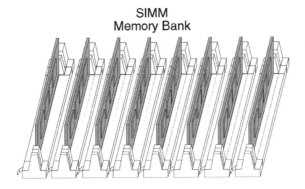

FIGURE 5.15 A SIMM memory bank.

To avoid wasting money, you should try to figure out exactly what your long-term memory goals are and purchase modules based on a plan. Some users think that they will save a bit of money by going with a 2 or 4Mb system, and find that the memory modules they bought must be discarded or given away when they upgrade the system to 8 or 16Mb.

Some vendors will accept RAM as trade-ins. Look in magazines like *Computer Shopper.*

NOTE

The only way you can know for sure just how your system board works with memory is to read the manual. It should have a section explaining how memory can be added, what types of memory modules can be used, and provide a list of tested and certified brands.

Ordering Chips

There are numerous mail-order houses providing discount chips, or you can go get them from your local store. Keep in mind that not all chips are created equal. There are different speeds, slightly different types of connectors, and, of course, differences in quality. The kinds listed in your documentation are those which are certified by your manufacturer to work in your system. You may be able to save money by using less expensive modules, not included on the list, but be aware that you do so with a certain element of risk, especially if you plan on adding more memory later. Minor timing differences can add up if you start mixing and matching modules from different vendors, especially if those vendors didn't spend quite enough time on quality control.

Once you have determined the type of chips and size and number of modules you'll need, it's time to do some shopping. Memory prices fluctuate, and there is often a 15% to 20% difference in cost between the lowest and highest prices available. Keep in mind that the lowest price may not always be a real bargain. Quality or technical support may not be as good as one of the more expensive vendors. I usually operate on the "20% rule" when buying any computer hardware. I evaluate the highest and lowest prices. I figure that they usually represent extra markup at the high end and corner-cutting at the low end. Unless I have an overriding reason to buy at either extreme, I usually stay within 20% of the middle of the price range. Once you have determined price and vendor, all that's left to do is place your order and then put the modules inside the case.

ADDING MORE MEMORY

SIMMs: Snap In and Forget It

The early PCs RAM consisted of groups of chips referred to as *DRAM* (Dynamic Random Access Memory). These were installed either directly into sockets on the motherboard, or on an expansion card. Several years ago engineers at Wang Computers designed the original *Single In-line Memory Module* (SIMM). This is a small card containing a row of chips, which provides anywhere from 1Mb to 16Mb of RAM, and which can be easily snapped in and out of a special slot on your motherboard or on an expansion card. Today, virtually all modern PCs are equipped with some form of SIMM bank.

The majority of 386, 486, and Pentium PCs use SIMMs with a 30-pin edge connector. Some newer units and proprietary designs use modules with 72 pins. When buying memory you should make sure that the type you are buying is designed to fit your machine and is appropriate for your class of computer.

NOTE

Some vendors use special expansion cards to seat memory, even SIMMs. These cards fit into a regular or special expansion slot, and the SIMM modules are snapped into place on that card. If your machine requires such a card and does not have available sockets on the motherboard, you will also have to buy a special card.

Adding the SIMM Chips

The hard part (except for making sure you use reasonable care) is over once the memory arrives. Memory chips are sensitive electronic devices. You have to be careful not to discharge static electricity from your fingers (or anything else) onto the card. This is especially a concern in dry, cool, or cold weather. We've already discussed how to remove the cover on your machine so I won't repeat those instructions now.

Once your memory arrives, assemble your basic tools. You'll need a screwdriver, and I also usually have a pen or a very small screwdriver available in case I have to adjust one of the SIMM's retaining latches. Place your computer in a convenient working position, with the cables disconnected, and remove the cover. Discharge any possible static electricity by touching one of the metal parts of the case. Once you've done that, open the package containing the memory. Most modules come individually-wrapped in a static resistant envelope.

Take one of the modules out. The lower side that will seat into the socket has a row of metal edge connectors, either gold or silver in color. Somewhere around the middle of that row of connectors there will be a cutout. This fits into a little raised portion in the middle of the socket so the module will only fit one way into the bank.

SIMMs must be inserted a specific way, in a specific order. Use your motherboard manual or the legends printed on the motherboard itself to determine which is the first position in the first bank of memory. Many motherboards start numbering with the number zero rather than one; if that's the case, you'll want to place the first module in Row zero of Bank zero. If the people who designed the board started counting at one, it will be Row one of Bank one. Don't worry, if you make a mistake here and put it in the wrong Bank, the worst scenario is that the system will be confused when it tries to access the memory and you'll have to repeat a couple of steps.

Once you have located the proper Bank, take a look at the way the socket that will hold the module is designed. You'll notice that it has little clips and projections on either side of the Bank. The projections are designed to fit in the two holes on the side of the module and secure it in place. The little plastic or metal latches on either side gently grip the module and keep it from moving once it's seated.

To get the module in place, you have to slide it in at an angle with the edge connectors in the slot, and the top of the module angled towards the back of the Bank. Using both thumbs or a thumb and forefinger, press down on the module, into the slot, while rotating the top so it clicks into place on the pin. In most cases you will hear a little click as the springs engage. On some machines, you may have to physically push the latches into place. Repeat this procedure until you have all the SIMMs properly seated. Refer to your manual to see if you have to set any jumpers or switches on the motherboard so that it will acknowledge the new memory. Make sure that all the SIMMs are all the same height and that they are all perfectly perpendicular to the motherboard (that last instruction may not apply to using a special expansion card, which might hold the modules at an angle). See Figure 5.16.

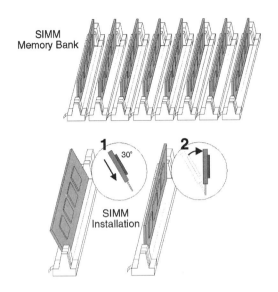

FIGURE 5.16 A standard SIMM bank with memory being installed.

Don't close the case yet, but go on and attach the cables and power leads, and turn on the machine. Watch the Power-On-Self-Test. This usually includes a memory test, which should show the same total amount of memory that you now have installed on the system (keep in mind that computers count funny. For each Mb of memory, the memory check should show 1024Kb of memory. Some machines may be off by 384Kb because of the way they handle part of the first Mb).

If your machine shows significantly less memory than what you expect, or if it doesn't go through the memory check properly, recheck the SIMMs and be sure they are seated properly. If necessary, remove them by reversing the procedure given above, starting at the back of the Bank first. Make sure all the SIMMs are tightly seated in their sockets. Then retry the memory check.

The next step is to run your system's CMOS Setup. Most machines today will automatically check the amount of memory, but many will report an error until you update Setup and confirm the new memory. Older machines may require that you enter the current amount of memory manually. Follow the instructions for setting CMOS values in your owner's manual.

Final Steps

If your computer does not see all of the memory that you've put in, you may have not seated one of the modules properly. Double-check to make sure that all are at the same height. If they are, try reseating them. If it still doesn't work, try reordering their position in the Bank; for instance, put the second one in slot one, three in two, four in three, and one in position four.

If that changes the amount of memory shown, but you still don't have all the memory, it is possible that one of the modules is damaged. If you can, locate another memory module and use it to replace one of the chips in succession until you've isolated the faulty module. When you've found it, contact the vendor you got the chip from and replace it.

SIPPs

SIPPs are a variation of the SIMM module. Instead of edge connectors like those found on SIMMs, SIPPs uses pins. Not many machines use SIPP memory; they work basically like SIMMs but are just placed straight down into a row of holes on the motherboard dedicated to this purpose. Like SIMMs, they must be matched to the machine and processor. Different kinds of SIPPs have different numbers of pins for connectors.

WARNING

Some vendors create SIPP and SIMM memory by using standard older DRAM chips, mounted on oversized module cards. Not only are the resultant products larger than the regular modules and therefore more likely to make it difficult to add expansion cards near them, but they are not as reliable. If you get any of these, you should return them immediately to the vendor you got them from.

Installing them is simple. Make sure that Pin 1 on the SIPP matches up with the Pin 1 hole on the motherboard; line the pins up precisely over the holes and insert by pushing downwards gently but firmly until the pins are seated. Removing SIPPs is just the reverse; place thumb and forefinger of each hand on either end of the SIPP and pull up gently.

DIP DRAM

NOTE

In some cases, you may have to remove a smaller-sized set of cache memory chips and install new ones. If you must remove older-style DIP chips, you may use one of two methods. If your tool kit came with a chip puller, you can use that to remove the chips. This tool resembles a wide pair of tweezers that don't come together, and usually has two little half-moon projections facing in at the bottom of each arm. Make sure you are grounded and work the two little moon shapes between the base of the chip and its mounting socket by squeezing the two sides together in one hand. Use the other hand to press gently down on the motherboard on either side of the socket, then pull straight up with the tool. If the chip is very firmly seated, you may have to rock back and forth on the long axis of the chip very gently and with a slight motion. If you are too rough, you may damage the soft solder pins on either side of the chip, which can very easily render it useless.

An alternate method is to gently work the blade of a small screwdriver in from either end of the chip, alternating ends and slowly rocking the blade underneath until the chip is loosened and you can pull it out.

You may have, or have inherited, an older PC which still uses Dual In-line Package DRAM. As with SIPPs and SIMMs, you must be sure that the speed of the memory matches the speed of your CPU and is supported by your motherboard. DIPs are a little bit more involved to install. Most DIPs are rectangular blocks of silicon that have very thin pins running down two sides of them. This pins have to be exactly seated in a mounting platform containing matching holes. In the unlikely event you have a machine using this form of RAM, refer to the instructions for upgrading the BIOS chip that follow. See Figure 5.17.

FIGURE 5.17 A Dual In-line Package chip being installed.

WARNING

Be extremely careful when placing this type of chip into its sockets. If you don't correctly line up all the pins into the little holes, and press down, the misaligned leads will be bent. In some cases, you can very carefully use your fingertips or a pair of tweezers to line the pins up again, but it's very easy to permanently damage the chip and make it unusable.

Installing Cache Memory

In all likelihood you will have ordered your motherboard with *cache*, and the cache chips will have come pre-installed. If not, you will have to mount them yourself or get a friend to do it. If you have never seated electronic components directly on a circuit board before, you may want to get a friend with experience to show you how it's done. While it is not difficult, it does take a gentle touch. If you want to do it by yourself, follow the steps outlined below.

Cache memory is sometimes distributed on modules similar to the SIMMs you just installed. Many systems still use individual chips to provide secondary cache. These are installed in banks, and you should refer to your system's manual for the exact placement of the chips on the motherboard. Based on the amount of cache you are installing, these chips must be properly oriented. You will find a little, moon-shaped cutout or indentation, or possibly a little bump, on one of the narrow sides of the chip, right on the edge of the top surface. All the chips need to be oriented the same way, and you should check with your manual to find out exactly how they should be positioned. Prongs are located along both long sides of the chip.

Once again, make sure you are properly grounded, and take the first chip gently between the thumb and first finger of each hand. Set the prongs facing away from you into the holes on the far side of the appropriate chip socket, raising the side towards you up at a very slight angle.

Press evenly and gently away from you and guide the prongs on the side towards you into their positions in the socket. In some cases you will need next to no angle at all to do this, in other cases you will need more. Be careful and make sure that all the pins go in their appropriate holes. Take care to make sure you don't bend any of them. If you bend one, you'll have to remove the chip, try to straighten the pin and try again. The pins are made of very soft metal and will fatigue or even break if you play with them too much.

Installing a Cache Module

Some motherboards use a *cache module* which is similar to the SIMMs described previously, but is often a slightly larger, click-in card. Refer to your motherboard manual for exact placement, and then follow the procedure outlined for SIMMs previously.

UPGRADING AND INSTALLING BIOS

Over time, the manufacturer of your system's motherboard may enhance the features contained in its BIOS, those you access by using the system's CMOS Setup routine. This is usually to take advantage of new devices, such as high-capacity floppy disk drives. One moderately recent instance of this kind of upgrade was the announcement of 2.88Mb floppy disks. Most BIOSes don't support these extended-capacity drives, and you must either upgrade the BIOS or use a special device driver. In other cases, the BIOS is enhanced because some problem was found in the current version. You usually have to contact your dealer or the motherboard manufacturer to learn about the availability of these upgrades and to order them.

Installing the BIOS

BIOSes are usually provided in one of two forms: as DIP chips similar to those mentioned above, or as a program which can be downloaded into the existing BIOS. The software upgrade is only available on machines having a special kind of chip to store the BIOS known as *flash* RAM. If you cannot determine which kind of BIOS you have based on the information in your motherboard manual, you should be able to find out from its manufacturer.

Updating Flash BIOS

This is a very simple procedure, especially if you have a modem. Most hardware vendors operate a bulletin-board service and will let you download the software directly into your machine. If you don't have access to a modem, you'll have to arrange to have the software shipped on disk.

Once the software arrives, you run the application using the instructions provided either in the information sheet or in a *Readme* file (the disk file with the latest information). You will usually need a formatted floppy disk to hold a Restore file which can be used if the new BIOS causes problems with your system. Once you have run the program, you will have to access your system's CMOS Setup and set new values following the instructions.

WARNING

Be sure to replace any jumpers that set a read-only state for the Flash BIOS. Failure to do so could ruin the flash chip, and kill the system until you could get a replacement. Check your motherboard manual for details, as each system has its own methods.

Updating DIP Chip BIOSes

To replace DIP-style BIOSes, you have to remove the old chip and replace it with the new one, following the procedures listed earlier for adding DIP-style memory. The only difference is that the BIOS chip will be larger, and therefore easier to work with than DRAM or cache memory modules. Once the new BIOS chip is installed, run your CMOS Setup program to set the values. Handle the old chip with care; if the new BIOS proves to be incompatible with your equipment, you'll have to reinstall it to get things working properly again.

MAKE IT EASY ON YOURSELF

Many years ago I picked up an adage from my Marine Corps Drill Instructor: "One way or the other you're going to keep at this until you get it right. Make it easy on yourselves." While there may seem to be a vast difference between a boot camp drill field and expanding a PC, they do have this one thing in common: you have to keep at it until you get it right; and there are two ways to do things, the easy way and the hard way. With PCs, the easy way of installing a card is to know what's in your system and how the different devices are set so that you can avoid conflicts.

In a simple setup, the default setting that the equipment came with will usually work the first time. Most people who read this book are probably planning on adding more than just a serial card to their machines. Over time you will probably acquire a number of gadgets, some of which may require a good bit of system resources or need intricate settings.

Doing It the Hard Way

Most users do things the hard way when it comes to integrating their system with a new product. They open the case, look at all the cards in there, and try to get an idea of what memory addresses or Interrupts might be free, adjust some settings to what they hope are conflict-free positions, install the card and hope the machine works. Sometimes they're lucky, everything works. Sometimes they're not and they spend the rest of the day fiddling with switches and jumpers. In even more obnoxious cases, things seem to work at first. It isn't until the case is closed and you're running your favorite application that things go awry, or perhaps you start getting random error messages that you can't quite figure out. You've landed in the Conflict Zone. Somewhere, an Interrupt, a DMA channel, or a memory address is nibbling at the stability of your system; and maybe you figure it out and maybe you don't. That's doing things the hard way.

The Easier Way

While nothing can make all your installations and tinkerings foolproof, being aware of how the different components of your PC are installed can save a lot of time and frustration. A very simple tool can be employed to keep track of your system's configuration and any idiosyncrasies. Included as Appendix B of this book is a PC Inventory form, which you can use to record vital data about your PC. This sheet of paper requires nothing more technical than a pen. It won't go down if you lose your hard disk, and you can keep it right at hand if you don't have any video and a support technician is asking you about your configuration.

The key to a good Inventory is keeping it up to date. Windows 95 and Windows NT users should make a hard-copy list of the system settings that are easily available in the Control Panel System or System Diagnostics section. For DOS and Windows 3.x users, two of the software programs included on the CD-ROM in the back of the book are very useful for maintaining an Inventory. WinSleuth Gold is a Windows program that does a reasonable job of going out and looking at Interrupts, memory addresses and standard hardware that is configured on your system. The shareware program, ASQ, from Qualitas, is designed to examine your system's memory map and use of system resources.

To some extent, these programs overlap and you may wonder why I included them both. Qualitas is one of the leading manufacturers of memory managers on the market. A more powerful version of ASQ is shipped with their program, 386 to the MAX. The shareware version on our CD-ROM can be used when you can't get into Windows to examine memory conflicts and quickly look at your configuration files and BIOS status. WinSleuth Gold can actually be used to test and benchmark your system. There are some devices that can fool it. Perhaps they don't respond when their Interrupt vector is queried by the program. In some cases memory management software might mask the proper setting. I use the combination of these programs, along with record keeping, every time I install a new piece of hardware to keep my Inventory up to date. The following paragraphs show you how to keep an accurate Inventory and use it when it comes time to install a new product.

Before proceeding, you'll probably want to make a photocopy of the Inventory form in Appendix B. I suggest making two or three at the same time. Then get a file folder and a pencil. The file folder can be used to also store printouts of your basic configuration files, AUTOEXEC.BAT and CONFIG.SYS, as well as any loose documentation pages that might come with some of the smaller cards, such as a serial card. One of the most frustrating things is to lose the little piece of paper that serves as a manual for some of the cheaper expansion cards. If you lose that information, it will be almost impossible to set the jumpers to disable a feature or change an IRQ.

It's also a good habit to keep the invoices and warranty cards from these products in the same file folder. That way if you ever have to contact a vendor for support, repair, or replacement, you'll have all the information in one place. I keep a folder like this for each machine on my network.

Starting an Inventory

What You'll Need

- ✔ One or more copies of the Inventory form from the back of the book
- ✔ Pencil (so you can go back and revise or correct entries)

✔ The manuals for your system and anything installed inside the case

✔ The CD-ROM from the back of the book or the System tools in the Windows NT or Windows 95 Control Panel

✔ A screwdriver and possibly a nut driver for opening your case and removing expansion cards

✔ Small flashlight and magnifying glass

Recording the Basics

The Inventory form includes information not only on the hardware, but also on the operating environment. Any of the information on the form that you know immediately can be filled in before actually opening up the case. It's a good idea to identify your system by name. This may sound funny if you only have one computer, but over time you may modify the motherboard or add a second system. You'll want to know which Inventory Sheet refers to which computer or reincarnation of a computer that you're dealing with.

I often name my machines by the type of motherboard in the case, or by the person who uses it the most. If you bought your machine already assembled, it's often a good idea to use the manufacturer's name for that product. This information can be recorded in the blank at the top of the Inventory Sheet. Next to that are entries for the type of CPU, its speed, the amount of RAM on the system, and the date it was put into service. The first section of the form includes the basic information about your computer's operating environment; the second contains the detailed settings for your expansion cards.

Also included in the basic section are blocks for recording what operating system is used and its version, the BIOS type and its revision number, your hard drive type and its capacity, the types of floppy drives installed on your system, the make and model of the motherboard, and the name and version of your memory manager. If you use an operating environment such as Microsoft Windows, that is not part of the operating system itself but is important to the way you use your computer, you can note it in the same line with your operating system.

If you only have one system this may seem like a bit of overkill; but these are all questions that a support technician may ask when you have a problem, and the Inventory will serve as an excellent record for insurance if the machine is stolen or damaged in a way covered by your policy.

Once you've completed this part, it's time to open the case so that you can verify the current settings of the cards inside. I have included several of the more common expansion cards at the top of the list in section two. These include your hard disk controller, video adapter, communications and printer ports. Some of these devices often are combined on one card. I usually make a listing of the settings for one entry and then just write that these settings are shared with named other peripherals on the sheet. Keep in mind that devices that share the same card can sometimes have their own Interrupts and memory addresses. If this is the case, be sure to write down each one in its own block.

An inset block on the form has been provided listing IRQs 1–15 and DMA channels 1–5. You can place an "X" over a number for each occupied location. This makes it an easy matter to scan the Inventory Sheet to find a free location for a new peripheral.

Taking Stock

The next step requires a little bit of homework. You'll have to identify the current settings for each card by inspecting the jumpers and DIP switches, and comparing the settings to the values in the documentation that came with the device. Some cards have labels on the back or markings next to jumpers that indicate the value of a setting. You might want to look for those to save time before going to the manual. While working inside the case, please follow all the anti-static precautions explained earlier. See Figure 5.18.

Inventory

Name of Computer_____   Date of Inventory _____

CPU type, speed _____   Date installed_____

Math coprocessor, overdrive, etc. _____   Date Installed _____

RAM Memory, amount, kind_____   Date installed _____

Operating system and environment and versions_____   _____

BIOS type, Revision Number _____   Date installed if appropriate _____

Hard Drive type, capacity_____   Date installed _____

Floppy Drive type, capacity_____   Dates installed_____

Motherboard Make and model_____   Date Installed _____

Memory Manager Program and Version Number_____   _____

Expansion Cards

Type	Vendor	IRQ	DMA	Memory Range	Date Installed	Driver(s)
Graphics Adapter						
I/O Card						
Hard disk Controller						
Floppy Drive controller						
SCSI Adapter						

IRQ's	1	2	3	4	5	6	7	8	9	10	11	12	13	14	15

DMA Channels	1	2	3	4	5

FIGURE 5.18 A sample Inventory Sheet.

The Inventory Sheet contains listings for common settings; most cards will not need to have all the blanks filled in. There's also a column for the name of any device driver used by the product, as well as a place to make remarks. You may need to refer to the product's documentation to ascertain the exact name of the device driver. The possible entries include the name of the card, the manufacturer's IRQ number, memory range, DMA channel, and date of installation.

Another trick you can use to make your life easier with this sheet is to turn the page over, and on the back write the name of each company, followed by their technical support number and their BBS service number. That way if you have to contact them, you just have to flip the form over and make the call.

Once you are done noting your cards in the Inventory, reassemble the case and reattach all cables and cords.

Checking Things Out with WinSleuth Gold

If you are a DOS or Windows 3.1x user you should already be familiar with WinSleuth Gold from using it to make the Dark and Stormy Night Disk described earlier in the book. Now we are going to use it to check out some of the basic characteristics of your system. Open the program by loading Windows and then clicking on its icon. Once WinSleuth Gold is loaded, click on the **Install** button and then choose **DMA/IRQ** Map from the button list on the right-hand side of the window. You should see a report similar to that shown in Figure 5.19.

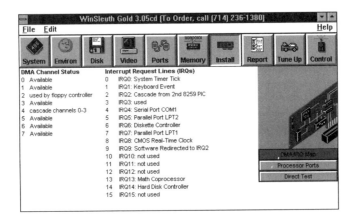

FIGURE 5.19 Inspecting the DMA/IRQ map.

This window shows the current status of available IRQs and DMA channels as reported to the program. It may not be a full listing, since some devices may not answer back properly. It will probably show some that you did not find in your Inventory. For example, in our figure, IRQ 13 shows that it is occupied by the math processor and IRQ 8 by the CMOS clock. Since these functions are not contained on an expansion card, you wouldn't have found them during your physical Inventory.

You can also use WinSleuth Gold to check the date of your BIOS, current CMOS settings, the operating system parameters, and descriptions of your hard disk and floppy drives, as well as information about your video controller, parallel ports, and memory usage. The majority of these reports can be printed by using the Report option. Any of these that you feel might be useful for future reference can be printed and stored in your file folder. For more information on WinSleuth Gold, complete documentation is included as a Microsoft Word file with the program.

You can also use ASQ to record much of this same information. By opening up the System Analysis menu, you can gain access to information about video, drives, and the detail of your CMOS Setup. ASQ has been included primarily to allow you to examine memory usage.

DEALING WITH TECHNICAL SUPPORT

A good Inventory and attention to detail can usually resolve most conflicts. In some cases the problems may be very subtle, or you may have actually come upon a flaw in the hardware's design or the software's functions. If you find yourself in a position where you can't isolate the problem, you've exhausted all the basic steps you can think of, or you think it's beyond your knowledge of the situation, it's time to call technical support.

To make things go as smoothly as possible, you should prepare for the support call by having the following things at hand:

✔ Your Inventory Sheet

✔ The version of any software involved and if necessary, your serial number and date of purchase

✔ The product's documentation

✔ A short description of the problem and exactly what seems to cause it

✔ A notepad and pen for jotting down instructions, etc.

✔ Your computer

The last item on the list may seem funny, but you should be seated at your computer (if possible) when you call technical support. If it's a hardware problem, you should also have the tools at hand to open your case, remove expansion cards, and adjust jumpers or DIP switches. In other words, you'll need a screwdriver and possibly a pair of tweezers or a hemostat. You also might want a magnifying glass and a small flashlight for reading small details printed on an expansion card or your motherboard.

In the event that the product is actually defective, you may have to obtain an RMA number (*Return Merchandise Authorization number*). If this is the case, you should write the vendor, the date, the product and the RMA number on the back of your Inventory Sheet. When you are given the RMA number, make sure you get the proper address and telephone number of the facility to which you are sending the product. This is not always the same as the address printed in the manual. If it's a major component, you should have kept the box and packing the product arrived in. Package it the way you received it and make sure that the RMA number is very visible on the outside of the package. In many cases if a product arrives at a repair facility without an RMA number, it is refused and returned to the sender without being opened.

Ask the technician how long the repair will take so you will have an idea of what to expect. Some manufacturers offer a "hot swap" option. In other words, they will go ahead and send a new unit out to you before your existing unit is received, you'll receive a new unit and they'll repair or discard the old one. You usually have to guarantee your return with a credit card, and if the product isn't returned within a set number of days, they will charge you the full retail price.

Support technicians are there to help you. They've probably heard every conceivable problem from the ridiculous to the obscure. Sometimes people forget very basic things when installing new equipment like turning the power back on or attaching a cable securely. In other cases they get a call from a user who is the first person to ever test their equipment in conjunction with some other piece of hardware. At that point, the caller becomes part of the quality assurance team, and resolving the problem is a part of improving the product. Reputable vendors are very interested in insuring the quality of their products. I judge the reputation of a product in large measure on the quality of its Technical Support and the willingness of the firm to offer complete support service.

CHAPTER SUMMARY

This chapter has covered the basic skills needed to work inside your system, how to install, remove, and troubleshoot expansion cards and other hardware components, and the procedures needed for taking and maintaining an accurate Inventory of your PC. We also covered how to contact technical support.

Expansion cards can be used to tailor your system to perform functions that go far beyond the basic entry-level PC. The following chapters include details on various sub-systems that can be enhanced using the procedures found in this chapter.

CHAPTER 6

MOTHERBOARDS— YOUR SYSTEM'S FOUNDATION

WHAT'S IN THIS CHAPTER

- ✔ What a Motherboard Does
- ✔ Motherboard Types and Features
- ✔ Choosing a Motherboard
- ✔ Installing and Replacing Motherboards
- ✔ Trouble-shooting a Motherboard

What This Chapter Is About

Your PC's motherboard is one of the defining characteristics of your system. It serves as the foundation of the entire machine. On most systems the motherboard is the home for all the other components. Its dimensions determine how many expansion cards can be seated and its electronic design defines what kinds of CPUs can be supported. This chapter focuses on the basic features of the motherboard and how to install and remove one.

What Is a Motherboard?

Your motherboard is a large fiberglass panel, usually located on the bottom of a desktop case, and on the side of a tower unit (see Figure 6.1). The rest of the system components are either attached to the board via cables, or mounted directly onto it. Power is fed to the rest of the system from the power supply via this board, and its expansion slots are the way we add new features to the machine. The motherboard takes up more floor space than anything else inside your PC; I refer to it the as the computer's foundation because, in both a physical and an engineering-design sense, this one component sets the functional limits of your system. Over the years several different designs of motherboards have arisen. Some of these changes involve little more than the physical size. As developments in technology allow using fewer and more powerful chips, there is less to be placed on the board, and boards shrink in size.

FIGURE 6.1 A typical motherboard.

Some of the differences evolved around how the different functions of the computer are organized; some designers put more things on the motherboard, and some rely more on placing functions on expansion cards. Let's look a little more closely at some of the factors which differentiate motherboard design.

These differences were made both to improve functionality and to provide a competitive edge either in price or performance for the company that produced them. Once upon a time motherboard design was a painstaking process, requiring months of planning and careful coordination with the suppliers who provided chips used in production. Those days are past. The pace of technology and fierce price competition has shifted the entire motherboard market. Once upon a time, the motherboard was one of the most expensive components in the system, often costing one third to half of the total purchase price; today you can buy motherboards wholesale for less than the cost of a mid-range display adapter. Part of the reason is the economics of scale, with many vendors producing lots of boards; another part of the reason is faster design; many motherboards have a total life-cycle from original sketch to retirement that lasts only about six weeks.

THERE STILL IS ROOM FOR QUALITY

The preceding paragraphs may make you think that all motherboards are alike and that they are simply a commodity item. The truth is, you still get what you pay for, although you may not have to pay quite as much as you used to. While writing this book, I tested several motherboards from various manufacturers. The most expensive of these cost three and a half times more than the cheapest one I examined. The top-of-the-line Micronics board offered a number of slick features, which I'll explain as we go through some of the basic motherboard components. It also exhibited a much higher benchmark score. These superiorities in design and performance are why Micronics motherboards are, as of this writing, the weapons of choice in my lab.

To see just what the performance difference was when the first edition of this book was written, I changed both the memory and the CPU from one board to another and used exactly the same video card, hard drive and SCSI host adapter. Using Norton Utilities System Information Benchmark, the inexpensive 486 clone scored a CPU benchmark score of 94.2; the high-end board with an identical configuration scored 141.8. This benchmark is a simple way to test how fast one system is compared to another. The more expensive Micronics board also exhibited better construction and more features. Those results allow me to state unequivocally that all motherboards are not created equal. The same results would appear if the testing where done today with newer motherboards and CPUs. While a cheap motherboard may run the same software, support the same operating system, and have the same number of slots, it may not be as robust. In other words: you get what you pay for. The extra money may not help if it just buys fancy ads in magazines, but if it goes into better design and engineering then you will get a product that is faster and easier to work with.

NOTE

Over the years several different terms have arisen for referring to motherboards. Some of these come from trying to be politically correct and remove the gender reference from these products. Others come from trying to indicate something about the board's design. IBM sometimes refers to this component as the *system board*. Another Big Blue acronym is *planar board*. Another term sometimes used is *backplane*. You have to be careful when somebody starts talking about backplanes; some companies, such as Zenith Data Systems, actually separate the motherboard on their systems into two separate parts. One board looks like a regular motherboard; the other, which holds the CPU and sometimes the memory circuits, looks like a regular expansion card; but neither component will work without the other. The idea behind this separate design was to make it easy to upgrade the CPU without having to replace the entire motherboard. That's a fine theory, but many times the replacements are not easy to install, and by the time you want to replace the CPU, you often need to replace the motherboard.

SOME MAJOR CONSIDERATIONS IN MOTHERBOARD DESIGN

To understand the differences between motherboards, it helps to understand the principal features in motherboard design; these affect how much the motherboard costs, what it can do for you, and how easy it is to upgrade. Refer to Figure 6.2 for an illustration of a typical motherboard layout.

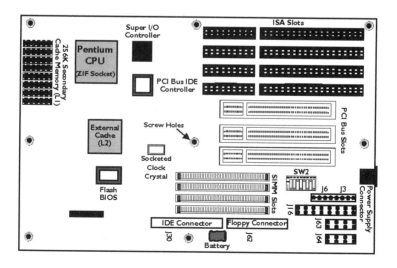

FIGURE 6.2 Diagram of a motherboard.

The Microprocessor

Rarely do end-users purchase a CPU directly from Intel or one of the other suppliers. Instead, they usually specify which CPU they want when purchasing a motherboard and obtain them as a matched set. Some motherboards have slots to allow for upgrading CPUs by adding an Intel Overdrive (a speed-doubling chip) or providing room for a numeric co-processor. We'll deal with these options in Chapter 7. If you are completely unfamiliar with the different types of CPU, you might want to read about them now, but you don't need detailed knowledge to understand the current discussion. Generally speaking, you should know what type of CPU you want to use before you go shopping for a motherboard; and for that matter, for a system as a whole.

Clock Speed

The separate backplane concept leads us to another interesting fact of motherboard life; most, but not all, motherboards are designed to work with a specific CPU, often operating at a specific speed. In other words, a motherboard design for a Pentium 90 CPU may not work with a Pentium 100 CPU even though both microprocessors are Pentiums. The number after the name indicates the processing speed in millions of cycles per second. There are a few motherboards available that can be used to seat a variety of both processors, but even here you should check things out before you buy. A related factor is power consumption. Newer processors require less power than the Intel Pentium 60 and older editions. As a result, boards designed for the newer chips are not backward-compatible.

Expansion Slots

The number of expansion slots available on your system determines how many add-in cards you can have. Some very limited boards offer only three or four slots. Most offer seven or eight; a few offer ten. The variations of expansion slot design are covered in Chapter 4.

Most modern motherboards offer at least one or two special high-speed slots based the Intel *PCI* standard, which stands for Peripheral Component Interconnect. Some older motherboards you might find in a flea market may use the VESA Local Bus (VLB) design. PCI is the bus of choice, offering ease of installation, reduced memory problems, a wider range of supported products, and often less expensive ones than other bus types. In general, your graphics display adapter, hard drive controller, SCSI host adapter, and network card are good choices for the power and simplicity of PCI. The remaining slots may be a combination of *ISA* (Industry Standard Architecture) or *EISA* (Enhanced Industry Standard Architecture) design. Most cards are ISA designs, while some high-end cards use the more expensive EISA bus. PCI has virtually eliminated the need for EISA in most systems.

The BIOS

The motherboard houses your system *BIOS* (Basic Input/ Output System). Some motherboards use a removable chip to provide BIOS services. When you want to upgrade the BIOS, it may cost you up to $40 or so for the replacement part. Better motherboards use *Flash BIOS*, which allows you to use a software routine to upgrade the BIOS without ever opening the case. It usually can be downloaded from the vendor's bulletin-board system for free.

Memory Banks

Virtually all modern motherboards provide sockets for installing Single In-line Memory Modules or *SIMMs*. A series of sockets is called a *bank*. You should match the maximum memory configuration available on the motherboard to your needs. Some older systems only provide sockets and logic circuits for 16Mb of RAM, which for serious power users is inadequate. You should look for a motherboard that will accommodate up to at least 64Mb of RAM. Not all SIMMs are created equal. Some have 72 positions on the edge connectors, others 30. A few use proprietary forms. There are also a few older motherboards that still rely on individual DRAM chips, or on

SIPP modules. It's generally best to pick ones that use the 72-pin (which is now the standard) over the older standard 30-pin model.

External Cache

Cache memory is short-term storage for recently-used commands or data. If the contents of a cache are needed again, it can be retrieved much quicker from the cache than from the disk it is normally drawn from. Motherboards vary in the amount and form of external cache used to support the CPU's operation. Some use a series of individual chips while others have modules. The details of cache memory were covered in Chapter 5; generally, with the motherboard you want to be sure that it will support the amount of cache memory you want. This is especially important with high-performance Pentium processors, as extra cache will significantly improve their performance.

NOTE

As vendors try to put more and more silicon on less and less motherboard area, things can get a bit cramped. Memory modules, cache and CPU heat sinks can rise far enough above the motherboard's surface to interfere with expansion card placement. If you plan on building a very heavily-configured system, you may want to investigate the exact layout of the board before making the purchase. I have seen some systems with eight expansion slots that could only comfortably seat four full-length expansion cards due to the placement of the memory modules and heat sinks.

I/O Ports

Many motherboards are equipped with built-in serial and parallel ports. This is a plus, since virtually all users will need at least one serial and one parallel port. By having them built onto the motherboard, you can directly attach cables to run the connection to the wall of the case. This not only saves about $30 for the cost of an I/O expansion card, but also frees up one of the expansion slots and usually improves system cooling.

Rechargeable CMOS Batteries, IDE Controllers and SCSI Host Adapters

There is also a trend towards building the hard-drive controller or a SCSI adapter directly onto the motherboard. Unless this feature exactly meets your needs, it probably won't do much good, but it won't hurt either. Of course, it may raise the price of your motherboard from $30 on up.

Some motherboards are equipped with a component that looks like a miniature blue or gray oil drum. This is actually a rechargeable battery. While the system is on, the battery is being constantly charged and is used to maintain the CMOS Setup when the unit is off. Generally speaking, you should also have a regular NiCad or alkaline battery pack (which usually comes with your case) attached to the motherboard as well. This is extra insurance that if you are gone for a long period of time, you won't lose your CMOS Setup. Of course, you'll still be prepared because you have the Dark and Stormy Night Disk that we prepared in Chapter 3. You didn't make one? If not, you should go back to Chapter 3 and make one now.

Plug and Play: Intelligent Configuration vs. Jumpers

Some motherboards are more elegantly-designed than others, allowing you to set more options via the system BIOS Setup or through auto-configuration. An example is a system that lets you mix and match memory modules (for instance a combination of 1Mb, 4Mb, and 16Mb SIMMs) without having to set jumpers on the motherboard.

One of the slickest advances in the past few years is the advent of Plug and Play. This is a feature that allows you to place a card into a slot, and the system itself "recognizes" it as, say, a CD-ROM drive, and automatically sets any DMA, IRQ, or I/O port assignments so that the new component will work without conflicting with existing components. Windows 95 appears to have added much of this capability via software alone. Plug and Play is not yet perfect, but has already delivered a healthy down payment on the promise of hassle-free system changes and upgrades. One of the most frustrating aspects of early PC design has been the necessity to throw those tiny little DIP switches, and pull and push those tiny little jumper pieces in order to get some new component to work. Thanks to Plug and Play technology, hours, even days, of lost time and temper because of these resource conflicts may be ending.

Bells and Whistles

Some motherboards offer more features than others; some of those features make more sense than others. The industry periodically seems to go through trends where manufacturers try to cram every conceivable option directly onto the motherboard. Some major manufacturers produce motherboards with virtually every system component built right in, hard disk controller, floppy controller, video adapter, I/O ports—the works.

Generally speaking, I like to see I/O ports and a floppy controller on the motherboard. I'm fond of rechargeable batteries and jumperless configuration. I tend to avoid built-in video or graphics adapters, on-board SCSI host adapters, and integrated coffee-makers. There are three reasons for this; the first is that by the time the motherboard has made it to market, somebody has already invented a better whatever-the-heck-it-is. When that happens I'm stuck trying to work around the obsolete device on the motherboard—which is always a pain. In addition, I'm paying for something I really don't want, and thirdly, if the darn thing breaks and I'm actually using it, half the time everything on the system goes down.

Coprocessor and Upgrade Sockets

Many motherboards are also equipped with upgrade sockets, or with 486 and older-style processor-based machines, sockets to seat a numeric coprocessor. With the 486, Intel started incorporating a numeric coprocessor directly inside the microprocessor itself. It then later backtracked to expand its market by providing crippled 486 chips known as the 486SX, which do not include a numeric coprocessor.

Unless you are on a very tight budget, you should buy the CPU you really want. In most cases, this is the fastest Pentium you can afford; then you don't need to worry about coprocessor sockets.

One other point about extra sockets for the true power-hungry user. There are Pentium and DEC Alpha-based boards that will seat more than one CPU, but you will have to use an operating system like Windows NT to take advantage of this feature. In reality his kind of exotic system is more suited to network servers than stand-alone workstations.

Dimensions

While the engineering on the motherboard may be far from standardized, certain features of a board's dimensions have to be, in order to allow case manufacturers to produce units that will accept the majority of motherboards on the market. Most motherboards fall into one of two categories; full-sized and "baby." Full-sized boards generally occupy almost the entire floor of the standard or tower-style case. While some baby cases will accept a full-sized board, I can tell you from personal experience that trying to squeeze one into a small case will be time-consuming and often an exercise in frustration and banged or scraped knuckles. In most cases, trying to lock down a large board in a small case will require backtracking as you find something you need is now under the power supply or the floppy drive bays, or requires running a cable in some awkward configuration.

While this is just an observation, and not based on any statistical evidence, I have found that full-sized boards are usually employed early in the cycle of motherboard design. That is, when 486/33's first came out, they were seated in the full-sized board. As that phase of technology matured, more of the support technology was miniaturized, allowing manufacturers to reduce the total motherboard area. Assuming that you are using a full-sized case, there's not much difference to you as an end-user between the board sizes. If you are using a small case, and you've already purchased it, it's generally a good idea to purchase a smaller-sized board.

All Those Other Chips and Circuits

We've basically covered all the essential components of the motherboard that you need to know about as an end-user. All the other chips on the board are there to support the stuff we've just talked about. Most motherboards have all but a few components permanently soldered into the fiberglass. Given the cost of the board itself, and the length of the warranties, it's usually not cost-effective to consider field repairs of the board itself.

INSTALLING A MOTHERBOARD

What You'll Need

- ✔ Motherboard
- ✔ Motherboard manual
- ✔ Mounting hardware
- ✔ Screwdriver
- ✔ Pair of needle-nosed pliers
- ✔ Tweezers
- ✔ Screws and spacers
- ✔ External battery pack
- ✔ A small flashlight is sometimes nice
- ✔ A magnifying glass is useful for reading the fine print screened onto the motherboard

Configuring the Motherboard

WARNING

Any time you handle the electronic components of your machine, you should protect it from static discharge. Usually all you have to do is touch the metal part of the case to make sure that you are not carrying a static charge that might be dissipated into the circuitry and cause damage. You should do this before opening up any static-protective envelopes, and repeat the procedure any time you take a step away from the machine, especially in cold, dry weather. If you have problems with static electricity buildup, you can also obtain a grounding strip that can be worn on the wrist to minimize and prevent static buildup.

You'll need your motherboard's manual. There should be a diagram, along with some instructions for setting jumpers and switches on the board; you'll need them for this step, as well as for connecting the different leads that come from the case to the board.

Hardware vendors use DIP switches and jumpers to set various options on their products. Figure 6.3 shows how one vendor indicates the settings for both; you need to check your motherboard's manual for any settings you need to adjust. If you bought the motherboard with the CPU and cache memory already installed, you may not have to make any adjustments at all. The required switches and jumpers will vary from board to board, so it's a good idea to go through and check each one before putting the board into the chassis. In some cases your manual may provide tables listing the different options and how they should be set. Sometimes they are displayed in the diagram itself. I'll mention some of the more common ones after a couple of explanations.

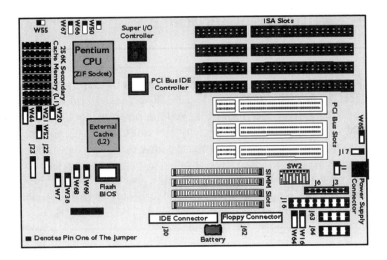

FIGURE 6.3 DIP switch and jumper block diagram.

DIP Switches

DIP switches look much like a miniature row of light switches and work much the same way; they can either be "on" or "off" to enable a certain feature. Since we are dealing with electronics, some suppliers like to make things a little more complicated. Instead of on or off, they may label their switches "open" and "closed." This sometimes confuses novices, especially when the vendor doesn't match terminology between the labels on the switch and the instructions in the documentation. If the manual says that Switch 1 should be on and the only label beside the numbers on the switch itself is "open," the switch will be in the "on" position when the handle of the switch is pushed away from the word "open." It helps to think of it this way: a switch is really a just a way to close or open a circuit. The switch is *on* when the circuit is closed and electricity can pass through the line. If you open the switch, it's *off* because the circuit is broken. See Figure 6.4.

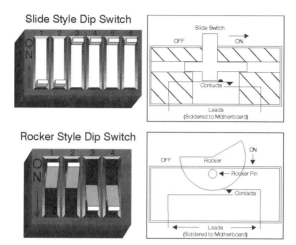

FIGURE 6.4 DIP switches.

Jumpers

Jumpers are really the most simple form of switch. The pins coming out of the motherboard are the poles, and the small conducting sleeve, called a *jumper*, is used to close the circuit. If there is no
jumper, the circuit is open or off. When you put the jumper on the
pins, it's closed, making the connection. Just as with DIP switches,
your manual may refer to jumper settings in a couple of different
ways. Keep in mind that *closed* and *on* are synonymous terms, and
so are *open* and *off*. Sometimes jumper switches are found as just a
pair of wires sticking up. Sometimes there are three-wire jumpers;
this allows setting two options, depending on which pair of pins
are actually covered by the jumper. The pins will usually be labeled
1, 2, and 3. Jumpering pins 1 and 2 selects one mode, while jumpering 2 and 3 chooses the other. Figure 6.5 shows an illustration of a
three-pin jumper.

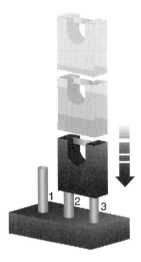

FIGURE 6.5 A three-pin jumper.

CPU Settings

If your motherboard will accept several different CPUs or a co-processor, there is probably a setting to select CPU speed, and to indicate the presence of any supplemental chips. Another common setting is to set the amount of RAM and type of memory chips used on the board. Most machines also require setting jumpers or DIP switches to indicate the amount of cache memory installed. Some machines are equipped with on-board parallel and serial ports and graphics adapters. Enabling or disabling these features often involves setting DIP switches or jumpers.

Installing Memory

Now it is time to install the memory on your motherboard if it didn't come with it already on-board. Most modern motherboards use *SIMM*s (Single In-line Memory Modules) as shown in Figure 6.6. Refer to your motherboard's manual and locate Bank 0 (computer people start counting at 0). Make sure you discharge any possible static by touching the case. Most SIMMs have a notch on one side of the unit, as shown in the figure. SIMMs only mount one way into the bank, so you may have to test to see just which way it fits. Insert the SIMM into the base of the socket at about a 30-degree angle. Place a thumb on either side and gently push the SIMM down and forward until it clicks into the socket guide.

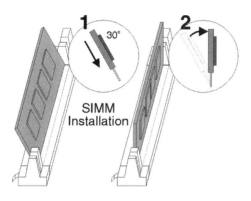

FIGURE 6.6 Installing a Single In-line Memory Module.

Repeat the process for the remaining modules. When you are finished, all modules should be standing perfectly upright and their heights should be exactly the same. If one module seems to be angled funny or sitting too high, it's installed improperly. Remove it by pressing the release tabs (at the base, away from the holes in the socket) and lift it out and away from the slot. If the misaligned SIMM is in the middle of the bank, you may have to remove the ones further outside to be able to get it free. Be sure all the SIMMs are seated properly before proceeding.

If possible, use SIMMs with silver-colored connections. The gold-plated versions are said by some motherboard vendors to be less reliable over time.

NOTE

Installing DRAM Memory Chips

Some older machines may use individual chips rather than memory modules. These are also assembled in banks or rows, usually eight or nine chips to a row. If your machine uses this system, refer to the manual for the exact placement of the bank and then use the same method detailed below for installing cache memory.

If you are paying money right now for a new motherboard that has DRAM, consider sending it back, since SIMMs are easier to work with, more reliable, and give better performance.

Installing Cache Memory

In all likelihood you will have ordered your motherboard with cache, and the cache chips will have come pre-installed. If not, you will have to mount them yourself or get a friend to do it. If you have never seated electronic components directly on a circuit board before, you may want to get a friend with experience to show you how it's done. While it is not difficult, it does take a gentle touch. If you want to do it by yourself, follow the steps outlined below, and refer to Figure 6.7.

FIGURE 6.7 Installing a chip.

Cache memory is sometimes distributed on modules similar to the SIMMs you just installed. Many systems still use individual chips to provide secondary cache. These are installed in banks and you should refer to your system's manual for the exact placement of the chips on the motherboard. Based on the amount of cache you are installing, these chips must be properly oriented. You will find a little moon-shaped cutout or indentation, or possibly a little bump on one of the narrow sides of the chip, right on the edge of the top surface. This indicates the primary pin side of the chip, and which way to properly place the chip in its socket. The other chips in the same bank should have the same orientation for reference. If you are uncertain, call the company's technical support department.

All the chips need to be oriented the same way and you should check with your manual to find out exactly how they should be positioned. Prongs are located along both long sides of the chip. Once again make sure you are properly grounded, and take the first chip gently between the thumb and first finger of one hand. Set the prongs facing away from you into the holes on the far side of the appropriate chip socket, raising the other side up towards you at a very slight angle. Press evenly and gently away from you and guide the prongs on the side towards you into their positions in the socket. In some cases you will need next to no angle at all to do this, in other cases you will need more. Be careful, and make sure that all the pins go into their appropriate holes. Take care to make sure you don't bend any of them. If you bend one, you'll have to remove the chip, try to straighten the pin and try again. The pins are made of very soft metal and will fatigue or even break off if you play with them too much.

Installing the CPU, Co-Processor, BIOS, or an Overdrive

CPUs and the BIOS, like the cache memory, should have come already installed on your motherboard. If they did not or you are upgrading one, you should refer to Appendix A for detailed instructions on how to place these components on motherboards. It's easiest to install them before mounting the motherboard in the case.

Mounting the Motherboard

The motherboard is like any electronic card in your PC; it's made of fiberglass and contains silicon chips. The motherboard has to sit slightly above the case to avoid shorting out the connections that stick through the bottom. This is accomplished by the use of Teflon spacers snapped through holes in the motherboard (see Figure 6.8). Then these spacers are locked into rails located on the bottom of the desktop-style case or on the right-hand side of the tower case.

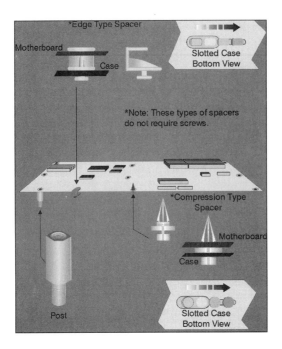

FIGURE 6.8 Details of a motherboard with typical spacers.

 Don't put the spacers in yet; you have to figure out exactly where they go.

NOTE

Two hexagonal screws, which can accept mounting screws on their tops, are used to fasten the board in place and to ground it to the chassis. Figure 6.9 shows a section of the case with the motherboard rail and the mounting screw. If your case does not already have these screws in place, you'll need to screw them in finger tight and then snug them down with a nut driver or a pair of pliers from a tool kit.

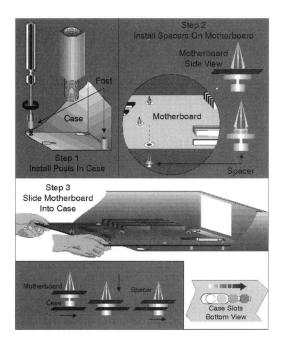

FIGURE 6.9 Mounting the motherboard in the case.

Locating the Position of the Retaining Screws and Spacers

Every time someone designs a new motherboard or chassis, it seems they feel they have to design a new way to arrange the location of the motherboard attachments; you may see a baby-style case with a full-size motherboard, or vice-versa. Or you may be fortunate enough to have both components designed appropriately. No matter which condition fits your situation, you will still have to "eyeball" exactly how the spacers and retaining screws must be placed in order to mount your motherboard. The easiest way is to gently lay the motherboard into position and then lift it off, seeing where the screws and spacers must go. If you have a tower case, you'll probably want to turn it on its side for this operation; then the motherboard will be mounted on the "bottom" of the case.

Ground yourself by touching the case and take your motherboard out of its protective plastic envelope. There should be at least two holes in the top of the motherboard with silver or gold collars around them made of solder. These are the holes for the mounting screws. Line up the motherboard so that the jack for the keyboard is lined up with the hole in the chassis for the keyboard plug. Then note where the spacing screws and retaining screws should go.

Move the motherboard out of the way and attach the screws. Once the screws are in place it's time to put in the spacers. Line up the motherboard so that both of the screw holes are positioned properly, then observe which spacer holes line up with the spacer retaining grooves in the case. There are two kinds of white Teflon spacers, as shown with a motherboard in Figure 6.10.

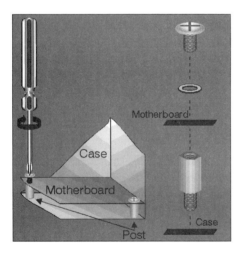

FIGURE 6.10 Mounting the motherboard.

Once you have noted the locations, set the motherboard on its edge and poke spacers from the bottom of the motherboard up to the top as shown in the Figure. If you have a full-sized motherboard you may also need to place two or three of the "C"-shaped spacers on the upper edge of the mounting rails. Once all the spacers are in place, position the motherboard over the rails and slide it into position until they lock. Now fasten the board into place with two retaining screws set into the hexagonal bases.

Attaching the Leads and Hooking Up the Switches

Now it's time to attach all the little wires running from the case to the motherboard. You'll probably want to open up the manual that came with the motherboard and find the diagram. These switches and *LED* (Light Emitting Diode) connectors are generally mounted into plastic sockets that look very much like jumpers, and they fit into jumper switch positions on the motherboard. Refer to your board's manual for the exact location of the switches. If you put them on backwards it won't hurt anything, but the function won't work properly, so it may take some trial and error. Unfortunately, it seems that no two cases use the same wiring colors nor any two motherboard manufacturers the same jumper positions; it's not possible for me to be able to give you precise instructions on how to hook up these connections. See Figure 6.11.

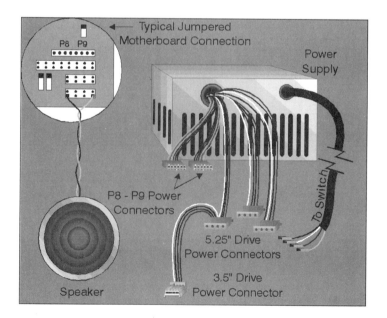

Figure 6.11 Connecting the wiring harness.

There are a number of wires from the case that have to be attached to the motherboard, and one that has to be attached to your hard disk controller. If you are very fortunate they will be labeled; the odds are you'll have to trace them back into the case to figure out exactly what their function is.

Most machines have leads to turn the power on, turn the Turbo function on and off, reset the system, and indicate when the hard drive is in operation, as well as one that hooks up the system's key lock.

Connecting the Power Supply to the Motherboard

Locate connectors P8 and P9 coming out of the power supply. They should be easy to spot. Both have six wires rather than the four that come with the other connectors. These plug into two jacks that are side by side, usually somewhere near the keyboard socket on your motherboard. P8 usually goes towards the rear. The way to know if you have them connected properly is to see that the black wires on each connector are next to each other. Figure 6.12 shows the connections being put into place. These connectors are also usually keyed so that they can only go one way.

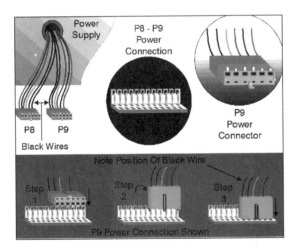

FIGURE 6.12 Installing the P8 and P9 power connectors.

Be sure to have the power connectors properly seated before applying power. If they haven't been installed correctly, you may damage the motherboard when power is turned on.

TROUBLESHOOTING A MOTHERBOARD

The real trick in troubleshooting possible motherboard problems is in isolating the problem. Before suspecting the motherboard, you should go through the usual diagnostic checklist.

Many times, users suspect a motherboard problem when in reality they've either just added something to the system and installed it improperly, or a conflict has developed between two pieces of software. Actual motherboard problems, though unusual, can be difficult to isolate. In some cases, the machine just doesn't seem to work at all. This could be the motherboard, but if you have just added a new expansion card, the machine may hang up because two devices on the system are trying to share the same Interrupt or address space (see Chapter 4 for details on solving these conflicts).

Have you just installed a new peripheral or software?

If so, it may be the culprit, rather than the motherboard.

Check the back of the case where the expansion cards sit.

Is it possible that any of the cards have worked loose from their slot due to moving the case or pulling on a cord? If you think one might be loose, don't reapply power to the machine; and if the machine is on, turn it off.

A loose card in an edge connector can severely damage the card, the motherboard, or both devices. With the power off, move the machine to where you can take off the cover and inspect all the cards.

Are you sure that you removed or fastened all screws while you were inside the machine, and that you didn't leave any tools in there?

If a loose screw or tool is closing a circuit between two solder joints on a board inside your machine, it could be shorting out the system. If you have any reason to suspect that's the problem, you need to immediately power down the system and check it out.

The easiest way is to remove the power cord and cables, then gently rock the case from side to side and listen for any loose items.

Is the unit getting power from the wall?

Trace the electrical circuit from the back of the machine all the way to the circuit breaker or fuse box. In other words, start by making sure that the power switch is in the *on* position. Do you have a green power-indicator light? Put your hand in the back and feel for the fan exhaust. If there's no air current, it may be the power supply or it may be a short since the motherboard is newly-installed. It can also be that you haven't turned on your surge protector or that circuit has blown a fuse or circuit breaker. Follow the cord all the way to the wall and make sure that you have a good circuit. It's not unknown to forget to plug the system back in after adding a new device and then wonder why things don't work.

Check all the cables going to and from your peripherals.

Are the keyboard and monitor properly attached?

Are there any functions during the Power-On-Self-Test?

If so, try to identify at which point the system locks up. For example, does it lock up right after finding the keyboard? In most cases the point at which the POST fails indicates which component in the system isn't working. In a majority of cases, the problem is not with the motherboard if you have just added a new device. In many cases, it's a conflict between the new device and some component already in your system. More rarely, but not impossible, something may have just died.

Remove all the expansion cards from your system, except for the card that contains your floppy disk controller and your display adapter, and any other cards that are required for basic operation. Attempt to boot from your Dark and Stormy Night Disk or a clean DOS disk. If this works, you've identified that there is a conflict. Add the removed cards one at a time until the machine refuses to boot. At this point you know that the card you've just installed is part of the problem. Refer to the documentation that came with your system and that card and identify the problem.

Check your Setup.

It's possible that you disabled or enabled some function that conflicts with the way your machine is actually set up. Remove the new accessory that you just installed.

If it gets to this point, refer to the diagnostic flow charts in the back of the book, and if those fail to help, call the technical support staff of the vendor who supplied your system or its motherboard.

Everything was working fine last night when you turned it off, but this morning nothing works.

Is the unit getting power from the wall?

Trace the electrical circuit from the back of the machine all the way to the circuit breaker or fuse box. In other words, start by making sure that the power switch is in the *on* position. Do you have a green power-indicator light? Put your hand in the back and feel for the fan exhaust. If there's no air current, it may be the power supply or it may be a short since the motherboard is newly-installed. It can also be that you haven't turned on your surge protector, or that a circuit has blown a fuse or breaker. Follow the cord all the way to the wall and make sure that you have a good circuit. It's not unknown for somebody to forget to plug the system back in after adding a new device and then wonder why things don't work.

Check the back of the case where the expansion cards sit.

Is it possible that one of the cards has worked loose from its slot due to moving the case or pulling on a cord? If you think one might be loose, don't reapply power to the machine; and if the machine is on, turn it off. A loose card in an edge connector can severely damage the card, the motherboard, or both devices. With the power off, move the machine to where you can take off the cover and inspect all the cards.

Check all the cables going to and from your peripherals.

Are the keyboard and monitor properly attached?

Are there any functions during the Power-On-Self-Test?

If so, try to identify at which point the system locks up. For example, does it lock up right after finding the keyboard? In most cases the point at which the POST fails indicates which component in the system isn't working. In a majority of cases the problem is not with the motherboard, if you have just added a new device. In many cases, it's a conflict between the new device and some component already in your system. More rare, but not impossible, something may have just died.

Check your Setup.

It's possible that you disabled or enabled some function that conflicts with the way your machine is actually set up. Remove the new accessory that you just installed.

If it gets to this point, refer to the diagnostic flow charts in the back of the book, and if those fail to help, call the technical support staff of the vendor who supplied your system or its motherboard. Have the machine open and the user manual at hand, with paper and pencil handy in case you need to take notes.

The machine comes up but behaves erratically.

Make sure that all the cable connections coming to the machine are properly attached. A loose monitor cable or other loose cord can cause these problems.

Boot from a basic DOS floppy disk.

If everything works fine, one of your drivers or your memory management is affecting things.

If you can't boot from your Dark and Stormy Night disk, try to get into your CMOS Setup.

Make sure that everything in there is properly configured. Power surges or other weird things in the night can sometimes reset things like your drive type number; if this happens, your system may hang during the POST or behave very erratically. Operating your system with an improper drive type setting can actually damage your hard disk.

Other Conditions Not Covered Above

The myriad of problems that is sometimes blamed on motherboards makes it impossible to discuss every sort of condition that might confront a user. If you don't feel that one of the above conditions matches your situation, refer to the diagnostic charts and error conditions contained in the Appendices.

REMOVING A MOTHERBOARD

Tools You'll Need

- ✔ Screwdriver
- ✔ Possibly a hemostat
- ✔ Goodie bag
- ✔ A cup or other container for screws and small parts
- ✔ A roll of masking tape and a pen

WARNING Any time you handle the electronic components of your machine, you should protect it from static discharge. Usually all you have to do is touch the metal part of the case to make sure that you are not carrying a static charge that might be dissipated into the circuitry and cause damage. You should do this before opening up any static-protective envelopes, and repeat the procedure any time you take a step away from the machine, especially in cold, dry weather. If you have problems with static electricity, you can also obtain a grounding strip that can be worn on the wrist to minimize and prevent static buildup.

STEP 1

Removing a motherboard is actually a fairly simple operation (unless you have a small or poorly-designed case). In any event, the steps are the same. First make sure that you remove power from the system, unplug and label the cables at the back of the case, and remove the case cover by unfastening the screws on the outside edges of the back of the case. Be careful not to remove the four screws inside the cover area that secure the power supply to the back wall of the system.

STEP 2

Remove all the expansion cards from their slots.

STEP 3

If you are planning on reinstalling the motherboard, you may want to use the masking tape to place labels on the wires leading from the motherboard to the various switches and LEDs on the case. The function should be marked on the motherboard itself. Just go ahead and fold a small piece of the tape over the wire near the connection and write an abbreviation on it for each function. Remove the wires by gently pulling them off the appropriate jumper. Do the same thing for the external battery pack. Locate the P8 and P9 connectors that carry power from the power supply to the motherboard and disconnect them. Figure 6.12, shown earlier in this chapter in the installation section, shows what these look like.

Check and remove any other cables or connections attaching the board to other components of the system, such as I/O ports or the hard drive.

STEP 4

Locate the two screws that attach the motherboard to the case. Remove them and put them into the little cup if you are placing another motherboard in the system, or into your goodie bag if you are not.

STEP 5

Gently slide the motherboard in the direction it moves freely. Depending on your case design, this could be in any one of the four directions. As it slides, use a slight upward pressure so that the spacers will disengage from the mounting rails. You may have to wiggle or angle the board to get it free and remove it from the case.

NOTE

In some smaller cases, you may have to remove a hard disk, floppy disk, or power supply in order to get access to the screws, or to get the board free from the case.

STEP 6

Once the board is clear of the case, you can remove the spacers if you are sending it off somewhere else, or you can use the spacers again. The board should be placed in a static-resistant envelope for safety.

CHAPTER SUMMARY

The motherboard is one of the defining components of your computer. It determines the size of the case needed, and the number of expansion slots available; how well it is designed will affect the performance of everything you put on it. This chapter has outlined the features manufacturers can design into motherboards, provided information on installation, operation, and troubleshooting, and shown how to install and remove the motherboard.

CHAPTER 7

CPU—THE BRAINS OF THE OPERATION

WHAT'S IN THIS CHAPTER

✔ The Central Processing Unit (Microprocessor)

✔ What the Microprocessor Does

✔ Co-processors and Overdrives

✔ Clock-Doubling Chips

✔ Choosing a Microprocessor

✔ Upgrading or Replacing a Microprocessor

✔ Replacing a Cooling Fan

255

What This Chapter Is About

The microprocessor makes the PC possible. This small wafer of silicon can perform the work or millions of transistors and in effect is a computer in its own right. This chapter focuses on the possibilities for upgrading microprocessors, explains the evolution of the Intel family of CPUs, and shows how to test, install and remove them.

What Is a Microprocessor?

Your system's microprocessor is a cross between a brain and an orchestra conductor. It actually performs all the calculations carried on by the machine. Some computers even have two or more processors, with the additional ones acting as extra brains; sort of the two-heads-are-better-than-one theory. By dividing up all the work the machine can operate faster. The conductor part of the job is just as important as the raw calculations. The other devices on the system request the CPU to perform functions. When a program wants to make use of the machine or have it do something, it does so by issuing one or more of a set of defined commands, which set the CPU in motion, and it then directs the function of the other devices in the system. We could get "twidget technical" at this point (*twidget* is a slang term for electronics technicians or engineers) but there is no real need to. Most users will never care about the inner workings of their CPU except to know what it can do for them and how fast it can run.

We will just peek inside the cover and see a bit of how it's arranged and get a simple overview of how it works, to take away some of the "black box" mystique. Figure 7.1 shows the Intel 486 microprocessor. Inside that small piece of silicon is a grid of circuits resembling the map of a large city. If we continue the map analogy, it can be divided up into neighborhoods. These neighborhoods are sub-units of the microprocessor, each with a dedicated purpose, just as within a city the planning commission might have reserved an area as an industrial park, another for retail operations, and designated other portions as residential. The exact layout is determined by the chip's engineers and all vary somewhat; however, there are some components that are common to all.

FIGURE 7.1 The Intel Pentium microprocessor.

✔ The Control Unit

This part of the chip exercises direct control over everything that goes on inside the processor and might be considered the hub of the entire computer.

✔ The Arithmetic Logic Unit

This is the number-crunching part of your CPU. It does all the numeric manipulations handled by the CPU. Some microprocessors and computers have a *floating point unit* to handle numbers involving decimal places or fractions. The ALU performs modifications on the data as directed by the control unit.

✔ The I/O Module

This module acts much like a traffic cop, routing commands in and out of the CPU and queuing instructions for execution.

The above list is a simplification. Engineers can break out these primary functions in several ways or group them, based on the chip's overall design. In its simplest form the CPU takes an instruction or a value passed to it by the operating system, internally acts upon the command or performs an operation on the data, and passes the result back to the system.

MOVING THE DATA AROUND

Now that you understand that there are different components inside the CPU and that the CPU has to send data in and out to the rest of the computer, we need to briefly look at the factors involved in how this data is passed.

You'll sometimes hear CPUs being referred to as "a 16-bit CPU" or "a 32-bit CPU," or "a 64-bit CPU." Keep in mind that a CPU is nothing more than a giant set of switches. These switches are used either to indicate "on" and "off" states (sort of an either/or situation), or to represent values stored as numbers. Let's say we wanted to store the letter "A;" we could give it a value as a number and the computer could interpret that and let us know that the value is an "A." Other numbers could be used to represent "B," "C," "D," and so on. It would be very difficult to represent very many things if all we had for numbers were zero and one; we'd only have two numbers. We would run into the same problem with only ten numbers available: zero through nine.

It's Just a Matter of 1, 2, 3—Isn't It?

When we're counting, what happens when we want to count above the number nine? We add another place to the left. By doing this, we can go up to the number 99, because each number in the left column is equal to ten in the right column. We use a similar system to increase the numbers we use inside a computer. Each wire carrying information can have a value of either zero or one. If two wires are linked together to carry a signal, we now have four combinations since each wire can have two possible values. Go to four wires and we have 16 possible combinations. A *bus* is a collection of wires used to transmit a number. It's sort of like a highway carrying information. Different components of your microprocessor get information off this bus.

Registers, Addresses, and Data Buses

Inside your CPU are two types of buses. The address bus defines the location in memory in which data is to be placed or where it is to be retrieved from. The total width of the *address bus* is very important because it determines the maximum number of available addresses, and therefore the total amount of memory the CPU—and the entire system—can directly manipulate. Each position in memory has to have one specific label, just like you have the address for your house. For example, a computer with 16 address lines can directly manipulate 65,536 different memory addresses.

Data Buses

The *data bus* is a similar bundle of wires used to transfer the data to and from the CPU. The wider the data bus, the more information that can be moved at a time and (if the software is capable) and the more complex the information can be. When you hear the term "32-bit CPU" it is usually referring to the data bus width of the CPU, because it gives a rough idea of the CPU's possible performance. The original IBM PC had a 8-bit-wide data bus, compared to 32 bits for the 486 and 64 bits for the Pentium.

When discussing the data bus, there are two numbers to keep in mind; one is the width of the *external data path*. This is the number of bits that can be moved between the CPU and other components of the computer such as RAM. The width of the *internal data path* refers to data that is actually moved just within the CPU itself. In some cases, the width of these two buses is the same; in others they're different.

Registers

A third characteristic of how a CPU can handle data is its *register size*. This refers to the width of the high-speed data storage area inside the CPU. The earliest PCs had 16-bit data registers, while the more recent Pentium microprocessor has a 64-bit register. The width and number of its registers determines the number of bits the CPU can work on at one time.

Early microprocessors had registers that were only four or eight bits wide. Modern CPUs have registers 32 or 64 bits wide. With a wider register, a CPU can manipulate more data with every operation. If used properly, a 64-bit register, such as those found in the Intel Pentium, can operate twice as fast as the older 486, which has a 32-bit register. Having more registers inside the microprocessor does not itself improve speed, since the microprocessor can only fetch data from one register at a time. The additional registers do however offer advantages to programmers if they use them efficiently, since there are more places to store data for execution.

Speed

Registers and bus width determine the majority of a CPU's potential performance. The *clock speed* determines how fast it can go. This is measured in *megahertz* (Mhz) or millionths of a second. This is sometimes referred to as *clock speed*. Inside your microprocessor is a timing device that is used to synchronize its operation. One spin of the clock is known as a *clock cycle*. Generally speaking, a microprocessor can execute one set of instructions with each clock cycle. The faster the clock cycle, the more instructions a second the CPU can execute and the faster data moves across the bus. The original IBM PC had a clock speed of 4.77Mhz. Today's fastest microprocessors, DEC Alphas, have speeds in excess of 270Mhz, while the Pentiums found in most systems run between 90 and 150Mhz. An increase in clock speed drastically improves performance, especially when matched with a wider bandwidth of the data bus and increased register size.

In reality, performing one set of instructions per clock cycle is an ideal. The way a chip is designed has a lot to do with how long it takes to operate an instruction. The details of these limitations are far too complex to go into here. Suffice it to say that clock speed is a relative indication of performance, but two chips operating at the same speed may not possess the same processing power.

Floating Point Operation

One of the difficulties in working with binary numbers as the basis for a computer model is the inability to work with fractions. It's hard to have a quarter of something when you are dealing with zeros and ones. In order to overcome this, the computer does a little bit of slight of hand. If it needs a quarter of something, it represents it as 25 (in reality, its binary equivalent) and then executes the command to put a decimal point in front of it. By moving the decimal point one place to the right, it can express two and a half. This technique of a moving decimal point gave rise to the term *floating point notation*. This kind of manipulation is more intensive than just handling the numbers directly. Early PCs could be equipped with an auxiliary microprocessor that was especially engineered just to handle these operations. They were called "math" or "numeric" co-processors. All Pentium and later Intel x86 family processors are equipped with built-in floating point units and have no use for a math co-processor.

It isn't enough for a computer just to be able to move numbers around. It has to be able to manipulate the data and also turn it into information. Data is just a value; information has meaning. If the computer knows that a given number equals "A" but can't report it as "A;" then it doesn't do the user much good. Information comes into the central processing unit and is stored in *a register*. This is sort of like a scratch pad. It stores the bit pattern until the microprocessor is done with it. Commands or instructions are used to manipulate the values in a register and to move them from one location to another. The microprocessor does its work by executing its instructions one at a time, moving data in and out of registers, or performing manipulations on the data in the register. In other words, a stream of data is constantly flowing into the CPU, through the data bus, being manipulated inside the central processor and then being sent back out, based on the instructions that are given to the CPU by the operating system and your applications.

Command Sets

Some CPUs have a wide range of commands available to programmers; others use a slimmed-down set. *Complex Instruction Set Computers* (CISCs) are the most common types used in PCs today. These are very complex designs because they can be operated using very complex instructions that offer a great deal of flexibility in programming. I'm not going to go into great detail about this since for our purposes it isn't really very important. The idea is to let you understand the basic difference between CISC processors and another kind you may hear about as you go looking around for the perfect computer, the RISC chip. This stands for *Reduced Instruction Set Computer*. In 1974 an IBM researcher named John Cocke designed the first processor based on the RISC concept. The idea is simple. For most purposes, 80% or so of a processor's command set is never used. If you can streamline the command set and the way functions are used to focus on the most commonly-used instructions, you can speed up performance and optimize the design. RISC processors are usually found in high-end workstations, costing a good bit more than the processors for most PCs.

Today, the dividing line between CISC and RISC processors is getting fuzzy, as newer designs incorporate RISC technology for some functions, but provide the flexibility of CISC design for others. The new Intel P6, which will one day replace the Pentium, is a hybrid CISC/RISC design.

Remember our discussion of speed up above? Because of their streamlined design, RISC-based microprocessors usually require fewer clock cycles to produce the same result as a CISC chip performing the same operation. For this reason, this design has become very popular in engineering and design-based workstations, which often perform well-defined functions over and over again.

In the Final Analysis

Some processors actually have two clock rates; one is the speed at which they perform internal operations, the other the rate at which they communicate with the outside world. For example, the

Intel family of chips include some designs that can operate internally two or three times faster than they communicate externally. As I write this I am sitting at a PC with a 486DX2/66. Externally, this microprocessor appears to the other components as a 33Mhz device (a megahertz equals one millionth of a second); internally, it is processing at 66Mhz, twice as fast.

There are some advantages to this kind of design. It can use motherboards designed to operate at 33Mhz, which are easier and therefore cheaper to build than one tuned to operate at faster speeds. Internally, it can carry out instructions faster than its 33Mhz sibling. Keep in mind that clock speed can't be used by itself to measure performance.

The faster the CPU's external communications, the faster and more expensive memory chips must be to keep up with it. A slower external speed allows the computer to be built with slower, and therefore less expensive, memory. While such a microprocessor may not offer all the performance of a CPU operating both internally and externally at a faster speed, in many applications it offers a real price-performance bargain.

Overall processor design affects what can be done during each clock cycle; clock speed just measures how fast that cycle is. It's a bit like moving things from point A to point B. If we wanted to get a load of furniture moved 100 miles, and one mover said that he would travel at 45 miles an hour while moving it, and the other said that he would go 60, at first glance it would appear that the faster would be the better choice. But what if the slower mover had a larger trailer that could make it in one trip, while the other mover had smaller capacity and had to make several round trips?

PROCESSING POWER FOR THE PC

So far our discussion of microprocessors has been general. Now it's time to look at the primary CPUs that are used for PC operation. While there are several manufacturers producing such chips, the vast majority are based on designs produced by Intel Corporation, which dominates the market. The Apple Macintosh uses a competing design based on the Motorola 68000 series; since this book focuses on IBM-compatible machines, we won't deal with that architecture here. There are some competing designs starting to emerge for PCs but as this book was being written, they were not generally available for evaluation.

Three companies, Advanced Micro Devices (AMD), Chips and Technologies (C&T), and Cyrix, offer clones of some of the popular Intel chips. Basically these competing processors are equivalent to certain products in the Intel line, and generally have less speed and fewer features than the Intel chips. IBM and Apple also produce a mass market PC CPU, called the PowerPC, but do not offer after-market sales and these chips are not compatible with the majority of motherboards. For those reasons, the following discussion will focus on the Intel family of microprocessors.

THE INTEL FAMILY OF MICROPROCESSORS

Today most PCs are shipped with some variation of Intel Pentium or 80486 microprocessors. They are the direct descendants of early Intel CPUs designed for calculators and personal computers. In order to understand their features and how to choose the one that's right for you, it's best to understand how they developed and what their distinguishing features are.

Intel has been manufacturing microprocessors since 1971, when they came out with the Intel 4004. This chip was designed to be used as the brains of a calculator, a 4-bit device that could represent 16 numbers and symbols. This was fine for math calculations, which only had to work with nine digits plus standard math symbols, but was far too under-powered to build a true PC. In 1974, Intel produced a more powerful design based on an 8-bit word (8 bits are commonly known as a word). This chip was the 8080. Zilog Corporation built a competing design known as a Z80. The 8-bit path provided enough room to handle 256 symbols, enough to represent the alphabet, punctuation, and numbers, and still had room left over for streamlined commands. Both chips could take advantage of an operating system known as *CP/M*, which stood for Control Program for Microprocessors.

A number of computers were designed around these chips, showing the potential of the microprocessors. Intel continued to work on refining the design and a few years later, IBM chose the 8088 to serve as the hub of its first PC. The 8088 had an internal 16-bit data path but only an 8-bit I/O function. This produced more internal processing power but maintained full compatibility with the CP/M operating system.

The Rise of the IBM PC

The combination of the IBM name and an existing pool of CP/M software helped fuel the original PC's success. But CP/M could not take full advantage of the machine's power. IBM commissioned Microsoft Corporation to produce a more advanced operating environment, which came to be known as MS DOS (disk operating system). It offered more flexibility but was still similar enough in design to make it easy for software vendors to migrate existing CP/M applications into the new environment.

The 8088, and its sibling, the 8086, could both address a full 1Mb of RAM; but the IBM engineers modified how the chip was used in a PC. They set aside the back 384K of RAM for use by system services, such as the display adapter which drives your monitor. When the original PC was designed, the first PCs were set up to ship with 16Kb of RAM, so the remaining 640K of the first Mb of memory that was left over seemed like an awful lot of space. If you've ever wondered where the notorious 640K-limit for conventional memory came from, now you know.

Today the 8088 is all but obsolete, and support for this chip and motherboards using it is rapidly disappearing. While it still is quite acceptable for basic applications such as straightforward word processing and for use possibly as a bulletin board system, time has passed this CPU by. Unless you're given one, or happen to have one lying around, it's not a good idea to even bother working with it.

The IBM PC soon spawned a series of look-alikes. This was because the machine was built with what was known as *open architecture*. Most of the components were off-the-shelf products available from several vendors. Anybody who wanted to could go out and buy the

Intel microprocessors and the other components and produce a product. While the number of people buying PCs increased and the number of software programs expanded, Intel was working on a more powerful replacement for the 8088, the 80286 (commonly referred to as the 286) and the IBM PC-AT.

AT stands for Advanced Technology, and IBM introduced the first machine using the 286 in 1984. The 286 operated at 6Mhz and could directly address up to 16Mb of RAM, by using a design in the chip called *protected-mode operation*. It offered a 16-bit data path, both internal and external. There are quite a few 286-based machines in operation but nobody has ever written an operating system that took full advantage of the 286 protected-mode operation. One of the reasons for the slow start of the 286 software was the fact that the 286 machine could run all the software written for the older 8088 machines. Another factor was confusion over what kind of operating system the ATs would eventually use. At the time, most people had very little understanding of how fast the pace of micro-processor development would become, and there was talk of having a new operating system that would take full advantage of the 16-bit operation within a couple of years. This slowed down interest in developing programs designed around the 286's 16-bit architecture until that new operating system should arrive.

Over its active lifetime the 286 was improved by various vendors until versions of the chip were available running at 12Mhz, twice the speed of the original design. In spite of this fact, the 286 was destined to have a very short period of time in the sun.

THE 386 AND THE BIRTH OF THE MODERN PC

In 1985, Intel upped the ante once again and signed the 286's death warrant with the release of a 16Mhz, 32-bit processor, the 80386. This new microprocessor was able to address four gigabytes of memory. With an *enhanced memory mode*, the 386 was able to run more than one application at the same time. A few years later, 386's were running up to 33Mhz and Intel introduced another variant on the chip design, the 386SX, and started calling the original design the 386DX. The original 386, now known as the 386DX, may have told us that the 286 was dying; the 386SX wrote its obituary.

The new chip was identical to the 386 except for the fact that it had a 16-bit external data path and cost about the same as the original 386. AMD produced a clone of the 386 running at 40Mhz, but by the time these chips started shipping in quantity, the next member of the family arrived on the scene, the 80486. As this book is written, new machines based on the 386 have all but disappeared. A few vendors still offer motherboards with this CPU, but for all intents and purposes, serious users have already moved on to the next generation.

The Intel 80486

In many respects the 486 looks very much like the older 386. Like its older sibling, the 486DX has a 32-bit data path and can access the same four gigabytes of memory. Like the 386, it is backwards-compatible and can run software designed for any of the earlier "80X86" family of processors. But when it comes to power, there's no comparing the two designs. At the tail end of its life, 386s operating at 33Mhz were made by Intel. The early 20- and 25Mhz 486s could keep up with it, in spite of their slower clock speed. The 486 includes 8K of internal cache, and the DX versions of the chip (we'll get to the other flavors in a minute) come equipped with a built-in math co-processor. Straight versions of the chip are available running up to 50Mhz. In general the 486 is obsolete, but if you want a solid machine to handle a BBS or straight file server, a used 486 in good shape might be a bargain. For serious work, Windows NT or multimedia applications, stick to the newer Pentiums.

Clock Doubling

To push the envelope even further, Intel offers clock-doubling versions of some chips even a triple-speed design. The 486DX2/66 operates internally at 66Mhz, but its external data path operates at 33Mhz. The *clock-doubling* chips offer improved speed without the need for a new motherboard. You can just unplug the old CPU and drop a new one in. The only difference is that things will work faster.

The 486SX

Probably to speed the demise of the older 386, Intel started offering an SX version of the 486. This chip is identical to the DX models, except that it does not have a functional math co-processor or floating point unit. Don't even bother with used machines based on this product.

Other Variations

Intel has produced a number of variations on their CPU designs, which have different letters after their name. These have different power consumption ratings and other factors, making them attractive to vendors building specialty machines such as laptop computers. As this is written, it is almost impossible to build your own laptop or notebook computer. Pentium prices have fallen enough so that buying the 486 isn't worth the savings.

The 486 Overdrive

Generally speaking, you buy a CPU matched to your motherboard. Clock-doubling chips changed that slightly. It is possible to buy one of the clock-doubling chips sold as an Overdrive, which plugs directly into your existing CPU socket. These are available from vendors and can be replaced using the instructions appearing later in this chapter. Given the fact CPUs are often 80% of the cost of the motherboard/CPU combination, you might want to consider just buying a DX2 with matching motherboard rather than the Overdrive upgrade kit. This way you can maintain your investment in the 486 chip that you've got. It can be used as the foundation of a new system, or as a spare in case your unit ever fails.

Readers who keep up with microprocessor design may have noticed that I've paid practically no attention to the 486DX/50. In my experience, this processor is much more difficult to use in a system. The 33Mhz motherboards have developed enough to be a very solid design. Clock-doubling chips use this same motherboard, and they arrived shortly after the 50Mhz model. As a result, I have heard many stories of compatibility issues especially in graphics adapters, hard disk controllers and SCSI host adapters. Since the 66Mhz model tends to offer better overall performance with few problems, I used to recommend it for machines over the 50Mhz model.

SOMEWHERE IN-BETWEEN

Intel offers an upgrade for 486 systems to provide some of the performance of the Pentium. This product, known as the P24T, is designed to fit in a special 238-pin socket. It's sort of a stepped-down Pentium. Given the price drops of the Pentium, why bother? Just get a new Pentium and motherboard for about $150 more.

The Intel Pentium, or, Whatever Happened to the 586?

A funny thing happened on the way to the market. It's very hard to trademark a number, and Intel really wanted to have the only use of the name for its hot new processor, which logic would suggest should have been named the 586. Instead Intel focused on a name that relates to the number five, the Pentium. This chip incorporates a host of design enhancements, including the ability to operate very well in conjunction with other Pentiums in the same system. Several vendors are now at work building super-servers incorporating a number of Pentiums in the same machine, and Microsoft's newest operating systems, Windows NT and Windows 95, are both designed to take advantage of this power.

Like the other chips in the family, the Pentium will run all the software ever designed for the series. The Pentium is the current pick of the litter, with a 64-bit data path, dual internal caches, and above-150Mhz speed potential. Think of it as a 486 on steroids. It includes a number of advanced design features, including separate caches for code and data that, along with its wider bus, offer enhanced performance. The 90Mhz and faster Pentiums have a 3.5-volt power demand, compared to the 5-volt requirement for slower models. This needn't bother you, except when choosing a mother-board. You have to be careful to match the proper type of board with the CPU.

The Pentium is hot, both in performance and in the heat it gener-ates. You need a good cooling system in your PC, and a mini-fan actually mounted on the processor, for safe operation. If you buy a new PC it should already have it included. If you upgrade, or build your own, make sure to get a cooling fan when you buy the Pentium.

Pundits are saying, as they always have, that the current proces-sor is only going to appeal to the fringe of power users and for use as a network server. I heard this same line of argument with the original 386, again with the 486, then with the Pentium. They are now starting the same line with the next in the line, the P6—and it isn't even on the market. My feeling is that the industry will take the same path as it has in the past. Over the first twelve months of a chip's existence, motherboards that use it will be refined and Intel will release alternate versions of the chip. The preceding CPU will start to be perceived as an entry-level system, and its retire-ment will begin as the successor, whatever it may be called, approaches the market.

CHOOSING A CPU

Choosing a microprocessor is more a matter of budget than anything else. In general, you don't want to buy the latest, greatest processor the week after it's been released. For one thing, you'd be forced to buy a system from one of the name-brand vendors and you'll pay a pre-mium for being the first kid on the block to have one. It takes several months for board designers to really start taking advantage of the new processor, and for software and accessories to catch up.

On the other hand, need is an elusive thing and you can never have too much power in your machine. The hottest chips will offer improved performance, and if you are planning to run graphics-intensive applications or use the machine as a network server, you should definitely consider the fastest chip you can afford. Consider a used machine, before the value of its processor makes it worth less that the sum of its parts.

REMOVING AND INSTALLING CPUs

In many machines the CPU is the most expensive single component, and it's certainly one you don't want to abuse. For this reason, you should use extreme care when removing or installing this chip. My discussion and the illustrations will show the Pentium but will apply equally well to the 386/486. Until Intel started promoting its Overdrive line, there was only one way to seat a CPU on a motherboard, but that has recently changed. The first step in either installing or removing a CPU is to determine what kind of socket is used on your board.

Locating the CPU or CPU Socket

Locating the CPU should be a fairly straightforward affair. The Pentium, 486, and the 386 CPUs are square designs, sometimes with one corner cut off at an angle. On machines without the new *Zero Insertion Force* or *ZIF socket* (Don't get the one for the CPU confused with the upgrade socket—check your manual for an exact drawing), the chip will completely cover its mounting pad. Chips up to the 486DX33 should be easy to locate. They'll have the word "Intel" (or other manufacturer) along with the name of the chip printed directly on the upper surface. Clock-doubled chips, such as the 486DX2/66 and the Pentium, have heat sinks mounted on the top of the chip; in some cases these will also have labeling—but not always. Figure 7.2 shows a picture of an Intel Pentium with its heat sink.

CPU Chip
With Heat Sink
Top View

CPU Chip
With Heat Sink
Side View

FIGURE 7.2 Intel Pentium with its heat sink.

If you are locating an empty socket for a CPU in a motherboard without one, refer to your motherboard documentation to locate the socket and determine its type.

WARNING

Many motherboards have the ability to seat CPUs of several different speeds, and some, like the Micronics M54E, can even handle more than one in the same box. Be sure to check your manual and adjust any jumpers that control the setting. Also, don't be tempted to rate a chip higher than the factory did. Some people boost the Pentium 90s to 100mHz and hope for the best. It may work, and it may lead to a system crash, or shorten the life of the processor—don't risk it.

Standard Sockets vs. Zero Insertion Force

Older motherboards, and some newer ones, come with standard, straight-push sockets for the CPU. Newer ones have Zero Insertion Force, or ZIF, sockets. The difference is quite simple; in the older sockets the chips are seated using pressure, and removing it involves using some kind of tool to free the pins from the socket. ZIF sockets have a hinge arm, which, in the down position, holds the CPU firmly in place. Raising the arm frees the chip and it can be pulled out easily with your fingers.

Removing a CPU

Tools You'll Need

✔ Screwdriver

✔ Motherboard manual

✔ Anti-static envelopes and/or pouch

✔ Box for the CPU

✔ Chip puller or an expansion slot cover (if you don't have a ZIF socket)

WARNING

Any time you handle the electronic components of your machine, you should protect them from static discharge. Usually all you have to do is touch the metal part of the case to make sure that you are not carrying a static charge that might be dissipated into the circuitry and cause damage. You should do this before opening up any static-protective envelopes, and repeat the procedure any time you take a step away from the machine, especially in cold, dry weather. If you have problems with static electricity buildup, you can also obtain a grounding strip that can be worn on the wrist to minimize and prevent it.

STEP 1

Exit any operating programs, turn off your computer and remove its power cord.

STEP 2

Remove the computer's cover by removing the screws around the edge of the case in back.

STEP 3

Either visually, or using a board manual, locate the CPU.

STEP 4

Remove any expansion card that may be in the way so that you can easily place your entire hand around the CPU and still have a couple of inches clearance on all sides.

Removing a ZIF Chip

STEP 5

If you have a Zero Insertion Force (ZIF) socket, there should either be a little lever on one side or the other of the CPU or a square bracket-shaped handle going around three sides of the CPU, as shown in Figure 7.3. Make sure you have grounded yourself so that you can't release static when you touch the CPU. Lift the handle and gently move it back as far as it will go on its hinge.

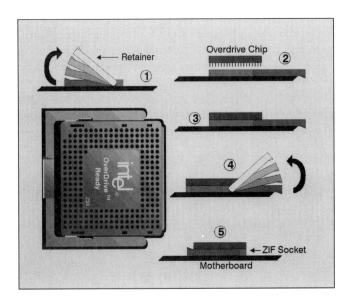

FIGURE 7.3 ZIF socket and retainer.

STEP 6

With a finger on either side of the CPU, gently lift straight up until it is clear of the socket.

STEP 7

Place the CPU immediately into a protective, anti-static container.

Removing a Non-ZIF Chip

STEP 5

If you don't have a ZIF socket, you'll have to work the CPU free of its moorings. All around the edge of the CPU are a series of delicate gold-plated pins. *It's important not to bend these pins.* If you don't have a special tool, you can use the expansion cover off the back of one of your system's slots to gently work it free. Start by working it very gently between the socket base and the bottom of the CPU in one corner as shown in Figure 7.4.

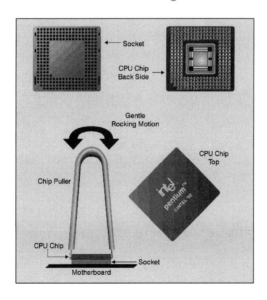

FIGURE 7.4 Working the CPU out of the socket.

STEP 6

Very carefully rock the tool back and forth and pry the chip lightly above the socket. Move to an opposite corner and repeat the process. Do this on all four corners until the chip is slightly free of the socket.

STEP 7

Now place the edge of the cover in the middle of one of the sides of the CPU and work it just a little bit higher up. Repeat on the other three sides. Continue this step until the CPU is worked completely free and you can lift it out.

Do not perform this step too quickly. If you pull the CPU too high on one side, you'll bend the pins on the other, possibly damaging a connector or making it more difficult to safely re-seat the CPU at another time.

WARNING

STEP 8

Once the CPU is completely free, place it immediately into an anti-static container.

Inserting a ZIF CPU onto the Motherboard

If you have a Zero Insertion Force socket, all you have to do is make sure the CPU is properly oriented.

STEP 1

Place it in position by lining up either the cut corner, or the little dot, with the matching side of the socket that houses Pin 1. If you are unsure of this positioning, check with your documentation or contact your motherboard manufacturer's technical support department.

Step 2

Raise the handle on the ZIF socket.

Step 3

Make sure you are properly grounded. Take the CPU out of its protective case.

Step 4

Inspect the bottom of the CPU and *make sure that all the pins on the bottom are straight and properly lined up*. If any of them are bent, they may splay out when you attempt to seat the CPU. If this happens, the CPU won't function; and if the pin is broken off or touches another pin, you may permanently damage the CPU.

Step 5

Carefully line up the pins and the holes so that the CPU is centered over the socket. Some of these sockets are designed to accept more than one kind of CPU, so you may have more holes than you need; just be sure that the CPU is centered.

Step 6

Gently ease the CPU into place, making sure that all the pins fit cleanly into position.

If for some reason the CPU does not slide easily into place, you either don't have the ZIF socket completely open, or you slightly bent one of the pins. *Do not use force*. If you bend one of the pins you may render the CPU useless.

STEP 7

Once the CPU is in place, close the latch on the socket.

Inserting a CPU into a Non-ZIF Socket

STEP 1

Locate the proper orientation of the CPU to the socket. This is usually done by matching the cut corner or dot in the CPU, with the angle corner or dot located on the innermost rim of the CPU socket. If you are unsure of this step, verify it, either by using your manual or by calling your motherboard's technical support department.

STEP 2

Make sure you are properly grounded. Take the CPU out of its protective case.

STEP 3

Inspect the bottom of the CPU and *make sure that all the pins on the bottom are straight and properly lined up.* If any of them are bent, they may splay out when you attempt to seat the CPU. If this happens, the CPU won't function; and if the pin is broken off or touches another pin, you may permanently damage the CPU.

STEP 4

Line up the pins exactly. Check from all sides and be sure that the rows are properly aligned with the sockets. If you go to the next step and push on the CPU's surface and things are not exactly lined up, you may permanently damage the CPU.

STEP 5

Use the thumbs and forefingers of both hands to seat the chip. Place one on each corner of the CPU and gently but firmly push the CPU into place.

WARNING

If you feel any unusual resistance, or if one side seems to be going down but the opposite side doesn't, *stop at once*. Double-check to make sure that all the pins are lined up properly with the holes and that nothing is obstructing them.

STEP 6

Push firmly until the CPU is fully down against the rim of the socket.

CPU CARE

In and of itself, a CPU requires no real maintenance. There are no moving parts and nothing to clean. However, there is one element always in your case that poses a threat to your CPU: *heat*. The more transistors and speed we pack into a CPU, the hotter it operates. Until the arrival of the 486DX2, a simple fan built into your PC's power supply was adequate to cool the system as long as the case was properly closed with all bays and expansion slots covered.

The faster 486 and Pentium chips have pushed the performance envelope up against the heat barrier. That is why these chips require heat sinks, and fans over the top. If your case's chassis is inadequately ventilated due to expansion cards, cables, etc., you may need to purchase an auxiliary fan for the case as well, or a more advanced power supply similar to those described later in the book. For more information, refer to Chapter 16.

Every so often listen to the sounds inside your machine. Pay careful attention to anything that sounds like a bearing wearing out. This is probably a fan. If it is the one on your CPU it should be replaced at once. If it is the power supply, swap it out for a new one that's covered later in the book. Here is how to remove and replace the CPU fan:

REMOVING/REPLACING A CPU FAN

Tools You'll Need

✔ New Fan Kit

✔ Screwdriver

✔ Anti-static envelopes and/or pouch

✔ Box for the CPU

✔ Chip puller or an expansion slot cover (if you don't have a ZIF socket)

WARNING

Any time you handle the electronic components of your machine, you should protect them from static discharge. Usually all you have to do is touch the metal part of the case to make sure that you are not carrying a static charge that might be dissipated into the circuitry and cause damage. You should do this before opening up any static-protective envelopes, and repeat the procedure any time you take a step away from the machine, especially in cold, dry weather. If you have problems with static electricity buildup, you can also obtain a grounding strip that can be worn on the wrist to minimize and prevent it.

Removing the Old Fan

STEP ONE

Open the case and unplug the power lead to the fan.

STEP TWO

Remove the CPU as described above.

Most fans are placed directly on the CPU with a pad of mounting adhesive that is supplied with the fan. A few are attached with clips. If you have the latter, just unhook the clip. If there is an adhesive, slip the edge of the knife between the top of the CPU and the base. Gently pry the fan off the top, and remove as much of the adhesive as you can. Don't worry, the top of the CPU is a cover plate. That doesn't mean you can jab into it, but reasonable care is all that is required.

Mounting a New Fan

STEP ONE

Make sure the fan is the right one for your CPU when you buy it.

STEP TWO

Identify if the new fan uses mounting adhesive or a clip—a few use both. Attach the fan over the top of the CPU.

STEP THREE

Place the CPU in its socket as described earlier in this chapter.

STEP FOUR

Connect the power lead to the fan.

STEP FIVE

Power up the system and visually check the operation of the fan. Make sure it is running smoothly. If you forget the plug the CPU will overheat—this condition could damage the CPU.

STEP SIX

Power down the PC and close up the case.

CHAPTER SUMMARY

The CPU is one of the most important factors in determining your system's performance and what software it can operate effectively. This chapter has focused on the different types of CPUs commonly used in personal computers, and the history of the Intel microprocessor. It has also presented the steps required to remove and replace the microprocessor on the motherboard, as well as how to replace a CPU fan.

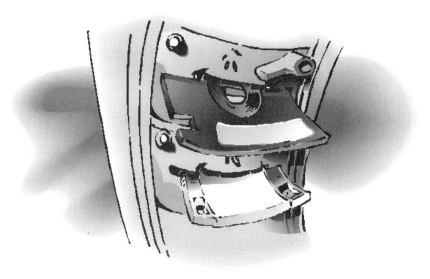

CHAPTER 8

WORKING WITH FLOPPY DRIVES

WHAT'S IN THIS CHAPTER

- ✔ Choosing a Floppy Drive Subsystem
- ✔ Explaining Controllers
- ✔ Installing Floppy Drives
- ✔ Drive Types
- ✔ Troubleshooting Floppy Drives

WHAT THIS CHAPTER IS ABOUT

Not that many years ago, hard drives were luxuries on PCs. In fact, early home machines were actually sold without floppy disk drives. Today no one would think of buying a serious machine without both. The floppy may not offer the storage space and speed of your hard disk drive, but it is indispensable for loading programs, sharing data with other users, and providing a back-up access to the operating system if the hard drive isn't working properly. This chapter covers floppy disk drives and with it the basics of magnetic storage and the considerations for selecting, installing and maintaining your system's floppy drives. We will cover other mass storage devices such as tape drives, CD-ROM, and optical drives in other chapters.

THE VENERABLE FLOPPY DRIVE

Owners of the original IBM PCs used 5.25-inch floppy disk drives as mass storage devices... yes, *mass* storage devices! Power-user systems were equipped with two 360k, 5.25-inch drives. Today virtually all PCs are equipped with fast hard drives, many having capacities of 1 Gb or more, and which cost not much more than one of those antique floppies. Yet the floppy drive has not outlived its usefulness. While more and more programs are distributed on CD-ROM, a large number are still shipped on floppies. The lowly floppy is also still the simplest network (sometimes referred to as a "sneaker-net"), because you walk between two computers with a disk, allowing an easy way of exchanging files between two machines. It is no longer a question of having a floppy disk drive; almost all systems today come with one 3.5-inch, 1.44 Mb floppy disk drive, and very likely, a CD-ROM drive as well; a few may have a 5.25-inch, 1.2Mb floppy drive as well, for backward compatibility with older programs. And of course there are still thousands and thousands of aging systems around with two of those giant 360- or 720k drives.

NOTE

Although the full name of the hardware device is "floppy disk drive," it is often shortened, as in "floppy disk," "floppy drive," or even just "floppy." The storage medium it uses is called a "floppy disk," a short form of "floppy diskette." Both device and diskette are typically called "disks." Often one has to tell which is meant by context, which usually isn't too hard. Just to further complicate matters a little, however, the storage medium used in a CD-ROM drive is also called a "disk"— but it is spelled with a "c" on the end, "d-i-s-c," and of course prounounced exactly the same as "disk"… Which I suppose only goes to show (again) that while computers are in their essence logical creations, humans aren't.

All PCs need a storage system, a place to hold programs and electronic information when they are not in use. Most use some form of magnetic medium similar to the technology used for video and audio cassette tapes. In fact, some of the very earliest home computers (like the Commodore VIC-20) used cassette tape drives; and even the very earliest IBM PCs assumed their owners would use cassettes! The regular cassette tapes did store the information adequately. Of course, "adequately" is a relative term. The major problem with tape is that it is a *sequential* device; that is, if the file you want is in the middle of the tape, you might wait several minutes for the drive to locate the information you wanted to use. Tape is also fragile—subject to breaks, crimps, jams, stretches, and drop-outs in the quality of the recording surface. Floppy and hard drives are *random access devices*, which means that they can go directly to any point on their surface to read information.

In effect, the recording surfaces of floppy and hard disks are a cross between a recording tape and a record or audio CD. A combination of revolving the disk and moving read/write heads over the surface is used to locate the data rapidly. Floppy diskettes are made from a flexible plastic which is coated on each side with a thin layer of magnetic sensitive material. By changing the magnetic properties of small portions of the material, it is possible to represent data. The intricacies of how the values are stored and retained is something no one but an engineer would ever use. The bottom line is, the computer can read the information on the disk as one of two values, either 0 or 1. As with all other information used by computers, in the final analysis, an individual piece of information is simply a binary number.

Floppy disks have three advantages over standard hard disks: the recording material is comparatively inexpensive, and the 3.5-inch disk itself, with its hard plastic shell, is relatively durable, and it is, as I said earlier, conveniently portable and can be easily removed from the drive. The floppy disk has two disadvantages compared to hard disks: the vastly smaller amount of information that it can store, and the comparatively longer time it takes to get it back to us.

Speed

Hard disks operate much faster than floppies. The actual recording surfaces of a hard disk are placed on a metal platter, instead of the more flexible, less-rigid film used for floppies, which is more, well, floppy. As a result, most hard disks can spin over 15 times faster, and some of the newest SCSI drives, over 30 times. Hard disks can also contain multiple platters in the same drive, with individual read/write heads for each recording surface. A typical floppy drive spins at 360 rpm, about 10 times faster than a high-fidelity record player. Slow hard drives spin at 3600 rpm. More advanced hard drives rotate at speeds of over 7800 rpm. The increase in speed, and the complexity of the more advanced electronics needed to operate at those speeds, are part of the reason for a hard drive's more expensive price tag.

While floppy drives are much faster than tape, they're still much slower in acquiring and reading data than a hard disk. Since all floppy drives are about equal in speed and all floppies of a given type (we'll give the types in a minute), store the same amount of data and have basically the same performance, there is little to concern ourselves with in buying a floppy drive except its size and price. Hard drives, on the other hand, come in a variety of types and with widely differing performance characteristics. We'll get into some of these differences in Chapter 9 to help you in deciding what type of unit to buy for your machine.

Size

There are two ways to describe size when it comes to computer disks. One is the actual physical size. Today most floppy and hard disks are sold in two *form factors* or sizes. Physical size is measured by the actual width of the drive itself, either 3.5 inches or 5.25 inches. Keep in mind that almost all software today is sold on either 3.5 inch disks or on CD-ROM, so you will only need to worry about

5.25 inch disks if you have old files you need to read stored on the "larger" media. The 3.5s are easier to carry, mail, and hold more data. Today, most 3.5-inch disks store 1.44Mb per disk. Both sides of the diskette are used to record data. Some 3.5s can hold up to 2.88Mb, but those are not widely used. As for the 5.25-inch drives, the standard capacity is 1.2Mb, slightly less than their more efficient smaller cousins. Both of these capacities are referred to as *high density*. You may also hear the terms "full-height" or "half-height." *Full-height* was the size of the old original IBM-PC drive slot or *bay*, which was 3.5 inches high (not wide). Today, all but the largest hard disks will usually fit in a *half-height* bay half as high as that, and some drives fit into spaces a quarter of that size.

More important than the physical size of the drive is its storage capacity, the amount of data that can be placed on its platters. For floppy drives, these sizes are fixed based on the size and type of the disk put into the drive. See Table 8.1.

TABLE 8.1 Common floppy disk sizes.

DISK SIZE	DISK TYPES	NUMBER OF CHARACTERS	EQUIVALENT # OF SINGLE-SPACED TYPED PAGES
5.25	360k	368,640	92
3.5	720k	737,280	184
5.25	1.2Mb	1,213,952	303
3.5	1.44Mb	1,457,664	364
3.5	2.88Mb	2,915,328	729

Evolution

The "high density" moniker is a product of an evolution. The original IBM 5.25-inch floppy stored only 160k. This was superseded by the double-density disk, which stored 320k. In the early days some manufacturers also sold some single-sided disks. These were disks on which testing was only performed on one side, reducing the cost of production. 3.5- (720k) and 5.25 (360k)-inch double-density disks are still in circulation. The difference in capacity is due to the difference in the quality of the magnetic coating. The finer the coating, the greater the ability to store information. At the present time, vendors also produce extra-high-density disks, as mentioned above. These are 3.5-inch disks that can store 2.88Mb. These floppies use a newer magnetic material that is able to store data much more efficiently than the earlier diskettes. These extra-high-density drives are also able to read disks created in the older drives.

In addition to the basic drive combinations mentioned above, there are some other alternatives when looking at a floppy drive. One option is a *dual-media* disk drive. These are slightly schizo-phrenic units that cram both a 3.5-inch and 5.25-inch drive into a single half-height slot. These units, at about $100, are about twice as expensive as a standard floppy disk drive, if you are considering putting both types of drives into a new or upgraded PC you might want to consider them. At this time, both Canon USA and TEAC are making these units.

Floppies are indispensable, but even the largest traditional floppy drives don't have enough space to store either large bitmap graphic files or large database files. One way to get around the limits of size for floppies for removable media is *floptical*. A floptical disk is a hybrid; it uses traditional floppy disk media and technology to place data on the disk, but has an optical device for positioning the heads. This provides a greater margin of accuracy, and therefore the ability to store greater amounts of data on a single disk. The original floptical unit provides about 21Mb of space on a single disk, but can't read existing 3.5-inch floppies. Some of the newer units can write a little over 20Mb and have the ability to read existing 3.5-inch disks. Be prepared to pay at least $350 for a floptical disk drive. The other drawback to floptical disks that offsets its advantage in size is the cost of disks, which is about $12 each—compared to a price of about a quarter apiece for 3.5-inch, 1.44Mb disks bought in bulk.

The Zip Drive

Another option for large cheap storage, in addition to having a traditional 3.5 floppy, is the Zip Drive from Bernoulli-Iomega. This is a special high-capacity drive that acts like a floppy, but can store up to 100MB of data. It is a neat SCSI-based device that can be used for backup, and to send large files between different sites. Many graphic and typesetting services are using them. These units were just coming to market as this book was being written, so I was not able to get one to test and install. Gary Bouton, who did the great cartoons at the start of each chapter, did, and he loves his.

Hard Shell/Soft Shell

Figure 8.1 shows the parts of a standard 5.25-inch floppy disk. The large center hole is where the spindle of the drive fits to actually rotate the disk during operation. The large open oval just below it has been cut out to allow access to the recording surface for the read/write heads. The notch in the upper right-hand quadrant is the *write-protect notch*. This is much like the tab on the back of a video or audio cassette. If the notch is uncovered, data can be written to the disk. If a piece of tape is placed over the notch, it will prevent data from being written to the disk.

FIGURE 8.1 A standard 5.25-inch floppy diskette.

Figure 8.2 shows a similar layout for a 3.5-inch diskette. The Macintosh and the IBM-PS/2 arrived with a different kind of floppy drive—the 3.5-inch hard shell. While the material inside the casing is basically the same, the mechanical operation of the drive and the shell of the diskette itself are different. The 3.5-inch drive has a metal door that flies over the head aperture hole to protect the disk's surface when it's not inside the drive. Instead of a hollow hole for the spindle, the diskette actually has a metal hub. The read/write notch has been replaced by a sliding plastic tab. When the hole is visible, the disk is *read-only*; when the hole is covered, you can read and write to it. A similar hole is present on the other side of high-density disks. If there is no hole on the other side, the disk is a 720k rather than a 1.44Mb.

FIGURE 8.2 A standard 3.5-inch floppy diskette.

The 3.5-inch design has many advantages over the 5.25; but both forms are still in common use. If you are building a new machine and do not have an existing collection of 5.25-inch floppies around, you should consider obtaining only one, or possibly two, high-density 3.5-inch drives. If you have a collection of the older disks, it's probably a good idea to consider installing both types in your machine. Several months ago, we converted all the machines in our lab, using the 3.5-inch drive as the primary, or A drive, and a 5.25 as the B drive. 1.2 or 1.44Mb floppy drives run between $45 and $70, depending on the source.

Extended-density 2.88Mb drives also use the same hard-shell design. At the present time the actual disks are a good bit more expensive than standard high-density 3.5-inch versions. It's hard to say whether the new format will actually catch on. Over the years, there have been several alternative disk sizes or formats that never gained popular acceptance. The 1.44Mb 3.5-inch size will probably maintain its dominant position for a good while.

Caring for Your Floppy Diskettes and Drives

Before we get into how to use and install floppy disk drives, I want to explain how to properly maintain them. The magnetic field generated by your monitor can weaken, and in some cases, even eliminate the charge used to record the data on your disks. The same is true for the magnets in the little paper-clip holders that are also found on many people's desks. Magnetic screwdrivers, the electric field generated by some telephones, fingerprints, coffee, Coke, and grease from french fries are among some of the common desktop and fingertip hazards that can destroy or severely injure disks. The operative word for caring for floppy disks is *care*. Handle them gently and don't store them under or alongside your monitor (one vendor actually sells a little case for holding disks up alongside your monitor). Keep them away from magnetic fields and put them away when they are not actually being used.

Formatting Floppy Disks

In order to use either a floppy or a hard drive your computer must know how to locate the information on the disk. Just telling it to get a file by the file name would not work very well. Imagine how difficult it would be to find a location in a large city if there were no street names or house numbers. Formatting is a bit like laying down a grid of streets and assigning precise locations for every point on the disk. To understand how a format works, we need to understand how the process is organized. There are three key terms: *sectors*, *tracks*, and *cylinders*. Figure 8.3 shows a diagram of a floppy disk with sectors and tracks displayed. Keep in mind that they aren't really *drawn* on the disk, it is just part of the magnetic organization of information.

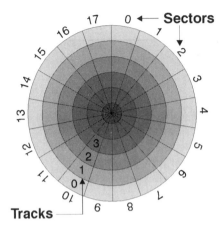

FIGURE 8.3 Floppy drive formatting organization.

The disk is divided into several circular tracks, much like the lanes on a running course at a Track and Field meet. The track is divided into sectors, and the sector is the actual storage location. MS-DOS sectors normally contain 512 bytes of data each. A single-sided disk has no cylinders. Dual-sided disks and hard disks with multiple platters have cylinders. This is nothing more than a way of referencing the relative location of a sector in a track to enable positioning and reading with the appropriate head when recovering data. In computer science counting is often begun with the number 0; cylinders and tracks are no exception. The first track is track 0 on side 0, the top side of the first platter. This is exactly opposite from track 0 on side 1, the bottom. On a hard disk with more than one platter, track 0 of side 2 would be the first track on the top side of the second platter.

When you format a disk, the machine is actually creating boundaries for the sectors and tracks. These boundaries actually take up usable space on the disk. So, once you've formatted a disk, you find that it has less usable space than you thought it would.

There are a couple of other terms you should understand when dealing with disks: one of these is the term *file allocation table*, or FAT. This is a list used by the operating system to determine what disk space is actually in use. When you erase a file, it is not immediately erased. Instead, the file allocation table is modified to show that area of the disk as "available" or "usable." As far as the operating system is concerned, the file no longer exists. Sooner or later that area of the disk will be overwritten with new data.

Another term you should be familiar with is *bootable*. When formatting a disk you can tell the operating system to make the floppy disk bootable. That means that you can actually use that disk to boot your system. In DOS, this is accomplished by using an /S switch (phrase) when using the Format command. For example, format a: /s /V. This command not only performs the format, but transfers the two hidden system files and command.com to the floppy disk. The /V switch also verifies that the data was properly written to disk. Covering all the intricacies of the formatting options of various operating systems is beyond the scope of this book. For more information on operating commands you should consult your system manual.

THE FLOPPY DISK SUB-SYSTEM

A floppy disk drive has to be integrated into the PC system. This involves three components: the drive itself, a controller card which passes the commands and data to and from the computer and the disk drive, and a cable to connect both of them. These are called the *floppy disk sub-system*.

When you ask the floppy drive to do something by a keystroke or clicking a mouse, that command has to be routed to the floppy drive and interpreted. This is handled by your computer's BIOS or *basic input/output system*. The BIOS is a set of programs usually contained in read-only memory (ROM) chips which contain basic instructions on how the computer deals with external devices, like floppy disks and hard disks. The *floppy disk controller* translates the commands from the BIOS into instructions that the drive can understand. On the other side, it translates the stream of signals from the floppy disk into data that can be read by the computer. The floppy disk controller is also the device that maintains knowledge of where the heads of the disk are actually located, and reads the track and sector information. It is also responsible for determining whether or not the disk is write-protected. Unless you are planning to design a floppy disk controller, you really don't have to understand any more about it than that.

Three Flavors of Floppy Disk Controllers

Floppy disk controllers for PCs come in three different styles: *combined*, *integrated*, and *stand-alone*. The original PC used a stand-alone controller, that is, it was contained on a separate card. Later models combined the *hard disk controller* (which performs similar functions for the hard drive) with the floppy disk controller on the same card. An integrated design builds the functions of the floppy disk controller directly into the system's motherboard. No matter what the design, a cable must be run from the floppy drive to either the floppy disk controller card or a floppy controller connection on the motherboard. Most PCs and floppy disk controllers are designed to support up to two floppy drives. Sophisticated controllers can handle more, but for most users, two drives are sufficient.

Most controllers can also support a combination of low- and high-density disks, in either 5.25- or 3.5-inch sizes. It should make no difference if you want to mix a high-density 5.25 and a low-density 3.5, or have matched 5.25- or 3.5-inch drives. At the present time most PCs do not automatically support the extended density 3.5-inch 2.88Mb-floppy drive. To use these devices you will probably have to upgrade your computer's BIOS, or use a special controller which comes with a special software driver program.

INSTALLING A FLOPPY DRIVE

Installing a floppy drive or adding a second drive to a system is fairly simple. You'll need the drive, an appropriate cable, a controller (if one is not already installed in your system), and appropriate mounting hardware (rails, spacers, etc.). For tools, you'll need a Philips-head screwdriver, perhaps a flat blade or torque screwdriver, and possibly a hemostat or tweezers to set the drive-select jumper.

Setting the Drive-Select Jumper

Convention has it that the first hard drive in a PC is designated as drive C. This allows room for up to two floppy drives to take the letters A and B. In order for the machine to "see" your floppy drives and assign a number, they must be properly configured, usually by using *jumpers* (small switch blocks) located on the floppy drive. The easiest way to set up floppies is to use a twisted-pair cable as shown in Figure 8.4. This allows you to determine the drive letter by its position on the cable, if the jumpers of any drive on the cable are set to identify it as the second drive. In other words, the drive on the last position on the cable is automatically assigned as drive 1. If you only have one drive in the system, you simply attach it to the end of the cable. Adding a second drive is done by attaching it to the middle position on the cable. If at some point in the future you need to reverse the drive positions, you don't even have to remove the drives from the case; simply swap positions on the cable.

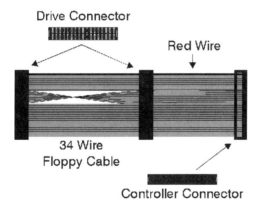

FIGURE 8.4 A twisted-pair floppy drive cable.

Setting the Jumpers

This is perhaps the only possibly confusing part of installing a floppy drive. For some reason vendors have never set up a standard for either the location of these jumpers, or the way they are designated.

Some start counting drives from 0, others from 1. Some use the labels DS0 and DS1, others use DS1 and 2; some others use bizarre designations based on the name of their favorite cousin, their post office box, or some other bit of arcane trivia that occurred to them as they were putting the labels on. To make matters even worse, some drives come configured to allow setting for three positions, others for four, and some include other jumper settings on the same block of pins. Unless you are already familiar with the drive and its jumpers, or can easily identify DS0 and 1 or DS1 and 2, you should refer to the instructions that came with your drive for setting the switches. If you are using twisted-pair cable (which I strongly recommend), you should use the little slide-on connecting blocks over the pins in order to set the drive selector for drive 2. If you see pins marked DS0 and DS1, set the DS1 position. If your floppy is marked DS1 and DS2, jumper the DS2 position. The same jumpering will apply to both floppy drives if you are installing more than one in your system. Refer to Figure 8.5.

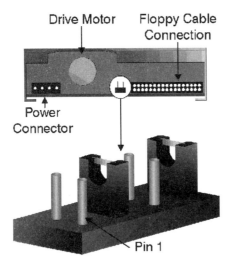

FIGURE 8.5   The back of a floppy disk drive and the drive-select jumper.

Installing the Drives in the Bay

3.5-Inch Drives

3.5-inch drives can be installed directly into a 3.5-inch bay in some newer cases. In some cases you may be provided with a mounting tray or mounting brackets. If that's true, you'll have to mount the drive in the tray or in the brackets and then slide that assembly into the bay, just as you would a 5.25-inch drive.

3.5-inch drives may have a smaller four-pronged connector on the back of the drive that resembles long jumper pins. These accept the specially-keyed power adapter that also will only slide in one way. If your power supply does not have this kind of connector, you will need an adapter, usually supplied with 3.5-inch drive kits.

Some 3.5-inch drives have controller cable connections identical to those for 5.25-inch drives; others use pin connections. Most of the latter have an adapter which will allow you to use a standard edge connector. Such an adapter slides over the pins of the drive and has an edge connector on the other side. This is usually the simplest way to attach the drive, since you can use standard twisted-pair cables without having to worry about the type of connections or the order in which the drives are placed.

5.25-Inch Drives

If you are mounting a 5.25-inch drive into a tower case, all you'll probably have to do is slide it into a bay from the front of the case (you'll have to remove the cover of the case first by unscrewing the screws at the back of the tower and removing the shroud). Once you have slid it into the bay, fasten it with four mounting screws through the slots on either side of the bay. Be sure not to use screws that are too long; they may penetrate through to the board on the floppy and damage it. Once the drive is fastened, attach a power lead plug from the power supply into the socket. This lead will have four wires, usually one red, one yellow, and two black. Most 5.25-inch drives will have a plug about 1 inch across which can only be seated one way, since two of the corners are rounded and the others are square cut (see Figure 8.6). Once the power supply is attached, attach one end of the cable to the controller. This also only fits one way. Some cables have plugs placed in the ends so that the cable will only fit one way over the edge connector, which looks a bit like the edge connector on an expansion card. Others do not. In either case the red stripe, or other color code that runs along one side of the cable, should go toward the side that has Pin 1 of the connector. This is almost always located on the side toward the power connection.

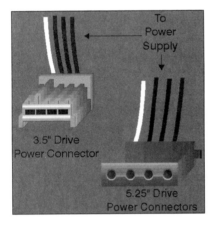

Figure 8.6 Power supply connectors.

If you are installing the drive in a desktop case, you will probably have to use some kind of mounting rail before sliding the drive into the bay. These are attached using two screws each.

Installing a Second Drive

If you are installing two drives in your system, the second drive is installed the same way as the first, and the drive-selection switches should be set the same way as the first drive. This is why we use the twisted-pair wire; see above. If we were to use straight wire, we would have to set each drive differently.

WARNING

Both floppy disk and some older hard disk drives use twisted pair cables. Floppy drive twisted-pair cables have a twisted-pair segment with seven wires, while hard disk cables have five. Be sure the cable you are using to attach your floppy is the right type.

Once you have all the drives attached to both the ribbon cable and the power cable, locate the pins on your floppy controller and attach the other end of the cable to it. It may be located on your motherboard, hard disk controller, or SCSI adapter. If you have an IDE-style hard drive (as discussed below), your floppy controller may be mounted on the IDE paddle-board, which often also contains your parallel and serial ports.

Modifying Setup

Any time you change the basic configuration of your PC, you have to modify your system's CMOS Setup. On AT, 386, and later machines, reset the values stored in your CMOS Setup. On the very early PCs (before the 286), you have to usually change jumpers on the motherboard. We won't deal with those older machines here. For 286 machines you will need a Setup disk. 386-based and later PCs access their Setup directly from the CMOS chip. In most cases, these machines will identify that the disk configuration is changed and will offer to run Setup the next time your machine is turned on. If yours doesn't, you'll need to use the appropriate keystrokes (see your owner's manual) to run the Setup utility.

Change the appropriate letter to match the drive type you have installed. For example, the first floppy drive (or drive A) equals 1.44Mb, 3.5-inch, etc. The screen should also show you how to exit and save your changes, such as hitting the **F10** or **Escape** key. It may also ask you to verify your changes by pressing the **Y** key after you have done this. At that point, your system should reboot and recognize the new drive or drives. Once that's completed, test your installation by placing a disk in the drive to see if you can read and write to it.

NOTE

Keep in mind that if a disk has not been formatted, your machine will not be able to read the disk until it has been formatted.

TROUBLESHOOTING FLOPPY DISK OPERATION

Floppy disk drives are fairly simple in construction. If a floppy disk isn't working right it's most likely the diskette itself. To evaluate this, place another disk that has been formatted and verified into the drive and attempt the same operation. This simple check will also verify another of the most common causes of disk failure: attempting to write to a disk when it was not actually placed in the drive, or the door was not closed. If both disks do not work properly, but work properly in another machine, then you may not have your system Setup working properly. Run the CMOS Setup utility described above and make sure you have the appropriate drive and drive type specified for your system.

If the system is properly configured, and the drives still don't work, then you may have a problem either with your cable or with the drive controller. Since cables are cheaper and easier to test, double-check your cabling and try again. Were all your connections tight, and were all the connections properly made? Were the drives properly connected to the power supply?

If you are using a twisted-pair cable, be sure that both floppy drives are set to drive type 2 (or your single drive if you only have one). If you are using non-twisted pair cable or a single drive cable, be sure that the drive is set appropriately to drive type 0 and 1 or 1 and 2, according to the way the manufacturer numbered the drives.

NOTE

If you have drives from two different manufacturers or two different size drives, one drive may start numbering at 0 and the other at 1. You must have both drives set to the second position, no matter what the numbering system is.

If everything is properly powered, selected, and cabled, and you know the cable is good and that the drives have been properly configured for your system Setup, then the remaining option is to try another disk controller. If your controller is embedded on the motherboard, you may be able to either de-select that controller using the system Setup, or it may automatically disengage itself if it detects another controller on the system. See your motherboard manual to find out.

If your floppy controller is integrated with your hard disk controller, you may have to replace the entire card. You can test this by getting another floppy controller of some sort and trying to boot the system using that card (remember, you don't have to have the hard disk attached to test the floppy drives). Depending on the cost of the failed component, you may want to investigate the possibility of repair, and you certainly want to double-check any possible warranty information that you may have.

CHAPTER SUMMARY

Though no longer the primary means of mass storage or backup on PCs, floppy disk drives in the 3.5-inch and older 5.25-inch size are still required on complete systems. The majority of software is still distributed on floppy disks as well as CD-ROM, and they are convenient for limited, cost-efficient storage and transfer of data. High-density 1.44Mb 3.5-inch drives have virually eliminated the need for the older 1.2Mb 5.25-inch models, and are preferred for upgrades and in new systems alike; extended-high-density drives (2.88Mb) and floptical drives (21Mb) are available at considerably higher prices. Floppy disks, especially the hard-shell 3.5-inch type, require only care, cleanliness, and an avoidance of magnetic fields to give long and reliable service. Installing a floppy disk drive requires understanding what type of floppy disk controller and cable you have or need, setting the jumpers on the controller and drive, and perhaps a little bit of mounting hardware. Typically, you will have to inform your system's BIOS (via your Setup utility) when you add or change drives. Floppy drives are also relatively easy to troubleshoot by checking settings, cables, connections, and substituting components.

CHAPTER 9

THE BIG CLOSET— HARD DRIVES

WHAT'S IN THIS CHAPTER

- ✔ Hard Disk Basics
- ✔ How Data Is Organized
- ✔ Types of Hard Disks
- ✔ Sorting Out the Alphabet Soup: EDSI, MFM, ISA, EISA, SCSI
- ✔ Installing Your Hard Drive
- ✔ Hard Drive Configuration
- ✔ Troubleshooting Your Hard Drive Sub-System

303

What This Chapter Is About

If the CPU can be called the brain of your personal computer, the hard disk might well be considered its heart. Throughout its life your hard disk is in continual motion. Modern hard drives rotate at speeds 10 to 20 times faster than floppy disks, up to 7800 rpm. They must be ready to locate and move data within milliseconds of your request. To these boxes you entrust all the work you do on your computer: letters, images, tax records, accounting data, the names and addresses of friends, your programs—everything you do with the machine that is worth keeping finds its way onto the platters of your hard disk. For that reason alone, it is worth obtaining the best hard disk you can, but that's not all. As with almost any other component of your system, the better the hardware, the better and more reliable its service.

NOTE In this discussion of hard disks and their controllers, I have not included references to different system expansion bus types (ISA, EISA, PCI, MCA). This is covered in Chapter 6, on motherboards. In general, if the bus offers faster performance and the controller is capable of taking advantage of it, you will get higher performance from advanced bus architecture. For example, there is a slight improvement gained when using an IDE or SCSI drive on a local bus with a local bus controller. If the hard drive is already working at maximum capacity or the controller is not capable of the advanced throughput, you won't see any speed improvement; you'll just be wasting money.

The Hard Disk Bottleneck

As discussed earlier in the book, RAM is fast. It does its work simply using electrical energy. Hard disks, however, use magnetic technology, motors, spinning platters, and coils to move their information, and that information has to travel along cables. The slower your hard disk, the longer you will wait for programs to load, for your system to come on line when you boot it, and even for the actual operation of programs. Microsoft Windows, for example, stores much of the information that it needs to operate on your hard disk, and when you do not have enough RAM available for an operation, it makes use of hard disk space as if it were RAM. Just as a group of people moving a heavy object can only move as fast as its slowest and weakest member, so your computer's operation is limited by the slowest component involved in any operation. Today's hard disks can acquire data about ten times faster than the earliest hard disks. This is due to better methods of storing and retrieving data, as well as basic hard disk design. But hard disk technology has not kept pace with CPU technology. On most systems the hard disk is still a bottleneck when it comes to performance.

Don't get me wrong, today's hard disks are marvels. My first hard disk had an 86-millisecond *access time*, and held 10 megabytes (Mb) (Access time is the minimum amount of time it takes for a hard disk to acquire data). The hard disk on my current system has a 10-millisecond (ms) access time, and stores 1.2Gb of data. Many new drives offer slightly slower performance, 12ms, and the average system being sold offers a 550Mb hard drive. Over the past ten years hard disks have increased in storage capacity and speed while decreasing significantly in price and physical size.

A Variety of Options

Buying a hard disk is one of the more important decisions you will make when assembling or upgrading a computer system, and it's not just a simple as choosing how large a drive you want and looking at how much it costs. In some respects, hard drives are much like very sophisticated floppy disks, but there are several different technologies used in their design and several different interfaces available for connecting them to your computer.

Hard Disk Basics

Before going into the intricacies of interfaces, it would be a help to understand how a hard disk works. Most hard disks have a sealed metal housing; a particle of dust, a hair, or other object basically too small to see could damage a hard disk. To prevent this from happening, hard drives are assembled in "Clean Rooms" that are controlled to even tighter standards than an operating room. The part that actually stores the information consists of one or more (usually more) metal disks that are coated with the magnetic recording material. These are all connected to a spindle or hub. The number of these platters and the quality of the magnetic recording material are the major factors involved in how much information can be recorded on your drive.

Some very large-capacity drives have as many as eight platters and can hold several *gigabytes* of data (one gigabyte equals one billion bytes). These drives are usually full-height 5.25-inch drives. These massive drives are generally used for network servers and high-performance graphics or engineering workstations. The average single-user PC usually has a single half-height hard disk ranging from between 380Mb to 1.2Gb, often with an access time of about 10-12 milliseconds.

Read/write heads are attached to moving arms, with at least one head for each recording surface. These heads align the magnetic particles on the disk, which indicate whether the value of a given position is 0 or 1, and can read the value of the information stored there by detecting the magnetic polarity of the particles on the platter. A device called a *head actuator* is used to move the arm across the platter to position the head quickly to any location on the disk.

The drive also contains a printed circuit board, which translates commands received from your computer into action, moving the head actuator into position to accurately read data. The board also issues the commands to read or write data as the computer directs, and has components that control the spinning of the drive, and to perform diagnostics to make sure that everything is working properly. See Figure 9.1.

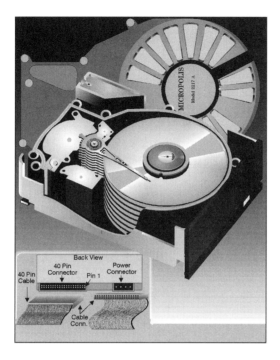

Back View

40 Pin
Connector   Power
                   Connector
Pin 1

40 Pin
Cable

Cable
Conn.

FIGURE 9.1 Hard disk construction.

How Data Is Organized

The data on a hard disk is organized in much the same way as on a floppy; the basic units of organization are tracks, sectors and cylinders. As you may have started reading the section on hard disks and ignored the section about floppies, I'll repeat some of that information here. A *track* is a band running in a circle around the disk as shown in Figure 9.2. These tracks are divided into short arcs called *sectors*. A sector is the basic storage unit and several sectors are grouped together into clusters. All of the tracks located at the same distance from the center of the spindle on each platter form a *cylinder*. Figure 9.2 shows this graphically.

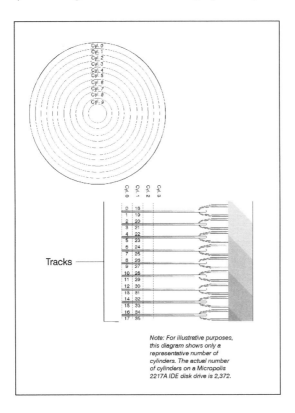

Note: For illustrative purposes, this diagram shows only a representative number of cylinders. The actual number of cylinders on a Micropolis 2217A IDE disk drive is 2,372.

FIGURE 9.2 Hard disk layout—tracks and cylinders.

This way of designing data on the disk presents some challenges for engineers. The closer you get to the spindle, the faster the data moves by the read/write head; the further out, the slower. It would be very complicated to adjust the spin of the drive to allow for the position of the head over the platter, so designers have taken several different approaches in adjusting to relative velocities. Discussing all the ins and outs of the various methods, such as constant linear velocity and zone bit recording, is both beyond the scope of this book and the likely attention span of its readers.

The thing to keep in mind is that newer drive technology makes use of advanced schemes for applying the physics involved in producing a hard drive. In other words, older drives use older technology which is not as efficient. The quality and ability of the recording medium is another factor in how much information a drive can store in how much space. Over the past several years, major hard disk vendors have produced both better techniques for managing data and better recording materials. While it is often possible to get deals on older-style drives, you may find that you are paying the price in performance as a trade-off for what you save in money. With that in mind, let's take a look at the different categories of disk drives and some of the buying options.

Types of Hard Disks

Hard disks can be divided into several families based on the technology used in their design, and how they are connected to the system. There are four basic families used on the PC. The most common is *IDE*, which stands for Integrated Drive Electronics. A recent variation is E-IDE (the E stands for Enhanced, and often offers more speed than plain IDE). *SCSI*, or Small Computer Systems Interface, is a more robust interface found on power-user machines and network servers. There are also two old (read all but extinct) methods; *MFM* (Modified Frequency Modulation) and *ESDI*, also known as the Enhanced Small Device Interface.

We'll look at each of these interfaces in turn, starting with the oldest. A bit of history will make it easier to understand both how hard drives developed, and how to separate the bargains from the bombs.

First let's define a few terms, then discuss the pros and cons of each family. It will make the following discussion much easier. There are two factors that control how well a hard disk performs: how fast the drive can access the data that your system is asking for, and how fast it can retrieve that data into the system. The first is listed usually as *access time*; the second as the *maximum data transfer rate*. The original PC-XT had drives with an 85-millisecond access time and a maximum transfer rate of under 5Mb per second. With the advent of 286-based machines, 40-millisecond access time became the norm, and with today's 486s and Pentiums, 10- to 12-millisecond access times (once considered impossible) are now pretty much standard. One of the reasons for the faster access time is the introduction of voice coil actuators to move and position the read/write heads. These replaced older stepper-motor technology.

The maximum transfer rate is determined by the type of interface being used, and the way the data is actually encoded on the disk.

The Hard Disk Sub-System

Your hard disk system has three primary components: the disk drive itself, your controller card (or in the case of SCSI, a card called a *host adapter*), and the cables. In some PCs the hard disk controller is built right onto the motherboard. The type of drive and the quality of its controller have as much if not more to do with overall performance than the mechanics of the drive itself. To get the maximum performance out of a hard disk, you must have a controller which matches disk speed and capability. Let's take a look at the different families of disks and their performance characteristics, and then discuss some purchasing considerations.

Bargain Basements In A Retirement Home— ESDI and MFM

MFM

The original PC hard disks were all based on the MFM method. This technique generally divides tracks into 17 sectors with 512 bytes in each sector and has transfer rates of about 5Mb per second. MFM technology is also sometimes referred to as the ST506 interface. The ST is based on the name Seagate Technology, the original company that produced the controller, and still a leading hard drive manufacturer.

Two variations of MFM are known as Run Length Limited or *RLL*, and Run Length Encoded (*RLE*). These use a special controller which formats up to 26 cylinders per track, allowing up to twice the data to be stored on the same size MFM drive. MFM and RLL/RLE drives are for all intents and purposes obsolete. Based on the way they store data, they cannot keep up with today's demand for high-capacity drives and have been superceded by newer methods which offer better performance, lower cost, and higher capacity. If you are considering building a starter system for a child or maybe a second or third system to run a bulletin board, you might be able to find an old 40Mb MFM drive with its controller that someone's willing to give you. Given the current inexpensive price and better performance of IDE drives, which we'll discuss shortly, buying an MFM drive today is a waste of money.

ESDI

The Enhanced Small Device Interface (ESDI; pronounced EZ-dee) was an improvement of MFM technology designed to provide higher capacity and better performance. Early ESDI drives offered 70 Mb of storage space at a time when MFM units provided about 40Mb. The last crop of ESDI drives offered about 1 gigabyte of space. These units require a special controller and are usually formatted with 34 sectors per track. Most have access speeds of 15 to 18 milliseconds, with data transfer rates of over 10 megabytes per second.

Until a few years ago, ESDI drives were considered good choices for power users and file servers. They offered good performance without the complications involved in using the newly emerging SCSI standard (which we'll discuss in a minute). While these drives may have more to offer than MFM-based units, they are still an aging technology and will soon be orphans so far as replacement parts and controllers are concerned. While I used a couple of ESDI drives in my lab until late in 1994, the same purchase warnings that I just gave for MFM drives also apply to ESDI.

INSTALLING AND CABLING MFM AND RLL SYSTEMS

With few exceptions, MFM, RLL, and ESDI drives use a separate hard disk controller—which also usually contains an integrated floppy disk controller as well. If you do have to work with one of these units, here are a few basics. Since very few readers of this book will probably deal with this technology in the future, I will be very brief. If you need more assistance with them, consult the owner's manual or contact the vendor.

Details of installing and formatting MFM and ESDI drives are very similar to those for SCSI and IDE systems. The physical structure of the drive itself is basically the same for all types. The difference is in how the controller functions are handled and in the way the data is actually organized on the disk. For this reason, I have given basic instructions on how to install and prepare a hard disk for use after the discussion of drive types.

Installing Controllers

ESDI and MFM controllers are usually designed to mimic MFM operations. The layout of all of the controllers is pretty much the same. If you set the controller on a table in front of you so that the *edge connector* (the gold pins on the bottom that slip into the slot on the motherboard) is facing towards you and the metal plate that goes in the slot at the back of the machine is to your right, you should see four groups of connector pins along the upper edge of the card on the side of the board away from you. Refer to Figure 9.3.

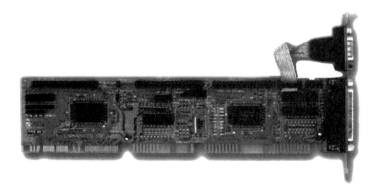

FIGURE 9.3

The rearmost set of pins is used to connect the floppy disk cables. This class of hard drive uses two cables to attach the hard drive to the controller. The next position of pins is used to connect the wide cable. This can either be a single-drive connection cable (which will then have one slotted connector at one end and the pins on the controller at the other), or in many cases a twisted-pair cable with five twisted wires. The installation for dual-drive setups using twisted-pair is identical to that described previously in Chapter 8 for floppy disks. These drives also use a smaller cable running from an edge connector on the back of the drive to the pins on the controller. Your card should have two of these blocks of pins in front of the wide connector. The one closest to the wide connector goes to the first or primary hard disk. This should be drive C, the one that your machine boots from. If you are installing a second physical hard disk, its smaller cable connects to the set of pins closer to the front.

Your controller card is likely to contain a number of jumpers. These control a variety of options, especially on ESDI cards. You should consult the manuals for your controller and for your hard disk before and during installation.

Mounting and jumpering the hard drive is similar to that described for floppies. Once again, you should consult your manual for specific details.

SCSI

The Small Computer Systems Interface is the most flexible of all the systems to attach hard drives and many other types of peripherals to a computer. Over time it will probably become the dominant technology for adding peripherals to your PC. Unlike other drive technology, SCSI is actually a complete expansion bus of its own, much like the part of your computer system that controls the expansion slots on your motherboard. A single SCSI channel can contain up to eight devices, numbered 0 through 7. On each channel you can mix and match any type of compatible device. For example, on the computer I used to write this book, I have a SCSI *host adapter* (what a SCSI controller is called) which manages an array of hard disks, a tape drive, two CD-ROMs, and a scanner. Using SCSI to connect the majority of peripherals in your machine will make integration easier and reduce the number of expansion slots you must use. See Figure 9.4.

FIGURE 9.4 A SCSI host adapter.

Another reason for SCSI's increasing popularity is its speed. It easily outruns any other method currently in use for getting data in and out of a computer. Low-end SCSI systems can transfer data at 5 megabytes per second. High-end systems get up to 40Mb per second, eight times faster than the PC's original MFM unit. If you are planning on adding a CD-ROM, scanner, tape drive, or multimedia capabilities to your PC, you should seriously consider using a SCSI hard disk.

One of the ways SCSI does its magic is by putting much of the intelligence for how a device works inside the device itself. In other words, the actual controller technology is built into each SCSI device, be it hard disk, CD-ROM, scanner, etc. The host adapter acts as a translator between the computer and the devices on the chain. Some SCSI host adapters currently available have three SCSI channels on a simile card and are able to control 21 devices. But even the simplest host adapter can control up to seven.

Is SCSI Worth It?

SCSI controllers range in price and quality from $50 to over $5,000. Generally speaking, a $200 SCSI controller will offer a significant improvement in performance over the cheaper kind of card that is often bundled with CD-ROMs or scanners. SCSI hard disks cost slightly more than a similar IDE drive, so if you are trying to keep to the barest budget and know you'll never expand in a way that will reduce the start-up cost of SCSI, then you'll probably want to consider using IDE. The next chapter presents a detailed look at SCSI technology, how it works, buying considerations, and how to build and integrate a SCSI system. If you are considering building a power-user system, working with graphics, multi-media or adding a CD-ROM, I heartily recommend you read it.

Information on installing and preparing SCSI hard drives for use comes later in this chapter. Information on SCSI host adapters and other devices is contained in Chapter 10.

IDE—A Hard Disk in Every PC

As PCs increased in power, and programs got more sophisticated (and bigger in size), users started to feel the need for bigger and faster hard disks at more reasonable prices. Where a few years ago a 350MB hard disk with an 18 millisecond access time cost around $2000, today you can buy an 850 Mb IDE (Integrated Drive Electronics) drive with a 10- to 12-millisecond access time (with adapter and cables) for about $250-300. This is about $100 cheaper than a comparable approach using a SCSI interface.

Unlike SCSI, the original IDE only allows you to connect two hard drives to your system and does not support other types of devices except CD-ROM drives. Like SCSI, IDE drives are intelligent. In other words, much of the electronics used to control the unit are housed inside the drive. Why does the I in IDE stand for integrated? The actual mechanics are integrated into the drive itself. A simple card called a *paddle board* connects the drive to the system using a 40-pin ribbon cable. Enhanced IDE or E-IDE offers improvements on IDE, with up to four devices, and even cache memory supported. See Figure 9.5.

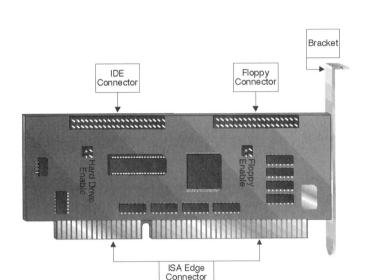

FIGURE 9.5 An IDE paddle board.

Current IDE drives offer transfer rates ranging from 1Mb to 4Mb per second, with capacities ranging from 80Mb to 1.6Gb. Today, the majority of new systems for single users are built using IDE drives. If you are planning on running Windows on a tight budget, consider a fast, 350 to 550Mb IDE drive. If possible, work into your system design, either by the motherboard or by the kind of paddle board you use, to use a *local bus*. This will offer you the best performance if you are going to use an IDE drive. As this was written, you could buy an 850Mb IDE hard drive for a little over $200; with many major business programs (to say nothing of Windows 95), requiring upwards of 100 Mb for full installations, and many DOS-based games setting up with 30Mb or more of space, it makes no sense to buy less than 850Mb if you are buying a new drive.

As mentioned above, if you plan to need more than 1.2 or 1.6Gb of mass storage, or plan on adding SCSI devices to your system such as a CD-ROM, seriously consider using a SCSI drive instead. IDE drives have some intelligence but they are not as snazzy as SCSI. In most cases the SCSI controller takes over total control of the bus, freeing up the CPU to do other things. IDE must wait for the CPU to perform reads and writes.

Some General IDE Buying Considerations

Since I'll be covering SCSI in the next chapter, and since I don't recommend purchasing MFM or ESDI drives, the rest of this chapter will be devoted to working with IDE drives and general hard disk installation, diagnostics, and maintenance. Specifics for installing SCSI peripherals are contained in the next chapter.

PHYSICAL DIMENSIONS

Advanced drives today offer capacities as high as 1.2 gigabytes in a case 1 inch high and 3.5 inches wide. Some older drives are still made to the old half-height 5.25-inch form factor, and a few larger-capacity drives are produced as full-height units. The size of the drive relative to its formatted capacity is a clue as to how modern it is. If you are looking for the best performance in drives of 1Gb or less, you're probably looking for one of the new 1-inch-high drives. Such units offer access times of 10 milliseconds or less and spin at 5,400 rpm. Plans are in the works for newer drives that spin at 7,200 rpm, offering even better performance, but as this is written they are not yet available. Prices range from $500 and up.

If you are on somewhat of a budget and are willing to wait a little bit longer for your hard disk, you can consider some of the older 3600-rpm units, which offer slower access time and are often larger. You can often obtain refurbished or reconditioned drives for under $100 if you are willing to be a notch or two behind the current technology.

WARRANTIES AND MEAN-TIME-BETWEEN-FAILURE

All disk drives die. That's a given. There is no guarantee as to just how long a given hard drive will last. One aged ESDI drive that I sold to a friend five years ago, after I had used it for a couple years, is still running fine. I have had other drives fail within a month. Brand name and type of construction are no guarantee. It's a good idea, whether buying drives new or reconditioned, to get at least a 90-day warranty, a year is even better. Most faulty electronic construction will fail within a few days, while the majority of subtle imperfections will generally result in failure within the first three months of operation. A 90-day warranty is a good way to insure yourself against sudden death during the shakedown period. In all likelihood, if it lasts that first three months, it should reach a normal old age.

Old age in electronic components is defined by a method known as "Mean-Time-Before-Failure" (*MTBF*). Manufacturers assign a MTBF based on the testing of several units, which are pushed to destruction. From this they assign an average value for how long these devices should last under normal use. MTBF is just a guideline, but it can be an indication of relative quality—especially if it is backed up by an appropriate warranty. IBM's Mass Storage division offers drives with MTBFs two to three times as long as their competitors, based in part on the construction technology and in part on the nature of the media they use for their recording surfaces.

BUYING A SECOND HARD DRIVE

If you are planning on installing more than one hard drive in a system, you must use care in making sure that the new drive is compatible with the existing disk sub-system. With SCSI sub-systems everything should be fine as long as the second drive is the same class of drives. For more information on SCSI drive types, see Chapter 10. With IDE systems, you must make sure that your new drive will work both with the existing paddle board and drive, and that the paddle board and drive are configured properly.

WHERE TO BUY

If you are building your own system, you probably (or should) feel reasonably comfortable with working in your own case and doing your own work. You can shop around in the back of computer magazines looking for mail-order houses that sell drives by direct mail. If you do this, be sure to check and make sure that the drive matches your needs and that you know about the warranties, and its previous history if it is used. Several firms offer used and reconditioned drives for sale with a reasonable warranty, and as long as you know what you are getting, these can be an alternative for bargain hunters.

If you are looking for the most recent technology and highest performance drives, you want to obtain drives from industry leaders such as IBM, Seagate, Conner, Maxtor, Micropolis, and Western Digital. It's a good idea to compare prices from several vendors for the different drive manufacturers. Then ask your salesperson to explain any differences in cost in relation to features. Key questions to ask and answers to be concerned about are: formatted capacity, maximum transfer rate, access time, controller requirements (and cost), warranty and Mean-Time-Between-Failure. Also check to see what components are provided with the drive: will you need to buy cables, mounting brackets, and a special or expensive type of adapter card?

If you need a little more hand-holding, you can probably obtain a comparable drive through a local computer store. If you are shopping for a new system, buy it with your hard drive already installed.

CHOOSING A CONTROLLER

In some respects your hard disk is only as good as its controller, much as a race horse is only as good as its jockey. If a jockey doesn't know how to manage the animal, judge the race, know when to hold back, and know when to go for the wire, the best horse in the world can't win the race. Of course, by the same token, the best jockey in the world would have a hard time bringing a lame nag across the finish line first. As in any relationship, the controller and the hard disk must be well-matched. Your supplier can help you by telling you what is required in a host adapter or controller. There are some basic considerations, and then added features. The most obvious issue is compatibility. You obviously can't attach an ESDI drive to a SCSI host adapter or an IDE drive to an MFM controller.

BASIC THROUGHPUT

Both drive and controller have a maximum rated throughput. If the controller does not match or exceed the rated throughput of the drive, you will not get all the performance your hard disk offers, and it may not even work at all. If the controller's maximum rate of throughput significantly exceeds that of your hard disk, it offers room for upgrading, but you may be spending more money than you need to.

NUMBER OF DRIVES SUPPORTED AND FLOPPY DRIVE SUPPORT

Some controllers can manage two drives, a few only one, and some several. Many hard disk interfaces also come with on-board floppy disk support. If your system has a built-in floppy disk controller mounted on the motherboard, you may not need to spend the $10 or $15 to duplicate this capability.

NOTE

If you do get a board with both types of controller on it, and also have a floppy controller on the motherboard, make sure that you can disable one of the floppy controllers. Otherwise they will both try to work, and neither will.

OTHER PERFORMANCE ISSUES

Some controllers and host adapters offer advanced features that can improve performance if matched to the right hard drive. It is beyond the scope of this book to detail all the possible combinations. If you are getting ready to buy a complete new hard disk system, you may want to check with recent coverage on hard disk and controller technology in *PC Magazine* or some other favorite computer periodical.

CACHING

One performance improver that I will discuss is *caching*. As I mentioned before, transfer rate and access speed are the two major factors in hard disk performance. Both of these factors have an upper limit defined by the very mechanical design of the devices. It takes time to locate the data and to move the head over the location where it is stored. And it takes more time to decode the information and move it to your system's RAM.

It is a basic fact of life that mechanical storage of any sort, be it magnetic, optical or some yet-undefined material, is slower than the electronic storage represented by memory chips. One approach to improved performance is to place frequently-used, or recently-used, data into memory. This form of storage is referred to as a *cache*.

Some controllers provide *hardware caching*, which is dedicated RAM on the controller used to store recently-retrieved information, or to gather information that the computer anticipates that you will need based on the last object it retrieved. If you are working with programs that read and write to the disk a lot, or if you work with large files such as a complex database or large graphics, caching can significantly improve performance. While some large computer systems put cache directly on the hard disk, a more likely location and one used by some advanced PC controllers is on the hard disk controller. For example, two of my more advanced systems, one used as a network file server and the other as an advanced graphics workstation, have 16Mb hardware caches on their SCSI host adapters.

Software cache uses some of your existing RAM, located on your motherboard, to perform caching. For the average user, a program like Smartdrive (which comes with Microsoft Windows), or caching software that is bundled with programs such as Qualitas 386 to the MAX, can give comparable performance. These performance-enhancers are built into Windows 95 and Windows NT. Hardware cache is more expensive: you are paying for more memory chips.

As a rule of thumb, very busy hard disk systems, like those used for file servers, can benefit from a hardware cache. Single-user systems might benefit from a hardware cache, but often can show the same improvement for less money by adding additional RAM onto the motherboard and implementing a software cache.

TAKING THE PLUNGE—ASSEMBLING A HARD DISK SUB-SYSTEM

Once you have done your research, it's time to buy, and then to assemble all the parts. In some cases you can obtain all the components from a single vendor, but you may need some additional parts that you'll have to obtain at your local computer store. Here's a check list:

✔ The drive with its accompanying manual or data sheet

✔ Mounting hardware or rails

✔ Appropriate cabling

✔ Hard disk controller or SCSI host adapter

✔ Your computer or motherboard documentation

✔ A screwdriver

✔ Tweezers or hemostat for jumpers

✔ A copy of your operating system

✔ A bootable floppy disk or operating system Setup disks

N O T E

This floppy disk must include not only Command.com but also Debug, Fdisk, and Format. If you are installing an operating system other than MS-DOS, consult your owner's manual to see what files you will need for booting a new system and partitioning and formatting a new hard disk. When buying an operating system make sure you have the most current version, and that it will work with your hardware. Some editions of MS-DOS and Windows 95 require a copy already on the drive; these are marked as "Upgrades," though sometimes in small print. Also look for the hologram on Microsoft products that identifies the real thing. Some OEMs sell versions that are meant to be sold ONLY as a part of a package with a new PC. These are illegal if bought separately, and are not properly supported.

✔ A Clean, static-free place to work

Physical Installation: An Overview

There are several steps you must take in installing a hard drive; it isn't just a matter of putting it inside the computer. You must make sure that the settings for the hard disk controller don't conflict with any other expansion card. If they do, your system won't boot. On many machines, the hard disk and floppy controllers are on the same card, so you may have to readjust the cabling or install floppy drives at the same time (if you are installing floppy drives, details of that procedure are contained in the previous chapter). You must physically mount the drive into a bay, and attach a power cable and a data cable. When that's done, you must formally introduce your drive to the system Setup stored in CMOS memory, and then format the drive so it can receive data. Once all this has been done, you must load your operating system onto the disk, and then, finally, programs and data files.

The physical hard disk just sits in your machine, but the data on it is in a constant state of flux. Once the hard disk is installed, you'll have to maintain it properly if you want it to operate at maximum efficiency. I'll cover these details after we get done with the installation.

Set Any Jumpers and Drive Selection Switches

Ground yourself by touching the case or some other metal object to discharge any possible static electricity. Then remove the drive from the packaging. It will probably be encased in an envelope of smoky plastic. This is an anti-static barrier. Save this and the packaging in case you ever have to send the drive back for repair or replacement.

IDE Configuration

You need to make sure that the switches on your IDE drive are set properly. If you are only installing one drive into the system, be sure that the drive type is set to *master*. If you are installing two drives, one must be set to master and one to *slave*. Refer to Figure 9.6. In general, you should buy matching IDE drives; not all drives can function as master and/or slave with drives from other vendors. The drive that you want to boot from should be set as the master. There may also be a jumper you have to set to determine whether or not there is a second drive in the system. Consult your drive manual.

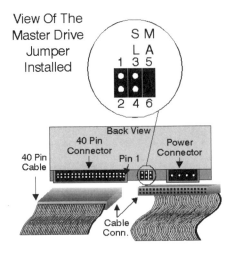

FIGURE 9.6 Setting IDE jumpers.

Setting Switches for a SCSI Drive

SCSI drives are different; they are a part of a collection of devices, even if that collection only consists of the drive and its host adapter. Each device on a SCSI chain must have one of eight unique ID numbers ranging from 0 to 7. On most systems you should set the ID number of the first hard disk on a SCSI chain to ID #0 and a second hard disk to ID #1. The device on either end of a SCSI chain should be terminated (for more discussion on termination and how to set up a complex SCSI chain see the next chapter). If you are only installing one hard drive, check the manual and set the appropriate jumper settings or place a resistor pack on the card—both procedures are simple and should be described in your manual—so that drive is terminated. Any other devices that will be cabled between the first hard drive and the host adapter must be set to unique ID's; in other words, you can't have two devices on the same SCSI chain with the same ID number, and they should not be terminated unless they are the devices on the end of the chain. Again, see Chapter 10 for more details.

Installing the Adapter Card

If you are replacing an existing hard disk controller, remove the old one from the case. This should be a simple matter of detaching any cables, removing the screw located on the mounting bracket, and then removing the card from its slot.

 NOTE If you are replacing existing components, you can save yourself some work by matching the settings on that device with those for the one you are installing. For example, if you are replacing a SCSI hard disk, ID #0 with termination, set up the new one the same way. I make it a habit to always set certain devices to the same values whenever possible. For example, I always set SCSI host adapters at IRQ 14 and if possible at address C800. Doing this not only reduces confusion during installation, but also makes it much easier to figure out what's available when installing new cards or trying to troubleshoot a difficult setup.

MFM and ESDI Drives

MFM and ESDI drives do not require termination, but you must set the drive number (one and two, or zero and one, depending on the way it is numbered), and on more advanced drives there may be other options which must be set to insure proper operation. Consult your drive manual and configure any jumpers appropriately.

INSTALLING THE DRIVE INTO THE SYSTEM

Preparing the Adapter (Controller, Paddle-Board, or Host Adapter Card)

Host adapters and controllers require a unique IRQ (Interrupt Request) and memory address (If you want more information on these terms, see Chapters 3 and 4). Since there are many ways to select these settings, you will have to refer to your manual for details. I will just give a few general guidelines here. Most ISA- and VL-bus-based cards use jumpers to configure these settings. EISA and MCA systems will have a reference disk, and configuration files will be used to select these options. If possible, use the old standard combinations of either IRQ 14 or 15 for the IRQ, and CC00 or C800 for the starting memory address. These are the options used most frequently by the original PC controller cards, and sticking to them makes it easier to reduce conflicts and eases installation of other peripherals.

N O T E   If you have created an inventory as suggested in the earlier chapters of this book, you should have a list that contains the addresses and IRQ settings for the different components already mounted in your system. Be sure you are not conflicting with one of these parameters. It will save you the hit-or-miss method to find an available combination. Once you find a combination, add it to your list. If you haven't already done so, this is a good time to start one.

The newer operating systems, many new cards, and latest motherboards offer Plug and Play installation and should be able to automatically configure IRQ and address settings. That does not mean you should ignore the creation of a hardware list! Not all devices work seamlessly, and some are more "Plug and Play-around."

You may also have to adjust settings to enable or disable the card's floppy disk controller and adjust DMA settings. It's always a good idea to read the installation section of the manual which came with your card for information on what settings are available. It's often possible to use advanced features on the better cards that will improve performance. One of the most common of these is cache.

Cache

If your controller incorporates hardware caching, you may have to set jumpers to enable, disable or otherwise configure the cache.

Installing the Card into the System

N O T E   Some systems are equipped with IDE connections built directly on the motherboard. If this is the case, your IDE setup will be controlled through the CMOS Setup—there will be no card to install. All you will have to do is attach the cable to the slot and enable the IDE function using your Setup routine. There are also a few motherboards that come equipped with on-board SCSI host adapters. For details on configuration, consult your owner's manual.

Unplug the computer and remove the cover. Make a diagram of existing cable connections (so that you can return to a working setup if necessary). Select an empty slot, preferably one closest to the hard drive. If you are installing into a hybrid system that has both local bus and ISA or local bus and EISA or other combinations of bus slots, this may not be possible. Don't screw the card down yet; you may have to take it out to set jumpers or make other modifications. Now attach all the appropriate cables. IDE drives are connected using a 40-pin connector. MFM drives and ESDI drives are connected using two cables. If you are attaching a SCSI card, you will probably have a 50-pin ribbon cable coming from your SCSI drive (or the preceding device on the chain). Once again, these cables should have a red stripe (sometimes it's blue) on one side or the other; this denotes Pin 1. Pin 1 usually faces towards the front of your computer, *away* from the mounting bracket on most systems. If you are not sure, double-check. Refer to Figure 9.7 for an illustration of hard drive cable types.

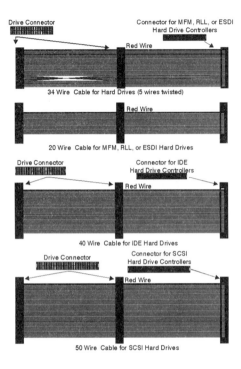

FIGURE 9.7 Hard drive cable types.

Testing the Installation and Setting CMOS

Once everything is properly cabled, attach the keyboard, monitor, mouse, and everything else you disconnected before, then plug the machine back in. Put the bootable disk in drive A and turn the machine on.

Run the Setup Routine

Now you need to introduce the hard drive to the system Setup. This is a very important step. You must invoke your system's Setup routine. Consult your user's manual for specific instructions. After the computer has completed its memory self-test, you should be able to directly access the program by holding down a key sequence; it might involve holding the delete key or pressing **Ctrl-Alt-Escape** or **Ctrl-Alt-S**. The exact key-strokes vary with the type of BIOS in your system. If you are not familiar with the procedure, watch your boot-up screen or check your manual before proceeding.

If you have read the earlier chapters in this book, you should be familiar with the CMOS in your system and have already created an inventory of the current Setup information. It is important to make sure that you use the appropriate drive type in the Setup screen for the drive you are installing. Failure to do so cannot only make your system unable to boot from the hard drive, but *may even damage the drive*. In order to properly work, your system usually needs to know several things about the drive's physical characteristics. These include the number of read/write heads, the number of cylinders, the number of tracks and the number of sectors per track. In other cases, your disk controller or host adapter may provide a translation, in which case the controller's manual will tell you exactly how to set the CMOS.

Setting Up MFM and ESDI Drives

If you have an MFM drive, there should be a drive type number established and included in the documentation which came with either your system or with the drive. Most ESDI controllers work by setting the drive type to 1. This tells the system that there is a drive physically present but does not give the correct information on the drive's physical characteristics. Translation is accomplished by the controller.

Setting Up IDE Drives

IDE drives may or may not have a supported number. In fact, most IDE drives won't fit into a standard drive list. They may put more sectors on the outer tracks than on the inner tracks. Although the Setup must be configured correctly, the information in it doesn't necessarily have to reflect accurately the physical configuration.

With IDE drives, in many cases all you have to do is select a drive from the BIOS list (that's the list of drive numbers recognized by your system's Setup program) that has the same number of sectors as the hard drive you are installing. If your BIOS doesn't have a drive type that matches the drive you are installing, you can choose to define the drive yourself. The values asked for include the number of cylinders, heads and often sectors per track. If the information isn't included in your manual, you may have to call your vendor to get this information.

To determine the number of sectors, multiply the number of cylinders times the number of sectors per track times the number of heads (this should be in your hard drive manual or written on its case) to get the drive's logical size. Then find a drive with an identical number or slightly smaller in size from the drive type list.

Setting Up SCSI Drives

SCSI drives, by definition, have all their talking to the system done for them by the host adapter. This makes handling the Setup very easy. Choose the **Not installed** or **No drive present** option for SCSI drives. Be aware that with a SCSI host adapter, if you want to boot from a SCSI drive you must also set the host adapter to pretend to be a standard AT-style controller mimicking the old MFM types. This should be covered in your manual and is usually pre-configured at the factory either by a jumper or in the controller's *firmware* (information permanently encoded on a chip at the factory).

Adding a Second Hard Drive

If you are adding a second hard drive to an existing system, you must go through the same Setup routine, setting values for the second hard disk as appropriate. If you are installing more than two drives into the system, consult your user's manual, because you'll probably have to use a software driver to enable your next disk to be seen by the system.

PREPARING THE NEW HARD DRIVE FOR USE

Hard drives require two separate formats. One is known as the low-level format. This provides the initial fingerprint used to identify the hard disk for a high-level (operating-system-level) format. Once the drive has received the low-level format, it can be divided into logical partitions. Each of these logical partitions can be treated as if it were a different drive with its own drive letter. DOS and WIndows will support logical hard drives all the way up to the letter Z.

Once the drive has been partitioned, it is then ready to receive the operating system format, which sets it up for use by that environment. It is possible to maintain two separate operating systems on one hard drive. In our test lab we have systems configured that share MS-DOS/Windows and OS/2, Windows NT and Windows 95, as well as one unit that is configured with both MS DOS/Windows and SCO UNIX. If you are planning to put more than one operating system onto a disk, you should consult both manuals before performing any partitioning or formatting operation. There may be special considerations both in working the partition and in how the boot information must be arranged.

Hard Disks Are Not Perfect

The magnetic material used to create your new hard drive is not perfect. In some cases the substrate did not adhere properly, in others it may not properly hold a magnetic field. For whatever reason your hard disk will contain a few bad tracks. The larger your hard disk the larger the list. The defect may occupy only a single sector but that entire track will be unusable because of it. During rigorous testing during manufacture these tracks were identified by the vendor. In some cases the information about the bad tracks is stored internally in the disk's firmware. In older drives like the MFM and ESDI types, this information is contained on a list, which should have been packaged with the drive. It is important not to write data to these bad tracks. If the bad track holds a program the program will probably crash; if it holds data the data will probably not be recoverable.

IDE hard drives are low-level formatted at the factory and this information is generally managed and noted there. SCSI drives are also usually low-level formatted at the factory, and SCSI often uses special tables to reorganize the logical location of these bad sectors, so once again the user doesn't have to do anything or has only to invoke a special program to take care of the problem. You should check your host adapter manual for more information.

Low-Level Formatting

A low-level format, as I mentioned before, prepares the drive to receive the operating system format. MFM and ESDI drives should be low-level formatted using an installation routine either provided with the drive or with the controller. See the appropriate manual for more information. Most SCSI and all IDE drives come low-level formatted from the factory.

N O T E

Do not low-level format any IDE drive without special software and without a good reason. If you feel you must low-level format an IDE drive, check with the manufacturer's technical support staff before proceeding. An improper low-level format may render the drive unusable.

If you must get into the BIOS to perform a low-level format, you will also probably need the DOS or other operating system's Debug command. Some SCSI drives provide special utilities for performing this step. They are usually provided with the host adapter or built into it. If you do need to provide a low-level format, it is almost an automatic operation using menus. Just be sure you understand the appropriate instructions that came with your hardware. As I mentioned before, all IDE and most SCSI drives do not require this step.

Partitioning

The next step in hard disk installation is to partition the drive. Even if you are only planning on having one large partition, you must still use Fdisk.

There are three basic steps:

✔ Dividing a disk into partitions: The exact way this is done will vary from operation system to operating system. In some cases you simply specify the percent of the drive that is to be used for each partition. In other cases, you must specify the number of cylinders or sectors to be used for each division.

✔ If you are dividing the drive into more than one partition, you must also create logical drives for subsequent partitions. Fdisk uses a series of menus for various options and is fairly easy to use. You might want to review the documentation that comes with your operating system before using it.

✔ The other job to do in Fdisk is to set which partition is active. This tells the machine which partition holds the boot information, usually drive C.

Performing the High-Level Format

Once you exit Fdisk the system will reboot. Since there is no operating system currently on the machine, the hard disk will have to be formatted. Boot from the floppy disk in drive A. Then issue the appropriate Format commands or follow any other installation requirements for your operating system. You want to make the first partition of your primary hard drive bootable, so that when you turn your system on, it comes up into DOS or Windows and is recognizing your hard drive. In DOS this is done by issuing the command: **format C: /s /v.** Follow the instructions in your manual for other operating systems, most are much like those for DOS. This process can take several minutes, even hours. When it is done you will see a note saying that the Format is complete and that the operating system has been transferred onto the hard disk. If you created more than one partition on your new hard disk, repeat the high-level format on the other portion without the /s and /v switches. In other words, just enter the command: **Format [drive letter]:**

I usually organize single drive systems with two logical drives. The first partition is used to hold the operating system and programs while I maintain data files on the second partition. This makes backing up your data a lot easier since you don't have to hunt all over your hard disk for it.

Hard disk organization and managing sub-directories is as much an art as a science. The more sub-directories you create, the easier it may become to locate individual files. The drawback is that as you build more sub-directories, it takes both you and your operating system longer to move through the disk. Some operating systems and software have limits to the number of nested sub-directories. Generally, if you are nesting more than three levels deep you are overdoing it.

LOADING THE OPERATING SYSTEM AND INSTALLING SOFTWARE

Once the disk has received a high-level format, you are ready to load the operating system and install your programs. Since the procedures for this will vary based on the operating system you use and your personal configuration, it is impossible to give detailed instructions in a book like this. There is one key piece of advice: *Make sure you keep a bootable floppy disk handy during the installation procedure.* It's very easy for something within your system to conflict, or write an incompatible command to one of your startup files. When this happens, your system may hang and you will need to use the floppy disk to get things running again.

FINISHING UP

Once you have installed all your software, run your primary program to make sure everything is working properly. When everything is functioning to your satisfaction, it's time to close the case back up, leaving the machine ready for regular operation. This is also a good time to make a backup of the contents of your hard disk, just in case.

TROUBLESHOOTING A HARD DISK INSTALLATION

In a perfect world, hard disk installation goes perfectly the first time. But—computers and their operators are far from perfect. If your hard disk fails to boot during installation, the odds are you have either improperly performed or overlooked one of the steps. The following is a check-list to help you work out what may have gone wrong.

Will the machine power up and perform the power-on self-test at all?

If the machine is stone cold dead, see if the fan is operating. If no rush of air is coming out of the fan grate, make sure that the machine is properly connected to a surge protector and the surge protector is properly turned on and connected to a working outlet. If the fan is working and you have a power light indicator on the machine, go to the next step.

The machine has power, but the drive lights for the hard or the floppy drive never come on or the system setup reports "no boot device" or "no floppy drive available."

This symptom usually appears if you have either not connected the drive cables, not connected power cables to the drives, or improperly installed or forgotten to install the floppy disk/hard disk controller or adapter. Make sure you have done all these steps properly. Refer to the instructions given earlier in this chapter. Make sure that the cables are attached properly; the red- or blue-striped part of the cable should be closest to Pin 1 on both ends. If all the cables, connections, and cards are installed properly, you may have a conflict with another device in the system. Remove all but the most necessary cards from your system and try to boot again.

If removing extraneous cards resolves the problem, replace them one at a time, re-booting after installing each. When the machine fails to boot, you've found the offender. Check its settings against the ones for your controller card, and change the settings for one or the other. The machine should now boot.

The drives are properly connected but you are unable to boot from either the floppy or the hard disk

This usually indicates either that your drives have not been properly installed into the CMOS Setup, or that they have not been properly formatted. Check the Setup and make sure that you have properly performed a Format /s on the appropriate drive.

"Drive Not Ready" or "Disk Boot Error" message.

This also could be a Setup error, or mean that the disk you put into the floppy drive has been installed improperly.

The system seems to see the drive but is behaving erratically or doesn't seem the right size.

These problems often show up if you set the wrong drive type. If you are installing a drive using a controller and drive combination that does not use regular numbers or requires "no disk present," you may not have installed according to the manufacturer's instructions. Refer to the manual which came with your controller or host adapter or consult the flowchart in the Appendix. *Remember, operating a drive with the wrong settings can damage your hardware.*

KEEPING YOUR HARD DISK HEALTHY

Hard disks are one of the most active components and one of the few truly mechanical devices in your system. As mentioned before, they are constantly spinning at a very high rpm with heads flying nonstop across the surface. During the course of a busy day, portions of a file may be moved from one section to another. MS DOS does not offer the world's most elegant system for organizing your hard disk, and many small errors can start to creep in, reducing both the integrity and the performance of your file system. Windows 95 has better options, and with the Plus Pack you can even automate hard disk care. I'm still waiting for a good set of utilities for Windows NT and long file names. If you use your system intensely you may need to take steps to optimize your hard disk every two to three days. Moderately-used systems can use such care every couple of weeks, while an infrequent user may only need to concern himself with such housekeeping tasks every month or two. These basic steps are outlined in Chapters 1 and 3 of this book but I'll repeat the highlights here. If you need more information, refer to those chapters.

Checkdisk and Scandisk

Improper program operation or having your system lock up while files are open can wreak havoc on portions of your filing system. Over time portions of the recording surface of your hard disk or floppy may become unstable. The DOS Chkdsk (checkdisk) command provides a basic tool for checking the integrity of your file system. In general you should use Scandisk, its more powerful sibling with Windows 95 and NT. From any command prompt or the icon in the Task Bar (but *not* from within Microsoft Windows 3.11 or earlier) type the command **Scandisk** or **Chkdsk**, and push **Return**. You can do a basic check or a through test of the drive with Scandisk, and it should be run at least once a week. With Chkdsk, if your DOS directory is in your search path, you should see a report similar to the one in Figure 9.8. The report for Scandisk and how it is formatted will be different, but provide much of the same information. See Figure 9.8.

```
Volume CONNER_1    created 05-14-1993 1:29p
Volume Serial Number is 1AC5-5BA5
Errors found, F parameter not specified
Corrections will not be written to disk

    1 lost allocation units found in 1 chains.
       8192 bytes disk space would be freed

 272457728 bytes total disk space
  63119360 bytes in 9 hidden files
   1597440 bytes in 195 directories
 121397248 bytes in 2766 user files
  86335488 bytes available on disk

      8192 bytes in each allocation unit
     33259 total allocation units on disk
     10539 available allocation units on disk

    655360 total bytes memory
    541888 bytes free
```

FIGURE 9.8 Chkdsk report.

The first line shows the volume label (if you assigned one) as well as the date and time on which the partition was formatted. The second line shows the serial number that was also assigned during formatting. The next five lines are standard reports showing both the total available space and a breakdown of the files and directories on the volume. Chkdsk also reports the total number of allocation units, how many are available, and the total amount of conventional memory and how much of that memory is free.

If Chkdsk finds lost clusters or other damaged files it will report the nature of these errors and offer to fix them, asking you for a Y or N (yes or no) response. And here we come to one of DOS's "gotchas."

The Case of the Phantom Switch

There is a wrinkle for MS-DOS users with **Chkdsk**. If you just typed **Chkdsk** all by itself and DOS asked if you wanted to fix errors, it will not really fix them, even if you say yes! For DOS to correct the errors you must use the command **Chkdsk**. If you use the command this way, DOS will attempt to save any data from the damaged files into the root directory of the drive you checked. You should run Chkdsk at least once a week, or any time your system unexpectedly bounces you out of a program or starts behaving erratically.

De-fragmenting Your Hard Disk

DOS is a very messy housekeeper, and the same is true for both Windows 95 and Windows NT with the DOS-style FAT (File Allocation Table, the "Table of Contents" of your hard disk). It will use bits and pieces of available space to store parts of a file. Depending on how tidy your disk was to begin with you may actually have pieces of a letter or a bitmap image stored in small groups all over your disk. While this doesn't bother DOS, it can slow down performance considerably. If you are a very intensive user of your machine you should use some form of disk optimizer or de-fragmenter every few days. The occasional user can get by with one every couple of months. If Microsoft Windows or a favorite program seems to be taking longer to load, or if the system seems to be making excessive calls to the hard disk to load a file, it is often an indication that the disk needs to be de-fragmented.

Starting with MS DOS 6.0, Microsoft began shipping a stripped-down version of the Norton Utilities Speed Disk. For more information on this program, consult your DOS users manual. There are a number of third party optimizers which offer more features than the DOS product, but it will do the job. For more explanation on potential third-party products and how to maintain a tidy hard disk, see Chapter 3. You can use the same program with Windows NT if you have a FAT-style file system, but beware. If you use long file names (ones that have more than the 8.3 format) the files will be renamed and the extra letters cut off. Windows 95 offers a Dfrag command that supports long file names. With the Window 95 Plus pack you can even set up the system to automatically run the test and make corrections.

If you use some form of cache or disk compression software to increase the apparent size of your hard disk, you may have trouble with optimization software. Since it is not uncommon for people to double up on the various caching and disk-saving routines, it is very easy to get into trouble. Double-check your users manuals or check with technical support if you are concerned about incompatibilities. Before you use a disk optimizer for the first time, or after reconfiguring your system with a new hard drive or controller or gift diagnostic software, you should back up all your data before de-fragmenting or testing your disk.

Diagnostic Software

Several vendors provide software that performs advanced diagnostics on hard disks, and will test their surface and even refresh a format without removing data. These can be very useful in checking out the health of your system. Once again, some software may conflict with more complicated configurations. You should always check for compatibility and do a complete backup before using these programs.

Viruses

There are some sick minds in the world. Some people seem to have nothing better to do with their lives than to try to make obnoxious programs which attempt to burrow into other people's computers. Some of these so-called viruses do nothing; others are relatively innocuous, wishing someone a happy birthday or writing a childish obscenity on your screen. Still others are very destructive, ripping into your hard disk structure, destroying data and making it unusable. These workings of twisted minds have even appeared on over-the-counter, shrink-wrapped software from major vendors and CD-ROM titles from major information houses. As a result, no one is truly safe from their presence, but a number of people do offer software that will check your disk and can repair or inoculate you from the damage of most viruses.

Backups

N O T E

As I've said before and will say again, it is not a matter of if your hard disk will fail, but when. Every time you power down your machine there is a risk that the hard disk will not start again, or that the critical file will no longer be usable. This doesn't happen every day, but it does happen and it will happen to you. The basic rule of thumb for backups: if it is more work to re-enter the file than to back it up, *back it up*. An even better gauge—could you afford to lose this file? If the answer is no, be sure it's backed up.

CHAPTER SUMMARY

A hard disk is rarely considered one of your system's most critical components. A decade ago, hard disks were considered a luxury or a tool for power users. Early PC hard disks offered capacities of 5 and 10Mb and people wondered what the home user would do with all that space. Today many new users are finding that 500Mb storage systems are barely enough to get by, and most power users are turning to systems offering 1Gb and beyond. These new drives are at price points lower than the smaller and slower drives of yesterday. As this book was being written, 1.9Gb megadrives were beginning to show up in the marketplace. Installing a new hard drive system does require several steps, but is something any careful and mildly adventurous PC user should be able to accomplish.

CHAPTER 10

THE FAST LANE—
SCSI, CD-ROM

WHAT'S IN THIS CHAPTER

- ✔ SCSI Technology
- ✔ High Performance Storage Systems
- ✔ CD-ROM Drives
- ✔ CD-Recordable Drives and Technology
- ✔ Installing and Managing SCSI Devices

WHAT THIS CHAPTER IS ABOUT

A PC can do a lot more than just crunch numbers and check your spelling. The same kind of CD that can bring lifelike music to your living room can also bring a wealth of information, images and even video to your PC. This chapter covers the basics of the Small Computer System Interface (SCSI), and connecting SCSI CD-ROM drives. Assembling a multimedia system is saved for Chapter 11. Our discussion will start with SCSI technology, since it offers the speed and flexibility needed for true multimedia and other high-performance uses of the PC. You can get a multimedia environment working with IDE technology, but if you want robust operation and are willing to build your own system, SCSI is the way to go.

WHAT IS SCSI AND WHY SHOULD I CARE?

If you are an aspiring power user desiring the fastest hard disk speeds available, or any user interested in adding a CD-ROM, a scanner, a tape drive, or a host of other interesting peripherals to your machine, you should be interested in SCSI. SCSI offers speed, simplicity and the ability to connect as many as seven (and possibly even more) devices using a single expansion card. The *Small Computer System Interface* also has the capability of data-transfer speeds of up to 40Mb per second. Adding additional devices onto the same SCSI chain is allegedly as easy as adding a cable to the new accessory and to the back of your machine.

Anyone considering a new or expanded PC should seriously consider basing it on SCSI technology. While a SCSI hard drive is slightly more expensive than competing IDE products, it offers much better performance. In addition, you can use the same card that runs your hard drive to connect the CD-ROM or other SCSI-compatible peripheral. If you are considering serious multimedia or graphics applications, such as animation or capturing live video, SCSI becomes a necessity. IDE drives top out at about 1.7 gigabytes (Gb), and you can only have two IDE drives on a single card. You can find SCSI hard drives in sizes greater than 4Gb and there are some host adapters available that will allow you to string up to 21 hard drives onto a single card! You can see why SCSI technology has become a favorite in large networks. If you are considering a CD-ROM drive keep in mind that most all these machines are based on SCSI technology. If you don't want one now you probably soon will. The odds are also excellent that a SCSI host adapter will also soon find its way into your system. See Figure 10.1.

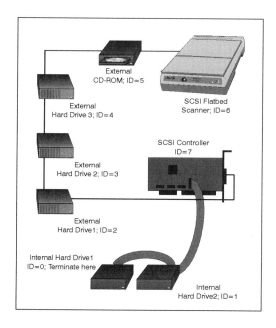

FIGURE 10.1 How a SCSI chain is constructed.

HOW SCSI WORKS

A SCSI *host adapter* (the proper name for the SCSI expansion card) actually runs an expansion bus of its own: data is transferred directly between all the units attached to the SCSI bus. Each device on the SCSI chain is "intelligent," having its own internal controller which can send, receive, and execute SCSI commands through the host adapter. A SCSI device can handle data internally almost any way it wants—as long as it can communicate with the host adapter using standard SCSI commands and formats. This gives SCSI incredible flexibility. Virtually any kind of device can be attached to a PC through a SCSI host adapter. If two years from now, somebody invents a wonderful new gadget and it's available in the SCSI design, odds are you can attach it to an existing host adapter with relative ease; it will still be a good idea to verify that any device is compatible with your host adapter before making a purchase.

There's another benefit to SCSI. If you look at the other areas in this book that deal with adding expansion cards to your system, you'll find constant references to avoiding Interrupt and address conflicts. Since only one card is needed to mount numerous devices in your machine, you only have to worry about installation conflicts with the host adapter alone. The number of available DMA (Direct Memory Access) channels and Interrupt requests (IRQ) on your PC are limited (for more information on DMA and IRQs see Chapter 4). When I converted one of my systems to SCSI, I was able to remove four expansion cards (the hard disk/floppy controller, scanner interface, tape interface, and CD-ROM card). These were replaced with one SCSI host adapter and for my efforts I gained three expansion slots, two free IRQs and better performance. So how does SCSI work?

SCSI IDs

Everything on the SCSI chain, including the adapter, has a unique ID number ranging from zero to seven. This number works much like a mail stop address, allowing data to be moved independent of the host PC to an addressee. You can place more than one SCSI host adapter into a PC, each with a maximum of seven devices. Some very fancy host adapters actually include more than one channel on a single card. Each channel can connect up to seven devices. Each adapter can run as a separate bus. SCSI devices can be mounted either inside the PC via a flat ribbon cable, or daisy-chained to a port on the back of the host adapter via external cable. Each end of the SCSI chain has to be terminated. A SCSI terminator is an electrical resistor that insures reliable communication by preventing excess signal noise on the line. If you only mount either internal or external devices onto a SCSI host adapter, then the last device on the chain and the host adapter itself are terminated. If you mount both internal and external devices, then the host adapter is unterminated and the farthest devices, both internal and external, are terminated.

A Bit of a Challenge

Configuring a SCSI system should be a snap. After all, there's just one card with relatively few jumpers and only one I/O and port address to worry about. On mini-computers, Macs, and UNIX workstations, SCSI support is built directly into the operating system, so integration is not much of a problem. But the PC has been different, and more diffi-cult. Windows 95 and Windows NT have changed much of that, but PCs still take a bit more care when it comes to SCSI—but the perfor-mance is well worth it.

Because of the way that the SCSI standard developed, many early devices were designed to work with specific host adapters. Getting them to work with other host adapters was almost impossible because the device drivers were designed for those specific combinations.

N O T E   In order to understand how SCSI works, and to be able to wisely buy SCSI devices, you need to understand a little bit about how SCSI developed and the performance potentials of its three variations. The following paragraphs offer a thumbnail sketch of how SCSI developed. The early days of SCSI were full of incompatibilities and proprietary solutions. Today SCSI is a much different matter. There are still some early SCSI products for sale and knowing how SCSI developed enables you to avoid getting stuck with a lemon.

The driver problem had its roots in the development of the original *ANSI* (American National Standards Institute) SCSI-1 standard, devel-oped in 1986. It called for a maximum 5Mb-per-second throughput over an 8-bit parallel data path on the SCSI bus (similar to the kind of 8-bit path used by printer ports). SCSI-1 was too vague. As long as a vendor made use of some SCSI command and had an 8-bit data path, the device could be called SCSI-compliant. The exact number and spe-cific commands were an issue for debate. Since SCSI can support all kinds of devices, a specific software driver is needed to handle commu-nications between the host-adapter and each device on the chain. This lack of detail in the standard opened up the floodgates for a tidal wave of driver and host adapter incompatibilities that prevented SCSI-1 from fulfilling its primary promise: that one host adapter could control up to seven peripheral devices of all kinds.

NOTE   You usually don't have to worry about driver incompatibility if you are adding a SCSI hard disk to your system, if the SCSI host adapter provides a BIOS Interrupt 13h replacement in its boot ROM. If a SCSI host ID of 0 or 1 is assigned to a hard drive, no special drivers are required because the host adapter will make the system think that it's a regular AT-style hard drive connection (if you have a hard drive larger than the maximum allowed by your operating system, often 2Gb (1Gb for older versions of DOS), you'll still need a special driver).

The Promise Renewed—The SCSI-2 Standard

Unlike bad movies, SCSI's sequels get better. Seeing the problems of SCSI-1, the standards committee went back to work to tighten up the specs, and while they were at it, increased the performance potential. In SCSI-2, a tighter command language leaves less room for proprietary host adapters. The committee also included new commands that provide for specific support for new devices in the future. They standardized some commands for devices already using the SCSI interface. One example is adding a "re-tension tape" command for tape drives. That way the command can be built right into the drive's *firmware* (hardware instructions) instead of having to be worked into a software driver. The SCSI-2 standard also offers improved speed.

The three performance protocols first introduced with SCSI-2 are labeled *Fast*, *Wide*, and *Fast-Wide*, and provide outstanding performance. Fast SCSI is twice as fast as the original specifications, offering a maximum transfer of up to 10Mb per second over either an 8- or 16-bit data path (in reality, achieving the maximum transfer rate is more likely over a 16-bit path). Wide SCSI provides for a data path of either 16- or 32-bits. It provides for throughput of up to 10Mb per second, again over either a 16- or 32-bit data path. Fast-Wide SCSI provides for up to 40Mb per second over a 32-bit path. Of course, you can't just get an old PC and expect this performance from Fast, Wide or Fast-Wide SCSI. You won't be able to get Wide and Fast-Wide SCSI performance unless you have a PC that supports local bus (either PCI or the now-obsolete VESA), EISA, or Micro-Channel architecture.

There is a good selection of fast hard drives offering 10Mb per second transfers and spinning at 5400 rpm or faster. Fast SCSI offers very good performance, always at least as good as the best Enhanced IDE designs, and often better. Plus you get the ability to add new non-drive or CD-ROM with virtually no pain—and SCSI is always a step ahead when it comes to power and features. The PCI interface is the method of choice for any SCSI system, providing the best throughput and the easiest installation.

SCSI-3, Enter Ultra SCSI and the Age of A La Carte

With SCSI-3 the standard has entered a new phase. The committee has decided that the SCSI-3 effort should be permanent, at least as permanent as anything ever gets in computer technology—but to get specifications out as quickly as possible. Instead of making one big change with a new standard that will take years to adopt, they are allowing sub-committees to release new developments on a fast track, by themselves, with oversight approval by the governing body as a whole. This lets developers produce hot new products that have industry support. We are seeing the first of the new products for SCSI-3 in the form of Ultra-SCSI. All of these adapters will be PCI—fussy PCI at that. Another reason to make sure your motherboard has the best PCI technology you can obtain.

Power systems can take advantage of some of the newer, more powerful, more exotic, and more expensive SCSI hardware. In my lab I have just added a new Ultra-SCSI (part of the SCSI-3 standard) Quantum Grand Prix 4Gb drive and a matching Qlogic PCI host adapter, providing burst speeds of up to 20Mb/sec. Ultra Wide SCSI-3 products are still in the works as this is written, and should offer 40Mb/sec burst transfers. Of course Ultra SCSI will cost more than traditional gear, but for the power-hungry, or performance-needy, this is the way to go. For stand-alone systems that don't require RAID technology (an array of several disks acting as one unit), Ultra SCSI is the wave of the future. See Figure 10.2.

FIGURE 10.2 Qlogic IQ PCI Ultra SCSI host adapter.

The nice thing about Ultra SCSI is that it uses the same cable connections and basic technology as SCSI-2 Fast or Wide, so you don't need new cables or other special gear, just the newer drive and adapter. I use the new system on my primary workstation, and it screams. It did take a bit of extra work to get the PCI bus working properly, but as the vendors get more experience with drivers and firmware, Ultra SCSI should become the choice of power users.

SCSI, RAID, AND SAFE STORAGE

SCSI offers another benefit to the paranoid—safe storage in the form of RAID systems. (Remember, just because you are paranoid, it doesn't mean there is no danger.) RAID stands for *Redundant Array of Independent Drives*. This is a sub-system of two or more disks that pretend to be just one device. The RAID can be a hardware RAID, that is, when the system is a hardware design; or it can be a software

RAID, where the devices are managed by the operating sytem or software drivers. The fastest RAIDs are Level 0, where the data is shared across several drives with no backup. It offers good performance and large amounts of storage space. If one drive fails, all go down. Level 5 is a common type for safety. The data is shared over at least three disks, but part of each drive holds backup data that can be used to rebuild the system if one drive fails. If two or more go down at once all data is lost. This is the safest type of hard drive system, but is slower than Level 0, and some storage space is wasted. The total space is divided by the number of disks, and that amount is lost to safety. In a 3Gb drive system only 2Gb are available for use. Windows NT has built-in software RAID. DPT makes very elegant high-performance caching controllers and drive systems for both Level 0 and 5 RAIDs. I use them on servers, and really admire the engineering and service they give. On the major server I have a SmartRAID for safety, with 24Mb of error-correcting cache. See Figure 10.3.

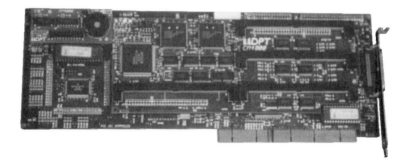

FIGURE 10.3 The DPT SmartRAID host adapter.

Mix and Match, and Sometimes Plug and Play

As long as you have the right software drivers (either built into your operating system, or provided by the vendor), a compatible host adapter, and an appropriate combination of cables, you can mix SCSI-1, SCSI-2, and SCSI-3 including the variations of Fast, Wide, and Fast-Wide, and even Ultra SCSI devices on the same chain. In order to do that you have to be aware of the different types of cables and connectors involved in the different variations of the standard. SCSI-1 devices use a 25-pin connector. It can look like either a RS-232 connector or a large Centronics printer adapter. SCSI-2 and Fast SCSI devices use 50-pin connectors, and Wide SCSI uses a 68-pin connector. SCSI-3 Ultra devices use the same connections as the Fast or Wide standard. Most of the added pins developed for the SCSI-2 standard provide grounding; some were added to allow room for future features which haven't been defined yet. The additional pins for Wide SCSI are needed for the extra bandwidth that that protocol offers.

The new smaller 50- and 69-pin SCSI D-shell connectors used as the external plugs on SCSI-2 and SCSI-3 adapters can be hard to tell apart. The trick is in how the cable is secured. The 50-pin style has a pair of clips that latch, while the 68-pin version makes use of knurled knobs on the cable end and screw-in receptacles on the adapter.

T I P

The trick in mixing SCSI devices is really just a matter of finding the right kind of cable, and making sure that they are the right length. It is NOT just a matter of, "Will it reach?" You should check your manual before buying a cable. The wrong length or poor quality can lead to problems. Check first and all should be well. Since the standard is backwards-compatible, it's easy to find 25-pin to 50-pin cables, but 68-pin Wide SCSI connectors are still scarce. Another difficulty is mixing Wide SCSI and Fast or regular SCSI on the same chain. For example, some vendors offer both 68-pin and 50-pin internal connectors, but only 50-pin or 68-pin external connectors on their adapter card. Because of this, you either have to have a pretty good idea of how you want your SCSI chain to work, or be ready to install more than one host adapter to mix Wide SCSI with other SCSI devices on the same system.

Better in the End

SCSI-2 brought about more changes than just speed. It also called for changes in the way termination was handled. SCSI-1 employed passive termination. SCSI-2 requires active termination, as does SCSI-3. The ins and outs of this can get pretty technical (you still have to have proper termination, but the hardware will do the work all by itself now—most of the time). All you really have to understand is that SCSI-2 and SCSI-3 terminators are designed to actively maintain the required voltage level on the chain. The standard also calls for better cable construction. These two much-needed enhancements both reduce the problems of line noise and signal loss, as well as making it much easier to get several devices working on the same chain (more about that later).

SCSI-3 is adding more speed and a simpler method of identifying the SCSI ID or a device—if it conforms to SCAM (*SCSI Configured Auto-Magically*—who said engineers don't have a sense of humor?). The SCAM system provides a common set of default IDs for common devices, like drives, CD-ROMs, and scanners. SCAM systems will automatically configure a SCSI chain if all the devices use the common IDs and the firmware is SCAM-compliant.

IN SEARCH OF A UNIVERSAL DRIVER

O.K. The SCSI standards set out all kinds of specifications concerning cabling, termination, and performance; but most of that is handled by the vendors. What they don't do is fix the one real challenge left in adding SCSI devices to your PC—operating system support. In order to attach a SCSI device to your machine, you have to have a program called a *device driver* that allows both pieces of hardware to talk to each other and to the host adapter. Some early SCSI devices used proprietary drivers to accomplish this. That fixed one problem (the two machines could talk to each other), but created another because the drivers were designed to work with one unique device and one operating system. It became virtually impossible to use the same host adapter to connect two different peripherals. Part of the problem is that DOS, and traditional PC disk storage, handles information in sectors, while SCSI moves data in blocks—sort of a bit like somebody giving distances in miles, when the other person is thinking their benefactor is speaking in kilometers. Several miles or kilometers down the road, they realize they are lost.

Today things are much better. The solution was found through using two sets of drivers, as shown in Figure 10.4, below. One driver provides communication between the operating system and the host adapter (this is known as the *Primary* or *Universal Driver*), the other (called the *Device Module*) provides the connection between the host adapter and an individual device on the SCSI chain. In most cases the Universal Driver should be on a disk which came with your host adapter. That same disk will also usually include installation utilities and device modules for common SCSI devices such as CD-ROMs. Drivers for other devices have to be obtained through a third-party source, if they are not provided with your operating system software (more about that shortly).

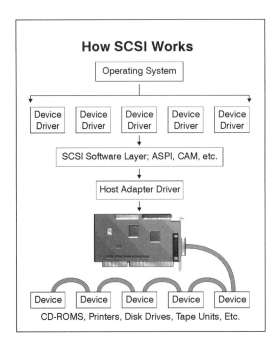

FIGURE 10.4 How SCSI works.

If you use more than one operating system on your machine, you'll need to have a separate universal driver for each one. The Universal Driver that works with DOS won't work with OS/2, Windows NT, Netware, or UNIX. The good news for Windows 95 and Windows NT users is that the Universal Driver for almost all popular adapters is built into the installation and Setup routines. All you have to do is follow the directions and select the right options. It is still a good idea to read the hardware manual for your new SCSI device and make sure that you have the latest driver. In many cases the software or even the firmware was updated after the operating system package was produced. In that case, the newer drive may be both more stable and faster.

Over the years three different brands of Universal Drivers have emerged. The earliest came from Microsoft Corporation. They called their panacea LADDR which stands for *Layered Device Driver Architecture*. About the only place you'll find LADDR used is in older versions of OS/2. As a result, few SCSI devices are equipped with LADDR device modules. The most popular approach is *ASPI* which stands for the *Advanced SCSI Programming Interface*. Originally the A in ASPI stood for Adaptec, the company which designed it, but they were smart enough to both license the protocol to other venders and change the name. While DOS doesn't have active support for ASPI, it is provided in OS/2, SCO UNIX and Windows NT. This is the most popular universal driver and virtually every device has a device module available for it. Operating systems that offer direct ASPI support will not require loading a separate universal driver, but you will still need a Device Module.

Theory has it that swapping ASPI-based cards and devices should be as simple as replacing the ASPI line in your CONFIG.SYS or loading a different driver. While I can't promise that it's always that easy, we tested a variety of cards and devices while we were writing this book and things worked basically as advertised. For example, we could move ASPI-compliant devices like a scanner, CD-ROM or external tape drive from machine to machine and even operating system to operating system. All we had to do was enable the device driver (the Universal Driver had already been loaded) and reboot the machine to be off and running. The one set of devices that did show problems was, of course, hard drives. The operating system is often not up to handling a different translation of the ASPI layer when it comes to the boot sector. For that reason you should always back up a drive before swapping out host adapters from different vendors.

Driving the Daisy Chain

The real trick to easy SCSI integration, especially under DOS, is in installing the device modules. The key is in finding a device module that is compatible with your host adapter. Until recently, that sometimes proved a bit of a challenge. Today it's fairly simple. Windows 95 comes with a range of popular drivers (but you may still need third party software and not all devices are supported. Third-party support varies with the device. In general the major players offer ASPI drivers for the major operating systems. Not all are really tweaked for the newer ones, but they are on the way. Older hardware may be orphaned, or supported via generic drivers with limited features. Corel Corporation, the same people who make CorelDRAW!, has become the general store on the SCSI frontier. They have designed and tested ASPI device modules and universal drivers for almost every conceivable SCSI device under DOS and Netware. They are working on products for Windows 95 and NT, but those were not announced as this book was being written. Their CorelSCSI and CorelSCSI Pro software includes an extensive range of modules for DOS, Windows, OS/2, and Netware. The device drivers include modules for CD-ROM, optical drives, *jukeboxes* (several CD-ROM readers in one cabinet), and a variety of other peripherals, including scanners.

CorelSCSI includes a nifty set of utilities, including virtually painless installation using an automated routine that works very well with most ASPI products. The utilities include diagnostic routines and inventory procedures for managing your SCSI adapters and chains under DOS, Windows, and Netware, as well a neat little program for using a CD-ROM drive as a regular audio player, allowing you to play standard music CDs right from your computer.

The other Universal Driver solution was produced as an alternative to ASPI by two competitors, Future Domain and NCR. They call their alternative *Common Access Method* (CAM). This approach is an ANSI-approved protocol that has the advantage of allowing several host adapters to be controlled from a single driver. OS/2, SCO UNIX, Windows 95 and Windows NT offer direct support for CAM within the operating system. While the real-world differences between CAM and ASPI are small, ASPI was here first. As a result, while you can get scores of device modules to work with ASPI host adapters, far fewer are available using a CAM protocol. That doesn't mean you should ignore host adapters from Future Domain or NCR if they fit your needs, because there is a CAM-to-ASPI converter available. Just be sure, if you want to use a CAM adapter with an ASPI device module, that the converter will work with your host adapter and that product.

SHOPPING FOR SCSI

The only possible expansion card that offers as much choice as a SCSI host adapter is possibly a graphics adapter. In addition to the choices between Fast, Wide and Fast-Wide protocols, you also can choose between single and multi-channel support (seven or more than seven devices per card), ASPI or CAM protocols, ease of installation, bundled device modules, and bus type.

Bus Type

The first consideration is finding a host adapter that will fit in your machine. Some form of SCSI host adapter is available for virtually every PC ever made (in fact, *every* computer ever made). If you have a machine with only standard ISA expansion slots, the choice is very simple, for only ISA-based cards will fit in your machine. There are cards available to fit both 8-bit and 16-bit slots. The 8-bit cards are usually inexpensive, designed to be bundled with devices like CD-ROM drives or scanners. They usually offer marginal performance and limited drivers beyond the device they were sold with. Many do not even support adding a hard drive to the chain.

In general, if you're planning on adding a SCSI sub-system to your PC, you should stick with products from name-brand vendors like Adaptec, Bus Logic, Future Domain, Always, DTP, and Qlogic. It's also a good idea to shop around for a card that offers support for Fast SCSI, and which comes bundled with drivers for CD-ROM as well as some easy form of installation. One of my favorites in this category is the Adaptec 2940, shown in Figure 10.5.

FIGURE 10.5 The Adaptec 2940 host adapter.

The really neat thing about this host adapter is its ease of installation. There are no jumpers to set; you simply have to set the I/O address information and a couple of other options contained on one DIP switch. The Adaptec Easy SCSI software which comes with it almost totally automates the installation. It identifies all the Adaptec products installed on your system and identifies their attached peripherals (they don't certify it to work with other brands, even those that use ASPI drivers). It then loads the appropriate device modules for supported products. It also can automatically shift termination on or off depending on whether it senses devices attached to the internal or external cables. The other major vendors are now providing similar firmware setup, with hot-key access during the boot cycle. Adaptec deserves a lot of credit for this innovation.

PCI and EISA

To get the maximum performance out of the SCSI standards with Fast-Wide drives or other peripherals, you'll have to move to an advanced bus architecture, such as that offered by EISA and PCI (for a full discussion of these architectures, please refer to the discussion in Chapter 5). At the time this book is written the PCI products were still under development. SCSI-1 and Fast SCSI-2 host adapters will not offer any real improvement in performance on an EISA machine running MS DOS. If you are running an advanced *multi-tasking, multi-threading* (see the Glossary for explanations of these terms) operating system such as Windows NT, UNIX, or OS/2, it's a different matter and you will get a definite boost with the right hardware.

If you are using SCSI on a network, you'll also see a real push from these advanced adapters. Most of the major vendors are working on high-powered chips (like the Adaptec Arrow) or actual co-processors such as DPT's use of the Motorola 68000 CPU, to offer even more power on board. These chips handle the entire bus, reducing the workload on the computer's own CPU. Again, you won't see as much of a change if you are using one of these cards in a single-user environment like DOS. With more complex operating systems you will see a boost from the extra power offered by the co-processor.

Several of these cards also offer additional options. For example, the Adaptec 2742 is similar in design to its cousin, the 2940, but offers two internal SCSI channels, allowing you to connect up to 14 devices to a single card. The DTP 3224SmartRAID, pictured earlier, offers up to 64Mb of dedicated error-correcting RAM cache and allows you to add a fault-tolerant RAID storage system (RAID stands for *Redundant Array* of *Independent Disks*, commonly used in networks. Several hard drives are chained together to look like one large disk. It is designed so if one of the drives fails, no data is lost and the system continues operating).

VL-Bus

VESA Local bus, or VL-BUS, as explained in Chapter 5, was once the bus of choice for power users. If you have a VL-B motherboard, consider upgrading it as well as the host adapter. If you just won't part with it, then a VL-B SCSI adapter will give better performance than an ISA-based one. Keep in mind that both VL-B and ISA are harder to install, and that ISA is slower.

Fast SCSI, Wide SCSI, or Fast-Wide SCSI? Or Even Ultra SCSI

While you can still buy SCSI-1-style hard drives, and even refurbished ones at a bargain price, they're not really an investment for the future. They do not offer the through-put or the improved design and faster speeds of SCSI-3 or even SCSI-2 drives. In fact, most IDE drives will out-perform the old SCSI units. As a result, you should be looking for a SCSI host adapter that will support, at the very least, Fast SCSI. If you are considering a network or very intensive large file transfers such as those encountered in high-end color graphics, you might want to consider Wide, Fast-Wide and the newer Ultra varieties as well. As I mentioned before, Ultra Wide SCSI technology is not really mature yet, so the safest bet at present is to go with Fast or Wide SCSI-2, or Ultra Fast SCSI-3. Once you've determined which one of the four protocols (Fast, Wide, Fast-Wide, or Ultra) you want to use, you can look at the other factors involved in buying (listed below).

T I P

There are a lot of bargains in the SCSI-2 drive market. The IBM 662, which was a *PC Magazine Editors'* Choice, is now available via remaindered resellers. If you want a solid drive on a budget, there are good buys—just check the older magazine reviews and get at least a 90-day warranty.

ASPI or CAM Protocol

For a while it looked like choosing between ASPI or CAM was a big deal, but for all intents and purposes, the choice has already been made by the industry. If for some reason your operating system offers direct embedded CAM support, and you plan on adding multiple host adapters, you might still want to consider a CAM-based product as an option. Given the CAM-to-ASPI converters mentioned above, as well as the virtual monopoly of third party support for ASPI, there are no other real considerations between the two approaches. Both ASPI and CAM installations have gotten a lot easier in the past year, as vendors offer products that can scan the SCSI chain, locate the connected devices, and automatically configure a system's drivers. More about that later.

Single and Multi-Channel Support

The average user will probably never connect more than the seven devices allowed on a single host adapter. If for some reason you're adding a variety of both internal and external devices or building a system for a large network involving a RAID, you might want to consider using a multi-channel card such as the Adaptec 2742T (*T* for *twin channel*), which offers two separate channels on the same card, or the DTP 3224 SmartRAID, which provides hardware RAID ability right on a host adapter.

SCSI, the Switching Power-House

Keep in mind that a SCSI host adapter is running its own expansion bus. In a true multitasking environment, that allows you to run a scanner, back up the tape, or perform other intensive I/O operations with devices directly on the SCSI chain with almost no demand on the host system CPU. Most host adapters offer their own *bus mastering* (devices use the bus only when they are moving data or commands; they unhook to process data, and can access memory without using the computer's standard DMA channel) within the SCSI bus (even on ISA systems). The fanciest offer coprocessors that support multitasking, allowing them to handle several requests from different devices at the same time. Advanced SCSI host adapters have the capability to shuffle 255 tasks at the same time. Adapters supporting command-tag queuing can accept several commands, place them in a queue, then rearrange their processing to provide maximum efficiency. Keep in mind that these advanced features only apply when you have more than one device attached to a host adapter.

Selecting a Host Adapter

If you are building a high-performance system or intending to build a multimedia system, you should seriously consider installing, and take care in selecting, a SCSI sub-system. Many devices such as scanners and CD-ROMs are often bundled with inexpensive (and low-performance) host adapters. A number of sound cards are also equipped with built-in SCSI ports. While these devices may allow you to connect SCSI peripherals, they won't offer the high performance that a well-engineered host adapter will provide. The SCSI chain is only as powerful as its weakest link. If you mount a high performance SCSI hard drive or one of the double-speed CD-ROMs to such a card, the system will not reach its full potential. An extra couple hundred dollars may double the performance in some cases. When choosing a host adapter, you should match it to the fastest device you plan on adding to the system.

Ease of Installation

Another consideration when choosing a host adapter, as with any peripheral, is ease in installation. If you already have a SCSI adapter in your installation—and you plan on keeping it in there—you should consider using either identical cards or obtaining another one from the same vendor. Some operating systems will not support having two Universal Drivers from different vendors on the same system. Another ease-of-installation consideration is just how well the card's mechanical and software setups are designed. A well-designed installation like those available with the Adaptec 1542C, mentioned above, can save you anywhere from a few minutes to a few hours frustration. On the other hand, if another card meets your needs better overall, that extra time spent piddling around setting jumpers and DIP switches may be paid back with several years of improved performance.

Bundled Drivers, Software, and Third-Party Support

Getting a host adapter to work with your system is only part of a SCSI installation. You also have to be able to get the adapter to talk to the Device Modules. As we've already discussed, that involves additional software. If you are buying the host adapter to work with a hard disk or a common SCSI peripheral such as a CD-ROM, you can probably save some money by finding a host adapter that throws in the device driver you need for free. If your device module needs are a bit more complicated, you'll probably have to spring for a kit. This is the same host adapter usually bundled with additional device modules or a third-party collection of modules such as CorelSCSI. In most cases the kits are provided with external and internal cables. When pricing out the purchase, don't forget to add in the worth of these extras and prices of the same components purchased alone. In most cases the kit is the better deal if you need the extras. If no one offers the correct device module with a host adapter, you'll have to obtain them from a third party. Corel and other vendors offer extensive stand-alone kits.

Building a SCSI Chain

When you install a floppy, a tape, or a hard drive in a system, the options are pretty well defined. But SCSI is a more open-ended affair. The only common denominator is the host adapter; beyond that you could be attaching a series of internal devices, external devices, or a mix of peripherals both inside and outside the case. I'll start by showing how a host adapter is installed (inserting remarks for all three possibilities) and then cover adding internal and external devices to the chain, before moving on to troubleshooting.

Installing a SCSI Host Adapter

What You'll Need

- ✔ The host adapter itself
- ✔ The appropriate internal or external cable(s) to install your peripheral(s)
- ✔ Appropriate software drivers
- ✔ Screwdriver

✔ Hemostat

✔ Tweezers or pliers for placing jumpers

✔ The card's documentation

✔ Your Inventory of the devices already installed on your system.

The basic procedure is straightforward. We install the SCSI host adapter, which serves as the expansion card for all the devices that will be connected to it. Then we add devices one at a time, install any required drivers and software, then test to make sure they work properly. Here we go.

Step 1

Turn off power to the system and remove the power cord. If you try to remove or install cards with the power turned on in the computer you may seriously injure the cards and/or the motherboard.

Step 2

Prepare to install the card. Remove the cover from your computer's case by removing the screws holding it along the back, outer edge of the machine. Touch the inside metal chassis to ground yourself. Now open the box that the card came in and remove the card from its protective envelope. Depending on the type of card, you will have one or more jumpers which should be checked, and which may need to be reset before installing.

Step 3: Setting Jumpers

Open the manual and identify any jumpers or DIP switches that have to be set. You will usually need to identify the BIOS address (usually in somewhere in the C000 to DFFF range) and an I/O port (usually in the 130h to 340h range). Your manual should tell you what combination of jumpers or DIP switches must be adjusted to select the proper range.

T I P

If you are installing a SCSI hard disk as your primary drive, you can simplify the installation by setting the host adapter address at one of those commonly used by standard AT-style hard disk controllers. Most systems use either C800 or CC00 as a starting address. I usually set the hard disk controllers on my system at C800 to minimize confusion. If you have another hard disk controller already in your system (SCSI or otherwise), be sure the new card is not set at the same address or your computer won't even boot.

If your SCSI card is equipped with an on-board floppy drive controller, there will also be jumper or switch settings to enable or disable it. If there is another floppy drive controller in the system it must be disabled if you want to access the floppy drive.

Step 4: Termination

Check in your user's manual for the instructions explaining how your host adapter deals with termination. In order to function properly the devices at either end of the SCSI chain MUST be terminated. That means that if you are attaching only internal or external devices (no matter how many) the host adapter must be terminated. If you are attaching both internal and external devices to a single host adapter, it will be in the middle of the chain; you have to disable termination. Older host adapters use either jumpers or more often, resistor packs to provide termination. If it's a jumper setting, simply place or remove a jumper as required for that card. If you have removable resistor packs, carefully pull them straight out, then remove them—if you are disabling termination. Place them in an envelope or small Ziploc bag and label it. If you ever need to reinstall the terminator, you'll have to be able to find it. Put them in your goodie bag.

Many newer host adapters provide automatic termination. You still have to terminate the devices at the end of the chain, but the host adapter itself will automatically switch into a terminated or unterminated condition during the boot process. If it is attached to only internal or external devices, it will enable its on-board termination. If it is attached to both internal and external devices, it will turn its own termination off. If your host adapter supports this feature, you shouldn't have to worry about its termination at all. Most SCSI host adapters with auto-termination also have a manual setting to override this feature. You'll see why when we cover troubleshooting.

NOTE

You should add SCSI devices to a chain one item at a time. If you are adding several devices to a system you should start with the host adapter terminated and then add all internal devices with the card terminated, then disable termination and add the external devices. Don't forget to power down the machine between each step, especially when adjusting DIP switches or jumpers. With SCSI devices there is an additional reason for powering down the machine: when the unit is first booted, the host adapter scans the SCSI bus and identifies all of the devices under its control. If you just plug the device into the end of the SCSI chain, you won't be able to use it because the host adapter, and therefore the computer, won't know it is there.

Step 5

If placing a host adapter in your system, locate a free expansion slot and remove the back cover plate. Once again touch the edge of the case to make sure that you aren't carrying any static charge, then with gentle pressure insert the card into the free slot. Use the screw that held the expansion plate cover to lock the card into place. Replace the cover on the computer. See Figure 10.6.

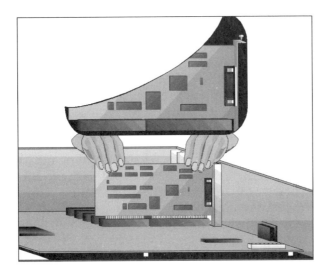

FIGURE 10.6 Installing a card into a slot.

Step 6: Installing the SCSI Device

The next step depends on what type and how many devices you are attaching to the new SCSI adapter. If one of the devices you are attaching is a hard drive, you should install it next.

Adding a Primary SCSI Hard Disk

As I mentioned in the general discussion of SCSI, the standard can support hard drives that are used as boot devices. This is done by mimicking the standard AT-style hard disk BIOS. In reality, the information on the hard disk is organized differently than with the standard MFM or RLL hard disk (refer to Chapter 9 for more detail). The host adapter will perform the translation if you have a disk smaller than 1Gb; you should not need any special drivers to attach one or two hard disks to your machine. The drive with ID 0 will be seen as the boot drive and the first partition on that drive will be assigned drive letter C. If you are installing a drive larger than one gigabyte, or more than two drives, you will need a software driver. If this applies to your situation, consult the documentation that came with both the host adapter and drive.

If you are installing an internal hard drive, mount the drive itself in the case as described in Chapter 9. Attach it to a 50-pin ribbon cable.

NOTE

When buying your SCSI cables, purchase those of high quality from a reliable source. Given SCSI's high performance and complex cabling demands, cheap cables can cause a lot of problems. If you are installing a Wide SCSI device it may require a 68-pin SCSI connector instead of a 50-pin.

The other end is attached to the 50-pin male connector on the upper edge of the host adapter itself. If you are installing more than one drive, all can be attached with the same ribbon cable. For sanity's sake, it's usually simplest to attach drive zero (which would also be SCSI ID zero) at the farthest end of the chain. That device should always be terminated. Consult your hard drive manual for instructions on how to enable termination. Any other drives or SCSI devices that are mounted closer to the host adapter than the farthest device should not have termination enabled.

Installing the Universal Driver

Depending on your operating system, you may need to install a *Universal Driver* (either ASCI or CAM). If you are adding a CD-ROM or any other device requiring a Device Module, you will have to load the Universal Driver. This will usually be accomplished automatically by using the installation software that comes with the host adapter. Some third-party products such as CorelSCSI Pro can also install ASPI managers for most popular cards. Once it's installed, you can use memory managers such as 386 to the MAX or QEMM to optimize your system's RAM. Be aware that some Universal Drivers do not work well (or in some cases, at all) if loaded into high memory.

Installing SCSI Peripherals

If you are installing more than one device, you should still add them to the SCSI chain one at a time. Let me give you a couple of examples to make things clear. If you are building a SCSI sub-system with both a hard drive and a CD-ROM, install the hard drive immediately after placing the adapter in the machine. Then come back, once the hard drive is up and running, and add the CD-ROM. If your immediate installation does not include a SCSI hard drive, and you are adding, let's say, a scanner and a CD-ROM to your system, pick one or the other and install it.

Installing the Device Module

Once the unit is installed and the system is rebooted, refer to the documentation for the host adapter, the new device, or your third-party SCSI software package for instructions on how to install any required device module drivers. If you are installing a CD-ROM under MS-DOS, you will also need to install the Microsoft CD-ROM software extension. This usually involves adding lines to both your CONFIG.SYS and AUTOEXEC.BAT files. For detailed instruction, consult your DOS manual or your CD-ROM or software manual.

TROUBLESHOOTING SCSI INSTALLATIONS: GETTING IT RIGHT THE FIRST TIME

SCSI installation should be as simple as plug-and-play. Attaching a single device to a matching host adapter is usually quite simple. When you start adding more devices, things get more complicated. If you are adding both internal and external devices or mixing new and old SCSI peripherals, odds are you'll run into a couple of snags along the way. Perseverance will lead to a smooth-running system that offers excellent performance. Here are my nine tips for getting things set up with a minimum of bother.

One: Start Simple

Rather than plugging a chain of peripherals into a SCSI card and then booting up, install the host adapter, then the first disk. After that install the devices one at a time and make sure that each device is working before moving on to the next. This may seem like a lot of extra work to the uninitiated, but in a complex setup, this is really the fastest way to proceed.

Two: Make a List

You should keep an up-to-date Inventory list of all the SCSI peripherals, their ID's, device drivers and the I/O and BIOS location of the host adapter. That way when you go to add another device to the chain or troubleshoot a pesky installation, you'll know exactly where everything should be set. SCSI devices with lower ID numbers usually have a higher priority when seeking attention from the host adapter. As a result, you should set your first hard disk to ID zero and the second at one. Host adapters are normally set to ID 7 and some operating systems (especially UNIX) expect to find them there. Some systems also expect other peripherals, such as the first CD-ROM, to have specific ID numbers. Be sure to check your software or adapter manual before installation. If you ignore these rules, the system will ignore your device.

Three: Start Inside

If possible install all internal units first, beginning with the hard disk. Then add one device at a time. After all the internal devices are on the chain, start with the externals. Keep in mind that you'll have to keep switching termination as you work on the external devices.

Four: Maintain Proper Termination

Any time you add or remove a device from the SCSI chain, you must adjust the termination. If you have only internal or external devices on the bus, the host adapter must be terminated on the side farthest away from the cabling. If you have both internal and external devices, you usually have to terminate both the first and last devices but not the SCSI host adapter in the middle.

Five: Use Quality Cabling

There are a variety of different SCSI cable connectors—25-pin adapters for SCSI-1, 50-pin varieties for SCSI-2 and a special 68-pin connector for Wide SCSI. Check the type of connection for the items you need to attach before buying cabling. Then buy quality cables that are well-shielded. It's also a good idea to buy as short a cable as possible to avoid signal noise, but keep in mind that all cable sections should be at least one foot in length. The maximum total cable length supported for a single host adapter under SCSI-1 or SCSI-2 is about 18 feet.

Six: Test the Installation

As you add each device to the system, turn on the computer and test it. Be sure all devices are properly cabled and attached to power before turning on the machine. Also be sure that any external devices are actually up and running before starting the boot process. If all the devices aren't powered on, when the SCSI host adapter scans the bus, it won't know the device is there when it's time to load the driver. Most newer host adapters will report all the devices they find during the boot cycle. Keep an eye on the monitor and make sure that everything on the bus is being seen. If one or more of the devices is missing, recheck to see that it is getting power, that it is properly cabled, and that two devices don't have the same ID number. Then you'll have to reboot the machine and watch to see if they are all recognized.

Seven: Make Sure All the Drivers Are Properly Installed and Loading

As your machine runs through its boot cycle and loads its device drivers, use the **Pause** key to halt the display. Make sure that all the device modules as well as the Universal Driver are loaded properly. Keep an eye open for statements like, `device driver not found`, `Improper line in config.sys`, etc. They indicate a problem. One of the most common reasons for a device not to work properly under SCSI is that the device module was either not properly loaded during boot-up, or not properly installed during installation.

Eight: Isolate Offending Devices

From the outside SCSI may seem like a bit of an arcane science, but it is one that has very well-defined rules. In reality it's a bit more like a neighborhood; if all else fails, try to isolate which device is causing the problem. It may be that a peripheral just won't work at a given ID number or it may not like its position on the chain. This may seem a little anthropomorphic, but it happens. There may be a conflict or the termination power may not be sufficient. If that's the case, you may have to add extra termination on the line. I've seen cases where even with both external and internal devices connected, the host adapter had to be terminated. While the rules say that you should only have to terminate the two end devices, sometimes the rules don't apply. Remember that you're more interested in a SCSI chain that works properly than exactly following the rules.

Nine: Optimizing the System

Once the SCSI chain is operating properly, use a memory manager such as HIMEM.SYS, Qualitas' 386 to the MAX or Quarterdeck's QEMM to recover the conventional memory used by the Device Modules and the Universal Driver. Keep in mind some Universal Drivers do not work when loaded into a high memory area. A complicated SCSI chain with all its drivers and the CD-ROM extension can easily consume more than 150K of conventional memory. Most of this can be recovered with a good memory manager.

CD-ROM Drives—A Window on the World

One of the most exciting developments in desktop computing was the adoption of *CD-ROM* (*Compact Disk—Read Only Memory*) technology for storing data. At first look that may seem like a pretty ho-hum development. So what, you can store 650 Mb of data on a little plastic platter. After all, hard disks can store much more than that and are much faster. The excitement comes from the fact that CD-ROM disks are cheap and easy to distribute since they are *removable media*. In other words, they're an excellent way to distribute large amounts of information and they can be mass-produced. For example, a whole encyclopedia that would normally take up the better part of a bookshelf can be stored on a single CD-ROM, and that information can be retrieved and cross-referenced using excellent search software that would be impossible to duplicate using regular bound volumes.

Not only that, but CD-ROM encyclopedias can also include sound clips, animation, and even live video when discussing a topic. Vast databases can be stored on CD-ROM. In my own lab I have silver platters that contain the entire contents of newspapers over a two-year period. I can easily search for a name, an event, or a subject and the computer can even suggest other possible areas of research based on my initial query. There's one company that produced all the phone books, both white and yellow pages, for the entire United States on five CD-ROMs. You can locate individual listings by name, phone number, or type of business. See Figure 10.7.

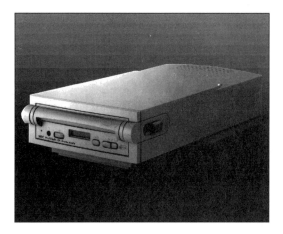

FIGURE 10.7 The NEC 6x multi spin external CD-ROM drive.

CD-ROMs can also play music, and can be used to distribute regular software. For example, Microsoft bundles its most popular office automation programs (Excel, Word, PowerPoint, Access, and Mail) all on a single CD-ROM with on-line documentation. CorelDRAW! is distributed on CD-ROM with a host of applications and fonts, some of which are not available in the version produced on floppy disk. You can obtain software that will allow you to play regular audio CDs directly from your PC's CD-ROM.

CD-ROMs are one of the key components involved in assembling a multimedia PC. If you want to get into the world of video, animation, and sound on your PC, you'll need a CD-ROM. More and more vendors are distributing software on CD-ROM as well. Kodak has a service, called *Photo-CD*, to process film at your local photo shop, then delivered as digital images on a CD-ROM that you can put into your computer or even display on your home TV screen (with a special CD-ROM reader made for the purpose).

How a CD-ROM Works

Just like a regular disk, a CD-ROM stores data as series of zeros and ones on a platter; unlike magnetic media, which arranges data in a series of even, concentric bands. CD-ROMs are organized in a single track that spirals from the center of the disk to its outside. The data is recorded as a series of pits burned into the underside surface of the platter. A laser beam is used to detect whether specific points on a disk are pitted or not and that information is translated into data that your computer can read.

Selecting a CD-ROM Drive

CD-ROM drives used in computers are very similar to those found on the shelves of hi-fi and electronic shops for home audio use. The only major difference is in its ability to be connected to a PC. The first question to answer when shopping for a computer CD-ROM player is whether to buy an internal or external version. Most vendors produce both types for each model. In general, external drives offer the same advantages as external modems. They don't take up space in your machine and they are easier to move around from one machine to another, or to keep if you are planning on selling your existing computer at some point in the future. Internal devices don't take up extra space on your desk or require their own power connection.

All CD-ROMs Are Not Created Equal

CD-ROMs are slower than hard drives, even the 6x devices. The newest models require about 45*ms* (*milliseconds*) to initially access a given point on the disk. Older drives may require up to 500ms (a full half-second) to perform the same task. Once the initial point has been reached, most CD-ROMs transfer data at about 150Kb per second. This is the same speed as a standard audio CD player. If you have the extra money, a multi-speed CD-ROM will perk up your system significantly when working with image files. PCs today can handle more in the way of live video clips and animation, and Windows 95 offers direct support for multimedia. You need a fast CD-ROM drive to take advantage of this technology. Slower units will produce jumps in images, along with pops and cracks in sound output.

Another dividing line in CD-ROMs is *multi-session* capabilities. Older drives were *single-session*; all the data was recorded at one time and is seen as one volume. Multi-session drives have the ability to read data that was laid down in several sequential sessions. At the present time this is not a big deal for the average end user.

CD-RECORDABLE DRIVES: DOUBLE DUTY AND LOTS OF FUN

There are devices available that allow you to create your own CD disks. These are not really CD-ROMs but *CD-R* or *CD Recordable*. These devices are now almost all manufactured as multi-session drives, allowing you to record part of a disk, use it and then record the rest later. The media cost about $15 each, and can store up to 650Mb of data, or about 74 minutes of music.

The cost of CD-R technology is dropping. The first unit I worked with in 1992 cost $18,000. Today the units are better, the software is easier, and the cost is way down. A good 2x speed unit is under $1,500. The software is under $100. If you are interested in CD-R check out the drives that are compatible with Corel's CD-Creator. This software lets you not only record data, but sound and traditional music CDs. It supports multi-session, and the newer CD-R drives can do double duty as a regular CD-ROM reader. But be sure to check out compatibility with your host adapter and operating system before you buy.

A final consideration, and one found in most of the multi-session drives, is the ability to support the new Kodak Photo CD format. This allows you to read disks produced with the Kodak film-to-digital imaging equipment mentioned above.

You may also hear the term *ISO 9660* bandied about, sometimes known as the *High Sierra* format. The ISO stands for *International Standards Organization*, which sponsored the committee that produced the document (number 9660) that sets out the accepted requirements for producing a CD-ROM product that will be compatible with other certified devices and discs. Basically, all micro-computer CD-ROMs produced for microcomputers, except those used on Apple Computers, are compatible with this standard. Unless you have a Macintosh, you don't really have to worry about compatibility.

Multi-session drives can read both single-session ISO 9660 and the newer multi-session extensions to the standard.

If you are on a limited budget and just have to have a CD-ROM now, it is possible to find older single-speed, single-session CD-ROMs at close-out prices, sometimes as low as about $150. This is sometimes as cheap as one-third of the price of a fancy, multi-speed multi-session CD-ROM drive. Keep in mind that you will not be able to take advantage of a host of new features, including the new Kodak Photo-CD, unless you get one of the newer models. Going on the cheap now may mean spending more cash later.

Installing a CD-ROM Drive

We will cover IDE CD-ROMs in the next chapter. If you are on a budget, IDE drives are an option, but the best technology and performance will belong to those who use SCSI. Placing an external CD-ROM on a system with an existing SCSI adapter is simple. Just decide where on the chain it will sit, assign it a unique SCSI ID and power down the system. Attach it to the SCSI chain using an appropriate cable and make sure that the last device on the string is properly terminated. Boot the machine and install the device module and if necessary the MSCDEX extension as described in the operating system documentation. *MSCDEX* stands for Microsoft CD-ROM Extensions. This is a driver that is loaded to allow DOS, which does normally have the ability to recognize CD-ROM discs, the read the files on one. If you run into any problems, refer to the troubleshooting tips above.

Internal CD-ROM Drives

Internal CD-ROMs are added to the system much like the installation of a SCSI hard disk. First make sure the device is assigned a unique ID number on the SCSI chain. Generally CD-ROMs are assigned numbers between three and six, depending on the other devices on the chain. If it is the only internal device on the system, it should be terminated and the host adapter should be unterminated. If other devices are placed further on the chain than the CD-ROM, make sure it is unterminated and that the last device on the chain is terminated.

Mounting the Drive in the System

What You Will Need

✔ The drive

✔ An appropriate cable

✔ Appropriate mounting hardware (rails, spacers, etc.).

✔ A Philips-head screwdriver

✔ A flat blade or torq screwdriver

✔ Possibly a hemostat or tweezers to set the drive select jumper

Now slide the drive into place and make sure that it is far enough back to fit a cover panel in front of it, that it doesn't obstruct any other drive bays, and that there is adequate spacing for ventilation.

In a desktop case there is usually some sort of retaining clip that often looks like a square washer. See Figure 10.8.

FIGURE 10.8 Mounting an internal CD-ROM drive.

Once you have all the drives attached to both the ribbon cable and the power cable, locate the pins on your hard disk controller or SCSI adapter. If you are placing a 5.25-inch drive in a tower case, all you'll probably have to do is slide it into a bay from the front of the case (you'll have to remove the cover of the case first by unscrewing the screws at the back of the tower and removing the shroud). Once you have slid it into the bay, fasten it with four mounting screws through the slots on either side of the bay. Be sure not to use screws that are too long. If you do, they may actually penetrate through to the board on the drive and damage it. Once the drive is fastened, plug in a power lead from the power supply. This lead will have four wires, usually one red, one yellow and two black. Most 5.25-inch drives will have a plug about 1 inch across which can only be seated one way, since two of the corners are rounded and the others are square cut. See Figure 10.9. Once the power supply is attached, attach one end of the cable that goes to the host adapter.

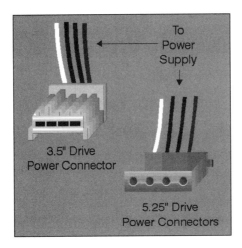

FIGURE 10.9 Drive power supply connectors.

If you are installing the drive into a desktop case, you will probably have to use some kind of mounting rail before sliding the drive into the bay. These are attached using two screws each.

CHAPTER SUMMARY

Your personal computer is a general-purpose tool. SCSI technology can make it much easier to add new components to your system. SCSI offers the best performance and ease of operation when it comes to hard drives, CD-ROM, scanners, and CD-Recordable technology. This chapter has outlined how SCSI works, and how you to add a SCSI chain and maintain it.

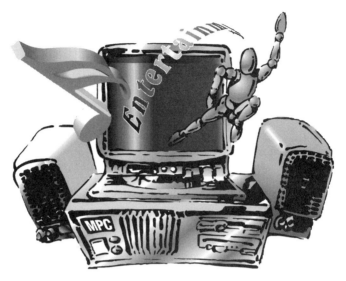

CHAPTER 11

THE MULTIMEDIA PC

WHAT'S IN THIS CHAPTER

- ✔ What is Multimedia?
- ✔ Why Upgrade to a Multimedia PC?
- ✔ How Much to Spend on an Upgrade
- ✔ Choosing Multimedia Upgrade Kits
- ✔ Adding Sound Cards
- ✔ Selecting and Installing CD-ROM Drives
- ✔ Speakers and Sound Value
- ✔ Motion Video

379

WHAT THIS CHAPTER IS ABOUT

A fully decked out multimedia PC is one of the most impressive and satisfying electronic appliances around these days. Unless you buy a complete system fully set up, however, you'll have some reading and thinking to do before you are ready to upgrade your existing PC. In fact, it may not even be worth trying it yourself, depending on a number of issues (which pretty much boil down to time, talent, and money).

In this chapter I'll explain the various components needed for multimedia, and how to go about selecting, installing, and tuning them up. These discussions should also help you shop for a multimedia system or an upgrade kit by spotlighting the range of products available and providing advice on what to seek out and what to avoid. If you already have a multimedia PC, reading this chapter will give you a deeper perspective on what makes it work than you'll get from reading your manuals, and give you the knowledge you'll need if you consider upgrading your *MPC* (Multimedia Personal Computer). Sooner or later you will have to do a little re-tuning or troubleshooting, things being what they are in the fast-changing PC world, and you'll find advice here to help you isolate problems, and fix them yourself or get more help.

WHAT IS MULTIMEDIA, ANYWAY?

As this book was being written, Windows 95 was newly released. It generated hype, commercials, and a slew of magazine covers dedicated to the importance of Windows 95. Microsoft sales shot up, and multimedia and the Internet became everyday buzzwords. Multimedia will remain a hot topic for several years. The reason? It brings an ever more convincing world of sound, color, and motion onto our PCs, and increases our intellectual and emotional involvement with the practical, informative, and entertaining programs we run on them.

The implicit goal of multimedia has always been the creation of a virtual illusion of human experience through rich sound, color, and motion on a PC. Something in our nature is attracted to realistic and controllable models of life, at bottom—the deep sense of creative play which is the essential impulse of all art. We have seen photography move from pale impressions in sepia or gray and white to color as rich as nature, and with Polaroid and digital technology, we can have our captured image in literally seconds, while we continue to look at the real scene. Then pictures got motion, and these "movies" became more realistic with the addition of sound, and finally a half century ago, added color to create an even richer illusion of reality. Larger screens, as wide as the theater itself, and wrap-around high-fidelity sound still make a movie theater an extremely powerful and immersive experience (if the software, er, film, has anything of value in it). Television has followed a similar path, from small black-and white sets to the miraculous 13-inch color sets of my youth. And in the mid-90s, "home theater" systems can have huge 36-inch and 48-inch screens and digital surround-sound systems which can break glass windows blocks away. Driven by an increasing population with an apparently insatiable demand for toys/appliances (choose one), technological research and continuous refinement of manufacturing approaches have combined to move a whole range of products towards the rich reproduction of sound, motion, and color; PC-based multimedia systems are part of this urge. A typical multimedia PC is shown in Figure 11.1.

FIGURE 11.1 A typical multimedia PC.

If we break the word *multimedia* apart, it means "multiple mediums," or more than one means of expression. Since even the most basic PC has some kind of video and monitor, and at least a fifty-cent internal speaker, by a long stretch it could be said to present us with both sound and visual images. But no one would call it a multimedia PC—for that we expect at least 256 colors on a tolerably sharp monitor, a sound card capable of high fidelity and speakers better than an AM radio, and, usually, a CD-ROM drive. We expect that such a system can play back video clips from CD-ROM, and keep up with most of the nifty games and other interactive programs pouring out of the gates. The system just outlined is really just an entry level one, however. If you have several thousand dollars to invest, you can buy a system good enough, not only to reproduce compelling multimedia, but even to produce your own high-quality multimedia programs, and even make your own CD-ROMs. If you can't afford to do that right now, like most of us, you may be able to work your way up by selective upgrading, by watching the PC marketplace and putting into practice what you've learned in this book.

WHERE IT'S BEEN

Before we take up the increasingly technical details of multimedia components and systems, let's look briefly at how multimedia grew.

PCs and Parallel Worlds

The IBM-PC compatible is now, in a full-blown MPC version, a very strong multimedia machine, but it has come to the party rather lately. In the early 1980s, the humble Commodore VIC-20 (with its then roomy 5Kb of RAM), and its once-dominant big brother the Commodore 64 (with an awesome 64 Kb), distinguished themselves by including chips which produced up to 16 colors and simple, entertaining sound. These machines, along with the early Atari and Radio Shack Color Computer (CoCo), were years ahead of the IBM-PC in what was then hot multimedia entertainment software (i.e., games).

IBM, after all, stands for *International Business Machines*, and its early PCs had businessmen, scientists, and accountants in mind as its users. And of course, these were serious people doing serious work, and they had no need or use for fancy color, much less good sound and motion...did they? Forget color, the first IBM-PCs offered a monochrome, text-only video card as an option! Then Microsoft brought out its first (and only) hit game, Flight Simulator, and since it offered an attempt to put you into an airplane cockpit and teach you to fly, it needed a video card that could put more than the alphabet up on the (green) screen. Enter a company called Hercules, which did an enormous business with its classic monochrome graphics adapter. IBM moved slowly, and brought out the CGA (*Color Graphics Adapter*) video standard in the mid-1980s, and toward the latter part of the decade, the EGA (*Extended Graphics Adapter*), and eventually the VGA (Video *Graphics Array*). During this time, while its color got better and better as third parties discovered there was brisk business in giving it better color than the VIC-20, and monitor makers likewise started beating IBM to the punch and offering something that didn't flicker noticeably, the PC continued to be worthy of sound which could only be called lame. IBM, which obviously never originally intended for the PC to be a multimedia machine, had designed it without such capabilities in mind. IBM's own engineers and others had to go through contortions to get hardware and software working towards multimedia.

Gradually IBM's control of the PC's design changes passed to third parties, and compatibles and clones started outselling and outperforming IBM's own PCs. Driven by consumer demand and competition from this decade's version of the Atari and Commodore, the Nintendo game machine and its offspring, the PC at last became the MPC (Multimedia Personal Computer). Meanwhile Commodore had brought out the Amiga in the mid-Eighties. Building on their earlier design, Commodore's engineers conceived of the Amiga as a high-powered multimedia machine from the beginning, and the Amiga, an immediate favorite of artists, video producers, and multimedia types, dominated the high-powered desktop in these areas until Commodore lost the long battle against IBM's ability to control the business market, and went into bankruptcy. Apple, which gained early ground in the personal computer field among hobbyists and educators, was, since the introduction of the Macintosh, the ease-of-use champion as well. With the color Mac, Apple took the lead in multimedia, and remains well-entrenched.

As multimedia began to take hold in a wider PC-based market, sound cards and video led the way. In 1994, many systems were based on the 486SX-25Mhz CPU, which was really much too slow, and, to make matters worse, these roughly $1500 systems had single-speed CD-ROM drives and video cards with a half Mb of memory. Five or ten-dollar speakers completed a system that typically produced grainy, halting video in small portions of the screen, and audio which was always trying to catch up. These systems were nonetheless fun for a while because of their novelty, and many of us knew that things would always get better technically and more affordable as well, for such has been our experience with electronic consumer goods for over half a century.

WHERE IT IS NOW

In the middle of the 1990s, things have gotten better. That same $1500 today will get you a system twice as good as little more than a year ago, and $2000 will buy you a quite impressive multimedia PC (at least compared to those 1994 systems). CD-ROM drives are now six times as fast as two years ago, and are finally capable of approaching realistic motion. The CD-ROM disc itself has become the medium of choice for the distribution of software, naturally enough for multimedia programs, with their huge audio and video files, but also for regular programs as well, whose size has grown to gargantuan proportions along with graphic user interfaces (i.e., Windows). Mass production is making it cheap to distribute these behemoth programs (some graphics and office "suites" want 100 or even close to 200Mb for full installations!) on CD-ROM; and just as it its older brother, the audio Compact Disc drove the LP record out of the stores, CD-ROM is putting a lot of pressure on floppy disk software distribution. The upshot is that the momentum for more (and better) multimedia is continuing to build. Today CD-ROM drives operate six to eight times as fast as the early units, and can even play full-length movies on your PC's screen.

MPC and MPC-2

As the PC evolves into a multimedia appliance, there are four important issues in its growth into a truly mass-market item: *cost, available software, technical performance,* and *ease-of-use.* The latter two supposedly have been addressed by an industry standard known as *MPC,* standing for Multimedia Personal Computer. Manufacturers attempted to provide hardware standards to let consumers know what was, and what wasn't, a suitable hardware configuration to run multimedia programs, and which software programs required such hardware. The idea is that a particular system, piece of software, or with a stretch even an individual component, could carry an MPC label, and the consumer could buy with the confidence that his MPC system or software could run at least basic multimedia programs. A good idea; but multimedia is essentially a cutting-edge resource hog in money and technology, and any standard which includes at least some older, slower systems will require a lowering of minimum standards. Many mass marketers often implemented their systems at the minimum low level to keep the price down; MPC usually stood for shaky video and stuttering audio. The resulting compromises, however desirable in the view of Sales and Marketing, have meant that MPC is a rather flabby standard, skewed towards the lower-price/earlier model machines.

The original (and now outdated) MPC standard (now called MPC-1 or MPC Level I) called for:

✔ 386-25Mhz Processor

✔ 4 Mb RAM

✔ 640x480x256-color VGA card

✔ 8-bit sound board

✔ A single-speed CD-ROM drive (Single-speed requires the ability to sustain an average data-transfer rate of 150Kb/sec)

Revised in 1994 as MPC-2 or MPC Level II, the upgraded standard required at least:

✔ 486-25Mhz Processor

✔ 800x600x65,535-color SVGA video card

✔   16-bit sound board

✔   A double-speed (2X, 300 Kb/sec) CD-ROM drive

Given the ever-increasing need for speed and power, the 3-to-6 month product-development cycles common in the industry, and the inherent nature of committees to be slow and compromising, the usual and predictable result has been that a standard is passing out of date by the time it is announced, at least as far as really exciting multimedia performance is concerned. If an MPC-3 emerges, you'll need to read it carefully, realizing that it looks backwards towards compatibility at least as much as forward towards new horizons. And, as we now know all too well, when "standards" are too loose, some manufacturers will modify them to wring a claimable improvement, often at the cost of ease-of-use and compatibility. The history of video card standards and SCSI standards, and indeed the history of the PC itself, illustrate this same lesson, and we must expect it to continue in the "Brave New World" of multimedia. MPC is helpful at a certain minimum level, but it doesn't guarantee either a high level of performance, or that everything with the letters MPC on it will even run at all.

Smaller is Better... Maybe

Another strong trend in the industry has been the success of engineers in miniaturizing more and more components for use in portable computers, laptops, and notebooks. The first "portable" PC, made by Compaq, weighed over 20 pounds and required a case the size of a medium suitcase to lug it around (and I do mean lug—watching someone try to carry one of these things onto an airplane was enough to make your back hurt! Not only was it heavy, its wedge-shaped, hard case added insult to injury, or vice versa). It was successful, however, and today a heavy portable weighs 7 pounds, and a notebook PC is often 4 pounds or under and is literally 8 x 11 inches and 1 inch thick. Multimedia fans have had to wait a long time for the technology to make a reasonably good VGA color screen to arrive; and it was so expensive, and not very exciting, in the last decade, that the phrase "multimedia portable PC" was all but unthinkable; it was certainly unobtainable. No longer. Portable PCs today can come with built-in CD-ROM drives, as well as hard disks close to 1 Gb, have 10-inch diagonal TFT color screens that are very crisp indeed, and contain built-in sound card capabilities and even small speakers. Naturally these are very expensive, $4,000—$6,000, but they are there and they work (In 1996 we may see entry-level machines at around $2000). Their only real shortcoming is the sound coming from rather tiny internal speakers.

Where it's Going

Prediction is always risky, especially in this wacky world of computers. It seems clear, however, that multimedia will continue to grow as a standard feature of PCs, and impressive multimedia at that. Let's take a moment to consider where hardware prices meet multimedia needs as this is written (we'll look at software in a moment). Hard disk prices have dropped to "unthinkable" levels, and you can now buy an IDE 1Gb drive for under $250. Strong video cards continue to drop in price, and before this book is again updated, 8x-speed CD-ROM drives will doubtless be found on entry-level machines. Diamond has a bundle with 8X drive, sound card, speakers, and a variety of multimedia titles for about $550 (street price). CD-ROM drives that hold and play multiple discs (called *jukeboxes*) have recently fallen to around $600 or even less. Excellent true color video cards are available for under $250. You can pay $100 or less today for a sound card that cost $400 two years ago. Speakers for multimedia systems, in contrast, have increased in price—because the quality has gotten better, and there is just so much manufacturers can do with small speakers and sell them for $20 or $40 apiece. High-end, high-fidelity multimedia sound systems are still around $250 and up, and you pay a lot for the engineering which goes into them.

Overall, these multimedia hardware component price trends make it clear that better and better multimedia will continue to get cheaper and cheaper in the next few years. The momentum of: consumer demand; improving quality for a given price; the fast product-development cycles of the consumer electronics industry, which now includes computers and especially, multimedia systems; and the bedrock human love of realistic toys I outlined above—all these trends make it seem inevitable that the time of critical mass for multimedia systems is here. I expect that the next edition of this book will assume that the majority of its readers will already have a multimedia system.

When it comes to software, the CD-ROM, as I implied above, has become for some huge programs the only practical way to distribute. If you've been around PCs for a few years, you may recall that when 3.5-inch floppy disks appeared, they of course held more than the trusty 5.25-inch disk, and they also cost more. So, when you bought a new program, it would come on the older, larger, cheaper disk(s). If you wanted or needed it on 3.5-inch disks, you could send in a card and the software company would send it (them) to you.

As 3.5-inch disks overtook their larger but smaller brothers, manufacturers shipped software on the smaller disks, and you could send in for the 5.25-inch flavor. The clock turns, and the wheel spins: software houses would rather send you one CD-ROM disc than 20 or 25 floppies for obvious reasons of economy and packaging, and, believe me, you'd rather have them do that than deal with all those floppies! So now you have to ask, and maybe pay extra, to get your software on even the 3.5-inch floppies. Some monster programs, like CorelDRAW! and some high-end games and shareware collections come on multiple CDs, and you must swap disks in and out as required (this inconvenience is one of the factors pushing the multiple-disc jukeboxes down in price and into the mass market).

The familiar economies of scale have kicked in, and you can now buy single CD-ROMs for $10 apiece, and collections which can bring the price of an individual disc down to $1.50 have started to appear! CD-ROM will probably overtake floppy disks as the preferred means of distribution; most new systems sold now have a CD-ROM built in, and technical improvements promise that in the near future CD-ROMs will be able to store several times the approximately 650 Mb they do today.

What does all this mean? Simply that the pressure towards more and more multimedia and more and more CD-ROMs seems irresistible. We stand at a point, wherein the hardware components to upgrade are more affordable than ever; wherein most new systems are not only multimedia-ready, but often include several CD-ROMs; wherein Windows 95, with its improved ability to recognize new hardware components, has begun what appears to be a fast-moving march to dominate the desktop of the PC; and wherein you will shortly be left behind as a PC user if you don't have at least a basic PC multimedia system.

WHY UPGRADE TO MULTIMEDIA?

The Moving Tide of Multimedia

If you've been following along during the overview of the subject on the preceding pages, you've got a good group of reasons to upgrade to multimedia, or perhaps get another PC with multimedia already included and set up. Here's a list which summarizes the above trends, and adds a few more ideas for your consideration.

- ✔ It makes using your system more attractive and fun

- ✔ It is required for increasing numbers of the best new programs

- ✔ It gives significantly better value than even a year ago

- ✔ It is built into many new systems

- ✔ It is increasingly easy to set up and use

- ✔ It is clearly the immediate future of computing

- ✔ It has the potential to teach children to enjoy using computers well

- ✔ It offers tremendous potential for interactive learning for all users

- ✔ It opens up the creation of original art

- ✔ It gives anyone the tools to do audio, video, audio-visual, and multimedia production

- ✔ It is now part of a consumer-driven, mass-market trend with unstoppable momentum

The Practical, the Possible, and the Practical Necessity

If adding a mouse or keyboard to your system is about the easiest thing you can do, upgrading a basic system to a multimedia screamer is one of the most challenging. This rather sobering fact is due to the complexity of components which make up a full-blown multimedia system—we're talking about adding another disk drive (CD-ROM), a sound card, a speaker system, a microphone, and possibly another controller card, possibly a motion video card... and this is before we have mentioned a CPU upgrade, a larger hard disk, a fast video card with lots of memory, and a better color monitor! If this begins to sound like a project on the order of, say, setting out to somehow cable and cobble together your TV, your component-quality stereo system, and your PC—well, you're getting the idea.

It's not likely that the majority of this book's readers will—or should—attempt to do an upgrade of the above complexity. Some of you probably will want to consider it, and if you've already replaced a component or two successfully, you should be equal to the task. If you've torn your system down and put it back, patched one together, or bought components and put a PC together yourself (see Chapter 20, *Building Your Own PC*), you can definitely do it. For these hardy souls, we'll give as much guidance as we can. Most of you, however, will properly decide you have reached a crossroads: you may want to: buy a new multimedia system, keeping your old PC as a spare/secondary system or selling it off; buy an upgrade kit with pre-matched components; or pay someone to upgrade it for you. We'll assume in the following discussion that you are at least considering doing it yourself. When the time comes will discuss the pros and cons of purchasing an upgrade kit. Even if you decide to buy a kit, that will be a more informed choice after going through the nuts-and-bolts discussion of multimedia upgrades, and you'll also be in a better position to buy a good kit. And if you decide you don't have the time or confidence to do your own upgrade, that too will be a more informed decision, and you'll be in better shape to choose a good person to do the work for you.

Plug and Play

One thing that has the potential to make installing multimedia add-ons like sound cards (one of the most difficult offenders) easier is the new Plug and Play (PnP) standard. It allows the system to automatically configure the components of a PC when a new item is added. You must have a PnP BIOS on the card, another in the PC on the motherboard, and a PnP-compatible operating system. Microsoft Windows 95 is compatible. But PnP is less than perfect. If it works, the new card will go in the first time, without setting jumpers. If not, you must use the options provided by the operating system. For more information on PnP options, see Chapter 2, on operating systems.

NOTE

If you decide you want to have someone else do your multimedia upgrade for you, some stores offer this service, especially if you bought the hardware there; if you bought several major components from them, try to get the installation thrown in. Otherwise, you can expect to pay $50 or more, and it may be well worth it to have someone else get the system working. If you try it yourself, get into trouble, and then want someone to straighten things out, they will probably want more money, and deserve it.

UPGRADE OR REPLACE? YOUR SECOND DECISION

Crossing the Line

If you have decided because of one or more of the above reasons that you want to upgrade a system to multimedia, or simply because you want to run a particular program and it requires multimedia, you now need to take a good look at three things: your vision, your system, and your budget. Each of these factors must be weighed according to your priorities, and then combined with the facts you gather from this book and from your own research. Yes, you really should do some! The PC industry changes rapidly when it comes to what features are the right ones for a given application, and it pays to shop for deals. It can be a lot of fun, and you'll increase your chances of a satisfying upgrade quite significantly—and save money.

Developing a Vision

Its a good idea to read reviews and test reports in magazines like *PC Magazine, Computer Shopper, CD-ROM Today*, and *Multimedia World*. If you belong to an online service such as Compuserve, America Online, or use the Internet, seek out the appropriate on-line conference groups to hear what users of specific products have to say about them. You can also check with vendor forums for product announcements and to ask questions, and price (or even buy) products in online shopping stores.

Caveat Emptor, Visitor Emptor

The best thing of all, of course, is to go see a few multimedia systems, especially those featuring components you're interested in. Nothing compares to actually seeing and hearing. This is easy to do in general, but may be hard in particular. As smaller computer stores have tended to disappear in favor of specialized stores, superstores like CompUSA and Computer City, office supply superstores like Office Depot and Office Max, and appliance and electronics chains have added multimedia systems and upgrade kits to their lines. You will probably be able to see and hear some multimedia systems, but a few cautions are in order. Obviously, they may not be able to demonstrate a particular CD-ROM drive, sound card and speaker setup you want to hear. In general these stores tend to sell mid- to low-end solutions—and you can buy better parts that improve performance and satisfaction. You may not be familiar with the program they are demonstrating, and it might be specially chosen or tweaked to highlight product strengths and mask weaknesses. And of course, you're looking at a monitor, video card, hard disk, CD-ROM drive, and CPU system which may be quite different from yours, which makes trying to compare the store's system to your present one with an upgrade, very questionable.

The quality of knowledge and advice you can get from a sales-person is likely to be quite variable; some are excellent and helpful, while as someone familiar with many of the concepts in this book, you may well know a good deal more than the salesperson about everything but prices and specifications. Occasionally, as befits mass market stores, you may run into cases where they are having specials on products you might not really want. They may be obsolete or of inferior quality. We'll talk more about this type of shopping in a following section. At this point, you'd be well advised not to buy something on your very first look. You're doing your research to get a concrete idea of what some products actually look and sound like.

Another approach to is to go see a system that a friend, relative, or friend of a friend has. Here you may get a more objective opinion; but you also may well not. Some people have enormous pride in their possessions and will sugar-coat everything; others may have had some installation or other hassles and hardly have a good thing to say about a basically fine system, or they may have problems with some program or other that have nothing to do with the performance of their multimedia components. If the friend is a good one, you can get a good idea if you'd be happy with a comparable system. Naturally, the same hardware cautions apply as above: you're looking at a lot of components probably different from yours.

Taking Stock

You also need to take a long, hard look at your system. If it is already beginning to feel cramped, outmoded, or underpowered, you'll have to take a long and hard look at whether you want to upgrade it piece by piece. Did you make the System Inventory as suggested in Chapter 5? Get it out or do it now. Even if you did one earlier, check it over and perhaps re-run some of the diagnostics we've included, such as Winsleuth Gold or ASQ, or run MSD if you're running DOS 5.0 or later. Consider these points as you look it over:

CPU: If it's an 386 or 486 say goodbye. Multimedia really needs a Pentium. You can, depending on your particular 386, upgrade to a 486, but weigh the cost carefully. If you have a 486 with the much-ballyhooed P24T Pentium upgrade socket, you can put a 60 or 75 Mhz Pentium chip into it, but again, Intel has priced these chips high enough to make you think about getting a new motherboard instead.

If you need clarification on terminology or the discussion of a particular component, refer to the Glossary or to the appropriate earlier chapter.

Memory: Even the early Scrooge-level multimedia systems gave you 4Mb RAM, and you're going to want to run Windows, as many of the best multimedia programs run only under Windows, and unless you've been way out in the bush with no radio or TV in recent months, you know that Windows 95 is coming on like gangbusters. Like Windows 3.1, it "requires" 4Mb and "recommends" 8Mb. Translation: it crawls with 4Mb and performs OK for single applications with 8Mb. If you have less than 4 Mb, your system is probably either unupgradable or not worth the money to do so. If you have at least 12 or 16Mb, you're in good shape.

Hard Drive: If it's less than about 540 Mb, you're likely to need a new one. Even though CD-ROMs have typically more space than that on them, some programs will nonetheless put 5 to 25Mb onto your hard drive just to get set up, and many will want 50 or 100 Mb. Even with the newer, faster CD-ROM drives, the data transfer rate from CD-ROM is much slower than from a hard disk, so even though some programs will allow you to run them from the CD-ROM, there is a performance penalty. Multimedia files are notorious space hogs, and can fill up a hard drive while you go get a drink from the 'fridge. With the price for a 1Gb drive under $300, there's small reason to run out of room.

Be sure your motherboard can support the new high-capacity E-IDE (*Enhanced IDE*, also known as *Fast ATA*) drives, or you'll also need to get an E-IDE controller board—if you go with IDE. If you plan of adding a scanner or CD-Recordable drive, consider SCSI and read the sections of this book that deal with it.

Video Card: If you're still getting by with VGA, reach for your checkbook or credit card. And if you have a SVGA (Super VGA) card with less than 2Mb RAM, you will need to get up to that level. Some cards are upgradable, some are not; and most video cards use more expensive types of memory, so tread carefully. A good multimedia card should be capable of at least 1024x768 resolution, and while much multimedia software maintains no more than 256 colors for compatibility with earlier VGA cards, some will benefit from more, and you'll be ready as the bar is raised. Good cards with 16.7 million colors can be found for about $100 more than cheap Super VGA, and are worth every penny.

Monitor: This should be at least a 15-inch model and have a dot pitch of 28mm or less. A 17-inch is worth the extra money if you can spring it, especially for multimedia. Remember, multimedia's specialty is super graphics and videos. If you're hoping to get by with your old 14-inch vanilla-VGA, do yourself a favor and get out the wallet again.

Sound Card, CD-ROM Drive, Speakers: Since these are the heart of the typical multimedia upgrade, I'm assuming you don't have them yet. If you do, evaluate them in light of their discussions in their own sections. You may find that replacing one or another of them will give you a significant improvement in multimedia performance, and for comparatively little cash.

Where the Money Meets the Multimedia

Remember how we said above that we are still paying the price for the fact that the IBM-PC was never designed to do the things we've got it doing now? Here's the point where we have to pony up for that—history has its price. If you've decided to upgrade, you obviously are going to spend some money. Only you can decide how much, but I'll try to help you sort out your options. Of course, your vision of your multimedia system has to come into play. If you must have a really hot system, the best thing is probably to buy one outright. If you can't afford two or three thousand dollars for the (current) latest-and-greatest, you may be able to upgrade your present PC gradually and affordably; and here's where your System Inventory comes into play, as discussed in the multimedia context above.

If you are looking at upgrading several major components of your PC, you can soon ring up close to the cost of a new system, at least an entry-level one. If you are, say, in reasonably good shape with a Pentium 60, 8Mb RAM, and an 850Mb hard drive, but have a 31mm dot pitch 14-inch monitor driven by a video card with 512k RAM, your system is an excellent candidate for a do-it-yourself upgrade. Since money is likely to be the major limiting factor (after all, it doesn't cost anything to have a vision or to Inventory your System), let's look at the issue from some typical upgrade possibilities at given dollar amounts, using representative costs for upgrading components. Here is where you'll have to use a little imagination; play with the possibilities, get a worksheet and pencil out.

If you own an older system, a 386 or an aging 486, consider a motherboard- or a "motherboard-plus" upgrade. Armed with this book and the $1500 it would take to buy an entry-level multimedia system, you could wind up with a much better system for the money, and you'd be able to recycle parts, plus have the satisfaction and confidence which comes from real work inside your own system. For $500 to $700, you could get a high-quality motherboard from, say, Micronics, with a fast Pentium, built-in E-IDE hard disk and CD-ROM controller, and built-in Com and parallel ports. You'd be able to reuse your case, power supply, keyboard, mouse, floppy drive, and depending on their multimedia suitability, your video card, monitor, and/or sound card. Less than $300 will buy a big, fast E-IDE hard drive. For the other $700-1,000, you could get a high-quality CD-ROM drive, good speakers, and perhaps upgrade another component, a video card or monitor perhaps. Chapters 6, 9, 12, and others appropriate to the component should guide you through the process, to wind up with a new-generation system with lots of multimedia muscle and flash.

T I P

You might take your System Inventory, put a sheet of lined or accounting paper up to its right edge, and draw an arrow from each component you need to upgrade over to the paper. Put a ballpark price for upgrading the component at the end of the arrow. Add up the column of ballparks, and you'll have a working figure for the cost of your proposed upgrade. You could use columns on the paper, and compare different levels of multimedia performance, or plan a series of upgrades to spread the cost over time.

Dialing for Dollars: How Much Can You Afford ?

N O T E

These figures are based on discounted or "street prices" current in later 1995. You should always check local stores, newspaper ads, and particularly the ads in computer magazines to get a feel for current prices. Change is certain, and most of it will be to your benefit. At least initially. Falling prices have a double edge: you are able to buy better gear than you could even a few months ago for the same money; but when it's time to sell older equipment, you'll not get much for it compared to how long you had it. This is especially true of components like sound and video cards, CD-ROM drives, hard disks, and CPUs, where the rate of innovation and change is greatest.

The $200 level: This will buy you an entry-level upgrade, with a double-speed CD-ROM drive, basic sound card, and (very) basic speakers. Or, it will buy you certain CPU upgrades, or, likely a better move, another 4Mb of RAM; in other words, this is either getting ready for an upgrade, or a bare-bones-budget upgrade.

The $300-400 level: A quad-speed CD-ROM drive and a good bundle of CD-ROMs. For the same money you could get a nice big hard drive, a very nice video card, or a new 15-inch color monitor (one of them, not all). If all you need is the multimedia components themselves, this will get you a decent Upgrade kit, with a better sound card and speakers, and possibly a 4x CD-ROM drive; this will buy you a decent, but not super, multimedia system.

The $500-800 level: Here's where the fun begins, providing you don't have to do too much preliminary upgrading. This will buy an impressively excellent sound system (card and speakers), or a superfast CD-ROM drive plus a good speaker system. Or a good 17-inch monitor, possibly with multimedia speakers built in (be sure to audition). Or an excellent video card and a quite nice upgrade kit. If you have to spend this much before you're buying the actual multimedia components, it's time to begin thinking about whether you want to put much more money than this into an older system.

Keep an eye out for bundles like the one from Diamond mentioned above. Other major players like Creative Labs also sell quality products at good prices. I recently tested a variety of these packages. The difference in a 6X or 8X CD-ROM for video and games is amazing.

The $1,000 level: If you can spend this amount on multimedia gear alone, you're going to have a wonderful system. This is the danger level if you have kids or work to do—it may be hard to keep people, including yourself, off the darn thing. If you also spend time online, you may need therapy if the system ever goes down. This money will get you a CD-ROM jukebox, a serious sound system, and enough software to make you anti-social for months. Or you could get a good upgrade kit and a 17-inch monitor.

The $1,200 level: Here you can get: a 17-inch monitor and an upgrade kit with a very fast CD-ROM drive. You could also upgrade several components of your base-level PC and get a decent kit or selection of components. But you must consider very seriously indeed whether an older system is worth this much money to upgrade. For $300 to $500 more, you could get a new system, with perhaps a few corners cut on monitor size or something similar. But your old system plus the upgrades probably wouldn't be sellable for the $1,200 you just put into it. If, on the other hand, you have a fast CPU, a good monitor, and a big hard drive, but need more memory, better video, and the actual multimedia components, you're in a pretty good position.

The $1500 level: If you're putting this kind of money into an existing system, I presume you've got it ready for top-drawer multimedia components already. Otherwise you'd be better off buying a new Pentium entry-level system, and upgrading it before too long. For $1500, you can get a top-flight CD-ROM or even a jukebox, and a sound system that's likely better than your stereo, or a real nice mix of video card, 17-inch monitor, and a top-drawer upgrade kit. Or, go get another $100 or so, and get a 21-inch monitor.

The $2000 level: This will buy you a good mail-order brand-new home system, or allow you to pretty much pick and

choose top-of-the line hardware. Unless, of course, you're looking to do some serious high-end graphics work, set up a video
studio, or produce your own multimedia. In that case, we are
leaving the boundaries of this book, which is concerned more
with the average PC owner's need to upgrade and maintain a
mainstream-level PC.

A La Carte, Kit, or KaBundle?

Another decision arrives: are you going to shop separately for your
multimedia components, or are you going to buy a kit? This decision is at least roughly analogous to the choice you make when
shopping for stereo gear. For decades the common wisdom was,
"If you're serious about audio, stick with separate components."
Manufacturers often make compromises in the quality of the individual components when they combine them. And you also are
stuck with what they chose for you. If you like their amp but not
their speakers, too bad. This was pretty good advice, and still has
considerable truth in the audio field. When it comes to total control over the components you buy, obviously you will hand pick
them and then choose a vendor. The range of kits available is
nowadays very wide, however. When the kit industry was young
not long ago, kits tended to be low-end in quality of components,
and the audiophile's advice above pretty much applied. But now
many of the hardware manufacturers themselves, especially the
sound card makers, are putting their middle-range and better products into a kit with a respectable CD-ROM drive, cables, instruction
manuals, installation software and drivers. Companies like Creative
Labs (Sound Blaster), Media Vision (ProAudio Spectrum), Diamond
Multimedia, Aztech (Sound Galaxy), and Turtle Beach have well-
established reputations for sound cards, and their kits are typically
worth a good look, especially if you like their sound cards. But
there are many others as well, sometimes featuring a name-brand
CD-ROM as the lead item; the multimedia upgrade kit is riding the
crest of the multimedia wave, and there is great variety. That's true
with prices, too; they can be as low as $130 and as high as $500
and beyond.

Getting It All Together: Kit Considerations

Let's take a close look at the issues involved in kit-buying. Doing so will open up the same sort of decisions you'll make if you go your own way, at least if you're going to upgrade thoughtfully. A "kit" is not as simple as it might first appear, and analyzing a kit is a good exercise, whether or not you decide to purchase it. This way, you'll learn about what's involved in choosing components, and if you decide to go with a kit, this will help you find the right one. Later we'll get into considerations of the separate components, especially CD-ROM drives, sound cards, and speakers, giving you some installation pointers.

Here are some points to keep in mind as you consider kits.

✔ Look carefully at the exact components. Often a name-brand unit will be coupled with a no-name. Check for specifications.

✔ Consider your usage. If you want to play a lot of DOS-based games, most of them are written for the Sound Blaster card. All cards should claim compatibility with Sound Blaster, but some actually license the chip-level code. If you are especially interested in high-quality music, look for a wavetable card with a MIDI interface. Some of these are not Sound-Blaster compatible!

✔ Is it a 16-bit card? If it isn't, don't buy it. You'll be disappointed in the lo-fi sound from an 8-bit card.

✔ If at all possible, audition the kit in a store. In any event, make sure you can return it if you're not satisfied.

✔ Be sure you know what kind of controller interface the CD-ROM has. If it's IDE or SCSI (most will be SCSI), you'll have more flexibility than if it's a proprietary one (more common than you think: Sony, Philips, Mitsumi, Panasonic). Some sound boards now have more than one interface built-in.

✔ Does it have mounting hardware for the CD-ROM drive?

✔ Is the CD-ROM drive an internal or external model? Most are internal, but there are a few external drives in kits. Make sure you have the one you want.

✔ The weakest link in upgrade kits, as with factory-based multimedia systems, are the speakers. Again, try to hear them, and don't expect too much. If the rest of the kit is solid, you can upgrade the speakers without losing much investment.

✔ Check for a microphone. If you want to add voice to presentations, use it in interactive music and learning CDs, or try out voice-recognition for dictation or commanding your PC, the basic mike you'll find in some kits will get you started.

✔ There has been an increasing trend to throw all sorts of CD-ROM bundles into the kits. Sometimes they are terrific, sometimes they're terrible. Check them out, but don't buy a mediocre upgrade kit to get a CD-ROM or two that look good.

✔ Find out if the vendor offers good technical support. If it's a retail store, look for those with on-site repair departments. Check the manufacturer's availability to offer support for the whole kit, not just their own unit. Look for an 800 number with night-time and weekend hours.

✔ Check the quality of the manuals. Look for an installation video.

✔ There are three main reasons to do your multimedia upgrade with a kit: convenience, compatibility of components, and cost-effectiveness.

This final point needs a little more discussion. Convenience and compatibility of components are very closely related; while it is convenient to pick up one box and have everything you need, it is also very convenient to have confidence that the two major components, the sound card and the CD-ROM drive, are matched well enough together to work. Incompatibilities are very inconvenient, and you increase your chances of a smooth and successful multimedia upgrade with the components guaranteed to work together. This has been historically the top reason to buy a kit. You can expect to save some money if you shop carefully, but remember that corners may well be cut. This market is very competitive, and you may find some special deals and bundles that really are good deals. Watch your step.

INSTALLING A KIT? READ ON...

Even if you buy a kit, which should come with well-done instructions, a Technical Support number, and possibly a README file on disk and an installation video, you will still benefit to read this chapter's sections describing the separate components, and installation and troubleshooting tips. The better you understand what you are doing, the smoother things will go, and the better any tune-up and troubleshooting will proceed. If you have an experienced friend, ask him or her to help. It's easy to miss a step or make a mistake, especially the first time.

SEPARATE ISSUES? HAND-PICKING YOUR MULTIMEDIA COMPONENTS

Perhaps you've decided to make your own decisions about your multimedia upgrade. We'll now consider the components separately. Just keep in mind that you are building a system, and they all have not only to work together, but should work well together.

Your PC Audio System

The phrase "PC audio system" was a dream at best and a joke at worst for most of the PC's history. You'll recall that the original system was intended for modest business and scientific work, and no one dreamed that it one day would, could, or should, rival a home stereo system, much less that it could be used to compose music and create and control what would have then been called "Audio-Visual Productions." The tinny little speaker that's still standard on a PC was really intended only to make a few clucks and beeps to inform the user of various system events like boot-up or a particular Morse-like error code. So to get much more than that out of a PC, we have to use its saving grace, the expansion bus, and dramatically expand its capabilities with a sound card, and send the card's output to an amplifier or to external speakers. From a few cards intended primarily to add arcade-like sounds to DOS-based games and play cute little melodies for children's programs, the possibilities have expanded indeed, to the point where some cards have on-board electronic synthesizers that need no apologies, and are in fact used by professional musicians and composers. Let's look at what sound cards have to do and how they do it, which, combined with your interests and budget, will give you a basis for picking one.

Adding a Sound Card—Your Computer's Voice-box

CD-ROMs and other multimedia sources can put sound in your machine, but that doesn't get it out to where you can hear it. The information contained in computerized sound is digitally formed, not the analog form that the human ear uses. In other words, the sound card must perform a digital-to-analog conversion similar to that performed by your video graphics adapter. The quality of the sound is determined by the card's sampling rate. The sampling rate is measured in bits, once again, similar to that used for graphics cards. The higher the number in bits, the more variations in sound can be represented as audio recorded or played through the system. See Figure 11.2.

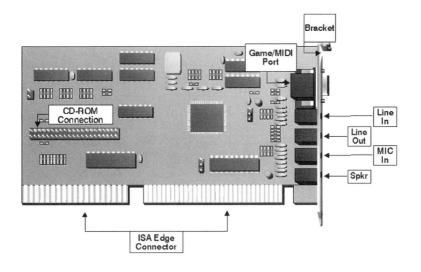

FIGURE 11.2 A high-end sound board.

By the same token, the higher the sampling rate, the more disk space per second is required to store the information. Most sound cards provide either 8- or 16-bit sampling depth. The sampling depth controls the dynamic range that the sound card can handle. A good 16-bit card can yield quality similar to that found on a CD. 8-bit cards are closer to that found with AM radio. There is no real reason today to buy an 8-bit card, since you can buy a basic 16-bit card for under $100, and a very decent 16-bit card for under $125. I have even seen the Media Vision ProAudio Spectrum, a very respectable 16-bit SCSI card with a boatload of utilities, selling for under $80! It definitely pays to shop around.

The sampling rate is a measure of how often the board actually records a source's analog wave. A general rule of thumb is that a sound card can produce a frequency no higher than half its sampling rate. Audio CD's have a sampling rate of 44.1 KHz. This reaches an upper limit of about 22,000 cycles per second, well beyond the upper limit of most people's hearing range, which rolls off sharply above 16,000Hz. High-fidelity sound is generally accepted to include a frequency response range of 20-20kHz, so most 16-bit cards should provide the basis for excellent sound. The quality of the sound you hear will depend much more on the quality of your amplifier and speakers than on the card.

Nuts and Bolts, Bits and Bytes, Waves and Tables

The actual quality of the sound card is determined by resolution, sampling rate, and by the quality of its synthesizer. Remember, computers only understand bits and bytes, and the sound card must have a way of turning them into actual sound waves that humans perceive as music and sound; in other words, your sound card must synthesize the sound waves. There are two common ways of doing this. One is called *FM Synthesis*. FM stands for *Frequency Modulation*, which means that a tone generator produces an electronic tone, which is then modulated or changed so as to synthesize analog sound waves, which can be amplified and sent to speakers. The more inexpensive boards use FM synthesis, which can do quite a good job when well-implemented. The most popular FM chip for

these cards is the Yamaha OPL-3. The other method of sound production is called *wavetable synthesis*, in which actual sound samples
(waves) are digitally recorded, compressed, and stored on a special
chip. The sound card then "looks up" the different recorded sounds
(instruments, etc.) in the "table" on the chip, and modifies them
according to the requirements of the sound, then amplifies them.
These chips were developed by top electronic synthesizer makers
such as Roland, E-mu, and Ensoniq, and are often as good as, or even
the same as, the chips they use in their keyboards and synth modules. Sound boards based on these chips, when properly matched to
other elements in your system, especially the speakers, will need no
apology as far as hi-fi stereo sound is concerned.

Let's consider a few other sound-board features you should
know about. The number of voices a board can generate refers to
the number of separate sound signals it can produce at the same
time, each corresponding more or less to an instrument. Here, the
more voices, the better: 11 used to be a common number, but you
should look for at least 20 nowadays, and 32 in the really good
boards. You will also see references to *polyphony*, which also
describes the number of separate sound-voices a card can generate.

Joysticks and MIDI

Virtually all sound boards conveniently provide you with a port
which can connect to a joystick; if you're already a gamer, you
almost certainly have a joystick already. This is a handy feature if
you intend to enjoy many of the contemporary multimedia games
and "edutainment" programs, many of which support joysticks.
Flight simulators, racing and battle games, and sports simulations
are available in enhanced (more scenarios and/or more features)
versions for CD-ROM, and are often optimized for joystick play.
The fact that this is still not included as a motherboard feature on
most PCs is one more example of the PC's backward heritage as a
rather limited, business-oriented machine. Your PC may well have
one on an I/O (Input/Output) board or on an IDE paddle board.
The port on some sound cards can also be used for MIDI, but not at

the same time as a joystick. Make sure that only one joystick port is enabled; if both are, neither will work. If you want to use the sound-card port for MIDI and you don't have another, you can buy a generic game-port card for $15 or so. These are short, 8-bit half-cards which can go into either an 8-bit slot or a 16-bit ISA slot.

Microsoft has come out with a great new joystick, in two flavors. The high-end unit is the equal of top of the line controllers like the ThrustMaster. If you are serious about games—this is the one to own. The Sidewinder 3D sells for about $60 via mail order. The standard Sidewinder is about $20 less.

Top-of-the-line boards have a *MIDI* (*Musical Instrument Digital Interface*) interface, an electronic musical standard which specifies sets of commands and the channels to send them over. This allows you to connect an electronic synthesizer or keyboard directly to your PC, which can then play sounds from a MIDI instrument or from the MIDI sound samples stored on the sound card. If you think all this is a bit much for right now, you're in luck, for many boards are themselves upgradable. For around $100, you can buy a plug-in module or a daughterboard with high-end features on it. But you have to pick an upgradable board initially.

Another exciting development is called *DSP*, for the Digital Signal Processor chip. This is actually a dedicated, highly-flexible microprocessor which can contain a number of functions. These are beginning to show up on the highest-price boards, where they will be used for recording-studio audio enhancements like echo and chorus. DSP chips can do a great deal more, however, and they are beginning to appear on high-end motherboards ready to assume the functions of modems and fax-modems, sound cards, telephony functions, and more. The potential is at hand to make separate cards for these and other familiar functions obsolete! At that point the PC will at last have the kind of built-in standard functionality it has needed all these years. The PC will have, in a critical element of design philosophy, caught up to the pioneering example set by Commodore and Apple long ago. Expect to pay a premium, if you want DSP in the shorter term; the newest, neatest stuff is almost always the most expensive.

A Blast from the Past, A Window into the Future

It's impossible to talk about PC sound boards without discussing Sound Blaster, and it also affords us the opportunity to provide a wider perspective on the past, present, and future of the multimedia PC. One of the earliest sound cards, Sound Blaster quickly became a standard as DOS game publishers supported it in droves. In DOS, a software engineer has to write a specific driver program for a particular device to interpret his commands for sound production. As we said above, IBM never conceived of the PC as a sound system, so when we wanted it to become one, every software company had to do the driver-writing job from the ground up; there were no standard rules to help—or to make one company's games sounds work with several different sound cards (which weren't standardized either). Writing drivers for hardware is neither quick, easy, nor fun, so most game developers, being in the game-writing and not the driver-writing business, chose to support the Sound Blaster from Creative Labs.

This *de facto* standard acquired such momentum that all but a few sound cards (like Microsoft's business-oriented Sound System) either license the technology from Creative Labs, or try to clone it. The latter approach is what is meant by the phrase "Sound-Blaster compatible" found on boxes and in ads. Some efforts are better than others, and if you play a lot of DOS-based games, you may be just as well off getting a board made by the originators. Creative Labs, which was busy making big money as the demand for multi-media systems started to build, lost momentum for a while, but has regained it and their best boards (such as the AWE 32) are right out there on the edge again. Windows, which largely relieved program developers from writing hardware device drivers by taking the function within the operating system where it belonged all along, has made Sound-Blaster compatibility much less important, and Windows 95, with significant strides towards true Plug and Play upgrades, should continue the trend. As multimedia systems gain the hardware muscle for better multimedia and the operating-system support, more and more programs are supporting more advanced standards, like MIDI. The enormously popular game MYST, is one very powerful example.

INSTALLING A SOUND BOARD

Before You Start

If you are also installing a SCSI CD-ROM drive at the same time as your sound card, or have one installed already, you must be sure you have the right cables and that the interfaces are compatible. If your CD-ROM drive uses an IDE interface, you can skip over the SCSI-specific instructions which follow; you will still require the correct audio cable. If your drive does have a SCSI interface (and up until recently, most do, because of faster performance; it remains to be seen if E-EIDE gains broad support from manufacturers) it will need a SCSI controller, called a *host adapter*. If you already have a SCSI system, you will add the CD-ROM into the SCSI chain as a new device, as explained below and in Chapter 10. If you don't, your sound card must provide one. Many do, but you need to know what type of SCSI your CD-ROM drive is, and pick the right cable; you may need some type of SCSI cable adapter as well.

 I strongly recommend that you consult Chapter 10 for a working knowledge of SCSI, especially concerning SCSI types and cables, IDs and terminations, and the section on CD-ROM drives. You really do need to know this stuff!

NOTE

A second cable will be needed to provide the audio signal from the CD-ROM to the sound card. In yet another example of the problems caused by lack of standards in the PC world, although the audio signal is standardized, the audio cable isn't. Or more exactly, the types of plugs and jacks it uses are not. Sound cards bought alone will usually not have a cable set in the box with them; the sound card manufacturers have no way of knowing what CD-ROM drive you have, so they don't include them. They will often be able to sell you a cable kit for a particular CD-ROM drive, once you know yourself and call them. This takes extra time and several dollars. Avoiding these frustrations is a big reason why upgrade kits are so popular—you don't have to go through the process of matching sound cards, CD-ROM drives, and their cables.

If you have an external CD-ROM drive, it should have come with a bracket which includes the jacks for the audio cable(s) and the SCSI cable. This bracket requires a slot on the back of your PC, though not an expansion slot per se. Investigate your slot configuration, usage, and availability to choose the best slot. You may have to rearrange some other boards. Consult Chapter 5 if you need information on installing, removing, and replacing expansion cards.

What You'll Need

✔ Small and large screwdrivers

✔ Cup or other container for screws and small parts

✔ Your System Inventory of currently-installed peripherals with their DMA, IRQ, and I/O assignments, and a piece of paper to log your installation step-by-step to aid in troubleshooting; your Dark and Stormy Night Disk, Windows Rescue Disk

✔ Sound board and installation manual; and CD-ROM drive manual if you have one

✔ Appropriate data and audio cables with the correct plugs on the ends (if you have or are installing a CD-ROM drive)

✔ Sound Board installation and utility software (and also for CD-ROM if you have one)

✔ Possibly a pair of pliers or hemostat for adjusting jumpers

Step 1

Review your sound card (and CD-ROM drive if you have one) installation instructions. Pay particular attention to diagrams and instructions for setting jumpers and switches. If you have a software installation disk, look for a Readme file, wherein the latest tips, warnings, and fixes are often provided by the maker's technical support.

Step 2

Begin to log your actions carefully, step-by-step, on a piece of paper. Power down the computer and disconnect the power cord and any other cable connections that might get in the way.

Step 3

Refer to your System Inventory, check the jumper and DIP switch settings to avoid DMA, IRQ, and port assignment conflicts (see Chapter 5), and adjust as needed. If you already are using a joystick, you'll want to disable the game port on your sound card; if two joystick ports are enabled, neither will work.

Step 4

Make sure you have taken steps to avoid static electricity. Remove the card and any accessories, along with the documentation, from the box the card came in.

If you are also installing a CD-ROM drive, you should probably install it first into its bay; remember you'll have to run the proper cables from the CD-ROM to the sound card, and it may be awkward to do the sound card first.

Step 5

Remove the cover from the case and then remove the edge cover from an appropriate slot.

Step 6

Install the card, using gentle but firm pressure to seat it in the expansion slot. See Figure 11.3.

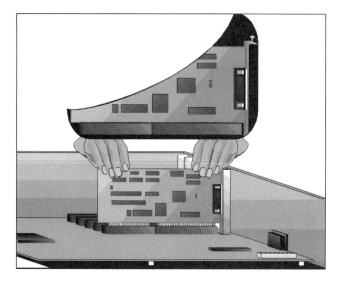

FIGURE 11.3 Installing a sound card.

Step 7

If you have a CD-ROM drive, connect the data and audio cables from the drive to the sound card. On the rear panel of your sound board there will be speaker jacks. Check the documentation which came with your board or the labels on the back plate for instructions on how to connect speakers.

Step 8

Install the software that will use the new card. Restart Windows or reboot the system as needed and run the program. Make sure the sound card is working properly. Test other devices, like a mouse or scanner. Make sure the new card is not interfering with their operation. Run a multimedia test or other program to see if everything is working. If not, carefully review all your steps. It is probably caused by a resource conflict (DMA, IRQ, I/O). Check your Readme files and manuals for trouble-shooting tips. If you still have problems, call technical support.

Step 9

Once you know that your sound board is operating properly, you can power down the system and replace your case cover.

A WORD ON THE MIKE: USING MICROPHONES

Most multimedia PC users will be satisfied with the microphones included in some CD-ROM upgrade kits. These are usually quite adequate for voice command and recording purposes, which do not require a very broad frequency-response curve and are relatively inexpensive to make. If you want to do studio-quality recording, invest $50 or $100 in a good mike. No matter how good the system itself or the announcer, you won't sound really good without a really good mike. Although the better multimedia upgrade sound cards and kits come with reasonably good audio mixing capabilities, and all sound cards can record sound to disk (where it takes up very large amounts of room), and although it's beyond our present scope to go deeply into the production side of multimedia, when shopping for a mike, you have to consider the *impedance* (a characteristic of electrical resistance), the pick-up type and pattern (some mikes are better for voice work, some for general work, some for instruments), and the *capacitance*. These characteristics have to be matched to the pre-amplifier in your sound card, and of course the plug on the end of the mike cord has to match the jack type on the sound card; usually this will be the sub-mini type. If not, adapters are easily available at electronics stores and music shops.

CD-ROM DRIVES

They've been around for about ten years, and only wildly popular for two. But the CD-ROM drive and its companion the CD-ROM disc, have been the "enabling technology" of what might be seriously called the *multimedia revolution*. These disc spinners, adapted from the Compact Disc Digital Audio format, were first used primarily to store scientific and research databases. With more storage capacity than the largest then-common hard disks, when they came out

CD-ROM drives went through the usual growing pains of struggling for standards and support, and emerged in the early 1990s, poised to be the vehicle of tremendous growth.

For more of the technical side of how CD-ROMs work, see their section in Chapter 10.

NOTE

It has long been an adage in the computer business that "software sells hardware." The best-known example of this is the mid-1980s introduction of Lotus 1-2-3, the spreadsheet-database-graphics program which convinced businesspeople that PCs were business tools, not curiosities; computers, monitors, printers, and other programs began to fly off the shelves, and a niche market became a mainstream phenomenon. The PC revolution achieved liftoff almost overnight.

CD-ROM has not had a single program which itself directly drove so many people to buy the hardware to run it, but several factors combined to set the stage for the explosive growth we have seen in the past year or so, and which promises to continue for several more. These reasons largely have to do with Windows, especially Version 3.1. That version got things functional and attractive enough so that people wanted to buy the hardware to run it. Graphics boards improved to meet the need to handle the huge amount of data the Windows graphic screens required; monitors got bigger, sharper, and more colorful to make using the graphic interface easier and more fun; and the need for bigger, faster hard drives to handle the huge files has led to the great bargains we enjoy today.

During this period the CD-ROM drive was, more or less, ready, and when people discovered that sound and video files played under Windows could make for more entertaining users of the computer, it provided a relatively cheap, reliable means of storing huge numbers of files on an inexpensive plastic disc. The technology of disc and drive was essentially right there to be borrowed from the audio industry, and off it went. As I said earlier, the CD-ROM is already beginning to replace the floppy drive in some systems, especially entry-level home and multimedia PCs and some multi media laptops, and a new system should not be considered without one installed. Multimedia aside, you don't want to be without one, so let's look briefly at the technical side, and move on to selecting and installing them.

Speeds and Specs and MPC

Today's CD-ROM drives are really a variation of the audio CD (compact disc) introduced in the early 1980's. In fact, with appropriate and universally-available software, a CD-ROM drive can play audio as well (a nice bonus to consider when picking or upgrading a multimedia system; it isn't only game sounds and incidental music you can enjoy hearing over your PC's audio sub-system). Virtually all CD-ROM drives, because of the nature of digital audio, are capable of high-fidelity stereo sound. What you actually hear will depend more on the quality of the other audio components in the chain, notably the sound card, its amplifier, any secondary amplifier, and your speaker system.

The original CD-ROM drives could transfer data at 150Kb per second (now called *single-speed* or *1x* drives), which given the huge amounts of data needed for graphic screens and multimedia sound and video files, quickly proved inadequate. Small windows with grainy, halting images, often accompanied by stuttering sound out of sync with the video, were popular more for their novelty than their ability to provide a convincing multimedia experience. Much of this lackluster performance was due to the slow 150Kb per second data transfer speed; remember that an average hard disk today, while slower than transfers using RAM, is still easily ten times as fast as that. Manufacturers have consistently attempted to provide better performance, and the first result was the *double-speed (2x)* drive, which logically enough, moved data at 300Kb per second. Soon afterwards, *triple-speed (3x)* drives appeared, but never found wide acceptance, probably because *quad-speed (4x)* drives which worked at 600Kb per second appeared not long afterward. For quite a time (in this industry) double-speed drives became standard in all but the most rock-bottom multimedia systems, but have been giving way to the quad-speed models since the even faster 6x and 8x drives have 'appeared. These new drives are finally getting fast enough to provide reasonably acceptable motion video. See Figure 11.4.

FIGURE 11.4 The NEC multi-CD changer.

Buying a CD-ROM Drive

The Faster the Better

As is probably obvious by now, speed is your first consideration when choosing a CD-ROM drive. You should consider a quad speed (4x) drive as the minimum acceptable configuration. There are now drives available for around $200 at this speed, and the price can be expected to continue to drop. 6x drives transfer data at 900 Kb per second and are a much better choice, but you'll likely need more than $400. These prices, too, are likely to drop considerably as economies of scale continue to operate. Be sure to check current newspapers and magazines like *Computer Shopper* for current prices before you buy. The first of the 8X drives are here, with speeds over 1.8 Mb a second. Watch out for access times. Some "hot" drives have slow access. IDE is slower than SCSI. In general, get a unit with at least 150ms for SCSI. Some IDEs are as slow as 235ms. This slows down program loads and can make data retrieval painful—even at 8x. It can be OK for video and most games.

NOTE

Much multimedia software is "optimized" for 256-color SVGA and 2x drives. More speed may be largely wasted on such software. But with 4x coming on as the entry-level, multimedia in general booming, and WIN95 making things easier (?), more and more CD-ROMs will start to support more color and 4x and above speeds.

Internal and External, Portable and Combo

As with modems, CD-ROM drives are available as both internal and external models, and similarly, the caseless internal models cost $75-$150 less than the external models. If you have the internal space, and don't anticipate moving your CD-ROM drive to other PCs, you can save some money with an internal model, especially if you are thinking about buying an upgrade kit, most of which come with internal models. If you have a laptop, or a system which accepts PCMCIA cards (PC cards), there are now portable CD-ROM drives available from Panasonic and Sony which look like (and are) modified portable CD-ROM audio players; of course they do play audio CDs too, and the Sony model can function independently as a portable audio CD player. These are, at this point, double-speed drives, and cost $125-$150 more than double-speed internal drives. Another portable CD-ROM approach is from MicroSolutions, the people who make the Backpack tape units; their Backpack 4x CD-ROM also uses your PC's parallel port for simple attachment and fast data transmission, and costs under $400. See Figure 11.5.

FIGURE 11.5 A portable CD-ROM drive.

One of the interesting choices available relatively recently is the multi-disc CD-ROM player, or *jukebox*. These units were introduced by Pioneer, well-known for innovative hardware in the audio industry, especially that dealing with lasers and audio (for example, laserdiscs, another form of multimedia). These first jukeboxes were external units, held six CD-ROM discs, and cost around $1200. They have been, predictably, dropping in price, and will probably settle at about half of that. Meanwhile, other familar companies in the audio field, like NEC and JVC, have entered the market with jukeboxes in the $400-$600 price range. Internal units which handle from 3 to 7 CD-ROM discs have recently appeared, and as they offer superior convenience, will probably rise quickly in popularity.

Why consider a multi-player jukebox, you say, if CD-ROMs can hold 650Mb of programs and data and A-V files, often in compressed form? Most of us humans like to follow the well-known, well-worn "path of least resistance" (read, convenience is King). Programmers are no exception, and it's faster and easier to write large-size program files (called "bloated code" in some quarters) than smaller, more space-efficient programs; so, applications themselves tend to grow. Also, we like lots of features these days, and they take room too. Remember, also, that multimedia and graphics files are huge, measured in megabytes rather than kilobytes. And, as more programs are available on CD-ROM, some only so, how nice to have several discs already loaded and ready to run.

There's another reason. Although several standard-length major encyclopedias can fit on a single CD-ROM disc, several games, like the groundbreaking *7th Guest* (if there is a single program which kick-started CD-ROM sales, this may be it), *Under a Killing Moon,* and *Wing Commander III,* are already multi-disk releases, and there are several multi-disk shareware sets around. Most of us would rather not disk-swap, especially if a new part of the haunted castle or another combat mission requires us to insert Disc 2 or Disc 3. That's even worse than the old 8-track audio tapes, which often interrupted a long, juicy jam with an enormous *clunk-a-chunk* and a pause which seemed to last forever. Jukeboxes should be *very* popular.

Caddy and Carry

Another feature to consider is whether to get a drive which uses a *caddy*. A caddy is a plastic case which holds the CD-ROM disc; you then push the caddy into the drive and it snaps down into place as do audio cassettes in car stereos. It is then ready to play (automatically if Windows 95 Autostart recognizes it). You push an **Eject** button, and the caddy pops back out of the drive. The other type of disc-loading system is the sliding drawer, quite familar on audio CD-ROM players. You push a button, the door opens; you push a button, the door closes. You must remember to be careful, though; you don't want to drag or hit the bottom of the disk on the corner of the door and scratch it.

The caddy system can add to the cost of a drive when you buy it, and you'll probably want to buy extra caddies as well. But the caddy system is intended for the protection of your disc, which, unlike an audio CD-ROM, can cost you in the hundreds of dollars if it is your master disk for a high-end program. At this point you wouldn't consider backing up 650Mb or so onto floppy disks, and you're unlikely to have a CD-R (which allows you to record your own CD-ROMs). So the purpose here is to protect the unprinted side of the disc, which holds the bits and bytes, from being scratched. One tiny chip or scratch in the wrong place, and a program or part of one could crash. This kind of damage is never good, since you have damaged your master copy of a program, or, if you are running it from the CD-ROM, perhaps cause it to bomb or refuse to run. You may have gotten the idea from the hype around the introduction of the audio CD-ROM that the discs are virtually indestructible; they are less subject to damage and not subject to wear, unlike the vinyl LP records they have replaced, but they are NOT immune to serious, even fatal damage. The basic idea here is, the less handling, the better. The caddy protects them from unnecessary handling (except when inserting and removing from the caddy, of course). You can also store frequently-used CD-ROMs in caddies, and, since the upper or label side shows through the clear plastic cover of the caddy, quickly pick out a CD-ROM for playing without handling it every time. This is an added safeguard if smaller children will be using the system—quite likely with multimedia systems. If you are going to use the CD-ROM disc on another system, caddies make an easy, safe way to transport the disc.

The downsides: caddies have come down in price somewhat, but they aren't exactly cheap, either—expect to pay $4-$5 apiece. Another, though rare, thing is that the little plastic tabs on a caddy, that you squeeze to allow the lid to open, can break off, ruining the caddy. If a part of a tab should break off while you're putting the caddy into the drive door, the caddy could jam in the drive.

Fortunately, your drive will probably have a small hole to push a paper clip into and open the door if it gets stuck or the power is off (the button which ejects the caddy requires power on some models, just a push on others). See Figure 11.6.

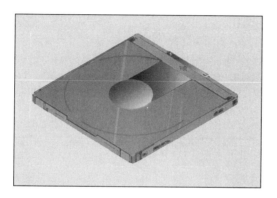

FIGURE 11.6 A CD-ROM caddy.

At the beginning of the CD-ROM's life, virtually all drives used the caddy system; now most seem not to, doubtless because it helps keep the price of what is now a mass-market piece of consumer electronic goods down. If you prefer one system over the other, this adds another little twist to your search.

Many caddy-less drives will not allow you to run a disc unless the drive is installed flat. If you put in in sideways—it won't run.

NOTE

On the Horizon (Coming Attractions)

Audio/CD merges: Since they are at bottom using the same technology, it is natural for Digital Audio and CD-ROM to merge. Typically, forward-looking artists and musicians like Todd Rungren, Peter Gabriel, Prince, The Residents, Bob Dylan, and Brian Eno are releasing CD-ROMs that have music tracks and music videos integrated with more static information, serach and reference capabilities, and games and amusements. Very likely this trend will spread, especially as storage and processing power continue to become cheaper. Already new hardware and software is appearing which can tell whether digital information on a CD is in audio or video format and play it back appropriately (if you try to play the wrong kind of track on an audio CD player, you can destroy your speakers).

Higher-capacity CD-ROMs: Having found wide acceptance, the CD's main limitations now are speed and capacity. The newer 6x and 8x drives are addressing the former need, and IBM has announced a higher-capacity CD-ROM which will hold up to 10 times the present capacity of 650Mb or so. The potential for such capacity at, eventually, a reasonable cost, along with the increasing affordability of CD-R (recording) units is tremendous.

WARNING

If you are installing, or have already installed, a sound card, be sure you have obtained the correct audio connection cable. These are not standardized. Your sound card manufacturer should be able to sell you a cable kit for your particular sound card and drive.

INSTALLING A CD-ROM DRIVE

Installing an External SCSI CD-ROM Drive

If you are already familiar with SCSI, placing an external CD-ROM on a system with an existing SCSI adapter is simple (if not, consult Chapter 10). Just decide where on the chain it will sit, assign it a unique SCSI ID and power down the system. Attach it to the SCSI chain using an appropriate cable and make sure that the last device on the string is properly terminated. With Windows 95 or NT, you are ready to go.

For DOS and oder versions of Windows, boot the machine and install the device module and if necessary the MSCDEX extensions, as described in the operating system documentation. *MSCDEX* stands for Microsoft CD-ROM Extensions. This is a device driver that is loaded to allow DOS, which does not normally have the ability to recognize CD-ROM drives, to recognize and read the files on one. If you run into any problems, refer to the troubleshooting tips in Chapter 10. See Figure 11.7.

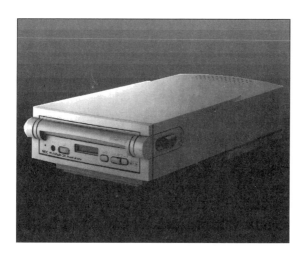

FIGURE 11.7 An external CD-ROM drive.

Internal SCSI CD-ROM Drives

Internal SCSI CD-ROM drives are added to the system much like the installation of a SCSI hard disk. First make sure the device is assigned a unique ID number on the SCSI chain. Generally CD-ROMs are assigned numbers between three and six, depending on the other devices on the chain. If it is the only internal device on the system, it should be terminated and the host adapter should be unterminated. If other devices are placed further on the chain than the CD-ROM, make sure it is unterminated and that the last device on the chain is terminated.

What You Will Need

✔ The drive and its manuals, including any software

✔ Your System Inventory with its list of previously-installed periph-erals and their DMA, IRQ, and I/O assignments. A piece of paper to log your installation steps. Your Dark and Stormy Night Disk, Windows Rescue Disk

✔ Appropriate power, data, and audio cables

✔ Appropriate mounting hardware (rails, spacers, etc.)

✔ A Philips-head screwdriver

✔ A flat blade or torq screwdriver

✔ Possibly a hemostat or tweezers to set the drive-select jumper

Read your installation manual, noting especially any diagrams or step-by-step instructions. Also check for a Readme file on your installation disk, which will often have late-breaking notes and workarounds for problems. Perform any preliminary steps as called for by the manufacturer.

Get out your System Inventory, which presumably you made when you read Chapter 5. You'll obviously be adding something to it, and you'll need its list of DMA, IRQ, and I/O assignments. Update your Dark and Stormy Night Disk or your Windows Rescue disk; if you haven't made one yet, make it now (see Chapter 3), before you start. Installation software for CD-ROM drives will need to modify your AUTOEXEC.BAT and CONFIG.SYS files, and you'll want to be able to start over if you need to do some tuning of DMA, IRQ, and I/O assignments (See Chapter 4 if you need help). A Windows Uninstall program might also prove extremely useful.

Get a piece of paper and carefully write down each step in the installation process as you make it. This log will be a blessing if you have to tune up, which you may well, or call Technical Support for help, enabling you to reread your vendor's instructions step-by-step and check to see if you followed them.

Uncable your system completely, then remove its cover. Take a few moments to check the layout of your system, and if it is an internal drive, plan where you'll put it. Make sure there is enough room to run power, data, and audio cables without strain. Then carefully unpack the drive, making sure to wear a static-cancelling strap or to touch your computer's chassis. Check the manual and make any preliminary preparations with jumpers and switches.

N O T E

If you're installing an external CD-ROM drive, skip the instructions for installation into the case. Your main concern is with cabling and terminations.

Slide the drive into place and make sure that it is far enough back to fit a cover panel in front of it, that it doesn't obstruct any other drive bays, and that there is adequate spacing for ventilation. This is the test fit. See Figure 11.8.

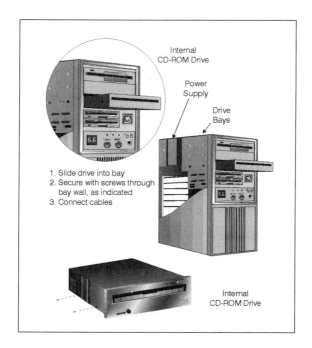

FIGURE 11.8 Installing a CD-ROM drive.

Now remove the drive and attach the mounting brackets and/or rails on the other side in the same orientation as the ones already installed. Now place the drive into the bay and fasten it down with screws. Regarding a tower case, you'll have to fasten the screws from the side of the case. In a desktop case there is usually some sort of retaining clip that often looks like a square washer. If you are installing the drive in a desktop case, you will probably have to use some kind of mounting rail before sliding the drive into the bay. These are attached using two screws each.

If you are placing a 5.25-inch drive into a tower case, all you'll probably have to do is slide it into a bay from the front of the case (you'll have to remove the cover of the case first by unscrewing the screws at the back of the tower and removing the shroud). Once you have slid it into the bay, fasten it with four mounting screws through the slots on either side of the bay. Be sure not to use screws that are too long. If you do, they may actually penetrate through to the board on the drive and damage it. Once the drive is fastened, plug in a power lead from the power supply. This lead will have four wires, usually one red, one yellow and two black. Most 5.25-inch drives will have a plug about 1 inch across which can only be seated one way, since two of the corners are rounded and the others are square cut. See Figure 11.9. Once you have attached the power cable to the drive, locate the pins on your hard disk controller or SCSI host adapter, and attach the data cable.

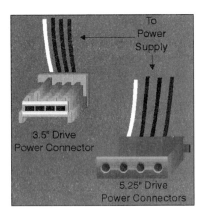

FIGURE 11.9 Connecting a power plug.

If you have a sound card, connect the audio cable to the sound card. Refer to the section earlier on installing sound cards.

Power up the system and load the software. You'll have to reboot for the changes to take effect; in DOS, watch your-boot-up screen to be sure MSCDEX loads. In Windows 3.1, you'll probably run a file called INSTALL, SETUP, or something similar, which will load the drivers and make necessary changes to WIN.INI and SYSTEM.INI. In Windows 95, the new Plug and Play capability may live up to its name and pre-release billing, find your drive, load your software, and reconfigure everything. Then again, it may not.

In all of these cases, you may have to check for the presence of the right device drivers, and for conflicts with system resources, and do some trial and error work. Record what you do and the results, so you can retrace your steps if needed. *Make only one change at a time, then test*. If it doesn't work, return to the previous setup so that you don't complicate matters and confusions further. Remember, you can call your vendor's Technical Support. It will help enormously if you have an accurate System Inventory and a log of your steps at hand when you call.

Installing an IDE CD-ROM Drive

This process is essentially like installing a SCSI drive, except you won't have to concern yourself with SCSI IDs and terminations. You'll want to get ready and proceed in basically the same way.

What You Will Need

✔ The drive and its manuals, including any software

✔ Appropriate power, data, and audio cables

✔ Your System Inventory with its list of previously-installed peripherals and their DMA, IRQ, and I/O assignments. A piece of paper to log your installation steps. Your Dark and Stormy Night Disk, Windows Rescue Disk

✔ Appropriate mounting hardware (rails, spacers, etc.)

✔ A Philips-head screwdriver

✔ A flat blade or torq screwdriver

✔ Possibly a hemostat or tweezers to set the drive-select jumper

Read your installation manual, noting especially any diagrams or step-by-step instructions. Also check for a Readme file on your installation disk, which will often have late-breaking notes and workarounds for problems. Perform any preliminary steps as called for by the manufacturer.

Get out your System Inventory, which presumably you made when you read Chapter 5. You'll obviously be adding something to it, and you'll need its list of DMA, IRQ, and I/O assignments. Update your Dark and Stormy Night Disk or your Windows Rescue disk; if you haven't made one yet, make it now (see Chapter 3), before you start. Installation software for CD-ROM drives will need to modify your AUTOEXEC.BAT and CONFIG.SYS files, and you'll want to be able to start over if you need to do some tuning of DMA, IRQ, and I/O assignments (See Chapter 4 if you need help). A Windows Uninstall program might also prove extremely useful.

Get a piece of paper and carefully write down each step in the installation process as you make it. This log will be a blessing if you have to tune up, which you may well, or call technical support for help, enabling you to reread your vendor's instructions step-by-step and check to see if you followed them.

Uncable your system completely, then remove its cover. Take a few moments to check the layout of your system, and if it's an internal drive, plan where you'll put it. Make sure there is enough room to run power, data, and audio cables without strain. Then carefully unpack the drive, making sure to wear a static-cancelling strap or to touch your computer's chassis. Check the manual and make any preliminary preparations with jumpers and switches.

If you're installing an external drive, skip the following instructions for installing into the case. Your main concern is with cabling the drive up properly.

NOTE

Slide the drive into place and make sure that it is far enough back to fit a cover panel in front of it, that it doesn't obstruct any other drive bays, and that there is adequate spacing for ventilation. This is the test fit. See Figure 11.8, earlier in this chapter.

Now remove the drive and attach the mounting brackets and/or rails on the other side in the same orientation as the ones already installed. Now place the drive into the bay and fasten it down with screws. Regarding a tower case, you'll have to fasten the screws from the side of the case. In a desktop case there is usually some sort of retaining clip that often looks like a square washer. If you are installing the drive in a desktop case, you will probably have to use some kind of mounting rail before sliding the drive into the bay. These are attached using two screws each.

If you are placing a 5.25-inch drive into a tower case, all you'll probably have to do is slide it into a bay from the front of the case (you'll have to remove the cover of the case first by unscrewing the screws at the back of the tower and removing the shroud). Once you have slid it into the bay, fasten it with four mounting screws through the slots on either side of the bay. Be sure not to use screws that are too long. If you do, they may actually penetrate through to the board on the drive and damage it. Once the drive is fastened, plug in a power lead from the power supply. This lead will have four wires, usually one red, one yellow and two black. Most 5.25-inch drives will have a plug about 1 inch across which can only be seated one way, since two of the corners are rounded and the others are square cut. See Figure 11.9, earlier. Once you have attached the power cable to the drive, locate the pins on your hard disk controller, and attach the data cable.

Power up the system and load the software. You'll have to reboot for the changes to take effect; in DOS, watch your-boot-up screen to be sure MSCDEX loads. In Windows 3.1, you'll probably run a file called INSTALL, SETUP, or something similar, which will load the drivers and make necessary changes to WIN.INI and SYSTEM.INI. In Windows 95, the new Plug and Play capability may live up to its name and pre-release billing, find your drive, load your software, and reconfigure everything. Then again, it may not.

In all of these cases, you may have to check for the presence of the right device drivers, and for conflicts with system resources, and do some trial and error work. Record what you do and the results, so you can retrace your steps if needed. *Make only one change at a time, then test.* If it doesn't work, return to the previous setup so that you don't complicate matters and confusions further. Remember, you can call your vendor's technical support. It will help enormously if you have an accurate System Inventory and a log of your steps at hand when you call.

Speakers—Your PC's Voice

Arriving at last at your speakers, your PC's digital sound splashes into the air and makes its bid to really ice the multimedia cake. Will it be a boom or a bust for better, balanced sound? Perhaps more than any other part of your multimedia PC, your speaker system's quality has really little to do with your PC as a computer. Evaluating speakers can be done pretty much the same way you'd upgrade your stereo system, by knowing how to match them to the rest of the audio system, what to seek and what to avoid, and by listening. After a brief bit of background, we'll try to show you how to do that.

A cynic with hi-fi experience would say that the speakers in many upgrade kits are, well, almost unspeakably bad. Of course, the quality of sound you get improves as you go up the price ladder, but the fact remains that the speakers are an attractive target for cost-cutting, especially in kits. See Figure 11.10. Some speakers cost as little as $20 per pair bought separately; anyone expecting rich, wide-range sound at that price probably thinks a 386DX-16 is

a good buy at $600 ($60, maybe). There are some good speakers at
$100 or less, and the high end, around $300, needs few apologies
even for audiophiles.

FIGURE 11.10 Typical inexpensive upgrade-kit speakers.

Round and Round, and it Comes out Here

If you read the high-fidelity magazines or hang out around audiophiles, it won't be too long before you read or hear someone say
that "this or that component is the most important, because... "
The sound reproduction chain consists of a sound source (say from
a cassette deck or a CD-ROM player), a preamplifier, an amplifier,
and the speaker system (here *system* means that usually there are at
least two speakers, carefully matched for balanced sound). Some
audio advisors will say spend a little more money on the speakers,
proportionately, if you are unable to flat-out buy or upgrade to the
audio system of your dreams all at once. After all, they say the
speakers are the final element in the chain, and the one you actually

hear. If they're bad, it doesn't matter if everything ahead of them in the chain is good, your system as a whole won't sound good. And they're right. But. Others will say, if the sound is not pure at the very beginning of the reproduction process, any imperfections will be literally amplified all along the way. There's truth here, also. And others make the case for the amplifier as most important, since it takes a very tiny signal and makes it thousands of times bigger, so any of its imperfections will have an enormous, proportionately large effect on what you actually hear. Who's right at last? That's a tough call, but since most of the sound coming from your PC has a digital origin, it's going to be pretty good; the quality of the preamp circuit on your sound card, and its amplifier circuit, will obviously have influence, but these are mostly standardized parts of decent quality. It's probably what happens to your audio signal after it leaves the Out jack on your sound card that makes the most difference.

Your sound card has a modest amplifier, which will put out a modest signal strength of 3 to 4 watts. This is enough to drive a pair of small, highly-efficient speakers without their own amp, but for really big and satisfying sound, they should have their own amplifier—which itself may be of dubious quality with inexpensive speakers. What you really need for really good sound is a good second amplifier, like your stereo amp, or a good multimedia speaker system with a good amp.

The Same, Only Different

This is one of the differences between multimedia speaker systems and regular stereo gear—the multimedia speakers will usually have their own amplifiers, and increasingly, tone controls built-in, while few stereo speakers systems are amplified, because that gives the owner less choice and ability to upgrade. A second difference is that multimedia speakers must be well-shielded electrically, so their magnets do not affect your PC's circuitry; this is why it is not a good idea to hook up just any old speakers you have around to your sound card, set them up by your PC, and let 'er rip. And the bigger the magnet, the bigger its field.

Battery powered speakers may not be shielded and are subject to declining performance and possibly may cause magnetic interference. $50 more for "powered speakers" may be worth it.

NOTE

Otherwise, what makes good speakers in the stereo system makes good speakers in the multimedia realm. Look for a wide frequency response, with little variation. The standard high fidelity range is 20-20kHz, but in practice, no small speaker set, excepting perhaps the 3-piece systems with separate subwoofers, will even approach 20Hz, which is so low it is felt more than heard anyway. Similarly, at the upper end of the spectrum, most people's ability (or desire) to hear sound much above 16,000Hz quickly diminishes. But little variation in sound level (*decibels*, or db) between 100Hz and 16,000Hz would indicate decent speakers. Distortion figures should be well under 10 per cent. One tip-off to mediocre speakers will be the lack of any real specifications at all, though decent-sounding speakers may not provide many either. High end speaker systems, such as those made by Altec-Lansing, Advent, Bose, Koss, and Cambridge should give you meaningful specs. As you may know, these represent some of the best names in the audio speaker market, and you should be happy with their multimedia product line.

Sound Shapes

Multimedia speakers systems come in many shapes and sizes. Picking which is right for you depends on your PC's physical setup, your ears, and your budget.

If you buy an upgrade kit, it will usually have speakers in it. You pay your money and plug them in. At least at first. If they are truly the weak link in your multimedia chain, you can always replace them. All you need is more money.

NOTE

Most multimedia speaker systems are fairly small, so they can sit next to or near your PC and not take up much room. It's difficult to get good sound out of small speakers, especially with the low or bass end of the audio spectrum, and especially when you turn them up. This is the quick way to spot low-end speakers in the store—crank them up, and if you grimace and they rattle and hum, they're not good. But PC multimedia fans can ride on audiophile's shoulders here also, as they do with the digital sound and video they get from the audio CD-ROM technology. Companies like Bose and Cambridge have revolutionized stereo speaker systems in recent years with drastic advances in speaker technology. *Satellite systems*, as they are called, are typically two small speakers, no bigger than a soft drink can, coupled with a subwoofer, a bass speaker in a small cabinet which you can put anywhere (bass is non-directional). These are literally astonishing in the size and quality of the sound they can produce—just as good as systems costing many times their $300 price (unless you need to entertain your neighbors as well as yourself). These systems are the cream of the multimedia crop, and you should at least audition them. Some of them are sold by mail with a 30-day moneyback guarantee. If you try these, you'll want them.

In the $100-150 range speakers systems seem to be appearing like video cards were as few years ago; since this multimedia market-place is exploding, as the marketing types say; there are countless firms, new and old, jumping into the fray. Try to hear what you buy first, if at all possible with program material you know. In a retail store you should be able to bring in a CD-ROM you know well, and play it using the demo PC's CD-player software through the speakers you're considering. If you can't do that, be sure you can return the speakers if you don't like them. Do this also if you're buying by direct mail from ads in magazines. After all, the best place to audition audio equipment is where you'll be using it.

Of course, you don't have to buy a special multimedia speaker system; if you want to use an existing stereo rig, it will work fine, with a couple of cautions. One, be sure it's capable of digital sound reproduction, especially the speakers. If they're approaching ten years old or more, use caution. Digital sound has terrific dynamic range, and you could blow out older speakers with a burst of high-volume game-noise. Second, keep the speakers at least a short distance away from the PC—they probably won't be magnetically shielded as multimedia speakers are. Beyond that, enjoy!

I should also mention a recent trend—monitors with multimedia speaker systems built in (or actually, onto the sides of the monitor cabinet). Viewsonic, one of the better monitor brands, is selling a unit featuring one of their high-quality 17-inch screens and two good size-speakers on the side of the case. Try before you buy, because you'll probably have these speakers a long time. This trend is likely to continue for the reasons I discussed at the beginning of the chapter—it's attractive and convenient. It is proving especially so to manufacturers who are aggressively courting the multimedia home market, like Acer, Compaq, and Packard-Bell, with entire multimedia systems priced from $1700 to $2400. By all means both see and hear these monitors if at all possible, and be sure you can return them if the speakers are too thin for your taste.

Another recent trend is 3-D sound. This is a combination of hardware and software which samples and uses subtly varying information in the two stereo signals to synthesize a signal which improves the sense of space. There are two companies leading the way: Q-Sound and SRS. Some manufacturers are beginning to ship higher-end cards, kits, and systems with this technology. How good is it, and is it worth it? It can be quite good indeed, especially with high-quality speakers, well-placed for effect. But as was the case with pseudo-stereo and later, pseudo-quad sound in the hi-fi world, and surround sound in the currently booming "home theater" market, the results will vary unpredictably, even with good hardware. This variation results from the fact that, unless software or signals are produced with special playback in mind, and most aren't, there is an element of chance in how successfully the SRS or Q-Sound can extract convincing details from any given source.

A MOVING TARGET: MOVIES ON YOUR PC

As computers got more powerful, they got closer to being able to play back color images and sound simultaneously, until now you can actually watch movies on a robustly-equipped PC. Color has been around for more than 10 years, decent sound for a bit less; what's taken so long? Why did you have to choose between a good used car and a PC which could handle what is sometimes called "motion video?" The answer is two-part: the business-oriented history of the PC I explained above, and the fact that the size of digitized image and sound files is enormous. High-capacity storage devices, fast transfer rates for those huge files, a CPU with brawn and speed, and a very fast video card are necessary, along with some very fancy software called *codecs* (for *co*mpression-*dec*ompression of sound and video files)—all these are necessary, and affordable, for video to be more than a novelty. And in fact, all the components are here. In one sense, that is the whole point of multimedia and the MPC standards; but if you've seen a single-speed CD-ROM drive struggling along trying to put more than a quarter-screen of grainy, jittery video on a monitor, with the sound out of sync and stuttering like a chicken, you'll realize we're not there yet. Quite. But we're getting closer. With a 6x CD-ROM and a fast 486 or Pentium and a good video card, a multimedia file in .AVI, .FLI, or QTW format can look well, almost convincing. Whether you want to upgrade to that level will depend on your budget and your level of interest. As far as sound is concerned, you can get quite good results with a 16-bit card and, especially, good speakers.

The fact is, video on a PC is still a maturing aspect of the technology; standards in both hardware and software are still evolving, and quickly, meaning that compromises in performance, limited program material, hard-to-solve conflicts and incompatibilities, and rapid product-introduction/upgrade cycles are quite inevitable. I recommend that you check recent issues of magazines like *Multimedia World*, *CD-ROM Today*, *PC Magazine*, and *Computer Shopper* for up-to-date tests and results. And make sure you can return any hardware components, like a hot video board with MPEG built-in, if things don't quite work in your system. What's MPEG? Now that we've laid out the landscape, let's look briefly at some present features, keeping in mind that the view will change rapidly.

NOTE

For some time there have been specialty cards which put a TV signal on your PC screen. This involves different video technology, and is beyond our present scope. Suffice it to say that these boards are there and they work, are not too expensive anymore, require strong multimedia-type hardware, and come with their own typical potential for fussiness. If you are interested, check recent PC or specialty magazines for reliable reviews and information.

Not as Simple as M-P-E-G

An organization of professionals called the *Motion Picture Experts Group* (*MPEG* for short), has been working on standards for video for years. MPEG-1 (which is what will be meant most of the time) is the current PC standard; MPEG-2 is the standard used for digital satellite transmission. It is not compatible with the MPEG-1 disk format, so don't wait for it to show up on the PC. MPEG-1 requires an MPEG-encoded CD-ROM holding (potentially) 74 minutes of 30 frames-per-second video at full-screen size. As with first attempts at SCSI, local bus, increases in modem transmission speed, PCMCIA cards, etc., MPEG-1 as an early standard is a bit loose, meaning it can be implemented in various ways, meaning you have to watch your step, every step of the way. There are basically three ways to get MPEG video at present.

✔ **Standalone hardware card.** This is usually an ISA card that attaches to an existing video board via its "feature connector." Of course, the existing board has to have one, and the two have to be compatible and will often be from the same manufacturer.

✔ **Adapter-MPEG combo board.** These are usually PCI or VESA video boards with at least 2 Mb of memory, and an MPEG chip built-in. These are getting common, and some cost little more than the video board itself. Some manufacturers like Diamond and VideoLogic use plug-in modules or daughtercards to add MPEG to video boards without requiring a slot to upgrade.

✔ **Software MPEG programs.** These require fast Pentiums to run well, or at all. The XING MPEG Player is currently on the rise, and Diamond, one of the leaders at the moment, is shipping some of their popular Viper Pro and Stealth 64 video cards with a special video-accelerating XING codec chip built onto the board.

CD-ROM software encoded for MPEG playback (i.e., movies) is beginning to appear, and game makers are experimenting with the technology as well. The CD-ROM drive feeds an MPEG data stream, which is decompressed to yield the equivalent of 30 frames per second, enough for convincing motion. High-end boards can do this in 24-bit (photo-realistic) color. Some boards will allow "motion video" (i.e., movies) and normal ("static") video on the same screen at the same time, some at different color depths. Some boards will output a standard TV signal (NTSC) for display on a TV monitor or recording on a VCR; some will also capture the video frames they play. All these boards will decode and synchronize audio, but the quality varies (it should be 16-bit).

MPEG, if properly done (remember all the industrial-strength components you need), does a good job; that's why it's gaining in popularity. It has the ability to match the throughput speed to its target device, it never drops frames, and some implementations have what are called good "pixel-interpolation algorithms," meaning the ability to enlarge an image to full-screen size without looking too grainy or off-color. But as I said above, there are many underlying technical details which must all be in line. Your board must support your MPEG-encoded CD-ROM format, and there are (of course!) different ones.

As you have doubtless realized, convincing video on your PC is possible now, and will get better. The requirements are quite stiff, making an initial or upgrade investment rather substantial. Incompatibilities abound, and they are changing quickly. It will greatly repay you to do some homework before deciding to buy something. Watch the magazines, audition systems if possible, and talk to people who have made the plunge.

CHAPTER SUMMARY

Multimedia on a PC involves fast, convincing color and sound. After a long history of gradual development, multimedia PCs are quickly becoming decent at the entry level, and most intended for the home and small-office market are multimedia systems. Upgrading an existing system requires careful analysis of your present system, your budget, and your vision before making a decision. Depending on what you already have, what you have to spend, and the level of performance you wish, you can decide whether to upgrade an existing system or buy a new one. You can spend between $150 and more than $2,000, so the decision requires some reading, shopping, thinking, and planning to be successful. We covered the facts and tradeoffs to help you decide what and where to buy, and then provided installation instructions for CD-ROM drives, sound cards, and speaker systems. Throughout we tried to give you background information on present and future technology, as well as prices current at the end of 1995, to help you upgrade to (or buy) a multimedia system with a minimum of fuss and a maximum of pleasure.

CHAPTER 12

SELECTING AND MAINTAINING A DISPLAY SYSTEM

WHAT'S IN THIS CHAPTER

- ✔ Matching Your Monitor and Graphic Adapter
- ✔ Dealing with Video Drivers
- ✔ Installing a Graphics Card
- ✔ Attaching a Monitor
- ✔ Calibrating a Monitor
- ✔ Troubleshooting Your Display

WHAT THIS CHAPTER IS ABOUT

Your video display system is the portion of your machine that you spend the most time with; you may spend a lot of time at the keyboard and handle your mouse a good deal, but while you are actively using your computer your attention is constantly on the monitor. Selecting the right combination of screen and graphics adapter is critical to your comfort, and will directly affect the types of application you can use, and in many cases, the quality of your output. If you use Windows or another graphic interface, it is also one of the single largest contributors to overall system performance. Advanced graphics adapters often require special drivers, and "minor" bugs in these drivers—or an improper installation—can bring your system to its knees. This is true even if the driver is included with the operating system. This chapter covers the essentials in selecting the right display system, installing it, and keeping it running properly.

THE DISPLAY SUB-SYSTEM

For most PC users, the letters and images on their computer screen are much like the water that comes out of the taps at the kitchen sink. It seems effortless. You turn a knob and you get water, hot or cold; you push a button and magically, letters and numbers, colors and images appear on your PC screen. The reality is much different. In both cases a large number of people and complex technology were required to bring both the stream of water and the stream of electrons to do your bidding. When water rages out of control in flood and storm, it can wreak havoc; when your video adapter, monitor or their attendant software break their normal boundaries, they can wreak havoc with the operation of your system. In order to wisely select and install a display sub-system, you need to have a basic understanding of how its components work, relate to each other, and interact with the rest of your system. Figure 12.1 shows the parts of a display sub-system.

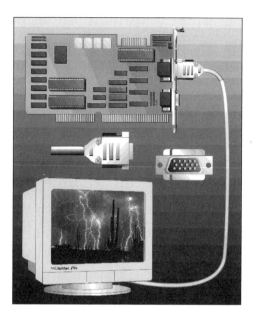

FIGURE 12.1 A display sub-system: video graphics adapter card, monitor, and cabling (showing connections).

Buying a Bundle

Many vendors and virtually all mail order houses sell computer systems with pre-assembled display systems. All display systems are not equal. A casual look at the ad may make it sound as simple as picking Super VGA, or just of selecting the maximum resolution and number of colors you want on the screen. Reality is much more complicated, due to the complexity of the technology. We can have a general discussion, enough to let you make an informed buying decision, without getting too carried away with technical terms.

As we discuss the individual components, you have to keep in mind that they work together. If you buy the best monitor in the world and attach it to a cheap video card, you'll get lousy results. If you buy an inexpensive monitor and attach it to a top-of-the-line graphics adapter, the same result will ensue; in fact, unless the graphics adapter can be stepped down to the level of your monitor, you may not get an image at all. Let's start with an overview of just how the display system works, and then we'll look at each of the major components in turn.

GETTING THE PICTURE

The monitor connected to your PC looks very much like a regular television set. The resemblance is more than superficial, because the hardware inside the case could be used as a TV set if it were attached to a tuner that could receive TV stations. But your monitor receives its signals from the cable that comes out of the back of your PC, signals that bear little resemblance to the standard network broadcast.

Here's a thumbnail description of how the process works. The operating system sends a stream of data in the form of binary numbers to the graphics adapter. This card processes these signals through a circuit known as a *digital-to-analog-converter* (DAC). The DAC then forwards an analog signal to the monitor. Color adapters send three signals: one for each of the primary colors, red, green and blue. They are passed to the monitor through a cable that connects the two components. The signal is received by an electron gun located inside the monitor. The gun then sends an electronic stream which varies in intensity based on the strength of the signal from the adapter card. This beam of energy is constantly moving back and forth across the monitor's picture tube in fine horizontal lines.

As the light strikes the back of the screen, it *excites* (lights up) a phosphor coating. In monochrome monitors, there's only one phosphor layer; color monitors have different layers for each primary color. A small mask, placed between the gun and the phosphor, tightly controls how large an area is illuminated. The result is a picture on the screen composed of tiny dots. These dots are called *picture elements* (or *pixels*). A single horizontal line of dots across the screen is called a *raster line*. An electro-magnet inside the monitor is used to sweep the active line down the screen. When the beam finishes painting the bottom line, the process is started over again at the top, and the image is repainted based on new information coming from the adapter card.

Color monitors usually use three electron guns, one for each primary color. Variations in intensity are used to produce the rest of the shades of the spectrum. This is a very brief explanation of the basics of how an image appears on your screen. There are many factors that contribute to the quality of the display and the number of colors available on the screen. In order to make an informed buying decision, you need to understand what some of these factors are.

Resolution and Color

One of the most important things in determining the quality of a display is its *resolution*. This is measured in pixels (as I mentioned, a pixel is the basic dot that is the smallest defined unit in the display). This is usually expressed by presenting the number of pixels displayed horizontally and vertically; for example, the basic VGA resolution is 640 pixels horizontally by 480 pixels vertically. While a few years ago, this resolution was considered excellent, today a good display adapter is capable of displaying a resolution of at least 1024 by 768. Top-of-the-line adapters can push the numbers to 1600 by 1200.

But straight resolution is only part of the picture. Another critical factor is the number of colors that can be displayed per pixel. Early display systems were *monochrome* in nature; that is, they could only display one color. The electron gun fired and as it passed across the line it either turned a given pixel on or left it off. Points struck by the energy emitted light, points that were not, did not. In order to accomplish this, the computer had only to send either a zero or one representing an "on" or "off" state. Monochrome monitors are said to be "one bit deep" because it takes one bit to describe each pixel on the screen (the bit can have a value of either zero or one). The number of bits it takes to display each pixel is called its *pixel depth*; The more depth, the more color. With four bits per pixel you get sixteen colors, with eight there are 256 possible colors. High-color displays allow either 15 or 16 bits per pixel, producing roughly 32,000 or 65,000 possible colors. True-color images, with photographic realism, are produced by 24-bit adapters, which can render up to 16.7 million colors per pixel.

Storing or manipulating those bits requires memory. You can determine the amount of memory required per given display by multiplying the horizontal resolution times the vertical resolution times the pixel depth. In other words, our basic VGA display would require slightly over 300,000 bits to display an image on the monitor. For true-color, (24-bit display), you need three times the memory of an 8-bit adapter. This is a major factor in the price of a graphics display card, and a bit later in this chapter I'll explain how some new memory designs can cut cost and improve performance at the same time.

That's All Fine in Theory, What Does It Mean to Me?

The real-world concern with resolution and color depth have to do with the kind of work you plan on using your PC for. If all you're ever going to do is use a DOS word processor, monochrome VGA with a resolution of 640 by 480 will probably meet your needs. The problem is that with the advent of Windows, with its use of color and fancy graphics, most applications and therefore most users require both more resolution and more color. If you plan on using Windows for simple tasks like word processing or spreadsheet operation, and you don't plan on having more than one application open at a time, then a standard VGA card with 256 colors will let you get by, but you will want better as soon as you see someone using a better system. Technology has gone far beyond the simple 256-color VGA card.

More Windows, Less Light

The original VGA cards were really a continuation of a series of graphics adapter standards that started when vendors first started to try to display graphics on a PC monitor. These basic devices are known as "dumb frame buffers" and you can generally pick up a simple VGA card today for about $30. They are called *frame buffers* because basically all they do is act as a buffer to hold the information that is then written onto the screen. They are called "dumb" because they have no intelligence: the computer's CPU has to do all the work of managing the video card. When all the CPU had to manage was a standard VGA resolution or less, that wasn't too much of a problem, although with the intensive graphics found in Windows, even that was becoming too much of a chore. At higher resolutions and with more colors on the screen, dumb frame buffer cards are totally out of their depth.

As Windows soared in popularity dumb frame buffers became one of the major bottlenecks in system performance. Users were actually waiting for the screen to be redrawn so they could get on with their work. Hardware vendors came up with several solutions. One of these was to use faster memory called *VRAM* or Video Random Access Memory. VRAM is dual-ported memory, which operates much faster than the DRAM (basically just like the standard memory chips found on your motherboard). One real drawback to VRAM is that it adds to the cost of the display adapter. VRAM by itself wasn't much of a solution. Early VRAM-based adapters still used dumb-frame-buffer technology. The CPU still had to do all the work, but data could be moved out much faster. VRAM and your system CPU still needed more help to get the job done.

Enter the Graphics Accelerators

An answer wasn't long in coming in the form of *fixed-function accelerators*. These are specialized graphics chips (sometimes referred to as "engines"), that are programmed to take over the work of calculating certain graphics functions that have to be drawn on the screen. They have two advantages: freeing the CPU to go back to crunching data and, if the designer has chosen the right things to optimize, speeding up the task itself, such as drawing a line or moving a block of pixels to a different location on the screen. At the time this chapter was written, the most powerful fixed-function accelerators were the Matrox MGA Millennium, and the Number Nine's 128-based boards.

These chips are matched with VRAM, or other special memory (more about that in a minute) to create graphics adapters that can offer ten to thirty times the performance of the standard dumb frame buffer card. If you work in a graphical environment like

Windows, and work with a lot of graphic-intensive applications, such cards can literally add hours to your work week by speeding up your display.

Co-processed Adapters

Co-processed boards were once the ultimate graphics solution, bringing a tremendous amount of muscle to bear on just one problem: making pixels march across the screen. When high-resolution 24-bit adapters first appeared, they were all co-processor designs. These products are actually full-fledged microprocessors that just handle the operation of the display. Today these have all but disappeared. They are occasionally found in special sales, or in older machines. The most popular of these come from Texas Instruments, with their 34020 CPU. This is a full 32-bit CPU and is like dedicating a 386 as a graphics engine. While there is real power in this design, it was too costly to survive the rush of less expensive and easier-to-operate accelerator boards. Most of the 34020 cards required a separate VGA card for non-Windows operation, and could literally take days to install because of their specialized drivers and finicky habits when it came to sharing memory with other system components. If you see a deal on one, ignore it. Today graphics accelerators dominate the market because they are easier to install, cheaper to build, and less demanding in their system memory needs.

BUYING MORE THAN JUST NUMBERS

Modern graphics adapter cards have become full-fledged sub-systems, outpacing the original design for display adapters planned for the PC. They offer blazing speed, resolutions up to 1600 by 1200, and now most boast at least some 24-bit color capabilities. All this horsepower allows us to edit color photographs directly on the screen, and provides the muscle needed for handling complex graphics applications. But power always comes at a price. These adapters require more memory, special drivers, are sometimes difficult to install, and the better ones carry price tags ranging from $300 to over $2,000.

When shopping for a new graphics adapter, you have to juggle a number of factors when making a purchasing decision. You can't just buy a graphics adapter, you have to also make sure that the monitor you attach it to is capable of supporting it. Here are the things we need to keep in mind when shopping for a graphics adapter; many of the following features listed for graphics adapters also apply to monitors, but they are easier to understand if we begin with a discussion of the cards.

Maximum Resolution

In general, the higher the resolution the better, but keep in mind that very high resolutions on a small monitor will produce very sharp, but very tiny images, especially text. In addition, some high resolutions require drivers tuned for large (read expensive) monitors. As a rule of thumb, 14-inch monitors will work well with 800 by 600 resolution. Most 14-inch monitors are incapable of supporting 24-bit color at resolutions greater than 640 by 480. 15- to 17-inch monitors can make use of 1024 by 768 resolution and many are capable of supporting up to 24-bit color at that resolution. Some 17-inch monitors can also manage 1600 by 1200 with 256 colors. 20-inch monitors and above are generally used for graphics-intensive operations such as CAD or desktop publishing. When looking at resolution, be cautious if you see the word *interlaced*.

Interlaced and Non-Interlaced Displays

Interlacing refers to the method used to draw the raster lines that create the image across the monitor. The difference is very simple: non-interlaced displays draw every line on the screen every time; interlaced displays draw only half of the lines with each pass. Then they come back and repeat their travel, drawing the other lines. Interlaced displays were designed to get higher resolution with less memory on the card, as they only have to manage half the pixels at one time; this saved the manufacturer some money. The problem is that this can lead to flicker. *Non-interlaced displays are always better.* (Good grief, there actually is an absolute statement you can make about graphics displays!) Many people will develop headaches after only a short working period of at an interlaced display. Just how bad flicker will be in an interlaced display depends a great deal on the system's refresh rate.

Refresh Rate

One of the things that determines how fast your video card must paint the screen is the *decay rate* of the monitor's phosphor. The phosphor can only emit light for a short period of time after it is charged by the electron gun. Different types of phosphors emit energy for different lengths of time; they decay at various rates. The card must repeat its path in time to re-energize the phosphor before it turns dark. The speed at which the screen is re-energized is called the *refresh rate*. This is expressed in *Hertz* (Hz), the number of times per second that the beam passes over the screen. Here's another absolute: *the higher the refresh rate, the better the image.*

The lowest acceptable refresh rate for standard VGA, 640 by 480, should be at least 60 Hz. 800 by 600 and above should be at least 70 Hz. Going below these rates will usually result in unacceptable flicker. If your card or monitor doesn't support certain minimums, they will be unable, just because of the physics, to draw higher resolutions. Many cards and monitors have the ability to work at different refresh rates or frequencies. In general, the more flexible your components are, the more likely you are to get solid performance. The better monitors generally cost more in part because of a wider range of refresh rates, and enhanced ability to synchronize with the signal coming from a video source.

Maximum Color

Five years ago most users, and the majority of experts, thought that 256 colors would be all that most users would ever need; after all, most applications used only 16 or 256 colors. But there are a number of factors pushing the desire for greater color depth. If you plan on using any color graphics applications such as CorelDRAW!, Adobe PhotoShop, PowerPoint, or Fractal Painter, and are planning on making a major purchase of a new graphics adapter, you should seriously consider buying one that supports 24-bit color. For this we have to look a little bit more into how color is displayed on the screen. 256-color adapters (also known as 8-bit boards) use a *look-up table* built into the display adapter when deciding which color to put on the screen. If you open the Windows Control Panel and choose **Color** (**Display** and then **Settings** in Windows 95) you will see the basic palette which is available for your monitor. See Figure 12.2.

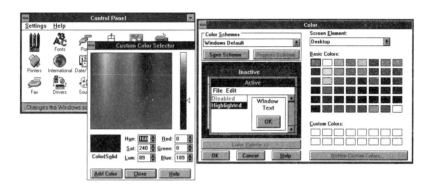

FIGURE 12.2 The Windows Control Panel ready to adjust colors.

The problem with 8-bit color is that if you want to work with realistic color images such as a color photograph, 256 colors just aren't enough. Some vendors will try to tell you that *high color* (otherwise known as 16-bit color, which offers 65,536 colors) will let you adequately edit photographic images on screen. In reality, 16-bit adapters do not let you see exactly what the final result will look like because they are still using a look-up table. 24-bit, or *true-color* adapters, actually provide 256 steps for each of the three primary colors; mixing and matching all the possible options gives you 16.7 million colors, which does allow enough precision for critical color graphics work. There's another advantage: 24-bit color provides a much smoother screen display than its weaker siblings. Gradient fills and subtle shifts of color in both illustrations and image-editing programs will show noticeable "banding" at lower color depths. Figure 12.3 shows the difference in appearance between two such images. Banding is also noticeable if the lower color depth is mixed with low resolution.

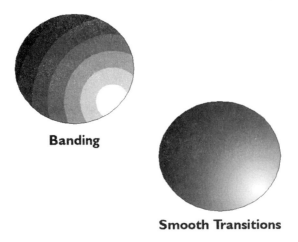

Banding

Smooth Transitions

FIGURE 12.3 Banding in graphic images.

Memory

To the casual observer memory may not seem like a big issue when dealing with display systems, but advanced adapters must have enough memory on the card to manage all the data displayed on the screen, as well as to have enough left over for their own internal operations. The original 16-color VGA card, with a resolution of 640 by 480, could get by with a paltry 256K of on-board DRAM (*Dynamic Random Access Memory*). A minimal 1Mb of DRAM should be considered standard for even the lowliest Windows accelerator. Serious users should shy away from anything with less than 2Mb of VRAM. Those interested in true-color operations should consider high-speed cards with at least 3 or 4Mb of VRAM and a maximum resolution of at least 1024 by 768.

Graphics cards have changed dramatically the past few years, but until recently a major component has remained the same: their memory chip. Low-end cards have been based on standard DRAM. Better boards with higher resolutions, color depths, and refresh rates were equipped with more expensive dual-ported VRAM. The new push for video playback and 3D for use with new multimedia software requires new technology, and the cost factor is adding emphasis—memory has become the most costly part of many graphics adapters.

Here is a run-down of the new types. Keep in mind that just how well they will work will depend of the ability of the engineers putting memory to use. *EDO (Extended Data Out) DRAM* has begun to appear as a replacement for system (i.e., motherboard) DRAM as well as in graphics cards. It improves overall memory performance by allowing valid data to persist through a longer portion of the overall memory cycle. The performance improvement is slight, compared to other new memory models, so expect to see it in cheaper cards, where it will eventually replace standard DRAM designs.

DRAM is rarely used in high-end cards, and EDO will not be able to compete with the existing performance of VRAM, so vendors are turning to other new types for their top-of-the-line products. VRAM is *dual-ported*; this means it has a second, read-only port in addition to having one like DRAM's read/write ("random") port. This allows the *RAMDAC* to handle refresh-related operations much faster than DRAM, or other single-port memory models. Several new dual-ported memory types are starting to appear. The first out is *WINRAM* or *WRAM* (Windows RAM), used in the Matrox MGA Millennium.

WRAM improves on DRAM, adding block-write and page-masking capabilities. These are two of its features specifically tuned to graphics adapter operations. Dual-color block write support produces very fast pattern and text fills, and its native ability to manage aligned BitBLTs gives a boost to video playback and 3D animation applications. WRAM offers significantly improved bandwidth and lets video applications coexist with more standard graphics types at high color depths and display resolutions. This has been a problem in older graphics cards. WRAM is somewhat more expensive than VRAM, and considerably more expensive than conventional DRAM. So WRAM will be used at the high end of the graphics market, and products based on EDO will be seen in mass-market products.

Another new memory technology may give them a run for the money. *RAMBUS* is a specification for memory with bus mastering (the RAMBUS Channel Master) and a new path (the RAMBUS Channel) between memory devices (the RAMBUS Channel Slaves).

A single RAMBUS Channel could provide exceptional bandwidth (up to 500 MB/s in burst mode) coupled with low voltage signaling methods that helps in reducing radio wave interference. Designers can produce multiple-channel versions, so the bandwidth potential is phenomenal. The drawback is huge development costs, so it will take time before we see a lot of cards using these chips.

The list of memory acronyms is going to get even longer. Other emerging technologies include SDRAM (Synchronous DRAM), SGRAM (Synchronous Graphics RAM), EDRAM (Enhanced DRAM), CDRAM (Cache DRAM), MDRAM (multi-bank DRAM), and RAMLink, a non-proprietary interface similar to RAMBUS. The best bet is to check out a copy of *PC Magazine*, or another trusted publication, for an informed opinion before jumping on a new product with your credit card or cash. Most products take some time to season, so it is not wise to run right out and get the first one on the market. Give it a month or two and watch for reports and reviews if you plan to buy a card based on one of the new memory types.

Getting On the Right Bus

The type of motherboard you have in your machine will also be a factor when it comes to choosing and using a graphics adapter. If your system only offers ISA-based expansion slots, you will not be able to take advantage of some of the hottest graphic cards around. For that you need either PCI local bus capability, or the older VESA local bus. It all comes down to a matter of how fast data can be moved to and from the graphics adapter. *Local bus* (be it VESA or PCI) allows the graphics adapter to be connected directly to the CPU, rather than having to go through the slower ISA or EISA expansion bus. In other words, the video card is going to be limited if you try to put it on one of the slower architectures.

Virtually all new motherboards come with two or three PCI slots, as well as built-in PCI IDE support for hard drives and CD-ROMs. PCI, which stands for *Peripheral Component Interconnect*, is a local bus standard designed by Intel and aimed directly at the Pentium marketplace. If you're considering a Pentium-based machine you should seriously examine PCI as the method for attaching video cards, hard disk controllers, SCSI host adapters and network interfaces to your system. Earmark one slot for a graphics adapter. The best candidates for the remainder are a SCSI card and a network adapter. Until some time in mid-1994, VL-Bus was more common than the PCI variety of high-performance interface connection. The reason local bus cards have come to dominate the market is performance and ease of use. They offer up to twenty times or more the speed of older ISA boards.

NOTE

A good example is the Matrox MGA. Using the PC Labs 3.11 Winmark test, a PCI version scored 90 million Winmarks, and a VL-Bus card scored 60 million Winmarks—compared to the same adapter with an ISA connector's rating of 39.8 million. All cards were tested on the same system using a Micronics Gemini motherboard with 16Mb of RAM. I used older test results because there was data available on all three types. The same spread would be seen with other benchmarks.

If you are planning on building a real power user's system, you should consider using the PCI architecture. The difference in the cost of the two types of cards is minimal compared to the speed boost you'll get and the difference in motherboard cost is insignificant. Another factor is ease of installation. The ISA and VLB cards do not use a shared memory address and IRQ assignment; PCI does. With PCI you can pop a card into a slot and load its drivers. With ISA and VLB you must locate a free address area and exclude it from other devices. This necessity has eased with Windows 95, which can usually handle most conflicts, but Interrupts can still present problems.

WARNING

In the early days of local bus, several vendors produced computers with their own proprietary video local bus design. You should avoid these systems like the plague, since the newer standardized local buses have taken over the market. As a result, these machines will not be able to use the vast majority of local bus video cards, and will rapidly be orphans. If you consider buying an older system, be sure to identify what type of local bus it has (if any).

Drivers

There's more to a video card or high-powered graphics adapter than its hardware. In order to manage all those pixels, access all the features of the engine, and run reliably under Windows and other operating environments, someone must write appropriate *drivers* (software programs) for each resolution and pixel depth. All drivers are not created equal. Some are written better than others and most are refined over time. Buggy drivers can lead to all kinds of problems, from funny artifacts on the screen (which can make something like screen captures or reading fine print a nightmare) to locking up the system with often-unpredictable results.

Who writes the drivers depends on who developed the graphics engines and who produced the board. These are not always the same people. Several years ago a vendor who shall remain nameless produced a very high-end and therefore expensive card. Given its potential horsepower, it should still be a major player today, but the company relied on the people who made the engine to produce the high-color and true-color drivers that the board really needed. Two years later, owners were still waiting for some of those drivers and the board faded away into obsolescence.

Several other boards were developed at the same time by several vendors based on the same engine. These manufacturers, however, chose to write their own drivers. While technology is now passing these boards by, they did reach their full potential. One of these companies, however, did not survive, and I have actually received mail from owners asking where they could obtain updated drivers. Unfortunately I had to tell them their chances were quite slim unless they could use generic drivers that might work with the underlying engine—but the chances were not good.

The most popular cards are directly supported by drivers that ship with the major applications, such as Windows, OS/2, and AUTOCAD. If your specific card is already listed as one of the drivers that comes with Microsoft Windows, odds are it has pretty good drivers. But, as with almost everything else in computerdom, you can't rely on that as a given. There are some generic drivers, such as those which support the aging Texas Instruments 34020 engine; while the driver is shipped directly with Windows, not all 34020-based cards will work with this driver. Many of the drivers included with Windows or other operating systems were developed by the card or engine manufacturers themselves, and supplied to Microsoft or another software vendor as a courtesy to both them and the user. In some cases, by the time the software ships, the drivers are updated. That means it is a good idea to check with a vendor for later drivers. Graphics adapter drivers are a VERY common source of system problems. These can include almost any kind of erratic behavior or crash. Most major manufacturers have forums on CompuServe, or a BBS system, where you can download their latest drivers. This alone is one great reason for having a modem.

VGA Support and Backward Compatibility

Fancy drivers are all well and good where they apply. But you still need support for character-based screens when you are running under DOS or when your system is on its way into Windows (or some other graphic-based user interface). Some graphics adapters come with built-in on-board VGA support. This may take the form of a real VGA chip actually built into the system, or it may be that VGA emulation was built into the engine. This can be a very handy feature, both because it enhances the compatibility of the product and it reduces the complexity of installation. If there is no on-board support you'll actually have to go out and get a VGA card to operate in modes not directly supported by the high-end card driver.

There are several older resolutions, which VGA supports, that are occasionally needed for working with older programs—especially some games. True VGA compatibility offers reasonable insurance that these programs will run with your souped-up system.

The above considerations let us draw some very basic but important lessons when buying a video card. The discussion below summarizes them, as well as other general buying considerations, in order of importance.

BUYING A VIDEO CARD

Does It Meet Your Needs?

The first step is to consider the types of applications you want to use the card with. If you are planning on high-powered graphics work, then you'll want a card with high-resolution and 24-bit color. If you'll only rarely look at 24-bit images to see what they look like, and do most of your work in less-intensive applications, you might want to shop for a card that offers good resolution and moderate color depth such as 1024 by 768 by 256-color and that possibly also has a driver that supports 800 by 600 by 24-bits. There will probably be a $200 difference between the prices of these two boards.

When considering needs, think what you might want to be doing in the future. If you plan on adding multimedia capability somewhere down the road, you may still want to opt for a hefty video card, anticipating your future needs.

Compatibility

Make sure that the card you are planning on buying is compatible with your existing hardware, or that you have the funds or the willingness to upgrade your system so that the card will work. In some cases you can actually do this in a piecemeal fashion; the card may work at a lower resolution or refresh rate with your existing monitor. But if your motherboard and monitor won't support the card (say you want to buy a PCI-based card but you have an ISA machine) you'll have to spend a bunch of money and a fair bit of time to get everything working right.

As mentioned above, drivers are a critical component of compatibility. Don't rely on promises, or the assumption that drivers that support your application or extra features will necessarily ever make it to market. The company could change its plans or run out of money before you ever get your drivers. On more than one occasion I have seen a vendor offer extras and even provide some of the hardware to support it and then change plans and never deliver. These cases have included things like compression modules, mouse ports, printer accelerators, and the ability to add extra memory. Always judge the board by how it works when you buy it. *PC Magazine* and other respected periodicals run regular reviews comparing different graphics adapters. They're a good starting point for narrowing your search.

For the next year or so, display adapters will continue to be one of the hottest segments in the hardware market. At the present time there is roughly one new video card per day, and a new engine announced every three or four weeks. While this pace of development may seem daunting when it comes to buying a card, it has brought us a lot of benefit. When I first reviewed 24-bit video cards, the average price for a somewhat slow and difficult-to-install board ran between $2,000 and $4,000. Today, faster and better-designed boards that match all the features found in those pioneers are available for street prices of about $700 or less.

WARNING

A few adapters require the use of special cables or use of a specific monitor. If this is the case, be sure that your combination of card and monitor are compatible. Some older monitors are based on a digital technology which goes under the abbreviation of TTL (Transistor to Transistor Logic). TTL technology has become obsolete, so if you are upgrading a card with an old monitor, be sure that both support today's analog technology and cabling.

Technical Support and Warranty

Given the complexity of graphics adapters and the rapid rate of change in the market, technical support should be a very real consideration when choosing a new card. You want to make sure you can get your new device up and running with a minimum of fuss, and that new drivers and spare parts will be available during its projected life-cycle. Keep an eye open for firms that offer toll-free 800-number support and don't charge extra for replacement drivers. Reliable firms should also offer bulletin board services for updating drivers and a reasonable warranty, at least a year.

On the other hand, I wouldn't put too much stock in the value of a five-year warranty. Most cards that last through the first 90 days will probably last through the five years, and possibly outlast the company that produced it. Video Seven, one of the leading lights of the industry in the days of the VGA card, offered a five-year warranty, no questions asked—and lived up to it. Lived up to it that is, until they went out of business.

The Price

Many people consider cost to be one of the most critical factors when buying computer components. Cost is a relative thing. In silicon as in most of the rest of life, there is no such thing as a free lunch. If a card is $15 or $20 cheaper than similar featured cards on the market, it may well give you poorer documentation. If it's $50 cheaper you'll probably pay for the technical support calls you'll have to make to get it running. If it's offering the same features of other cards costing $100 or $200 more, you'll have to seriously ask yourself where they cut corners, or if the other vendors in the market are seriously gouging you.

My rule of thumb with cost is that 80% of the vendors should probably be within 10% of each other's price. The ones at the very low end are probably cutting corners they shouldn't, while the ones at the very top of the list are either charging you for their fancy advertising or, in rare cases, have discovered a new technology that no one else has caught onto yet.

Benchmarks

Many people put a lot of emphasis on benchmark scores when shopping for a video adapter. While benchmarks are a reasonable indication of the relative speed of one graphics adapter to another, my opinion is that *they should only be used as an indicator*. This opinion is based on several considerations. The first is how benchmarks are designed; most of them rapidly repeat a range of specialized instructions designed to measure how fast the display system can handle the tasks. Very few people will constantly draw two or three hundred straight lines in a row, or type "the quick brown fox jumped over the lazy dog." Again, most benchmarks are designed to focus on higher scores based on what its designer thinks relates to the needs of the average user, but his idea of an average user and an individual's real requirements and work habits can be far apart. The third problem comes from the pressure on video vendors to obtain good benchmark scores. Some vendors will reverse-engineer benchmark tests and design drivers, and in some cases, even modify firmware just to get good benchmark scores.

During my testing for magazine reviews I have more than once found a vendor cheating to raise scores. There are two problems with this behavior; one is obvious: it becomes harder to trust benchmark scores as a valid way to compare the relative performance of competing products. The second is more insidious. If a vendor is taking all this time to tweak a project just to get the numbers, they are hindering the card's ability to perform real-world applications, and wasting R&D (Research and Development) money that would be better spent on valuable product development.

Installing a Display Adapter

What You'll Need

✔ Screwdriver

✔ Small cup for holding screws and other miscellaneous parts

✔ Graphics adapter card

✔ Software drivers and installation files, especially a "Readme" file

✔ Card Manual; possibly your system manual

✔ Small flashlight and a magnifying glass

✔ Tweezers of hemostat for setting jumpers

It's also a good idea to make sure you have a current copy of your Dark and Stormy Night disk. Some of the more advanced graphics adapters may install drivers that are incompatible with applications or other hardware on your system. If this happens, you may not be able to boot using the configuration files on your hard disk and may have to boot from a floppy. You can then used your DSND to copy back your old files.

STEP 1

Power down the computer and disconnect the power cord and any other cable connections that might get in the way. If you try to remove or install cards with the power turned on in the computer, you may seriously injure the cards and/or the motherboard.

STEP 2

Remove the cover from the case. See Figure 12.4.

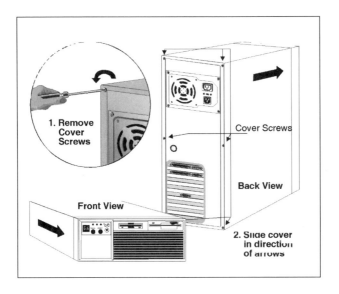

FIGURE 12.4 Removing the cover from your case.

STEP 3

Once the cover is off, you need to locate the proper type of expansion slot for the type of card you are installing. If you have a very old or very inexpensive display adapter it may fit in an 8-bit slot. Most ISA-based graphics adapters will require a 16-bit slot. If you have a VL-based card or a PCI card, it will require a special local bus slot. Figure 12.5 shows details of what these different type slots look like. Remove the end cover (expansion plate cover) from an appropriate slot, as shown in Figure 12.6.

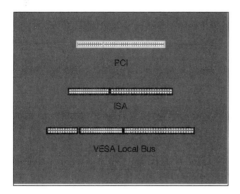

FIGURE 12.5 PCI, regular (ISA) and VL bus slots.

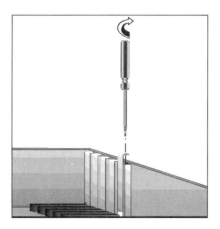

FIGURE 12.6 Removing the expansion plate cover.

WARNING

If you are installing either a VL-Bus or an EISA card, take extra care to make sure that you push the card straight down into the slot. Installing or removing these cards at an angle can possibly jam the card and damage the edge connector or motherboard.

STEP 4

Make sure you discharge any possible static by touching the case. Now open the box that the graphics adapter came in and remove the card from its protective envelope. See Figure 12.7.

FIGURE 12.7 A typical video graphic adapter card.

STEP 5

Before proceeding with the actual installation, check the manual and determine if you need to set any Interrupts, DIP switches or jumpers. Some adapters will be able to use the standard VGA addresses and will not require any modification. Some will be Interrupt-driven and require both an IRQ and a memory address. If this is the case, refer to your System Inventory to find free locations. Then modify the jumpers or switches as shown in your user's manual. A few cards, especially those with hardware compression built in, may also require assignment of a DMA (Direct Memory Access) channel. Refer to Figure 12.8.

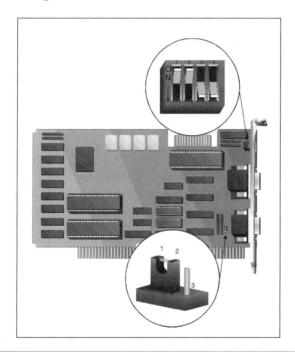

FIGURE 12.8 Setting DIP switches and jumpers.

If you are installing a video card that does not have on-board VGA support, or planning to install two graphics adapters to configure a dual monitor set-up, you will also need to attach the correct VGA pass-through cable onto their pin or edge-style "feature-connector" posts, shown in Figure 12.9.

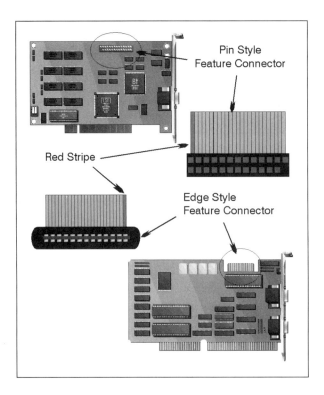

FIGURE 12.9 A VGA card showing feature connectors.

STEP 6

Now that the card is installed properly into the case, connect the monitor cables. Most cards will work directly with your regular monitor cables. This is usually a 15-pin *DSUB*-type, as shown in Figure 12.10. This should be attached to the matching connector on the video card. Some cables are permanently attached to the monitor, others may require connecting the monitor at both ends. Older monitors may have an analog/TTL switch. Virtually all adapters today are analog. Be sure that if this switch exists that it is set properly. Having it set in the wrong position could possibly damage the monitor.

FIGURE 12.10 A 15-pin cable.

Some high-end cards ship with special cables with *BNC* connectors (a sort of twist-on, twist-off connector used in some video applications, as well as for some network installations using Thin Ethernet). This kind of connection offers more bandwidth. If your card came with such a cable, and your monitor supports the connection, you should use it; see Figure 12.11. Generally speaking, only the higher-end monitors have these connections. The exact way these lines are attached to the back of the monitor will vary, based on the type of synchronization used by the system. There are two types, separate and composite. Figure 12.11 shows how the connections are attached for both types. The other end of the cable that goes to the video card should be the standard DSUB type of connector.

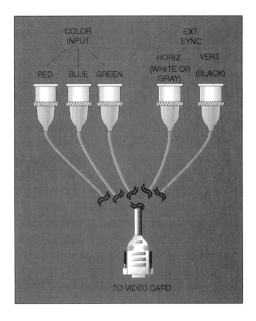

FIGURE 12.11 BNC monitor cables and connections.

STEP 7

Before turning on the monitor, double-check the manual for any special requirements. Some units require selecting either internal or external synchronization, or require other special settings.

Installing Drivers and Testing the Installation

STEP 1

Once you have verified that all the switches are set correctly, that the connections are properly made, and the cables properly attached to the monitor, turn on the monitor and boot the PC.

Assuming that you don't have any memory or address conflicts, you should get the normal C:> prompt, or your operating system welcome screen.

STEP 2

Install or configure (depending on the operating system version) the driver software for Windows and any other applications you plan on running, following the instructions that came with your graphics adapter. Be sure to look at any "Readme" type of file on your installation disks. Such files often have later and more helpful information than the printed manuals. Test all the software that you have installed drivers for and make sure everything works.

STEP 3

DOS: Then use your favorite memory manager software, be it DOS 6.0's MemoryMaker, Qualitas 386 to the MAX or Quarterdeck's QEMM to optimize memory usage on your system.

Windows 95, Windows NT, and OS/2: Use the Display settings available in the Control Panel to select screen savers, resolution, and other options.

NOTE

If you are using a non-PCI graphics adapter under an older 16-bit version of Windows (Windows 3.11 or older) that makes use of a specific memory address (for example C800-CFFF), it's usually necessary to exclude this area from Windows memory management by placing the following line

EMMExclude=C800-CFFF

into the [386ENH] section of your SYSTEM.INI file. This keeps Windows from trying to place things into the video display section of memory, which could cause your system to lock up or crash. Check your user's manual for any additional requirements that might be needed to either make your system run smoothly with your new card or to make use of its advanced features.

STEP 4

Once you are sure everything is working properly, go ahead and install any exotic optional features that your card might possess, such as a mouse driver, video grabber, compression, or other accessory. Most video cards don't have these exotic options; in that case, just go on to the next step.

STEP 5

Replace the cover and place any spare screws, parts or anything else into your goodies bag for future use.

STEP 6

Make a new Dark And Stormy Night disk as described in Chapter 3 so that you will have backup copies of all these settings. Under DOS You'll want to save copies of your CONFIG.SYS, AUTOEXEC.BAT, SYSTEM.INI, and WINDOWS.INI (the last two files are for Windows users only) off onto your bootable floppy. For other operating systems, be sure to create a new Rescue Disk.

THE MONITOR

We have already talked about monitors as part of the display sub-system team; let's now take a closer look at monitors as the separate piece of equipment they are when you buy one. As you know, a monitor produces an image by firing a beam of electrons from a gun located at the back of the set onto a coating of phosphorus on the inside of the glass in the front (see Figure 12.12). Some monitors have a single gun, others have several. The electron beam scans rapidly in a horizontal line down the length of the tube. When the beam reaches the bottom line, it returns to the top and starts the scan all over again.

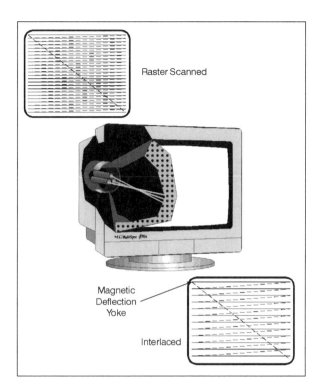

Raster Scanned

Magnetic
Deflection
Yoke

Interlaced

FIGURE 12.12 How a monitor forms an image.

As the beam strikes the phosphor, light is emitted. Color monitors normally use three phosphors, one that emits red light, another green and the third blue. By combining these phosphors, we can create all the other colors in the spectrum. To prevent stray radiation from lighting up the phosphor screen improperly, the electron beams are passed through a mask. Most tubes use a dot mask. The somewhat more expensive Sony Trinitron uses a series of vertical stripes to form their mask. This type of tube has been available both in commercial TV sets and monitors for years and offers a very sharp picture. You can also buy the same technology from other vendors who have licensed the technology from Sony. A lot of Japanese companies use the same method.

How Many Colors Do You Need?

The earliest PC monitors were much like model T's. Henry Ford would sell you a car in any color you wanted as long as it was black. Likewise, the first PC monitors offered you the option of green. That's because they only possessed a single phosphor coating inside the tube. Variety crept in with the addition of amber monitors and later, paper-white screens. These types of monitors are still available. If you have no reason to use color in your work you can save a modest amount of money by sticking to a monochrome monitor.

On the other hand, as the PC world gets more and more into photo-realistic images and graphical environments, you'll probably feel left out if you don't have a dazzling display. The reason monochrome monitors are so much less expensive is that there's only one color of phosphor and a much simpler electron gun design. If you opt for a monochrome display, you'll be limited in your selection. It's easy to find 14-inch or 15-inch green and amber displays. There are also some specialized CAD and desktop-publishing display systems available, but these are generally as expensive as going with a decent mid-range color display system.

The maximum number of colors available on a color monitor will actually be determined by the monitor's maximum scanning frequency and the video adapter it is attached to. It's always important to match a monitor to the intended display adapter, so you will have to know the exact requirements of your graphics adapter for a specific resolution and color depth if you plan on choosing a monitor for that option.

Picture Size

One of the major factors that determine the price of a monitor is the size of its picture. The same thing is true of TV sets. This is because it is much more difficult to build a 21-inch picture tube than it is to build a 14- or even a 17-inch model. Over time this is changing with the increasing demand for larger systems, driven by Microsoft Windows. If you are not a regular Windows user or haven't yet become accustomed to using more than one application at the same time, it may be hard to understand why anyone would want to sit in front of a 21-inch picture tube unless they were trying to lay out something like newspaper pages or engineering drawings. Large monitors offer several advantages. If you are working in Windows, you have a larger on-screen desktop, which makes it much easier to juggle several applications on the screen. To really take advantage of this, you need a sharper (higher resolution) image which is generally easier on the eye, adding to your comfort level.

Large monitors are often the pride of their manufacturer and so they often include the newest features and extra options not found on their smaller counterparts. The drawback is that going from say, a 17-inch monitor to a 21-inch monitor can sometimes double or triple the price. Another drawback to large monitors is that, at very high resolution, the type may be very small and even though it's sharp, you may need glasses to read it.

Graphics adapter manufacturers have come up with some interesting utilities for getting around this problem (we'll cover that shortly). If you are planning on buying a large monitor, you should shop carefully. Most people can do quite well with a 17-inch or even smaller monitor, depending upon the types of applications they use. Coupled with the right adapter card, a 17-inch monitor will easily support three or four open applications under Windows, and the better ones can handle resolutions up to 1600 by 1200 with 16.7 million colors.

Dot Pitch

The technical term for a horizontal line created by the electron gun is a *raster* line. Just how well this line is drawn has a lot to do with the quality of the picture you'll see, how comfortable it is on your eyes, and the cost of the monitor. In a color monitor, as we have already explained, each dot in the raster line is made up of three dots created by the glowing red, green, and blue phosphorus as it is hit by the electron beam. The closer the dots sit together, the sharper the picture. The term *dot pitch* is used to describe the distance between two phosphor dots of the same color on the raster line above or below it. Most good monitors have a dot pitch no larger than 0.28 millimeters (mm). Cheaper monitors have dot pitches of 0.31mm or greater. If you are doing critical work or spend a lot of time in front of a monitor, a tight dot pitch can have a major bearing on how accurate your work is and how comfortable your eyes will be.

Scanning Frequency

The scanning frequency of a monitor is the speed with which it can scan from one corner to another. There are usually two numbers provided: one is the *horizontal scan rate*, which is measured in kilohertz (Khz). This is the time it takes the monitor to scan from the leftmost edge of the screen to the right edge. Generally speaking, for critical applications, you want a horizontal scan rate of 60- to 75KHz. The *vertical scan rate* is the actual refresh rate of the monitor. In other words, the time it takes to actually complete a full scan from one upper corner to the opposite lower corner, drawing a complete picture across the tube.

Generally speaking, a minimum acceptable vertical scan rate is 60Hz; you'll want at least 72Hz at your standard working resolution to avoid flicker and eye strain. Current Swedish MPR II standards, which are designed with the health of the user in mind, call for a standard refresh rate of 80Hz. It's a good idea to pay for the highest refresh rate you can afford. Not only will it be more comfortable on your eyes, but the monitor should be compatible with newer cards for a longer period of time than those with a lower rate.

Some monitors are shipped as *fixed-frequency* devices. That means they only work at one rate. These are less expensive than *multi-frequency* monitors but *multisync* monitors are more flexible and are generally able to work with a wider range of video cards. Not all cards and monitors perform exactly as the numbers listed in the manual. The ability to adjust to varying frequencies allows a monitor to lock on a picture more accurately.

WARNING

If you are looking for a multiscanning monitor along the lines of the original Multisync developed by NEC, be careful if you are shopping with less well-known vendors. Many monitors marketed as multi-frequency devices are not true multi-scanning monitors. There's a big difference. True multi-scanning or multisync monitors have the ability to automatically lock onto the frequency provided by the display adapter. Multi-frequency devices are limited to certain specific scan rates and do not have the ability to automatically adjust, the way a true multi-scanning monitor does. If you obtain both a low-budget monitor and an inexpensive or poorly-designed graphics adapter, you may find that the two devices cannot really lock in properly at some (or possibly all) resolutions.

Screen Types

One of the buzzwords in monitor design is "flat tube display" or "flat square screen." This type of monitor has a picture tube that is designed with an almost flat picture area. This feature reduces the amount of glare on the screen and shows less distortion at the edges. A less-expensive approach is the older round-tube design. This is less costly to make but is more prone to glare and distortion.

NOT ALL MONITORS ARE CREATED EQUAL

There are a large number of variables when it comes to choosing a monitor. In addition to scan rate and some of the other considerations discussed above, you also have to contend with the engineering that went into producing the device. There are several different kinds of phosphors in use, some of which can produce better images with sharper definition and more consistent color. Monitors can always have different ranges of control over brightness, contrast, and fine color adjustments. It is difficult to go into all the possible options. Check to see large-scale comparative tests as done by leading computer magazines, such as *PC Magazine*, *Byte*, and *Computer Shopper*.

Some monitors use digital controls, others analog, to adjust things like brightness, color, and image positioning. Some monitors also offer special controls to minimize visual aberrations such as "pin-cushioning" reduction, which can control distortions but sometimes make the image take on somewhat of a bow-tie effect.

Some monitors and video cards also offer some form of color calibration. While not necessary for general purpose work, calibration can be a big issue if you are going to use some form of color output device, be it a printer or photographic output. This is because a specific color displayed on the screen may not accurately match the one produced by the graphics adapter or produced by the final output device. If you are working with critical applications such as logo design or color photography, improper color correction can be very expensive. Imagine what would happen if you were running the color in a major college's yearbook and the school colors showed up improperly, or if the skin tones in photographs came up with a greenish cast.

The most sophisticated monitors also include dedicated processors which will automatically remember display parameters for certain applications or resolutions. This can be a very handy feature if you are constantly jumping around to different resolutions or pixel depths, or moving out of one operating environment such as Windows to DOS or Windows to AUTOCAD.

ENVIRONMENTAL AND ERGONOMIC STANDARDS

There has been much discussion and even more controversy recently over magnetic and other radiation emitted by computer displays. The Swedish Government has set strict standards for the control of these emissions, as well as ergonomic designs to reduce eyestrain and other workplace hazards. Checking to make sure that your new monitor meets the current Swedish standard (MPR II) is a good way to insure your own safety. Be aware that virtually all monitors produce more emissions to the side or back of the unit than toward the front.

THE BASIC BUYING DECISION

With many PC components, parts are just parts. Many vendors buy components from the same sources and assemble them in virtually identical ways. Monitors and display adapters are an exception to this. There are reasons that vendors such as NEC, Nanao, and Sony have come to enjoy excellent reputations among users. It's a good idea to review round-ups of monitors when making a buying decision.

Even within a top-of-the-line company, there are variances in quality and features in individual models. As a rule of thumb, go for the highest refresh rate with the most features that fit your budget, and match picture size to the kind of work you will be doing. For serious Windows-style applications, a 17-inch monitor is generally preferable to a 14- or 15-inch unit. But most users will have no real reason to spring enough money to move up to a 20- or 21-inch display.

NOTE

These days you should insist on at least a 15-inch monitor.

INSTALLING A MONITOR

Basically, the description on installing the graphics adapter given above covers the majority of steps involved in installing a monitor. You should make sure that the device is in a secure position where it is not easily tipped over or where it will not exert too much weight on whatever it's resting on. Large monitors can easily weigh 40 pounds or more.

When installing the monitor, be sure to read the owner's manual before setting up the unit to make sure that you understand the cabling and the use of all the auxiliary controls. Many monitors offer a degaussing button. This is to clear magnetic interference that can build up over time and distort the picture. Be sure you check the manufacturer's recommendations for using this button before playing with it. Some monitors can be damaged by excessive or improper use of this control.

TROUBLESHOOTING A VIDEO INSTALLATION

Problems with the video system range from the simple to the sublime. In some cases it's nothing more than a bad connection. At its extreme it can be an incompatibility in a driver or in your system's memory management. It can be difficult to isolate and time-consuming to resolve. The following check list can serve as a guide for isolating display-related problems. If your specific case is not resolved using the following steps, you should refer to the manuals that came with your equipment or to the vendor's technical support. Also consult the flowcharts in Appendix G of this book. Following these steps before you make the phone call can simplify matters when you get the technician on the line.

Display System Check List

No Video At All and You Haven't Been Messing Around In Your System.

STEP 1

If you have just turned on the machine, or if the video went down all at once while you were in an application, make sure that the system is still getting power by checking to make sure that all the appropriate power switches are in the "on" position, that the equipment is properly plugged in (all the way back to the wall socket), and that the circuit the system is on is actually getting electrical power. There are cases on record of people calling support technicians and asking why there was no display on the screen because their entire building was suffering a power outage.

STEP 2

If everything is getting power, make sure that the system is actually running. Place your hand over the fan in the power supply. If you don't feel a flow of air, the power supply may be bad, or something may be shorted out in the system itself. If this is true, there may be no problem with your display system at all.

STEP 3

Make sure that the video card is fully seated in its slot. If the card seems to be loose when you check the monitor cable, it may have worked loose from its expansion slot. Be careful, you're just trying to see if it might be loose, NOT trying to make it loose. If it appears like it might be loose, power down the system at once, remove the cover and properly seat the card. A loose card's edge connector can conceivably short out the card, the slot or the motherboard.

STEP 4

Make sure that the monitor is properly cabled to the display adapter. If the cable isn't fully seated it may look like it's properly attached, but may not be sending a signal to the monitor. Double-check to make sure that all the settings on the monitor such as sync type, mode, and other possible options that might have been misadjusted are in their proper orientation. Try adjusting the brightness and contrast controls. It may be that they have gotten set so low that the picture is not visible on the screen.

STEP 5

After you have gone through the above steps, try rebooting the machine.

STEP 6

Do you get any video at all during any portion of the boot process? If so, you may have a memory or driver conflict. Get out a Dark and Stormy Night disk or a plain, bootable DOS disk and try to bring the system up using that disk. You can use a DOS boot disk, even if your hard disk runs on another operating system, like Windows 95 or OS/2. If you can boot from the floppy, you have a software problem, or a display driver problem. Be sure that your system is configured to boot from the floppy. If not, adjust your CMOS Setup so it will. If the PC is seeking drive C first, it won't.

STEP 7

If the system seems to boot, you get the beep and you can see it recognize the floppies, the hard drive, etc., but you get no video, it's most likely a hardware conflict. Before proceeding, try taking the card out and replacing it with another video adapter, preferably a plain vanilla VGA card. Your other option is to try resetting the address, Interrupts, and if necessary, DMA channels (one at a time) and see if you get video that way. You can also try to selectively remove other cards that you think might be causing the conflict from the system; once you have isolated the card, try to find memory addresses, IRQs, or DMA channels that do not conflict. On PCI systems, check the CMOS Setup. On most systems, all the PCI cards share one Interrupt. This usually avoids conflicts, but you may have also set a non-PCI card to the same location.

Step 8

Once you solve the basic problem, you may have to go and reset software or drivers before everything will run properly with the new configuration. You may also have to rework any memory management software if you are running under DOS.

NOTE

If you are operating with two video cards in the system, either because one doesn't have on-board VGA or to set up a dual-monitor system, the trouble could also lie in problems between the two cards or their cabling. Make sure that the VGA pass-through cable is properly seated (refer back to Figure 12.9), and that all switches, especially those concerning video pass-through, are properly set.

No Video, and You Have Just Been Adding New Hardware and/or Software

The most likely option is that there is a hardware conflict if you are getting no video at all. Double-check your Setup to make sure you don't have a direct conflict in DMA, IRQ or address between two or more cards. If you can't immediately isolate a conflict, remove all the cards except the video card and the hard disk/floppy controller. If you have video now, it was a conflict with one of the cards you removed.

Replace them one at a time until you install one that locks up the system again. There's your offender. Adjust the settings between the two cards (the video adapter and the one that was locking things up) until you get things resolved. If the problem persists even after you remove all those cards, try booting after removing the hard disk/floppy controller, if you get video then, that was the offender. You'll have to move either its own or the video card's settings until you find a compatible combination.

You Can See Things When It Starts To Boot but...

...things lock up or you can't get into one or more of your programs even though things work fine under DOS.

This is most likely due to a software incompatibility but it could be a problem with your system BIOS Setup. In some cases, your Setup has different values for monochrome, 80-column, color, VGA, and special adapters. Check your user's manual for your motherboard and find out how to access the Setup program.

If your system Setup is OK, the problem is most likely with one of your drivers or your system memory management. If you are using a memory manager, such as Qualitas 386 to the MAX, Quarterdeck's QEMM or even DOS's EMM386.SYS, memory management may be the root of your problem. Edit your CONFIG.SYS and AUTOEXEC.BAT files, removing any unnecessary calls for drivers or applications. Reboot the system with this minimal configuration and see if the problem goes away. This may take a bit of juggling since you may not have as much memory as is needed to run applications such as Windows.

If this seems to solve the problem, you'll have to experiment with your memory management settings.

If you are using a graphics adapter under DOS that makes use of a specific memory address (for example C800-CFFF) it's usually necessary to exclude this area from Windows' memory management (only worry about this with versions of Windows other than Windows 95 or NT) by placing the following line:

NOTE

EMMExclude=C800-CFFF

into the [**386ENH**] section of your **SYSTEM.INI** file. This keeps Windows from trying to place things into the video display section of memory, which could cause your system to lock up or crash. Check your user's manual for any additional requirements that might be needed to either make your system run smoothly with your new card or to make use of its advanced features.

You could still have a problem with some more subtle memory conflicts, or an Interrupt problem, such as your video card banging into areas used by your mouse or your hard disk controller. Update your Inventory and try experimenting first with removing drivers for other applications, such as your mouse, until you resolve conflicts.

The Black Screen of Death and Things That Go Bump in the Night

The above protocols cover the more standard approaches to solving display system problems, but designing a display and creating a driver is not a simple task. The open design of the PC and its huge market brings all kinds of players into the arena trying to sell us new goodies. The result is a dynamic environment with constant change, and improving toys with lower prices. The downside is incompatibility and the need to constantly refine both our configuration and the vendor's software.

Some video cards and certain programs (especially Windows and other graphical environments) can run out of system resources due to poor design on the part of either a software developer or a hardware manufacturer. One common culprit is the screen saver. These programs can tie up system resources, or rapidly make a number of demands, which can overload a driver. Another problem can be certain drawing modes, especially in graphics programs, that can likewise overload system resources. In Windows 95 and Windows NT the problem may be related to a program designed to run under older versions of Windows, or under DOS. If this is the case, try a newer driver, and notify the maker of the card.

Try to isolate what you were doing when the system crashed or when things got funny. Try duplicating the problem and see if you can pinpoint what triggered it. Contact your vendor and see if other people have been reporting the problem and whether or not they have a fix or a work-around. Find out when new drivers will be released or if one is available now.

While we should be able to expect rock-solid products, even major names in the business are known to ship early or to not have done all their homework. When you first install a new display system it's a good idea to save your work regularly. I make it a habit to save a file before opening another application or attempting to print, just as a matter of safety.

CHAPTER SUMMARY

A computer's display system is one of the most critical components when it comes to performance. It also is a determining factor in what kind of applications you can use and how well-suited it is to working with graphics files. Keeping your display system up to date and well-tuned can make you more productive and reduce the risk of eye-strain.

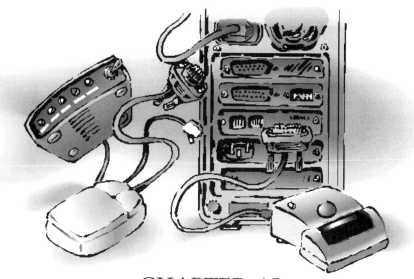

CHAPTER 13

MICE, KEYBOARDS, AND MORE— INPUT DEVICES

WHAT'S IN THIS CHAPTER

- ✔ Installing and Maintaining Keyboards
- ✔ Pointing Devices
- ✔ Choosing a Mouse or Trackball
- ✔ Bus and Serial interfaces
- ✔ Graphics Tablets

✔ Scanners

✔ Desktop vs. Hand Held Scanners

✔ Optical Character Recognition (OCR)

✔ Voice Recognition Systems and Special Needs Options

WHAT THIS CHAPTER IS ABOUT

There is a very basic fact about computers—before you can get information out, you must put information in. While most people use a keyboard as their principal means of talking to their computer, we can also use a mouse, tablet or trackball to communicate our commands and to draw directly on the screen. This chapter covers the fundamentals of selecting, installing and maintaining keyboards, mice, and other input devices. All are similar in one respect: they issue a signal that the computer can interpret as either a command or as usable data. Many people take the lowly keyboard or the click of a mouse button for granted, but there is a wide variety in quality and features involved in their design. While these devices may seem to work with minimal fuss, think of what it would be like if you sat down at your keyboard— and it didn't work.

Of course, the keyboard is not the only way to get data into a PC. *Voice recognition* software, combined with a sound card and microphone, can turn a PC into a transcriber. *Scanners* act as the eyes of a PC, giving it the ability to see images and read text. *Optical Character Recognition* (OCR) software can be used to convert printed text into a form that can be edited in a word processor. *Imaging software* lets us scan photographs, line art, and other pictures into the machine so that they can be incorporated into our document or enhanced using editing software. With an appropriate scanner and the right program, you can turn your PC into a digital darkroom. This chapter also helps you choose a scanner appropriate to your needs and discusses the software available for them.

Installing a new keyboard is as simple as plugging the cord of a light into a wall socket, and most of the time installing a mouse is only a little more involved. The projects discussed in this chapter will require no more tools than a screwdriver, and often not that.

THE KEYBOARD

While your PC's keyboard may closely resemble the layout of a standard typewriter, it is not just a device for making letters and numbers appear on the screen. It is a tool used to issue most of the commands we give our computers, and the navigator that lets us roam through our storage system. While science-fiction movies have computers that can take direct dictation from the human voice, and there are rudimentary programs giving voice recognition for the PC, full-fledged voice-operated computers are still a tool for the future.

The quality of your keyboard has a direct bearing on your level of comfort in using it. If its keys are awkwardly-placed, or the size or touch aren't properly designed for your hand, you'll be much more likely to make mistakes or be slowed down while using it. Typing is a repetitive action requiring fine muscle-motor control. An improperly-made keyboard or one improperly used can actually cause serious physical injury. Some vendors design special keyboards or accessories to minimize risks for heavy users; other vendors provide specially-designed keyboards for disabled individuals so that they can use the computer to lead productive lives. A typical keyboard is shown in Figure 13.1.

FIGURE 13.1 A typical PC keyboard.

How Keyboards Work

In principle, all keyboards work the same. They are a collection of switches. When you press a switch, an electrical signal is sent to the computer. That signal is interpreted as a binary value. The specific value will be looked up in a special table of characters, and the corresponding character or action in that table is then represented on the screen and stored in the computer's RAM. There are four primary types of switches used in computer keyboards: *capacitive*, *conductive*, *mechanical*, and *membrane*.

Mechanical Switch Keyboards

This is probably the most common form of keyboard. In general it has the closest look and feel to a traditional typewriter keyboard. There is a familiar click as you depress a key, and a positive tactile sensation as you use it. A positive tension is produced by a coil spring hidden inside each key, which rests on a plunger. As your finger presses down, a contact is closed, completing the circuit and sending a signal (as illustrated in Figure 13.2). Mechanical keyboards are a bit more complicated to manufacture than some other forms because of the number of parts involved. This is offset by the high-quality feel and precise response.

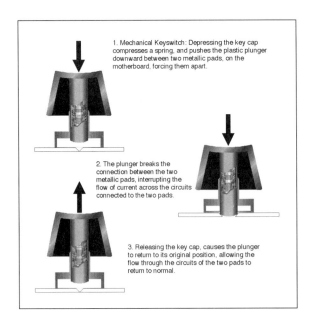

1. Mechanical Keyswitch: Depressing the key cap compresses a spring, and pushes the plastic plunger downward between two metallic pads, on the motherboard, forcing them apart.

2. The plunger breaks the connection between the two metallic pads, interrupting the flow of current across the circuits connected to the two pads.

3. Releasing the key cap, causes the plunger to return to its original position, allowing the flow through the circuits of the two pads to return to normal.

FIGURE 13.2 A mechanical keyboard switch.

Membrane Switch Keyboards

Membrane switches have a very small number of parts. This type of keyboard has a membrane, hence the name, underneath the key. When the key is touched, pressure is exerted against the membrane, closing the switch (See Figure 13.3). Cheap membrane keyboards have an inferior touch to them and are not suitable for heavy use. Newer membrane technology uses a spring/plunger design with a positive feel that approaches that of traditional mechanical designs. Some PCs that rely on membrane keyboards in their design incorporate a speaker-click for feedback to the typist, mimicking the mechanical sound of a key being depressed.

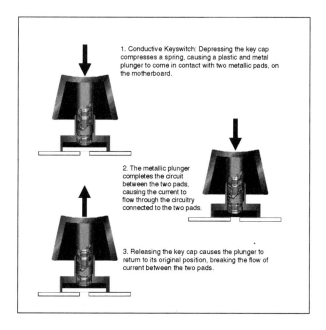

1. Conductive Keyswitch: Depressing the key cap compresses a spring, causing a plastic and metal plunger to come in contact with two metallic pads, on the motherboard.

2. The metallic plunger completes the circuit between the two pads, causing the current to flow through the circuitry connected to the two pads.

3. Releasing the key cap causes the plunger to return to its original position, breaking the flow of current between the two pads.

FIGURE 13.3 A membrane keyboard switch.

Capacitive Switch Keyboards

Capacitive keyboards operate by detecting a change in the electrical impulse. When a key is pressed down, a non-conducting pad is forced against two circuits resting underneath the key. This produces a change in the electrical impulse, signaling that a particular key is depressed. This design is more complex than the other types of computer keyboards. See Figure 13.4.

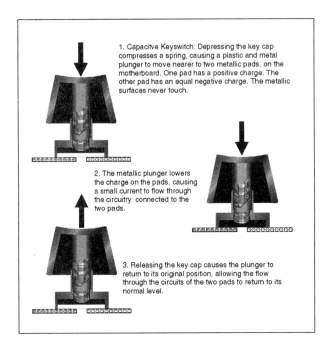

FIGURE 13.4 A capacitive keyboard switch.

Conductive Keyboards

You've probably seen, and maybe even used, keyboards that seem to have a rubber sheath with raised dots for each key. These are conductive keyboards, sometimes referred to as "rubber dome" or "sheath" keyboards. Each of the raised rubber spots contains carbon. When you depress the key, the carbon is pressed down to complete a circuit located underneath (See Figure 13.5). These are generally used for point of sale, cash registers, and for tourist kiosks, as they can be completely covered, and are resistant to liquid spills. As a rule, this form of keyboard is unsuitable for general typing operations.

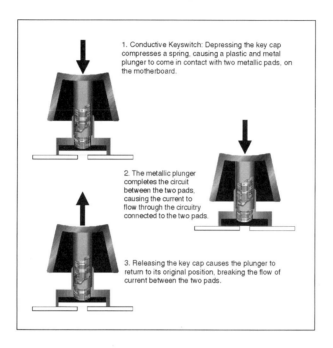

1. Conductive Keyswitch: Depressing the key cap compresses a spring, causing a plastic and metal plunger to come in contact with two metallic pads, on the motherboard.

2. The metallic plunger completes the circuit between the two pads, causing the current to flow through the circuitry connected to the two pads.

3. Releasing the key cap causes the plunger to return to its original position, breaking the flow of current between the two pads.

FIGURE 13.5 A conductive keyboard switch.

Keyboard Layout

Standard Keys

Figure 13.6 shows a typical AT-style keyboard layout. The wide bar in the lower left-hand center is the space bar; above it in a V-shape, the standard typewriter alpha-numeric keyboard appears. Depending on the model you buy, the keys may be arranged in the standard *qwerty* format, or, less frequently, in the optional Dvorak or an international layout offering different placement of keys. On some keyboards the standard alpha-numeric keys are a lighter color, compared to a darker beige or brownish color for the command and function keys.

Figure 13.6 A typical AT-style PC keyboard.

Command and Manipulation Keys

Alongside these standard keys are others some familiar and some new to the novice user. The Tab, Caps-Lock, Shift, and Backspace keys work almost identically to those found on a standard typewriter. The Control, Alternate, and Escape keys are used like additional shift keys, usually combined with standard keys to issue commands to the computer. For readers unfamiliar with the design and use of the computer keyboard, I have detailed the basic layout and function of the keys in the paragraphs below. If you are not a novice user, you'll probably want to skip on to the next heading, where we'll discuss the ins and out of choosing a keyboard.

The Function Keys

The Function keys do invoke specific actions, but can also be used by programs as shortcut keys, allowing the user to issue commands with a single push. Early keyboards placed ten Function keys on the left side in two rows, as in Figure 13.1; most modern units have twelve across the top. If you do a lot of touch typing you might want to investigate models that still have the Function set on the left, which is less disruptive of good hand placement.

The Cursor Pad

The keys of the cursor pad are used to navigate the screen. A flashing bar or block indicates the current active cursor position on the screen; this is the point at which any typing performed will be entered on the display. The cursor keys, usually indicated by arrows, let us move the cursor position as desired. Some older keyboards do not have a separate cursor pad, and the very earliest ones may require the use of various alpha-numeric keys, along with one of the command keys, to move the cursor. If you have one of these units, you need a new machine and the old one belongs in a museum. See Figure 13.7.

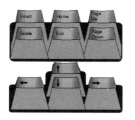

Inverse "T"
Cursor

Combination
Cursor/Numeric
Keypad

FIGURE 13.7 A cursor pad.

Many programs also support express-navigation keys, also found on the cursor pad. These include Page Up and Page Down, which scroll and display a page on the screen at a time, and the Home and End keys, which can move to the very top or bottom of a file. The Insert and Delete keys are usually also found on this keypad.

The Numeric Keypad

A calculator-style block of keys is often included on modern keyboards. This allows the rapid entry of strings of numbers, as well as the standard arithmetic symbols (+, –, =, ÷).

The Enter or Return Key

New users often confuse the return key with the traditional type-writer carriage return. Most computer programs will automatically wrap text to the line below when the edge of the display is reached, so a carriage return symbol is used only to show the end of a para-graph. The Enter key not only places a typewriter-like hard carriage return into a text document, but is also used to signal the computer that a command sequence is complete and should be executed.

CHOOSING A KEYBOARD

There are four things to consider when choosing a keyboard: com-patibility, comfort, cost, and features. Keyboards range in price from a low of about $19, with most name-brand keyboards costing in the $75 to $125 range. Exotic, ergonomic designs and special keyboards for handicapped users can exceed these numbers many times over. It's a good idea to spend some time investigating your keyboard purchase, not so much from a cost standpoint, but for how it's going to work for you. A keyboard that is uncomfortable or difficult to use can make working at your computer difficult. Keys that are placed too close together, exotic placements, or a small Enter key can be frustrating, to say the least.

Compatibility

There are three compatibility issues when it comes to keyboards. The original IBM-XT is not compatible with all the later AT, 386, 486, etc. models. Some third-party vendors produce keyboards that have a switch, allowing them to be used with either type of machine. In general, all keyboards produced today are AT-style keyboards. The only time to be concerned about this is when buying a used key-board: make sure it's compatible with your machine.

A second real compatibility issue is how the keyboard attaches to your computer. Most PCs use a 5-pin DIN-style (*DIN* is the acronym for the German national standards institute which set the specifications) connector, as shown in Figure 13.8. Some compact IBM PS/2 and a few other manufactures use a smaller 6-pin connector resembling that of a PS/2 Mouse connector. Be sure that the keyboard and your motherboard have appropriate fittings so that they can be connected.

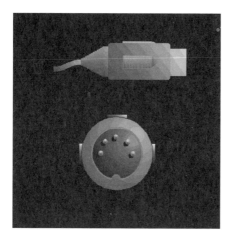

FIGURE 13.8 A DIN-style keyboard cable connector.

A semi-compatibility issue is the length of the cord. If you are attaching your new keyboard to a tower case that rests across the desk from where you will be using it, or if you like to lean back in your chair, you may need a keyboard with a longer cable. Some manufacturers are more generous than others. If the keyboard of your dreams comes with a shorter cable, you can usually find an extension in most computer shops.

The only other real compatibility concern is with software. Virtually all keyboards use the standard original keyboard layout; some specialty keyboards, made for specific programs like WordPerfect, offer additional keys that allow you to execute multi-keystroke commands by pressing a single button. Probably the most popular extended-set keyboard is the Northgate Omni-Key. It not only has the traditional function keys along the left side, but has another row of function keys across the top. These function keys can be programmed to perform *Shift/Function* key and *Control/Function* key actions with a single stroke. It also allows you to shift the placement of the Control and Key-lock functions.

Comfort

Comfort is both an objective and a subjective topic. Poor keyboard design, as mentioned before, can actually lead to injury. The computer age has increased the incidence of *Carpal Tunnel Syndrome* and other *Repetitive Stress Injury* (RSI). If you are continually executing the same motions over and over again, you are at risk of RSI.

Generally speaking, you should take a break every hour or so and rest your hands and wrists for at least five minutes. There are also exercises, such as shaking your hands and wrists as if trying to shake off water, that can be performed to reduce the risk of RSI. Since this is not a medical book, you should consult with your health care provider for exercises which might be of use. The carpal tunnel is a place in your wrist where the radial nerve, which runs down your arm, passes into your hand. Carpal Tunnel Syndrome is pain produced when the tendons are over-used, which results in swelling and pain. In some cases, the ailment can last for months, making it impossible to type; in extreme cases, surgery is needed.

The computer keyboard is much easier to use than a traditional typewriter, and doesn't require carriage returns or inserting paper into the machine. As a result, typists often sit for hours just keying-in, and the position of the keyboard may also be a contributing factor to RSI. If you do a lot of keyboarding without breaks, you should seek advice on how to minimize risk. There are a number of products available, such as wrist supports and specially-designed keyboards, that can help. One company, Fox Bay, makes a line of pads and cushions that can be used with both keyboards and mice. Forminco is another company that has entered the office comfort business. They make a series of products including complete work-stations and even massaging foot-rests, to reduce the risk of stress injuries.

Ergonomic Keyboards

Microsoft offers the most widely-known of the ergonomic keyboards, providing a more natural alignment of hand position and wrist support in a single design. It is called, naturally, the *Microsoft Natural Keyboard*, and is shown in Figure 13.9. I find that these devices work a lot better for those who touch-type. They have the ability to work with the new layouts, while those of us who hunt and peck seem to be slowed down by the shift in key locations. The result for me, the new boards add up to sore wrists. To each his or her own. If you do a lot of typing they may well be worth the money, about $100.

FIGURE 13.9 Microsoft Natural Keyboard.

Special Keyboards for the Disabled

Ergonomic design is aimed at reducing the possibility of your keyboard injuring you with improper use, but there is another class of keyboard and input device which helps you if your hands are already injured or don't function normally. In fact, the computer has opened a new world of work, communication, and pleasure for many people with physical disabilities. IBM and other vendors provide a variety of special input devices for people who for one reason or another do not have normal use of their hands. Given the variety and scope of such alternative input devices, it is beyond the scope of this book to discuss them in detail. If you or someone you know needs such devices, you should check with an appropriate health care provider as well as one of these manufacturers for assistance in selecting the device that's right for your needs.

Cost

Keyboards range in price from a low of about $20 for low-quality imports to over $1000 for high-end ergonomic design. When selecting a keyboard the most important consideration is comfort. The comfort of your keyboard and the way it suits your typing technique will have a direct impact on your productivity and how well you like sitting down to use your computer. Keyboards, probably more than any other component of your computer, are a matter of individual taste. Keyboards like the Northgate Omni-Key 101 have a crisp feel, an audible click, and programmable keys that allow you to shift the location of some of the keys to suit individual working styles. Such keyboards generally cost in the $90 to $150 range.

Features: Bells and Whistles

In addition to the standard keys, a number of vendors, including Lexmark (an IBM company) and KeyTronic, produce products that incorporate track-balls or that have additional keys. There are also several different ways the cursor pad can be arranged. These include a cross shape and the inverted T. The cross shape is found on keyboards that have numeric keypads doubling as cursor controls. The problem with the cross shape is that there is a key in the middle that has nothing to do with cursor movement. When your hand is resting on the keypad, your left and right fingers control the side to side movement very easily, but your middle finger must travel farther than is needed to move the cursor up and down. Keyboards with an inverted T have dedicated cursor controls using only four keys, three across the bottom and one directly above the one in the middle. Several studies have shown that this arrangement is both faster and easier on the fingers.

Built-In Trackballs

One KeyTronic keyboard incorporates a keyboard wrist pad and pointing device all in one unit. While I will save the general discussion of trackballs for later on in the chapter, this is a good example of how some vendors are producing integrated designs. While I personally prefer a mouse, I find this kind of arrangement does offer the advantage of reducing how far my hands have to travel to move the pointer, just simply a matter of dropping a thumb back from the spacebar onto the roller. Lexmark and other vendors offer versions with the trackball roller built right into the keyboard itself. This is also a popular design on some laptop and notebook computers.

INSTALLING A KEYBOARD

As I mentioned at the beginning of the chapter, this is probably one of the easiest procedures in the PC world. On most machines, the keyboard is plugged directly into a socket on the motherboard, usually with a 6- or 5-pin DIN connector. This socket is accessible through a hole cut into the case at the back, so that the operation can be conducted without opening the machine. Some PS/2 and Compaq models have a smaller DIN connector, which is plugged into a socket located on the outside of the computer case.

Step 1

Turn off the computer. Then unplug the existing keyboard if it is present. Note the size of the connector, the number of pins and their position. Most DIN connectors are equipped with some sort of key structure, making sure that the connector can only be inserted in one way. Look at the connector and its matching slot. There is usually a plastic square that projects out with the pins from the end of the cable, and a corresponding hole in the fitting on the computer. All you have to do is line them up to get a proper fit.

Step 2

Find the manual for your keyboard. Note any DIP switches or toggle switches that must be set to match it up with your type of computer. If you are unsure about how to do this, refer to "Setting Switches" in Chapter 6. As mentioned before, some keyboards can be used with either the old-style XT and the newer AT-style machines. If the switches are set wrong, the keyboard will not operate.

Some keyboards allow you to define certain key functions and their locations by setting DIP switches. If your device supports these features and you want to use them, consult your owner's manual. Once this is completed, you are ready to attach the keyboard to the computer.

Step 3

Line the pins of the keyboard's connector up with the socket on the computer. Gently push the connector into place. If it doesn't go smoothly, rotate it slightly while applying gentle pressure. Do not force it. Excessive force could bend or break either one of the pins or the socket on the motherboard. This is especially true with the newer, smaller cables, which have very fine pins. The cost of repairing such a cable will often exceed the value of the keyboard. Reasonable care is all that's needed, but do exercise care.

Step 4

Turn the power onto the computer and watch the screen as the computer goes through its Power-On-Self-Test. If your keyboard is not properly switched or connected, the POST will indicate a keyboard failure or a keyboard error. In all likelihood it should work fine the first time. If it doesn't, try reseating the cable and if it is seated properly, check the setting on the DIP switches or toggle switch.

KEYBOARD MAINTENANCE AND TROUBLESHOOTING

Keep It Clean

Keyboards require very little maintenance. In fact, you shouldn't feed them or give them anything to drink. The most common cause of keyboard problems stems from eating or drinking while sitting at your computer. Crumbs from sandwiches, bits of potato chips, and popcorn hulls can get between the keypad and the switches underneath them. These can result in keys that don't operate properly when depressed. If you have a keyboard that allows you to remove the keycaps by pulling directly up (most do) you can do so and remove any foreign matter underneath them. Keep in mind, an ounce of prevention is worth two hours of cure. Better to not eat and drink next to your keyboard. Some of the larger keys, like the Space key and the Return key, may also have secondary springs and latches underneath them. If you have to get such a key off, consult your owner's manual or the manufacturer's technical support department before proceeding. Some keyboards have very small springs lying directly under the keypad. Be careful when taking the key off so that you do not lose the spring or have it hit you in the eye when you remove the key.

If you have to remove several keys, you may want to place them on a counter-top in the same orientation in which you removed them. There are many different ways to lay out a keyboard, especially the Control, Alt, Shift, and Tab keys. If you put a key into the wrong position, you may have to spend several minutes pecking about finding out where it should go. It's a lot easier to get it right the first time.

Spills

Cookie crumbs are one thing, coffee, Cokes and prune juice quite another. Hot and sugary liquids can destroy a keyboard. In event of this catastrophe, one manufacturer has recommended immediately putting the keyboard under cold running water. Be sure you power down the computer and detach the keyboard before trying that! You may have to disassemble the unit to allow it to properly dry. Most keyboards are enclosed in their case with several screws placed around the edges of the underside of the case. If you have to disassemble your keyboard, proceed slowly; place the screws as you remove them in a cup or some other container so they don't get lost. Once the case is released, you may find that there are other screws that hold additional components to the board the keys rest on. Given the many differences in design, it is impossible to give detailed instructions for disassembly of your keyboard. If the proper steps aren't obvious, you may have to contact technical support for assistance. If you have a inexpensive imported keyboard, there may not be any technical support that you can reach, other than the dealer from whom you bought the device.

WARNING While it may help to use a blow dryer to speed evaporation of the water, use it only on low or no heat. It's possible that the heat generated by the high setting could destroy connections or delicate electronic parts.

Keyboard Covers

There are two basic kinds of covers you can get for your keyboard to protect it from spills. One is basically a dust cover; when you are not using your keyboard, you can cover it up. These don't offer much protection, as the keyboard is in more danger when there are human beings around it than when it is sitting there idle. The second kind is a clear membrane that molds itself to the upper surface of the keyboard, allowing you to actually use it when it is covered. This can protect your keyboard from spills and crumbs but many people find the feel of the cover a distraction. As with almost everything regarding keyboards, covers are a matter of personal preference.

BIOS Upgrades

Many keyboards also have a replaceable BIOS chip located somewhere on the circuit board underneath the keys, but which is concealed by the design of the case. Over time the manufacturer may redesign the BIOS to improve compatibility with other system components, or to offer improved features, such as programmable keys. It is sometimes possible to re-work the design of a keyboard by replacing the BIOS. For example, the Northgate Omni-Key has gone through several BIOS revisions to change the function of certain keys, including the cursor pad. I actually obtained an older BIOS from them for one of my keyboards to change part of the cursor function back to the way it had been on an earlier model.

THE MOUSE AND OTHER POINTING DEVICES

In the early days of the PC, the keyboard was the only input device you needed. Unless you were doing some kind of sophisticated graphics work, like *computer-aided design* (CAD) you didn't need a mouse or graphics tablet. As graphic applications became available, mice started appearing next to the computers of illustrators and desktop publishers, but few applications really took advantage of the desktop rodents. All that has changed. Microsoft Windows has probably done more for the status of mice in our society than Walt Disney. Today a pointing device is considered an indispensable part of most systems. You can't effectively use a graphical interface such a Windows, OS/2 or X-Windows without the ability to point and click, drag and drop your objects on the screen.

Not All Mice are Created Equal

From the outside all mice look much the same. While they may have different shapes and some have more buttons than others, all are designed to rest under your palm and have buttons in the front. All serve one basic purpose: they move a cursor across the display as your hand moves the mouse on the desk. But looks can be deceiving. There are several different ways to make a mouse operate, and not all of us have the same size hands, or even use the same one to operate a mouse. Those distinctions can have a great deal to do with how well a mouse suits your needs; one mouse doesn't fit all. Vendors have to make trade-offs; a mouse for a man with large hands will not suit a child and a left-handed person may find the button placement on a right-handed mouse tiring.

Just as with keyboards, using a mouse improperly can lead to Repetitive Stress Injury. Many newer mice are incorporating shapes and button placements based on ergonomic studies, to produce a shape that will be comfortable for the average user. Since different engineers will have different definitions of "average," it pays to shop for a mouse with as much concern for comfort as for your pocketbook. There is also the issue of software compatibility. Some vendors provide a variety of drivers and utilities and some do not. Prices for a mouse can range from less than $10 to several hundred.

How a Mouse Works

To an engineer the most obvious distinction might be in how the mouse works. There is no magic in the way the pointer travels as you move the mouse. The device communicates the direction and the amount of travel to the PC. There are three methods used to do that: *optical*, *optical-mechanical* and *mechanical*. The optical variety uses a special mouse pad that has a fine patchwork of horizontal and vertical lines. LEDs (Light Emitting Diodes) shine onto the surface, and receptive transistors note movement over the grid, which is then converted into X,Y coordinates in the software drivers. Since there are no moving parts other than the buttons, optical mice are the most reliable. The drawbacks are in having to use a special pad, and in the strict one-to-one ratio of movement. See Figure 13.10.

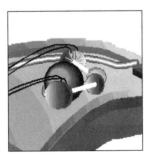

FIGURE 13.10 Cut away view of a typical mouse..

Mechanical mice use a set of spinning wheels to detect motion. Tiny wire brushes work with a series of metal contacts placed on the wheels to measure hand movements. While this type of mouse is inexpensive, it is less accurate than other methods and more prone to problems with dirt, dust, and weak parts.

The majority of today's mice are opto-mechanical and don't require a special pad. They have light-sensitive semi-conductors, which work with slotted wheels attached to rollers that touch a ball inside the mouse. The slots produce flickers of light as the mouse is moved, which translate into cursor movement. Since you can use it on any surface and it doesn't require a one-to-one ratio, these devices offer a more flexible response and will work on a variety of surfaces. The down side is the addition of delicate moving parts, along with balls and rollers, that can pick up dirt and grime.

How Many Buttons Do You Need?

Most PC mice sport two and some, three buttons. Until very recently, few software programs took advantage of more than one. Mac users for years have gotten along with just one button. Mouse commands are basically a combination of clicks, or of holding down a mouse button and then moving the device. Logitech and Mouse Systems provide drivers with their mice that let you customize the second (and sometimes the third) button as a hot-key shortcut. Newer editions of software, such as Windows 95, are starting to make use of the right button for pop-up menus and pre-defined functions. CAD users and others interested in 3-D graphics may find a three-button mouse indispensable, since those applications make extensive use of them for complex navigation and object-manipulation commands.

Most users will find that two buttons will serve them admirably. If you are very fond of using macros and customizing your operating environment (and have a lot of manual dexterity) you may find the third button useful. Personally, I find that the way a mouse feels in my hand and how easy it feels to depress the button is more important than the number of buttons. Button placement to me is more important than number. If it is hard for me to comfortably or accurately click a button, it makes it much more difficult to use a program.

Resolution

One term you'll hear in relation to mice is that of *resolution*. This is an indication of their ability to interpret distance. The higher the resolution (measured in *dots per inch* or *dpi*), the finer the sensitivity and more control over movement. The first PC mice were 200-dpi devices. Today most range from 300 to 400 dpi, with some offering 700 dpi and above.

Higher numbers translate into faster on-screen movement of the pointer. Most mice can be tuned to move sharply without fine resolution by adjusting a ballistic variable via the control panel. This lets you have fine control of the cursor when the mouse is moved slowly, but increases the rate of travel when you move your hand quickly. Many mice also offer a variety of other controls as part of their driver. Figure 13.11 shows the Windows 3.1 Control Panel for the Microsoft mouse.

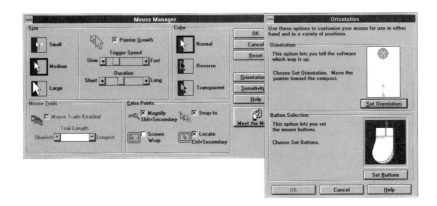

FIGURE 13.11 The software control panel for the Microsoft mouse.

Be wary of claims of very high resolution. Some mice use software to simulate resolution of 1000 dpi or more. For most users 400 dpi will be more than satisfactory. If you need very find control for graphic applications, you may want to consider adding a digitizing pad (discussed later in this chapter) to your system as well as a mouse. Of course, there's more to control than just resolution. To get a mouse to work on your system, you need a software driver. Some vendors, mostly those selling mice from about $35 to $50, offer one that will give you a mouse cursor under Windows and not much more. For more money, you get more features. The better mice come with control panels that allow you to swap buttons, increase resolution, and even map mouse clicks to the application's macro language.

Software compatibility is a major issue when choosing a mouse. Virtually all mice have Windows compatibility and that usually isn't much of a problem, but getting your mouse to work with other applications (or other operating environments) may often not be possible without special drivers. It's a good idea to check for drivers for any special applications you need before making a purchase.

More than Just a Matter of Comfort

Major vendors like Microsoft and Logitech redesigned the shape of their mice a few years ago at great cost. They didn't do it just for eye appeal. We tend to be mousing around more than we used to, and that can lead to health problems. There is a lot more attention being paid today as to how well a mouse fits its user's hands and work methods. Vendors may be civic-minded, or they may want to fend off possible lawsuits. These new editions are supposed to reduce hand and wrist Repetitive Stress Injuries such as tendonitis and Carpal Tunnel Syndrome (CTS). These can be painful and often long-term problems that have been associated with the use of computer keyboards and mice because of the constant small movements needed for typing and clicking buttons. RSI can keep a worker off the payroll for months. CTS is an inflammation of the wrist that can require surgery. In 1992 the number of RSI injuries reported to the U.S. Department of Labor was 800% higher than in 1982, when the IBM-PC went on sale.

There are several things you can do to reduce the risk of RSI, according to experts. One is to make sure that your hardware is properly positioned to avoid strain. Your family physician or physical therapist can probably provide brochures that show how to do this. Others are to take frequent short breaks, and to not ignore pain. Several vendors make a variety of accessories similar to those for keyboards. One of the more elaborate such gadgets is the Mouse Arena from Forminco. This is a combination wrist-support, mouse pad, and cord control, as can be seen in Figure 13.12.

FIGURE 13.12 The Mouse Arena.

Making a Connection

While I'll save the actual discussion of how to install a mouse, trackball or other pointing device until later in the chapter, you need to understand how they are attached to the PC before we move on. Some computers are equipped with a mouse port already built in (such as IBM PS/2's and many laptops or notebooks). Serial mice get their name from the fact that they are attached to one of your computer's serial or Com ports. Bus mice come with their own expansion card. If you have a free Com port, you may want to get a serial mouse. You can attach it without even opening the case and it won't take up a slot. If you don't want to lose one of your Com ports to your pointing device, then a bus mouse is probably the way to go, unless you have a mouse port already built into your system. See Figure 13.13.

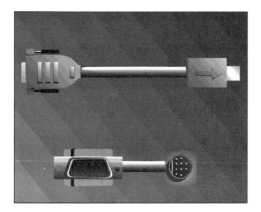

FIGURE 13.13 A bus mouse connector.

A variation on the serial mouse is the (almost) cordless mouse. These devices use a small infrared or radio-sensing unit to transmit signals through a serial port into the PC. The sending unit is housed in the mouse itself. This allows you to have a device that requires no cords directly where you are working, but you will pay a bit more for the privilege. Because of the extra electronics, some of these units tend to be a bit heavier. As with anything else with mice, it becomes a matter of personal preference.

A BRIEF RODENT ROUND-UP

As mentioned before, all mice are not created equal, but which mouse is right for you depends as much on how it fits in your hand as the features that come in the box. Before we cover how to attach a mouse to your system, I'd like to give you an idea of some of the types of devices that are available. The following pages contain thumbnail reviews of a number of mice currently available from the major vendors. Microsoft and Logitech control a lion's share of the mouse market in this country. Microsoft offers one basic design while Logitech offers a series. Another well-known name is Mouse Systems.

The following list of players is by no means complete, but it will give you a reasonable idea of what is available and highlight some of the more noteworthy products.

Appoint's Gulliver and MousePen

Appoint has been known for years for building mice that don't look like mice. Their first product, the MousePen, looks very much like a stylus for a digitizing pad but a bit more square in design, with the buttons located roughly where your forefinger would rest on a pencil (See Figure 13.14). It's sibling, the Gulliver, is a very compact pointing device roughly the same size and almost identical in appearance to an artist's wedge-shaped eraser. You can use the Gulliver like a normal mouse. The primary button is on the leading edge of the device, with a smaller button placed farther back. It's also possible to use the Gulliver like a trackball by flipping it over on its back. Appoint products are a bit different from the average mouse, but well-designed and very suited for switching off between a desktop unit and a laptop or notebook. Appoint is also working on a cordless version of the Gulliver which we had a chance to *beta test* (pre-release evaluation) while this book was in production.

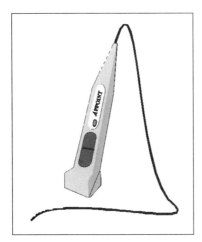

FIGURE 13.14 Appoint's MousePen.

The KeyTronic Mouse

Don't look for a ball on the bottom of this mouse; instead you'll find two teflon feet on the underside. These serve as optical-mechanical sensors. KeyTronic claims this design makes it almost impervious to dirt and grime and so easier to maintain and more accurate. It is available in both two and three-button versions and can be used either on a Com port or with a PS/2 style connection.

The Logitech Litter

Logitech makes a variety of mice; the mainstay being the MouseMan series. These are well-suited for people with medium- to large-sized hands, and come in two- and three-button versions. All of these are shipped as serial mice and have adapters so they can be used in the PS/2 port. There's also a reversed edition available for left-handed users.

The MouseMan ships with a full set of utilities, as well as drivers that are compatible with the Microsoft Mouse. Sophisticated controls allow you to adjust how the mouse behaves on the screen and configure the second and third button to automatically invoke program commands. See Figure 13.15.

FIGURE 13.15 Logitech's MouseMan.

Their cordless version of the MouseMan is available for $110. It has the same basic appearance, but is angled a little more sharply in the back. If you turn the cordless version over, you'll find that it has to have a battery and uses a much smaller ball, set over to one side, than the traditional MouseMan. If you do an awful lot of intensive mouse work you may find the cordless version a bit tiring.

KidzMouse

One of the most unique is Logitech's KIDZ Mouse. Shipped in a box that resembles a piece of swiss cheese, it looks like a mouse with green ears for buttons, two raised bumps for eyes, a very pointy nose and a small rounded body. Unlike most mice its cord curves around from the back like a tail. It's also the only mouse I've ever seen that comes with a dinosaur game for teaching basic reading skills. While researching this chapter, I presented the mouse to my three-year old daughter, who exclaimed both her delight with its appearance and her preference for the way it fitted her hand. Preschoolers will love this mouse but adults find it a bit small. In order to allow for this, Logitech has made it possible to use two mice on the same system.

First Mouse

This in an entry-level three-button mouse from LogiTech which does not have the fancy ergonomic design or all the sophisticated software controls of its siblings. If you are shopping on a budget and want a brand-name, this mouse may pass; but keep in mind that if you spend a lot of time working with a mouse, except for those with very small hands, this mouse may not be comfortable over time.

The Redmond Rodent

Microsoft says it spent $10 million in ergonomic and user input when designing its latest version of its famous white mouse (Version 2.0). At first appearance it may seem that this mouse is a bit bulky, but it fits the hand well and is almost equally suited for left or right-hand use. It also possesses one of the most positive but not difficult button clicks of any of the pointing devices I've used over the years. It is available in both a bus version with its own adapter card or with a serial connector. This is the unit that almost all the PCs in my lab have attached. See Figure 13.16.

FIGURE 13.16 Microsoft Mouse 2.0.

The Series from Mouse Systems

While Mouse Systems may not have the market share of the two industry leaders, it does produce some interesting products. The most notable of its offerings is the PC Mouse 3D (See Figure 13.17). If you are really into buttons and are a frustrated top-gunner, this may be the mouse for you. If you include the two switches located on the left side of the device, it offers six buttons. Inside Windows and other supported software such as AUTOCAD, you can control not only the horizontal and vertical movements of your pointer, but yaw and pitch as well. While the last two may only be of real use in CAD and other 3-D applications, Mouse Systems has included customization software that allows you to write macros to invoke commands by using a specific mouse click, rather than having to go to a menu and find them. This is a very light-weight optical mouse with excellent control and a comfortable fit for small to somewhat larger than medium hands. You may find yourself at a disadvantage if you are a lefty because of the two buttons located on the left-hand side.

FIGURE 13.17 The 3D mouse.

If you don't need all the fancy gadgets on the 3D but like the ergonomics, try the New Mouse. This uses the same Mouse Systems case minus the roller ball found at the front of the 3D, and lacking some of its more advanced controls. On the plus side, you get a very ergonomically-pleasing case, along with excellent setup software.

PC Mouse, PC Mouse III, and the White Mouse

If you have a small hand, you might be satisfied with one of these three. The PC Mice use serial connections; one sports two buttons, the other three. If you have large hands, you will probably find this design too small and the mouse click a bit difficult. All three products share the same basic shape. The buttons can be reversed for those who are left-handed. If you are looking for just a plain mouse, these ought to fit your needs, but don't expect any bells and whistles.

TRACKBALLS—A DIFFERENT POINT OF VIEW

The trackball is an alternative to a mouse. In reality a trackball is not much more than a mechanical mouse twisted around, so the buttons are still on the top and the ball that is normally on the bottom is now where it can be operated by the thumb or by the palm of the hand. They work almost exactly the same, in that you move the cursor on the screen by rolling the ball, usually with your thumb, sometimes with the palm of your hand. Figure 13.18 shows the TrackMan. Microsoft offers a version called the BallPoint, which is designed to be used primarily with portable computers since it can be clamped onto the side.

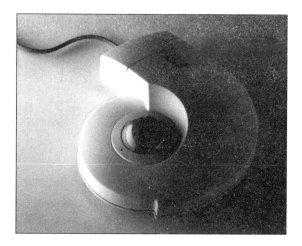

FIGURE 13.18 The Logitech TrackMan.

Trackballs are installed and maintained just like mice so we'll cover their care and maintenance at the same time later in this chapter.

Trackballs have one distinct advantage over mice: they require very little desk space. Whereas you have to pick up a mouse and move it, the trackball stays stationary. With a mouse you must keep at least a 6-by-6-inch grid open on your desktop to use it effectively. Another advantage is that as long as you have not been eating sticky foods, the ball should not get gummed up over time from rolling over the surface of your desk or pad, as mice often do.

THE TOUCHPAD

This is a pointing device that is finding its way onto laptops, and then migrating to the owner's desktop machine. Instead of a moving device, you move your finger over a pad that detects the change in location. While there are buttons, a tap on the surface will serve the same purpose as a click. It takes a bit of getting used to, but there are no moving parts. This is a real option to the trackball for those with limited desk space. One of the stand-alone units is shown in Figure 13.19.

FIGURE 13.19 A touchpad.

THE NO-MOUSE MOUSE AND OTHER VARIATIONS ON A THEME

Periodically some inventor comes up with an idea for a better mouse, assuming that the world will beat a track to his or her door. These include mice that are shaped like pens with a small ball in the tip so you can in effect write your way across the screen, and there is even a no-mouse mouse available from Abacus Software. This is a software emulator that uses the cursor keys to move the mouse cursor across the screen. While Windows will let you use the cursor keys to move the mouse, the No-Mouse mouse will let you configure custom set-ups to control tracking speed and the rate of acceleration, as well as allowing you to configure certain keys for diagonal configuration, so you will not have to mouse over and up. The no-mouse is primarily useful for those who travel and don't want to drag along a mouse. If you do much work under Windows or do any graphics, you will find that such an approach does not offer the flexibility found in the hardware.

INSTALLING A MOUSE ,TRACKBALL, OR TOUCHPAD

Installing a mouse is generally a simple task. If you have a serial mouse and are attaching it to a Com port, you probably won't even have to open the case. The same is true if you have an appropriate mouse port. If you have to install an adapter card you will need a screwdriver both to get into your case and for the expansion slot cover.

Step 1

Determine the kind of connection you will be using. Mice attach either to a Com port, to a specialized bus card, or to a PS/2 style adapter.

Installing a Serial Mouse

Step 2

Make sure the Com port you wish to use is free. If you do not have a free Com slot on your machine and need to add an I/O card, refer to the section on I/O cards and communications in Chapter 14.

Step 3

Identify the Com port you wish to use and plug the connector on the mouse into it. You may have to use an adapter if your mouse is designed to fit into several different styles of connections. See your instruction manual.

Step 4

Locate the installation disk for your mouse and install its software (if the machine is off, boot it first). Some mice use drivers that can be invoked without re-booting the machine. Others place a line in your CONFIG.SYS file and have to be rebooted.

Step 5

If you plan on using the mouse under Microsoft Windows, you'll also want to run the Windows Setup program from the Windows directory (or from Microsoft's Setup disks if you are doing a new Windows installation). See your Microsoft Windows or mouse manual for more instructions.

Step 6

Once the driver is properly loaded into memory, load a program that uses the mouse and make sure the cursor works properly. Use the mouse utilities or mouse control panel under Windows to customize the setting for clicking speed, rate of travel, etc. Redo your Dark and Stormy Night Disk.

The PS/2 Connector Mouse

PS/2 style mice have their own special connection port. Some of these mice can also be attached to a Com port with an appropriate adapter, often included with the mouse. The basic instructions are as above. Locate your port, make sure the connector is properly oriented and push it in gently. The pins on this kind of connector tend to be fragile, so be careful that you don't bend them by trying to force it when they are not perfectly lined up. Once the mouse is installed, go ahead and load the software according to the instructions in your user's manual.

N O T E

You can use a serial mouse with a PS/2-style port by obtaining a special adapter. This will let you use the same serial mouse for a desktop, and attach it to a laptop with a PS/2 port.

Installing a Bus Mouse

Installing a bus mouse is a little more complicated than working with a serial or PS/2-style connection because you have to install an adapter card. The majority of mouse cards today are either half-slot or smaller. The one from Microsoft seen in Figure 13.20 is a good example.

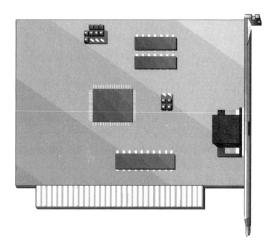

FIGURE 13.20 Microsoft bus mouse adapter card.

What You'll Need

✔ Screwdriver

✔ Small cup for holding screws and other miscellaneous parts

✔ Mouse kit including card, mouse, software, and manual

Step 1

Locate a free Interrupt address (IRQ). As discussed in Chapter 5, a mouse card will require a free Interrupt to be able to communicate with your computer. If you don't have a second printer port, and not many cards in your system, Interrupt (IRQ) 5 should be available. If you are not sure, use the software contained on the disk in the back of the book, some other utility, or refer to the Inventory Sheet discussed in Chapter 5, if you created one. Before opening the case you should know which Interrupts are available on your system. It's usually easier to get this done using software before turning off your computer.

Step 2

Turn off power to the system and remove the power cord. If you try to remove or install cards with the power turned on, you may seriously injure the cards and/or the motherboard.

Step 3

Prepare to install the card. Remove the cover from your computer's case by removing the screws holding it along the back, outer edge of the machine. Touch the inside metal chassis to ground yourself; this will prevent creating a static-electricity spark that might damage a chip. Now open the box that the mouse came in and remove the card from its protective envelope. Depending on the type of card, you will have one or more jumpers which should be checked and which may need to be reset before installing. I'll give you some of the details here for a Microsoft Mouse. If you are using another type, or a later version, you may need to refer to your manual for additional instructions.

Step 4: Port Selection

Microsoft refers to their bus mouse card as an *InPort adapter*. If you are only installing one such card in your system, you can leave the port selection switch set for primary InPort. This is handled with a three-pin jumper block. Make sure the jumper is covering the two pins on the side that says "pri InPort." Unless you are installing a card in the last slot of an old IBM-XT computer, you should have the jumper block labeled *XT Slot 8* (another three-jumper block) jumper over the two pins next to the label "normal."

For most users, the only really important jumper will be to set the Interrupt. If you don't have an active second printer port, IRQ 5 is usually a good choice—unless you have already used it for something else on your system. The Microsoft bus mouse card allows you to place a jumper to select IRQs 2, 3, 4, and 5. IRQs 3 and 4 are normally used by your system's Com ports and unless you can disable one of those, choosing these positions can cause a conflict. IRQ 2 does have some function related to a floppy controller, but is not likely to cause conflict. Once you set the jumpers, you are ready to install the card into the machine. If your card has any other jumpers or DIP switches, you should check your user's manual before proceeding to the next step.

Step 5

Locate a free expansion slot and remove the back cover plate. Once again touch the edge of the case to make sure that you aren't carrying any static charge, then with gentle pressure insert the card into the free slot. Use the screw that held the expansion plate cover to lock the card into place. Replace the cover on the computer. See Figure 13.21.

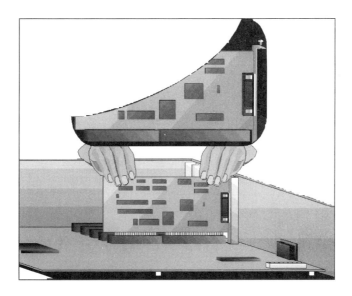

FIGURE 13.21 Installing a card into a slot.

Step 6

With gentle pressure, insert the connector for the mouse into the hole in the back of the expansion card. Reconnect power to the computer and reboot the machine.

Step 7

With the disk which came with the mouse, follow the instructions in your user's manual to install the drivers for the applications you wish to use with the mouse. Some mice use drivers that can be invoked without re-booting the machine; others place a line in your CONFIG.SYS file and require rebooting.

If you plan on using the mouse under Microsoft Windows, you'll also want to run the Windows Setup program from the Windows directory (or from Microsoft's Setup disks if you are doing a new Windows installation). See your Microsoft Windows or mouse manual for more instructions. Redo your Dark and Stormy Night Disk.

GRAPHICS TABLETS

The mouse is fine for navigating around Windows and for simple graphics applications. However, if you are planning on doing serious graphics illustration or lots of bitmap editing, you may want to consider adding a graphics tablet to your system, possibly in addition to your mouse. Graphics tablets, sometimes called *digitizers*, use either a pen-shaped stylus or a puck on a special pad to move the cursor on the screen. The stylus provides basically the same control as using a pen or brush, but that's not the only difference. Most mice use relative positioning; in other words, they interpret the movements of your hand relative to the movement of the cursor across the screen. A one-inch movement of your hand may result in a four-inch movement across the screen. Digitizers, on the other hand, can be set up for absolute values. For instance, if you draw a one-eighth-of-an-inch line across the pad with the stylus, a line the same length will be drawn inside the program you are working with.

More advanced tablets like that from Wacom, shown in Figure 13.22, and Cal-Comp also offer pressure-sensitive controls. In other words, if you push harder down on the writing surface, that will be translated into a different response on the screen, mimicking real artistic tools. In order to use the pressure-sensitive features, you have to have software that supports them, such as Fractal Design Painter. This program mimics many of the sophisticated artist's tools found in a fully-stocked art supply store. Pressing harder with the stylus, with the software set to imitate a calligraphy brush, modifies not only the stroke of the pen, but also the amount of ink that appears to be left on the page. Since the program can provide the appearance of textured papers, a lighter or heavier touch will also affect the amount of patterning that is seen in the final drawing.

FIGURE 13.22 The Wacom tablet.

The puck looks very much like a mouse and is designed to work in conjunction with the digitizing tablet. Like a mouse, the puck has buttons that are pressed to send commands or to draw shapes on the screen. Most common PC pucks have four buttons, although some have more than a dozen. Styluses are generally used by those interested in doing artistic kinds of drawing on the PC, while the puck is used more for CAD-style applications. Most pucks have a cross-hair assembly in front of the buttons, which can be used for pin-point accuracy.

You do not have to choose just one kind of pointing device to use with a graphics tablet. Some illustrators will keep both pressure- and non-pressure-sensitive styluses, as well as a puck, close at hand; all three can be used by the same digitizing tablet. Wacom offers additional control, allowing you to move back and forth between a regular mouse and the digitizing tools.

There are a variety of styles of digitizing tablets available. Wacom, for example, offers both a small and a large size. The 6-by-9-inch format is suitable for general work, while for engineering applications or large-scale drawings, they also make one which is 12 by 18 inches. The larger format is also available in a version that uses a static charge to hold a piece of paper flat against its surface.

Some digitizing tablets require a cord attached to the pen or puck that is moved around the surface; others offer cordless technology, which, while more expensive, offers more flexibility and finer control, since the cord doesn't get in your way.

Installing a Graphics Tablet

Most graphics tablets are serial devices and install very much the same way as the serial mouse procedure outlined above. Because of their added feature set, and more complicated electrical structure, you may have to work a bit harder at installing special drivers, especially for Windows. Because of the way they are designed, they also require a special power adapter similar to the AC adapter for many electrical products like answering machines, tape recorders and modems. Some, such as the large Wacom tablet, have large banks of DIP switches which must be set according to the diagrams in the user's manual. Some also may require a special adapter card. The guidelines given above will help you through the basic steps, but be sure to follow the guidelines in your user's manual.

MAINTAINING YOUR MOUSE OR TRACKBALL

Preventive Maintenance

Most mice and all trackballs use some combination of rollers and a rubber, teflon, or plastic ball to measure movement. If your mouse starts to behave erratically, it may be that a piece of foreign material has gotten either on the ball's surface, or grime has gummed up the rollers. Keeping the surface of the table or mouse pad clean will help reduce this problem.

Mouse Movement is Erratic

If you notice your mouse behaving erratically, first brush off the surface of the desk under the mouse and turn it over to see if there is anything stuck on the surface of the ball. You can roll the ball with your finger. Next you should see a circular or oval plate around the ball, usually with arrows indicating the way it can be pushed, or rotated, to release it. See Figure 13.23. Turn the plate as appropriate.

FIGURE 13.23 Close-up of a mouse ball assembly.

Now put your other hand on the bottom of the mouse and turn both hands over. Lift the mouse up gently. The plate and ball should now be in the lower hand and free of the mouse. Set the mouse down and inspect the entire surface of the ball. Use a lint-free cloth to wipe any particles off its surface. Set it aside and pick up the mouse with the ball opening facing you. With the edge of your thumb, very gently rotate and scrape the surface of the rollers. There'll be two or three of them. Turn the mouse back over and shake out any residue once you've finished that. Place the ball back in position, and re-secure the plate back on top of it. Your mouse should now work normally.

Mouse Fails to Operate

New Installation

If you have just installed a new mouse and it doesn't work, it's usually due to one of three things. Either there is a conflict between its card or Com port and some other device in your system; the software driver isn't loaded properly; or the cable isn't properly connected. Check the last first. Physically remove and replace the mouse cable, gently. Then reboot your system and see if the mouse works. If that doesn't work, try reloading the software driver; use diagnostics like those included in the back of the book, and see if they report a mouse being present. If the mouse still isn't working or the mouse isn't reported present, then you need to check for possible hardware conflicts.

Existing Mouse Suddenly Stops Working

Have You Installed New Hardware or Software?

If you have just installed new software which uses a mouse, it may have replaced your usual mouse driver with its own mouse driver, or it may have removed your mouse driver altogether. If you followed the steps for the Dark and Stormy Night disk, you should have copies of your old CONFIG.SYS and AUTOEXEC.BAT files. Compare the old files with those currently on your machine to see if they have been changed in any way, or to see if the new ones contain a new mouse driver that may be conflicting with the old one. If all that seems in order, proceed to the next heading.

You Haven't Recently Installed Any New Hardware or Software

Check your mouse cable to make sure it is still connected. Check the underside of the mouse to make sure the ball isn't locked and can move freely. If neither of these steps works, try reloading the mouse software from the installation disk or, in the case of Windows, from the Windows Setup utility.

VOICE RECOGNITION SYSTEMS

Don't think computers can't hear? Voice recognition systems (VRS) are a combination of sound card, microphone, and software that can translate your speech into words in a word processor or into commands to operate a program. You can't expect to be able to talk in your normal manner; the computer compares what you say to a dictionary. Command and control programs match the signal to a list of commands in a dictionary. This type of software is much simpler than a dictation system. I write much of the material in my books using Dragon Dictate. This is a full-fledged VRS that has a 60,000 word dictionary and can be trained to recognize your voice and almost any word or phrase you use. It takes about 45 minutes to condition it for personal use—and you must train it. Anyone else wanting to use it must train it as well.

Once a VRS is installed you can command it to accept input from a word processor, or any other supported programs. Keep in mind that continuous speech—that is, talking as you normally do, is about two years off. Until then, these systems will be of interest to those who do a lot of keyboarding and are willing to learn to talk like a machine. How-are-you-today-question mark—like that. For information on sound cards see Chapter 11, on multimedia. Most of the newer VRS programs will work with third-party cards, but before buying either a VRS or sound card, you should check articles in the major computer magazines for current trends and features in VRS technology.

SCANNERS—THE EYES OF YOUR COMPUTER

Computers can't read, and they can't see pictures. but a scanner can let your computer take in the images of pictures, and convert hard-copy pages into editable text. Choosing a scanner is not as simple as just deciding how much money you want to spend. There are several different types and the way they work can have a direct impact, not only upon the kind of material that they can handle but on the performance of the rest of your system as well. There are two types of scanners, *reflective* and *transparency*. Transparency, or slide, scanners are used to bring in images from slide material, i.e. transparent. Reflective scanners are made to scan material such as paper or photographs. In general, the operating technology is the same. In fact, some reflective scanners can also be used to scan transparencies by reversing the light source: That's the major difference, on which side of the material is the light source. To simplify the material in this section of the chapter, I will base my remarks primarily on reflective scanners.

Scanners can broadly be broken down into three categories, the first of which is *hand-held* scanners. These are designed for limited use by people who occasionally need to scan a piece of art work in for a desktop publishing program or who occasionally want to convert a small amount of typewritten material into editable text. Scanners average in price from about $200 to $1,000. The low cost of a good HP ScanJet has dropped to about $500, so the desire for hand-held models is waning fast. See Figure 13.24.

FIGURE 13.24 Logitech's ScanMan hand-held scanner.

What's Involved

Adding a scanner to your system generally involves installing an expansion card, as well as placing a software driver into your CONFIG. SYS file, or into the Windows Control Panel. Some scanners require the use of a proprietary interface card, while the best ones generally make use of a SCSI host adapter (for more information about SCSI see Chapter 10). It may need anywhere from 1.5 to 8Mb of hard disk space for the programs needed to operate it. Individual full-page scanned images can eat up anywhere from 1 to 100+Mb of hard disk space. While scanners are a bit more work than some other peripherals you can add, they greatly expand functionality, especially if you are interested in graphics.

Flat-bed scanners, the second type, are the work-horses of desktop publishers, and people who do a fair bit of *Optical Character Recognition* (OCR—that's the fancy name for converting hard copy into editable text). Flat-bed scanners range in price from $300 to several thousand dollars. Drum scanners, the third type, are expensive units designed for demanding pre-press work, and can cost from $14,000 on up—way up. We'll focus our attention on hand-held and flat-bed scanners. Let's take a quick look at how they work. Another use for scanners is as an input device for a fax. You can scan material into the computer, and then send it out with a fax-capable modem. See Figure 13.25.

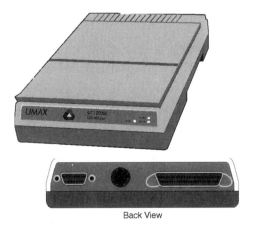

Back View

FIGURE 13.25 A typical flat-bed scanner.

There are several other things which set scanners apart besides whether they are hand-held, flat-bed, or drum scanners. Some scanners can only handle pure black-and-white images, not even able to capture shades of gray. More advanced scanners can handle 250 colors or shades or gray (8-bit—don't worry about the bits, I'll explain all this later in the chapter). While this may be an improvement, it still can't handle the range of tones found in a color photograph. For that you need one of the more advanced scanners that can handle 16.7 million colors (24-bit). Some scanners can also produce images with higher resolution, giving you the ability to provide both more detail and more accurate color.

What you need—exactly what kind of scanner, how many colors it can handle, and at what resolution is something only you can decide. If all you want to do is convert hard copy into text pages, a black-and-white scanner with an automatic sheet-feeding attachment can handle the job. If you want to capture black and white photographs, also referred to as *grayscale*, you'll need a scanner capable of handling 256 colors. For users needing full-color realism, you'll need the full 24-bit scanner.

I mentioned that you can't just treat the scanner by itself when adding one to your system. To work with color images, you'll have to have an appropriate color monitor and display adapter. Scanned images can also eat up a lot of disk space. A one-page monochrome image takes up about 1Mb of disk space; a full-color image of the same size will eat up over 100Mb of disk space. If you plan on getting into full-color graphics, you should be prepared to invest in, or have access to, at least a Pentium-90 system with a large, fast hard drive and a fast, 24-bit color display.

HOW PC SCANNERS WORK

The following paragraphs explain the basic technology involved in producing black-and-white and color scanned images. While it gets just a little bit technical, it does help you understand the issues in both attaching and using scanners. While the discussion of image size and color depth does involve binary numbers, you don't have to understand how binary numbers work to understand how scanners work, or the material presented below.

The basic principle behind most hand-held and flat-bed scanners is very similar to that of a copy machine. A light source, usually a fluorescent lamp, is passed underneath a sheet of paper lying face down on a sheet of glass. The light is reflected through a succession of mirrors into a lens focused on a series of light-sensitive diodes, known as *Charge-Coupled Devices* (CCD). The lighter areas of a page reflect more light, the darker areas less. The more light reflected off the surface, the greater the voltage passing out of the CCD into an analog-to-digital converter. This converts the voltage into a number that can be used by the computer to reference that point in the scan.

The scanning is conducted in a series of lines down the page. The number of dots per inch in each line that the scanner can measure is called its *resolution*. Most desktop scanners today have resolutions between 300 and 600 dots per inch. The information about the page is stored in a bit-map file. Each dot has a binary number attached to it. For a black-and-white image, commonly referred to as line art, you only need one bit per pixel to define a point as being either black or white. This is sometimes referred to as a monochrome image. If each bit can have two states, the value is 2^1.

An 8-bit image, or 2^8 power, gives you 256 possible combinations. These scanners are capable of handling black-and-white photographs or providing a "reasonable" color image. 24-bit scanners, or 2 to the 24th power, allow us to represent 16.7 million colors, which is adequate for handling lifelike color photographs.

Color scanners use a series of filters, usually red, green and blue, to measure the different color values in an image. Most scanners use one pass of the light over the image to record the data for each filter. This is why color images can be so much larger than monochrome images. In other words, for a monochrome image the machine is only storing one bit of data per pixel, whereas it has to store 24 bits per pixel for a true-color image.

The Scanner Interface

As you can see from the above paragraphs, scanners move a huge amount of information into the computer. Some vendors use a modified parallel interface on an expansion card with a custom cable to connect the scanner to the computer. Others make use of SCSI adapters to accomplish the same task. The advantage of the proprietary solution is that everything comes out of the box already configured for that particular scanner; it's disadvantages are that the software driver and card may be difficult to integrate with your existing system, and that the card takes up another slot. A SCSI host adapter can connect up to seven devices to your PC. The system I used when writing this book had a hard drive, tape drive, scanner and two CD-ROMs attached to a single card and it still wasn't full. In addition, my high-performance SCSI controller out-performed both the proprietary card that came with an earlier scanner and the inexpensive SCSI card that came with the scanner that I now use. If you already have a SCSI card in your machine and a compatible driver, you may not even have to open up the computer to install your scanner.

Scanner Software

Image Editing

While some scanner software will operate on 386 and even on older 286 machines, it is not advisable. For serious imaging and OCR work you should have at least a 486DX CPU. Given the low cost of the Pentium, consider at least a good 90 mHz machine for serious graphics work, with a large SCSI hard drive and a really good graphics adapter. For occasional work you can get by with a 486/66. These programs use a tremendous amount of system resources and can create very large swap (holding) files and may tax a system's display and hard disks to the limit. They provide a lot of power and open up whole new vistas to your computer, but to use them with any degree of speed and comfort you have to have the right hardware.

Just like everything else in a computer, without the proper software instructions, hardware is just so much plastic, silicon, fiberglass and wire. Scanner software involves several layers; the drivers, which are usually loaded into your Windows control panel settings, or for DOS, into the CONFIG.SYS file, let the scanner and your operating system talk to each other. Different programs are used to scan in images and perform optical character recognition. Both types of programs can send instructions to the scanner to scan a page, and most also have primary controls to adjust the brightness, contrast, and in some cases, the color quality of the images being scanned.

Image editing software is used to scan pictures, from line art to color photographs, into your machine. They are also called *bit-map editors*, or *paint programs*. They can allow you to scan images into a file and then manipulate it. You can adjust the contrast, the brightness, soften it, shift its color, and perform a variety of special effects, depending on the capabilities of your program. These programs directly manipulate the individual pixels. Leading programs in this field include Adobe PhotoShop, shown in Figure 13.26; Aldus PhotoStyler, and MicroGrafix Picture Publisher. When shopping for a scanner or an image editor, make sure that you match its capabilities to that of your system and your scanner—as well as the features that you want it to have. Some programs are well-suited to handling 8-bit, 256-color images, while others have all the color-correcting capabilities to handle 24-bit photo-realistic images.

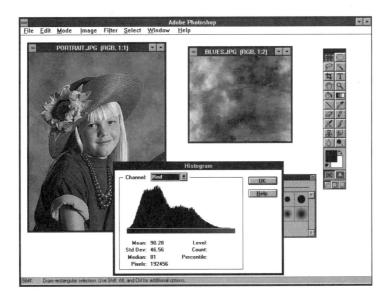

FIGURE 13.26 Adobe PhotoShop at work.

OCR Software

OCR software also controls the scanner directly and scans in a bit-map image. The magic is in what happens next. The program is designed to analyze the patterns of dots, and determine which ones are letters and what those letters are. It then can build another file with its interpretation of the document in editable text. There are several different types of *engines* (fast, powerful programs) that are used to do these conversions. The simplest can do little more than scan monospaced, typewritten pages; the most modern can scan and recognize almost any font and maintain the original document's formatting. In other words, it will also capture things like indentations, tabs, bold, underlines, etc. and the size of the type. Some of these programs also have the ability to capture the graphics on the page at the same time.

ExperVision TypeReader is an example of one of the full-featured programs. Some earlier versions of the software are bundled with popular scanners. An example of a TypeReader is shown in Figure 13.27. Pressing the **Auto** button in the upper left-hand corner with the mouse causes the software to read the current page into the scanner and perform its conversion. If you have an automatic sheet feeder, a number of pages can be handled automatically at the same time. Otherwise you have to click an **OK** button to scan each page.

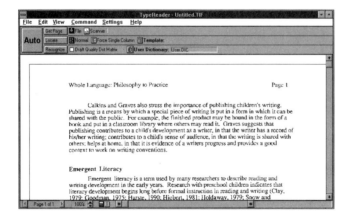

FIGURE 13.27 TypeReader in action.

Other major venders in this field are Calera, makers of WordScan Plus, which was originally designed to be used in large-scale professional scanning systems; and Caere, makers of OmniPage. If you are interested in OCR capabilities, you may find that you can buy a scanner with one of these programs already included. Be aware that the software may be a stripped-down version, so check the features carefully. *PC Magazine* periodically does roundups of scanners, image editing, and OCR software, so a trip to your bookshelf or library might be in order when you start shopping.

INSTALLING A SCANNER

Adding a scanner to your system usually requires adding an expansion card into a free slot, installing software drivers and using anywhere from one to 10+Mb of hard disk space for its software. If you already have a SCSI card installed on your system, you should consider purchasing a scanner that also uses a SCSI interface. If you follow the guidelines listed in Chapter 10 for designing a SCSI system, there's a good chance you'll be able to just attach your new scanner to that system without even having to open the computer case. If that is the case, refer to Chapter 10 for instructions on adding a device to your SCSI chain, and follow the instructions in your manual for installing the operating software. If you are not attaching it to a SCSI host adapter, follow the instructions below.

Preparation

What You'll Need

✔ A screwdriver for removing the cover of the computer case

✔ The scanner, its expansion card, and cable

✔ The scanner's power supply, and its operating software

Step 1

If you are installing the scanner on a fairly simple system, in all like-lihood you can use the default settings for the scanner's expansion card just as they come from the box. Most scanners will require an I/O address (usually in the 100h to 330h range—if these numbers seem strange or unfamiliar, refer to the discussion on installing cards in Chapter 5) and possibly an Interrupt (IRQ) and in some cases a DMA (Direct Memory Access) channel. If you have a number of expansion cards already in the system such as a tape drive, SCSI host adapter, or fax card, you should check that the default settings for your scanner do not conflict with any of these. The software program contained on the disk in the back of the book and the Inventory method described in Chapter 5 can make this task fairly simple.

Step 2

Exit any operating programs, turn off your computer and remove its power cord.

Step 3

Remove the computer's cover by removing the screws around the edge of the case in back.

Step 4

Set any required DIP switches or jumpers on the expansion card. Take a look at the card and decide which slot it would fit in best. Keep in mind that some systems have components on the motherboard which make it difficult to use certain slots with a full-sized card. If you have a full-sized card it might not fit in the slot near the computer's memory modules. Remove the screw holding in the back plate of the expansion slot you are going to use and then firmly, but gently, place the card into the slot, as shown in Figure 13.28.

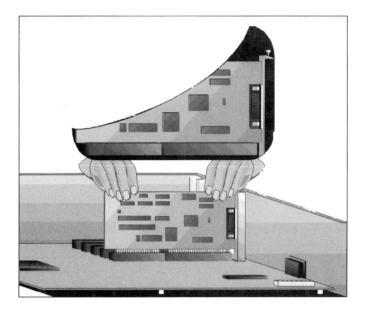

FIGURE 13.28 Placing the expansion card into the slot.

Step 5

Check your user's manual for any required set-up steps for the scanner. Most flat-bed scanners have a shipping lock, either in the form of a tab or a screw, that must be released or removed before the scanner can operate. Check your manual for any other necessary steps. You may have to install the scanner's florescent bulb or *platen cover* (the platen is the glass that you rest the paper on). Individual setup requirements will vary, so check your owner's manual.

WARNING

Attempting to operate the scanner with the shipping lock in place may damage the scanner mechanism or burn out the motor. Double-check the lock condition before powering the scanner up. Make sure it is refitted before moving the scanner or shipping it.

Step 6

Use the same screw that held in the cover plate to hold down the card. Set up the scanner in a location within range of the cable and attach the cable to the expansion card. Attach the power cord as needed.

Step 7

Turn on the scanner.

Most scanners, especially SCSI scanners, have to be powered on and have completed their own self-test before they can be recognized by the system. If you are going to use your scanner, even to install the software, be sure it's powered on before you boot or reboot your system.

Step 8

Power on your computer and observe the Power-On-Self-Test. If your computer doesn't boot properly, you probably have a conflict between the new card and one of the other expansion cards in your system. Before proceeding on that assumption, make sure that you have connected everything properly. If you have a problem, review the Inventory of your system and resolve the conflict by either changing the address of the scanner card, or adjusting the configuration of the other card that's causing the conflict. Refer to the card or device's manual for details on setting the address. Repeat this step as necessary until all conflicts are resolved.

Keep notes as you work if you run into a conflict. Record the existing settings of any card you change and then the new settings. That way you can easily return things to their original state if something didn't work. Only change one setting at a time. If you make several changes at once you may introduce new conflicts and end up going in circles.

Step 9

Once the computer is booted successfully, install the scanner driver and application per the manufacturer's instructions.

Step 10

Test the scanner with the software. It should operate without problems.

Run the software that came with your scanner and make sure that it can successfully complete a scan using that program. If it does, exit all applications, power down your equipment and replace the cover. Then update your Dark and Stormy Night disk.

TROUBLESHOOTING A SCANNER INSTALLATION

If you've installed a scanner and it doesn't work, and you know there are no conflicts with the interface card, then the problem has to be in the software setup. If the scanner does not do anything when you try to scan with the software, it is most likely due to improper installation of the driver. Reboot your machine and watch carefully for any remarks during the boot process relating to the scanner. You may get a message telling you that no scanner was found or that the driver failed to load. Make sure that the driver is properly installed and try again.

It is also possible that there is a hidden conflict that allows your system to boot but prevents your computer from talking to the scanner. Consult your owner's manual or the vendor's technical support department if you can't easily solve the difficulty.

MAINTAINING YOUR SCANNER

Scanners require very little in the way of maintenance, but they do require a bit of care. You should be sure to save the shipping carton it came in, as well as the shipping lock, in case you have to return it for repair. Another reason to save the box is that some vendors have, in the past, offered substantial trade-ins for new models if you return the existing scanner with all its manuals and accessories in the original carton. The old scanners are then given to schools or other non-profit organizations.

If your scanner does not have an automatic shut-off feature for the light, you should power down the unit when it is not being used. The heat buildup in the scanner can gradually shorten the life of the bulb and isn't that good for the scanner. If your unit does have an automatic power-down feature, you can leave it on all the time.

Other cautions include only cleaning the glass when it is necessary; cleaning even with a very soft cloth scratches glass and this will reduce the clarity of the scanned image. Another obvious but sometimes-overlooked safety precaution is: don't place heavy objects on top of the scanner.

CHAPTER SUMMARY

Keyboards and mice are the devices we use to talk to our computers. Scanners let us show our computer the world, giving it the ability to read and turn pictures into images that we can use in our documents. The quality and care that we put into selecting, installing, and maintaining our input devices has a direct bearing on how comfortable and productive we are when we use our PC.

CHAPTER 14

CONNECTING PCs— MODEMS, FAXES, AND THE INTERNET

WHAT'S IN THIS CHAPTER

- ✔ Parallel and Serial Ports
- ✔ Modems
- ✔ Fax Cards
- ✔ Installing I/O Cards
- ✔ Null-Modem Connections

✔ Electronic Mail

✔ On-Line Services

✔ Networks

WHAT THIS CHAPTER IS ABOUT

The PC by itself is a pretty powerful tool, but without the ability to connect it to other devices it is unable to talk or listen. We covered some input devices earlier (your system's keyboard and mouse) and will cover some additional output devices later (printers). In this chapter we cover telecommunications and the physical ports, both serial and parallel, that let your machine communicate with the outside world. This chapter covers the selection and installation of modems, fax equipment, and software tools that can turn your machine into a window to the world of electronic communications. Your PC and modem can be used to send and receive electronic mail, access thousands of programs that others are willing to share, and send and receive mail from around the world.

HOW COMPUTERS COMMUNICATE

To the uninitiated, computers seem magical. With the right software it seems you can do almost anything with a PC: compose letters, record sound and pictures, edit video images, and maintain vast storehouses of information. In reality, computers are very simple-minded beings, only able to count using two numbers, 0 and 1. All PC communications, whether it's to your printer at the end of a 6-foot cable or to another PC thousands of miles away, involve nothing more than moving a string of 0's and 1's from point A to point B.

Your Computer's I/O Ports

Most PCs have communications ports, also known as *I/O*, for Input/Output devices. The two most common types of I/O ports are serial and parallel. *Serial ports* transport data one number at a time, much like a one-lane road. This type of port, also referred to as a *Com port*, is commonly used for PC-to-PC communications using a device called a modem, which I'll explain shortly. The other common port is called a *parallel port*, most often used to send data from a PC to a printer. It allows a much faster transfer rate because it can transmit several bytes of data at the same time, in parallel, much like a multi-lane highway can have several cars traveling side-by-side down the road at the same time. See Figure 14.1.

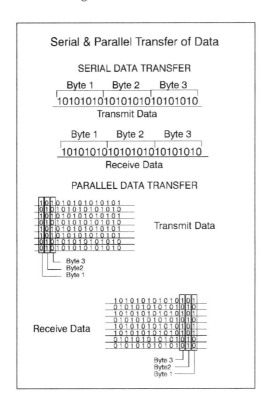

FIGURE 14.1 Serial and parallel data transfers.

Serial and parallel ports can be installed in PCs in several different ways. Some motherboards come with two serial and one parallel port already installed. Another option is to purchase an expansion card, which can contain one or more of the ports. Some accessories, like internal modems or fax cards, are equipped with their own communications port built right into the card. No matter what method is used, all I/O ports follow certain standard conventions. One of the things which sometimes makes dealing with communications difficult, is that some vendors' interpretations of the standards are a bit different from others.

The Parallel Port

We'll start with the easy one first. *Parallel ports*, also commonly referred to as *printer ports*, are fairly simple to deal with. While there are other ways to attach a printer to your PC, unless you are working on a network the parallel port is still the best way to do it. While there are a few eccentric types of parallel connections out there, most printers use a standard style of connection named after the company that first promoted it, Centronics. The connection is usually one of two 25-pin connectors similar to those shown in Figure 14.2.

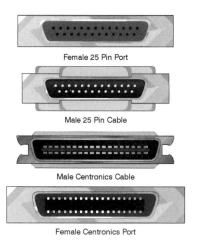

Female 25 Pin Port

Male 25 Pin Cable

Male Centronics Cable

Female Centronics Port

FIGURE 14.2 Parallel connectors.

As you can see, one side has 25 pins. This connection usually attaches to the PC. The other, somewhat unusual female connector is attached to the printer. One limitation of the parallel port which has kept it from being used for a number of things, such as PC-to-PC communications over a distance, is *cross-talk*. All electrical circuits generate electrical noise. If you place several wires within a single cable, as you do in parallel connections, there will be some noise generated within the cable. Generally speaking, parallel cables over about 10 feet will generate too much noise to be reliable. This usually is not much of a problem, since you really don't want your printer much more than 10 feet away from the computer it is attached to anyway.

One-Way or Two-Way Communication

The original parallel connection was designed to be a one-way street, with the PC sending data to the printer. Some more advanced printers today (mainly those designed for use on a network) have the ability to send messages back to their hosts. This is known as a *bi-directional* parallel port. At the present time the average end-user doesn't need to worry about bi-directional ports.

ADDING A PARALLEL PORT TO YOUR SYSTEM

In most cases, parallel ports are added into a system as part of an I/O card, which may have one or two I/O ports on it. In some cases, you may want to add an additional parallel port to handle a second printer. If you need to do this, you can move on down to the discussion on adding I/O cards, because the basic procedure and considerations are the same. Standard convention has it that the first parallel port in a PC will use Interrupt (IRQ) 7 and the second parallel port will use IRQ 5. Most I/O cards come equipped to allow positioning parallel ports at either of those Interrupts, and possibly others. If you plan on adding more than two parallel ports to a system, you should make sure that both the card and the system have enough free Interrupts to support them.

SERIAL PORTS

If you hang around people involved with PC communications very much, you soon learn that there are all kinds of different names and nomenclatures for the lowly serial port. They can be referred to as the Com port, serial port, and sometimes as an *RS-232* connection (based on the Electronic Industry Association's identification number for the standard serial port). One of the problems with serial ports is that the standard is sometimes very loosely interpreted. For one thing, there are two basic types of connector for the one port: some cards use 9-pin connectors, others 25-pin. As a result, a whole new market has grown up that provides adapters which convert between the 9- and 25-pin connectors. They are interchangeable—more or less. The reason I say more or less is that there are still a few vendors who use exotic cabling connections that don't exactly match, pin for pin, those used in the standard. Ten years ago this was a real problem, but thankfully now most vendors are realizing that if they try to go their own way, nobody else will follow.

The basic thing to keep in mind when selecting serial ports to add to your system is that you must make sure that you have some way of properly making the 9- or 25-pin connection to whatever peripheral you plan to attach. If you head off to the computer store to get a cable to attach to a modem, make sure you know what combination of 9- and 25-pin connectors you need and which ends have to be male and female. One of the annoying facts of life is that vendors seem to arbitrarily adopt male and female connectors when setting up their serial connections. Most PCs use male connectors on the computer itself but modems and other devices use a variety of male and female serial connectors. See Figure 14.3.

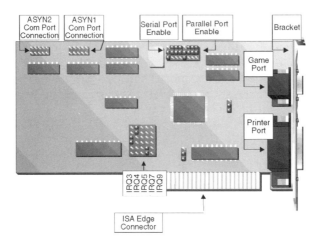

FIGURE 14.3 Standard I/O card.

You might think that a serial connection would only need one line, since only one signal is being sent or received at any one time. But there are a lot of things that can happen to that byte of information as it travels across the wire. In order to make sure that data gets there successfully, additional lines are used to send supplemental signals and perform other housekeeping chores. To the casual observer, serial communications may seem very simple, but in order to insure that what is received is exactly the same as what is sent requires a lot of behind-the-scenes work. We'll talk more about some of these techniques when we discuss modems and telecommunications later in the chapter. For right now we'll focus on how to install a standard serial card (using the word "standard" somewhat loosely) in your machine.

All Serial Ports are Not Created Equal

If you are planning on using your serial port to connect a high-speed modem (which you probably will), you should make sure that your serial port is equipped with a 16550 *UART* chip. The UART, which stands for Universal Asynchronous Receiver/Transmitter (don't worry about the big words), is much more sophisticated than the preceding 16450 and 8250 UARTs. If you are going to be doing very simple work you can get by with a card equipped with a 15450 but totally avoid those using the 8250. The 8250 is an 8-byte chip and is unable to keep handle modern telecommunications. Both the 16450 and 16550 UART are 16-byte devices. The newer 16550 is much more sophisticated, and designed to handle the extra workload of operating under a multi-tasking environment like Microsoft Windows, OS/2, or UNIX. There are even more powerful serial port cards from vendors like StarGate. These require special drivers for the operating system, so you should check for compatibility before buying. Also keep in mind that ultra-high-speed cards require matching devices at the other end of the connection.

INSTALLING AN I/O CARD

I/O cards come in a variety of configurations ranging in price from $15 to about $145 and more, depending on the quality, number and types of ports involved, and how much somebody thinks they can charge for them. The simplest cards have a single port on them, be it serial or parallel. Today the majority of cards come as multiport devices. Common combinations include: two serial; one serial and one parallel; two serial and one parallel; two serial and two parallel; and two serial, one parallel and one game port.

NOTE Game ports are specialized connectors used to attach joysticks to a PC for playing games such as Flight Simulator. If you plan on using a joystick you probably want to get an I/O card with a game port attached. The installation procedures are the same as for other I/O cards, just note any special considerations included in the documentation for handling the additional port.

Given the varieties of possible configuration, it might seem that installing I/O ports is difficult, but in most cases it is pretty straightforward. The only real problem comes with the variety of ways that such cards can be constructed. There is no uniformity in the combination of DIP switches and jumpers, and most of these cards are inexpensive imports with limited documentation, often in broken English. The key to successful I/O card installation lies in keeping it simple.

Basic I/O Card Design

Most I/O combo cards have one 9-pin male serial connection and one 25-pin female parallel connection on the card itself. The additional ports, such as another 9-pin or 25-pin serial connection and a second printer port or game port, are usually connected by means of a ribbon cable and attached to the mounting bracket plate, as shown in Figure 14.4.

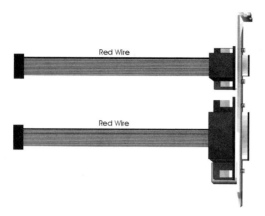

Red Wire

Red Wire

FIGURE 14.4 A port-mounting bracket plate with ribbon cables.

Before you go shopping, decide on exactly the sort of ports you need and then buy a matching card. Be aware that if you go to the local computer shop, they may only stock one or two types of card so you may have to buy ports that you won't use.

Installation Procedures

What You'll Need

✔ Small and large screwdrivers

✔ Cup or other container for screws and small parts

✔ Inventory of currently installed peripherals

✔ I/O card kit

✔ Possibly a pair of pliers or hemostat for adjusting jumpers

✔ Small flashlight and magnifying glass

If you plan on immediately attaching devices to the I/O card, you will also need the appropriate cables and any required 9- to 25-pin adapters.

Step 1

Power down the computer and disconnect the power cord and any other cable connections that might get in the way.

Step 2

Remove the card and any accessories along with the documentation from the box the card came in. If you currently have no I/O ports in the machine, the *defaults* (pre-chosen settings) will probably work fine. If you have any devices such as a mouse or an internal modem card using IRQs 3, 4, 5, or 7, you'll need to adjust the settings to resolve any conflicts. IRQ 4 is used by Com one, IRQ 3 is used by Com 2, IRQ 7 is used by a parallel port (LPT 1) LPT 2 uses Com 5. Bus mice commonly use Com 5. If you are installing additional Com 3 or Com 4 ports or have an internal modem, you may have to do a bit of juggling. Com 3 frequently shares the same IRQ as Com 1 and Com 4 with Com 2. Depending on the card, you may have to set one or more DIP switches or adjust one or more jumpers if there are possible conflicts.

Step 3

Remove the cover from the case and then remove the edge cover from an appropriate slot.

Step 4

If you have a single card (with no accessory plate attached by ribbon cables), simply install the card into the free slot using a gentle, downward push to seat the edge connector squarely into the slot. See Figure 14.5.

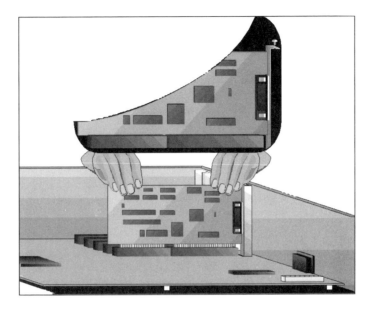

FIGURE 14.5 Fitting a card into a slot.

Step 5

If you do have a unit with additional ports attached by ribbon cables, you have three options; one is to not install the additional ports if you don't need them. Keep in mind that while most people won't need a second parallel port, it's a good idea to have two Com ports available. If you are not installing all the ports, you may want to disable the IRQ settings for the ports you aren't going to install. Refer to the card's documentation to do this.

If you want to leave the extra ports attached directly to the plate, attach the cable for the port to the appropriate pins on the card. Be sure to connect the side of the cable with the red (or blue) stripe to the side marked as Pin 1 on the card. See Figure 14.6.

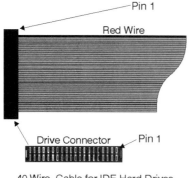

Pin 1

Red Wire

Drive Connector   Pin 1

40 Wire Cable for IDE Hard Drives

FIGURE 14.6 The edge strip and Pin 1.

Step 6

If your case has openings for I/O ports built into the back of the unit, you can remove the appropriate 9- or 25-pin plate covers and mount the ports there. Use a nut driver or needle-nosed pliers to remove the hexagonal screws on either side of the port connector, and use the same screws to mount it to the back of the case. You'll have to remove the existing covers over the holes in the case. In some cases this will mean removing a screw, in others you will have to physically poke the hole out with a screwdriver. In either case, make sure you hold one hand on the other side to catch the cover when it falls out. You don't want it wedging between the case and the motherboard.

Step 7

Once all the ports are installed, immediately attach any peripherals that you plan on connecting to the port. Reconnect the power cord and boot your machine.

Step 8

Use the diagnostic supplied on the CD-ROM in this book or another utility, such as PC Tools, or Norton Utilities' System Information, to make sure that the ports are seen by the system and are active. If you have already attached a printer, you may want to try printing something and if it's a modem, try using communications software such as ProComm Plus or Windows Terminal to talk to the modem (see the appropriate instruction manual). If your software check shows that everything is working, you're all set. If it doesn't, you probably have an Interrupt conflict with something else on your system. If you completed the Inventory Sheet as discussed in Chapter 5, finding this shouldn't be much of a problem. If not you'll have to make an Inventory now and resolve any conflict.

Step 9

Once you are sure everything is working, replace the cover and place any spare screws, parts, or anything else into your goodies bag for future use.

With your new ports installed you are ready to attach modems, printers, and other devices to allow your PC to talk to the world, or at least your printer on the end of the cable. For more information on printers refer to Chapter 18. Right now we are going to move on to a discussion of modems and telecommunications.

MODEMS AND TELECOMMUNICATING

In the early days of the PC, modems were both slow and expensive. Today 14,400-baud modems with built-in fax-receive capabilities can be purchased mail order for under $100. Modems let your PC communicate over telephone lines with other computers, and in some cases, with fax machines. The word "modem" is actually a contraction for "*mo*dulator/*dem*odulator." PCs do all their work digitally, working with discrete signals representing numbers. Telephone lines are analog devices designed to carry the human voice. A *modem* is a device that converts outgoing numbers into tones that can be carried over a telephone line. Modems also convert incoming analog sounds into their digital equivalents so that the computer can absorb them.

When you create a connection between two PCs using modems, they go through a series of procedures called "handshaking," sort of like a formal introduction. If you were to convert these into more-or-less human speech, the conversation would sound something like this: One modem dials the other, and waits for it to answer. If the other modem answers the phone, it listens for a tone. As soon as the modem starting the call hears the line pick up, it gives that initial tone. Sort of like, "Hello, would you like to talk?" The next sequence of tones sort of set up the language, "How would you like to talk?" Different quality modems can talk at different speeds and use different techniques to make sure that data gets across the line successfully (we'll talk about that in a minute).

A MATTER OF CONTROL

While you can put a modem inside your computer, it's actually a separate device no matter where it resides; the two devices may use the same letters and words (binary numbers) but they speak different languages. In the early days each manufacturer had his own set of command words to control the modem. These are very simple and often very English-like commands, things like "open the telephone line," "dial tone," etc. In the early 1980s one command set, that used by Hayes Communications, became the *de facto* standard. Today most modems offer some degree of Hayes compatibility. That means they support the use of the Hayes command language. Keep in mind that the Hayes command set is often only a starting point. Your modem may offer a series of features that goes beyond that defined by those commands. It's a good idea, when shopping for modem software, to make sure that the package fully supports all the features of your modem.

Types of Communications Software

In order to communicate properly, both modems must be in the proper mode and working at the proper speed; if you were listening in to the conversation you would hear something comparable to a series of clicks, whistles and static. Once the handshaking portion is done, the two modems have adjusted to each other and they are ready to accept commands from either computer to send and receive data. About the only time anyone ever uses direct commands to the modem is to test it. Virtually all modem operations are conducted using software.

General Purpose Products

In order to use the modem, you must either send commands directly to it by directing them through the Com port, or by using one of a number of telecommunications programs such as ProComm Plus, CrossTalk, WinComm, or BitCom. These are the Swiss Army knives of telecommunications. They can be used to transfer files between computers, connect with remote on-line services, send electronic mail, automatically dial the phone for regular voice communication, and allow you to chat with someone on a remote system in real time by typing your responses to his/her comments. Figure 14.7 shows ProComm Plus for Windows, a popular general-purpose program.

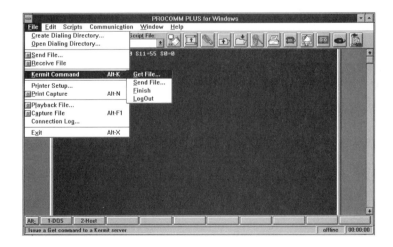

FIGURE 14.7 Procomm Plus for Windows.

Online Service Software

Over the past several years, a number of service companies have sprung up, offering a variety of on-line services for computer users with modems. They offer services such as electronic mail (e-mail), special interest groups with on-line conferencing, bulletin boards, specialty software, electronic shopping, weather, news and stock quotations, on-line multi-player games, and electronic software support.

The largest of these is Compuserve Information Services, operated by H & R Block. Other providers include America Online, Prodigy, Genie, and Dow-Jones News Retrieval Service. Many of these services have specialized software that allows easy automation for transferring messages and e-mail, as well as a friendly interface for navigating the service and communicating with other users. Figure 14.8 shows Compuserve WINCIM, which stands for *Compuserve Information Manager for Windows.*

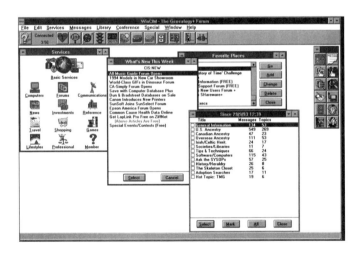

FIGURE 14.8 Compuserve's WINCIM.

Personal Information Managers

These software products serve as a combination Rolodex and personal secretary. You can keep track of schedules, appointments, to-do lists, and manage telephone logs. When used with a modem, these packages will automatically dial numbers and record the length of the conversation, along with notes on who you talked to and what the topic of the conversation was.

Bulletin Board Services and the Internet

You don't have to be a communications giant to operate an on-line service. There are a wide number of programs ranging from the very inexpensive ($30 to $50) to the outrageous, that allow you to set up a computer as a dial-in service. These services, known as *Bulletin Board Systems* (BBS), can handle electronic mail, automatic file transfer, electronic messaging, and even electronic shopping. Some users even set up dedicated PCs to handle nothing but BBS traffic and charge for the service. A large number of people operate BBSes part-time for personal satisfaction and to interact with like-minded users. Bulletin boards are set up for all kinds of special interests by all kinds of people. There are magazines and books dedicated to BBS phenomena if you want to try to find others with similar interests. Several organizations have sprung up, providing interlinking services between bulletin boards, and forming in effect, a national electronic mail service.

Not all bulletin boards are run out of someone's home/office. The *Internet* is a vast conglomeration of universities, corporations, government agencies, and lately, individuals and companies, that operate a rather free-wheeling network of networks, linking computers both large and small all around the world. Most of the Internet hosts operate under the UNIX environment, but it is possible to obtain software and access the Internet system with a home computer through services such as CompuServe and America Online. Your local bookstores will have several titles related to the variety of services available, and on how to access the Internet.

Electronic Mail

Some phone service vendors, such as MCI, now offer extensive electronic mail services. You can send anything from short messages to a series of word processing files, spreadsheets or presentation files directly from your computer to another user who has an account on that system via modem. If you want to send a hard copy, they will also print your file and mail it from the closest Post Office. Other options include having them transmitted as faxes or telexes for users without computers or who prefer a permanent physical record.

Buying a Modem

As I mentioned before, you have to have a modem for your PC to talk to the outside world. Your first decision is whether to go with an internal or external type of device. *Internal modems* are less expensive—the manufacturer doesn't have to provide a case or a power supply for the modem since those necessities are handled by the PC itself. Internal modems come with all the features available in external devices and they have their own built-in serial port. That makes selection sound pretty simple. After all, it's cheaper, and it offers more. What a deal! Appearances can be deceiving. See Figure 14.9.

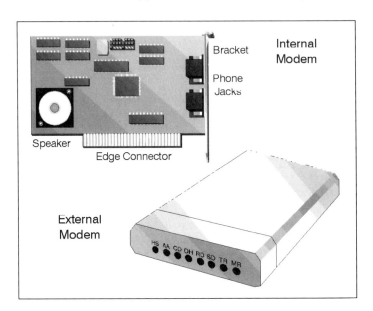

FIGURE 14.9 Internal and external modems.

External modems have some advantages too. Unlike internal modems, external versions can be easily moved from one PC to another or even shared with other types of computers like a Macintosh. Most external modems offer a series of status lights across their front panel which indicate various conditions while the modem is in operation. Given the fact that telecommunications is not an exact science, it's often nice to know if you still have an active connection, and if data is being transmitted between the machines. Another plus in favor of external vs. internal is ease of installation. If you have an external unit, installation is usually no more effort then plugging in the cable to both the modem and the serial port on your PC and attaching the power supply and the connection to your telephone line. The real problem with internal modems is their built-in serial port, since it can conflict with the serial ports already installed on your machine or with some other device. Getting things working right may involve a bit of playing around, and, depending upon your system's configuration, may even involve disabling one of your existing serial ports to make the thing work. In the final analysis, internal vs. external is a matter of personal preference. Personally, I tend towards external units.

FAX OR FAX/MODEM

Over the past few years more and more modems have come equipped with standard Group III (I'll explain this "group" business in just a minute) facsimile capabilities built in. Initially these *fax/modems* were a good bit more expensive than a plain modem, but today they usually don't cost anything extra. Be careful when shopping for a fax modem, because there is more involved in sending faxes from your PC than simple telecommunications. Fax/modems come in two flavors: receive-only and send/receive. These work just as the name implies: a *receive-only fax/modem* can send and receive normal modem communications, but it can only receive incoming faxes. *Send/receive* units can both send and receive faxes. When shopping around, you may also notice that there are some cards that promote their fax capabilities over modem operations. These are generally designed to be used as network or stand-alone fax servers rather than as a general purpose telecommunications device. Dollar for dollar, the general PC user is probably better off with a regular external modem with fax capabilities.

NOTE

The "group" business mentioned earlier comes from the naming conventions of the international organization that sets up standards for telecommunication, telex, and fax operation. This organization was known as the International Consultative Committee for Telephony and Telegraphy. This is a French group organized under the United Nations, so CCITT is the abbreviation of their name in French. They are responsible for most of the jargon involved with modems that I'll explain shortly. The Group designation is set up by the Committee to explain how the fax machines work, and what kind or compression and error correction they must use, as well as some general standards for performance.

There are two categories of faxes currently in use, Group III and Group IV. Virtually all PC modems today support the CCITT Group III standards. a Group III fax usually operates at about 9600 baud and is the backbone of modern office fax technology. Group IV fax is a newer standard which offers greater compression (efficient "packing" of data) but is at present in limited use. A good number of plain-paper faxes use the newer Group IV standard.

Fax capabilities in a modem can be quite useful, even if you have an existing fax machine. Some software allows you to send a fax directly from a word processor, spreadsheet or other application, just as if you were sending the file to a regular printer. The result at the other end is a much cleaner fax. Receiving fax transmissions inside your PC has pluses as well. You get a cleaner copy and, with the appropriate software, you can actually convert the fax file into editable text, which can then be imported into a word processor. When shopping for fax software keep in mind that some programs may tie up your machine while a fax is being received and you may have to juggle printer setups a little bit more.

Speed and Accuracy

Once you've worked through the basic decisions of internal and external, fax and no fax, you can start looking at the basic features of the class of modem you've decided upon. The first consideration, as with many things in PCs, is speed. My first modem was a 300-baud (see note that follows) device based on the standard set up by Bell Telephone. Sending a simple file containing nothing more than word processing data would take longer than I now like to remember. Over the intervening years, speeds have improved. Today's modems offer speeds of 9600 and above. A 9600-baud modem, rapidly becoming the standard, produces transmissions of about 1200 characters per second.

Baud rate is the number of times a line changes its electrical state during telecommunications. While it's not exactly interchangeable with bytes per second, they're really fairly equal. This is the standard unit of measurement for how fast the unit operates. The number of bytes per second (bps) divided by 8 gives you the number of characters per second. In other words, under ideal conditions 300 baud would translate into about 32 characters per second (yes, I know the math works out to 37.5 but you have to allow for error correction and the vagary of the phone line quality).

We don't just move text over modem lines. Many people also exchange computer programs and graphics. The difference between a 300-baud and 9600-baud modem can mean the difference between tying up your machine (and running up your phone bill) for more than an hour or more vs. running the tab for eight to twelve minutes for files in the half-Mb range.

There is more to speed than just the raw ability of the modem to move data; as speed increases, the need for two modems to be able to talk cleanly to each other becomes imperative. If two people are talking in a quiet room late at night, it's very easy to understand each other. If the same two people are driving down a busy highway in a convertible with the top down, communication is a bit more difficult. 300-baud transmissions are like the quiet room; the faster a modem operates, the more susceptible it is to line noise, just like our convertible speeding down a busy highway. To overcome these problems, modem manufacturers provide advanced chip sets that incorporate CCITT standards for error correction and fancier handshaking protocols. These are generally referred to as *V-DOT* (Department of Transportation) standards since they all use the letter V. If you are planning on buying a high-speed modem, you should be at least somewhat familiar with the features offered by the different V-DOT standards. Unless you never plan on calling long distance, you should consider a high-speed modem. Even though they cost a couple of hundred dollars more than their slower siblings, it doesn't take long, calling long distance, to run up a huge phone bill when you are shopping at 2400 baud.

Error Correction and Data Compression

In a perfect world, two identical modems would connect two computers over a perfectly clear telephone line. In reality our modern telephone system is not well-equipped to handle telecommunications. Companies which rely on long distance computer-to-computer links often fork out large sums of money to guarantee dedicated, high-quality telephone lines for their exclusive use. The average small business or personal PC owner could not afford such luxury. If you are dialing into one of the major services like CompuServe, you may not have to worry about this too much. They offer local connections through such telephone nets from almost every medium-to-major metropolitan area in the United States.

There are two ways modem manufacturers have made life easier and data more secure for the average user. The first is through *error correction*. Error correction *algorithms* have been designed that check and make sure that the information received is the same as the information sent. In some cases these are embedded in software known as *exchange protocols*. They are also available in hardware, built into the chips in your modem as *firmware*. Software protocols only require that both systems are running software that knows how to work with that protocol. The better your software program, the more protocols it is likely to support. Common varieties to look for in a package include XModem, YModem, ZModem, Kermit, and Sealink. The Compuserve B format, also known as CISB, has also become quite popular. Hardware protocols are a little more involved since both modems must actually have compatible interpretation chips built into them. Several industry standards have become popular and are described below.

Data compression serves two purposes. The faster you can move data from point A to point B, the less time you tie up your computer and the less money you pay to the telephone company. Depending on the type of file, data compression can cut the size of the transfer in half. It uses fancy algorithms that encode the data and a reverse procedure is used at the other end to expand it. Once again, there are both hardware and software solutions. Most bulletin boards and on-line services offer programs like PKZIP and LHARC. The user compresses the file using the software and the person receiving the file runs a companion program to uncompress it. Since there's less data actually being transferred across the line, the risk of errors and the need for correction is also reduced. Hardware compression is more involved, since the code for both packing and unpacking the file must reside in the hardware provided with the modem. With this method both modems must have the same firmware before compression can be used.

V-DOT Standards

NOTE

The following list of standards may seem a little bit convoluted. Keep in mind that they were designed by a committee, and standards committees are notorious for convoluted negotiations designed to satisfy a number of special interests. If you are buying a modem today and you want high performance, you probably want a unit that incorporates V.42 bis and MNP 5 protocols. If you want to know more about what you are buying, the following list will provide at least a basic introduction to what all the gobbledygook nomenclature is about. To really understand all the intricacies of these standards you would need a background in telecommunications and possibly an advanced degree in math or computer science.

The V.32 Standard

This standard provides protocols to allow two-way signaling at speeds up to 9600 bps over standard telephone lines. The problem with V.32 is the fact that the CCITT left out any provisions for error correction.

V.32 bis

This is a revision of the original V-DOT 32 standard, which allows for transfers up to 14,400 bps.

V.42 and V.42 bis Standard

If you ever see the acronym *LAPM*, it stands for the Linked Access Procedure for Modem. This is the primary protocol described in V.42. V.42 bis adds data compression using the Lempel-Ziv algorithm. This is a popular means of compressing files used by such popular shareware (try-before-buy) programs such as LHARC or PKZIP. The V.42 bis standard allows transfers (at least in theory) of up to 38,400 bps, based on the degree to which the file can be compressed during transfer.

MNP 4 and MNP 5

While these two standards are not actually defined by CCITT, they are often included in the feature set of high-speed modems. MNP stands for the *Microcom Networking Protocol*. MNP 4 provides advanced error correction, while MNP 5 provides compression. In fact, MNP 5 can compress files to almost half their original size.

All These Standards Are Great, But...

When you go shopping for a modem it's easy to be beguiled by claims of super high speed and error correction using the standards listed above. In addition to the alphabet soup in the preceding list, several vendors offer their own enhancements to improve transfers over dirty phone lines and to pack files tightly as they are being sent. Using modems like U.S. Robotics Couriers can offer speeds up to 28,800 bps but only when working with a similar modem on the other end. The standards are great. Data compression is fantastic, but they only work when both modems support the same protocols and speed, and when your telephone line is clean. If the modem on the other end is slower or doesn't support the compression protocol they can't be used, and if the phone line is dirty, the modem may have to slow down to make sure everything gets across properly. I've seen very high speed modems slow to a crawl when confronted by a bad telephone connection.

Another possible problem is, if you have to connect to someone with a very slow modem, like an old 300- or 1200-baud unit, it may not even be able to make the connection. If you are not planning on getting seriously involved in telecommunications or running a bulletin board, the 9600- or 14,400-baud modem with fax capabilities will probably meet your needs.

When Is a Modem Not a Modem?

If you want to connect two PCs that are located fairly close to each other, for instance on adjacent desks, or to connect your regular PC to a notebook or laptop computer that you take on the road, you don't even need a modem. Your local computer store can provide you with a *null-modem* cable or a no-modem adapter that can be put on any serial cable. This is simply a device that reverses certain wires in the cable structure so that the device can imitate two modems working over a telephone line. Special linking software is available or you can use regular telecommunications software like ProComm Plus or Windows Terminal. In some cases you will have to specify that it is a direct connection, or set up one unit as a master and the other computer as a slave. Check with your software manual for more information.

INSTALLING A MODEM

Internal Modems

What You'll Need

✔ Small and large screwdrivers

✔ Cup or other container for screws and small parts

✔ Inventory of currently installed peripherals

✔ Modem card

✔ Possibly a pair of pliers or hemostat for adjusting jumpers

✔ Small flashlight and magnifying glass

Step 1

Power down the computer and disconnect the power cord and any other cable connections that might get in the way.

Step 2

Remove the card and any accessories, along with the documentation, from the box the card came in. If you have any devices such as a mouse using IRQs 3 or 4, you'll need to adjust the settings to resolve any conflicts.

WARNING

Some older PC systems may only be able to recognize two serial ports. In that case you'll have to actually disable one of your existing Com ports to get the internal modem to work. The only two other solutions you have are to replace the motherboard with a new one which supports four Com ports, or go to an external modem.

Some newer PCs allow you to disable/enable and change the IRQ settings of your Com ports using your CMOS Setup routine or through a configuration utility. Refer to your system or motherboard documentation for more details.

With internal modems you may also have to set an internal jumper or DIP switch for tone or pulse dialing. Depending on the card, you may have to set one or more DIP switches or adjust one or more jumpers if there are conflicts. See Figure 14.10.

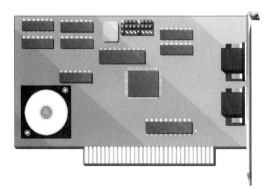

FIGURE 14.10 An internal modem.

Step 3

Remove the cover from the case and then remove the edge cover from an appropriate slot.

Step 4

Install the card using gentle but firm pressure to seat it into the expansion slot. See Figure 14.11.

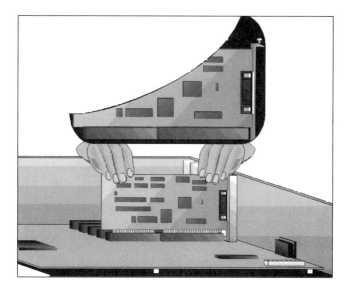

FIGURE 14.11 Installing a modem card.

Step 5

On the rear panel of your modem should be two telephone jacks. Check the documentation which came with your modem or the labels on the back plate. One should be "line in" or "line" and the other "line out" or "phone." Attach a standard single-line telephone cable with modular jacks into the "line in" connection and plug the other end of the cable into a telephone wall jack. You can use the other connection to run a line to a regular telephone handset, which can be used any time the modem is not actually sending or receiving—even if the computer is not turned on.

WARNING

Telephone lines and transformers are often the victims of lightning strikes, which can cause a surge of electricity to come down the line. The phone line you are attaching to your modem opens up the risk of a severe power surge if such a strike occurs in your vicinity. Several surge protectors are available that offer protection for phone lines. Some are included in the standard multi-plug units that are used for PCs; some are available strictly for phone-line attachment. Regular surge protectors are cheap insurance. You should seriously consider adding one to your system.

Step 6

Turn on your computer and install your telecommunications software. Make sure that during the installation or once it is set up, you set the options for the appropriate Com port for which you set your modem, Com 1, Com 2, Com 3, or Com 4. Without this information, it may seem that the modem isn't operating even when properly configured, because the software is sending the information to the wrong port.

Step 7

Check your software manual for a listing of manual dialing procedures. This allows you to use your modem as a regular phone dialer, or to manually set up a phone number for a connection. Use it and try to dial your own phone number, the one the line is connected to. If everything is set up properly, you should hear the internal speaker acquire a dial tone and then a series of beeps or clicks as the number is dialed. This tells you that the outgoing connection is working properly. To fully test the modem, you should dial into a bulletin board service or another computer and actually upload or download a file. Many modems come with free-trial connect time for one of the major online services, and most software companies now offer on-line bulletin boards for updates and product information. Check the user's manual; it probably includes a phone number and dialing instructions.

NOTE

This book primarily deals with hardware issues even though I do discuss some software. There are a number of issues in telecommunications that are beyond the scope of this book. The documentation which came with your modem and communications software should have information about proper settings. Basically you have to tell the software how you want these settings defined. While they may seem complicated, you don't really have to understand exactly what they all mean. Terms such as *parity* and *stop bits* relate to how the information is transferred between the two machines. All you really need to know is how to make your settings match the settings on the machine you're talking to. Usually the instructions for connecting to a service or a bulletin board will include which settings you should use. Your software package usually includes a dialing directory that allows you to record the settings for a given number in a menu or dialog box. Refer to your manual for more instructions.

Step 8

Once you know that your modem is operating properly, you can power down the system and replace your case cover. Keep in mind that, if you have to turn the machine around to replace the cover, it's now attached to a telephone line.

Installing an External Modem

What You'll Need

✔ Modem

✔ Software

✔ Serial cable with appropriate connectors

✔ Telephone line

✔ Power supply

Step 1

Unpack the modem and check the owner's manual to make sure all the appropriate parts are there as described in the manual.

Step 2

Check the manual to see if there are any switch settings that must be set prior to installation, for example, for tone or pulse dialing or setup compatibility modes (the need to do this is rare, but a misfit here could lead to frustration if you think the modem is broken when all it needs is a setting change).

Step 3

Attach the appropriate end of the cable to the appropriate Com port on your PC and the other to the connector on the back of the modem.

Step 4

On the rear panel of your modem should be two telephone jacks. Check the documentation which came with your modem or the labels on the back plate. One should be "line in" or "line" and the other "line out" or "phone." Attach a standard single-line telephone cable with modular jacks into the "line in" connection and plug the other end of the cable into a telephone wall jack. You can use the other connection to run a line to a regular telephone hand set which can be used any time the modem is not actually sending or receiving—even if the computer is not turned on.

WARNING

Telephone lines and transformers are often the victim of lightning strikes, which can cause a surge of electricity to come down the line. The phone line you are attaching to your modem opens up the risk of a severe power surge if such a strike occurs in your vicinity. Several surge protectors are available that offer protection for phone lines; some are included in the standard multi-plug units that are used for PCs; some are available strictly for phone-line attachment. Regular surge protectors are cheap insurance. You should seriously consider adding one to your system.

Step 5

Connect the power supply.

Step 6

Turn on your computer and install your telecommunications software. Make sure that during the installation or once it is set up, you set the options for the appropriate Com port for which you set your modem, Com 1, Com 2, Com 3, or Com 4. Without this information, it may seem that the modem isn't operating even when properly configured because the software is sending the information to the wrong port. See Figure 14.12.

FIGURE 14.12 Detail of external modem connections.

Step 7

Check your software manual for a listing of manual dialing procedures. This allows you to use your modem as a regular phone dialer or to manually set up a phone number for a connection. Use it and try to dial your own phone number, the one the line is connected to. If everything is set up properly, you should hear the internal speaker acquire a dial tone and then a series of beeps or clicks as the number is dialed. This tells you that the outgoing connection is working properly. To fully test the modem, you should dial into a bulletin board service or another computer and actually upload or download a file. Many modems come with free-trial connect time for one of the major online services, and most software companies now offer on-line bulletin boards for updates and product information. Check the user's manual; it probably includes a phone number and dialing instructions.

NOTE

This book primarily deals with hardware issues even though I do discuss some software. There are a number of issues in telecommunications that are beyond the scope of this book. The documentation which came with your modem and communications software should have information about proper settings. Basically you have to tell the software how you want these settings defined. While they may seem complicated, you don't really have to understand exactly what they all mean. Terms such as *parity* and *stop bits* relate to how the information is transferred between the two machines. All you really need to know is how to make your settings match the settings on the machine you're talking to. Usually the instructions for connecting to a service or a bulletin board will include which settings you should use. Your software package usually includes a dialing directory that allows you to record the settings for a given number in a menu or dialog box. Refer to your manual for more instructions.

INSTALLING A FAX CARD

Dedicated fax cards, such as the Intel SatisFAXion, follow the same procedure as the one detailed above for an internal modem.

TROUBLESHOOTING MODEM AND FAX-CARD OPERATION

Even with a properly-installed modem you may find you have difficulty connecting two systems. Ninety percent of the time this is due to some simple oversight or incompatibility in the setup between the two machines. Five percent of the time the difficulties are due to problems in the quality of the telephone line being used. The other five percent the problem is either due to faulty hardware or to incompatibilities between the two devices. If you are having difficulty, work through the steps given below in the order they are presented.

Step 1: Check the Cables

Given the number of connections—cable, power supply, telephone lines, and given the fact that people often pull on the telephone attached to a modem or shift the computer attached to a modem around a bit, it's very easy for one or another of the cables to either work loose or become completely disconnected. I've often found myself able to dial into a service but not able to maintain a connection or receive files because the cable had worked partially loose.

Step 2: Com Port Designations

Check to make sure you're using the right Com port as defined in your communications software package and make sure that Com port is enabled. If you have recently installed another device into your computer, it may be using an Interrupt normally reserved for the Com port. If that's the case, you'll have to reinstall one device or the other to resolve that issue.

Step 3: Check the Communications Settings

If you can dial out to a remote line but all you get on the screen is gibberish, the problem is most likely due to incompatible settings between the two systems. Try adjusting the setting or contacting the service to be sure you are using the right parameters.

Step 4: If You Can't Maintain a Connection or Transmission

In some cases, you can dial a line but not hold a connection; or if a connection is made, transmission is very slow. This could be due to one of several things: a noisy telephone line, unsupported error correction or compression protocols, or incompatible hardware. If you have a voice line for the remote system you are trying to connect to, you can try dialing it to see if the connection is any better, or you can disconnect and try data connection a bit later in hopes that the line will clear up.

Step 5: Double-Check Your Software

The final possibility is that you do not have your software set up properly or that a file has become corrupted. If you are trying to download a file, make sure that the path set for storing downloaded information actually exists. Some programs will not allow you to have two files with the same name; if you are downloading a file, make sure you don't have another file in that directory with the same name.

Step 6: If All Else Fails

If at this point you are still having trouble, you'll just have to examine everything. Remember that as a last resort you can call the technical support staff for either the hardware or the software.

BEYOND MODEMS

Networking

Modems aren't the only way to connect two PCs. A much more sophisticated solution is known as *networking*. A network allows you to connect a number of PCs, including those of different design, such as mainframes, minis, PCs, and Macintoshes. The networked computers can share devices such as printers, CD-ROMs, and modems—depending on the type of network you have. Networks can be divided into two types, *dedicated* and *peer-to-peer*.

NOTE

As operating systems get bigger and offer more services, they offer varying amounts of networking capability, built-in. Windows for Workgroups, Windows 95, and Windows NT are well-known examples. Products such as Novell Netware and Artisoft's Lantastic are among successful networking software systems. Choosing and implementing a network is a subject for a book of its own. In this chapter, we will give an overview of networks, then, keeping our primary focus on hardware, we'll explain how to install a network interface card.

Computers on a *local area network* (LAN) require the use of a special network card, which acts a bit like a modem, and cables to connect those cards. There are several different methods for running the cabling. A full discussion of network options is beyond the scope of this book. Our focus here will be limited to an explanation of the basic types of networks and how you could install a network card in a single system to connect it to a network.

Dedicated Networks

Novell's NetWare is the primary example of dedicated network environment software. On a *dedicated network* one or more PCs are set up as servers. A *server* provides services to computers attached to it, but can not be used to run any application other than the network itself. The advantage of a dedicated server is in the ability to concentrate resources in a central hub. The server can contain very large storage systems, and be connected to high-performance printers and other peripherals that might be too expensive to dedicate to a single user. The server manages access to the resources and can also be used to control security. Administrators can determine who can use what resources and what files they can see. Dedicated networks can require more time to administrate and more training than their peer-to-peer rivals. On the other hand, they offer more control and quite often better performance—if they are properly configured with the right hardware.

Peer-To-Peer Networks

Usually simpler than a dedicated server is a *peer-to-peer* environment, such as Microsoft Windows for Workgroups or Artisoft LANtastic. These networks do not require a dedicated server. Each computer on the system can be set up to act as both a server and a client. This allows you to easily move files between machines, and share resources such as printers and CD-ROM drives. The exact features will vary from network to network. Peer-to-peer networks are well-suited for small networks or those which do not require some of the elaborate security procedures found in dedicated systems. Peer-to-peer networks do not have the concentrated muscle in a server that a dedicated environment does, so while they offer more flexibility, if several users are trying to access a resource off one computer, that system's performance may slow down significantly. Peer-to-peer networks are very effective for small-to-medium sized workgroups that want to share files frequently, and which occasionally may need to use common programs and devices such as a printer.

NETWORK CONNECTIONS

There are three things involved in connecting a computer to a network: *cabling*, the *network interface* card (NIC), and the *network software*.

Network Software

All the machines on the network must have software to both use the network itself, and to act as a *device driver* to talk to the network interface card. Just how this software will work and how much it will tie up in the way of your computer's memory resources will vary from program to program. If you plan on using a network, you will also probably want to investigate memory management software to improve system performance. For more information on memory management programs, see Chapter 4.

Network Interface Cards

There are a wide number of network card manufacturers and several different varieties of cards. These can be divided up by the type of protocols they use and the kind of cabling used to attach them. The two most common types of cards are those which use IBM *token-ring* protocols and those that use EtherNet. Since the basic installation procedures are the same for both and since most small networks use EtherNet, we'll focus on those types here.

EtherNet is both a method and hardware. It is a method for sending information between computers in packets, much like an envelope holds information going through the mail. Each computer on the system has a unique address, and information can run through the wire to and from any machine on the network. EtherNet connections can be used with both dedicated and peer-to-peer networks. EtherNet cards, such as that shown in Figure 14.13, are installed very much like internal modems. The primary buying considerations are compatibility with the software you plan to use, speed, and ease of installation. All the factors involved in network speed and its performance are beyond the scope of this book; for more information consult either magazines on networking or a book specifically written on the topic. For exact compatibility advice you should check the manual for your network software before purchasing any network adapter card.

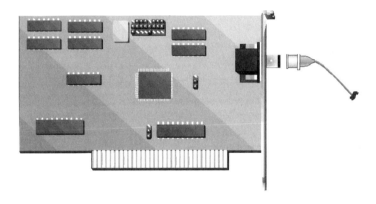

FIGURE 14.13 An Ethernet network interface card and thin Ethernet cable and connector.

Network Cabling

EtherNet cabling comes in three flavors; thick yellow garden hose (sometimes referred to as frozen yellow garden hose. The real name is *thick EtherNet* but almost everybody refers to it by one of the preceding two names because of how hard it is to work with. As a result it's not normally used for small network installation, so we're not going to talk about it any more). *Thin EtherNet* (also referred to as "thin net" or "cheaper net") and *twisted-pair* are the two other types.

Thin EtherNet is available in both predetermined lengths and custom lengths at most computer stores. It is similar to the coaxial cable used to string cable TV, but it is slightly different in thickness and uses a bayonet-type snap-on connector. It is strung from adapter card to adapter card using a T-shaped connector. The connectors at each end of the line are also fitted with a terminating plug on the open side of the T. Twisted-pair cables use thick phone line and modular jacks. They are normally connected through a repeater hub.

If you are planning on putting up a small network with five or fewer computers, the simplest solution is probably to go with thin net since you won't need a hub to connect the machines. There are a number of good books available on designing network connections. If you need more information, you should consult one of them or take a short class provided by Novell or another vendor on network connectability.

INSTALLING AN ETHERNET CARD

EtherNet installations are fairly simple unless you already have a number of expansion cards in your computer. They require both an Interrupt (IRQ) and a memory address, usually in the range between 110H and 380H. If you don't already have a second serial port in your machine or can disable it, a good choice is often IRQ 3 and address 300H, which are the default for many popular cards.

What You'll Need

✔ Small and large screwdrivers

✔ Cup or other container for screws and small parts

✔ Inventory of currently installed peripherals

✔ Network interface card with appropriate cable

✔ Ts and terminating fittings

✔ Possibly a pair of pliers or hemostat for adjusting jumpers

Step 1

Power down the computer and disconnect the power cord and any other cable connections that might get in the way.

Step 2

Remove the card and any accessories, along with the documentation from the box the card came in. Check that all the appropriate parts are there. Check your inventory to determine if you need to reset any jumpers. Depending on the card, you may have to set one or more DIP switches or adjust one or more jumpers if there are conflicts.

Step 3

Remove the cover from the case and then remove the edge cover from an appropriate slot.

Step 4

Install the card using gentle but firm pressure to seat it into the expansion slot.

Step 5

On the rear panel of your EtherNet card you should find the bayonet connector. Place the T fitting on the connector and place one end of your EtherNet cable into the connector. If this PC will be the last one in line, attach the termination fitting. Otherwise, connect the second cable.

Step 6

Turn on your computer and install your networking software.

Step 7

Check your software manual for the proper procedures for logging on to the network and accessing another machine, and test to see that the network is functioning. If you have any problems, check all the cable attachments on the PC you are working on *and* on the PC(s) that comprise the whole network.

Step 8

Once you know that your network is operating properly, you can power down the system and replace your case cover. Keep in mind that the EtherNet cabling is somewhat delicate—use care when moving your machine around. If you must move the machine much, first detach the EtherNet cables and replace them after the case is in its permanent position.

CHAPTER SUMMARY

Your PC can open a whole new world of communications for both business and pleasure. Online services and Bulletin Boards provide access to programs, news, and other people around the world with similar interests to yours. The PC can serve as a FAX machine and electronic mailbox. All you need to get started is a modem and the right software.

CHAPTER 15

PLAYING IT SAFE— CHOOSING AND ADDING A BACKUP SYSTEM

WHAT'S IN THIS CHAPTER...

- ✔ Preserving Your Data
- ✔ Choosing A Backup Strategy
- ✔ Tape Drives
- ✔ Tape Vs. Floppy Vs. Optical Backups
- ✔ Backup Software

579

WHAT THIS CHAPTER IS ABOUT

This chapter covers backing up your data. It describes the different kinds of backup systems available and provides information on how to choose a system that meets your needs, as well as basic installation instructions and how to maintain your backup library.

WHAT, ME WORRY?

It isn't a matter of if it's going to happen, but when. Sooner or later your hard disk is going to die, or you are going to erase a critical file, or you're going to turn on your PC and instead of the friendly, familiar beep, all you're going to hear is "whir, thunk." You will have just become the victim of a data disaster.

Your PC's hardware and all the programs in fancy boxes are just tools. The most valuable thing in your PC is the data you create with it. Unfortunately, computers are mechanical things and mechanical things fail. When they fail you run the risk of losing your data. Then there's human error. It's all too easy to think you are in an unnecessary sub-directory, and type `erase *.*` only to find out after you hit the **Return** key that you are in the root directory and you've just deleted all your startup files and device drivers.

There's only one way to overcome the potential disaster of such an event: good backup. The mission of a good backup is simple: there should be a usable copy of a deleted or corrupted file readily available when you need it. Backup systems range from the simple to the complex, and from the inexpensive to the extravagant.

DEVISING BACKUP STRATEGIES

Determining a backup strategy involves figuring out what you need to back up, how often it needs to be done, and what you need to do it—as well as how much you are willing to spend.

Selective Backup

There are several basic categories of backup. The simplest form is the selective backup. With this method, you just back up the specific files that are too important to lose. You can also use a selective backup to make copies of all related files once the project is completed. For example, when I finish writing this book, I'll make a selective backup onto tape of all the related files, and when it comes time to re-write, the files will be easy to find. In the meantime, I can take the files off my hard disk so they aren't getting in the way or running the risk of being damaged.

Small-volume selective backups are easily done to floppy disk. The only problem is that most people don't do selective backups on a regular basis.

Using Floppies

The simplest back up strategy is to back up important data files to floppy disk as you create them. The elegance of this system is its simplicity. You already have a floppy drive on your system, and disks are cheap. Unfortunately, few people actually save important data on a regular schedule. So when disaster strikes, they probably won't have a backup of the files they need.

Even if you are fanatical in maintaining proper backup of your data files as you create them, all you have is a partial backup. In the event of a total disk failure, you will still have to go through the trouble of reloading first your programs, and then your backup data files, before you can continue using the computer. The alternative is to make a total backup.

It is possible to make a total backup of your disk using floppies. In fact the DOS Backup and Restore commands were designed to allow you to do this. But if you have even a 200Mb hard disk, backing it up using 1.4 Mb floppies can be a tedious, if not mind-numbing, experience. Practically speaking, total backups using floppies and the DOS commands are a thing of the past. There are third-party programs such as FastBack and Norton Backup which will use floppies and offer data compression, but even so, for serious work, floppies are just not a practical alternative for total backup. The easiest way to maintain some form of backup using floppies is to create a sub-directory for your data files and then maintain that religiously.

A Simple Backup Strategy

The programs you load on your hard disk can be reinstalled from the disks you originally used to load them, so the important thing is to back up your actual working files. I use a sub-directory on my hard disk called DATA, and then make sub-directories either by projects or by the files stored there. For example, I have a separate sub-directory for spreadsheets, another for word-processing files, and another for graphic images. For book projects, I make a separate sub-directory for each book, and then individual sub-directories within it for each chapter. In and of itself, doing this doesn't back up any data, but it does keep your working files organized so they can be easily backed up. This is a good habit to develop even if you have some kind of fancy backup system.

It then becomes a simple matter to make copies of your files. If you wish to make a total copy of all the files contained in your data sub-directory, and there aren't too many to fit on a single disk, all you have to do is either use the menu options in Windows 95, drag and drop the directory in older versions of Windows, or use the DOS **Xcopy** command. To do the last, first place a formatted disk into your floppy drive, and then type the following command: **xcopy** `c:\data\*.* /s`. Of course, this assumes that the **xcopy** command is in your search path or in the same directory, and that your files are in a sub-directory called DATA on your C: drive. If you've placed them somewhere else, just modify the command appropriately. The /s option indicates that DOS should copy not only the current sub-directory, but also all the ones underneath it along with all their files.

If you have more files than will fit on one disk, you will probably want to use either the DOS Backup command or third-party software. These programs have the ability to use the DOS *archive bit*. This is a hidden marker which is attached to a file to indicate whether it has been backed up, or if it has been modified since the last time it was backed up. Such programs can create *archive volumes* spanning several disks, but you need to make sure you have enough formatted floppy disks before you start to use them. Going into all the details of such software is beyond the scope of this book; however, the names of several vendors are listed in the Resource Guide. *PC Magazine* and other computer periodicals regularly offer articles comparing different products in this category.

A single copy on floppies stored in the same location as your computer is not total security. For one thing, the file you need may be on a floppy that is on the verge of failure itself, and, furthermore, if disaster struck in the form of a fire that destroyed not only your computer but your backups, your data would still be lost forever. To be totally secure, your backup strategy must also call for a copy of critical files in another location.

Image or Mirror Backup

Mirror backup involves making a total backup of an entire disk or storage system. It is usually done using a tape drive or a second hard disk. Every file on the disk is saved. Given the size of today's hard disks, doing mirror backup using floppies is generally not a viable alternative. If you have a complex system, it is a good idea to have a mirror backup. If you are replacing your primary hard disk, a mirror backup is both the easiest and fastest way to get everything back up and running. All you have to do is install and partition the new hard drive and then restore all the files. I've been back at work after installing a new 1.2Gb hard disk in less than an hour from the time the new drive arrived.

Incremental and Archival Backups

If you already have a mirror of your entire disk or your data sub-directory, incremental backups can be used to add new versions of existing files and files created since the last mirror backup. This is usually done using backup software. The process can be automated so that it is handled at some time when you are not using the computer.

Incremental backups replace older versions of a file with updated versions; they cannot be done manually and require sophisticated software.

Archival backup differs from incremental backup in that old files are not deleted; both original and modified copies are maintained on the backup media. The advantage is that you can go back and get earlier copies of a file, but the disadvantage is that you'll accumulate more and more tape or backup disks.

ADVANCED BACKUP STRATEGIES: TAPE AND BEYOND

Floppies are tedious. It takes a long time to make a backup on floppies, and then they must be labeled and stored. Very few people make the effort to create proper backups using floppies. A more popular method for keeping secure backups is to use tape. The most common form of PC backup tape systems use some variation of the cassette tape. Tape drives are available from several vendors at prices starting at about $150. These tapes offer several advantages. Not only are these units relatively inexpensive, but so are the tapes. A cassette roughly the size of a standard audio cassette can hold up to 340Mb of data and costs about $20. Larger tapes about half as thick as a videotape can store from 2 to 4Gb at a cost between $30 and $45. Another option is *DAT* (Digital Audio Tape), which is a music format that has been adapted to work with a computer. These can also store about 4Gb on a $12-$20 cartridge, but the cost of the unit is a bit more expensive. On the plus side, they are a lot faster when it comes to recovering the files to restore them. These units are generally bundled with their own backup software that can be set to automatically back up all the files on a hard disk, or to turn on at some obscure hour of the night and back up all the files that you changed or created that day.

Hardware is a Determining Factor

If the only backup equipment you have is your floppy disk drive, it's a safe bet that you won't be making regular mirror backups. If you are like most users you probably won't get around to making backups at all. At best you'll occasionally save a copy of an occasional important letter or report to floppy disk. Your attitude about backup will probably change the first time you have a disaster and can't recover a number of files that you need. As you go looking for hard copies or searching disks in the hopes that maybe you saved a version of it onto a floppy disk, your mind will probably be going over how you *can* afford an automatic backup system.

Since dedicated tape drives start at about $150 and come with automated software, it might be wise to take some of the money you save by maintaining and/or building your own machine and buy a tape unit now. Figure 15.1 shows two types of backup drive.

FIGURE 15.1 Internal and external tape backup drives.

Buying Backup Hardware

Any type of storage medium that can be connected to a PC can be used as a backup device. These include cassette tapes, large reel-to-reel nine-track units, writable optical drives, and even video recorders. We'll examine the different classes of hardware first, and then examine the pros and cons of the different types.

Firms like Colorado Memory Systems (CMS), Archive, and Connor make a variety of relatively inexpensive backup solutions (I'll focus on CMS since that's what I'm most familiar with, but you'll probably want to shop around before making a final decision). The simplest tape unit, the Jumbo 350, installs almost exactly like a floppy drive; in fact, it can be attached to your floppy drive controller. It doesn't work like another floppy drive; rather, its backup software takes charge when it's controlling the tape drive.

These units are a bit like erector sets; the basic unit comes as an internal drive that is attached using a regular floppy cable. If you want better performance, for an extra fee the company will sell you a high-speed controller card that is dedicated to the use of the tape drive. This card can cut the time of a backup by two-thirds. CMS units use QIC 40 and QIC 80 cassettes, and can store up to 340Mb by using data compression. They are about the size of a standard audio tape with a metal plate on the bottom. CMS bundles software with it that works with both Windows and DOS; an extra fee buys software for other operating systems such as UNIX or Netware. QIC 40 and 80 drives can generally be installed in either 3.5- or 5.25-inch drive bays.

You can also share one tape drive between several machines. CMS offers a case for their internal drive, or you can buy one already assembled as an external unit. If you want to use them this way, you should buy an adapter card for each machine. Then all you have to do is to move the unit to the machine you want to back up and perform the operation. If you're using one of these tape units on the Novell network, it is possible to back up the file server from a standard workstation.

Parallel-Port Type Tape Drives

There is another option besides using the floppy-controller type of tape drive. There are QIC tape-based units such as the CMS Tracker 250. Just like the Jumbo 250, this unit uses a QIC 80 250Mb tape, and has two connectors at the rear which act as a printer pass-through: you connect your system's printer port to the drive and then connect the printer to the tape unit. Your printer will still function normally as long as you are not backing up the tape (in which case your computer is busy anyway).

If you are only backing up one computer, the Jumbo with a floppy controller is probably a better alternative, since the Tracker costs a good bit more, starting at about $260 street price using a QIC 40 cassette. The Tracker's advantage comes when you use it to serve more than one machine since it is likely all your machines will have a printer port, and there is no need for an expansion card. This unit is also very handy if you have to back up a laptop, which doesn't have accessible floppy drive connections, but usually does have a printer port. In all other respects, the Tracker series is identical to the Jumbo 350 editions.

Large-Capacity QIC Drives

Recently, vendors have started to market larger format magnum-style QIC tape drives, such as the CMS Powertape unit. These cassettes look much like the QIC 80's but have a length and width similar to that of a standard video cassette. CMS currently markets three units, one which can hold 2Gb of data and another with a 4Gb capacity. These are generally available as kits starting at about $700. Unlike the Jumbo series, the Powertape uses a SCSI 2 interface (for more information on SCSI, see Chapter 10). The Powertape bundles are shipped with an Adaptec 1510 controller and software for operating under DOS and Windows, and for backing up Novell Netware from a workstation.

Just as with their lower-priced drives, CMS offers an external enclosure for the Powertape series, so you can move the unit and back up any machine that has a SCSI host adapter and software installed. The Adaptec 1510 is an old controller. If you have a new SCSI host adapter installed in your machine, you will probably get better performance using it. I've used the Powertape series with a variety of ASPI-based SCSI adapters without problems (like I said, if SCSI is unclear, check Chapter 10).

The software that comes with the unit allows you to select total or partial backup, and even choose specific individual files to be included or excluded from the run. It is also possible to schedule unattended backups at regular times.

Digital Audio and 8 Millimeter Tape Units

The types of drives we have been talking about use a stationary recording head similar to that found in standard audio cassette recorders. *Digital Audio Tape* (DAT) is a different animal. It uses a *helical-scan device* similar to that found in VCRs. Stationary-head drives pass the tape in front of the head; helical-scan units have rotating heads inside a helical drum. The tape is wound around the drum, which can travel at speeds of up to 2000 rpm.

The same technology is used in camcorder design. Exabyte Corporation sells a backup drive that uses the same 8mm cassettes as those used in camcorders for video recording. Another helical-scan product is a video-track backup system. This uses a proprietary expansion card which allows your PC to back up directly onto a standard VHS videotape (unlike the Exabyte System that can only do digital backup). At the present time, helical-scan units probably cost too much for home or small office use.

Unlike regular analog audio tape, DAT is well suited for use as a backup medium. Some units can hold up to 5Gb of uncompressed data on a single tape, which costs between $15 and $60 depending on length.

Optical Devices

There are a variety of optical storage drives that can be used for backup (see Figure 15.2). These include *WORM* (Write Once, Read Many), *Read/Write Optical*, and *CD-R* (Compact Disc, Write Once). Optical devices offer speeds between that of a floppy drive and that of a hard disk, along with excellent shelf-life. The data is actually burned on with a laser and is much less likely to be damaged.

FIGURE 15.2 Optical drive.

WORM drives and Read/Write drives are similar in design. They have removable optical cartridges which cost about $150 each, and can generally store about 1Gb per cartridge (500Mb on a side). WORM units are excellent for archival storage. When a file is written to the platter, it is there forever. You can't erase it, but you can write another copy of the same file; the drive will normally allow you to see only the most recent copy, but you can go back and look at and restore earlier versions if desired.

Read/Writable drives fall into two categories: *Phase-Change* (P-C) and *Magneto-Optical* (M-O). Magneto-Optical drives, as the name implies, use a combination of both magnetic and optical technology to position and write data. These are somewhat slower than P-C drives because they require two passes to write data. P-C units use a more powerful beam and can write data in one pass, but the drawback is that there is less stability in the recording surface. As a rule, P-C drives can sustain only about 2/3 the read/write of an M-O unit, roughly about 100,000 transactions. This seems like a lot, and it is if you are only using the device for backup; in that case, it will probably work just fine. If you are using the drive to actually store and run program files, it may be another matter. Many programs and operating environments, such as Microsoft Windows, are constantly reading and writing small amounts of information to disk. These units range in price from about $1800 to over $4000. In our lab we have a Panasonic 7010 combination drive. This unit can access and use both WORM and P-C cartridges but costs about $4000.

PURCHASING CONSIDERATIONS

Floppy-based 1/4" tape units like the Jumbo 350 offer an inexpensive means of automating your backup. They're reliable, have good warranties, and are easy to use and install. The disadvantage is lack of speed. A basic unit without a dedicated expansion card can only write as fast as your floppy drive, which by current standards is very slow. With the supplemental card things are better, but not as efficient as the more powerful units. For a home user with only one or two machines to back up and without a lot of hard disk storage (i.e., no more than 500Mb), these units are an excellent choice.

If you have a couple of machines and don't have to back up very large hard disks, or if you have both a desktop and a portable machine, the parallel port-based unit offers somewhat better performance as well as portability.

For those of us who have higher capacity drives, tape units based on SCSI interfaces offer better speed and more capacity. Since you can buy five or six QIC-based units for one Powertape, this probably isn't a good strategy for a typical user. Helical-scan units offer high speed and high capacity, but are probably beyond both the needs and budget of most home and small business users.

DEDICATED BACKUP SOFTWARE

Most of the units mentioned above come with their own backup software, and the newer versions of Windows also sport their own backup routines. Third-party vendors offer products like Norton

Backup and FastBack Plus. Some of these programs offer additional features and can support the drives mentioned earlier. In some cases they offer better compression algorithms, advanced data verification and repair, and the ability to write complex scripts to automatically back up data from several disks.

THE BOTTOM LINE ABOUT BACKUP

The most important thing about backups is that you have them when you need them. The only way to do that is to find a system that is not only reliable, but easy to use on a regular basis. If you don't intend to buy a dedicated tape drive or other device for backup, at least make sure you make regular copies of your important data files.

INSTALLATION

With such a wide variety of options for backup, giving detailed instructions for installation is impossible. But there are a few things to keep in mind. In earlier parts of the book we discussed potential address and operating conflicts between different peripherals inside a PC. If you have a very complicated installation, and already have most, if not all, of your expansion slots full, you may be forced to use an external device or one that can take advantage of an existing expansion card, such as a floppy disk controller, printer port, or SCSI host adapter.

Another thing to keep in mind is that a tape unit, in general, must be electrically grounded. If you have a tower case, this is generally not a problem since the unit will be bolted directly onto the frame of the case. If you are installing a unit which uses plastic rails, you may have to attach a ground wire. The ground wire is usually a green wire with an eyelet on it, which may come attached to the drive or be included in the packaging. If you have plastic rails, be sure to attach this wire to the drive and then screw it down to bare metal on the case itself.

A FINAL CAUTION

Before trusting your backup installation, make a test run. I've seen installations in which, apparently, all the data was written, but it couldn't be restored properly to disk. The best way to do the test is to make a TEST subdirectory and copy (not move) several program and data files into it. Then use your backup software to make an archival copy. Make another sub-directory and restore the files there. Then make sure that all the files are still usable and work properly.

Once everything is installed and tested, all you have to do is get into the habit of making regular backups. If you do this properly, you won't have to worry about losing your data. If you get lazy, you are certain to get a painful reminder at some point in the future.

CHAPTER SUMMARY

People who don't back up their data systematically and regularly are vulnerable to assorted disasters, most typically hard disk failure. Organize your data sub-directories to make backing up simpler and shorter, and strongly consider at least a relatively inexpensive tape backup unit. There is a wide range of products and prices available for the small and gigantic system alike, enabling the prudent user to pick an appropriate level of data insurance. Sophisticated backup software is available which makes backing up efficient and even automated, and provides valuable insurance against data disaster.

CHAPTER 16

POWER STATION

WHAT'S IN THIS CHAPTER...

✔ Buying a Power Supply

✔ Replacing a Power Supply

✔ Maintaining a Proper Environment

✔ Uninterruptible Power Supplies

✔ Surge Protection

WHAT THIS CHAPTER IS ABOUT

Personal computers are electronic devices. While they require very little electrical current, they require current that is high quality and free of disruptions. This chapter covers evaluating, purchasing, and replacing power supplies, surge protectors, cooling sub-systems, and how to keep your PC from running afoul of the local utility. We'll then move on to the PC's operating environment, and cover maintenance strategies.

THE TRUE POWER USER

It's an old saying that a PC cannot have too much speed, too much memory, or too large a hard disk. There's lots of concern over data security, protection from viruses and the worry of a hard disk crash. Few users pay much attention to the one component most likely to fail and often the cause of random errors and system lockup—the *power supply*.

It's Not Plug and Play

One of the reasons that we don't think much about our power supply is that it doesn't seem to take any effort. After all, we just plug the cord in the wall and turn on the machine and it works, right? Like many things in life, the PC power supply looks simple but is really complex. Your power company puts out tremendous amounts of alternating current over thick wires. They come into your house and step down to lower voltages and are routed to wall sockets.

When that current hits the back of your PC it has to be converted to a very finely-tuned direct current precisely matched with the needs of the delicate electronic components inside. Your power supply must not only convert the power, but also provide enough to meet the maximum demands, which usually occur when your machine powers up. It must bring all your hard disks up to operating speed and operate the floppy drives, as well as provide general operating current. Most PCs also rely on it for cooling, since it contains the system's primary fan and exhaust port. If your power supply isn't doing its job, you can run into a variety of problems that aren't easy to track down. These include erratic read/write errors on the hard drive, failing to boot, overheating, and funny noises. Your PC's power supply is one of its weakest components, with one of the most demanding jobs. Cheap power supplies often cost about $30, less than half of their more expensive counterparts. The cost of a power supply is somewhat indicative of its quality, although you should use features and Underwriter Laboratories (UL) certification as more reliable gauges than price. Also, don't forget that power supplies come with different wattages. Obviously a 400-watt power supply is going to cost more than a 200-watt power supply. See Figure 16.1.

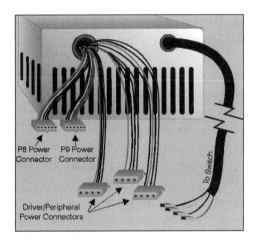

FIGURE 16.1 A common PC power supply.

Good power supplies with enough juice are well worth the extra money. Not only do they offer better power, but also protect the chips and circuits of your PC—and they handle drops in current better. I once had four PCs running without backup power, and the lights flickered off for a fraction of a second. Two machines had less-expensive power supplies, two had Silencer units from PC Power and Cooling. Those two stayed on, the other two crashed. The difference in price was about $70 for both. The result of this lesson? I replaced the cheap units, and now only use quality supplies.

Power Supply Connections

Most modern power supplies come with four different kinds of power connectors. The ones that connect older hard drives, tape drives, and other mass storage devices are about 1-inch square by 1/3-inch thick, and have a four-pin recessed male connector with one red, one yellow, and two black wires. Two of the four sides will be rounded so that the plug can only be fitted one way into the matching connector on the back of the device it powers. Attaching these can sometimes be a bit of a pain, as some vendors don't solidly lock the pins into the plug, and they wobble around a bit. It may take a little bit of wiggling to get this kind of connector to fit properly. If it seems that it isn't going in, double-check to make sure that you are putting it in correctly: they only go one way.

T I P   One trick I use with wobbley connectors is to hold the plastic hood with my thumb and forefinger, then use the rest of fingers and palm of that hand to stretch the wires tight. This seats the leads on the plug in their sockets. A little wiggle and the connection is made.

Newer 3.5-inch floppy drives require a smaller, solid four-pin female connector just about 1/2-inch square. These usually have a ridge and a locking pin so that they can only go in one direction. If you have to use an adapter to convert one to another, be sure that you put it on with the proper orientation. All power fittings are designed to connect only one way.

Your power supply should also have two rather strange-looking rectangular connectors with six wires each. Two wires on these connectors will be black. These are used to provide power to the motherboard at the P8 and P9 motherboard connectors. Some larger supplies may have three of these connectors. Two are as listed above, the third is for some server-style motherboards that can (but don't have to) use three. If you find an extra, check with the manuals for both the power supply and your motherboard. For more details on connecting these plugs see the chapter discussing the device or board you are attaching.

The final connectors that come off a power supply usually are a series of flat, female jacks coming out of one shielded cable. These are the leads that go to the main power switch for your computer. There should be blue, white, brown, black, and green connectors. Different switches may require different colored connectors to work properly. Be very careful and make sure that you follow the directions that came with your switch (usually provided with the case. PC Power and Cooling power supplies provide a key card on the main wire). Improper wiring could damage either the switch or your system, so if you're not sure, find out before you turn on the power.

BUYING A POWER SUPPLY

Once upon a time, when all computers came in one of two or three kinds of case, ordering a power supply was simple: you told the salesman what you wanted, named your computer, and they sent it to you. Today there are a wide variety of power supplies available. In some cases you may have to provide measurements to the vendors.

As a rule of thumb, it's a good idea to have twice as much power available from the power supply as the maximum needed by your system during normal operation, and even going beyond that isn't a bad idea. For example, if your machine normally uses about 110 watts of power, a 230- or a 270-watt power supply is adequate. Not having enough wattage can overload the unit and produce excess heat. Your motherboard will require somewhere between 15 and 20 watts of power, floppy drives 5 to 20 watts each, hard disks from as low as 3.5 to over 50 watts each, and figure about 10 for each full-size expansion card. Keep in mind that you will probably continue adding new toys, so keep some leeway in your evaluation. As a rule of thumb, a basic PC can get by with about a 220- to 230-watt power supply, while a power user's machine should have at least a 250- to 270-watt; with several hard drives, at least a 300-watt supply. Servers, and other machines that will have multiple drives and the like may need 450 watts or so. Also, make sure that it has enough plugs for what you need to connect (If it doesn't, you can always add additional connections with a Y-connector, but that adds cost and is not as elegant).

If you are a paranoid type, or a system administrator that can't stand a computer crash, you can also buy an alarm that will sound (or even beep you) if the heat in a case goes above a certain point. These are available from better power supply vendors. They also sell the little fans that sit on most modern CPUs. For more on that subject see Chapter 7.

DIAGNOSING A POWER SUPPLY

Is the Unit Plugged In?

Strange as it may seem, a very common complaint comes from people who try to run their PC without plugging it in. I was actually called to one client's office on four separate occasions because they had failed to turn on the surge protector, or failed to plug in either the computer or monitor. Do not assume that it is plugged in even if you are sure that you recently plugged it in yourself. Double-check before proceeding.

Even if the unit is plugged in, it still may not be getting power. It may be attached to a surge protector that is turned off or you may have blown a circuit breaker at the wall or fuse box. To test this, unplug it and plug in some other device that you know is working, such as a lamp, blow dryer, etc., into the same socket.

Other Types of Failure

Power supply problems fall into three categories: easy to identify, suspicious, and best guess. The easy to identify are almost the scariest: smoke or a burned smell comes from your power supply. This is a rather horrific indicator that something is wrong inside your computer. Quite often the damage will have extended beyond the power supply. A less-severe indication of a need to replace the power supply is a change in the cooling characteristics (without the smoke) or a failure of the fan to work.

NOTE

If you have a Silencer model from PC Power and Cooling it is sometimes hard to tell whether the unit is working or not without putting your hand back to see if there is air coming out. A good habit to get into is to put your hand near the fan every time you turn your machine on. Just because you have a power light doesn't mean that you are getting proper fan function. Another good habit is to put your hand back there just before you turn the machine off. If the air coming out is warm, something is wrong with your cooling system. If it is hot, there is definitely a problem. If you leave your machine on all the time, when you quit work you should check to see that the fan is running.

Weird Failures

If the computer seems to have a mind of its own when you turn it on or off, or if you get occasional memory errors but the memory seems to check OK (see the section on memory in Chapter 4), it may well be your power supply. Other indicators are if the machine seems to sort of lurch into motion, if it has trouble spinning up hard drives, or if the floppy drive seems to "sink" a while coming up to speed.

NOTE

These last three symptoms may not indicate that your power supply is bad, it may just not be up to the job you are asking it to do. See the discussion of typical power needs under "Buying a Power Supply," earlier in this chapter. If you have just added a new device, make sure the connections are good, and re-examine your power requirements.

The final possibilities are that your local power utility is putting out very "dirty" power, or the wiring in your house is not adequate to the task. You want to evaluate this before replacing the power supply. If your electricity is not "clean," you can use an UPS (*Uninterruptible Power Supply*) that has line conditioning hardware in it between your wall socket and the power supply. If the difficulty goes away, your power supply is probably all right.

If the computer sometimes freezes up while you are working, or just resets itself without cause, it may be the power supply, but it could also be a high-powered graphics adapter with driver problems, a bad memory chip, or a memory manager causing problems. If the problem recurs by repeatedly running a program or executing a command, it's probably your machine's software configuration or a troublesome peripheral rather than the power supply. You will probably want to check these things before proceeding to remove the power supply. To test the condition, boot without the memory manager or without using all the features of the video card, or try checking the memory before proceeding.

In some cases the power supply may be in good order but not operating. This can happen if there is a short on your motherboard. To test power supply function, you have to detach it from the other devices in the computer.

REMOVING THE POWER SUPPLY

WARNING

PC power supplies can hold an electrical charge even when the machine is turned off. With the exception of the fan, there are no user-repairable parts inside the power supply. When it's the fan going bad, its usually wisest to just replace the whole power supply. For this reason, I will not explain any steps in disassembling the power supply (*Don't Do It!*), simply how to remove and reinstall it.

Tools Needed

✔ Philips screwdriver
✔ Pencil and paper to note positions of wires, connectors, etc.

Step 1

Remove all cabling from the back of the computer. You should disconnect the keyboard, monitor, mouse, power cord, and any other cables attached to your computer case.

Step 2

Place the computer where you can work on it; a sturdy flat table is best. With your screwdriver, remove the screws used to close the cover of the case. They should be located on the back of the case. Place them in a can, jar, or zip-lock bag so you don't lose them. Remove the computer's cover and set it aside.

The power supply is easy to locate. It will be a big silver metal box usually toward the right-hand rear corner of desktop-style cases. An exception is in some smaller cases, where it may be located in the rear center. In tower cases it's almost always found up high on the back. Figure 16.2 shows a desktop case with the power supply.

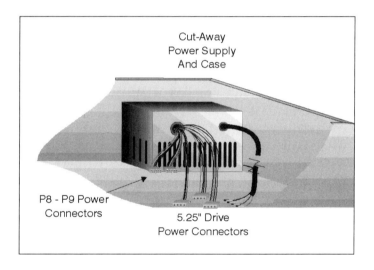

FIGURE 16.2 Desktop case and power supply.

Step 3

Remove all cables coming from the power supply to all your drives, the motherboard, and any other peripheral which is powered directly from the power supply.

The wires from the power supply come out in a "trunk" from one side or the other of the unit. Just keep following the trunk from the power supply to your machine until you have removed all the connectors.

NOTE

Create an accurate diagram of the connections *before* removing wires and connectors. You probably won't remember how they were connected, and putting them back incorrectly could damage components and/or incur frustrating delays. Pay particular attention to any color coding on wires, and to the Pin 1 position on connectors and plugs.

WARNING

Step 4

Disconnect the power switch. In most machines, the power switch is connected directly to the power supply and all connections are inside of it. If your power supply is like this, go on to the next step. If not, locate your power switch and disconnect the wires coming off it, after marking down the position of the different colored wires on the switch.

It's important to properly re-wire the switch according to the color-coded wires. Most will have five wires, one a ground, as well as a brown, black, white, and blue one. They must go back *exactly* the way they came off when you install the new power supply or replace this one.

WARNING

Step 5

Locate the screws on the back of your case that hold the power supply in place. There are usually four of them placed at the corners of the power supply. Place these screws in your container with the ones from the case cover. Don't remove the ones to the fan. They don't hold the power supply in place and you don't need to remove them.

Step 6

Carefully lift out the power supply. If it doesn't come out easily, hold it with one hand and use the other hand to help figure out why it isn't coming free. If it won't come loose, either one of the cables is wrapped around another one, or it is still attached to a drive or the motherboard. If you tug it free you may damage the connector or whatever it is attached to.

TESTING A NEW OR REMOVED POWER SUPPLY

A new power supply, or one which has been removed because it is suspect, should be tested before it is either installed or returned. This is fairly easy.

Step 1

Without attaching the power supply to any other device, attach a power cord to the back of it.

Step 2

Make sure the supply is switched off and plug the cord into a wall socket. Now turn the supply on and see if the fan is operating. If it is now but wasn't operating *before* you took it out of the computer, you may have a short circuit in the system. There are a couple of ways you can try to isolate this. One is to attach another power supply to the existing computer. If it shows the same problem, there is probably a short. Or you can attach this power supply to another working computer; if it works fine, once again the problem is probably a short.

To attach a power supply to a computer, you do not have to screw the unit down. Just attach the motherboard connectors, a hard drive and a floppy connector, and then turn on the switch.

NOTE If your power supply has an external switch rather than one mounted inside the unit itself, you'll have to attach it to the switch to turn it on and off.

If the power supply has been producing intermittent problems or overheating, it will probably have to be replaced. It isn't just a matter of whether it turns the fan, but whether or not it produces clean and consistent power. If you feel that the unit may have been under-powered before and that was the cause of your problem, be sure you get a powerful enough unit to overcome your difficulties. Going up a notch or two in power rating, say from 230 to 270 or even 300 watts is often only about a 25% increase in the cost of the unit and buys you an extra measure of protection.

INSTALLING OR REPLACING THE POWER SUPPLY

Step 1

Test the power supply to make sure it functions outside the case. Plug it into the wall and turn on the switch. Is the fan running smoothly and without excessive or strange noises? If it is you can install it in the case. If not, call your vendor and ask for another one.

Step 2

Place the unit in its position inside the case with no power cord attached; don't screw it down yet.

Step 3

Attach the connector plugs P8 and P9 that carry power to the mother-board. These are two large rectangular plugs having six wires each. The easiest way to make sure that you are placing them correctly is to make sure that the two black wires in each plug are next to each other. The connectors should be located near the keyboard socket on the motherboard. Figure 16.3 shows the P8 and P9 plugs being installed.

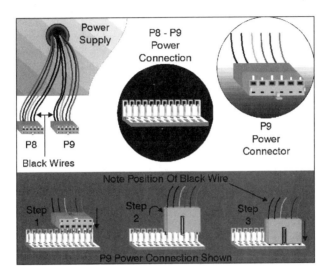

FIGURE 16.3 P8 and P9 power plugs being connected.

There are two slightly different styles of connectors for the P8 and P9 plugs. If they match exactly, you should be able to slide them on with no trouble. If they don't, they will still work but will take just a little bit of jiggling. Once you have them in place, check them to make sure that the combination has the four black wires in the middle. If it does not, take them off and place them properly (otherwise you could damage the motherboard).

Step 4

Now plug in all the cables attached to the power supply to the drives they serve.

Step 5

If your power supply uses a remote switch (one that's not physically mounted on or in the power supply) you'll have to reattach and possibly remount the switch. This involves attaching the five wires (one being the ground) exactly as they were on the unit before you removed it (refer to the diagram you made in Step 3 of "Removing the Power Supply"). If this is a new installation, be sure to consult your documentation to make sure you get the color coding exactly right.

Step 6

Make sure the power is switched off; attach a power cord, preferably through a surge protector to a wall outlet; and power up the unit. Make sure the fan is operating and that the Power On Self Test operates properly (see Chapter 2).

Step 7

If everything seems to be working correctly, screw the power supply down again. Consult your diagram and documentation, and do a careful visual inspection of the system, testing all connections for tightness. Make sure that no stray tools or screws are in the case or under the motherboard—they could cause a short circuit, and ruin your work (and your day). Finally, replace the cover and screw it back on.

OUT OF THE GLASS CASTLE

Computers are a part of the world around them. They draw electricity from the local utility company, and that power can be disrupted by storms and heavy demands. Sensitive electronic parts must be kept within a certain operating temperature range. If the chips on your computer circuit boards get too hot, it shortens their life; if they get very hot it may even destroy them. Extreme swings in temperature are not good for them either, which is why some people leave their computers on all the time. It is important to maintain the proper temperature inside your computer's case and to make sure that the outside air is not so warm that it adds to the problem. While your PC may be comfortable at standard room temperature, and work fine with the power that comes out of the local wall socket, your PC's power supply and its operating environment is not something to take for granted.

In the heyday of the mainframe, corporate computers were kept in sterile environments working in air-conditioned comfort, breathing filtered air and using carefully-regulated power. While computers have become hardier, smaller, and less expensive, they still need a somewhat controlled environment. When setting up your PC you should try to avoid extreme heat and cold, especially heat. I remember one winter seeing the image on the monitor of a Macintosh actually start to shimmy in an hourglass shape because the temperature in the room was high enough to overheat the machine's circuits.

Unlike the PC, the Macintosh did not have a fan to help cool the internal air. Most of the PCs in my laboratory actually have two fans. Today's microprocessors generate a lot of heat and the newer ones even have heat sinks built into them.

You can also help reduce the amount of heat inside your computer by not placing it in direct sunlight, or at least leave it in a position that is shaded for most of the day. These same basic precautions also apply to your monitor and any other external components, such as a CD-ROM or printer. You should place your PC so that none of its air intake or outlets are blocked, and so that there is a reasonable flow of air around the machine. A layer of dust inside it can act as an insulator, building up heat—not to mention that dust can get into floppy disks or into lubrication, literally gumming up the works. So you should also try to minimize the amount of dust in the environment near your machine.

A Healthy Diet

Your computer lives on electricity. While its 200- to 270-watt power supply may not consume much more electricity than a strong light bulb, it is much more finicky than a reading lamp. Some communities have very good power supplies with very few fluctuations in the strength of the current and very few power outages. Other users are less fortunate, living in areas where frequent storms or limited resources result in a loss of power.

You may think that you are getting 115-volt alternating current from that plug in the wall, but that current may be alternating more than you are aware. At its worst, your power may fail completely because of mechanical problems at a sub-station, a downed power line, or an electrical storm. There are three basic problems that can occur: *over-voltage*, *under-voltage*, and *line noise*.

The Dangers of Over-Voltage

Severe over-voltage, as from a nearby lightning strike, can literally fry the internal components of your PC. Your PC's circuitry is designed to handle a reasonable fluctuation of the power coming into it; lightning strikes can often produce a surge in power of over 20,000 volts. If your machine is the recipient of a surge like this, about all you can do is hope your insurance is paid up. If a severe thunderstorm is known to be in your area it is a good idea to stop work and power down your machine.

Not all surges are quite so dramatic. Spikes and surges are often produced on local lines due to fluctuations in the amount of current provided by your local utility. Spikes are very short-lived jumps in the power supply, sometimes lasting only for about a billionth of a second. These can cause difficulties with your computer's RAM, producing erratic program behavior, or if you are writing to disk, may cause an error with the file being written. Surges are much longer-lived, sometimes several milliseconds! Well, that may not seem like a long time to us, but it extends the time that your computer is under stress.

Surge Protection

Surge protectors come in a variety of forms. They are devices designed to stop over-voltage from reaching your PC. The most common type is the *metal oxide varistor* (MOV). These short out the excess voltage (usually referred to as *clamping*). Of course, the electricity has to go somewhere, and in this case it will be transferred into heat. A very large over-voltage can actually melt the MOV.

Even without something as flashy as a lightning strike, MOVs will wear out over time due to smaller over-voltages that occur regularly in most power systems. Sometimes a MOV unit will just stop working, leaving your PC susceptible to damage. In other cases the unit can conceivably start a fire when it fails. As a rule, it's a good idea to replace this type of surge protector every three or four years. Your local computer shop should carry an assortment of these devices, and can help you in selecting one that is appropriate for your needs. The primary considerations are how fast they can work and how large an over-voltage they can dissipate. Faster clamping times and higher power-absorption abilities are better. The better the abilities, as usual, the higher the cost.

Almost all PC's have some sort of built-in surge protection. This is sort of like a fuse or a circuit breaker. If too much power comes down the line, this component will fail, sacrificing itself rather than having the whole computer go down. That's a neat trick, but it's still going to mean a trip to the repair shop so that the circuit can be replaced. And, who knows, it may not function quickly enough. For that reason, you should purchase an external surge protection device. These come in several varieties and range in cost from about $10 on up.

Some surge protectors plug directly into the wall, offering two to six outlets. Curtis offer a series of Safe-Bloc units with different ratings. In general, the more expensive, the fancier the surge protection. With most of these devices, an indicator light shows that the unit is functioning properly. If a surge is detected, the unit will clamp down in an attempt to keep the power from damaging the devices plugged into it.

QBS and a number of other vendors offer power strips with surge protection built into them. Some of these even provide connections for phone lines so that you can protect your modem from surges. Another form of surge protector is found in switch consoles that double as monitor stands, allowing you to selectively turn on and off different computer components as long as they are connected by separate power cords. See Figure 16.4.

FIGURE 16.4 An assortment of surge protectors.

WARNING

Surge protectors are safety devices; they are not a guarantee. If you have a lightning strike near your house on a nearby generator, the odds are very good that the current will blow out your average surge protector and keep right on going. Surge protectors don't fix all electrical line problems. They can't add extra power if there isn't enough there for proper function.

It's a good idea to save all critical data and power down your equipment, then unplug the power leads from the wall socket, any time severe weather is in your area.

NOTE

There's another thing to consider when placing surge protectors: you may not have enough power on a given circuit to use all of the outlets that are provided on the surge protector. Keep in mind that just adding more outlets does not add more total electricity. If the socket into which you plug your computer has had problems in the past with blown fuses or popped circuit breakers, you should consider another location, or possibly, modifications to your wiring.

Under-Voltage and Power Failures—It's Not Always a Matter of Too Much

Brown-outs and black-outs can also cause problems with PCs. Under-voltage occurs when the power fed to the machine falls below the level it's designed for. Your PC can usually compensate for a 15% to 20% under- or over-voltage without any real problem. Voltage regulators are generally included with power conditioning devices combined with surge protection and, often, a standby power supply.

UPS DELIVERS

While surge protectors offer some measure of security against line problems, a good *Uninterruptible Power Supply* (UPS) offers surge protection as well as on-line battery back-up. In other words, in the event of an under-voltage or a complete failure of power, the UPS provides back-up power. Just how long the power will last depends on the unit you purchase. UPSes are based on battery power. When the power fails, the UPS switches over to battery power, thus keeping your PC on-line. In the past UPSes included a hefty measure of line-conditioning circuitry to protect equipment. Recent changes in UPS technology have reduced the cost of these units but reduced their inherent noise-handling capabilities. Most newer units do, however, have some sort of surge suppression built in. See Figure 16.5.

FIGURE 16.5 A typical UPS.

Choosing a Surge Protector or an UPS

All home systems should at least be on a surge suppressor and that surge suppressor should be changed at least every three or four years. The $20 or $30 is cheap insurance. UPSes that provide 10 to 15 minutes of standby power can be had in the $200 to $300 range. While this may seem a bit high for some users, others will consider it cheap insurance if the information they are working with is valuable. Remember, when the power goes off, the information stored in your computer's memory goes with it—and precious data may be damaged as well.

I have Deltec UPS units on my primary computers. The servers have 600-watt units that offer 30 minutes or so of backup power. Once I came home just after the power went out, and the monitors were the only lights in the room. The UPSes were sounding the alarm. Now I have added a serial connection to the UPSes on my two servers that communicates with their Windows NT operating system. If the power goes off for more than a set period of time, the UPS software will close running programs, then shut down the systems. It can also report on the condition of the UPS and its battery.

We are also impressed with the Back-UPS Pro line from American Power Conversion (APC). These unites have similar sophisticated features, and safety and shut-down software tailored for Windows 95 and 3.1.

GETTING WIRED

We have talked about the wires coming from the wall to the surge protector and the power going into your computer. Now let's talk about that spaghetti salad that comes out the back of your machine. If all you have attached to your computer is a monitor, a mouse, a keyboard, and a printer, you can still have a fair number of cables dangling on the back of your desk: that's four power cords, and at least four cables. It's a good idea to minimize how intertwined the cables become and it's an excellent idea to make sure all those cables and connectors are properly secured. I've had calls from more than one user convinced that they had a printer problem when the difficulty was really a loose cable. Make sure that your cables are long enough to provide some slack when the devices they are collecting are in their normal positions. Cables that are too short can be pulled loose or bent so that they weaken the wires inside. Extreme stress can also result in damage to the connectors themselves.

CHAPTER SUMMARY

Clean, steady power is vital to the safe and reliable operation of a PC. Power supplies are often ignored or taken for granted—until they fail. The wise user will make sure his/her supply is large enough, and habitually monitor its performance. Suspect or failed units can be tested and replaced by most users. Surge protectors help to clean up electrical current and guard against dangerous variations in live voltage, and every PC should have a new one every three or four years. The most cautious user will also provide an Uninterruptible Power Supply (UPS) to protect against brown-outs and power outages, which can damage data and even electronic components. Computer security in the broadest sense involves making sure that the PC's surroundings and operating conditions promote reliability.

CHAPTER 17

THE BIG BOX

WHAT'S IN THIS CHAPTER...

- ✔ Choosing a Case
- ✔ Design Considerations
- ✔ FCC Certification
- ✔ Accessories
- ✔ Radio Interference

WHAT THIS CHAPTER IS ABOUT

The case is your computer's home. It is the determining factor in how much space your machine will take up on or by your desk, and sets the limit of practical expandability. If you want a real power-user machine equipped with lots of drives and hosts of accessories, you don't want a baby-size PC case. If your heart's desire is a tidy machine that will sit unobtrusively on a corner of your desk, you won't be happy with a giant tower containing 16 drive bays and a power supply that momentarily dims the house-lights as it comes to life. Cases are a major factor in maintaining proper cooling and determine how easy it is to add new accessories or effect repairs. This chapter focuses on buying considerations, and how to set up a case for building a new system, as well as FCC requirements as applied to home-built computers.

CROSSING THE LINE

Buying a new case separates you from the casual computer enthusiast. It's an indication that you are going to build one from scratch, or at the very least tear down your existing machine and build a new one. There are very few maintenance considerations with PC cases. Assuming that you haven't allowed an existing one to rust out, or you didn't back into it with a fork-lift, the case should last for the life of your machine. But it is possible to outgrow one.

A case is your PC's protection against the outside world. Just like the roof and walls of your house protect you from the elements, letting you live in a dry, temperature-maintained environment, the case provides the same service to the delicate electronic components that are the heart of your machine. It also protects nearby TVs and radios from possible interference from your computer.

Since we rarely replace the case, it's important to take care when buying one. If it has cramped quarters—making it difficult to work inside—you will find yourself frustrated when adding or replacing cards. If it has sharp edges, you're more likely to get cut when working inside it. The positioning of the drive bays and the space allowed for motherboard placement will determine how easy it is to attach cables and power supplies, or make repairs. It can be a real pain to have just about assembled a new machine and find out that you have to run out to the local computer store for a floppy drive cable because the case makes the existing one too short.

A NOTE ABOUT THE FCC

At first it might be hard to understand why the FCC has an interest in personal computers. After all, they just sit on your desk, and without a modem they don't talk to anybody. The FCC was originally chartered to make sure that radio stations in a given area didn't interfere with each other. They accomplished this by assigning channels so that no two stations in a given area were broadcasting on the same wavelength. What many people don't realize is that all electrical devices generate radio signals. Your PC can interfere with radio, television and even telephone communication. In my own office I have a laser printer at just about an arm's reach from where I'm sitting. If I'm talking on the telephone and reach over to pull a sheet of paper out of the printer, as my hand passes over the printer I can hear a high-pitched whine in the telephone ear piece. The noise is being generated by the laser printer.

This kind of noise is the reason that the FCC requires that PCs be certified. There are two classifications: one for business operation and another for home or portable use. Business requirements are more lax than home or portable usage because the FCC assumes that fewer people will be watching TV or listening to the radio in their office environments than in their homes. PCs can be found in either environment, and therefore the FCC has mandated that all PCs be certified to the more rigid non-commercial standard.

Generally speaking, if you are building a computer for home use, you don't have to worry about FCC certification. Certification can be an expensive process, but if you're not marketing and offering it for sale, and if you are making it in quantities of five or less for your own use, you don't have to get certification. If you are building a computer from a kit where all the parts were sold to you as a unit, that kit must be certified. But if you are just going to build a machine for your own use, your real concern is not with getting an FCC certificate, but in making sure that your new machine won't interfere with your or your neighbors' TV and radio reception. If your new computer starts bothering your neighbor's evening with Jay Leno or Ted Koppel you may have to take steps to remedy the problem.

A better case can pay for itself in subtle ways if you live in a city. The case is a major factor in suppressing *radio frequency interference* (RFI). Units with heavy steel cases go a long way toward cutting down interference. A highly conductive paint, which often includes silver, is sometimes also used and is often needed on cases containing a lot of plastic. Inexpensive cases are sometimes cheaper because the manufacturer scrimps on the thickness of the metal and the quality of the finish. The poor quality finish can also make the case more prone to rust damage, especially since most cases are made overseas and spend the first few weeks of their lives in the hold of a cargo ship on the Pacific. The price difference between a good case and a medium case is probably $20 to $35; between a poor case and a good case it may be $50 or $60, depending on the size of the case. Over the life of the average PC this difference in cost works out to about a cup of coffee a day. Keep in mind that the vendor who scrimped on metal and paint costs has probably also cut corners on the quality of switches and how much time is spent on quality control inspection.

CHOOSING A CASE

A Wide Selection

When selecting a case, quality is a concern. But before you can evaluate the quality of the contenders, you have to determine just what kind of case you need. Cases come in a wide selection of shapes and sizes. They can be broadly broken down into three classifications: tower, full size desktop, and compact cases. Each has advantages and disadvantages.

Choosing which one is right for your needs involves several considerations; if all you need is enough room for your motherboard, two floppies (or one floppy and a CD-ROM drive), a small hard drive, and room for a couple of expansion cards, a small case will suit your needs just fine. If you are planning on assembling a heavy-duty graphics workstation or network server, you may have to turn to a tower case. Tower cases are also handy if you want to maximize your desktop area because they take up less room on it, or can sit on the floor next to it.

Keep in mind that case size can have a lot to do with what you can put into it and how easy it is to work inside. Compact cases can be devilishly hard to work in and are often more difficult to keep cool. Not all cases are designed to accept full-sized motherboards, and new processes are frequently delivered on large motherboards. If you need a lot of expansion slots, a tower or full-sized case may be a must, as some compact cases do not provide access to a full eight expansion slots.

If you are buying a case, it should come with an accessory pack. This should include cover plates for empty drive bays and for the back panel for empty expansion slots. It should also include all the screws, spacers, and wiring needed to install a motherboard in the case and wire up the appropriate switches. For desktop cases, and some compact cases, it should also include adequate mounting rails for disk drives. It should also include a battery pack to power the CMOS setup chip. If your case has a keylock on it, the accessory pack should also include two keys.

WARNING

Unless you feel an overweening need for security, put them somewhere safe and leave them there. Leaving them in the key lock invites problems. If one is turned slightly, it can freeze your keyboard and you'll probably check all kinds of things before you think to check the position of the key. If you have young children in the house, they may think the key is fun to play with, turn the switch and take the keys off and hide them somewhere. Many newer systems offer password protection as a means of preventing someone from accessing your data, and that is probably a better approach.

Tower Cases

Tower cases offer maximum room for expandability (see Figure 17.1). Standard towers have between six and eight half-size drive bays, room for 8 to 10 expansion slots and are designed to sit on the floor. Mid-size towers have fewer drive bays and fit well on a desk. There are also jumbo units that can seat 16 drives, and come with two power supplies.

FIGURE 17.1 A tower case.

Check the dimensions in Table 17.1 for dimensions of the basic units. Regular towers are slightly larger than a standard desktop case turned up on its side. This size is excellent for power users who want easy access to add or remove disk drives and expansion cards, or for people who don't want a machine taking up a lot of room on their desk. These units tend to be a little bit more expensive than their desktop counterparts, about $20-$45, depending on features and quality. If you are in an environment with a lot of dusty foot traffic, they may not be as good a choice because they will tend to accumulate more dust. With 486 and Pentium processors it is generally a good idea to get a second fan if you are using a tower to be sure there is adequate airflow for cooling. Adding drives in towers is usually easier because they don't require mounting rails; drives are screwed directly onto the interior of the case itself.

TABLE 17.1 Standard case dimensions.

TYPICAL DIMENSIONS FOR DESKTOP AND TOWER SYSTEMS (IN INCHES)			
TYPE	HEIGHT	WIDTH	DEPTH
Desktop AT	6.5	21.3	18.5
Baby AT	6	14.5	17
Standard Tower	26	8	18
Mini-Tower	14	8	18

If you choose to use a tower case, make sure that you obtain floppy and hard disk cables that are long enough to reach from the uppermost bay in the tower and still have a little bit of slack when pulled all the way down to the third expansion slot location. If you don't, you may find that your cables won't reach or that they may pull loose during use, requiring you to open the case and replace them. The same thing is true of your power supply. It needs to have long enough connectors to reach the motherboard and farthest drive bay. I have run into several case and power supply combinations that made it very difficult to comfortably plug in all the peripherals.

Working with Tower Cases

Most towers have a plastic front bezel mounted over steel ribs, with four to six openings for drive bays in the upper portion of the front. Bays that are not used are covered with plastic snap-in plates. The bays in most tower cases are designed to accommodate drives 5.25-inches wide. Since you will probably want to use at least one 3.5 floppy drive and will probably have hard drives 3.5 inches wide, you will need adapters to mount them in the case. The better manufacturers include at least one 3.5 floppy mounting rack, but you will probably have to buy the hard disk mounting rack separately. An option is to buy a 3.5 inch mounting kit that comes with mounting hardware, or buy a kit—drive and mounting gear together. In a tower case the motherboard is perpendicular to the floor, usually against the right wall as you face the unit, with the expansion slots in the lower back left-hand side of the unit.

Be sure to specify to your dealer whether you need floppy drive or hard drive mounting brackets when buying parts for placing 3.5 drives in 5.25 bays. For some obscure reason the computer industry has standardized on two different mounting configurations for 3.5-inch floppy and hard drives. If you get the wrong one, the screw positions won't fit. It's also a good idea to buy mounting brackets that come with the screws that you'll need.

Opening the Case

Almost all tower cases unscrew from the rear using either five, six, or eight screws. When you unscrew them keep them separate from the other screws you remove from the case, since typically they use a different thread from the others used in the construction. Some cases have a decorative bezel (or plastic frame) on the back that covers the screws. Simply pull this loose, or insert the blade of a flat screwdriver and turn it slightly to remove the bezel from the back. Once all the screws are removed, take off the cover. Most work like this: lift the back of the case cover up until it is at about a 30 to 45 degree angle, and pull up and away from the body of the case. This shroud is designed to tuck inside the front bezel, so you will have to unhook the front lip of the cover from the notch in the front. Some cases slide off towards the back, with runners along the bottom side of the case. These should slide backwards with ease, but be sure that your drive cables are not caught in the case fittings as you slide the cover back. There are a few towers, like those sold by Compaq, that open using a side panel. Screws are fitted along the top and side. Access to the interior is gained by removing the screws and sliding the panel out. In general, assembly is easier with the full-shroud type of case, since you have full and easy access to the entire inside.

When replacing the case, reverse the process, inserting the leading edge first under the front bezel and then gently lower the back until it gets into position. As it gets closer be sure not to catch any power cords or drive cables or other wiring between the case cover and the rest of the case. If you don't, you may find that a hard disk doesn't boot or a light doesn't come on, and if you do it often enough you may actually short out the wiring. It usually takes a little fiddling to get the case to fit snugly. Be gentle, and be sure to get a proper fit. If you screw the unit down without a proper fit you will warp the case slightly and then it won't fit well in the future. If your unit does have a rear bezel, don't forget to reattach it before you put the rear cables back on, the power cord, etc. It is also usually a good idea to power the unit up before buttoning everything down to make sure that it still works.

Some Other Points about Tower Cases

As with every case, towers need a good airflow. Their power supplies are usually mounted high in the back and so that's where you'll find both the power cord and the cooling fan. Usually this is an exhaust fan and air is brought in either from the front, or sometimes through the base of the unit. Many tower cases also have a plastic stand or feet to raise them slightly off the floor. These are usually attached with four or six screws. The kind with a permanent stand are better than those with the little plastic feet angled out on ears or ratchets. The latter kind are too easy to break if you are moving the machine around to get at a power cord or if someone leans up against them. Since tower cases usually sit alongside of the desk, you also have to consider how long your mouse, keyboard, and monitor cables are. In general you want to make sure that they are long enough to reach all the way from the lowest point of the tower to the far side of your desk. You don't want to be adjusting a monitor and find that you've pulled the cable loose from its setting or damaged a pin. Your local computer store should be able to provide you with extension cables for external devices. Make sure you know what kind of pin fittings you need before you leave. For internal cables, you'll just have to buy a new one that's long enough if you didn't get one of adequate length in the first place.

Standard AT-Style Cases

A standard AT-style case, like the one pictured in Figure 17.2, is like a tower case laid on its side and set onto your desktop. The motherboard is on the bottom of the case, usually on the left-hand side. A regular AT case should be able to accept a full-sized motherboard and have room for at least four half-height 5.25-inch drives. If you are going to be doing a lot of expansion or be in and out of your case a lot and want a desktop unit, a full-size AT case is a good choice (unless you have very little space). It offers the easiest general access.

FIGURE 17.2 A standard AT-style case.

Most AT cases have the power supply and fan in the back right-hand side of the case as you face it, and the power switch is a toggle switch located either on the right rear corner of the case or nearby. It's important to keep the rear and front of the case free of obstructions to ensure good airflow and proper cooling.

Opening the Case

AT-style cases usually have a front bezel with a shroud which fits over the top and sides. The shroud is usually secured at the back by five to eight screws. To open the case, remove these screws. On some cases you remove the shroud by sliding it backwards after unhinging it from the bezel by lifting it slightly at the back. Other cases, usually those with power switches on the right side, require that you slide the entire shroud forward. This can get a bit tricky and may take just a little bit of wiggling to remove the cover. When you are removing the screws make sure you don't remove the four screws that hold the power supply in place, just the screws that are actually screwed through the shroud itself.

In general you don't have to worry about cable lengths with standard cases since, being standard, they are what determined how long these cables should be. When buying a standard case, make sure that you get a proper accessory pack and that it has enough rails for all the drives you are likely to install. Ideally it should have a set of rails for each half-height bay.

Desktop cases offer something that tower-type units can't—the ability to double as a monitor stand. But this feature comes at a price. A standard unit can easily eat up half the free space on your desktop, which must also support your keyboard and mouse. If you are someone who spends a fair bit of time tinkering with the inside of your machine, you will probably find it more than a passing annoyance to relocate your monitor every time you crack your case open. External cable lengths for mouse, keyboard, and monitor don't pose a problem with standard cases since they rarely need to be more than 18 to 24 inches long.

Compact Cases

Most motherboard designs today are built on a "baby board" or half-size form factor which is not as wide as the full-size board. This has allowed case manufacturers to build designs with smaller footprints on the desktop, which are commonly referred to as "baby AT-style" or mini-tower cases, as shown in Figure 17.3. The increasing use of 3.5-inch drives has added to designers' abilities to build smaller cases, sometimes half the width or height of standard-style boxes. If you don't plan on having to get inside your computer and don't plan on adding a lot of peripherals, compact cases can save both space and money. The basic types mimic the standard style cases. You can check out the dimensions in Table 17.1.

FIGURE 17.3 A mini-tower case.

The quality of these cases varies, as with standard boxes. Keep in mind that extra reinforcement in the form of additional supports may make the case even harder to work in. We have one compact case in our test lab which is so tightly designed that it is almost impossible to get drives located in the rear bay in and out. Accessory pack considerations are similar to those mentioned for the standard cases.

Accessing Compact Cases

Compact cases can vary widely in how the cover is removed, and also in the placing of switches and drive bays, so it would be impossible to detail all the options. Your best bet when looking for a compact case is to examine the internal design carefully, and even try placing and removing drives in them before purchasing. Another consideration is airflow. Very tight cases with lots of cables can have restricted airflow, raising the heat level inside the case.

SOME OTHER CONSIDERATIONS

In final analysis, much of the decision when buying a case comes down to personal preference. Some people who would be better served by a tower are wooed by a compact design's smaller footprint. Others, who will never need the extra room in a tower, enjoy the fact that it sits on the floor rather than on their desk and use its upper surface as a tabletop for their telephones. As mentioned in the beginning of the chapter, a little extra money will buy a case that probably produces less radio interference and a tighter assembly. The extra expense many also provide a unit with better finish and thicker walls.

I/O Ports

Many cases, especially towers, come with cutouts for 25-pin and 9-pin I/O connectors. These let you run cables from on-board serial and parallel connectors to the outside of the case. Cheaper cases have literal cutouts that you have to push out, much like the dies cut into electrical supply boxes; better cases have plates that can be screwed in or out. This is much better, because if you reconfigure the system you can once again seal the openings. Extra openings in a case can degrade the airflow and actually raise the temperature inside the case—not good.

When adding to or removing components from a case, as with any computer part, put all the spare screws, nuts, jumpers and other fittings in a sealed baggie and keep them with your tools. In time you will accumulate a very useful collection of assorted hardware. Make sure to clear only unnecessary jumpers when giving an old board away; the new owner may need to reconfigure the board.

Power Supplies

Many vendors will sell you a matched case and power supply. Unless you know and trust that manufacturer, it's usually best to get your own power supply. The power supply is one of the most critical, and often least thought-about components of good PC operation. Inadequate power supplies can cause all sorts of problems, which are often very hard to diagnose. For more information on power supplies refer to Chapter 16.

Connecting Lights and Switches

The case also comes with the wiring tree that has the LED indicators and external option switches, like those for reset and turbo operation. Towers and baby cases will also be equipped with the external toggle switch that is used to turn your machine on and off. I explain how to attach those in the chapter on motherboards (Chapter 6).

Speakers

While a PC speaker may seem crude compared to the sound cards found on multimedia PCs, keep in mind that the basic PC speaker is designed to provide information during boot, before any sound card comes into operation. Be sure to get a speaker when you purchase your case. In most cases this will be part of the regular purchase price.

The speaker may be already installed in your case or may have come in a separate box. Generally speaking, speakers have two wires coming off into a 4-wire plastic block. A few have two individual teeny, tiny connectors which are a real pain to install.

External Batteries

In the goody bag that came with your case you should receive an external battery connector for your system's CMOS chip. If you don't know what a CMOS is, refer to the chapter on motherboards (Chapter 6). This battery provides external power for your system's set-up information when the computer is turned off. Today many motherboards offer on-board rechargeable batteries, usually a blue or red barrel-looking device. Even if this is present you should attach an external battery. The 4-pin connector is usually located near the keyboard socket on the motherboard. The more expensive battery packs are lithium cells; cheaper units often have just a flat plastic case where you can place four AA batteries. One set of batteries should last about a year, some longer.

On the back of the battery pack you should find a velcro pad with adhesive. This is used to attach the battery to the case. You simply pull the protective strip from the outside portion of the velcro and then press the assembly onto a vacant portion of the case wall. Don't do this before installing the motherboard. That way you can make sure that the pack is placed close enough to connect the wires without stressing them.

WARNING

Installing the battery leads backwards on the motherboard may cause the CPU to lose power even when another on-board battery is present. If this happens your computer will reset to default and forget all your special set-up information. Many battery connectors have one end plugged and many motherboards have one pin removed to make sure that you don't make this mistake. If you're not sure, you might want to leave the case open and the machine powered down overnight to test and make sure before closing up the case.

Lights, Switches, and Motherboard Connections

Somewhere on the front of your case is the control console. In tower cases the controls and indicators are usually clustered together. In many AT-style cases, the power switch is on the side or the back of the machine while the buttons and indicator lights are on the front. Almost all modern PCs have a power-on light, a Turbo mode indicator light, a hard disk activity light, and a Reset button.

All of these devices are connected to the motherboard using a wiring tree, with the exception of the power switch. The power switch is connected directly to the power supply, usually located in the back of the machine. The others should come connected to the appropriate positions on the case and if you are lucky, have labels. If they don't, you'll have to trace them back to what they come from, see what they are attached to, and connect them properly to the motherboard. Details for this operation are included in the section on installing the motherboard in Chapter 6.

The Power On Light

This is usually a green LED which indicates that the power supply has been turned on and a power-good signal is being returned by the motherboard.

The Hard Disk Activity Light

This is a very useful light which should flash any time there is hard disk activity detected by the system. These are usually red in color.

The Reset Button

This switch provides a function similar to that of the Control/ Alternate/Delete combination in DOS. Pressing and releasing it will cause your system to reboot without needing to turn the power switch off and on. As a general rule, if you want to reboot and cannot use the keyboard for some reason, you should use the Reset button if possible. This puts a lot less stress on the computer's electronics and the hard disk motor. Many machines place the Reset and Turbo buttons very close together, so if your Turbo button is connected, be careful until you get used to their relative positions.

Power Switch

Some power switches are simply push-in, push-out buttons, others are rocker switches, while some of the older ones mounted on the side of the case look like industrial electrical switches. Something that confuses many new users are the markings on some power switches. Instead of on or off, they are generally marked with 1 and 0. One indicates a closed switch and an on position, 0 indicates an open switch or off position.

The Turbo Switch

In addition to the switches and lights mentioned before, most cases are equipped with a Turbo button. This connects to the mother-board and allows you to slow down the speed of the machine in the event that some piece of software can't support the high-speed setting of the CPU. Many motherboards today are jumpering this switch so that it is permanently set in the high-speed position. Very few software applications require this setting, mostly games.

Connecting Switches and Lights

If you are very lucky, you will have leads from your switches and lights that are marked, and if you are extremely lucky you will have one which also shows which is Pin 1. If you're extremely fortunate it will also be easy to identify Pin 1 for all the connections on the motherboard. If all those above conditions are met, I'd like to know who the vendors are, drop me a note. If not, you'll get to play the match-up-the-wires game.

Since these go to LEDs and switches, most have to be oriented properly to work. If you have the connections backwards the light won't flash or the function won't operate. This is often a matter of trial and error. It seems every case assembler has his own favorite colors for everything. Very few provide proper labeling. So trial and error is the order of the day.

The manual that should have come with your motherboard probably had a diagram indicating the position of the various jumpers for attaching the LEDs. More considerate vendors label the motherboard fittings; others number them but provide a key in the manual.

COOLING SYSTEMS

The fan in your PC does a lot more than just move air around. It controls the amount of heat retained inside the case, and how hot the vital CPU and other chips become during operation. Cheap systems and weak fans can reduce the life of your PC and cause erratic behavior. Using a quality power supply can help. You should also make sure that the case is properly closed up. If you use your computer without the cover on for long periods of time, or don't replace all the expansion slot or drive bay covers, the flow of air will not move as the designers planned. I also make it a habit to place a hand over the fan outlet when I boot the machine—just to make sure it is running. That's a bit like keeping an eye on the water and oil pressure gauges of a car. Think of what happens to your car without coolant and oil—think of your PC without proper cooling. Enough said.

Secondary Fans and Heat Sinks

If you have a very hot system, any Pentium, or a 486/DX2 processor, you should have a secondary fan or an additional heat sink to reduce the operating temperatures inside the case and on the surface of the CPU. Several vendors, like PC Power and Cooling, offer products. Since there are a wide variety of computers and CPU combinations, you should consult a vendor about which ones are suitable for your system. Most are very easy to install.

CHAPTER SUMMARY

Besides the basic function of housing your system's components, your choice of case affects your workspace, the amount of cooling your system gets, and the ease (or difficulty) of repairs and upgrading. Choosing a tower, AT-style desktop, or compact case depends on personal taste, available space, and the number of expansion slots and drive bays you need or plan to use. There are many varieties and many vendors—consider quality of construction as well as price. Make sure you have an adequate fan; consider a secondary fan for high-powered (hot) systems.

CHAPTER 18

SELECTING AND MAINTAINING A PRINTER

WHAT'S IN THIS CHAPTER

- ✔ Choosing a Printer
- ✔ Installing Printer Drivers
- ✔ Dot Matrix Printers
- ✔ Laser Printers
- ✔ Ink-Jet Printers
- ✔ Printer Accessories
- ✔ Basic Printer Maintenance

633

WHAT THIS CHAPTER IS ABOUT

There was a time when some experts believed that the word processor and personal computer would bring us into the age of the paperless office. While that may someday yet happen, the personal computer has actually *increased* the amount of paper we use, and the printer has become a mainstay of the American office. This chapter deals with choosing the printer that is right for your needs, how to install it, and how to keep it happily humming along. Many software firms find up to 90% of requests for support are somehow related to printer problems, many of which can be easily prevented. This chapter will show you the basic steps required to get a printer up and running, as well as provide tips on how to keep your printer from failing due to poor maintenance or mishandling.

CHOOSING A PRINTER

There is no one-size-fits-all printer. In order to select the device right for your needs, you must be able to provide the answers to several questions. Once you have a clear idea of what your own needs and budget limitations are, you can then select from a wide range of products. The shopping advice here is generic. It will help you narrow your search down to a defined set of features based on things like print quality, graphics capability, and plain old speed.

Each year hardware vendors produce more than 100 new printers, and models are constantly being upgraded and improved. Every November, *PC Magazine* publishes its printer blockbuster issue. This issue includes a series of articles explaining current trends in the printer market, along with short reviews of products that have been released in the past year. While the articles may be short, they are the result of rigorous testing. Each printer is checked for ease of installation, speed, and its ability to successfully print test files designed to insure that it meets accepted industry standards. I suggest that you use the basic considerations given in this chapter coupled with the detailed product information contained in Issue 20 of that magazine when you go shopping for a printer.

How a Printer Works

It's easy to think of a printer as part of a disembodied typewriter (Remember typewriters?): you type on the keyboard just as you would on a typewriter. When you use the **Print** command, that information is transferred to the printer and comes out as a finished page. It looks pretty simple. But one of the reasons people have difficulty with printers is that we're actually talking about making two different devices, the computer and the printer, act as if they were really one machine. When you don't get a page out of the printer, it is often the result of a failure to communicate.

Printer Modes

Line printers, which include most simple dot matrix printers, accept data from the computer as a series of binary numbers, and match those numbers to the ASCII character set (*ASCII* stands for American Standard Code for Information Interchange, the name of the organization that specified the numbers used to define the character set). Many printers today still allow you to send character data directly to the printer using the ASCII character set. To do this, they have to print using either the currently selected or a *default* font (a built-in font automatically chosen), usually in a fixed *monospaced* size.

Part of the 256 ASCII character set includes elements for creating simple graphics such as bars, lines, double-lines, corners, and the like. While these are fine for rudimentary graphics, they leave a lot to be desired when it comes to printing fancy charts or photographs. In many cases you can use the printer's line print mode to send a text file, or the contents of the current screen on the monitor, directly to the printer. To see if your printer supports this feature, from the DOS prompt use the **DIR** command to scroll the listing of the current sub-directory onto your screen. Then try either pressing the **Print Screen** button on your keyboard, or the **Shift/Print Screen** combination. If your printer is capable of this function, you should get the screen contents on a sheet of paper displayed in the current system font.

You may have to press a key or a combination to eject your page.

All of that is very exciting, but leaves a lot to be desired when printing formatted documents such as business letters or handling graphics. That's where printer drivers and page-description languages come in.

PRINTER LANGUAGES

Your computer and its printer speak different languages. Your word processor or graphics package uses its own internal language to paint the image on a page. Your printer needs to describe the entire page in its own language based on the way *it* works. There has to be an interpreter in order for them to talk to each other. This interpreter is the *printer driver*.

Your software program must have an appropriate printer driver for the printer you plan to use. In the early days of PCs, each printer had its own unique driver, creating a real nightmare for both software developers and for users, because if the software did not have an appropriate printer driver, it could not be used with that printer. To some extent this is still true. Your software product must have a driver that supports your printer. But the advent of standard printer languages has made life a lot easier. If you primarily work under Microsoft Windows, and Windows has a driver for your printer, then you should have very little difficulty getting a new printer to work with any of your Windows programs.

PostScript vs. PCL

Most laser printers today support either one or both of the common *page-descriptions languages* (PDL) (complex programs which tell a printer how to produce output). If you are considering using your laser printer for graphics, or plan on sending output to a typesetting service bureau, you should seriously consider a printer that supports Adobe's PostScript PDL. If most of your work will be done in text, then you can consider a non-PostScript printer that supports Hewlett-Packard Printer Control Language (PCL). Many printers today support both, even the ones from Hewlett-Packard. When choosing a printer with several languages, you will find that some are *emulations*—in other words the printer can support some of the PDLs, but they are not native. If you are very picky about high-end printing, then make sure a PostScript printer has a real Adobe PostScript engine. If not, check the magazine reviews concerning how robust the printer you are considering is when handling the language you plan to use. More about that in a minute.

PRINTER DRIVERS

Most PC printers have one or more high-level languages built in that allow control of the device's advanced features. Just what these languages are capable of will vary depending upon the type of printer and from printer to printer. Software manufacturers include drivers for the major brands of printer with their packages. A large number of drivers are also provided with all the versions of Microsoft Windows. Printer vendors periodically update drivers themselves for Windows and other popular applications like WordPerfect, Lotus 1-2-3 and database applications. These drivers usually allow you to: define typefaces; use format commands such as bold, center and underline; and control graphics output. Many printers also support *plotter emulations*, which allow you to use your printer as if it were a Hewlett-Packard plotter. Unless you are into applications that use *plotters* (basically, automatic pen drawing machines) such as an engineering or a drafting program, don't worry about whether or not your printer supports HPGL.

PDLs—The Super Printer Drivers

In the mid-1980s, Adobe Systems changed the way the printer market was defined forever when they released the PostScript *Page Description Language*. PostScript is a very complex programming language designed to produce sophisticated graphics and *scalable* fonts (that means that the size of the letters can be resized at will).

Adobe began licensing PostScript interpreters that could be embedded in almost any output device, including laser printers, wax thermal color printers, and very high-resolution photo-typesetting equipment. Since the interpretation is all handled by the device, any piece of equipment equipped with a PostScript interpreter can theoretically print the file no matter what package produced it or what computer that package was running on. PostScript has become the *de facto* standard for high quality output and is supported by virtually every major software application and operating system with the exception of MS-DOS.

Let me clarify that. You can't send the DOS **Print Screen** command directly to a PostScript printer, unless it's also equipped with line printer capabilities, but programs running under DOS can use a PostScript driver to talk to a PostScript printer. Microsoft Windows also includes a generic PostScript driver as well as specialty drivers for the more popular PostScript printers. Many high-end graphics programs including CorelDRAW!, Fractal Design Painter and Sketcher, and Micrografix Designer only reach their full potential when used in conjunction with a PostScript printer.

Several organizations, including Zenographics and Pacific Data Systems, provide after-market products that can be used to turn non-PostScript printers into PostScript-capable devices.

Since PostScript is an independent page-description language, as mentioned before, files can be printed on any compatible device. They can also be resized or printed at different resolutions without loss of quality.

Hewlett-Packard Printer Control Language

While PostScript printers dominate the graphics market, the most popular laser printer on the planet is probably the HP Laser Jet. It uses HP's *PCL* (Printer Control Language), which provides control over both fonts and graphics. PCL is really more of a fancy printer command set rather than a true page-description language. It was originally introduced with the company's lines of ink-jet printers, but has been expanded and adapted five times. That explains why the current version is called *PCL5*. It includes the ability to handle scalable fonts, and has additional line drawing commands that were lacking in its predecessors. PCL also allows you to have multiple fonts on the same page and to use downloaded fonts. These may seem similar to the features in PostScript but there is a big difference. PCL is *device dependent*; it must be re-done for each model of printer. At the present time, it only works with 300 to 600 *dpi* (dots per inch) laser printers, although that may change soon. If you do not need sophisticated graphics and are only going to work with a single laser printer—and are not going to send your output to a high-resolution device—a straight PCL printer may meet all your needs. As I mentioned before, many printers are now available with both PostScript and PCL, providing the best of both worlds. It all depends on your budget.

TYPES OF PRINTERS

Over the past several years, printer manufacturers have designed several technologies for producing *hard-copy* (printed) pages. Three different categories have emerged as popular choices: *dot matrix*, *laser*, and *ink-jet*. Another category, *wax transfer*, has become popular for high-quality color work. Let's look at each of these technologies in turn.

Dot Matrix

Dot matrix printers work using a ribbon similar to that found in typewriters. Instead of having individual keys that strike the ribbon, the printer uses a series of needles that are fired from a head, through the ribbon, forcing ink onto the page. Dot matrix printers can be broken down into two groups: 9-pin and 24-pin models. A good 9-pin printer can produce output essentially equal to a medium-quality typewriter. The 24-pin models offer much higher quality output. In fact, many of the 9-pin models have trouble even forming some characters with descenders, such as "q," "g," and "p." They have poor output quality compared to other forms of printers, but have two distinct advantages. They are cheap, with some models selling in the $130 range, and they actually strike the print surface.

If you have to use multipart forms or produce carbon copies, then you are almost forced into using a dot matrix printer. On the down side (in addition to relatively poor print quality), dot matrix printers are loud. Remember, when the printer is operating, those pins are constantly striking the roller and the head is moving back and forth at high speed on a pulley and belt. See Figure 18.1.

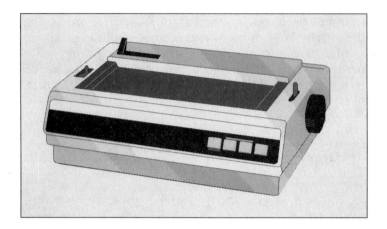

FIGURE 18.1 A dot matrix printer.

The speed of a dot matrix printer is measured in characters per second (*cps*) and a good dot matrix printer can type faster than the fastest typist. Most dot matrix printers today are also *bi-directional*. That means that they print going in both directions, left to right and right to left—there's no time wasted repositioning the print head to the left margin.

Dot matrix printers offer only a limited number of type styles in very few sizes. There are some programs available that will let you obtain scalable fonts from a dot matrix printer, but this involves using the printer in its graphic mode, which can be very slow. It can also take several minutes to get a full page of graphics out of a dot matrix printer.

To produce a graphic image on a dot matrix printer, your program must be able to control the firing of each pin individually all the way across the page. As just mentioned, this can drastically slow down the performance of your printer. Once again, 24-pin units have an advantage over 9-pin, as they can define a finer number of dots per inch than their 9-pin siblings.

The drop in laser prices and advent of more reliable ink-jet models over the past few years has all but eliminated the market for dot-matrix devices. If you decide to buy a dot matrix printer you should make sure it supports either the Epson or IBM command set. These are the closest things to standards for a dot matrix printer and will provide the most flexibility. Unless you are on a very limited budget or have to print multipart forms, you should probably consider using either an ink jet or a laser printer.

Ink-Jet Printers

Ink-jet printers also use print head technology but instead of pins striking a ribbon, the ink jet actually squirts ink directly onto the paper. Early ink-jet models were plagued with heads that gummed up with the ink, but that problem's been solved and they are extremely popular due to their compact size and quiet operation. This is especially true for use in combination with laptops. Ink-jet quality rivals that of many laser printers. Another advantage of ink-jet technology is its ability to print in color at relatively low cost; so low in fact, that prices (and sales) of monochrome ink-jets have dropped sharply. This makes monochrome ink-jets excellent buys if you only need black output. Several color models, including one from Hewlett-Packard, are excellent for producing presentation overheads and color charts. See Figure 18.2. One drawback with ink-jets is in their cost per print compared to lasers. The ink cartridges add dramatically to the expense of using them. Ink-jet refill kits can lower this cost, but require careful use. Four-color, rather than three-color, ink-jet printers also allow you to replace (or refill) the black ink cartridge separately, which saves money as well as giving you truer blacks. Don't get ink-jet cartridges wet; their ink tends to run.

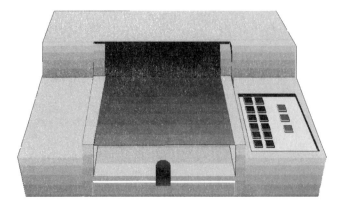

FIGURE 18.2 An HP ink-jet printer.

Laser Printers

Since the mid-1980s the printer of choice for serious business and graphics applications (except for some high-end color uses) has been the *laser printer*. These devices use a technology very similar to photocopy machines. Laser printers work by passing a laser beam over a photo-sensitive drum. This changes the electrical charge of sections of the drum based on light and dark portions of the final image. As the drum moves it picks up very fine pieces of black plastic called *toner*, which are then transferred to the paper passing through the machine. A heated roller melts the plastic into the page, making it permanent. Modern laser printers offer resolutions from 300 dots per inch—about twice that of the best dot matrix printers—to 1200 dots per inch, rivaling the output of photo-type-setting machines. See Figure 18.3.

FIGURE 18.3 A laser printer.

The performance of a laser printer is generally measured in pages per minute. High-speed network laser printers costing tens of thousands of dollars can produce in excess of 20 pages per minute. General business-quality lasers are rated at 8-12 pages per minute, while inexpensive (under $400) models designed for home and small office use are rated at 4-6 pages per minute. That doesn't mean that if you do a four-page document it will necessarily be printed in one minute's time; the rating is based on the mechanical limitations of the unit. A complex page of graphics can take several minutes to print, while a page of average text may be fairly close to the rated numbers.

FONTS AND RESOLUTION

Laser printers have made most of us very aware of print quality. The old days of hard-to-read computer printouts have given way to almost typeset-quality output. At the core of this revolution is the laser printer's ability to produce high-quality fonts. In reality a laser printer is much like a very sophisticated dot matrix: they are both *raster* devices. That means that the image, be it an individual character or the whole page, is made up of a matrix of dots. Imagine a line running from left to right made by touching a felt-tipped pen in a row of dots. The smaller the dots the finer the line. In effect, this is how printer resolution works. 24-pin dot matrix printers can manage about 180 dots per inch as a maximum resolution. Most laser printers range between 300 and 800 dots per inch, while sophisticated high-end typesetters can manage something in the vicinity of 1200 dots per inch. The higher the resolution, the smoother the line, especially diagonal lines like those found in the letters "A" and "V."

Printer fonts are generally handled in one of two ways: *bit-map* or *outline*. In a bit-map font, characters are defined in terms of a square grid. For instance, if we were defining the letter "X," two lines would be drawn, one from the upper right corner to the lower left corner, and one from the upper left corner to the lower right corner. This may seem like a simple way of handling things, but there is a problem. Take the letter "G." If we want to make that letter "G" twice as big to add emphasis in a document, with bit-map fonts we have to draw the entire letter from scratch. In other words, for each typeface and each point size and each variation of a typeface, the manufacturer has to define and store the entire font, dot by dot. See Figure 18.4.

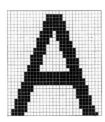

FIGURE 18.4 A bit-mapped letter.

There is a better way. PostScript fonts and the newer Microsoft TrueType fonts, embedded within the design of Windows, describe characters as mathematical descriptions—*outlines*—rather than individual dots. If you want to redefine a letter to be larger, all you have to do is include a command which says "make it bigger." You can even turn it upside down just by saying, in effect, "turn upside down." Sophisticated font languages like those included in PostScript can handle these tasks with ease. The space required in memory for storing outline fonts is greater than for a single bit-map font, but storing an entire family of outline fonts (bold, italic, bold-italic) requires much less space than storing the same amount of font information for bit-maps. See Figure 18.5.

CENTURY OLDSTYLE—FONT FAMILY

Normal	ABCDEFGHIJKLMNOPQRSTUVWXYZ abcdefghijklmnopqrstuvwxyz0123456789 ?@#$%^&*()_+=~{}[]\\:;"'/<>,.
Bold	**ABCDEFGHIJKLMNOPQRSTUVWXYZ** **abcdefghijklmnopqrstu vwxyz0123456789** **?@#$%^&*()_+=~{}[]\\:;"'/<>,.**
Italic	*ABCDEFGHIJKLMNOPQRSTUVWXYZ* *abcdefghijklmnopqrstuvwxyz0123456789* *?@#$%^&*()_+=~{}[]\\:;"'/<>,.*
Bold Italic	**ABCDEFGHIJKLMNOPQRSTUVWXYZ** **abcdefghijklmnopqrstuvwxyz0123456789** **?@#$%^&*()_+=~{}[]\\:;"'/<>,.**

FIGURE 18.5 A font family.

Generally speaking, if you want a range of quality fonts, it's best to go with the technology that allows you to use outline fonts. If most of your work is not done inside Windows, you may need to go with a PostScript printer or some sort of PostScript emulation to access outline fonts. If you are working inside Windows or OS/2, outline font capability is built directly into your operating environment. See Figure 18.6.

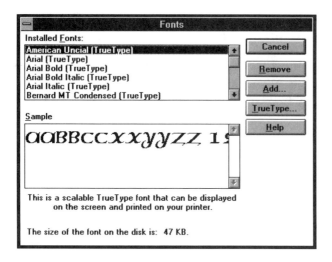

FIGURE 18.6 Windows font control panel.

PAGE SIZE, MEMORY, AND STORAGE SPACE

The maximum size paper your printer can handle is defined by the width of its print area. For a dot matrix printer, that area is defined by the width of the page, which is based on the width of the area where the print head travels and is generally measured in columns. Standard letter-width paper is generally associated with 80-column printers. Wide carriage is 132 columns. Laser printers define area by paper sizes and are dependent upon the amount of memory they have as to what paper sizes they can use. The memory factor comes into play because the laser printer must be able to calculate the bit-map image for the entire page in order to be able to print it. The wider or longer the page, the more memory required. When buying a laser printer you should consider the maximum page size allowed, and also inquire as to how easy and expensive it is to upgrade memory capacity in case you need to change. Most personal laser printers can handle letter-sized pages while some network and specialty printers offer paper paths as wide as a tabloid, 11 by 17 inches.

IMAGE ENHANCEMENT

If you plan on using your laser printer to produce near-photographic output, you should also be aware of image-enhancement technology. Different vendors use different acronyms, but is it basically a way of manipulating a laser printer's engine to produce cleaner half-tone images. Keep in mind that to produce really good half-tones you will need a fairly high-resolution device having about 600 to 1200 dpi resolution. For really clean half-tones you can also output your image to a PostScript file and have it printed on a high-quality type-setter. There are a number of service bureaus that can take your files and produce either film or photographic-style output.

COLOR PRINTING

Over the past few years, a variety of techniques for producing color with computer printers have been tried. These have included color ribbons for dot matrix printers and colored toners for lasers, as well as a variety of ways of splattering colored inks on paper. At the high end of the color printing spectrum, however, are color page printers. In general these devices are not affordable unless you have a serious need for color print output. The HP Color Jet Printer is an ink-jet device with street prices roughly the same as an inexpensive laser printer. It has been joined by very capable models from other major manufacturers such as Canon and Epson, and color printing is now within almost everyone's reach (see the earlier section on ink-jet printers). On the other hand, the fancier wax models, using either thermal transfers or the even more exotic dye-transfer method start in the $5,000 to $10,000 range and go up from there. These printers use either wax or plastic substances to create the colors, which are usually transferred from a roll of gel using some type of heat process. They require special papers and have very expensive per-print costs compared to other computer print technology. On the plus side, the results can be very dramatic, with the better units rivaling the appearance of photographs unless you look very carefully. If you are on a real budget, some dot matrix printers can handle limited colors, but won't produce as clean a copy as the wax and laser models.

OTHER OPTIONS

There are a variety of special options available for printers, depending on their type and the inventiveness of the company's engineers. Most dot matrix printers can be equipped to take both regular cut-sheet paper and perforated paper, allowing the unit to use continuous rolls while printing a long series of documents or multi-page reports without human assistance. Laser printers can be configured with more memory, different types of paper trays, special envelope carriers, font cartridges, network connections, and even collators and stapling machines. To detail all the possible options is far beyond the scope of this chapter. When shopping for a printer it's a good idea to examine all the options that might suit your needs but not be swayed by features that you'll never use.

PRINTER INTERFACES

Most printers are attached to stand-alone computers via the standard parallel printer port (for more information on printer ports see Chapter 14). A few devices are still connected using serial ports, which provide much slower service. Network printers are often connected directly to a network server using a parallel port, but a more elegant solution is to place them on the network using EtherNet or standard twisted-pair network connections.

If you have several computers to connect and don't want to deal with the issues involved in setting up a network, there are multiple-switch boxes available which will allow you to attach several computers to a single printer; manual boxes will require that you get up and physically turn a switch to determine which computer is able to talk to the printer. More elegant electronic switch boxes automatically scan continuously to see if one of the computers on its line is requesting service. The only real drawback to this approach is that if more than one user attempts to send data at the same time, the second will be told that the printer is not responding and the job will not be handled.

Do not ever use a manual switch box to share a laser printer. This can result in severe damage to the printer from line surges. Electronic switches can be used, or a local area network.

DOT MATRIX INSTALLATION AND MAINTENANCE

The instructions listed below for installation are generic and intended to help you understand the installation process more clearly. If the order of steps presented here varies in any way from those offered in the installation manual for your printer, you should always defer to the manufacturer's instructions.

What You'll Need

✔ The printer itself

✔ The appropriate cable

✔ Software drivers for the programs you wish to use

✔ Paper and ribbon

✔ Possibly a small screwdriver

Step 1

Unpack the printer. Carefully open the printer's box and remove it and all its accessories. Then locate the printer's manual or quick-start guide. Save the packing material in case you ever have to send the printer back for repairs.

Step 2

The manual or quick-start guide should contain a list of parts that were supposed to come with the printer. Make sure you have all the components.

Step 3

Check and assemble the printer. Many dot matrix printers come with various locks that prevent the head from being damaged during transit or keep the pulleys from moving. These must be removed prior to powering the unit on in order to prevent possible damage.

Step 4

Refer to the manual to see if there are any DIP switches that must be set to make the unit compatible with your software and to set the data board. Many dot matrix printers come with both serial and parallel connections and use DIP switches to determine which port is active. Some printers allows you to set different emulation modes, such as Epson and IBM ProPrinter, and these are also controlled with DIP switch settings. You may want to use a small screwdriver or ball-point pen to adjust the DIP switches. See Figure 18.7.

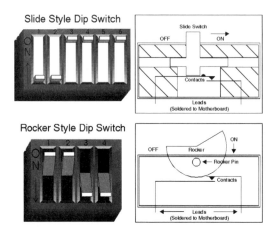

FIGURE 18.7 A set of printer DIP switches.

Step 5

Insert the ribbon. Refer to the user's guide for precise steps on how to insert the ribbon. Most modern dot matrix printers use cartridges rather than spool ribbons. See Figure 18.8.

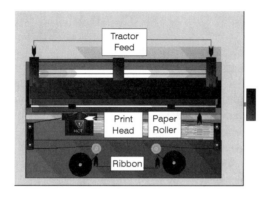

FIGURE 18.8 Inside a dot matrix printer.

Step 6

Assemble the paper feed. Your dot matrix printer will be equipped with (either and possibly both) manual and power-driven (commonly known as *tractor-feed*) paper guides. Refer to the manual for instruction.

Many dot matrix printers have the ability to print with different levels of force or spacing between the print head and the platen, depending upon the type of paper being used. Make sure this setting is correctly adjusted for your configuration. Improper spacing can result in improper paper travel and possible permanent damage to the printhead and/or platen.

Step 7

Attach the power cord to a wall socket and to the printer. Insert the paper according to the manual's instructions, and perform its Power-On-Self-Test. Most dot matrix printers offer some kind of control to automatically run through and test their various features. This is usually done by holding down some combination of control panel buttons when the unit is turned on. Identify what these are and perform the task.

N O T E

The Power-On-Self-Test is a very handy tool not only to make sure that your new printer is working right, but also to see what features it has and what the fonts look like. It's also a handy tool if at some point your printer doesn't seem to be responding to a print command. If the POST works, but the unit isn't working properly under your software, then it probably means that you either have a bad connection or that you have a problem with the printer driver. It is also possible that you have selected the wrong driver.

Step 8

Attach the cables to the printer and the computer, and place paper in the printer.

Step 9

Proceed to install software drivers and enjoy your new printer.

Dot Matrix Maintenance

The majority of dot matrix machines are fairly rugged and under normal use all you should have to do is to periodically replace the ink ribbon and the paper supply. It's a good idea when you replace the ribbon to dust out or vacuum the paper lint that accumulates.

It's a good idea to keep a reference sheet from a page printed shortly after you have changed the printer ribbon. Many people fail to notice how light their print is becoming until long after other people are frustrated at trying to read their letters.

Over a period of time your printhead will start to wear; eventually it will die. For many printers this is a user-changeable part and a new print head can be ordered from your printer's technical support department. In many cases installing a new printhead is only a matter of opening the lid on the printer, removing a couple of screws and plugging in a new cable after putting in the new print head. The replacement should come with adequate installation instructions.

LASER PRINTER INSTALLATION AND MAINTENANCE

What You'll Need

✔ The printer

✔ The appropriate cable

✔ Software drivers for the programs you wish to use

✔ Paper

✔ Toner

✔ Possibly a small screwdriver

Step 1

Unpack the printer. Carefully open the printer's box and remove it and all its accessories. Then locate the printer's manual or quick-start guide. Save the packing material in case you ever have to send the printer back for repairs.

Step 2

The manual or quick-start guide should contain a list of parts that were supposed to come with the printer. Make sure you have all the components. Keep a bag handy for any parts that have to be removed. You will need them if you ever have to ship the unit off for repair.

Step 3

Check and assemble the printer. Many laser printers come with various locks that prevent the internal moving parts from being damaged during transit or to keep the pulleys from moving. These must be removed prior to powering the unit on to prevent possible damage.

Step 4

Refer to the manual to see if there are any DIP switches that must be set to make the unit compatible with your software or to select the active I/O port. Check your manual for any settings you may have to make before the unit can be powered up. While most laser printers offer several different connections (often parallel, serial and AppleTalk), most modern laser printers can automatically switch and recognize which one is being used.

Step 5

Open the toner cartridge kit. It may have come in the box with the printer or in a box of its own. The toner assembly typically contains all the periodic maintenance parts for your printer, as well as the actual imaging material that forms the letters and graphics on the page. The instructions will probably tell you to place a felt bar inside the printer to collect excess toner off a drum, and to clean several components during this phase of the installation. Open the door or top of your printer and follow these instructions provided with the kit. See Figure 18.9.

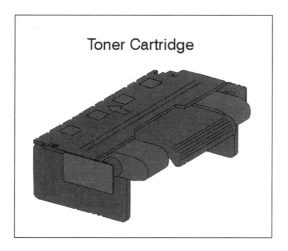

Toner Cartridge

FIGURE 18.9 A typical laser toner cartridge.

WARNING

If the laser printer you are working with has been turned on, some of the rollers may be very hot—hot enough to cause you harm. Be very careful when working inside the printer. One of the steps usually involves using a Q-tip to clean a very thin wire inside the printer. *If you break or damage this wire, you'll have to have the printer repaired.* Be very careful when performing this step. See Figure 18.10. Also be very careful to never expose to light any of the shutters inside the toner cartridge itself. The drums are photosensitive and will deteriorate if exposed to bright light. Avoid spilling any toner material; it is a very fine plastic power and very hard to clean up.

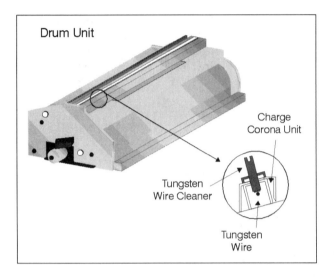

FIGURE 18.10 Cleaning the fuser wire.

Insert the toner cartridge into its carriage. Once it's fully seated, find the plastic tab that is used to seal the cartridge until it's installed. Holding the cartridge in place with one hand, pull the tab away from the cartridge with the other hand. This removes the plastic seal. Once it's clear of the printer, discard it, and close the lid of the printer.

Step 6

Install the paper tray. Among the items which came with your printer will be two or more pieces that form the assembly of the paper tray. Following the instructions which probably appear on the guide itself, or in the manual, assemble the carrier and place it in the printer. Place paper into the tray.

Step 7

If your printer requires any accessory cartridges or cards to be installed, follow the instructions that came with the accessory for installing them.

Step 8

Attach the power cord to a wall socket and to the printer and perform its Power-On-Self-Test. Most printers offer some kind of control to automatically run through and test their various features. This is usually done by holding down some combination of control panel buttons when the unit is turned on. Identify what these are and perform the task.

Step 9

Install software drivers. Printer drivers will vary from application to application. If you are using a graphical interface like Microsoft Windows, OS/2 or X-Windows, you will probably have one master driver that will cover all supported applications. This is usually done through some form of control panel. Figure 18.11 shows one of the printer set-up dialog boxes from Microsoft Windows.

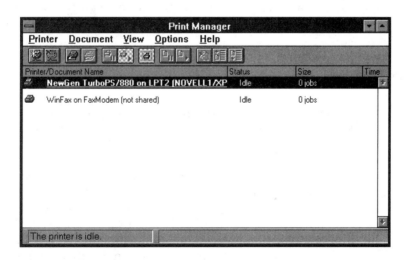

FIGURE 18.11 Windows Print Manager dialog box.

Accessing Your Printer's Other Features

Depending on your printer and its options, some of the device's more advanced features may be accessed using either software drivers or the control located on the unit itself. If your printer doesn't seem to be delivering all the power you thought it should, make sure that the options are properly enabled. Many printers come equipped with draft or low-resolution modes and require enabling commands to access image-enhancement technology.

Selecting Printer Paper

Not all computer paper is the same. Several vendors make special papers designed for laser printing that look much better than standard typing paper. Also, some less-expensive papers build up dust much quicker, which is not good for your printer. Consult your owner's manual to be sure that the paper you are using is supported. A trip to a local office supply store will probably reveal several papers that will let you get the maximum performance and best appearance out of your printer.

Printing Envelopes and Labels

Envelopes and labels present special challenges to a printer. They are both trickier to format and are not normally designed the same as regular paper. When using labels, be sure to get the kind that are designed for your type of printer. Using the improper kind of label can not only make it more difficult to get the print properly positioned, but labels may actually work loose during the printing process and gum up the works. Check with your manual and find out if there is a special door or method of feeding envelopes through the machine and use it. Failure to follow proper procedures for printing labels can result in spending the afternoon picking gooey bits of paper out of the inside of your machine. The adhesive has also been known to destroy dot matrix printer heads.

Preventive Maintenance and Troubleshooting

Once your printer is properly set up and the drivers are configured, it should require little in the way of care. You should keep an eye on toner or ink quality. If a laser begins to print unevenly, take the toner out and rock it gently from side to side to move the toner around. This will often help squeak a little extra life out of a declining cartridge. Uneven printing is often the result of improper paper or paper that has become too damp. Try using paper from a different stock and see if it makes a difference.

Splotches or Flecks of Black on Laser Print Output

Splotches on laser print paper are usually an invitation for an afternoon with the innards of your unit. Turn off the machine, open its cover and inspect the bottom of its inner bay. You will probably find a collection of toner loose inside the machine. This usually happens when someone improperly replaces a toner cartridge. Remove the toner cartridge very gently to avoid spilling any more than is necessary. You may want to put some paper or a sheet down before doing this. Toner is very fine and no fun to get out of fiber. Make sure that all the shutters on the toner cartridge are properly closed, and then inspect the inside of the printer for any spills. Most computer stores carry very small vacuums that can be used to remove spilled toner. Be very careful when working around the very fine wires inside. If the toner has really gotten all around inside the case, you may want to take it in for cleaning. I have taken portions of a laser printer apart to clean out toner, but there are a lot of little springs and pieces, and if one of them is not put back properly you could tear up the unit.

The Printer Doesn't Print

If you are in your application and your printer was working before and all at once it stops, make sure it's turned on, then check the cable connection. If everything is connected, make sure you have the right driver selected and that the software is printing to the right printer port. If everything seems fine, power everything off and power it back on (don't forget to save your work). Now try printing again. It's possible the printer or the program was just confused.

If things still don't work, you may have to reload the driver. Before doing that you might want to try the Power-On-Self-Test to make sure that the printer is printing properly, and you might want to try printing from another application. If the other application prints, you just have a problem with that driver.

If you are printing from Windows or some other general operating environment, make sure that you have not accidentally deselected the printer or told it to pause for some reason without realizing it.

INK-JET PRINTER INSTALLATION AND MAINTENANCE

What You'll Need

✔ The printer itself

✔ The appropriate cable

✔ Software drivers for the programs you wish to use

✔ Paper

✔ Cartridge

✔ Possibly a small screwdriver

Step 1

Unpack the printer. Carefully open the printer's box and remove it and all its accessories. Then locate the printer's manual or quick-start guide. Save the packing material in case you ever have to send the printer back for repairs.

Step 2

The manual or quick-start guide should contain a list of parts that were supposed to come with the printer. Make sure you have all the components.

Step 3

Check and assemble the printer. Many ink-jet printers come with various locks that prevent the internal moving parts from being damaged during transit or to keep the pulleys from moving. These must be removed prior to powering the unit on to prevent possible damage.

Step 4

Refer to the manual to see if there are any DIP switches that must be set to make the unit compatible with your software and to set the data board. Check your manual for any settings you may have to make before the unit can be powered up.

Step 5

Open the container with the ink and containers or cartridge. Check with your owner's manual to fill (if necessary) and prepare the inking apparatus. When this is done, open the door or top of your printer and install the unit following these instructions provided with the kit.

Step 6

Install the paper tray. Among the items which came with your printer will be two or more pieces that form the assembly of the paper tray. Following the instructions which probably appear on the guide itself, or in the manual, assemble the carrier and place it in the printer.

Step 7

If your printer requires any accessory cartridges or cards to be installed, follow the instructions that came with the accessory for installing them.

Step 8

Attach the power cord to a wall socket and to the printer, and perform its Power-On-Self-Test. Most printers offer some kind of control to automatically run through and test their various features. This is usually done by holding down some combination of control panel buttons when the unit is turned on. Identify what these are and perform the task.

Step 9

Install software drivers. Printer drivers will vary from application to application. If you are using a graphical interface like Microsoft Windows, OS/2, or X-Windows, you will probably have one master driver that will cover all supported applications. This is usually done through some form of control panel. Figure 18.12 shows one of the printer set-up dialog boxes from Microsoft Windows 3.1.

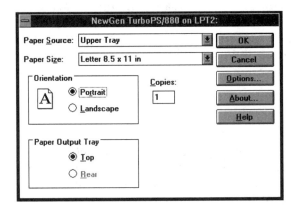

FIGURE 18.12 Windows Printer Setup dialog box.

CHAPTER SUMMARY

While choosing the perfect printer for your needs requires some figuring, the variety of printers available means that you should be able to find a printer that will do your job within your budget. Assembling a printer out of its shipping box involves several steps, but it is generally a pretty straightforward task. Connecting the printer to your computer is one of the easiest jobs you're likely to hit and, once you've installed the appropriate software drivers, you'll be ready to go.

CHAPTER 19

A BIT ABOUT LAPTOPS

WHAT'S IN THIS CHAPTER

- ✔ Laptop Differences
- ✔ Care and Feeding
- ✔ Upgrade Options
- ✔ Installing PC (PCMCIA) Cards
- ✔ The Briefcase Concept

WHAT THIS CHAPTER IS ABOUT

Laptops and notebook computers are a fact of life in the modern business world. This chapter covers the methods you can use to make your laptop work better with your base machine, at home or at work. The focus is not on what laptop to buy; that is beyond the scope of this book. Instead you will find tools and tips on how to get the most out of your folding machine, a rundown of upgrade options, and how to keep it healthy.

ONE FOR THE ROAD, OR, GOOD THINGS COME IN SMALL PACKAGES

The first portables were also known as *luggables*. My first one in 1983 was a 29-pound $6,000 Columbia Data Products 8088-based PC with two floppies, a 6-inch amber screen, 512Kb of RAM, and a case the size of a large sewing machine. Today I have a $3,000 486-based Toshiba with 8Mb RAM, 512Mb hard drive, 10-inch color display, and a new wonder, the *PC Card* slot. This is an opening in the machine that takes a credit-card-size expansion device like a modem or a network adapter. It is used as a road machine, and a backup. It is often plugged into our home network. The modern laptop looks like the device shown in Figure 19.1.

FIGURE 19.1 A typical laptop computer.

The portable market spans a range of computers running a gamut from network servers with 64Mb of RAM to palm-tops with minuscule keyboards or pen-based screens. Our discussion focuses on the middle ground; machines that have most of the features of a desktop computer, including a standard keyboard, and can be easily made to work with a regular computer that is used for most of your work. The assumption is that you do have a desktop (or tower) PC, and that is why you bought this book.

Palm-tops are great as a general-purpose memo pad and phone list; they do not yet have the power or keyboard for serious software applications. *Notebooks* are smaller than one inch thick and are great for basic business applications. Some have built-in floppies, some don't. *Laptops* are true miniature desktops, and cost like it.

The Road Warrior Survival Kit

Your portable is your computer away from home, and a backup if the main unit is down for some reason. That means that it needs the same care as the big system, and then some. In the first few chapters of this book we covered how to create Dark and Stormy Night Disks (*DSND*), how to keep a hard disk tuned, and how and why to keep good records of your system. Those rules all apply for portables as well. Here are some basics and why they are part of the Road Warrior Survival Kit.

✔ **Carrying Case**—This should have room for the AC power supply, a spare battery, disks, PC Cards, and other basics you need on the road. The best ones have extra support under the handle. With some laptops weighing in at over nine pounds, you don't want the handle falling off at the wrong moment. It should also allow easy access, not just for use on board the plane, but to get it out for a hand check. The case should also offer protection for the display screen, since this is the most fragile and expensive part of most laptops.

T I P

If possible, avoid letting airport security run your laptop through the X-ray scanner. The coil in that gadget can disrupt the format on the hard drive as much as the metal detector. Make sure you have a good charge on the battery, since they will make you turn it on at the checkpoint to show that your machine is a working portable computer, and not a disguised bomb.

✔ **Boot and Data Disks**—It is a good idea to carry a DSND, plus any very important files you need at the other end, and a copy of your schedule and phone directory files on disk. That way you can at least do some work if the hard drive has problems on a trip. Also make sure that software that must access dial-in services has the right settings for your destination.

✔ **Modem, Network Card, Printer, CD-ROM**—All of these are options, depending on what you need the laptop for. Some multimedia presentations also require a sound card, and even a projection display. Just what comes under this category is up to individual preference and need. There are also wireless mice that can let you operate the machine from a podium.

✔ **Spare Battery**—This is a good idea on long trips. Don't charge it every time it is a little down. The battery will work best if it is run all the way down before recharging. There should be more information on how to get the most out of your particular type in the computer manual.

✔ **Power Cords, Modem Cords, Telephone Cord**—Keep a set of appropriate cords in the case. Make sure you can connect to any outside service before you leave.

✔ **Identification**—Make sure you have a copy of the machine's serial number in a safe place *at home*. Laptops have a high ticket value and are portable. They attract thieves. An extra business card—not a label with a home address—is a good extra to tuck into a pocket of the case, and to attach to the underside of the machine.

T I P

It's a good idea to check for connection information and the phone numbers for any remote services (like CompuServe or the Internet) before heading out on a trip. I always add a session setting for the new location in WinCim and other access software at least a day in advance. Have a copy of your service contract agency's phone number in case you need (shudder) repairs on the road.

UPGRADING: A MATTER OF LIMITED OPTIONS

What are the major differences between the laptop and a desktop unit? Size is obvious. The engineering to get the goodies into a small package requires a fairly closed system. In short, all the parts are custom-fitted from the ground up. That means special memory modules, and things like display adapters and sound cards, are generally built right onto the motherboard. Floppies and hard drives are not usually user upgrades on portables. There are some exceptions, like the IBM Thinkpad shown in Figure 19.2. But even there, the add-ons are IBM parts as a rule—not items you can get at just any computer store.

FIGURE 19.2 The IBM Thinkpad.

But with a little planning and careful shopping, even the most closed-system laptop can be upgraded by its owner. The trick for maximizing your upgrade options is to shop with an eye to the future. Just which method you choose will depend on the way you plan to use the machine. There are basically three approaches for adding extras—cheaper options than manufacturer-supplied parts—the docking station, the PC Card slots, and portable machine's standard external ports. Let's look at each.

THE BASICS

Most portables have at least a pair of serial ports and one printer port. These can be used for more than modems and printers; they can also add networking and even SCSI connections for machines with no other means of attachment. Xircom makes a device that attaches to the printer port and provides both twisted-pair and thinnet Ethernet support. Adaptec has a division that has a similar SCSI port adapter. Both devices have a pass-through design that allows the same port to still provide a printer connection. With these gadgets you can add a network, a CD-ROM, and even a tape drive or scanner.

To hook them up you must enable the printer port (most portables have a means of disabling the printer port to conserve power), then connect the device and add the drivers. Windows 95 has drivers for these things, but will not automatically see them with its *PnP* (Plug and Play) feature. Go to the Control Panel and choose **Add/Remove Hardware**, then load the driver. When you reboot it should be on the system.

Modems and fax-modems are easy to add to a portable system this way; just hook them up to the serial port. Many such devices also require a battery, or a power connection. There is a better way to handle almost any expansion on a newer machine: the *PC Card slot.*

A really good set of options are external keyboard, mouse, and monitor connections. I am actually writing this part of the chapter in a hotel room. There is a standard keyboard plugged into my laptop, making it much easier to type. If we had had room on the trip, a regular monitor would have made for better display quality.

A Step Beyond

The slickest solution is the PC Card, previously known as a *PCMCIA* slot. These allow the insertion of credit-card-size expansion cards. I keep a combination network and fax-modem card in one, and often add a SCSI card in the second. You can get a wide range of products, including memory modules, hard drives and sound cards, for these slots. The better portables have at least two slots. You need to check your manual to find out how to access and power them. Like ports, they are often disabled to conserve battery life. Most are concealed by a plate when not in use. The IBM Thinkpad has a pin under the keyboard that has to be removed to access the slot. Most machines have a snap-on plate that can be removed or opened to expose the slot.

There are only a few cautions with PC Card operations. The first, make sure that the type of card is compatible with your machine and operating system before you buy it. Never use force when inserting one, and always use care with any special cables that attach to the card. These cables are usually fitted with small connectors, and are expensive to replace.

Check your manual for the proper procedure for adding a PC Card product. Here are some basic guidelines:

Remove the card slot cover from the machine.

Remove the card from its protective case and place the case in a safe place.

Slide the card into a free and compatible PC Card slot (as shown in Figure 19.3).

Attach any cover plate.

Attach any special cables required to use the slot.

Load any drivers and follow any steps required by your machine or operating system to make the card active.

Set up any software that uses the card to work with it.

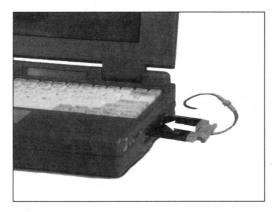

FIGURE 19.3 Installing a PC Card in a laptop.

Home Base: The Docking Station

The third expansion option is the most complex, and expensive: the *docking station*. This is a special expansion box that seats the portable and is often equipped with standard expansion slots, and maybe a CD-ROM drive and sound card with speakers. See Figure 19.4 The exact configuration depends on the vendor and the options that are already designed into your portable machine. Docking stations are attached to the laptop by means of a special connector in the laptop, and are not interchangeable between brands—often not even between models. If you are planning on adding one, make sure the right model is available.

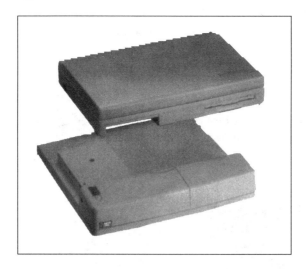

FIGURE 19.4 A laptop docking station.

The advantage of a docking station is the ability to use it and a laptop as is if they were a regular desktop computer. However, the combination is not necessarily one, and the docking station may only have two or three slots, have only ISA slots, and be expensive. Using this kind of hardware is an individual decision, and the wide range of options make any further discussion of it far beyond the scope of this book.

THE BRIEFCASE CONCEPT

I think of my laptop as a means of taking work and information with me on the road. All of my working files, schedules, phone logs and numbers, and some hobby stuff—like a genealogy program and a game or two—are on the disk. When I get ready for a trip, all of that has to be updated.

The old-fashioned way to handle these updates is to make a copy of the file on floppy disk, and move it between the desktop PC and the portable. There are other options. An easier way is via a laplink program that lets you connect the two machines via a cable. The next step up is a network card. Then the laptop can be connected to the host network, and the files copied with ease.

The problem with all of the above methods is *version control*. That is the technical term for keeping track of revisions to a file, and making sure you have the most complete and current version. What is needed is a way to use a master record to track the file, or to use a single master copy that can be automatically updated when the laptop is connected to the network.

Windows 95 has a Briefcase utility that will handle the tracking of a file. It has a Wizard tool that makes it easy to step up the transfer, using the operating system's built-in networking functions. Figure 19.5 shows a screen shot of the Briefcase Wizard's opening dialog box. For more information on this useful tool, check the Windows 95 documentation.

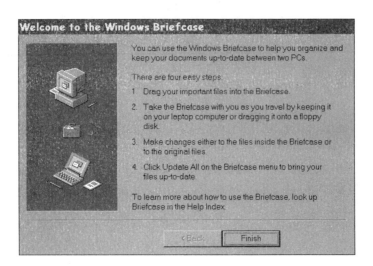

FIGURE 19.5 The Windows 95 Briefcase Wizard.

I also use a *PIM (Personal Information Manager)* that has an automatic master file function. By using a utility, a special copy of the program's master file is used for all remote sites. Copies are used on the road. Any time the master is accessed and it does not contain all the information in the copy, it is updated; if the copy is less complete, it is refreshed. That lets me work from any site, and keep all my records up to date.

Several shareware PIMs are included on the CD-ROM at the back of this book. you can use them to plan your taxes, life insurance, finances, and other personal needs. See the instructions in Appendix I for specific directions on accessing these programs.

Another trick that can help: keep all of your working word processing and spreadsheet files in a data directory by task. Then you can find and move the files you need on the road with ease. The real key to a good road trip with a portable PC is *planning*, and making sure to take the tools and files you need with you.

CHAPTER SUMMARY

Portable computers are not as easy to expand as a desktop or tower-style PC. There are several ways to add functions like networking, communications, and multimedia support. Just which one is right for you will depend on the type of machine you have, your budget, and what it is you want to upgrade. A few basic skills, like tracking the common files in use on both machines, can make your trips more productive and enjoyable.

CHAPTER 20

BUILDING
YOUR OWN PC

WHAT'S IN THIS CHAPTER

- ✔ Assembling an Entire PC
- ✔ Obtaining Components
- ✔ Safety Precautions
- ✔ Step-by-Step Assembly Instructions

WHAT THIS CHAPTER IS ABOUT

Most of the chapters in this book focus on the individual sub-systems of a PC; this chapter explains how to build a new machine from parts. It assumes a minimum amount of mechanical aptitude. You should be at ease with using a screwdriver and have a basic understanding of how components fit together. If you're the kind of person who wouldn't have any serious problems performing an oil change on your car, or assembling a child's toy using the instructions found on the box, you shouldn't have any trouble here. The following pages give step-by-step instructions on how to perform the actual assembly. Detailed direction for performing steps like formatting a hard disk or setting drive-select jumpers on a floppy are included in earlier chapters in the book. Building an entire system is not difficult, as long as you have a basic understanding of what you are doing and proceed in an organized manner. If you are very new to computers, or are not comfortable in working with the inside of a computer, you might want to get a more experienced friend to watch over your shoulder or give you a hand. The first time you assemble one it should not take more than an hour to an hour and a half, once all the components are assembled and ready to be installed. I've had a lot of practice and can put one together in a half-hour. If you are totally unfamiliar with the process and are starting with completely brand-new components, it might take three hours to get everything up and running when you add in the time for formatting the hard disk and loading the operating system. In return for your effort you get exactly the PC you want, know the quality of all the components, gain a comfortable familiarity with the innards of your system, and save money in the bargain.

SKILLS REQUIRED

No exotic tools nor elaborate skills are required to assemble a personal computer. There is really no need for electrical or electronics experience, as almost all the components are designed to either be fastened in with screws or connected with cables or snap-on fasteners. It is important not to use excessive force when mounting parts onto the system, and to avoid the possibility of discharging static electricity—

simply ground yourself by touching the case or some other metal object before handling circuit boards or other electronic parts.

Getting Ready

Obviously, before you can assemble a machine you have to decide what you are going to build and where to obtain the parts. The earlier chapters of the book should aid you in deciding which features are of importance for your own needs, and, together with the Glossary, explain any terms or concepts which aren't clear. In this edition of the book, most users will be considering building some version of a 486- or Pentium-based machine and probably plan to run Windows on it.

With that in mind, I have assembled a generic parts list that anticipates the needs of such a user. In the Appendix in the back of this book is a parts list which you can use as an aid in shopping, and to keep track of where and when you obtained your parts, and how long the warranty runs. Appendix B is an inventory form which you can use to record installation settings, which will help both in putting the machine together initially, and when performing upgrades or troubleshooting.

The following instructions, coupled with the documentation that comes with each of the parts, should give you enough information to perform the assembly. With some components, (especially the case) documentation will be sparse, but you should be able to figure out how the pieces fit together. During those steps of the assembly where you might become confused, I've tried to provide more detail. If at any time you feel you need more information about a given sub-assembly, refer to the appropriate chapter earlier in the book for more detailed information.

Required Tools

For the most part you can assemble a PC with nothing more than a medium and small Philips-head screwdriver and a small flat-blade screwdriver. While this minimal set of instruments will do the job, for about $15 or so you can buy a small PC repair kit that will make the job a lot easier. These generally include large and small screwdrivers, nut drivers, torq drivers, a pair of tweezers, a chip puller, and a plastic tube for holding spare screws and small parts. See Figure 20.1.

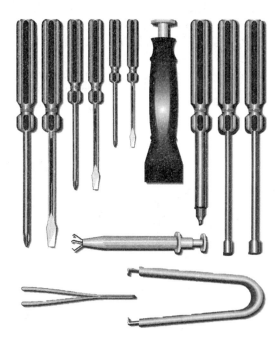

FIGURE 20.1 A PC tool kit.

You might also want to add a pair of needle-nosed pliers and a hemostat, which can usually be found at any electronics store or a Radio Shack. If you plan on doing a lot of this kind of work or have some other possible use for it, a real luxury is a rechargeable electric screwdriver, which can really speed up the job. You can find one at discount stores for about $20. You'll also want a reasonably clean and illuminated workspace; the top of a desk or the kitchen table should work just fine. A magnifying glass and a small flashlight with a tight beam can be helpful for close work.

A List of Major Players

The following list includes the generic components needed to assemble a complete PC. In some cases, I'll elaborate just a little bit and note any sub-assemblies that are necessary. If your vendor didn't supply these parts you can usually find them in a local computer shop.

✔ A Case

   Should be equipped with a:

   ✔ PC speaker

   ✔ Power Supply

   ✔ Wiring harness for the wires that connect LEDs and switches

   ✔ Mounting hardware for disk drives (if required)

   ✔ Cover plates for empty drive bays and expansion slots

   ✔ Remote power switch (if needed)

   ✔ Fasteners

   ✔ Motherboard spacers

   ✔ Battery Pack

✔ Batteries for Battery Pack

✔ Power Cord

✔ Surge Protector

✔ Motherboard with CPU and BIOS

✔ Cache memory (optional)

✔ RAM Memory (either SIMMs or DRAM chips)

✔ Floppy Disk Drive(s)

✔ Appropriate floppy drive cable

✔ Hard Drive

✔ Appropriate cable(s)

✔ Display Adapter Card

✔ Monitor With Cable and Power Cord

✔ Hard Disk Controller or SCSI Host Adapter

✔ I/O Card with Parallel and Serial Ports

✔ Keyboard

✔ Serial or Bus Mouse

✔ Copy of MS-DOS or Other Desired Operating System

✔ Copy of Microsoft Windows (optional)

✔ Floppy Disks

Miscellaneous Parts

It's a good idea to stop by your local computer shop and ask them if they can give you some miscellaneous screws and a couple of jumpers. With a brand new case and cards you shouldn't need them, but I have run into situations where I was a screw short or I needed a jumper when there weren't enough provided on the card.

In addition to the parts listed above, you should also keep a goodie bag. This can take the form of a Ziplock bag or you can get fancy and get some kind of small metal box or plastic case at your local discount store. It is used to store all the miscellaneous parts, like the extra accessories and screws that came with the case, or jumpers that you remove from expansion cards, so that you'll have them handy if you need to reconfigure your PC or build another machine.

While you're working, you should keep a can or cup handy. This is used to hold any screws, fasteners or jumpers as you remove them; that way they are handy when you have to put them back in and when you are done working, any remaining contents can be put in your goodie bag.

THE ASSEMBLY

Work Area Preparation

Put all the boxes, tools, and miscellaneous parts all within easy reach. Take the case out of its packing box and put it onto the workspace. It's advisable to get rid of any coffee cups, soft drinks, snacks, small children, pets, and other potential interruptions or disasters before beginning work.

WARNING

If your current home environment tends to build up static electricity, it's a good idea to routinely ground yourself and your tools before handling any components, and maybe work in your bare feet. This is not a time for building up static electrical discharges. Such jolts can actually damage the electronic components in your computer.

Never use force. One of the basic laws of mechanics is not to force something where it doesn't want to go. While we must sometimes break this rule, it's generally not a good idea except as an utter last resort. In the case of PC assembly, most of the pieces should go together without fuss. If you are having trouble fitting something into place, there may be a cable in the way, and forcing the fit could damage something. Don't feel nervous about working inside the case; just remember to use care and common sense.

Remove the cover from the case by taking out the retaining screws located in the back. The screws should all be located right around the edge of the case. Be careful not to remove the four screws holding in the power supply, if you purchased the case with a power supply already installed. Place the screws into the goodie bag. Figure 20.2 gives an approximation of the screw placement. This will vary from case to case, but finding the right screws should be pretty easy.

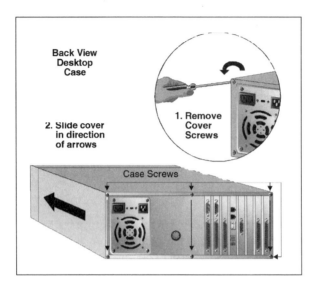

FIGURE 20.2 Remove the cover screws.

Installing the Speaker

Usually the speaker will be shipped already installed in the case as a standard part. If it came loose in a box, you'll have to find out where it attaches. It may be held in the case with a retaining clip, or slide into a couple of raised hooks on the bottom of the case (in a desktop case). Most tower cases and many desktop units mount the speaker behind a plastic grill that holds the guide for the expansion cards. It's usually mounted in the lower front of the case. You may also have to mount this retainer. It generally just snaps into the front on four little hooks.

Configuring the Motherboard

You'll need your motherboard's manual. There should be a diagram, along with some instructions for setting jumpers and switches on the board. You'll need that for this step, as well as for connecting the different leads that come from the case to the board.

Hardware vendors use DIP switches and jumpers to set various options on their products. You need to check your motherboard's manual for any settings you need to adjust. If you bought the motherboard with the CPU and cache memory already installed, you may not have to make any adjustments at all. The required switches and jumpers will vary from board to board, so it's a good idea to go through and check each one before putting the board in the chassis. I'll mention some of the more common settings in the list below. Figure 20.3 shows a sample motherboard diagram similar to one you might find in your documentation.

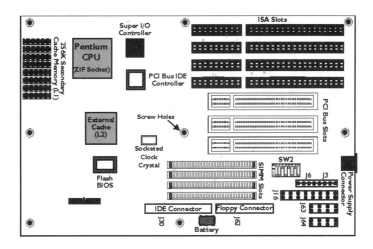

FIGURE 20.3 Diagram of a Micronics motherboard.

In some cases your manual may provide tables listing the different options and how they should be set. Sometimes they are displayed in the diagram itself.

DIP Switches

DIP switches look much like a miniature row of light switches and work much the same way. They can either be on or off to enable a certain feature. Since we are dealing with electronics, some suppliers like to make things a little more complicated. Instead of "on" or "off," they may label their switches "open" and "closed." This sometimes confuses novices, especially when the vendor doesn't match terminology between the labels on the switch and the instructions in the documentation. If the manual says that Switch 1 should be on, and the only label beside the numbers on the switch itself is "open," the switch will be in the "on" position when the handle of the switch is pushed away from the word "open." It helps to think of it this way: a switch is really a circuit. The switch is *on* when the circuit is closed and electricity can pass through the line; if you open the circuit, it's *off* because the circuit is broken. See Figure 20.4.

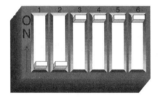

FIGURE 20.4 A DIP Switch.

Jumpers

Jumpers are really a very simple form of switch. The pins coming out of the motherboard are the poles and the small conducting sleeve, called a *jumper*, is used to close the circuit. If there is no jumper, the circuit is open (or off). When you put the jumper on the pins, it's closed, making the connection. Just as with DIP switches, your manual may refer to jumper settings in a couple of different ways. Keep in mind that "closed" and "on" are synonymous terms, and so are "off" and "open." Sometimes jumper switches are found as just a pair of wires sticking up; sometimes there are three wire jumpers. This allows setting two options, depending on which pair of pins are actually covered by the jumper. The pins will usually be labeled 1, 2, and 3. Jumpering pins 1 and 2 selects one mode, while jumpering 2 and 3 chooses the other. Figure 20.5 shows an illustration of a three-pin jumper switch.

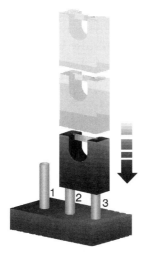

FIGURE 20.5 A three-pin jumper switch.

CPU Settings

If your motherboard has the ability to accept several different CPUs or a co-processor, there is probably a setting to select CPU speed and to indicate the presence of any supplemental chips. Another common setting is for the amount of RAM and type of memory chip used on the board. Most machines also require setting jumpers or DIP switches to indicate the amount of cache memory installed. Some machines are equipped with on-board parallel and serial ports and graphics adapters; enabling or disabling these features often involves setting DIP switches or jumpers.

Installing Memory

Now it is time to install the memory onto your motherboard if it didn't come with it already mounted. Most modern motherboards use SIMMs (Single In-line Memory Modules) as shown in Figure 20.6. Refer to your motherboard's manual and locate Bank 0 (computer people start counting at 0). Make sure you discharge any possible static by touching the case. Most SIMMs have a notch on one side of the unit. SIMMs only mount one way into the bank, so you may have to test to see just which way they fit. Insert the SIMM into the base of the socket at about a 30-degree angle. Place a thumb on either side and gently push the SIMM down and forward until it clicks into the socket guide.

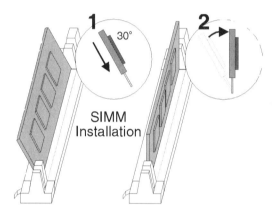

FIGURE 20.6 Installing a Single In-line Memory Module (SIMM).

Most state-of-the-art motherboards use 72-pin SIMMs, while older units were rigged for 30-pin modules. Be sure to purchase the right ones for your system. Also buy the ones with tin-silver looking-connections. The gold ones may look richer, but they are more prone to problems.

WARNING

Repeat the process for the remaining modules. When you are finished, all modules should be standing perfectly upright and their heights should be exactly the same. If one module seems to be angled funny or sitting too high, it's installed improperly. Remove it by pressing the release tabs at the base away from the holes in the socket, and lift it out and away from the slot. If the SIMM is one in the middle of the bank you may have to remove the ones further outside to be able to get it free. Be sure all the SIMMs are seated properly before proceeding.

Installing DRAM Memory Chips

Some older machines may use individual chips rather than memory modules. These are also assembled in banks or rows, usually eight or nine chips to a row. If your machine uses this system, refer to the manual for the exact placement of the bank, and then use the same method detailed below for installing cache memory.

If you are paying money right now for a new motherboard that has DRAM, consider sending it back, since SIMMs are easier to work with, are more reliable, and give better performance.

Installing Cache Memory

In all likelihood you will have ordered your motherboard with cache, and cache chips will have come pre-installed. If not, you will have to mount them yourself or get a friend to do it. If you have never seated electronic components directly onto a circuit board before, you may want to get a friend with experience to show you how it's done. While it is not difficult, it does take a gentle touch. If you want to do it by yourself, follow the steps outlined below.

Cache memory is sometimes distributed on modules similar to the SIMMs you just installed, but many systems still use individual chips to provide secondary cache. These are installed in banks and you should refer to your system's manual for the exact placement of the chips on the motherboard. Based on the amount of cache you are installing, these chips must be properly oriented. You will find a little moon-shaped cutout or indentation, or possibly a little bump on one of the narrow sides of the chip, right on the edge of the top surface.

All the chips need to be oriented the same way, and you should check with your manual to find out exactly how they should be positioned. Prongs are located along both long sides of the chip. Once again, make sure you are properly grounded and take the first chip gently between the thumb and first finger of each hand. Set the prongs facing away from you into the holes on the far side of the appropriate chip socket, raising the side towards you up at a very slight angle. Press evenly and gently away from you and guide the prongs on the side towards you into their positions in the socket. In some cases you will need next to no angle at all to do this, in other cases you will need more. Be careful and make sure that all the prongs go into their appropriate holes. Take care to make sure you don't bend any of them. If you bend one, you'll have to remove the chip. Try to straighten the prong and try again. The prongs are made of very soft metal and will fatigue or even break off if you play with them too much. Refer to Figure 20.7.

FIGURE 20.7 Installing a chip.

Installing the CPU, Co-processor, BIOS, or Overdrive

CPUs and the BIOS, like the cache memory, should have come already installed on your motherboard. If they did not or you are upgrading one, you should refer to Chapter 7 for detailed instructions on how to place these components onto motherboards; it's easiest to install them before mounting the motherboard in the case.

Mounting the Motherboard

The motherboard is like any electronic card in your PC; it's made of fiberglass and contains silicon chips. The motherboard has to sit slightly above the case to avoid shorting out the connections that stick through the bottom. This is accomplished by the use of Teflon spacers, which are snapped through holes in the motherboard. Then these spacers are locked into rails located on the bottom of the desktop-style case or on the right-hand side of the tower case. Figure 20.8 shows the detail of a motherboard with a spacer.

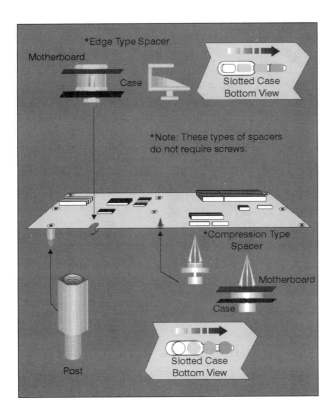

FIGURE 20.8 Detail of a motherboard with a spacer.

Don't put the spacers in yet; you still have to figure out exactly where they go.

NOTE

Two hexagonal screws, which can accept mounting screws on their tops, are used to fasten the board in place and ground it to the chassis. Figure 20.9 shows a section of the case with the motherboard rail and the mounting screw. If your case does not already have these screws in place, you'll need to screw them in finger tight and then snug them down with a nut driver from a tool kit or a pair of pliers.

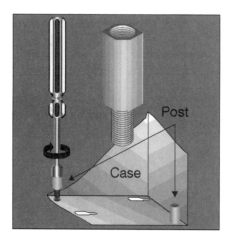

FIGURE 20.9 Mounting the motherboard in the case.

Locating the Position of the Retaining Screws and Spacers

Every time someone designs a new motherboard or chassis, it seems as if they have to design a new way to arrange the location of the motherboard attachments. You may have a baby-style case with a full-size motherboard, or vice versa. Or you may be fortunate enough to have both components designed the same size. No matter which, you will still have to "eyeball" exactly how the spacers and retaining screws must be placed to mount your motherboard. The easiest way is to gently lay the motherboard into position and then lift it off, seeing where the screws and spacers should be placed.

If you have a tower case, you'll probably want to turn it on its side so that, for this operation, the motherboard will be mounted onto the "bottom" of the case. Ground yourself by touching the case and take your motherboard out of its protective plastic envelope. There should be at least two holes in the top of the motherboard with silver or gold collars around them made of solder. These are the holes for the mounting screws. Position the motherboard so that the jack for the keyboard is lined up with the hole in the chassis for the keyboard plug. Then note where the spacing screws and retaining screws should go.

Move the motherboard out of the way and attach the screws. Once the screws are in place, it's time to put in the spacers. Line up the motherboard so both of the screw holes are positioned properly, then observe which spacer holes line up with spacer-retaining grooves in the case. Note the white Teflon spacers, shown with a motherboard in Figure 20.10.

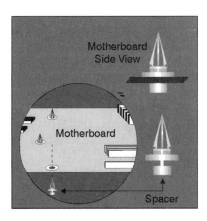

FIGURE 20.10 Mounting the motherboard.

Once you have noted the locations, sit the motherboard onto its edge and poke spacers from the bottom of the motherboard up to the top as shown in the Figure. If you have a full-sized motherboard you may also need to place two or three of the "C"-shaped spacers onto the upper edge of the mounting rails. Once all the spacers are in place, position the motherboard over the rails and slide it into position until they lock.

Now fasten the board into place with the two retaining screws set into the hexagonal bases.

Attaching the Leads and Hooking Up the Switches

Now it's time to attach all the little wires running from the case to the motherboard. You'll probably want to open up the manual that came with the motherboard and find the diagram. These switches and LED connectors are generally mounted into plastic sockets that look very much like jumpers, and they fit into jumper-switch positions on the motherboard. Refer to your board's manual for the exact location of the switches. If you put them on backwards it won't hurt anything, but the function won't work properly, so it may take some trial and error. Unfortunately, it seems that no two cases use the same wiring colors, nor any two motherboard manufacturers the same jumper positions, so it's not possible for me to give you precise instructions on how to hook up these connections.

There are a number of wires that lead from the case that have to be attached to the motherboard, and one that has to be attached to your hard disk controller. If you are very fortunate they will be labeled. Odds are you'll have to trace them back into the case to figure out exactly what their function is.

Most machines have leads for: power being turned on, turbo operation, turning turbo function on and off, resetting the system, and indicating when the hard drive is in operation, as well as one that hooks up the system's key lock.

Mounting the Power Supply

Our next step is to mount the power supply into the case. (If you purchased the case with the power supply already installed, you can move on to the next step, which explains how to connect the power supply to the motherboard). This is a very straightforward task. Simply locate the openings in the case for the fan and the power plugs. On some desktop units you may have to slide two retaining screws into receiving wells on the floor of the chassis. If you have to do this, it should be fairly obvious. Then, simply secure the power supply by fastening it to the wall of the chassis with four screws in the pre-drilled holes.

WARNING

Be sure that the switch is in the "off" position and that no cable is running from the power supply to the wall socket at this time.

Connecting the Power Supply to the Motherboard

Locate connectors P8 and P9 coming out of the power supply. They should be easy to spot. Both have six wires rather than the four that come with the other connectors. These plug into two jacks that are side by side, usually somewhere near the keyboard socket, on your motherboard. P8 usually goes towards the rear. The way to know if you have it connected properly is that the black wires on each connector adjoin each other when they are mounted into their sockets. Figure 20.11 shows the connections being put into place. These connectors are also usually keyed so that they can only go one way. Be *sure* to have them properly seated before applying power; if they haven't been installed correctly, *you may damage the motherboard when power is turned on.*

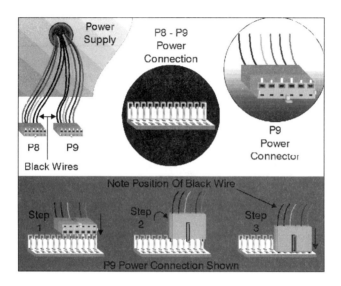

FIGURE 20.11 Installing the P8 and P9 power connectors.

Installing the Hard Drive into the Chassis

Now it's time to mount your hard disk or hard drive into the case. I'm just going to cover the basics here. If you need more detail on cabling or for jumper settings, please refer to Chapters 8 and 9 on storage systems for more information on both hard drives and floppies.

Drive placement will depend upon how many drives you're going to have in your system. Generally speaking, the uppermost drive bay should be reserved for the primary floppy drive. In some cases, a 3.5-inch exposed drive bay is reserved for the first 3.5-inch floppy, and in that case you will have limited choice as to where to place drives. If you are installing a second floppy, it should go into the drive bay below that. If you have a tape unit, it can go into the bay below the last floppy. Any remaining bays are available to install your hard disk.

I usually install hard drives first. This makes it easier to attach cables, because the floppies are usually placed over the hard disk position. In fact, the easiest way is to install from the bottom up when it comes to drives. Refer to Figure 20.12.

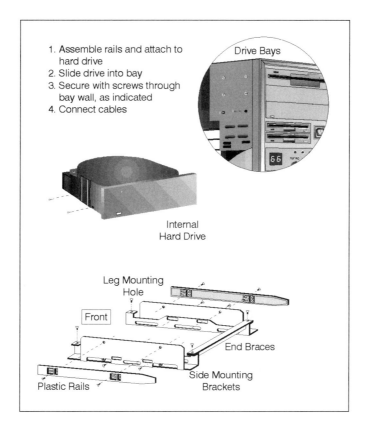

1. Assemble rails and attach to hard drive
2. Slide drive into bay
3. Secure with screws through bay wall, as indicated
4. Connect cables

Drive Bays

Internal Hard Drive

Leg Mounting Hole

Front

End Braces

Plastic Rails

Side Mounting Brackets

FIGURE 20.12 Mounting a hard drive.

If you are installing into a desktop case, you may have to attach plastic rails to the side of your drive. This is done using two screws, which should be found in the goodies bag which came with your case, or, in the case of a generous manufacturer, with the mounting kit that came with your drive. If you are installing a 3.5-inch hard drive into a 5.25-inch bay, you will also need an adapter mounting kit. Screw the rails and/or the adapter onto one side of the drive.

WARNING

Be careful not to overtighten screws into either a hard disk or a floppy disk. In some cases the screws will be too long for the job at hand and may actually screw into the circuit board of the drive or into the casing of the unit itself, thus damaging your drive.

Now slide the drive into place and make sure that it is far enough back to put a cover panel in front of it, that it doesn't obstruct any other drive bays, and that there is adequate spacing for ventilation.

It's generally a good idea, if you have three bays available in your machine, to leave one bay empty on either side of a hard disk. If you don't have that many free bays, try to at least leave one free on the side where the drive's circuit board is; this allows better cooling and relieves stress on the drive and on your entire system.

Now remove the drive and attach the mounting brackets and/or rails on the other side in the same orientation as the ones already installed. Next, place the drive into the bay and fasten it down with screws. With a tower case, you'll have to fasten the screws from the side of the case. In a desktop case there is usually some sort of retaining clip that usually looks like a square washer.

Attaching the Power Cable to the Hard Drive

All hard drives require a power connector. This is one of the leads coming off the power supply. One side of this plug will be slightly rounded, so it can only be mounted one way. Find the power plug at the back of your hard drive and connect the lead. We'll attach the data cables later. Install any additional hard drives the same way. Refer to Figure 20.13

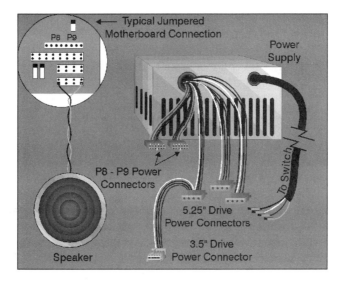

FIGURE 20.13 Connecting the wiring harness.

Installing the Floppy Drives

Your floppy drive(s) are installed in the case the same way the hard drive was. Use the appropriate mounting hardware and slide them into a drive rail and secure them. Then attach the power connectors.

If you are not sure of the drive number settings or how to check them, refer to Chapter 8 on floppy disks for information on how to configure them and what kind of cables you'll need.

Installing the Expansion Cards

Now it is time to add the expansion cards. For a simple system this may mean nothing more than plugging in your floppy and hard disk controller and placing your video adapter into a free expansion slot. If that's the case, you can just go ahead and make the connections, following the instructions listed further below.

If you are adding several cards, such as a mouse, SCSI host adapter, and maybe a sound card or scanner, life is a little more complicated. Even in a simple installation, it's a good idea to keep a written record of what's installed in your machine and how your expansion cards are configured. To help you do this, I have provided an Inventory Sheet in Appendix B in the back of this book. You should probably make a copy of it that you can write on while you are finishing the assembly.

If you are unfamiliar with Interrupt requests and memory addresses, you should review the material in Chapter 5 on adding expansion cards. I'll just give an abbreviated refresher right now. All the devices in your machine that request service from the CPU have an Interrupt number. This is sort of like a flag saying, "I need attention now." If two devices share the same Interrupt, it causes a conflict, which may result in the device not being seen (your mouse may not work because it's using the same Interrupt as your communications port), or in some cases it may hang up the system so that it doesn't even boot when you turn it on.

Many cards also require a memory address and again a conflict can cause erratic behavior or lock up your system. Some expansion cards also will make use of your system's Direct Memory Access (DMA) channels, which is the ability to write data directly into the system memory. If two devices share the same DMA channel they can also cause problems.

We'll try to avoid these possible conflicts by making a list of the settings for each card. Refer to Chapter 5 for standard Interrupt settings; keep in mind, these are generally-accepted standards and may not be the same for your system. That way you can quickly scan the list and see if two devices share the same setting. If they do, you have to change one of them to enable both of them to work. Maintaining this list will allow you to add new cards at a later date with a minimum of fuss. Most cards use jumpers or DIP switches to set Interrupts and memory addresses or to enable DMA transfers. Some newer cards allow these settings to be configured using software.

N O T E

If you are installing cards in an EISA-based machine or a PS/2 with a Micro-Channel Architecture bus (MCA), setting the cards will be done using configuration software. You may still need to make sure there are some jumpers to be set on your expansion cards, but addresses and Interrupts are set using your computer's Configure utility. For both types of machines, you should have received a disk with your system that contains the software. On EISA machines, this is known as the *Configuration diskette,* and the program you have to run is named CF.EXE. You will also need configuration files for each EISA-based expansion card. If you are installing ISA-based cards in an EISA system (if this "ISA, EISA" stuff is getting confusing, see Chapter 6 on motherboards. If you have an ISA-based system, why are you reading this note?), you will still have to set the jumper switches, just as if you were installing them on a standard ISA motherboard.

Since it is almost impossible to build your own PS/2-style machine, I am not going to explain how to do the initial configuration. If you have such a device, consult your owner's manual.

Placing the Expansion Cards Inside the Case

Now that I've explained the basic procedure for adjusting expansion card settings, it's time to actually start putting the individual cards inside the case. You'll need the manuals which came with your different expansion cards, and probably your motherboard documentation. Start with your hard disk controller or IDE paddle board. In some cases this will be built right into the motherboard and you will just have to refer to your system's default settings. If it is not mounted on the motherboard, go to your card's manual and locate the current default settings for the IRQ (this is normally IRQ 14 or 15) and address space (this is normally CC00 or C800). If you are using a SCSI host adapter to drive your hard disk and floppies, you can avoid some potential problems by setting them at one of the IRQ and address spaces I just mentioned.

Now repeat the process for your video adapter, mouse, and any other cards you are installing in your machine, as you set their jumpers, write down the setting in your log. Once you've finished this step, insert the cards into their expansion slots. As a rule it's a good idea to place your hard disk/floppy controller closest to the drives. If you have a VL-BUS-based system, you'll have to place VL-based cards into those slots; if you don't have VL-based cards they can be used to seat regular ISA-based expansion cards.

NOTE

PCI card slots are not all created equal. Check your manual or the technical support line of the vendor for information on which slot is first to get requests to move data; it should be the one where you locate your hard drive controller or SCSI card, then the next slot over should get the network adapter, and the next the graphics or display card. If it is a network server, you might want to position the network board in the place of honor.

WARNING

Use caution when placing VL-Bus cards. Be sure to push the card straight down into the slot; *do not angle it*. Given the length of these cards and the way the edge connectors are constructed, if you put these cards in at an angle it is possible to jam them in the case or damage the cards.

Attaching the Internal Cables

Now we are ready to attach the cards to their respective devices. Start with the hard disk first. If you have an IDE hard drive, there should be a flat ribbon cable with a female 40-pin connector. SCSI drives are attached using a 50-pin ribbon cable. Older MFM and ESDI drives use two cables. Figure 20.14 illustrates the various types of drive-connecting cables. The outermost wire of one side of the ribbon should be color-coded, usually red but sometimes blue. In most cases this is a solid band of color, although some vendors use a light set of stripes to mark the wire. The side with the red indicates the side that goes towards Pin 1 of whatever device is connected. This is standard procedure for ribbon cables.

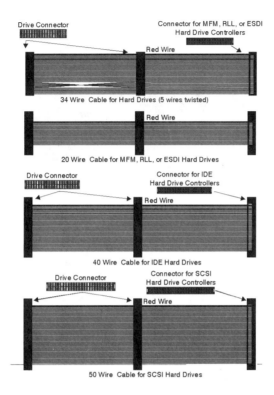

FIGURE 20.14 Standard hard disk cables.

It's important to attach both ends of the cable to the appropriate Pin 1. If you don't, the device won't work properly and you may damage your system. Many ribbon cables are rigged with a raised portion in the middle so that they can only be installed one way. As a rule of thumb, Pin 1 with hard disks and floppy drives is almost always located on the side towards the drive's power cable. On hard disk and floppy controllers, Pin 1 usually faces away from the edge plate in back. If you lie the card down with the edge connector pointing towards you and the metal plate on the right, the front of the card is on your left; see Figure 20.15.

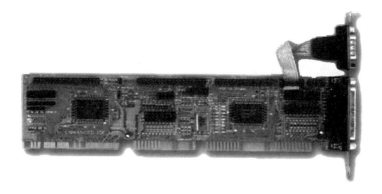

FIGURE 20.15 A disk controller card.

If you are installing older MFM- or ESD-style hard drives, refer to Chapter 9 on hard disks for more information on cabling.

NOTE

Since there are different kinds of hard drive and floppy drive controllers, refer to your documentation to find out where to connect drive cables. As a rule, most combination controllers place the floppy controller pins at the top edge of the card, towards the back, nearest the expansion plate cover.

Attaching the Floppy Drive Cables

If you have two floppy drives, you'll probably be using a twisted ribbon cable. If you are attaching a single floppy drive, you may be using either a single drive ribbon cable or a twisted ribbon cable. If you are using the latter, simply ignore the middle connector; see Figure 20.16 for floppy drive cable types.

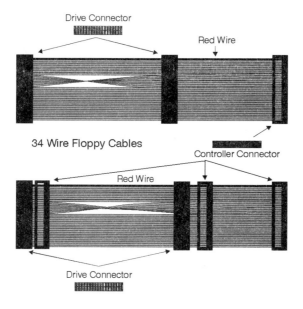

Drive Connector

Red Wire

34 Wire Floppy Cables

Controller Connector

Red Wire

Drive Connector

FIGURE 20.16 Floppy drive cable types.

Be sure you are using a floppy drive cable (once again, refer to Figure 20.16). Twisted ribbon cables for floppy drives and hard drives are *not* interchangeable.

Connecting the Peripherals

Now we are going to finish connecting the other expansion cards to their peripherals. If you have a bus mouse, it should have its own card. Plug the mouse cord into the back of that card. It will only go one way. If you have a serial mouse, it will have to be plugged into one of your computer's serial ports. Almost all mice come with 9-pin connectors, but some also have a 9-to 25-pin adapter. If you are plugging it into a 25-pin Com port, you will have to use the extra fitting. Make a note of which port you plugged it into on your Inventory sheet. You'll need that information later when installing the mouse.

Next connect the power cord from your monitor to the surge protector (or wall outlet, if you are living dangerously). Then attach the monitor cable to the display adapter and monitor. See Figure 20.17 for the different kinds of connectors and how they are attached.

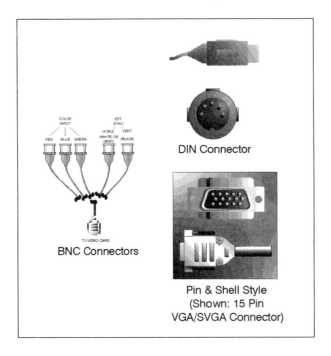

FIGURE 20.17 Types of monitor cable connectors.

Next attach the keyboard. It should have a round plug with crescent-shaped pins inside of it. If it doesn't go in easily, rotate it until it does. Don't try to force it. You'll damage either the motherboard or the connector.

Now attach any other peripherals as appropriate.

N O T E

If you are using a SCSI host adapter as a disk controller, you must make sure that the card is properly terminated. If it is not, your hard disk may not operate when you first turn it on. If you need more information, refer to Chapter 20 on SCSI.

TAKING A TEST DRIVE

We're almost ready to turn it on. Make sure the main power switch is turned off, as well as the one on your surge protector. Attach the power cord from the back of your PC to the surge protector, and turn on the switches to both your monitor and your PC, and then switch on the surge protector. Place your hand at the back of the machine where the fan exhaust is. You should feel a cool breeze. That indicates that your unit is getting power, that you haven't shorted something out, and that the power supply is working.

If You Don't Have Power

There should probably also be green "power good" indicator lights lit up on both the monitor and the computer. If you have a Turbo light and it is functioning properly, you should also see a yellow Turbo indicator light. If you don't have fan operation, turn the power off and make sure that you have connected all the cords properly that provide power to the unit. If you have power to the monitor but not to the PC, you may be shorting out the power supply somehow, or not have it properly connected. It's also possible that you didn't properly connect the main switch to the power supply.

Warming Up

Your computer should now go through its Power-On-Self-Test. You'll probably hear a beep and see the lights come on the floppy drive and the indicator lights flash on in the keyboard. During the POST the computer will probably find out that there are devices on the motherboard that it didn't know were there, since it's never been told using the **Setup** utilities. Keep watching the monitor. At some point you should get a message saying `incorrect setup` or `incorrect data` in CMOS. The exact wording of the message will depend on the exact kind of BIOS you have on your motherboard.

The message should indicate what key or combination of keys you have to push to enter your Setup utility. Do that and you should see the menu for your system's CMOS Setup. Follow the instructions in your motherboard manual for making the entries in these screens match the configuration in your system. For more information, see the detailed instructions earlier in this book.

At this point, if your hard disk has not already been formatted and set up in another computer, you will need a bootable operating system disk or the Install disk which came with the operating system you have selected. Place this in your first floppy drive and exit the Setup utility, saving your new settings.

The computer should boot and you should see the A: prompt. Follow the instructions provided with your operating system for installing it onto your hard disk. See Chapter 2. For help in partitioning your hard disk and configuring your system's memory, see Chapters 5 and 9 in the book.

If your computer is hung at one place or another in the Power-On-Self-Test or is not operating as you expected, refer to the section on the POST in Chapter 3 or the appropriate troubleshooting guides in the appropriate chapter, based on the problem you are encountering.

CHAPTER SUMMARY

Assembling a system from scratch is actually fairly simple. While I have given elaborate details in the preceding narrative, it is much like giving directions to drive to a place you've never been before: it often seems as if it takes more time to describe landmarks than it takes to drive there. Even a novice should be able to assemble a brand-new machine and be using it in no more than an hour or two, assuming all of the parts were obtained and in good working order before he or she began.

When you figure that you should save yourself at least a couple hundred dollars by assembling your own machine and get better quality in the bargain, your hourly rate of return is very nice indeed.

APPENDIX A

A QUICK START

This Appendix contains the basic steps for the procedures outlined in the book. You can use them as a reference when working in your machine to quickly locate the steps for a given operation. For more discussion or troubleshooting, refer to the appropriate chapter.

WORK AREA PREPARATION

Put all the boxes, tools, and miscellaneous parts within easy reach. Take the new equipment out of its packing box and put it on the workspace. It's advisable to get rid of any coffee cups, soft drinks, snacks, small children, pets, and other potential interruptions or disasters before beginning work.

GETTING INTO THE CASE

Follow these steps any time you must open the case of your computer.

1. Turn off power to the system, unplug it from your surge protector, and remove the power cord. If you try to remove or install cards with the power turned on in the computer, you may seriously injure the cards and/or the motherboards.

2. Remove all the cables from your machine. You may need to use a small screwdriver to remove some of the cable connections. If you aren't sure where they go, label them with masking tape.

3. Remove the cover from your computer's case by removing the screws holding it along the back, outer edge of the machine (not those holding the fan). Slide it off; you may need to tip it.

4. Touch the inside metal chassis to ground yourself.

INSTALLING AN EXPANSION CARD

What You'll Need

✔ The expansion card itself

✔ The appropriate internal or external cable(s) to install your peripheral(s)

✔ Appropriate software drivers

✔ Screwdrivers, flat-head and Philips

✔ Hemostat

✔ Tweezers or pliers for placing jumpers

✔ The card's documentation

✔ Small flashlight and magnifying glass

1. Follow the instructions for preparing your workspace and getting into the case given at the beginning of this Appendix.

2. Open the box that the expansion card came in and remove the card from its protective envelope. Depending on the type of card, you will have one or more jumpers which should be checked, and which may need to be reset before installing. You will need to refer to the expansion card's manual for additional instructions, and possibly a Readme file on an installation disk.

3. Open the manual and identify any jumpers or DIP switches that have to be set. You will usually need to identify what the BIOS address and I/O port are. Your manual should tell you what combination of jumpers or DIP switches must be adjusted to select the proper range.

4. Locate a free expansion slot and remove the back cover plate.

5. Once again touch the edge of the case to make sure that you aren't carrying any static charge, then with gentle pressure insert the card into the free slot. You may find it helps to hold the card at a slight angle while you line the edge connector up with the slot. Then straighten it to the perpendicular and gently push it into place.

6. Use the screw that held the expansion plate cover to lock the card into place.

7. If the card should be attached to another device, attach the appropriate cable to both the expansion card and the internal or external device it functions with.

INSTALLING DRIVERS AND TESTING THE INSTALLATION

1. Once you have verified that all the switches are set correctly, that the connections are properly made, and the cables properly attached, you are ready to turn the machine back on. Turn on any peripheral device that relates to the card's function as well.

2. Install the driver software for your operating system and any other applications you plan on running, following the instruc-

tions that came with the expansion card. Test all the software that you have installed drivers for and make sure everything works. If you are installing the card on a Windows 95 machine, boot the PC and see if Windows will recognize it. You will need the Windows 95 disks or CD-ROM and the drivers that came with the new card.

3. Replace the cover and place any spare screws, parts or anything else in your goodies bag for future use.

4. Make a new Dark and Stormy Night Disk or Windows Rescue Disk as described in Chapter 3, so that you will have backup copies of all the new settings. For DOS users: you'll want to save copies of your CONFIG.SYS, AUTOEXEC.BAT, SYSTEM.INI, and WINDOWS.INI (the last two files are for Windows version 3.xx users only) off onto your bootable floppy.

REMOVING AN EXPANSION CARD

1. Follow the instructions for preparing your workspace and for getting into the case given at the beginning of this Appendix.

2. Remove the screw that holds the mounting bracket to the case. Once again touch the edge of the case to make sure that you aren't carrying any static charge, and remove the card by pulling gently but firmly straight up on it.

3. Place the card into a static-resistant envelope.

4. If you are not inserting another card into the slot, replace the cover plate and screw it down.

INSTALLING A DAUGHTER BOARD

If your expansion card comes with a daughter board that you wish to use, follow this procedure to install it. Daughter cards usually connect by using a series of pins similar to jumpers on one card, and a female fitting on the other to slide into.

1. Follow the instructions for preparing your workspace and for getting into the case given at the beginning of this Appendix.

2. Remove the card from the system, if necessary, using the procedure outlined earlier.

3. Be careful to avoid static electricity by grounding yourself before opening any protective envelopes or touching any of the electronic components inside the case.

4. Follow the instructions that came with the card for setting any switches required to recognize the new hardware, and assemble the pieces as defined in the product's documentation.

5. You may need to attach some form of cabling to the two cards. If so, be sure to follow any instructions for specific orientation of the cable. In most cases, this will involve making sure that the side of a ribbon cable with a red stripe on it is closest to pin 1 on both cards.

6. Once you've finished this assembly, place it in the machine, using the procedure for installing expansion cards.

ADDING SIMM MEMORY

What You'll Need

✔ Screwdrivers, flat-head and Philips

✔ Small flashlight

✔ Have a pen or a very small screwdriver available, in case you have to adjust one of the SIMMs' retaining bank locks

1. Follow the instructions for preparing your workspace and for getting into the case given at the beginning of this Appendix.

2. Open the package containing the memory. *Ensure it is the right type and speed.* Most modules come individually wrapped in a static-resistant envelope.

3. Take one of the modules out. The lower side that will seat into the socket has a row of metal edge connectors, either gold or silver in color. Somewhere around the middle of that row of connectors there will be a cutout. This fits into a little raised portion in the middle of the socket so the module will only fit one way into the bank.

4. SIMMs must be inserted a specific way, in a specific order. Use your motherboard manual or the legends printed on the motherboard itself to determine which is the first position of the first bank of memory. Many motherboards start numbering with the number zero rather than one. If that's the case, you'll want to place the first module in row zero of bank zero.

5. Once you have located the proper bank, take a look at the way the socket that will hold the module is designed. You'll notice that it has little clips and projections on either side of the bank. The projections are designed to fit in the two holes on the side of the module and secure it in place. The little plastic or metal latches on either side gently grip the module and keep it from moving once it's seated.

6. To put the module into place, you have to slide it in at an angle to the edge connectors in the slot, with the top of the module angled towards the back of the bank.

7. Using both thumbs or a thumb and forefinger, press the module down into the slot, while rotating the top so it clicks into place. In most cases you will hear a little click as the springs engage. On some machines, you may have to physically push the latches into place. Repeat this procedure until you have all the SIMMs properly seated. Refer to your manual to see if you have to set any jumpers or switches on the motherboard so that it will acknowledge the new memory. Make sure that the SIMMs are all the same height, and that they are all perfectly perpendicular to the motherboard. (That last instruction may not apply to using a special expansion card, which might hold the modules at an angle.)

8. Attach the cables and power leads, and turn on the machine. Watch the Power-On-Self-Test. This usually includes a memory

test, which should show the same amount of memory as installed on the system. Keep in mind that computers count funny. For each Mb of memory, the memory check should show 1024Kb of memory; some machines may be off by 384Kb because of the way they handle part of the first Mb of memory.

9. If your machine shows significantly less memory than you expect, or if it doesn't go through the memory check properly, recheck the SIMMs and be sure they are seated correctly. If necessary, remove them by reversing the procedure given above, starting at the back of the bank first. Make sure all the SIMMs are tightly seated in their sockets. Then retry the memory check.

10. Automatically check the amount of memory, but many will report an error until you update Setup and confirm the new memory. Older machines may require that you enter the current amount of memory manually. Follow the instructions for setting CMOS values in your owner's manual.

    The next step is to run your system's CMOS Setup. Most machines today will automatically check the amount of memory. Many will report an error until you update Setup and confirm the new memory. Older machines may require that you enter the current amount of memory manually. Follow the instructions for setting CMOS values in your owner's manual.

11. If your computer does not see all of the memory that you've put in, you may have not seated one of the modules properly. Double-check to make sure that all are at the same height. If they are, try re-seating them. If that still doesn't work, try re-ordering their position in the bank. For instance, put the second one in slot one, three in two, four in three and one in position four.

12. If that changes the amount of memory shown, but you still don't have all the memory, it is possible that one of the modules is damaged. If you can, locate another memory module and use it to replace one of the chips in succession until you've isolated the faulty module. When you've found it, contact the vendor you got the chip from and replace it.

INSTALLING SIPPS MEMORY MODULES

1. Follow the instructions for preparing your workspace and for getting into the case given at the beginning of this Appendix.

2. Review the instructions above for installing SIPPs. Most apply here. Note Step 3 below.

3. Make sure that Pin 1 on the SIPP matches up with the Pin 1 hole on the motherboard. Line the pins up precisely over the holes and insert by pushing downward gently but firmly until the pins are seated. Removing SIPPs is just the reverse: place thumb and forefinger of each hand on either end of the SIPP and pull up gently.

INSTALLING DRAM

1. Follow the instructions for preparing your workspace and for getting into the case given at the beginning of this Appendix.

2. In some cases, you may have to replace a smaller-sized set of memory chips and install new ones. If you must remove older-style DIP chips, you may use one of two methods. If your tool kit came with a chip puller, you can use that to remove the chips. This tool resembles a wide pair of tweezers that don't come together, and usually have two little half-moon projections facing in at the bottom of each arm. Make sure you are grounded, and work the two little moon shapes between the base of the chip and its mounting socket by squeezing the two sides together in one hand.

   Use the other hand to press gently down on the motherboard on either side of the socket, then pull straight up with the tool. If the chip is very firmly seated, you may have to rock slightly back and forth on the long axis of the chip very gently. If you are too rough, you may damage the soft solder pins on either side of the chip, which can very easily render it useless.

3. An alternate method is to gently work the blade of a small screwdriver in from either end of the chip, alternating sides and slowly rocking the blade underneath it until the chip is loosened and you can pull it out.

4. *Ensure that you have the right type and speed of chip.* Make sure that all the pins on the bottom of the chip are pointing straight down and are evenly spaced. If not, *very gently* straighten them with a pin straightener, if your tool kit has one, or a fingertip.

5. Note the half-moon indentation at one end of a chip. This will identify the Pin 1 end of the chip. Locate the proper socket on your motherboard or memory board, referring to the diagram in its manual and any markings on the circuit board itself. Line the chip up properly, and put one line of pins at an angle above one row of socket holes. Gently ease the very ends of the pins into the socket holes, and rotate the chip so that the second row of pins can slide into its matching row of holes. Then, using gentle finger or thumb pressure, push down a little. Usually one side of pins will slide in a little further. Push the higher side down, then push alternate sides until the chip is firmly seated in its socket. Inspect it closely to make sure that all the pins are in the holes. Be careful to make sure that all the pins go in their appropriate holes. Take care to make sure you don't bend any of them. If you bend one, you'll have to remove the chip, try to straighten the pin and try again. The pins are made of very soft metal and will fatigue if you play with them too much.

6. Follow Steps 8 through 12 in the section "Adding SIMM Memory," earlier, allowing for the fact that you are installing DRAM chips, not SIMM modules.

INSTALLING CACHE MEMORY

1. Follow the instructions for preparing your workspace and for getting into the case given at the beginning of this Appendix.

2. Cache memory is sometimes distributed on modules similar to the SIMMs, and should be installed using the procedure for

installing SIMMs. Many systems still use individual DRAM chips to provide secondary cache. These are installed in banks and you should refer to your system's manual for the exact placement of the chips on the motherboard. These chips must be properly oriented based on the amount of cache you are installing. You will find a little, moon-shaped cutout or indentation, or possibly a little bump, on one of the narrow sides of the chip right on the edge of the top surface.

3. All the chips need to be oriented the same way, and you should check with your manual to find out exactly how they should be positioned. Prongs are located along both long sides of the chip.

4. Once again, make sure you are properly grounded, and take the first chip gently between the thumb and first finger of each hand. Set the prongs facing away from you into the holes on the far side of the appropriate chip socket, raising the other side, towards you, up at a very slight angle.

5. Press evenly and gently away from you and guide the prongs on the side towards you into their positions in the socket. In some cases you will need next to no angle at all to do this, in other cases you will need more. Be careful to make sure that all the pins go in their appropriate holes. Take care to make sure you don't bend any of them. If you bend one, you'll have to remove the chip, try to straighten the pin and try again. The pins are made of very soft metal and will fatigue if you play with them too much.

INSTALLING A BIOS

Updating Flash BIOS

This is a very simple procedure, especially if you have a modem. Most hardware vendors operate a Bulletin-Board Service and will let you download the software directly into your machine. If you don't have access to a modem, you'll have to arrange to have the software shipped on disk.

Once the software arrives, you run the application using the instructions provided either in the information sheet or in a Readme file. You will usually need a formatted floppy disk to hold a Restore file, which can be used if the new BIOS causes problems with your system. Once you have run the program, you will have to access your system's CMOS Setup and set new values following the instructions.

Updating Non-Flash BIOSes

To replace this type of BIOS you have to remove the old chip and replace it with the new one, following the procedures listed earlier for adding DRAM-style memory. The only difference is that the BIOS chip will be larger, and therefore easier to work with than DRAM or cache memory modules. Once the new BIOS chip is installed, run your CMOS Setup program to set the values. Handle the old chip with care; if the new BIOS proves to be incompatible with your equipment, you'll have to reinstall it to get things working properly again.

INSTALLING A MOTHERBOARD

What You'll Need

- ✔ Motherboard
- ✔ Motherboard manual
- ✔ Mounting hardware
- ✔ Screwdrivers, flat-head and Philips
- ✔ Pair of needle-nosed pliers
- ✔ Tweezers
- ✔ Screws and spacers
- ✔ External battery pack
- ✔ A small flashlight is sometimes handy

✔ A magnifying glass is useful for reading the fine print on the motherboard

Configuring the Motherboard

1. Remove the motherboard from its packing and place it on a clear, grounded workspace.

2. Set DIP switches and jumpers to configure the motherboard appropriately, using the documentation which came with it.

3. If your motherboard will accept several different CPUs or a Coprocessor, there is probably a setting to select CPU speed and to indicate the presence of any supplemental chips. Another common setting is the amount of RAM and type of memory chips used on the board. Most machines also require setting jumpers or DIP switches to indicate the amount of cache memory installed. Some machines are equipped with on-board parallel and serial ports and graphics adapters. Enabling or disabling these features often involves setting DIP switches or jumpers.

4. Install the CPU, Coprocessor, BIOS, or Overdrive. CPUs and the BIOS, like the cache memory, should have come already installed on your motherboard. If they did not or you are upgrading one, you should refer to the headings on "Installing a CPU" later in this Appendix for detailed instructions on how to place these components on motherboards. It's easiest to install them before mounting the motherboard in the case.

5. Follow the instructions for preparing your workspace and for getting into the case given at the beginning of this Appendix.

6. Prepare to mount the motherboard.

    The motherboard has to sit slightly above the case to avoid shorting out the connections that stick through the bottom. This is accomplished by the use of Teflon spacers which are snapped through holes in the motherboard. Then these spacers are locked into rails located on the bottom of the desktop style case, or on the right-hand side of the tower case.

    Two hexagonal screws, which can accept mounting screws on their tops, are used to fasten the board in place and ground it to the chassis. If your case does not already have these screws in place, you'll need to screw them in finger tight and then snug them down with a nut driver or a pair of pliers from a tool kit.

7. Locate the position of the retaining screws and spacers.

    You will have to eyeball exactly how the spacers and retaining screws must be placed to mount your motherboard. The easiest way is to gently lie the motherboard in position, and then lift it off, seeing where the screws and spacers should be placed.

    If you have a tower case, you'll probably want to turn it on its side so that for this operation the motherboard will be mounted on the "bottom" of the case. Ground yourself by touching the case and take your motherboard out of its protective plastic envelope. There should be at least two holes in the top of the motherboard with silver or gold collars around them made of solder. These are the holes for the mounting screws. Line up the motherboard so that the jack for the keyboard is lined up with the hole in the chassis for the keyboard plug. Then note where the spacing screws and retaining screws should go.

8. Move the motherboard out of the way and attach the screws. Once the screws are in place it's time to put in the spacers. Line up the motherboard so both of the screw holes are positioned properly, then observe which spacer holes line up with spacer retaining grooves in the case.

9. Once you have noted the locations, set the motherboard on its edge and poke spacers from the bottom of the motherboard up to the top. If you have a full-sized motherboard you may also need to place two or three of the "C" shaped spacers on the upper edge of the mounting rails.

10. Once all the spacers are in place, position the motherboard over the rails and slide it into position until they lock.

11. Now fasten the board into place with the two retaining screws set into the hexagonal bases.

12. Attach all the little wires running from the case to the motherboard. You'll probably want to open up the manual that came with the motherboard and find the diagram. These switches and LED connectors are generally mounted into plastic sockets that look very much like jumpers, and they fit into jumper

switch positions on the motherboard. Refer to your board's manual for the exact location of the switches. If you put them on backwards you won't hurt anything, but the function won't work properly, so it may take some trial-and-error.

There are a number of wires that lead from the case that have to be attached to the motherboard, and one that has to be attached to your hard disk controller. If you are very fortunate they will be labeled. Odds are you'll have to trace them back into the case to figure out exactly what their function is.

Most machines have power leads, leads for Turbo operation, turning Turbo function on and off, resetting the system, and indicating when the hard drive is in operation, as well as one that hooks up the system's key lock.

13. Locate connectors P8 and P9 coming out of the power supply. They should be easy to spot. Both have six wires rather than the four that come with the other connectors. These plug into two jacks that are side by side, usually somewhere near the keyboard socket on your motherboard. P8 usually goes towards the rear. The way to know if you have it connected properly is that the black wires on each connector are adjacent when they are mounted in their sockets. These connectors are also usually keyed, so that they can only go one way. Be sure to have them properly seated before applying power. If they haven't been installed correctly, you may damage the motherboard when power is turned on.

REMOVING A MOTHERBOARD

What You'll Need

✔ Screwdrivers, flat-head and Philips

✔ Possibly a hemostat, tweezers, or small pliers

✔ Goodie bag

✔ A cup or other container for screws and small parts

✔ A roll of masking tape

✔ A pen and a small flashlight

1. Follow the instructions for preparing your workspace and for getting into the case given at the beginning of this Appendix.

2. Remove all the expansion cards from their slots.

3. If you are planning on re-installing the motherboard, you may want to use the masking tape to label the wires leading from the motherboard to the various switches and LEDs on the case. The function should be marked on the motherboard itself. Just go ahead and label a small piece of the tape, then fold it over the wire near the connection. Remove the wires by gently pulling them off the appropriate jumper. Do the same thing for the external battery pack. Locate the P8 and P9 connectors that carry power from the power supply to the motherboard and disconnect them. Check and remove any other cables or connections attaching the board to other components of the system, such as I/O ports or the hard drive.

4. Locate the two screws that attach the motherboard to the case. Remove them and place them in the little cup if you are placing another motherboard in the system, in your goodie bag if you are not.

5. Gently slide the motherboard in the direction it moves freely. Depending on your case design, this could be in any one of the four directions. As it slides, use a slight upward pressure so that the spacers will disengage from the mounting rails. You may have to wiggle or angle the board to get it free and remove it from the case.

6. Once the board is clear of the case, you can remove the spacers if you are sending it off somewhere else, or you can use the spacers again. The board should be placed in a static-resistant envelope for safety.

REMOVING A CPU

What You'll Need

✔ Screwdriver

✔ Motherboard manual

✔ Anti-static envelopes and/or pouch

✔ Box for the CPU

✔ Chip puller or an expansion slot cover (if you don't have a ZIF socket, which has a small lever to help install or remove the chip)

1. Follow the instructions for preparing your workspace and for getting into the case given at the beginning of this Appendix.

2. Either visually, or using a board manual, locate the CPU.

3. Remove any expansion card that may be in the way so that you can easily place your entire hand around the CPU and still have a couple of inches clear on all sides.

Removing a ZIF Chip

1. Repeat steps 1, 2, and 3 for "Removing a CPU."

4. If you have a Zero Insertion Force (ZIF) socket, there should either be a little lever on one side or the other of the CPU, or a square bracket-shaped handle going around three sides of the CPU. Make sure you have grounded yourself so that you can't release static when you touch the CPU. Lift the handle and gently move it back as far as it will go on its hinge.

5. With a finger on either side of the CPU, gently lift straight up until it is clear of the socket.

6. Place the CPU immediately into a protective, anti-static container.

Removing a Non-ZIF Chip

1. Repeat steps 1, 2, and 3 for "Removing a CPU."

4. If you don't have a ZIF socket, you'll have to work the CPU free of its moorings. All around the edge of the CPU are a series of delicate gold-plated pins. It's important not to bend these pins. If you don't have a special tool, you can use the expansion cover off the

back of one of your system's slots to gently work it free. Start by working it very gently between the socket base and the bottom of the CPU in one corner.

5. Very carefully rock the tool back and forth and pry the chip lightly above the socket. Move to an opposite corner and repeat the process. Do this on all four corners until the chip is slightly free of the socket.

6. Now place the edge of the cover in the middle of one of the sides of the CPU and work it just a little bit higher up. Repeat on the other three sides. Continue this step until the CPU is worked completely free and you can lift it out.

7. Once the CPU is completely free, place it immediately in an anti-static container.

INSERTING A CPU INTO A ZIF SOCKET

1. Follow the instructions for preparing your workspace and for getting into the case given at the beginning of this Appendix.

2. Either visually, or using a motherboard manual, locate the CPU.

3. Remove any expansion card that may be in the way so that you can easily place your entire hand around the CPU and still have a couple of inches clear on all sides.

4. Place the chip in position by lining up either the cut corner, or the little dot, located on the innermost rim of the CPU, with the matching side of the socket that houses Pin 1. If you are unsure of this positioning, check with your documentation or contact your motherboard manufacturer's technical support department.

5. Raise the handle on the ZIF socket.

6. Make sure you are properly grounded. Take the CPU out of its protective case.

7. Inspect the bottom of the CPU and make sure that all the pins on the bottom are straight and properly lined up. If any of them are bent, they may splay out when you attempt to seat the CPU. If this happens, the CPU won't function; and if the

pin is broken off or touches another pin, you may permanently damage the CPU.

8. Carefully line up the pins and the holes so that the CPU is centered over the socket. Some of these sockets are designed to accept more than one kind of CPU so you may have more holes than you need; just be sure that the CPU is centered.

9. Gently ease the CPU into place, making sure that all the pins cleanly fit into position.

    If for some reason the CPU does not slide easily into place, you either don't have the ZIF socket completely open, or you slightly bent one of the pins. Do not use force. If you bend one of the pins you may render the CPU useless.

10. Once the CPU is in place, close the latch on the socket.

INSERTING A CPU INTO A NON-ZIF SOCKET ON THE MOTHERBOARD

1. Follow the instructions for preparing your workspace and for getting into the case given at the beginning of this Appendix.

2. Either visually, or using a motherboard manual, locate the CPU.

3. Remove any expansion card that may be in the way so that you can easily place your entire hand around the CPU and still have a couple of inches clear on all sides.

4. Locate the proper orientation of the CPU to the socket. This is usually done by matching the cut corner or dot on the CPU with the angled corner that indicates Pin 1, located on the innermost rim of the CPU socket. If you are unsure of this step, verify it either by using your manual or by calling your motherboard's manufacturer's technical support department.

5. Make sure you are properly grounded. Take the CPU out of its protective case.

6. Inspect the bottom of the CPU and make sure that all the pins on the bottom are straight and properly lined up. If any of them

are bent, they may splay out when you attempt to seat the CPU. If this happens, the CPU won't function; and if the pin is broken off or touches another pin, you may permanently damage the CPU.

7. Line up the pins exactly. Check from all sides and be sure that the rows are properly aligned with the sockets. If you go to the next step and push on the CPU's surface and things are not exactly lined up, you may permanently damage the CPU.

8. Use the thumbs and forefingers of both hands to seat the chip. Place one on each corner of the CPU and gently but firmly push the CPU into place.

9. Push firmly until the CPU is fully down against the rim of the socket.

INSTALLING A FLOPPY DRIVE

1. Follow the instructions for preparing your workspace and for getting into the case given at the beginning of this Appendix.

2. Set the drive-select jumper.

    Unless you are already familiar with the drive and its jumpers or can easily identify DS0 and DS1 (or DS1 and DS2), you should probably refer to the instructions that came with your drive for setting the switches. If you are using twisted ribbon cable (which I strongly recommend), you should set the drive selector type for drive 2. If you see pins marked DS0 and DS1, jumper the DS1 position. If your floppy is marked DS1 and DS2, jumper the DS2 position. The same jumpering will apply to both floppy drives if you are installing more than one in your system.

3. Install the drives into the bay. To place a 5.25-inch drive into the bay, all you'll probably have to do is slide it into a bay from the front of the case (you'll have to remove the cover of the case first by unscrewing the screws at the back of the tower and removing the shroud). With 3.5-inch models you may have to mount the drive into a bracket if your case does not have a 3.5-inch bay. It is easy to figure out; just take care to not twist a screw into the drive.

The bracket may consist of a pair of metal plates, or may be a single plastic shroud. Once it is attached the rest of the procedure is the same as for a 5.25-inch device.

4. Once you have slid the drive into the bay, fasten it with four mounting screws through the slots on either side of the bay. Be sure not to use screws that are too long. If you use long screws they may actually penetrate through to the board on the floppy and damage it.

5. Once the drive is fastened, attach a power lead from the power supply into the plug. This lead will have four wires, usually one red, one yellow and two blacks. Most 5.25-inch drives will have a plug about 1 inch across which can only be seated one way, since two of the corners are rounded and the others are square-cut.

   3.5-inch drives may have a smaller four-pronged connector on the back of the drive that resembles long jumper pins. These accept the specially-keyed power adapter that also will only slide in one way. If your power supply does not have this kind of connector, you will need an adapter, which is usually supplied with 3.5-inch drive kits.

6. Attach the end of the cable that goes to the controller. This also only fits one way. Some cables have plugs placed in the ends so that the cable will only fit one way over the edge connector, which looks a bit like the edge connectors on an expansion card. Others do not. In either case, the red stripe, or other color code that runs along one side of the cable, should go towards the side that has Pin 1 of the connector. This is almost always located on the side toward the power connection.

   Some 3.5-inch drives have controller-cable connections identical to those for 5.25-inch drives. Others use pin connections. Most of the latter do have an adapter which allows you to use a standard edge connector. Such an adapter slides over the pins of the drive and has an edge connector on the other side. This is usually the simplest way to attach the drive. That way you can use standard twisted-ribbon cables, without having to worry about the type of connections or the order in which the drives are attached.

7. Modify the system CMOS Setup, then test the new drive to make sure it operates. Once everything is tested, replace the computer's cover.

INSTALLING A SECOND DRIVE

If you are installing two drives into your system, the second drive is installed the same way as the first, and the drive selection switches should be set the same way as the first drive, i.e. both as the second drive (keep in mind the vagaries of drive selection switches mentioned above). This is why we use the twisted-ribbon cable. If we use straight cable, we would have to set each drive differently. See Chapter 8 for more information.

Once you have all the drives attached to both the ribbon cable and the power cable, locate the pins on your floppy controller and attach the other end of the cable to it. It may be located on your motherboard, or on your hard disk controller, or SCSI adapter. If you have an IDE-style hard drive (as discussed below), your floppy controller may be attached to the IDE paddle-board, which often also contains your parallel and serial ports.

INSTALLING A HARD DRIVE

What You'll Need

✔ The drive, with its accompanying manual or data sheet /or installation disk / Readme file)

✔ Mounting hardware or rails

✔ Appropriate cabling

✔ Hard disk controller or SCSI host adapter

✔ Your computer or motherboard documentation

✔ Screwdrivers, flat-head and Philips

✔ Tweezers or hemostat for jumpers

✔ A copy of your operating system

✔ A bootable floppy disk

✔ This floppy disk must include not only COMMAND.COM, but also DEBUG, FDISK, and FORMAT. If you are installing an operating system other than MS-DOS, consult your owner's manual as to what files you will need for booting a new system, and partitioning and formatting a new hard disk.

✔ Clean, static-free place to work

1. Follow the instructions for preparing your workspace and for getting into the case given at the beginning of this Appendix.

2. Ground yourself by touching the case or some other metal object to discharge any possible static electricity. Then remove the drive from the packaging. It will probably be encased in an envelope of smoky plastic. This is an anti-static barrier. Save this and the packaging in case you ever have to send the drive back for repair or replacement.

3. Consulting your manual, set any jumpers and drive selection switches.

4. Installing the adapter card.

   If you are replacing an existing hard disk controller, remove the old one from the case. This should be a simple matter of unscrewing the mounting bracket, and then removing the card from its slot and detaching any cables.

5. Install the drive into the case. Drive placement will depend upon how many drives you're going to have in your system. Generally speaking, the uppermost drive bay should be reserved for the primary floppy drive. In some cases, a 3.5-inch exposed drive bay is reserved for the first 3.5-inch floppy, and in that case you will have a limited choice as to where to place drives. If you are installing a second floppy, it should go into the drive bay below that. If you have a tape unit it can go into the bay below the last floppy. Any remaining bays are available for your hard disk.

   If you are installing into a desktop case, you may have to attach plastic rails to the side of your drive. This is done using two screws which should be found in the goodies bag which came with your case or, in the case of a generous manufacturer, with the mounting kit that came with your drive. If you are installing a 3.5-inch hard drive into a 5.25-inch bay, you will also need an adapter mounting kit. Screw the rails and/or the adapter onto one side of the drive.

6. Now slide the drive into place, and make sure that it is far enough back to fit a cover panel in front of it, that it doesn't obstruct any other drive bays, and that there is adequate spacing for ventilation.

7. Now remove the drive and attach the mounting brackets and/or rails onto the other side in the same orientation as the ones already installed. Next, place the drive into the bay and fasten it down with screws. With a tower case, you'll have to fasten the screws from the side of the case. In a desktop case there is usually some sort of retaining clip that often looks like a square washer.

8. If you are installing two hard drives into your system, the second drive is installed the same way as the first, and the drive-selection switches should be set the same way as the first drive, i.e. both as the second drive (keep in mind the vagaries of drive selection switches mentioned above; see the explanation under "Installing a Floppy Drive" in this Appendix). This is why we use the twisted-ribbon cable. If we use straight cables, we would have to set each drive differently.

9. Once you have all the drives attached to both the ribbon cable and the power cable, locate the pins on your hard disk controller or SCSI adapter and plug the ribbon cable onto them.

10. Modify Setup.

INSTALLING THE ADAPTER (CONTROLLER, PADDLE-BOARD, OR HOST ADAPTER CARD)

1. Follow the instructions for preparing your workspace and for getting into the case given at the beginning of this Appendix.

2. Host adapters and controllers require a unique IRQ (Interrupt Request) and memory address (if you want more information

on these terms, see Chapters 4 and 5). Since there are many way to select these settings, you will have to refer to your manual for details; I will just give a few general guidelines here. Most ISA and VL-Bus-based cards use jumpers to configure these settings. EISA and MCA systems will have a reference disk, and configuration files will be used to select these options. If possible, use the old standard combinations of either IRQ 14 or 15 for the IRQ, and CC00 or C800 for the starting memory address. These are the options used most frequently by the original PC controller cards, and sticking to them makes it easier to reduce conflict and eases installation of other peripherals.

3. You may also have to adjust settings to enable or disable the card's floppy disk controller and DMA settings. It's always a good idea to read the installation section of the manual which came with your card for information on what settings are available.

4. If your controller incorporates hardware caching, you may have to set jumpers to enable, disable, or otherwise configure the cache.

5. Install the card in the system, following the steps outlined earlier for "Installing an Expansion Card" (The third topic in this Appendix).

6. Now attach all the appropriate cables. If you are attaching a SCSI card you will probably have a 50-pin ribbon cable coming from your SCSI drive (or the preceding device on the chain). Once again, these cables should have a red stripe (sometimes it's blue) on one side or the other; this denotes Pin 1. Pin 1 usually faces towards the front of your computer, away from your mounting bracket on most systems. If you are not sure, double-check.

    IDE drives are connected using a 40-pin connector. MFM drives and ESDI drives are connected using two cables.

7. Attach the keyboard, monitor, mouse, and everything else you have disconnected and plug the machine back in. Put the bootable disk in drive A: and turn the machine on.

8. Invoke your system's Setup routine.

ADDING A SECOND HARD DRIVE

If you are adding a second hard drive to an existing system, you must go through the same Setup routine, setting values for the second hard disk as appropriate. If you are installing more than two drives in the system, consult your user's manual, because you'll probably have to use a software driver utility to enable your disk to be seen by the system.

PREPARING THE NEW HARD DRIVE FOR USE

1. A low-level format prepares the drive to receive the operating system format. MFM and ESDI drives should be low-level formatted using an installation routine provided either with the drive or with the controller. See the appropriate manual for more information. Most SCSI and all IDE drives come low-level formatted from the factory.

2. Dividing a disk into partitions: The exact way this is done will vary from operating system to operating system. In some cases you simply specify the percent of the drive that is to be used for each partition. In other cases, you must specify the number of cylinders or sectors to be used for each division.

3. If you are dividing the drive into more than one portion, you must also create logical drives for subsequent portions. FDISK uses a series of menus for various options and is fairly easy to use. You might want to review the documentation that comes with your operating system before using it.

4. The other job to do in FDISK is to set which partition is active. This tells the machine which partition holds the boot information, usually drive C.

5. Once you exit FDISK, the system will reboot. Since there is no operating system currently on the machine, the hard disk will have to be formatted. Boot from the floppy disk in drive A. Then issue the appropriate FORMAT commands or follow any other installation requirements for your operating system. If you want to make the first partition of your primary hard drive bootable, in DOS this is done by issuing the command: **Format C: /s /v.** This process can take several minutes. When it is done you will see a note saying that the format is complete and the system has been transferred. If you created more than one partition on your new hard disk, repeat the high-level format on the other partition without the /s and /v switches. In other words, just enter the command: **Format [drive letter]:**

INSTALLING A SCSI HOST ADAPTER, HARD DISK AND/OR PERIPHERALS

What You'll Need

✔ The host adapter itself

✔ The appropriate internal or external cable(s) to install your peripheral(s)

✔ Appropriate software drivers

✔ Screwdriver

✔ Hemostat

✔ Tweezers or pliers for placing jumpers

✔ The card's documentation, including any Readme files on disk

✔ Your Inventory of the devices already installed on your System

1. Follow the instructions for preparing your workspace and for getting into the case given at the beginning of this Appendix.

2. Install the host adapter with termination enabled and jumpers set as required.

   Check in your user's manual for the instructions explaining how your host adapter deals with termination. In order to function properly, the devices at either end of the SCSI chain MUST be terminated. That means that if you are only attaching internal or external devices (no matter how many), the host adapter must be terminated. If you are attaching both internal and external devices to a single host adapter, it will be in the middle of the chain; you have to disable termination on it.

   Many newer host adapters provide automatic termination. You still have to terminate the devices at the end of the chain, but the host adapter itself will automatically switch into a terminated or unterminated condition during the boot process.

3. Attach internal devices to the SCSI chain.

4. If you are installing an internal hard drive, mount the drive itself into the case as described above in the section on "Installing a Hard Drive."

5. Attach it to a 50-pin ribbon cable.

6. The other end of the cable is attached to the 50-pin male connector on the upper edge of the host adapter itself. If you are installing more than one drive, all can be attached with the same ribbon cable. For sanity's sake, it's usually simplest to attach Drive Zero (which would also be SCSI ID zero) at the farthest end of the chain. That device should always be terminated. Consult your hard drive manual for instructions on how to enable termination. Any other drives or SCSI devices that are mounted closer to the host adapter than the farthest device should not have termination enabled.

7. Install SCSI peripherals one at a time.

8. Install the device module software.

   Once the unit is installed and the system is rebooted, refer to the documentation for the host adapter, the new device, or your third-party SCSI software package for instructions on how to install any required device module drivers.

9. Install the universal driver.

    Depending on your operating system, you may need to install a universal driver (either ASCI or CAM). If you are adding a CD-ROM or any other device requiring a device module, you will have to load the universal driver.

INSTALLING A SOUND BOARD

Before You Start

If you are also installing a SCSI CD-ROM drive at the same time as your sound card, or have one installed already, you must be sure you have the right cables and that the interfaces are compatible. If your CD-ROM drive uses an IDE interface, you can skip over the SCSI-specific instructions which follow; you will still require the correct audio cable. If your drive does have a SCSI interface it will need a SCSI controller, called a *host adapter*. If you already have a SCSI system, you will add the CD-ROM into the SCSI chain as a new device. If you don't, your sound card must provide one. Many do, but you need to know what type of SCSI your CD-ROM drive is, and pick the right cable; you may need some type of SCSI cable adapter as well.

A second cable will be needed to provide the audio signal from the CD-ROM to the sound card. In yet another example of the problems caused by lack of standards in the PC world, although the audio signal is standardized, the audio cable isn't. Or more exactly, the types of plugs and jacks it uses are not. Sound cards bought alone will usually not have a cable set in the box with them; the sound card manufacturers have no way of knowing what CD-ROM drive you have, so they don't include them. They will often be able to sell you a cable kit for a particular CD-ROM drive, once you know yourself and call them. This takes extra time and several dollars. Avoiding these frustrations is a big reason why upgrade kits are so popular—you don't have to go through the process of matching sound cards, CD-ROM drives, and their cables.

What You'll Need

✔ Small and large screwdrivers, flat-head and Philips

✔ Cup or other container for screws and small parts

✔ Your System Inventory of currently-installed peripherals with their DMA, IRQ, and I/O assignments, and a piece of paper to log your installation step-by-step to aid in troubleshooting; your Dark and Stormy Night Disk, Windows Rescue Disk

✔ Sound board and installation manual; and CD-ROM drive manual if you have one

✔ Appropriate data and audio cables with the correct plugs on the ends (if you have or are installing a CD-ROM drive)

✔ Sound Board installation and utility software (and also for CD-ROM if you have one)

✔ Possibly a pair of pliers or hemostat for adjusting jumpers

1. Review your sound card (and CD-ROM drive if you have one) installation instructions. Pay particular attention to diagrams and instructions for setting jumpers and switches. If you have a software installation disk, look for a Readme file, wherein the latest tips, warnings, and fixes are often provided by the maker's technical support.

2. Begin to log your actions carefully, step-by-step, on a piece of paper. Power down the computer and disconnect the power cord and any other cable connections that might get in the way.

3. Refer to your System Inventory, check the jumper and DIP switch settings to avoid DMA, IRQ, and port assignment conflicts (see Chapter 5), and adjust as needed. If you already are using a joystick, you'll want to disable the game port on your sound card; if two joystick ports are enabled, neither will work.

4. Make sure you have taken steps to avoid static electricity. Remove the card and any accessories, along with the documentation, from the box the card came in.

If you are also installing a CD-ROM drive, you should probably install it first into its bay; remember you'll have to run the proper cables from the CD-ROM to the sound card, and it may be awkward to do the sound card first.

5. Remove the cover from the case and then remove the edge cover from an appropriate slot.

6. Install the card, using gentle but firm pressure to seat it in the expansion slot.

7. If you have a CD-ROM drive, connect the data and audio cables from the drive to the sound card. On the rear panel of your sound board there will be speaker jacks. Check the documentation which came with your board or the labels on the back plate for instructions on how to connect speakers.

8. Install the software that will use the new card. Restart Windows or reboot the system as needed and run the program. Make sure the sound card is working properly. Test other devices, like a mouse or scanner. Make sure the new card is not interfering with their operation. Run a multimedia test or other program to see if everything is working. If not, carefully review all your steps. It is probably caused by a resource conflict (DMA, IRQ, I/O). Check your Readme files and manuals for trouble-shooting tips. If you still have problems, call technical support.

9. Once you know that your sound board is operating properly, you can power down the system and replace your case cover.

INSTALLING A DISPLAY ADAPTER

What You'll Need

✔ Screwdrivers, flat-had and Philips

✔ Small cup for holding screws and other miscellaneous parts

✔ Graphics adapter card

✔ Software and manual, including Readme files on disk

✔ It's also a good idea to make sure you have a current copy of your Dark and Stormy Night disk. Some of the more advanced graphics adapters may install drivers that are incompatible with applications or other hardware on your system. If this happens, you may not be able to boot using the configuration files on your hard disk and may have to boot from a floppy.

1. Follow the instructions for preparing your workspace and for getting into the case given at the beginning of this Appendix.

2. Follow the instructions for "Installing an Expansion Card," given above in the third section of this Appendix.

3. Before proceeding with the actual installation, check the manual and determine if you need to set any Interrupts, DIP switches or jumpers. A few cards, especially those with hardware compression built in, may also require assignment of a DMA (Direct Memory Access) channel. Under Windows 95, these chores should be handled for you by its Plug and Play capability and the Add New Hardware Wizard, especially if you have a card made in 1995 or later.

4. Now that the card is installed properly in the case, connect the monitor cables.

   Some high-end cards ship with special cables with *BNC connectors* (a sort of twist-on, twist-off connector used in some video applications, as well as for some network installations using Thin EtherNet). This kind of connection offers more bandwidth. If your card came with such a cable, and your monitor supports the connection, you should use it.

5. Before turning on the monitor, double-check the manual for any special requirements. Some units require selecting either internal or external synchronization or require other special settings.

6. Once you have verified that all the switches are set correctly, that the connections are properly made, and the cables properly attached to the monitor, turn on the monitor and boot the PC. Assuming that you don't have any memory or address conflicts, you should get the normal C:> prompt.

7. Install the driver software for Windows and any other applications you plan on running, following the instructions that came with your graphics adapter. Test all the software that you have installed drivers for and make sure everything works. Under Windows 95, the Add New Hardware Wizard should make this virtually automatic.

8. Then use your favorite memory manager software, be it DOS 6.0's MemoryMaker, Qualitas' 386 to the MAX or Quarterdeck's QEMM to optimize memory usage on your system. Under Windows 95, this should be handled by its Plug and Play capability.

9. Once you are sure everything is working properly, go ahead and install any exotic options that your card might possess, such as a mouse, video grabber, compression, or other accessory. Most video cards don't have these exotic options; in that case, just go on to the next step.

10. Replace the cover and place any spare screws, parts, or anything else in your goodies bag for future use.

11. Make a new Dark and Stormy Night Disk as described earlier in Chapter 3, so that you will have backup copies of all these settings. You'll want to save copies of your CONFIG.SYS, AUTOEXEC.BAT, SYSTEM.INI, and WINDOWS.INI (the last two files are for Windows 3.x users only) off onto your bootable floppy. Windows 95 users should make a new Startup or Rescue Disk.

INSTALLING A KEYBOARD

1. Turn off the computer. Then unplug the existing keyboard if it is present. Note the size of the connector, the number of pins and their position. Most DIN connectors are equipped with some sort of key structure so that the connector can only be inserted in one way.

2. Find the manual for your keyboard. Note any DIP switches or toggle switches that must be set to match it up with your type of computer. Some keyboards can be used with either the old-style XT and the newer AT-style machines. If the switches are set wrong, the keyboard will not operate.

Some keyboards allow you to define certain key functions and their locations by setting DIP switches. If your device supports these features and you want to use them, consult your owner's manual. Once this is completed you are actually ready to attach the keyboard to the computer.

3. Line the pins of the keyboard's connector up with the socket on the computer. Gently push the connector into place. If it doesn't go smoothly, rotate it slightly while applying gentle pressure. Do not force it. Excessive force could bend or break either one of the pins or the socket on the motherboard. This is especially true with the newer, smaller cables, which have very fine pins. The cost of repairing such a cable will often exceed the value of the keyboard. Reasonable care is all that's needed, but do exercise care.

4. Power on the computer and watch the screen as the computer goes through its Power-On-Self-Test. If your keyboard is not properly switched or connected, the POST will indicate a keyboard failure or a keyboard error. In all likelihood it should work fine the first time. If it doesn't, try reseating the cable and if it is seated properly, check the setting on the DIP switches or toggle switch.

INSTALLING A MOUSE OR TRACKBALL

1. Determine the kind of connection you will be using. Mice attach either to a Com port, to a specialized bus card, or to a PS/2 style adapter.

To Install a Serial Mouse or PS/2 Mouse

1. Follow step 1 for "Installing a Mouse or Trackball."

2. Make sure the Com port you wish to use is free. If you do not have a free Com port on your machine and need to add an I/O card, refer to the section on I/O cards and communications in Chapter 14.

3. Identify the Com port you wish to use and plug the connector on the mouse into it. You may have to use an adapter if your mouse is designed to plug into several different styles of connection. See your instruction manual.

4. Locate the installation disk for your mouse and install its software (if the machine if off, boot it first). Some mice use drivers that can be invoked without rebooting the machine. Others place a line in your CONFIG.SYS file and you must reboot.

5. If you plan on using the mouse under Microsoft Windows 3.x, you'll also want to run the Windows Setup program from the Windows directory (or from Microsoft's master disks if you are doing a new Windows installation). See your Microsoft Windows or Mouse manual for more instructions. Under Windows 95 this can be handled via Add New Hardware.

6. Once the driver is properly loaded into memory, load a program that uses the mouse and make sure the cursor works properly. Use the mouse utilities or mouse Control Panel under Windows to customize the setting for clicking speed, rate of travel, etc. Redo your Dark and Stormy Night disk or your Windows Rescue Disk.

To Install a PS/2-Connection Mouse

1. Follow step 1 for "Installing a Mouse or Trackball."

2. PS/2-connection mice have their own special connection port. Some of these mice can also be attached to a Com port with an appropriate adapter, which is usually included with the mouse. The basic instructions are as above. Locate your port, make sure the connector is properly oriented and push it in gently. The pins on this kind of connector tend to be fragile, so be careful that you don't bend them by trying to force it when they are not perfectly lined up.

3. Once the mouse is installed go ahead and load the software according to the instructions in your user's manual.

To Install a Bus Mouse

1. Follow step 1 for "Installing a Mouse or Trackball."

2. Follow the instructions for preparing your workspace and for getting into the case given at the beginning of this Appendix.

3. Follow the instructions for "Installing an Expansion Card" given in the third section of this Appendix.

4. Locate a free Interrupt. As discussed in Chapter 11, a mouse card will require a free Interrupt to be able to communicate with your computer. If you don't have a second printer port, and not many cards in your system, Interrupt (IRQ) 5 should be available.

5. Port selection:

   Microsoft refers to their bus mouse card as an *InPort Adapter*. If you are only installing one such card in your system, you can leave the port-selection switch set for Primary InPort. This is handled with a three-pin jumper block. Make sure the jumper is covering the two pins on the side that says "pri InPort." Unless you are installing a card in the last slot of an old IBM-XT computer, you should have the jumper block labeled "XT Slot 8" (another three-jumper block) jumpered over the two pins next to the label "normal."

6. Locate a free expansion slot and remove the back cover plate. Once again, touch the edge of the case to make sure that you aren't carrying any static charge, then with gentle pressure insert the card into the free slot. Use the screw that held the expansion plate cover to lock the card into place. Replace the cover on the computer.

7. With gentle pressure, insert the connector for the mouse into the hole in the back of the expansion card. Reconnect power to the computer and reboot the machine.

8. Using the disk which came with the mouse, follow the instructions in your user's manual to install the mouse drivers for the applications you wish to use. Some mice use drivers that can be invoked without rebooting the machine. Others place a line in your Config.sys file and you must reboot.

INSTALLING A SCANNER

What You'll Need

✔ Screwdrivers, flat-head and Philips

✔ The scanner

✔ Expansion card and cable

✔ The scanner's power supply

✔ Installation and operating software, including Readme files on disk

1. Follow the instructions for preparing your workspace and for getting into the case given at the beginning of this Appendix.

2. Follow the instructions for "Installing an Expansion Card" given earlier in the third section of this Appendix.

3. If you are installing the scanner on a fairly simple system, in all likelihood you can use the default settings for the scanner's expansion card just as they come from the box. Most scanners will require an I/O address (usually in the 100h to 330h range; "h" indicates Hexadecimal notation—see the Glossary and Chapter 4) and possibly an Interrupt (IRQ) and in some cases a DMA (Direct Memory Access) channel. If you have a number of expansion cards already in the system such as a tape drive, SCSI host adapter, or fax card, you should check that the default settings for your scanner do not conflict with any of these. The software program contained on the disc in the back of the book and the System Inventory method described earlier in Chapter 4 can make this task fairly simple.

4. Check your user's manual for any required set-up steps for the scanner. Most flat-bed scanners have a shipping lock either in the form of a tab or a screw that must be released or removed before the scanner can operate. Check your manual for any other necessary steps. You may have to install the scanner's florescent bulb or platen cover (the platen is the glass that you

rest the paper on). Individual set-up requirements will vary, so check your owner's manual.

5. Use the same screw to hold down the card. Set up the scanner in a location within range of the cable and attach the cable to the expansion card. Attach the power cord as needed.

6. Turn on the scanner.

7. Power on your computer and observe the Power-On-Self-Test. If your computer doesn't boot properly, you probably have a conflict between the new card and one of the other expansion cards in your system. Before proceeding on that assumption, make sure that you have connected everything properly. If you have a problem, review your System Inventory and resolve the conflict by either changing the address of the scanner card or adjusting the configuration of the other card that's causing the conflict. Repeat this step as necessary until all conflicts are resolved. Windows 95 users may avoid problems if Plug and Play works via the Add New Hardware Wizard.

8. Once the computer is booted successfully, install the scanner driver and application per the manufacturer's instructions.

9. Test the scanner with the software. It should operate without a problem. Run the software that came with your scanner and make sure that it can successfully complete a scan using that program. If it does, exit all applications, power down your equipment and replace the cover.

INSTALLING AN INTERNAL MODEM

What You'll Need

✔ Small and large screwdrivers, flat-head and Philips

✔ Cup or other container for screws and small parts

✔ System Inventory of currently-installed peripherals

✔ Modem card

✔ Possibly a pair of pliers or hemostat for adjusting jumpers

✔ Modem installation manual and possibly, disk, with Readme file

✔ Telephone Line

1. Follow the instructions for preparing your workspace and for getting into the case given at the beginning of this Appendix.

2. Follow the instructions for "Installing an Expansion Card" given above in the third section of this Appendix.

3. Set the port address.

4. With internal modems you may also have to set an internal jumper or DIP switch for tone or pulse dialing. Depending on the card you have, you may have to set one or more DIP switches or adjust one or more jumpers if there are possible conflicts.

5. On the rear panel of your modem should be two telephone jacks. Check the manual which came with your modem or the labels on the back plate. One should be "line in" or "line" and the other "line out" or "phone." Attach a standard single-line telephone cable with modular jacks into the "line in" connection, and plug the other end of the cable into a telephone wall jack. You can use the other connection to run a line to a regular telephone handset, which can be used any time the modem is not actually sending or receiving (even if the computer is not turned on).

6. Turn on your computer and install your telecommunications software. Make sure that during the installation or once it is set up, you set the options for the appropriate Com port for which you set your modem (Com 1, Com 2, Com 3, or Com 4). Without this information, it may seem that the modem isn't operating even when properly configured, because the software is sending the information to the wrong port.

7. Test your modem using your telecommunications software.

8. Once you know that your modem is operating properly, you can power down the system and replace your case cover. Keep in mind that, if you have to turn the machine around to replace the cover, it's now attached to a telephone line!

INSTALLING AN EXTERNAL MODEM

What You'll Need

✔ Screwdrivers, flat-head and Philips

✔ Modem

✔ Software and Manual, including possibly a Readme file on disk

✔ Serial cable with appropriate connectors

✔ Telephone line

✔ Power supply

1. Unpack the modem and check the owner's manual to make sure all the appropriate parts are there as described in the manual.

2. Check the manual to see if there are any switch settings that must be set prior to installation (for example, for tone or pulse dialing or setup compatibility modes). The need to do this is rare, but a misfit here could lead to frustration if you think the modem is broken when all it needs is a setting change.

3. Attach the appropriate end of the cable to the appropriate Com port on your PC and the other to the connector on the back of the modem.

4. On the rear panel of your modem should be two telephone jacks. Check the manuals which came with your modem or labels on the back plate. One should be "line in" or "line" and the other "line out" or "phone." Attach a standard single-line telephone cable with modular jacks into the "line" in connection, and plug the other end of the cable into a telephone wall jack. You can use the other connection to run a line to a regular telephone handset, which can be used any time the modem is not actually sending or receiving (even if the computer is not turned on).

5. Connect the power supply.

6. Turn on your computer and install your telecommunications software. Make sure that during the installation or once it is set

up, you set the options for the appropriate Com port for which you set your modem (Com 1, Com 2, Com 3, or Com 4). Without this information, it may seem that the modem isn't operating even when properly configured, because the software is sending the information to the wrong port.

7. Test your modem using your telecommunications software.

INSTALLING A FAX CARD

Dedicated fax cards, such as the Intel SatisFAXion, follow the same procedure as the one detailed earlier for an internal modem.

INSTALLING AN ETHERNET CARD

EtherNet installations are fairly simple, unless you already have a number of expansion cards in your computer. They require both an interrupt (IRQ) and memory address, usually in the range between 110h ("h" denotes Hexadecimal notation—see the Glossary and Chapter 4) and 380h. If you don't already have a second serial port in your machine, or if you can disable it, a good choice is often IRQ 3 and address 300h, which are the defaults for many popular cards.

What You'll Need

- ✔ Small and large screwdrivers, flat-head and Philips
- ✔ Cup or other container for screws and small parts
- ✔ System Inventory of currently-installed peripherals
- ✔ Network interface card with appropriate cable
- ✔ T-fittings and termination fitting
- ✔ Possibly a pair of pliers or a hemostat for adjusting jumpers
- ✔ Installation manual, including software and Readme files

1. Follow the instructions for preparing your workspace and for getting into the case given at the beginning of this Appendix.

2. Follow the instructions for "Installing an Expansion Card" given above in the third section of this Appendix.

3. On the rear panel of your EtherNet card you should find the bayonet connector. Place the T fitting on the connector and place one end of your Ethernet cable into the connector. If this PC will be the last one in line, attach the termination fitting. Otherwise, connect the second cable.

4. Turn on your computer and install your networking software.

5. Check your software manual for the proper procedures for logging on to the network and accessing another machine, and test to see that the network is functioning. If you have any problems, check all the cable attachments on the PC you are working on and on the PC(s) that comprise the whole network.

6. Once you know that your network is operating properly, you can power down the system and replace your case cover. Keep in mind that the Ethernet cabling is somewhat delicate, and use care when moving your machine around. If you must move the machine much, first detach the EtherNet cables; replace them after the case is in its permanent position.

DOT MATRIX PRINTER INSTALLATION AND MAINTENANCE

What You'll Need

✔ The printer itself

✔ Manual and installation disk with Readme file

✔ The appropriate cable

✔ Software drivers for the programs you wish to use

✔ Paper

✔ Ribbon

✔ Possibly a small screwdriver

1. Unpack the printer. Carefully open the printer's box and remove it and all its accessories. Then locate the printer's manual or quick-start guide. Save the packing material in case you ever have to send the printer back for repairs.

2. The manual or quick-start guide should contain a list of parts that were supposed to come with the printer. Make sure you have all the components.

3. Check and assemble the printer. Many dot matrix printers come with various locks that prevent the head from being damaged during transit or to keep the pulleys from moving. These must be removed prior to powering the unit on to prevent possible damage.

4. Refer to the manual to see if there are any DIP switches that must be set to make the unit compatible with your software and to set the data board. Many dot matrix printers come with both serial and parallel connections and use DIP switches to determine which port is active. Some printers allow you to set different emulation modes, such as Epson and IBM ProPrinter, and these are also controlled with DIP switch settings. You may want to use a small screwdriver or a ball-point pen to adjust the DIP switches.

5. Insert the ribbon. Refer to the user's guide for precise steps on how to insert the ribbon. Most modern dot matrix printers use cartridges rather than spool ribbons.

6. Assemble the paper feed. Your dot matrix printer will be equipped with either (and possibly both) manual and power-driven (commonly known as *tractor feed*) paper guides. Refer to the manual for instruction.

7. Attach the power cord to a wall socket and to the printer. Insert the paper according to the manual's instructions, and perform its Power-On-Self-Test. Most dot matrix printers offer some kind of control to automatically run through and test their various features. This is usually done by holding down some combination of

control panel buttons when the unit is turned on. Identify what these are and perform the task.

8. Attach the cables to the printer and the computer.

9. Proceed to install software drivers and enjoy your new printer.

LASER PRINTER INSTALLATION AND MAINTENANCE

What You'll Need

✔ The printer itself

✔ The appropriate cable

✔ Installation manual and software, perhaps a Readme file

✔ Software drivers for the programs you wish to use

✔ Paper

✔ Toner

✔ Possibly a small screwdriver

1. Unpack the printer. Carefully open the printer's box and remove it and all its accessories. Then locate the printer's manual or quick-start guide. Save the packing material in case you ever have to send the printer back for repairs.

2. The manual or quick-start guide should contain a list of parts that were supposed to come with the printer. Make sure you have all the components.

3. Check and assemble the printer. Many laser printers come with various locks that prevent the internal moving parts from being damaged during transit or to keep the pulleys from moving. These must be removed prior to powering the unit on to prevent possible damage.

4. Refer to the manual to see if there are any DIP switches that must be set to make the unit compatible with your software and to set

the data board. Check your manual for any settings you may have to make before the unit can be powered up. While most laser printers offer several different connections (often parallel, serial and AppleTalk) most modern laser printers can automatically switch and recognize which one is being used.

5. Open the toner cartridge kit. It may have come in the box in the printer or in a box of its own. The toner assembly sometimes contains all the periodic maintenance parts for your printer as well as the actual imaging material that forms the letters and graphics on the page. The instructions will probably tell you to place a felt bar inside the printer to collect excess toner off a drum, and to clean several components during this phase of the installation. Open the door or top of your printer and follow these instructions provided with the kit.

   Insert the toner cartridge into its carriage, or the printer, if directed. Find the plastic tab that is used to seal the cartridge until it's installed in the printer. Holding the cartridge in place with one hand, pull the tab away from the cartridge with the other hand. This removes the plastic seal. Follow your directions. Discard it, install the cartridge if need be, and close the lid of the printer.

6. Install the paper tray. Among the items which came with your printer will be two or more pieces that help make up the paper-handling system. Following the instructions which appear on the guide itself, or in the manual, assemble these pieces and install them if needed.

7. If your printer requires any accessory cartridges or cards to be installed, follow the instructions that came with the accessory for installing them.

8. Attach the power cord to a wall socket and to the printer and perform its Power-On-Self-Test. Most printers offer some kind of control to automatically run through and test their various features. This is usually done by holding down some combination of control panel buttons when the unit is turned on. Identify what these are and perform the task.

9. Install software drivers. Printer drivers will vary from application to application. If you are using a graphical interface like Microsoft Windows, OS/2 or X-Windows, you will probably have

one master driver that will cover all supported applications. This is usually done through some form of Control Panel. In Windows 95 it can be done through the Printers folder or with the Add New Hardware Wizard.

Ink Jet Printer Installation and Maintenance

What You'll Need

✔ The printer itself

✔ The appropriate cable

✔ Manual and installation software, including Readme file

✔ Software drivers for the programs you wish to use

✔ Paper

✔ Ink

✔ Possibly a small screwdriver

1. Unpack the printer. Carefully open the printer's box and remove it and all its accessories. Then locate the printer's manual or quick-start guide. Save the packing material in case you ever have to send the printer back for repairs.

2. The manual or quick-start guide should contain a list of parts that were supposed to come with the printer. Make sure you have all the components.

3. Check and assemble the printer. Many ink jet printers come with various locks that prevent the internal moving parts from being damaged during transit or to keep the pulleys from moving. These must be removed prior to powering the unit on to prevent possible damage.

4. Refer to the manual to see if there are any DIP switches that must be set to make the unit compatible with your software and to set the data board. Check your manual for any settings you may have to make before the unit can be powered up.

5. Open the container with the ink and containers. Check with your owner's manual to fill (if necessary) and prepare the inking apparatus. When this is done, open the door or top of your printer and install the unit following the instructions provided with the kit.

6. Install the paper tray. Among the items which came with your printer may be two or more pieces that make up the paper-handling assembly. Following the instructions which appear on the guide itself, or in the manual, assemble these pieces and install them if needed.

7. If your printer requires any accessory cartridges or cards to be installed, follow the instructions that came with the accessory for installing them.

8. Attach the power cord to a wall socket and to the printer and perform its Power-On-Self-Test. Most printers offer some kind of control to automatically run through and test their various features. This is usually done by holding down some combination of control panel buttons when the unit is turned on. Identify what these are and perform the task.

9. Install software drivers. Printer drivers will vary from application to application. If you are using a graphical interface like Microsoft Windows, OS/2 or X-Windows, you will probably have one master driver that will cover all supported applications. This is usually done through some form of Control Panel. In Windows 95 it can be done through the Printers folder or with the Add New Hardware Wizard.

INSTALLATION PROCEDURES FOR I/O CARDS

What You'll Need

✔ Small and large screwdrivers

✔ Cup or other container for screws and small parts

✔ Inventory of currently-installed peripherals

✔ I/O card kit, manuals, and any installation and Readme files

✔ Possibly a pair of pliers or hemostat for adjusting jumpers

If you plan on immediately attaching devices to the I/O card you will also need the appropriate cables and any required 9- to 25-pin adapters.

1. Follow the instructions for preparing your workspace and for getting into the case given at the beginning of this Appendix.

2. Follow the instructions for "Installing an Expansion Card" given above in the third section of this Appendix.

3. Install ports to the back of the case and attach ribbon cables.

    If you have a unit with internal printer ports attached by ribbon cables, you have three options. One is to not install the additional ports if you don't need them. Keep in mind that while most people won't need a second parallel port, it's a good idea to have two Com ports available. If you are not installing all the ports, you may want to disable the IRQ settings for the ports you aren't going to install. Refer to the card's documentation to do this.

    If you want to leave the extra ports attached directly to the plate, attach the cable for the port to the appropriate pin on the card. Be sure to connect the side of the cable with the red (or blue) stripe to the side marked as Pin 1 on the card.

4. If your case has openings for I/O ports built into the back of the unit, you can remove the appropriate 9- or 25-pin plate covers and mount the ports there. Use a nut driver or needle-nosed pliers to remove the hexagonal screws on either side of the port connector and use the same screws to mount it to the back of the case. You'll have to remove the existing covers over the holes in the case. In some cases, this will mean removing a screw, in others you will have to physically poke the hole out with a screwdriver. In either case, make sure you hold one hand on the other side to catch the cover when it falls out. You don't want it wedging between the case and the motherboard.

5. Once all the ports are installed attach any peripherals that you plan on connecting immediately to the port. Reconnect the power cord and boot your machine.

6. Use the ASQ or other diagnostic supplied on the disc in this book, or another utility such as PC Tools, or Norton Utilities' System Information to make sure that the ports are seen by the system and are active. If you have already attached a printer, you may want to try printing something and if it's a modem, using communications software such as ProComm Plus or Windows Terminal to talk to the modem (see the appropriate instruction manual). If your software check shows that everything is working, you're all set. If it doesn't, you probably have an Interrupt conflict with something else on your system. If you completed the System Inventory as discussed in Chapter 4, finding this shouldn't be much of a problem. If not, you'll have to make an Inventory now and resolve any conflict. Windows 95 should resolve any conflicts by itself, or at least point them out to you.

7. Once you are sure everything is working, replace the cover and place any spare screws, parts or anything else in your goodies bag for future use.

REMOVING THE POWER SUPPLY

What You'll Need

✔ Philips screwdriver
✔ Masking tape

1. Follow the instructions for preparing your workspace and for getting into the case given at the beginning of this Appendix.

2. Remove all cables coming from the power supply to all your drives, the motherboard, and any other peripheral power directly from the power supply. Label them with masking tape.

3. Disconnect the power switch.

4. Locate the screws on the back of your case that hold the power supply in place and remove them.

5. Carefully lift out the power supply. If it doesn't come out easily, hold it with one hand and use the other hand to help figure out why it isn't coming free.

INSTALLING OR REPLACING THE POWER SUPPLY

1. Follow the instructions for preparing your workspace and for getting into the case given at the beginning of this Appendix.

2. Test the power supply by plugging it in and watching for the fan to run.

3. Place the unit in its position inside the case with no power cord attached; don't screw it down yet.

4. Attach the power connectors P8 and P9 to the motherboard.

5. Now attach all the power supply cables to the disk drives.

6. If your power supply uses a remote switch (one that's not physically mounted on or in the power supply) you'll have to reattach, and possibly remount, the switch.

7. Make sure the power is switched off, attach a power cord, preferably through a surge protector to a wall outlet, and power up the unit. Make sure the fan is operating and that the Power-On-Self-Test operates properly.

TESTING A NEW OR REMOVED POWER SUPPLY

1. Without attaching the power supply to any other device, attach a power cord to the back of the unit.

2. Make sure the unit is switched off and plug the cord into a wall socket. Now turn the unit on and see if the fan is operating. To attach a power supply to a computer for testing, you do not have to screw the unit down. Just attach the motherboard connectors, a hard drive and a floppy connector and then turn on the switch.

APPENDIX B

BLANK FORMS

SCSI List

Name of Computer _____ Date of Inventory _____

SCSI Host Adapter: _____ Standard: _____

Manufacturer: _____

Date Installed: _____ Terminated: Y N

SCSI Hard Drive I, capacity _____ Date Installed _____

Number: 0 1 2 3 4 5 6 7 _____ Terminated: Y N

SCSI Hard Drive II, capacity _____ Date Installed _____

Number: 0 1 2 3 4 5 6 7 _____ Terminated: Y N

Other Internal SCSI Devices

Tape Backup Unit: Make: _____ Date installed _____

Number: 0 1 2 3 4 5 6 7 _____ Terminated: Y N

Make: _____ Date installed _____

Number: 0 1 2 3 4 5 6 7 _____ Terminated: Y N

Make: _____ Date installed _____

Number: 0 1 2 3 4 5 6 7 _____ Terminated: Y N

External SCSI Devices

Make: _____Date installed _____Number: 0 1 2 3 4 5 6 7 _____Terminated: Y N

Make: _____Date installed _____Number: 0 1 2 3 4 5 6 7 _____Terminated: Y N

Make: _____Date installed _____Number: 0 1 2 3 4 5 6 7 _____Terminated: Y N

Make: _____Date installed _____Number: 0 1 2 3 4 5 6 7 _____Terminated: Y N

Make: _____Date installed _____Number: 0 1 2 3 4 5 6 7 _____Terminated: Y N

Make: _____Date installed _____Number: 0 1 2 3 4 5 6 7 _____Terminated: Y N

Make: _____Date installed _____Number: 0 1 2 3 4 5 6 7 _____Terminated: Y N

IRQs	1	2	3	4	5	6	7	8	9	10	11	12	13	14	15
DMA Channels	1	2	3	4	5										

INVENTORY

Name of Computer _____Date of Inventory _____

CPU type, speed _____Date Installed _____

Math coprocessor, overdrive, etc. _____Date Installed _____

RAM Memory, amount, kind_____Date Installed _____

Operating System and environment versions_____

BIOS type, Revision Number _____Date Installed, if appropriate _____

Hard Drive type, capacity_____Date Installed _____

Floppy Drive type, capacity _____Date Installed _____

CD-ROM Drive Make and model _____Type_____Date Installed _____

Motherboard Make and model _____Date Installed _____

Memory Manager Program and Version Number _____

Expansion Cards

Type	Vendor	IRQ	DMA	Memory Range	Date Installed	Driver(s)
Graphics Adapter						
I/O Card						
Hard Disk Controller						
Floppy Drive Controller						
SCSI Adapter						
Sound Card						

IRQs   1   2   3   4   5   6   7   8   9   10   11   12   13   14   15
DMA Channels   1   2   3   4   5

APPENDIX C

RESOURCE LIST

Adaptec, Inc.
691 S. Milpitas Blvd.
Milpitas, CA 95035
408/945-8600
Adaptec Easy SCSI, Arrow, Hard disk controllers

Adobe Systems, Inc.
1585 Charleston Rd.
Mountain View, CA 94039-7900
800/833-6687
Adobe PhotoShop

Advanced Micro Devices (AMD)
901 Compton Pl. POB 3453
Sunnyvale, CA 94088
800/222-9323

Aldus Corp.
411 First Avenue, South
Seattle, WA 98104-2871
800/333-2538
206/628-2320
Aldus PhotoStyler

Always Technology Corp.
31336 Via Colinas, Suite 101
Westlake Village, CA 91362
818/597-1400
SCSI accessories

American Megatrends, Inc.
6145-F Northbelt Parkway
Norcross, GA 30071
800/828-9264
404/263-8181
Motherboards and chips

Appian Technology, Inc.
477 North Matilda Ave.
Sunnyvale, CA 94088
800/727-7426
408/730-5400
Video card

Apple Computers Inc.
20525 Mariani Ave.
Cupertino, CA 95014
800/776-2333
408/996-1010
Computers

Applied Learning Corporation
1376 Glen Hardie Rd.
Wayne, PA 19087
215/688-6866
Mice, educational software

Appoint, Ind.
4473 Willow Rd., Suite 110
Pleasanton, CA 94588
800/448-1184
510/463-3003
Gulliver and MousePen

Artisoft, Inc.
2202 North Forbes Blvd.
Tuscon, AZ 85745
800/610-0001
602/670-7100
Networking products

Autodesk, Inc
2320 Marinship Way
Saulsilito, CA 94965
800/445-5415
415/332-2344
CAD/CAM software

Bus Logic
4151 Burton Dr.
Santa Clara, CA 95054
408/492-9090
747 host adapter

Caere Corp.
100 Cooper Court
Los Gatos, CA 95030
800/535-7226
408/395-7000
OmniPage

Cal-Comp, Inc.
2411 West La Palma Ave.
Anaheim, CA 92801
800/932-1212
714/821-2000
Digitizing tablets

Calera Recognition Systems, Inc.
475 Potrero Ave.
Sunnyvale, CA 94086-4118
800/422-5372
408/720-8300
WordScan Plus

Colorado Memory Systems
800 South Taft Ave.
Loveland, CO 80537
800/845-7905
Tape backups

Command Software
1061 East Indiantown Rd.,
Suite 500, Jupiter, FL 33477
800/423-9147
407/575-3200
FPROT

Compaq Computer Corp.
20555 State Hwy. 249
Houston, TX 77070
800/345-1518
713/374-0670

Compuserve Inc.
5000 Arlington Center Blvd.
Columbus, OH 43220
800/848-8199
614/457-8600
Information service, WINCIM

Connor Peripherals
3081 Zanker Rd.
San Jose, CA 95134
408/456-4500
Hard drives

Corel Corporation
1600 Carling Ave.
Ottawa, Ontario, CANADA K1Z
8R7
800/836-3729
613/728-8200
*CorelSCSI and CorelSCSI Pro,
CorelDRAW!*

Dariana Software
5241 Lincoln Ave., Suite D5
Cyprus, CA 90630
800/892-9950
Fax 704/236-1390
WinSleuth Gold Plus

Datastorm Technologies, Inc.
46710 Fremont Blvd.
Fremont, CA 94538-6538
510/651-5580
*ProComm Plus,
ProComm Plus for Windows*

**Distributed Processing
Technology**
140 Candace Dr.
Maitland, FL 32751
800/322-4378
407/830-5522

Eastman Kodak Company
343 State St.
Rochester, NY 14650
800/242-2424
716/724-4000
Photo CD

Ergo-Nomics, Inc.
POB 964
South Hampton, PA 18966
215/357-5124
Miscellaneous Ergonomic Products

Ergonomic Solutions
POB 7052
Plainesville, CT 06062
203/793-0445
Miscellaneous Ergonomic products

Exabyte Corporation
1685 38th St.
Boulder, CO 80301
800/ EXABYTE
Backup systems

ExperVision, Inc.
3590 N. First St.
San Jose, CA 95134
800/732-3897
408/428-9988
TypeReader, FastBack Plus

Fox Bay Industries
4150 B Place, NW, Suite 101
Auburn, WA 98001
800/874-8527
206/941-9155
Ergonomic devices, PC Add-ons

Fractal Design Corp.
334 Spreckels Dr., Suite F
Aptos, CA 93005
800/647-7443
408/688-8800
Fractal Design Painter

Future Domain Corp.
2801 McGaw Ave.
Irvine, CA 92714
800/879-7599
SCSI products

Hewlett-Packard
3000 Hanover St.
Palo Alto, CA 94304
800/752-0900
415/857-1501
*HP Scan Jet, Hewlett Packard plotter,
HP Laser Jet, HP Color Jet Printer*

IBM
One Old Orchard Road
Armonk, NY 10504
800/426-3333
PS/2 and other computers

Intel Corporation
2200 Mission College Blvd.
Santa Clara, CA 95052-8119
408/765-8080
Intel SatisFAXion

Kinesis Corporation
915 118th Ave., SE
Bellevue, WA 98005
206/455-9220
Ergonomic products

**Landmark Research
International Corp.**
703 Grand Central Street
Clearwater, FL 34616
1/800/683-6696
813/443-1331
Fax 813/443-6603
Diagnostic utilities

Lexmark International, Inc.
740 New Circle Rd. NW
Lexington, KY 40511
800/358-5835
606/232-2000
Printers, keyboards

Logitec, Inc.
6505 Kaiser Dr.
Fremont, CA 94555
800/231-7717
510/795-8500
MouseMan, TrackMan, Kidz mouse

Matrox Electronics, Ltd.
1055 St. Regis Blvd.
Dorval, Quebec, CANADA H9P 2T4
800/361-4903
514/685-2630
Video products

MCI Communications Corp.
1650 Tysons Blvd.
McLean, VA 22102
800/333-1000
703/506-6000
Electronic mail services

Micrografix, Inc.
1303 East Arapaho Rd.
Richardson, TX 75081
800/487-2116
214/234-1769
MicroGrafix Picture Publisher

Micronics Computers Inc.
232 East Warren Ave.
Fremont, CA 94539
510/651-2300
Motherboards

Microsoft Corp.
One Microsoft Way
Redmond, WA 98052-6399
800/426-9400
206/882-8080
Excel, Word, Power Point,
Access, Mail, Microsoft Sound
System, Windows, OS/2, Terminal,
Microsoft Windows for Workgroups

Mouse Systems
47505 Seabridge Dr.
Fremont, CA 94538
510/656-1117
First Mouse PC Mouse 3D/6D.
PC Mouse, PC Mouse III, and the
White Mouse, New Mouse

Nanao USA Corp.
23535 Telo Ave.
Torrance, CA 90505
800/800-5202
310/525-5202
Monitors

NCR Corp.
1700 S. Patterson Blvd.
Dayton, OH 45479
800/637-2600
513/445-5000

NEC Technologies
1414 Massachusetts Ave.
Boxborough, MA 01719
800/632-4636
Computers, CD-ROMs, monitors

Novell, Inc.
122 East 1700 South
Provo, UT 84606
800/453-1267
801/429-7000
NetWare, LAN operating system
software, DR DOS 6.0

Northgate Computer Systems
141 N. Jonathan Blvd.
Chaska, MN 55318
800/858-8819
612/361-5000
Omni Key keyboard

Pacific Data Products
9125 Rehco Rd.
San Diego, CA 92121
619/552-0880
Modems, printers, plotters

Panasonic Communications and Systems Company
2 Panasonic Way
Secaucus, NJ 07094
800/742-8086
201/348-7000
Monitors, CD-ROMS, Optical disks,
scanners, computers

PC Magazine (Ziff-Davis Communications)
(subscriptions)
POB 51524
Boulder, CO 80321

PC Power and Cooling
5995 Avenida Encinas
Carlsbad, CA 92008
800/722-6555
Fax 619/931-6988
Power supplies

Phoenix Technologies, Ltd.
846 University Ave.
Norwood, MA 02062
800/344-7200
617/551-4000
BIOS

Qualitas
7101 Wisconsin Ave., Suite 1386
Bethesda, MD 20814
800/733-1377
ASQ. 386 to the MAX

Quantech International
83 Boston Post Rd.
Sudbury, MA 01776
800/438-5336

Quarterdeck Office Systems
150 Pico Blvd.
Santa Monica, CA 90405
800/354-3222
310/392-9851
QEMM, Manifest

Sony Corp. of America
3300 Zanker Rd.
San Jose, CA 95134
800/352-7669
408/432-0190
Monitors

Symantec
10201 Torre Avenue
Cupertino, CA 95014
408/253-9600
Fax 408/252-4694
*The Norton Utilities,
Norton Backup*

Texas Instruments Inc.
POB 655474
Dallas, TX 75265
800/527-3500
214/995-2011
34020 CPU

U.S. Robotics, Inc.
8100 N. McCormick Blvd.
Skokie, IL 60076
800/342-5877
Modems, Courier modems

UltraStor Corp.
15 Hammond, Suite 310
Irvine, CA 92718
714/581-4100
SCSI host adapter

Wacom Technology Corp.
501 SE Columbia Shores Blvd.,
Suite 300, Vancouver, WA 98661
800/922-6613
206/750-8882
Digitizing tablets

Weitek Corp.
1060 East Arques Ave.
Sunnyvale, CA 94086
408/738-8400
  Chips

WordPerfect Corp.
1555 North Technology Way
Orem, UT 84057-2399
800/451-5151
801/225-5000

Xerox Imaging Systems, Inc.
9 Centennial Dr.
Peabody, MA 01960
800/248-6550
508/977-2000
  X/Windows

Zenographics
4 Executive Circle, Suite 200
Irvine, CA 92714
800/366-7494
714/851-6352

APPENDIX D

NUMERIC ERROR CODES

Most PCs use numeric error codes. The following list of these numeric codes includes the official name of the BIOS error each number denotes, and some suggestions to help you track down the cause of the error and fix it.

If the error message you get on your screen contains text, look it up in Appendix E.

NOTE

Numeric Error Code   Associated Text Message

101   System Interrupt Failed

In XTs this means you have trouble with the motherboard. For others, it might be an Interrupt conflict or the motherboard.

102   System Timer Failed

The timer chip on the motherboard is bad. You may have to replace the motherboard.

103   System Timer Interrupt Failed

Chances are the motherboard will have to be replaced.

104   Protected Mode Operation Failed

Occurs only on AT-style machines. This can be a bad motherboard or a bad keyboard. Check the keyboard switch. If that doesn't work, replace the motherboard.

105   Command Not Accepted
                                       Keyboard Communication Failure

Bad keyboard or keyboard controller chip.

106   Post Logic Test Problem

A bad motherboard or a faulty card can cause this error. Turn off the computer and remove all cards except the video adapter and attempt to reboot. If this is successful, replace the other cards one at a time until you find the one causing the failure. If the computer won't boot with only the video adapter installed, try another video card. If it still will not boot, the motherboard is probably bad. This is a catch-all message for errors occurring during the Power On Self-Test which aren't covered by other numeric codes.

107   NMI Test Failed

The CPU chip has failed. You may be able to replace the CPU. Otherwise, a new motherboard with CPU will be required.

108   Failed System Timer Test

The timer chip on the motherboard is bad. It or the motherboard must be replaced.

Numeric Error Code   Associated Text Message

109	Problem With First 64K Ram

Bad memory chips must be replaced or the motherboard replaced.

161	System Option Not Set Or Possible Bad Battery
162	System Option Not Set, Or Invalid Checksum, Or Configuration Incorrect
163	Time And Date Not Set

In the case of codes 161, 162, and 163, your CMOS memory has forgotten the computer's Setup. Typically, you must replace the battery, then redo your Setup using the information on your system inventory list. If replacing the battery does not fix this error, the power supply may be bad. Attach a working power supply and attempt to reboot. If it still gives you this error message, a failing RTC-CMOS chip can cause this. Replace the chip or the motherboard.

164	Memory Size Error

CMOS may have forgotten your Setup. Rerun the Setup program and reconfigure your CMOS, using the information on your system inventory list. If this doesn't fix the problem, open your case and gently push down on all the memory chips to see that they are properly seated. If it still won't boot, you can carefully remove the chips, take them to your computer store for testing and replace any that are bad. Other possibilities include a bad power supply or, rarely, a bad motherboard.

201	Memory Error

In XT machines, this error code indicates that the RAM on the motherboard is functioning incorrectly. Remove the RAM chips and have them tested. For AT-style machines, this indicates that there is one or more bad memory chips. First turn off the computer and gently push down on all the memory chips to see that they are properly seated. If it still won't boot, you can carefully remove the chips, take them to your computer store for testing and replace any that are bad. If no memory is bad, you'll probably have to replace the motherboard.

Numeric Error Code	Associated Text Message
202	Memory Address Error Lines 0–15
203	Memory Address Error Lines 16–23

You have one or more bad memory chips. First turn off the computer and gently push down on all the memory chips to see that they are properly seated. If it still won't boot, you can carefully remove the chips, take them to your computer store for testing and replace any that are bad.

301	Keyboard Error

Turn off the machine and check the keyboard cable connections carefully. Also check to see that there is nothing resting on the keyboard, pressing down a key. If this doesn't work, you'll probably have to replace the keyboard.

302	System Unit Key Lock Is Locked

Either the key has been turned in the lock or the jumper wires have accidentally been disconnected from the lock or the motherboard (have you installed something new that took you inside the case?). This error may also occur if there is a key stuck in the "on" position or if the switch in the lock is faulty. Check all of these possibilities.

NOTE If you don't commonly use the lock on the computer, take the keys out of the machine and keep them in your goodie bag. This prevents accidents and practical jokes.

303	Keyboard Or System Unit Error
304	Keyboard Or System Unit Error, Keyboard Clockline Error

This indicates that the keyboard is not sending appropriate responses during the Power-On-Self-Test. Check all keyboard connections and, if you have one, the AT/XT switch on the keyboard. Also check for a key stuck in the "on" position. Either the cord or the keyboard could be bad.

Numeric Error Code   Associated Text Message

401   CRT Error #1

Occurs in XT machines and indicates that the monochrome display adapter is bad. Turn off the machine and check to see that it is properly seated in the slot. If that isn't it, replace it.

501   CRT Error #2

Applies to only XT machines and indicates that the Color Graphics Adapter is bad. Turn off the machine and check to see that it is properly seated in the slot. If that isn't it, replace it.

601   Disk Error

Most commonly seen if you have removed a drive and haven't updated your CMOS. If this might be the case, enter your CMOS Setup and remove that drive from it. Can also be caused by a bad disk, drive or controller card. If you haven't removed a drive, turn the machine off and check all the drive cables, and see if the controller is properly seated.

602   Disk Boot Record Error

Begin tracking this down by attempting to boot again using your Dark and Stormy Night Disk. If possible, test the disk on another computer to be sure the disk is good. If that doesn't work, turn the machine off, open the case and check all your drive cables. If this doesn't work, remove the first floppy drive (update your CMOS when attempting the reboot). Check each of your drives this way. If the machine still won't boot, replace the controller and try again.

1701   Hard Disk Failure

Don't panic, there are several things to check. Turn off the machine and check all the power and cable connections to the hard drive. If this doesn't solve the problem, double-check the drive-select jumper on the disk and see that it is properly set (see Chapter 9). After that, check the settings on the controller and/or try another controller. Only if all else fails should you begin to suspect your hard drive has crashed. 1701 errors may vary from manufacturer to manufacturer. Check the manuals that came with your controller and hard drive for more exact information.

Numeric Error Code   Associated Text Message

1780   Disk 0 Failure

"Disk 0" is always the first physical hard disk and is always drive C. This error, however, refers to the entire disk regardless of any partitioning.

Turn off the machine and check all the power and cable connections to the hard drive. If this doesn't solve the problem, double-check the drive-select jumper on the disk and see that it is properly set (see Chapter 9). After that, check the settings on the controller and/or try another controller. Only if all else fails should you begin to suspect your hard drive has crashed.

1781   Disk 1 Failure

"Disk 1" is the second actual hard drive regardless of letter name.

Turn off the machine and check all the power and cable connections to the hard drive. If this doesn't solve the problem, double check the drive select jumper on the disk and see that it is properly set (See Chapter 8). After than, check the settings on the controller and/or try another controller. Only if all else fails should you begin to suspect your hard drive has crashed.

1782   Disk Controller Failure

This almost certainly indicates a bad controller. However, you may first turn off the computer, remove the case, and check on all disk cabling. Be sure that all ribbon cables have the side with the red or blue stripe going to Pin 1. Also check to see that the controller is properly seated in the slot. If this doesn't work and you have recently installed a new card into your computer, take the newly installed card out and attempt to reboot. If the computer boots, the new card probably has its BIOS ROM at the controller's address. Find a new address for your new card and try it out.

Numeric Error Code   Associated Text Message

1790   Disk 0 Error

"Disk 0" is always the first physical hard disk and is always drive C. This error, however, refers to the entire disk regardless of any partitioning.

Turn off the machine and check all the power and cable connections to the hard drive. If this doesn't solve the problem, double-check the drive-select jumper on the disk and see that it is properly set (see Chapter 9). After that, check the settings on the controller and/or try another controller. Only if all else fails should you begin to suspect your hard drive has crashed.

1791   Disk 1 Error

"Disk 1" is the second actual hard drive regardless of letter name.

Turn off the machine and check all the power and cable connections to the hard drive. If this doesn't solve the problem, double-check the drive-select jumper on the disk and see that it is properly set (see Chapter 9). After that, check the settings on the controller and/or try another controller. Only if all else fails should you begin to suspect your hard drive has crashed.

TEXT ERROR MESSAGES

Text error messages are more common than numeric error codes. They vary slightly depending on the exact flavor of BIOS in your machine. The wording you see may vary slightly from that given here. Remember that when you see "NNN" in this Appendix, it stands for whatever series of actual numbers your system reports. Similarly, "X" (or "XX," etc.) stands for either the numbers or letters reported by your system.

DOS also produces some text error messages and we have included many of them also. Again, different editions of DOS may vary the wording slightly. The following list of text error codes includes a short explanation of the error, and some suggestions to help you track down the cause of the error and fix it.

128K NOT OK, PARITY DISABLED

The first 128K of RAM failed in the Power-On-Self-Test. Turn off the computer and then try rebooting. Next open your case, and gently push down on all the memory chips to see if they are properly seated. If it still won't boot, you can carefully remove the chips, take them to your computer store for testing, and replace any that are bad.

You can also try moving the chips serving as part of the first 128K and exchanging them with other memory chips. You will have to consult the manual for your motherboard to find the appropriate banks of chips. This error can also be caused by a bad motherboard.

`8042 GATE-A20 ERROR`

This is usually a bad keyboard.

`8087 NMI AT XXX.XXX. TYPE (S)HUT OFF NMI, (R)EBOOT, OTHER KEYS TO CONTINUE`

There is a problem with the math coprocessor 8087 chip. It must be tested and replaced if bad. To save your work, type **S** and you may temporarily continue with your work. Save, shut the system down, and test the chip.

`ACCESS DENIED`

You attempted to over-write a protected, read-only, or locked file. If you were writing to a floppy, check to see if it is write-protected. Should a floppy drive give you this message with several unprotected disks, the part of the drive that finds the notch may be broken. If the file is write-protected or read only, save under another name or take steps to take the protection off the file. You may get this message if you are trying to open a directory as if it were a file.

`ADDRESS LINE SHORT!`

Turn off the computer and gently press on the memory chips to make sure they are properly seated. If the problem continues, you may try replacing the memory or simply replace the motherboard. It is slightly more likely that it is the motherboard, but testing the memory may let you save the cost of a new one.

`ALLOCATION ERROR, SIZE ADJUSTED`

This may happen when you run CHKDSK. The utility found that either the file was larger or smaller than the directory entry called for. If the file was longer than the entry, the file was cut off to match the directory. If the file was shorter, the directory entry was adjusted. Using PCTools' DISKFIX or Norton's Disk Doctor will save more of your data than DOS does.

WARNING

This can happen occasionally, but if it happens more than once in six or so months, your hard disk is acting up. Back everything up and use a diagnostic/repair utility.

ATTEMPTED WRITE-PROTECT VIOLATION

This message is received if you try to format a disk that is write-protected. Should a floppy drive give you this message with several unprotected disks, the part of the drive that finds the notch may be broken.

BAD DMA PORT = XX

Your DMA chip has failed the Power-On-Self-Test. You will almost certainly have to replace the motherboard.

BAD OR MISSING COMMAND INTERPRETER

DOS has lost the path to your COMMAND.COM file. This message is sometimes received if you try to boot from a non-system disk. Check your CONFIG.SYS and AUTOEXEC.BAT files against your actual files and make sure that you have the correct path. You might also check to make sure that your DOS shell program also has the COMMAND.COM path information. (If your CONFIG.SYS reads SHELL=C:\DOS\COMMAND.COM C:\DOS\ /P, for instance, check to be sure that the file actually is in the C:\DOS\ directory.)

N O T E

If you are using a network copy of COMMAND.COM from the file server, log off the network and reboot.

BAD PARTITION TABLE

Hopefully, you'll only get this message if you've just run FDISK. It means that you did the low-level format improperly. Run FDISK again, referring to the instructions in Chapter 9. If FDISK was run correctly, you have a bad hard disk. If you have not run FDISK on the hard drive in question, you could have a virus. Run your virus checker and follow the instructions in the owner's manual to fix the situation (it is just barely possible that a malfunctioning controller is causing this message; try putting in another controller).

NNNK BASE MEMORY

This is not an error; your PC is just telling you how much system memory it found.

BASE MEMORY SIZE = NNK

This is not an error; your PC is just telling you how much system memory it found.

BUS TIMEOUT NMI AT SLOT X

This message only occurs on EISA-based PCs. Run your configuration utility, making certain that you have correctly configured all your EISA boards. If this doesn't fix matters, the adapter card in the slot number given in the error message is almost certainly at fault.

C: DRIVE ERROR

Something is wrong with your CMOS Setup; check your configuration.

C: DRIVE FAILURE

If you have just been working inside your computer, turn it off and check out the cables, controller, etc. If you haven't been inside the case, press **F1** to try a reboot. If this works, run your disk utilities to check our your hard drive, just in case. If this doesn't work, get out your Dark and Stormy Night Disk and boot from it. When the machine is up, change to your hard drive and see if you can see the directories. Run the CMOS Setup to see that everything is set correctly. If it still won't boot, you may have to reformat the drive (that's why FORMAT.COM and FDISK.EXE are on your DSND). If you've kept backups, it will probably just be a bit time-consuming. If nothing can find your hard disk, you can try calling technical support to see if you have some strange conflict. And last of all, you may have to replace your hard drive or the hard drive controller.

There are methods of recovering data from an inoperative hard drive, at least under many circumstances. If you are not backed up, you may want to consider this. Usually this job is done by a specialist. Check for names and addresses in your favorite computer magazine.

NOTE

CACHE MEMORY BAD, DO NOT ENABLE CACHE!

Turn off the computer, remove the case and gently press the cache memory chips down to be sure they are properly seated. Try rebooting. Run AMIDiag (if you have it) since this is an AMI BIOS error message. If not, replace the cache memory chips. It's possible although not likely, that the cache controller chip on the motherboard is bad, requiring replacement of the motherboard.

CMOS SYSTEM OPTIONS NOT SET

Your CMOS chip forgot your Setup. Run Setup and reconfigure using the information on your system inventory sheet. Check or replace your CMOS batteries.

A few older machines require a Setup floppy disk. Be sure to use the right Setup utility for your particular machine.

NOTE

CMOS TIME & DATE NOT SET

Run your CMOS Setup and check the configuration. For older computers, see the note above.

COM PORT DOES NOT EXIST

You have specified a non-enabled Com port. Turn off the machine, remove the case, and check the cabling from the I/O card to the serial ports. If this doesn't solve the problem, run a diagnostics program such as Norton Utilities, CheckIt, or QAPlus to make sure that your computer recognizes the Com port you specified.

CONFIGURATION ERROR FOR SLOT N

This is an EISA message. You may have just added an EISA card and failed to configure it properly, you may have accidentally unplugged your CMOS battery, or the battery is low. If the battery is bad or low, replace it. In any case, you must run your EISA configuration utility.

CONVERT DIRECTORY TO FILE?

Tell CHKDSKN for "no" or you will lose the whole directory. Use a disk utility program such as Norton Utilities or PC Tools DISKFIX to save the directory and its file.

CONVERT DIRECTORY TO FILE (Y/N)?

If CHKDSK finds lost chains when inspecting your disk, it will ask this question. Lost chains are collections of data clusters that are not attached to any known file. These lost chains are rarely significant. They are usually leftovers from some mass file deletions. It's generally better to run CHKDSK with the /F option. Then the program will correct the errors as it checks your disk. If you think the data in the lost chains might be important, you can use PC Tools or Norton's Disk Doctor instead, as they are more careful than CHKDSK.

D: DRIVE ERROR

Your second physical hard disk, regardless of letter designations, is improperly set up in CMOS. Access the CMOS Setup and correct this problem.

D: DRIVE FAILURE
DATA ERROR READING DRIVE X

This is generally caused by an older hard disk getting very slightly out of alignment. Use a hard disk utility program (such as PCTools'

DISKFIX, SpinRite II, Norton's Disk Doctor, QA/WIN, or QA Plus) to get the files reoriented. This is not a serious problem so long as you do the housecleaning before some data gets lost.

DECREASING AVAILABLE MEMORY

This message usually appears with other messages indicating that there is a memory error or an error in the CMOS Setup. Check the other message on the screen.

DISK BAD

Some part of the hard disk system isn't responding properly. Turn the computer off and remove the case. Check all the cables and power connections and attempt to reboot. Listen carefully during the boot cycle and see if you can hear the hard disk spinning. If you aren't sure, you can put a finger on the case to see if you can feel the vibration. You can even try unplugging the power connector from the disk and plugging it back in to make sure if it is spinning or not (currently, hard disks have a fairly noisy spin and it's pretty easy to tell). If it is spinning, check out the controller. You may have to replace the hard disk and /or the controller.

DISK BOOT ERROR, REPLACE AND STRIKE KEY TO RETRY

You probably left a disk in one of the drives. If a non-bootable disk is in the A: drive, you will get this message. If there isn't a floppy disk in any of the bays, get out your Dark and Stormy Night Disk and reboot. Check to see if your DOS system files are where they are supposed to be. If they appear to be there, use a disk utility program (such as PCTools' DISKFIX, SpinRite II, Norton's Disk Doctor, QA/WIN, or QA Plus) to check the files in the DOS directory. Reload DOS if any are damaged.

DISK CONFIGURATION ERROR

Your CMOS Setup is incorrect. Enter the CMOS Setup utility and use the information on your system inventory sheet to check the settings.

On older machines that use a Setup program on a floppy disk to work with CMOS, this error may indicate that you are using a Setup disk that is newer than your BIOS ROM. Either get the proper Setup disk or upgrade your ROM.

DISK DRIVE 0 SEEK FAILURE

Turn off the computer, remove the case and check the A: drive cables first. Then check your CMOS Setup to make sure that all your drives are listed correctly and that you haven't removed a drive and forgotten to tell CMOS.

On XT machines, this message may be due to a bad or unformatted disk.

DISK DRIVE 1 SEEK FAILURE

Turn off the computer, remove the case and check the B: drive cables first. Then check your CMOS Setup to make sure that all your drives are listed correctly and that you haven't removed a drive and forgotten to tell CMOS.

DISK DRIVE RESET FAILED

Your disk controller card is bad.

DISK ERROR READING (OR WRITING) DRIVE X

This is generally caused by an older hard disk getting very slightly out of alignment. Use a hard disk utility program (such as PCTools' DISKFIX, SpinRite II, Norton's Disk Doctor, QA/WIN, or QA Plus) to get the files reoriented. This is not a serious problem so long as you do the housecleaning before some data gets lost.

DISK ERROR READING (OR WRITING) FAT

You have a bad sector on your FAT table. Luckily, DOS keeps two FAT tables and it will just go to using the backup copy. However, if something happens now, there isn't any backup. If it's a floppy disk, transfer all the files to another disk and throw the first one away. If it is a hard disk, run PCTools' DISKFIX or SpinRite II on the drive.

DISK BOOT FAILURE

The boot disk in drive A: is probably bad. Try booting from another disk. If you have recently been working inside the computer, turn it off, take off the case, and check all the cables and connections. If that isn't it, you may have to replace the controller or the disk in question.

DISK DRIVE FAILURE OR DISKETTE DRIVE X FAILURE
DISK DRIVE 0 SEEK FAILURE

Turn off the computer, remove the case and check the A drive cables first. Then check your CMOS Setup to make sure that all your drives are listed correctly and that you haven't removed a drive and forgotten to tell CMOS.

On XT machines, this message may be due to a bad or unformatted disk.

NOTE

DISKETTE READ FAILURE

The boot disk in drive A: is probably bad. Try booting from another disk. If you have recently been working inside the computer, turn it off, take off the case, and check all the cables and connections. If that isn't it, you may have to replace the controller or the disk in question.

DISK READ FAILURE—STRIKE F1 TO RETRY BOOT

The boot disk in drive A: is probably bad. Try booting from another disk. If you have recently been working inside the computer, turn it off, take off the case, and check all the cables and connections. If that isn't it, you may have to replace the controller or the disk in question.

DISPLAY ADAPTER FAILED; USING ALTERNATE

The mono/color jumper on the motherboard has been improperly set. Use your owner's manual to reset this jumper properly.

DISPLAY SWITCH NOT SET PROPERLY

The mono/color jumper on the motherboard has been improperly set. Use your owner's manual to reset this jumper properly.

DIVIDED OVERFLOW

Reboot your computer. If one application gives you this message more than once or twice, contact technical support for that software.

DMA ERROR OR DMA 1 ERROR OR DMA 2 ERROR

The DMA chip has failed. You will probably have to replace the motherboard.

(.) (..) DOES NOT EXIST

Your current directory—(.)—or the parent directory—(..)—is messed up. Run an appropriate disk utility like SpinRite II or PCTools' DISKFIX. This should correct the problem. It may be an early warning of hard disk problems; back up all your data and run disk diagnostic/repair utilities.

DRIVE NOT READY ABORT, RETRY, IGNORE, FAIL?

OR

DRIVE X NOT READY. MAKE SURE A DISK IS INSERTED INTO THE DRIVE AND THE DOOR IS CLOSED

If this is a floppy drive, make sure that there is a disk in the drive, that the disk is right-side up and that the door or latch is closed. If the disk works in another drive, turn the machine off, remove the case, and check the cables and power connections to the disk drive. If the floppy won't work in any drive, use Norton Disk Doctor or PCTools' DISKFIX to repair the disk.

NOTE
If you have a SCSI or ESDI controller, it may be having trouble communicating with the motherboard, usually from timing incompatibilities. Try pressing **R**(etry). Usually this will get things going again, although you'll likely see the message from time to time. If **R**(etry) doesn't work, boot from your Dark and Stormy Night Disk and run an appropriate utility to test the hard drive.

EISA CMOS CHECKSUM FAILURE

OR

EISA CMOS INOPERATIONAL

Either the Checksum for your EISA CMOS showed that data was corrupted or there's a read/write error in the CMOS. A low battery is the likeliest culprit. Run the Setup program and replace the batteries.

(.) (..) ENTRY HAS A BAD ATTRIBUTE (OR LINK OR SIZE)

The current directory or the parent directory can't be accessed. Run SpinRite II or PCTools' DISKFIX to correct the problem. This can be an early warning of upcoming hard disk problems.

ERROR READING/WRITING THE PARTITION TABLE

Hopefully, you'll only get this message if you've just run FDISK. It means that you did the low-level format improperly. Run FDISK again, referring to the instructions in Chapter 9. If FDISK was run correctly, you have a bad hard disk. If you have not run FDISK on the hard drive in question, you could have a virus. Run your virus checker and follow the instructions in the owner's manual to fix the situation (it is just barely possible that a malfunctioning controller is causing this message. Try putting in another controller).

ERRORS FOUND; DISK X FAILED INITIALIZATION

Some part of the hard disk system isn't responding properly. Turn the computer off and remove the case. Check all the cables and power connections and attempt to reboot. Check to be sure the ribbon cables are connected properly. Double-check the Drive Select jumper on the hard disk. Substitute a controller card you know is working. You may have to replace the hard disk and/or the controller.

ERRORS FOUND, F PARAMETER NOT SPECIFIED. CORRECTIONS WILL NOT BE WRITTEN TO DISK

If CHKDSK finds lost chains when inspecting your disk, it will give this message. *Lost chains* are collections of data clusters that are not attached to any known file. These lost chains are rarely significant. They are usually leftovers from some mass file deletions. It's generally better to run CHKDSK with the /F option. Then the program will correct the errors as it checks your disk. If you think the data in the lost chains might be important, you can use PCTools or Norton's Disk Doctor instead, as they are more careful than CHKDSK.

ERRORS FOUND; INCORRECT CONFIGURATION INFORMATION MEMORY
SIZE MISCOMPARE

Probably CMOS has forgotten your Setup. Run Setup and reconfigure, using the information on your system inventory sheet. Try booting again. If this fails, turn off the computer, remove the case and gently press the memory chips down to be sure they are properly seated. Try rebooting. If it still won't boot, you can carefully remove the chips, take them to your computer store for testing and replace any that are bad. Other possibilities include a bad power supply or, rarely, a bad motherboard.

ERRORS ON LIST DEVICE INDICATE THAT IT MAY BE OFF-LINE.
PLEASE CHECK IT

The printer isn't responding. Make sure it is turned on, and properly plugged into the wall socket and the printer. Check the cable from the computer to the printer. If this doesn't solve the problem, turn the machine off, remove the case, and check the leads from the I/O card to the port sockets. If this doesn't help, you probably have a bad port, cable, or I/O card.

ERROR WRITING FAT

You have a bad sector on your FAT table. Luckily, DOS keeps two FAT tables and it will just go to using the backup copy. However, if something happens now, there isn't any backup. If it's a floppy disk, transfer all the files to another disk and throw the first one away. If it is a hard disk, run PCTools' DISKFIX or SpinRite II on the drive.

NNK EXPANDED MEMORY

An informational message telling you that you have NNNK of expanded memory.

EXPANSION BOARD DISABLED AT SLOT X

An informational message on EISA machines that slot X has been disabled in the configuration.

EXPANSION BOARD NMI AT SLOT X

You have real trouble with the adapter in the designated slot. Take the card out and check it over. You may have to call the manufacturer of the board for technical support.

EXPANSION BOARD NOT READY AT SLOT X

In EISA machines this tells you that you configured it for an adapter in the designated slot, but it cannot find the board. Turn off the machine, remove the cover, and check carefully to make sure that the board is properly seated.

NNN EXTENDED MEMORY

An informational message telling you that you have NNNK of extended memory.

EXTENDED MEMORY SIZE=NNNNNK

An informational message telling you that you have NNNK of extended memory.

FAIL-SAFE TIMER NMI

In EISA machines this indicates that some device is hogging the bus. This may be just a glitch; try rebooting. If you still get this error, turn off the computer, remove the case, and remove the adapter card you most recently installed or the most high-tech card you have. If that doesn't help, remove another card. Continue this until you find the offender. You'll have to substitute video adapters and controllers you know are good if this testing doesn't produce results quickly. When you find the offending card, check your owner's manual and the appropriate troubleshooting section in this book. Then call technical support for that card. If you are unable to identify a bad card, it's probably the motherboard.

FAIL-SAFE TIMER NMI INOPERATIONAL

The timer on your EISA board has failed and you will have to replace the motherboard.

FDD CONTROLLER FAILURE

This usually means that your floppy drive and/or controller are bad. However, you should first turn off the computer, remove the case, and check on all disk cabling. Be sure that all ribbon cables have the side with the red or blue stripe going to Pin 1. Also check to see that the controller is properly seated in the slot.

FDD A IS NOT INSTALLED
FDD B IS NOT INSTALLED

The computer can't find your floppy disk controller. Turn off the computer, remove the case, and check on all disk cabling. Be sure that all ribbon cables have the side with the red or blue stripe going to Pin 1. Also check to see that the controller is properly seated in the slot.

FILE ALLOCATION TABLE BAD

OR

FILE ALLOCATION TABLE BAD DRIVE X

There is a problem with your FAT table. Run Norton Disk Doctor or PCTools' DISKFIX to attempt to save your data.

FIRST CLUSTER NUMBER IS INVALID, ENTRY TRUNCATED

CHKDSK has, in effect, deleted your file. It is only a name in the directory. Run your hard disk diagnostic and repair utility and resolve to do your disk housekeeping more regularly. This file is probably lost for good.

FIXED DISK CONFIGURATION ERROR

There's something wrong in the CMOS Setup. Check your Setup information using information from your inventory. Some old machines can't recognize all the newer types of disks—and remember that some older machines need a separate Setup disk. You must use the original disk, as later versions will store information your computer can't use.

```
FIXED DISK CONTROLLER FAILURE
FIXED DISK FAILURE
FIXED DISK READ FAILURE
```

If you have just been working inside your computer, turn it off and check out the cables, controller, etc. If you haven't been inside the case, press **F1** to try a reboot. If this works, run your disk utilities to check our your hard drive just in case. If this doesn't work, get out your Dark and Stormy Night Disk and boot from it. When the machine is up, change to your hard drive and see if you can see the directories. Run the CMOS Setup to see that everything is set correctly. If it still won't boot, you may have to reformat the drive (that's why FORMAT.COM and FDISK.EXE are on your DSND). If you've kept backups, it will probably just be a bit time-consuming. If nothing can find your hard disk, you can try calling technical support to see if you have some strange conflict. And last of all, you may have to replace your hard drive or the hard drive controller.

There are methods of recovering data from an inoperative hard drive, at least under many circumstances. If you are not backed up, you may want to consider this. Usually this job is done by a specialist. Check for names and addresses in your favorite computer magazine.

NOTE

```
GATE A20 FAILURE
```

AT clones only: the computer failed to switch into protected mode. Check to see that your keyboard switch is set properly. Also can be a bad motherboard.

```
GENERAL FAILURE READING (OR WRITING) DRIVE X: (A)BORT,
(R)ETRY, (I)IGNORE?
```

Press **I**. If drive now works, run a diagnostic check on it (however, SCSI disks will sometimes send this message on a regular basis when nothing is actually wrong). If drive **I** does not work, press A:.

If it is a floppy drive, first try another disk. Check out the drive cables and controller.

HARD DISK CONFIGURATION ERROR

There's something wrong in the CMOS Setup. Check your Setup information using information from your inventory. Some old machines can't recognize all the newer types of disks—and remember that some older machines need a separate Setup disk. You must use the original disk, as later versions will store information your computer can't use.

HARD DISK FAILURE

If you have just been working inside your computer, turn it off and check out the cables, controller, etc. If you haven't been inside the case, press **F1** to try a reboot. If this works, run your disk utilities to check our your hard drive just in case. If this doesn't work, get out your Dark and Stormy Night Disk and boot from it. When the machine is up, change to your hard drive and see if you can see the directories. Run the CMOS Setup to see that everything is set correctly. If it still won't boot, you may have to reformat the drive (that's why FORMAT.COM and FDISK.EXE are on your DSND). If you've kept backups, it will probably just be a bit time-consuming. If nothing can find your hard disk, you can try calling technical support to see if you have some strange conflict. And last of all, you may have to replace your hard drive or the hard drive controller.

NOTE

There are methods of recovering data from an inoperative hard drive, at least under many circumstances. If you are not backed up, you may want to consider this. Usually this job is done by a specialist. Check for names and addresses in your favorite computer magazine.

HAS INVALID CLUSTER, FILE TRUNCATED

CHKDSK has found a bad (or nonexistent) cluster and erased it. Run PCTools' DISKFIX or Norton's Disk Doctor to put your hard disk in better order.

This can happen occasionally, but if it happens more than once in six or so months, your hard disk is acting up. Back everything up and use a diagnostic/repair utility.

NOTE

ID INFORMATION MISMATCH FOR SLOT N

Your EISA has lost the configuration (or you added an expansion card and didn't reconfigure). Run the CF utility. If this keeps happening when you haven't been working in the machine, you may need to replace your backup batteries.

INFINITE RETRY ON PARALLEL PRINTER TIMEOUT

Your printer isn't responding; check to see that it is plugged in, turned on, and that the cable is firmly connected at both ends.

INSUFFICIENT MEMORY

This is a software error. Windows users are familiar with it. Tune up your memory management, close some applications or TSRs (*Terminate and Stay Resident*, programs that hide until you call them up with a special key combination).

INTERNAL CACHE TEST FAILED—CACHE IS DISABLED

Reboot your computer. If you get the message again, use a utility to test your CPU. It may have failed.

INTERNAL ERROR

This is a software message; check your DOS manual.

INTERNAL STACK OVERFLOW

This is generally a software error; check your DOS manual. If the error continues, run a check on your conventional memory.

```
INTR1 ERROR
INTR2 ERROR
```

The interrupt controller logic has failed. Replace the motherboard.

```
INVALID BOOT DISKETTE
```

The computer can't boot from the floppy drive. Did you leave a disk in the drive? If so, take it out and reboot the computer. If not, try using your Dark and Stormy Night disk. If possible, test your disk in another computer. If it is not the disk, it could be a bad floppy drive or a bad controller. If you have had some error messages earlier on this particular drive, it's probably bad.

```
INVALID CONFIGURATION INFORMATION. PLEASE RUN SETUP PROGRAM
```

(If there are other error messages up at the same time as this one, deal with them first.) Run your CMOS Setup and make sure that you've got everything set up exactly right, using the information on your inventory sheet. If this occurs again after you've had the computer turned off, replace the backup batteries and see if that takes care of things. Another possibility is that your power supply is going bad. Very rarely the CMOS chip is bad; if it is, replace it or the motherboard.

```
INVALID CONFIGURATION INFORMATION FOR SLOT X
INVALID EISA CONFIGURATION STORAGE. PLEASE RUN THE
CONFIGURATION UTILITY
```

Run your EISA configuration utility and check your Setup. You may need to replace your backup batteries.

```
I/O CARD PARITY ERROR AT XXX(R)
```

OR

```
I/O CARD PARITY INTERRUPT AT XXX.XXX
TYPE (S)HUT OFF NMI, (R)EBOOT, OTHER KEYS TO CONTINUE
```

OR

```
I/O CARD PARITY INTERRUPT AT XXX.XXX
TYPE (S)HUT OFF NMI, (R)EBOOT, OTHER KEYS TO CONTINUE
```

Use the (S) alternative if you need to save a file. You have a bad expansion card. Test by either taking out all the cards except the video adapter and the disk controller and replacing one by one, or take them out one at a time (Be sure you turn off and unplug the machine EACH time). If you are still getting the message, try to test with another video adapter, and then with another disk controller. Replace or fix the bad card. If you absolutely can't find a bad card, it may be the motherboard.

```
KEYBOARD BAD
```

The keyboard failed the Power-On-Self-Test. Turn the computer off and check to see that the cables are properly connected at both ends. If your keyboard has the AT switch, check to be sure it's in the right position. Try another keyboard cable. If none of these work, the keyboard is bad and must be replaced.

```
KEYBOARD CLOCK LINE FAILURE
```

OR

```
KEYBOARD DATA LINE FAILURE
```

OR

```
KEYBOARD CONTROLLER FAILURE
```

OR

```
KEYBOARD STUCK KEY FAILURE
```

The keyboard is not responding properly to the Power-On-Self-Test. Turn the computer off and check to see that the cables are properly connected at both ends. If your keyboard has the AT switch, check to be sure it's in the right position. If this doesn't work, the keyboard is bad and must be replaced.

KEYBOARD ERROR

If you have American MegaTrends, Inc. AMI BIOS, your keyboard may be incompatible. Check your documentation. You can set the keyboard to Not Installed in your CMOS Setup and see what happens.

LAST BOOT INCOMPLETE

Caused by a malfunctioning chip in the Intel 82335 chip set used in some ATs. Run the Setup program and watch the memory and EMS configuration parameters.

X LOST CLUSTER(S) FOUND IN Y CHAINS
CONVERT LOST CHAINS TO FILES (Y/N)

If CHKDSK finds lost chains when inspecting your disk, it will ask this question. Lost chains are collections of data clusters that are not attached to any known file. These lost chains are rarely significant. They are usually leftovers from some mass file deletions. If you want to check the data, answer "Y" and examine the files CHKDSK then creates with an ASCII text editor; if not, answer "N" and the data will be lost. It's generally better to run CHKDSK with the /F option. Then the program will correct the errors as it checks your disk. If you think the data in the lost chains might be important, you can use PCTools or Norton's Disk Doctor instead, as they are more careful than CHKDSK.

MEMORY ADDRESS LINE FAILURE AT XXX.XXX, READ HEX VALUE XXX, EXPECTING XXX

Despite the explicitness of the message, there's nothing to do but replace the motherboard.

MEMORY ALLOCATION ERROR. CANNOT LOAD DOS, SYSTEM HALTED.

This is a software error, check your DOS manual. Your boot directory may be damaged. Boot from your Dark and Stormy Night disk and run SYS to copy the DOS hidden files and COMMAND.COM to your hard disk.

```
MEMORY DATA LINE FAILURE AT XXXX.XXXX, READ XXXX, EXPECTING XXXX
```

OR

```
MEMORY FAILURE AT XXXX.XXXX, READ XXXX, EXPECTING XXXX
```

This is caused by a bad or slow memory chip. The first hexadecimal number tells you which row contains the bad chip(s). You can have the memory tested and replace any bad chips. You can also run your diagnostic utilities and see what the problem is.

```
MEMORY HIGH ADDRESS FAILURE AT XXXX.XXXX, READ XXXX,
EXPECTING XXXX
```

The motherboard is bad and must be replaced.

```
MEMORY DOUBLE WORD LOGIC FAILURE AT (HEX VALUE), READ (HEX
VALUE), EXPECTING (HEX VALUE)
```

This is caused by a bad or slow memory chip. The first hexadecimal number tells you which row contains the bad chip(s). You can have the memory tested and replace any bad chips. You can also run your diagnostic utilities and see what the problem is.

```
MEMORY ODD/EVEN LOGIC FAILURE AT (HEX VALUE), READ (HEX
VALUE), EXPECTING (HEX VALUE)
```

The motherboard is bad and must be replaced.

```
MEMORY PARITY ERROR AT (HEX VALUE)
```

There is a bad memory chip, either data storage memory, or a memory chip dedicated to parity checking. You can have the memory tested and replace any bad chips. You can also run your diagnostic utilities and see what the problem is.

```
MEMORY PARITY NMI AT XXX.XXX; TYPE (S)HUT OFF NMI, (R)EBOOT,
OTHER KEYS TO CONTINUE
```

OR

```
MEMORY PARITY INTERRUPT AT XXX.XXX; TYPE (S)HUT OFF NMI,
(R)EBOOT, OTHER KEYS TO CONTINUE
```

Usually caused by a bad memory chip. Use the S option if you need to save a file. You can have the memory tested and replace any bad chips. You can also run your diagnostic utilities and see what the problem is. If no chip tests bad, it could be your disk controller or power supply.

```
MEMORY TESTS TERMINATED BY KEYSTROKE
```

On many machines you can stop the memory test by hitting the space bar. This merely reports that you have done this, and goes on booting up.

```
MEMORY WRITE/READ FAILURE AT (HEX VALUE), READ (HEX VALUE),
EXPECTING (HEX VALUE)
```

There is a bad memory chip. You can have the memory tested and replace any bad chips. You can also run your diagnostic utilities and see what the problem is.

```
NO BOOT DEVICE AVAILABLE—STRIKE F1 TO RETRY BOOT
```

First check your floppy drive; did you leave a disk in there? If so, take it out and try again. If you have been working inside the case, turn the computer off, disconnect the power, and check all your cables and power connections. Try again. If it still can't boot off the hard drive, boot from your Dark and Stormy Night disk.

If you have not been working on the machine, press **F1** to try booting again.

In any case, if it does boot, use your favorite utilities to check out the hard drive so as to catch any problem before it gets worse. Also check out your boot files and use SYS to copy the hidden files and COMMAND.COM from your DSND to your hard drive.

If the computer can't see your hard drive at all, check out your CMOS Setup to see that everything is set the way it should be. If it still won't boot, you may have to reformat the drive (that's why FORMAT.COM and FDISK.EXE are on your DSND). If you've kept

backups, it will probably just be a bit time-consuming. If nothing
can find your hard disk, you can try calling technical support to see
if you have some strange conflict. And last of all, you may have to
replace your hard drive or your hard disk controller.

There are methods of recovering data from an inoperative hard drive, at least
under many circumstances. If you are not backed up, you may want to consider this. Usually this job is done by a specialist. Check for names and addresses in
your favorite computer magazine.

NOTE

NO FAIL SAFE TIMER NMI

The fail-safe timer on your EISA motherboard has failed. Run your
favorite utility to check it out; if it has, you'll have to replace the
motherboard.

NO SCAN CODE FROM THE KEYBOARD

This occurs only on XT clones. Check out cable connections and the
AT switch on the keyboard. Try another keyboard cable, or another
keyboard.

NO SOFTWARE PORT NMI

Run QAPlus or QA/Win or your favorite utility to check this out. If it
is true, you'll have to replace the motherboard.

NON-DOS DISK ERROR READING (OR WRITING) DRIVE X

The boot track on the indicated disk is dead. If it's your hard drive,
boot from your Dark and Stormy Night disk and see if you can run
SpinRite II, PCTools' DISKFIX or Norton's Disk Doctor and fix it. It's
unlikely that you can, but it's worth a try.

NON-SYSTEM DISK OR DISK ERROR. REPLACE AND STRIKE ANY KEY
WHEN READY

Did you forget a disk in the floppy drive? Remove it and try again. If
it won't boot, the DOS boot files on your hard disk may have been
damaged. Boot using your Dark and Stormy Night disk and run SYS

to transfer the hidden DOS files and COMMAND.COM to your hard drive. Then check out the hard drive with your favorite utility.

NO TIME TICK INTERRUPT

The timer chip can't get the Interrupt controller to send it the 0 Interrupt. You'll have to replace the motherboard.

NOT A BOOT DISK—STRIKE F1 TO RETRY BOOT

Did you forget a disk in the floppy drive? Remove it and try again. If it won't boot, the DOS boot files on your hard disk may have been damaged. Boot using your Dark and Stormy Night disk and run SYS to transfer the hidden DOS files and COMMAND.COM to your hard drive. Then check out the hard drive with your favorite utility.

If you can't boot from the floppy drive, it can be a bad drive or a bad controller.

NOT ENOUGH MEMORY

This is a software message. Check your DOS manual and work on your memory management.

NOT READY READING DRIVE X

OR

NOT READY ERROR READING (OR WRITING) DRIVE X

Usually this happens when you've changed to a drive and the door is not closed (or latched). Check it out. If this doesn't work, try several different disks. You may have a bad drive or the closed-door sensor in the drive may be bad. In older versions of DOS, you sometimes got this message if the printer was off-line.

(HEX VALUE) OPTIONAL ROM BAD CHECKSUM = (HEX VALUE)

The ROM on an expansion card is bad. Check your inventory to see what card is supposed to be at that location. Turn the computer off and take that card out. Try rebooting. You may have to test the other cards anyway. When you determine the offending device, install a new expansion card.

OUT OF ENVIRONMENT SPACE

This is a software error. Check your DOS manual.

PARITY CHECK 1

Many expansion cards these days have memory, and one of them just failed the test. Test by either taking out all the cards except the video adapter and the disk controller and replacing one by one—or take them out one at a time. (Be sure you turn off and unplug the machine EACH time.) If you are still getting the message, try to test with another video adapter, and then with another disk controller. Replace or fix the bad card.

PARITY CHECK 2

You'll only get this from an XT clone. There is a bad memory chip. You can have the memory tested and replace any bad chips. You can also run your diagnostic utilities and see what the problem is.

POINTER DEVICE FAILURE

If you have a PS/2-style mouse port, this has failed. Turn the machine off and check to see that the mouse if properly connected. If this does not work, see if you received a testing utility with your mouse (or other pointing device) and run it.

PRINTER ERROR

Is the printer plugged in? Turned on? Are the cables properly connected? Try turning the PC and the printer off and on a time or two to completely reset everything. Try another printer cable. This could also be a software message—check your application manual.

PROBABLY NON-DOS DISK. CONTINUE (Y/N)

DOS cannot recognize this disk. It may have been formatted by another operating system. If it is your hard drive, thunderstorms sometimes write gibberish on hard drives. Using your Dark and

Stormy Night disk (if necessary), boot and use SpinRite II, PCTools' DISKFIX, or Norton's Disk Doctor to see if you can recover the data. You may have to reformat the disk. Use your virus checker to make sure that nothing has infected your boot sectors.

PROCESSING CANNOT CONTINUE

Occurs if you try to run CHKDSK without sufficient memory. More memory must be added in order to run the utility.

RAM BAD

You'll need to test your RAM memory chips and replace the bad ones. If there are no bad chips, the motherboard is bad.

RAM BUS TIMEOUT

The BIOS provided by American Megatrends, Inc. displays this message when a reply to a signal has been delayed. This is frequently just a glitch, so try rebooting. If you get this message, it's probably a DMA conflict. Turn off the computer, remove the case and remove the adapter card you most recently installed, or the most high-tech card you have. If that doesn't help, remove another card. Continue this until you find the offender. You'll have to substitute video adapters and controllers you know are good if this testing doesn't produce results quickly. When you find the offending card, check your owner's manual and the appropriate troubleshooting section in this book. Then call technical support for that card. If you are unable to identify a bad card, it's probably the motherboard.

READ FAULT ERROR READING DRIVE X

If this is a floppy drive, check to see that the disk is in the drive right, not upside down, and that the door (or latch) is closed. If you still have the error run SpinRite II, PCTools' DISKFIX, or Norton's Disk Doctor to see if you can recover the data. You may have to reformat the disk. Use your virus checker to make sure that nothing has infected your boot sectors.

```
REAL TIME CLOCK FAILURE
```

Either the clock or the battery has failed. Run the Setup program and check your CMOS settings. Replace the backup batteries. If this is not the case, your power supply may be failing. Very occasionally it's a problem with the motherboard.

```
RESUME—F1 KEY
```

An error has occurred. Press **F1**.

```
ROM
ROM BAD SUM =
ROM BAD CHECKSUM =
```

If you have an XT, the system ROM BIOS is bad.

```
ROM ERROR
```

Your BIOS ROM is dead and gone. Replace it. It's possible the whole motherboard is bad.

```
XX = SCANCODE, CHECK KEYBOARD
```

The computer is receiving bad messages from your keyboard. Check the connections and make sure there isn't a key sticking. Check the AT switch to make sure it's correctly set. Try another keyboard or another cable.

```
SECTOR NOT FOUND ERROR READING (OR WRITING) DRIVE X
```

OR

```
SEEK ERROR READING (OR WRITING) DRIVE X
```

If this is a floppy drive, check to see that the disk is in the drive right, not upside down, and that the door (or latch) is closed. If you still have the error run SpinRite II, PCTools' DISKFIX, or Norton's Disk Doctor to see if you can recover the data. You may have to reformat the disk. Use your virus checker to make sure that nothing has infected your boot sectors.

SHARING VIOLATION READING DRIVE X

This is a software error. Check your DOS manual.

SHUTDOWN FAILURE

Applies to XT clones only. The computer failed to switch into protected mode. Check the keyboard, particularly the AT switch. You may need a new motherboard (or a newer, bigger, computer).

NNK STANDARD MEMORY

A report on your working standard memory.

STRIKE THE F1 KEY TO CONTINUE

An error was detected in the Power-On-Self-Test. Check for the error message and fix whatever was wrong. You can press **F1** to go on and try to boot, particularly if you were booting from a floppy drive.

KEYBOARD ERROR

OR

STUCK KEY SCANCODE = XX

A key is stuck on your keyboard. If you can't find the key at once, try pressing them one after another until you identify it.

TARGET DISK IS WRITE PROTECTED

You were trying to write on a disk with the write-protect window covered. If you really do want to write to that disk, remove the write-protect tape, move the slide on a 3.5" disk (or put a piece of write-protect tape over the unfunctional right-side hole). It is possible that the sensor in the drive is bad and "sees" all disks as write-protected.

```
TIMER OR INTERRUPT CONTROLLER BAD
```

OR

```
TIMER CHIP COUNTER 2 FAILED
```

Either the timer chip or the Interrupt controller has failed. Replace your motherboard.

```
TIMER-OF-DAY CLOCK STOPPED
```

OR

```
TIME-OF-DAY NOT SET UP—PLEASE RUN SETUP PROGRAM
```

Either the clock or the battery has failed. Run the Setup program and check your CMOS settings. Replace the backup batteries. If this is not the cause, your power supply may be failing. Very occasionally it's a problem with the motherboard.

```
TIMER CHIP COUNTER 2 FAILED
TIMER OR INTERRUPT CONTROLLER BAD
```

The timer (or Interrupt controller) chip is bad, you'll have to replace the motherboard.

```
TRACK 0 BAD—DISK UNUSABLE
```

If you are trying to format a 1.2Mb floppy in a 360K drive (or the other way around) you can get this message. The disk also may be bad (throw it away if it's a floppy). If you get this message on your hard drive, you'll have to do the same thing as with a floppy—throw it away and put in a new one.

```
UNEXPECTED HW INTERRUPT AT XXH AT XXXX.XXXX. TYPE (S)HUT OFF
NMI, (R)EBOOT, OTHER KEYS TO CONTINUE
```

OR

```
UNEXPECTED SW INTERRUPT AT XXH AT XXXX.XXXX. TYPE (S)HUT OFF
NMI, (R)EBOOT, OTHER KEYS TO CONTINUE
```

The system BIOS has detected an error. Check out your device drivers first as this frequently turns out to be a software problem. What the computer means by the message is that it's getting an Interrupt where it doesn't expect it. Check your inventory list for the most likely culprit.

```
UNEXPECTED INTERRUPT IN PROTECTED MODE
```

This can be caused by a bad expansion card or a bad motherboard. Check your expansion cards first. Test by either taking out all the cards except the video adapter and the disk controller and replacing one by one—or take them out one at a time. (Be sure you turn off and unplug the machine EACH time.) If you are still getting the message, try to test with another video adapter, and then with another disk controller. Replace or fix the bad card. It is possible that it is a bad motherboard.

```
UNLOCK SYSTEM UNIT KEYLOCK
```

Either the key has been turned in the lock or the jumper wires have accidentally been disconnected from the lock or the motherboard. (Have you installed something new that took you inside the case?) This error may also occur if there is a key stuck in the on position or if the switch in the lock is faulty. Check all of these possibilities.

```
UNRECOVERABLE ERROR IN DIRECTORY. CONVERT DIRECTORY TO
FILE (Y/N)
```

Press **N** to avoid losing everything. Run SpinRite II, PCTools' DISK-FIX, or Norton's Disk Doctor to see if you can recover the data. Use your virus checker to make sure that nothing has infected your disk.

```
UNRECOVERABLE READ (OR WRITE) ERROR ON DRIVE X
```

If this is a floppy drive, check to see that the disk is in the drive correctly, right side up and that the door or latch is closed. If that doesn't fix it, run SpinRite II, PCTools' DISKFIX, or Norton's Disk Doctor to see if you can recover the data. Use your virus checker to make sure that nothing has infected your disk.

WRITE FAULT ERROR WRITING DRIVE X

If it's a floppy drive, check to see that the door is properly closed or the latch is in the closed position. It is possible that the drive sensor is bad, and it can't tell that the door is closed (or the drive may be bad). It is possible that DOS is sending this message because your printer is off-line.

WRITE PROTECT ERROR WRITING DRIVE X

You were trying to write on a disk with the write-protect window covered. If you really do want to write to that disk, remove the write-protect tape, move the slide on a 3.5" disk (or put a piece of write-protect tape over the unfunctional right-side hole). It is possible that the sensor in the drive is bad and "sees" all disks as write-protected.

APPENDIX F

BEEP ERROR CODES

Industry Standard Architecture (ISA) 286/386/486-bus computers and Extended Industry Standard Architecture (EISA) computers use beep codes for errors that are so severe that they prevent video display. Each BIOS ROM manufacturer is free to build into the BIOS ROM chip on the motherboard whatever beep codes they wish. Listed here are beep codes for the American Megatrends, Inc. BIOS, and for the Phoenix BIOS since they produce the chips most computers use. American Megatrends, Inc. BIOS (AMIBIOS) use a series of long beeps to signal fatal errors and those beep codes are also listed.

Most computers beep once when booted, but yours may usually beep several times and still boot fine. If the video display comes up, you shouldn't try to look up the beep codes. If there's an error, either the numerical or text designations will appear on your screen and you can look them up in Appendix D or E. If you do get a series of beeps and no video, you'll probably have to boot the machine again to determine the code it is sending. If you have an American Megatrends BIOS, you will get a single series of one to eleven beeps. For a Phoenix BIOS, the beeps will come in sets of one to four beeps, each set separated by a pause.

AMERICAN MEGATRENDS, INC. BIOS ROM BEEP CODES

One Beep: Refresh Failure

There is faulty memory refresh circuitry on your motherboard. This can be caused by bad memory chips, a bad DMA chip, or bad memory-addressing chips on the motherboard. You can turn the system off and check to be sure that all memory chips and SIMM strips are properly seated.

NOTE

Remember, many, if not all, PCs will beep once or twice during a normal boot.

Two Beeps: Parity Error

For some reason the RAM isn't responding to the CPU. You can turn the system off and check to be sure that all memory chips and SIMM strips are properly seated.

Three Beeps: Base 64K Memory Failure

Can be caused by either bad memory chips or a bad motherboard. You can turn the system off and check to be sure that all memory chips and SIMM strips are properly seated. On some motherboards, you can try swapping the high and low memory chips.

Four Beeps: Timer Not Operational

Memory failure in the first 64K of RAM or a malfunctioning timer 1. You can try replacing the first 64K of memory to see whether it's the chips or the motherboard (if the memory is socketed).

Five Beeps: Processor Error

The CPU is not responding. You could check to see if the CPU is properly seated. If that doesn't fix it, you'll need a new one—or a complete new motherboard.

Six Beeps: 8042—Gate A20 Failure

Either keyboard problems or a bad motherboard cause this message. Try attaching a working keyboard. Or replace the keyboard controller or the fuse in the keyboard if there is one.

Seven Beeps: Processor Exception Interrupt Error

The CPU chip is dead. Check to see that it is properly seated. If that's not it, you'll need a new CPU (usually a whole new motherboard is a better idea, depending on the age of your system, your needs, and your budget).

Eight Beeps: Display Memory Read/Write Error

The video card is bad or missing or its memory is bad. Check to see that it's properly seated. Otherwise, get a new graphics adapter card.

Nine Beeps: ROM Checksum Error

BIOS chip is bad and must be replaced.

Ten Beeps: CMOS Shutdown Register Read/Write Error

When your machine boots, it transfers into protected mode and then back. This error occurs when the machine is unable to transfer back into work mode. You'll have to replace the motherboard.

Eleven Beeps: Cache Memory Bad— Do Not Enable Cache

The test of the cache memory failed and cache memory is disabled. You can try checking to see that the cache memory is properly seated on the motherboard, then replace the cache memory (or the motherboard).

PHOENIX BIOS ROM BEEP CODES

1-1-3: CMOS Write/Read Failure

The computer is unable to read the configuration that should be stored in CMOS. Replace the motherboard.

1-1-4: ROM BIOS Checksum Error

The BIOS ROM has been damaged and you'll have to replace it.

1-2-1: Programmable Interval Timer Failure

There is a bad timer chip on the motherboard and it will have to be replaced.

1-2-2: DMA Initialization Failure
1-2-3 DMA Page Register Write/Read Failure

The DMA chip is bad and you'll have to replace the motherboard. If you are sure the motherboard is good, there is an outside chance that one of your expansion cards is causing this. If you think this might be the case, take out all the cards except the video and controller and try booting. If you can get it to boot, replace the cards one at a time until you identify the culprit. (Remember not to remove or replace cards except when the computer is turned off and unplugged).

1-3-1: RAM Refresh Verification Failure

There is faulty memory refresh circuitry on your motherboard. This can be caused by bad memory chips, a bad DMA chip, or bad memory-addressing chips on the motherboard. You can turn the system off and check to be sure that all memory chips and SIMM strips are properly seated.

1-3-3: First 64K RAM Chip Or Data Line Failure, Multi-Bit

Can be caused by either bad memory chips or a bad motherboard. You can turn the system off and check to be sure that all memory chips and SIMM strips are properly seated. On some motherboards, you can try swapping the high and low memory chips.

1-3-4: First 64K Odd/Even Logic Failure
1-4-1: Address Line Failure First 64K of RAM

You have a bad motherboard and it will have to be replaced.

1-4-2: Parity Failure First 64K of RAM

You have a bad memory chip; it could be either a data-storing chip or one of the dedicated-parity checking chips. You can test the memory chips to try to avoid replacing the motherboard.

1-4-3: Fail-Safe Timer Failure

The fail-safe timer on your EISA motherboard failed; replace the motherboard.

1-4-4: Software NMI Port Failure

This software port allows the EISA software to talk to the EISA expansion cards; replace the motherboard.

2-1-1;
2-1-2; Bit "0" First 64K RAM Failure
2-1-3; Bit "1" First 64K RAM Failure
2-1-4; Bit "2" First 64K RAM Failure
2-2-1; Bit "3" First 64K RAM Failure
2-2-2; Bit "4" First 64K RAM Failure
2-2-3; Bit "5" First 64K RAM Failure
2-2-4: Bit "6" First 64K RAM Failure
2-3-1; Bit "7" First 64K RAM Failure
2-3-2; Bit "8" First 64K RAM Failure
2-3-3; Bit "9" First 64K RAM Failure
2-3-4; Bit "10" First 64K RAM Failure
2-4-1; Bit "12" First 64K RAM Failure
2-4-2; Bit "13" First 64K RAM Failure
2-4-3; Bit "14" First 64K RAM Failure
2-4-4: Bit "15" First 64K RAM Failure

This code tells you that a specific memory chip has failed. It's best to test all memory chips to see if the culprit can be identified and replaced.

3-1-1: Slave DMA Register Failure
3-1-2: Master DMA Register Failure

You have a bad DMA chip and will have to replace the motherboard.

3-2-4: Keyboard Controller Test Failure

The keyboard, cable or controller is bad. You can try attaching a good keyboard. Do check to see that the AT/XT switch is set right (if your keyboard has one).

3-3-4: Screen Initialization Failure

Usually means that there is no graphics adapter in the machine and one will have to be installed.

3-4-1: Screen Retrace Test Failure

The chip on your graphics adapter is failing and the card will have to be replaced.

3-4-2: Screen Retrace Test Failure

Your graphics adapter won't reset the retrace bit within the allotted time. You'll have to replace the card.

4-2-1: Timer Tick Failure

Timer chip can't get the Interrupt controller chip to send Interrupt 0. You have a bad motherboard.

4-2-2: Shutdown Test Failure

Either keyboard problems or a bad motherboard cause this message. Try attaching a working keyboard, or replace the keyboard controller or the fuse in the keyboard if there is one.

4-2-3: Gate A20 Failure

Either Keyboard problems or a bad motherboard cause this message. First check the AT/XT switch on your keyboard (if it has one). Try attaching a working keyboard, or replace the keyboard controller, or the fuse in the keyboard if there is one.

4-2-4: Unexpected Interrupt in Protected Mode

Either a bad expansion card or a bad motherboard causes this error. Take out all the cards except the video and controller and try booting. If it won't boot, replace the video card. If you can get it to boot, replace the cards one at a time until you identify the culprit (Remember not to remove or replace cards except when the computer is turned off and unplugged).

4-3-1: RAM Test Address Failure

Chips responsible for memory address logic have failed; replace motherboard.

4-3-2: Programmable Interval Timer Channel 2 Test Failure

The programmable interval timer is used to refresh memory—you'll have to replace the motherboard.

4-3-3: Interval Timer Channel 2 Failure

Timer chip has failed; you'll have to replace the motherboard.

4-3-4: Time Of Day Clock Failure

Run the computer's Setup program. If that doesn't work, replace batteries and try again. If that doesn't help, it is likely to be a failing power supply, replace it. On rare occasions this does signal a bad motherboard.

4-4-1: Serial Port Test Failure
4-4-2: Parallel Port Test Failure
4-4-3: Math Co-processor Failure

In all three cases, the indicated component has failed and must be replaced.

APPENDIX G

TROUBLESHOOTING FLOW CHARTS

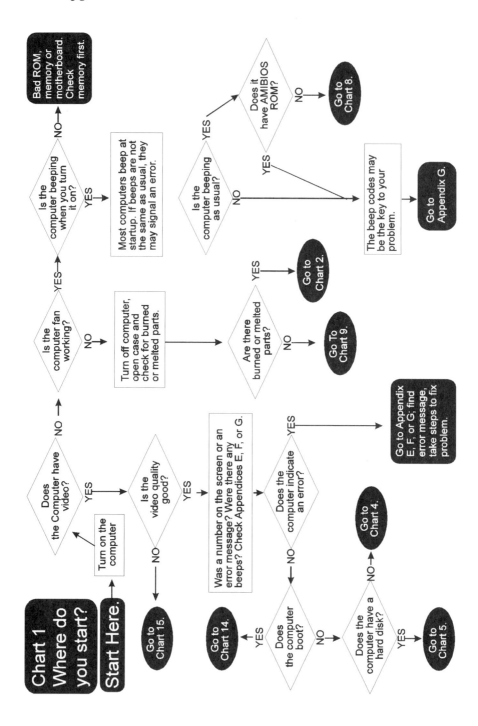

Chart 1
Where do you start?

Start Here.

Turn on the computer

Does the Computer have video?

NO → Is the computer fan working?

NO → Turn off computer, open case and check for burned or melted parts.

Are there burned or melted parts?

YES → Go to Chart 2.

NO → Go To Chart 9.

YES → Is the computer beeping when you turn it on?

NO → Bad ROM, memory or motherboard. Check memory first.

YES → Most computers beep at startup. If beeps are not the same as usual, they may signal an error.

Is the computer beeping as usual?

YES → Does it have AMIBIOS ROM?

YES → The beep codes may be the key to your problem.

NO → Go to Chart 8.

NO → The beep codes may be the key to your problem.

Go to Appendix G.

YES → Is the video quality good?

NO → Go to Chart 15.

YES → Was a number on the screen or an error message? Were there any beeps? Check Appendices E, F, or G.

Does the computer indicate an error?

YES → Go to Appendix E, F, or G; find error message, take steps to fix problem.

NO → Does the computer boot?

YES → Go to Chart 14.

NO → Does the computer have a hard disk?

NO → Go to Chart 4.

YES → Go to Chart 5.

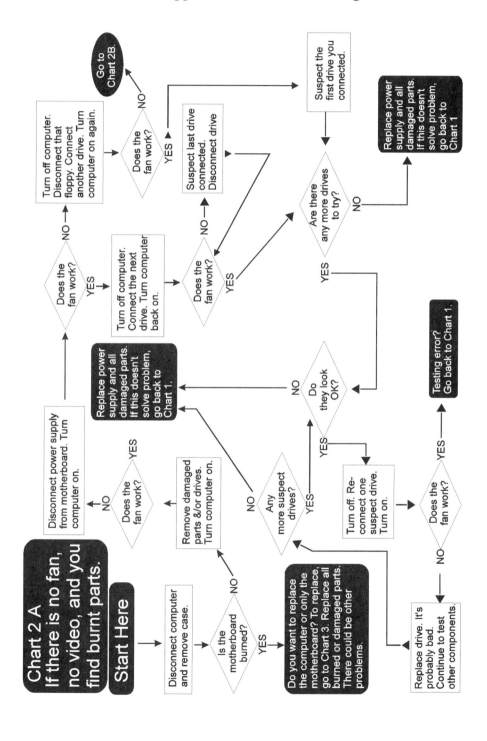

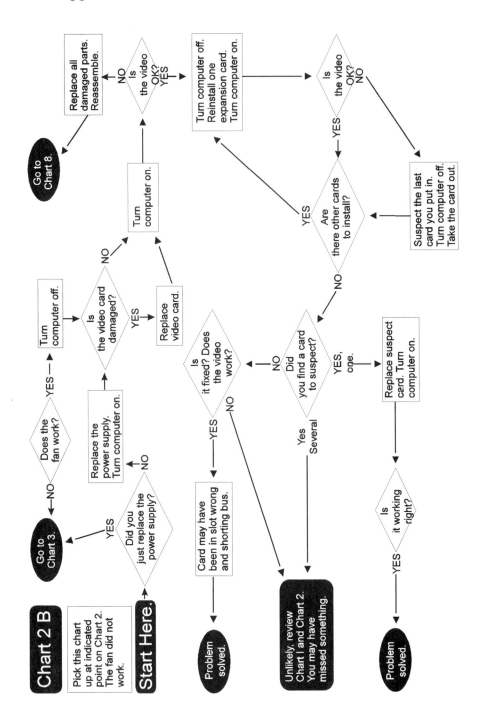

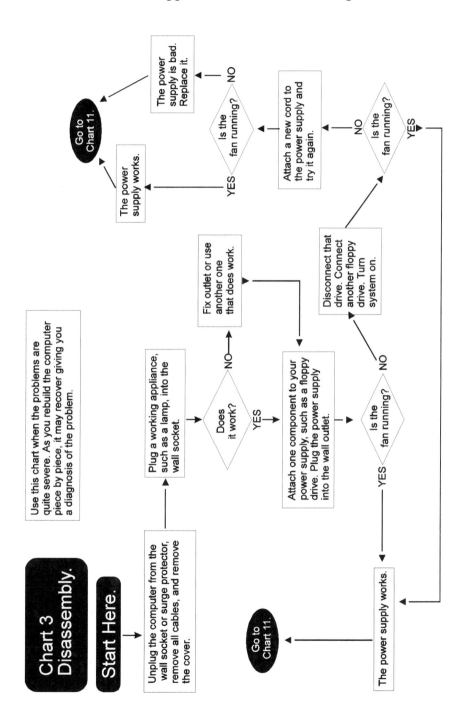

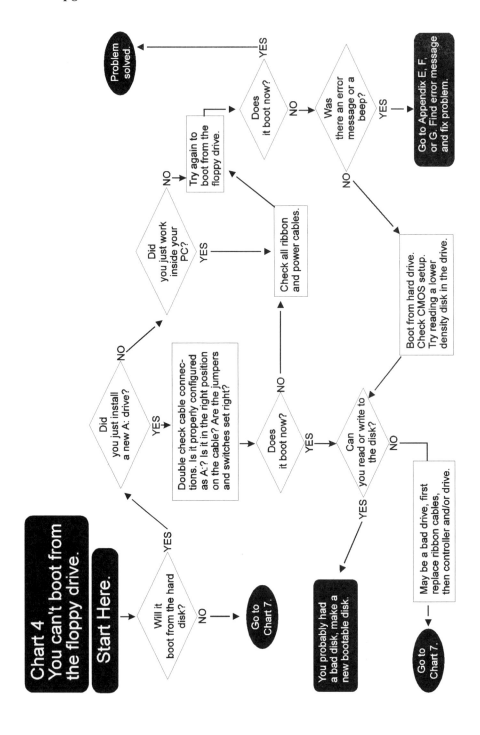

Chart 4
You can't boot from the floppy drive.

Start Here.

Will it boot from the hard disk?

YES → Did you just install a new A: drive?

NO → Go to Chart 7.

Did you just install a new A: drive?

YES → Double check cable connections. Is it properly configured as A:? Is it in the right position on the cable? Are the jumpers and switches set right?

NO → Did you just work inside your PC?

Double check cable connections... → Does it boot now?

Does it boot now?

YES → Can you read or write to the disk?

NO → Check all ribbon and power cables.

Did you just work inside your PC?

YES → Check all ribbon and power cables.

NO → Try again to boot from the floppy drive.

Try again to boot from the floppy drive. → Does it boot now?

Does it boot now?

YES → Problem solved.

NO → Was there an error message or a beep?

Was there an error message or a beep?

YES → Go to Appendix E, F, or G. Find error message and fix problem.

NO → Boot from hard drive. Check CMOS setup. Try reading a lower density disk in the drive.

Can you read or write to the disk?

YES → You probably had a bad disk, make a new bootable disk.

NO → May be a bad drive, first replace ribbon cables, then controller and/or drive.

May be a bad drive... → Go to Chart 7.

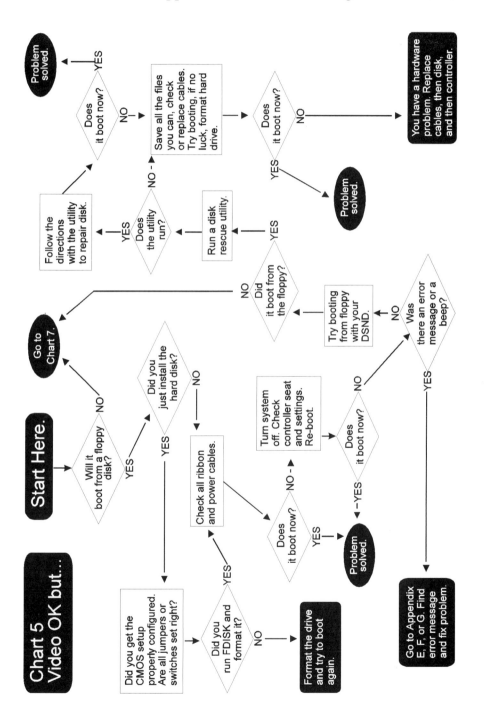

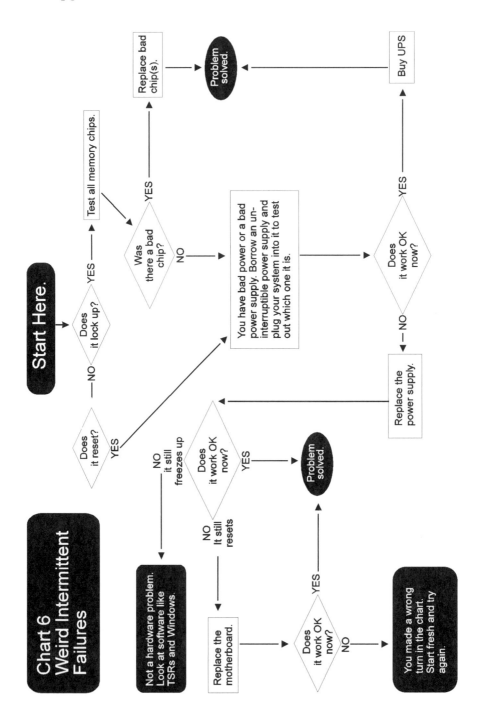

**Chart 6
Weird Intermittent
Failures**

Start Here.

Does it lock up?

YES — Test all memory chips.

Was there a bad chip? — YES — Replace bad chip(s). → Problem solved.

NO

You have bad power or a bad power supply. Borrow an un-interruptible power supply and plug your system into it to test out which one it is.

Does it work OK now? — YES — Buy UPS → Problem solved.

NO — Replace the power supply.

Does it reset?

NO

YES

NO it still freezes up — Not a hardware problem. Look at software like TSRs and Windows.

Does it work OK now? — YES — Problem solved.

NO It still resets

Replace the motherboard.

Does it work OK now? — YES — Problem solved.

NO — You made a wrong turn in the chart. Start fresh and try again.

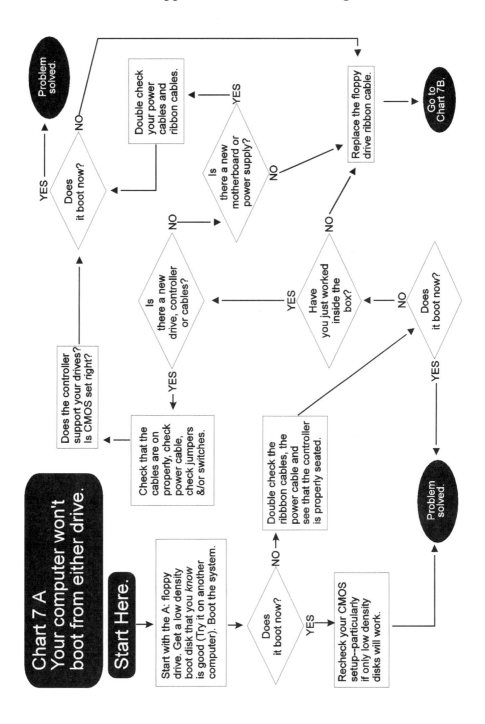

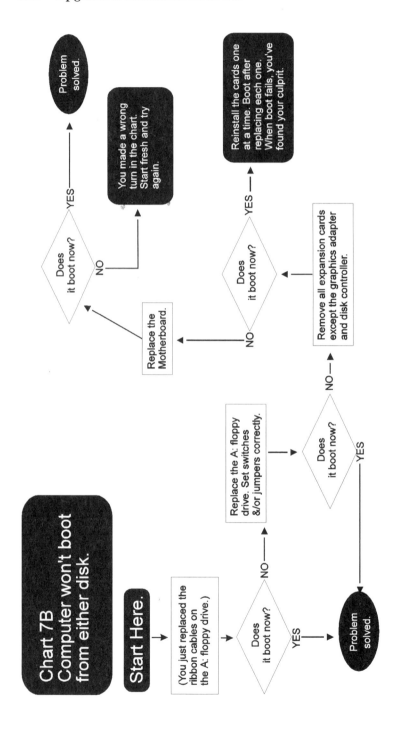

Chart 7B
Computer won't boot from either disk.

Start Here.

(You just replaced the ribbon cables on the A: floppy drive.)

Does it boot now?

NO — Replace the A: floppy drive. Set switches &/or jumpers correctly.

YES — Problem solved.

Does it boot now?

YES — Problem solved.

NO — Remove all expansion cards except the graphics adapter and disk controller.

Does it boot now?

YES — Reinstall the cards one at a time. Boot after replacing each one. When boot fails, you've found your culprit.

NO — Replace the Motherboard.

Does it boot now?

NO — You made a wrong turn in the chart. Start fresh and try again.

YES — Problem solved.

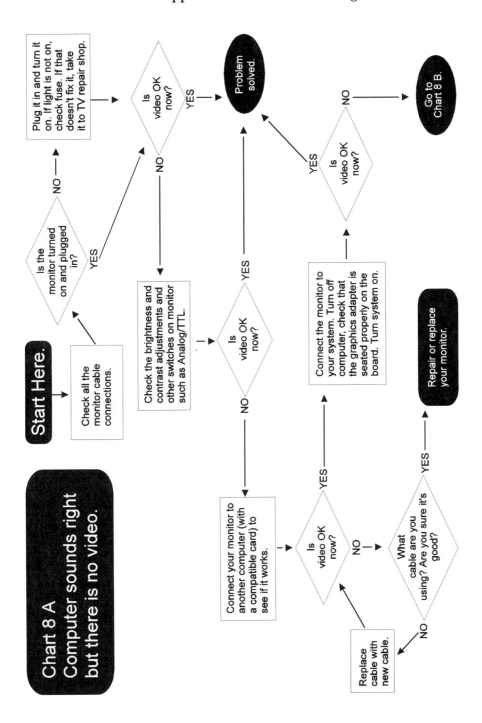

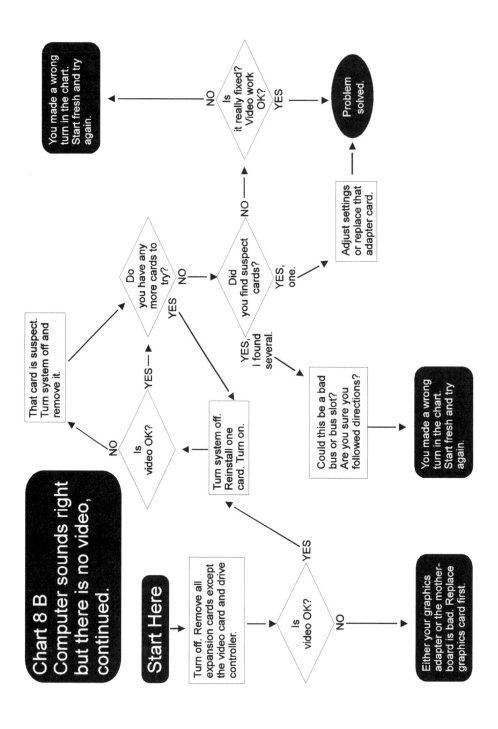

Chart 8 B
Computer sounds right but there is no video, continued.

Start Here

Turn off. Remove all expansion cards except the video card and drive controller.

Is video OK?

YES

NO

Either your graphics adapter or the mother-board is bad. Replace graphics card first.

Turn system off. Reinstall one card. Turn on.

Is video OK?

NO

YES —

That card is suspect. Turn system off and remove it.

Do you have any more cards to try?

YES

NO

Did you find suspect cards?

YES, one.

YES, I found several.

Could this be a bad bus or bus slot? Are you sure you followed directions?

You made a wrong turn in the chart. Start fresh and try again.

Adjust settings or replace that adapter card.

NO

Is it really fixed? Video work OK?

NO

YES

Problem solved.

You made a wrong turn in the chart. Start fresh and try again.

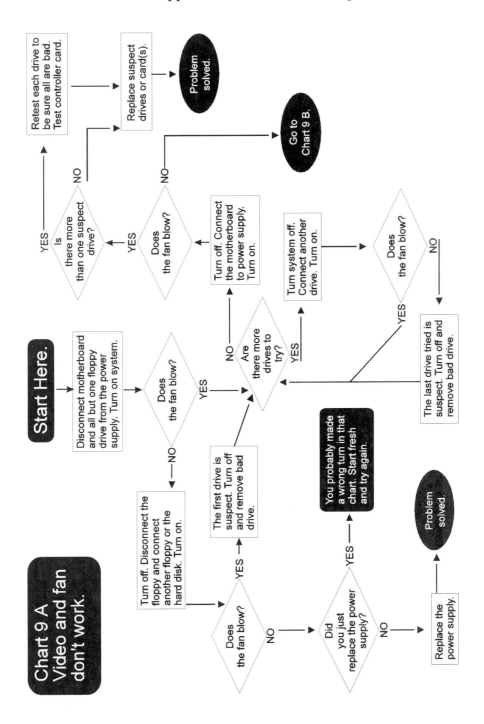

Chart 9 A
Video and fan don't work.

Start Here.

Disconnect motherboard and all but one floppy drive from the power supply. Turn on system.

Does the fan blow?

NO — Turn off. Disconnect the floppy and connect another floppy or the hard disk. Turn on.

Does the fan blow?

YES → The first drive is suspect. Turn off and remove bad drive.

NO → Did you just replace the power supply?

YES → You probably made a wrong turn in that chart. Start fresh and try again.

NO → Replace the power supply.

Problem solved.

Are there more drives to try?

NO → Turn off. Connect the motherboard to power supply. Turn on.

YES → Turn system off. Connect another drive. Turn on.

Does the fan blow?

NO → The last drive tried is suspect. Turn off and remove bad drive.

YES

Does the fan blow?

YES → Is there more than one suspect drive?

YES → Retest each drive to be sure all are bad. Test controller card.

NO → Replace suspect drives or card(s).

Problem solved.

NO → Go to Chart 9 B.

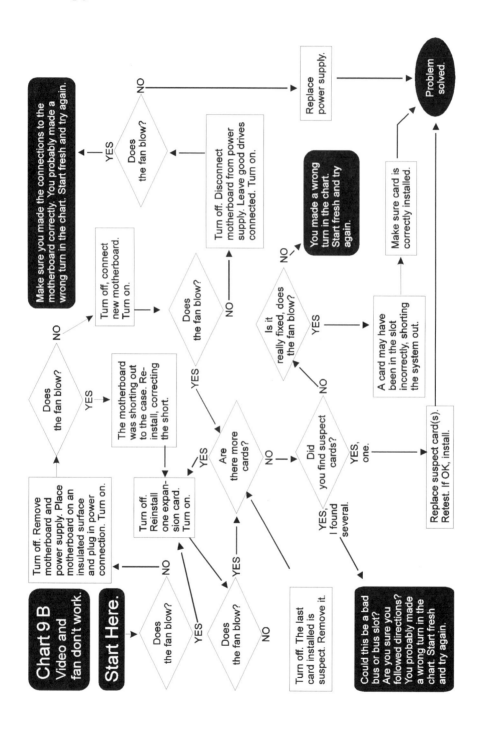

Chart 9 B
Video and fan don't work.

Start Here.

Turn off. Remove motherboard and power supply. Place motherboard on an insulated surface and plug in power connection. Turn on.

Does the fan blow?

NO

YES

Does the fan blow?

NO

YES

The motherboard was shorting out to the case. Reinstall, correcting the short.

Turn off, connect new motherboard. Turn on.

Does the fan blow?

YES

NO

Make sure you made the connections to the motherboard correctly. You probably made a wrong turn in the chart. Start fresh and try again.

Does the fan blow?

YES

NO

Replace power supply.

Turn off. Disconnect motherboard from power supply. Leave good drives connected. Turn on.

Does the fan blow?

YES

NO

Turn off. Reinstall one expansion card. Turn on.

Are there more cards?

YES

NO

Does the fan blow?

YES

NO

Turn off. The last card installed is suspect. Remove it.

Did you find suspect cards?

YES, one.

YES, I found several.

NO

Is it really fixed, does the fan blow?

YES

NO

A card may have been in the slot incorrectly, shorting the system out.

You made a wrong turn in the chart. Start fresh and try again.

Make sure card is correctly installed.

Replace suspect card(s). Retest. If OK, install.

Problem solved.

Could this be a bad bus or bus slot? Are you sure you followed directions? You probably made a wrong turn in the chart. Start fresh and try again.

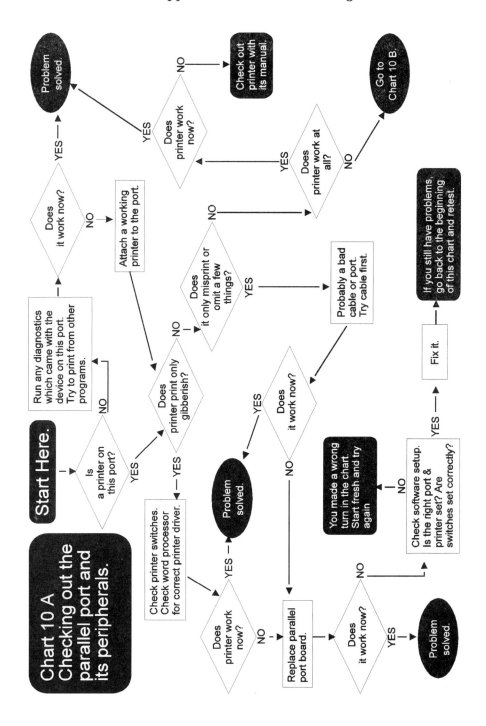

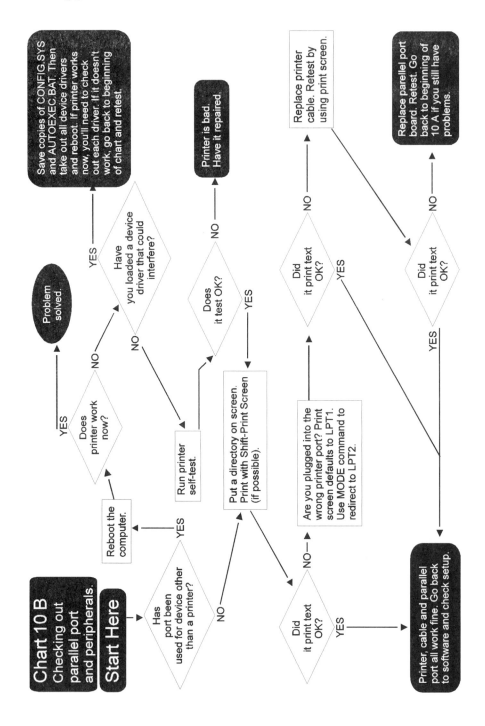

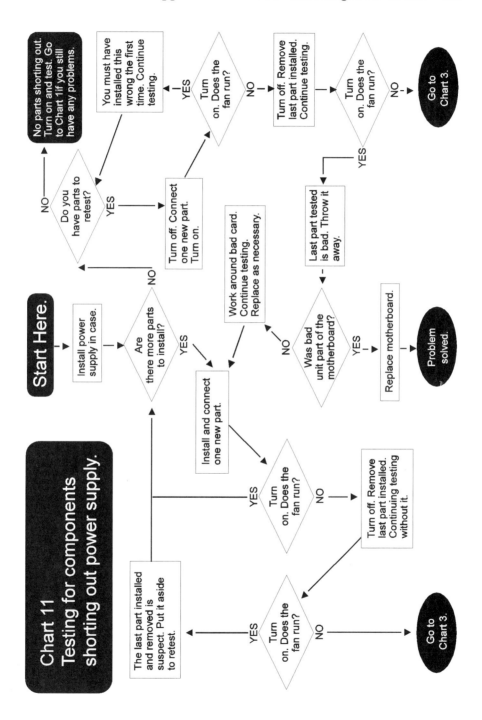

Start Here.

Chart 11
Testing for components shorting out power supply.

Install power supply in case.

Are there more parts to install?

Install and connect one new part.

Turn on. Does the fan run?

YES → Turn on. Does the fan run?

NO → Turn off. Remove last part installed. Continuing testing without it.

Turn on. Does the fan run?

YES → The last part installed and removed is suspect. Put it aside to retest.

NO → Go to Chart 3.

Do you have parts to retest?

NO → No parts shorting out. Turn on and test. Go to Chart 1 if you still have any problems.

YES → Turn off. Connect one new part. Turn on.

Turn on. Does the fan run?

YES → You must have installed this wrong the first time. Continue testing.

NO → Turn off. Remove last part installed. Continue testing.

Turn on. Does the fan run?

NO → Go to Chart 3.

YES → Last part tested is bad. Throw it away.

Work around bad card. Continue testing. Replace as necessary.

Was bad unit part of the motherboard?

NO → Work around bad card. Continue testing. Replace as necessary.

YES → Replace motherboard. → Problem solved.

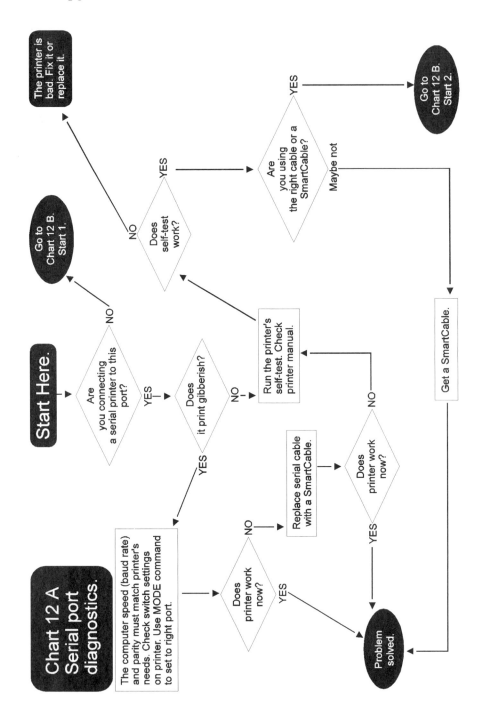

Chart 12 A
Serial port
diagnostics.

Start Here.

Are you connecting a serial printer to this port?

YES → The computer speed (baud rate) and parity must match printer's needs. Check switch settings on printer. Use MODE command to set to right port.

Does it print gibberish?

YES → The computer speed (baud rate) and parity must match printer's needs. Check switch settings on printer. Use MODE command to set to right port.

Does printer work now?

YES → Problem solved.

NO → Replace serial cable with a SmartCable.

Does printer work now?

YES → Problem solved.

NO → Run the printer's self-test. Check printer manual.

Does it print gibberish?
NO → Run the printer's self-test. Check printer manual.

NO → Go to Chart 12 B. Start 1.

Does self-test work?

YES → Are you using the right cable or a SmartCable?

NO → The printer is bad. Fix it or replace it.

Are you using the right cable or a SmartCable?

YES → Go to Chart 12 B. Start 2.

Maybe not → Get a SmartCable.

Get a SmartCable. → Problem solved.

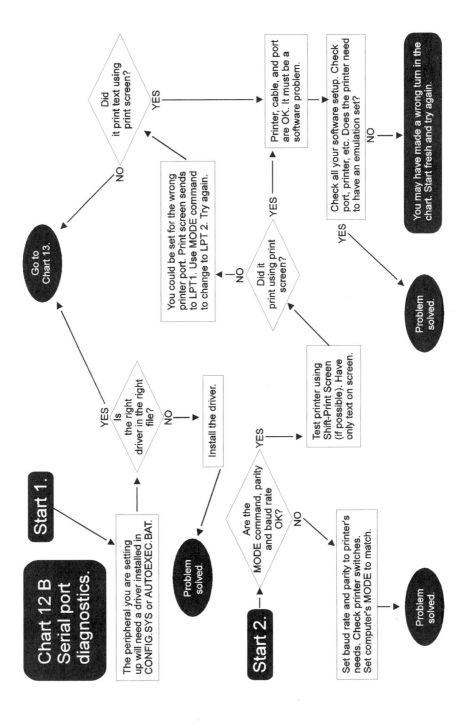

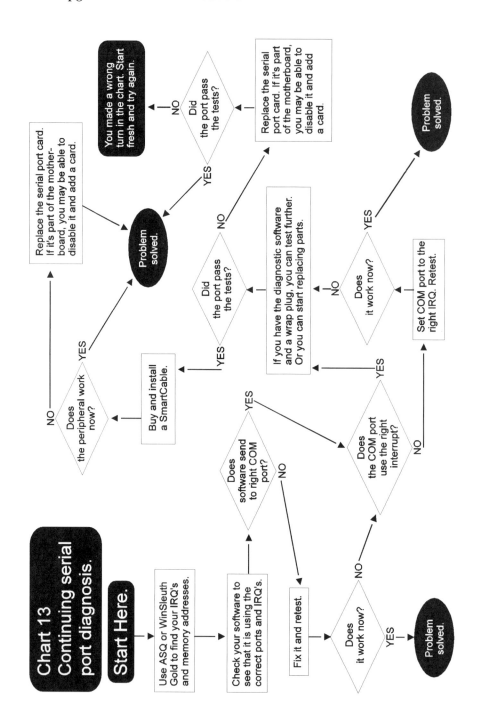

Chart 13
Continuing serial port diagnosis.

Start Here.

Use ASQ or WinSleuth Gold to find your IRQ's and memory addresses.

Check your software to see that it is using the correct ports and IRQ's.

Does software send to right COM port?

YES → Does the COM port use the right interrupt?

NO → Fix it and retest.

Does it work now?

YES → Problem solved.

NO →

Does the COM port use the right interrupt?

YES → If you have the diagnostic software and a wrap plug, you can test further. Or you can start replacing parts.

NO → Set COM port to the right IRQ. Retest.

Does it work now?

YES → Problem solved.

NO → If you have the diagnostic software and a wrap plug, you can test further. Or you can start replacing parts.

Did the port pass the tests?

YES → Buy and install a SmartCable.

NO → Replace the serial port card. If it's part of the motherboard, you may be able to disable it and add a card.

Did the port pass the tests?

YES → You made a wrong turn in the chart. Start fresh and try again.

NO → Replace the serial port card. If it's part of the motherboard, you may be able to disable it and add a card.

Does the peripheral work now?

YES → Problem solved.

NO → Replace the serial port card. If it's part of the motherboard, you may be able to disable it and add a card.

Problem solved.

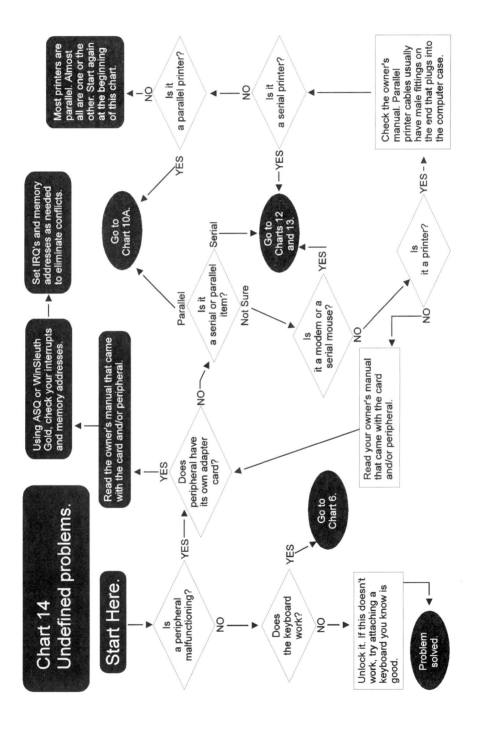

Chart 14
Undefined problems.

Start Here.

Is a peripheral malfunctioning?

YES → Does peripheral have its own adapter card?

YES → Read the owner's manual that came with the card and/or peripheral.

Using ASQ or WinSleuth Gold, check your interrupts and memory addresses.

Set IRQ's and memory addresses as needed to eliminate conflicts.

NO → Is it a serial or parallel item?

Parallel → Go to Chart 10A.

Is it a parallel printer?

YES →

NO → Most printers are parallel. Almost all are one or the other. Start again at the beginning of this chart.

Serial → Go to Charts 12 and 13.

Not Sure → Is it a modem or a serial mouse?

YES → Go to Charts 12 and 13.

Is it a serial printer?

YES →

NO →

NO → Is it a printer?

YES → Check the owner's manual. Parallel printer cables usually have male fittings on the end that plugs into the computer case.

NO → Read your owner's manual that came with the card and/or peripheral.

NO → Does the keyboard work?

YES → Go to Chart 6.

NO → Unlock it. If this doesn't work, try attaching a keyboard you know is good.

Problem solved.

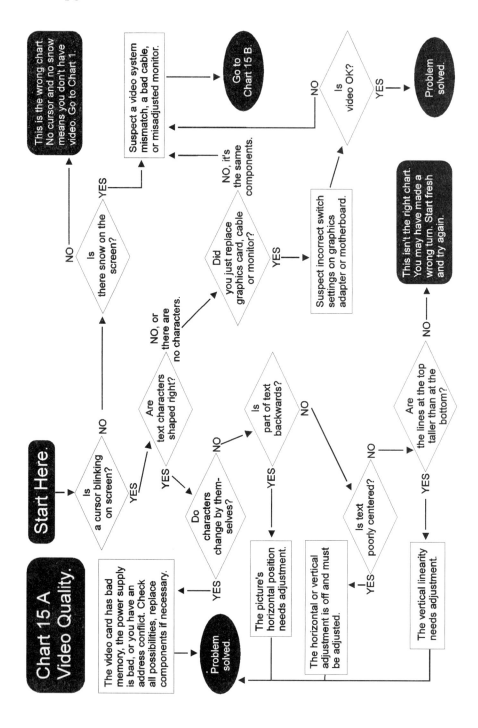

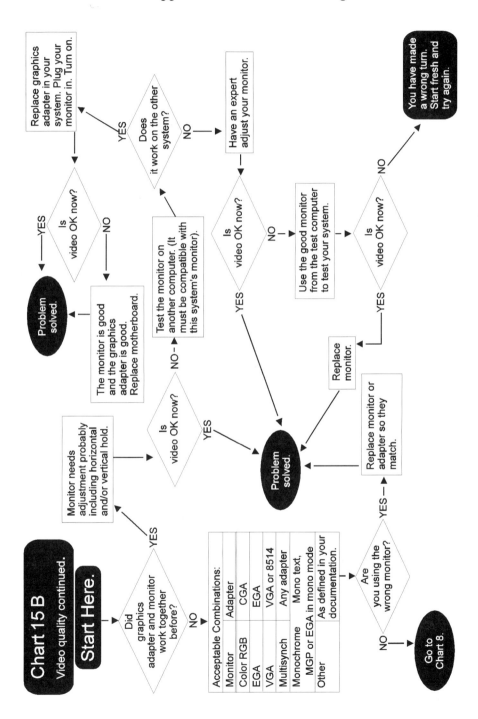

Chart 15 B
Video quality continued.

Start Here.

Did graphics adapter and monitor work together before?

YES → Monitor needs adjustment probably including horizontal and/or vertical hold.

Is video OK now?

YES → Problem solved.

NO → The monitor is good and the graphics adapter is good. Replace motherboard.

Replace graphics adapter in your system. Plug your monitor in. Turn on.

Is video OK now?

NO → Test the monitor on another computer. (It must be compatible with this system's monitor).

Does it work on the other system?

YES → Replace graphics adapter in your system. Plug your monitor in. Turn on.

NO → Have an expert adjust your monitor.

Is video OK now?

YES → Problem solved.

NO → You have made a wrong turn. Start fresh and try again.

Use the good monitor from the test computer to test your system.

Is video OK now?

YES → Replace monitor.

NO → You have made a wrong turn. Start fresh and try again.

NO → Acceptable Combinations:

Monitor	Adapter
Color RGB	CGA
EGA	EGA
VGA	VGA or 8514
Multisynch	Any adapter
Monochrome	Mono text, MGP or EGA in mono mode
Other	As defined in your documentation.

Are you using the wrong monitor?

YES → Replace monitor or adapter so they match.

NO → Go to Chart 8.

Problem solved.

APPENDIX H
GLOSSARY

486DX

> This microprocessor has a 32-bit data path and can address four gigabytes of memory. It is backwards-compatible and can run software designed for any of the earlier 80X86 (the "X" is the specific number, such as 2 or 3) family of processors. Straight versions of the chip are available, running up to 50Mhz. Clock-doubled versions reach 66Mhz, others (DX4) reach 100Mhz.

80386

> A 16MHz-to-40MHz, 32-bit microprocessor able to address four gigabytes of memory.

Access time

How fast a disk drive or CD-ROM drive can access the data that your system is asking for.

Address bus/Address

The data transfer circuits to the locations (addresses) in memory at which data is to be put or from which it is to be retrieved. Each position in memory has to have a specific location. The total width of the address bus is very important, because it determines the maximum number of available address combinations, and therefore the maximum amount of memory the CPU, and in turn the entire system, can directly manipulate. For example, a computer with 16 address lines can directly manipulate 65,536 different memory addresses.

Algorithm

A complex formula used to analyze or process data, often to condense, compress or expand it.

Analog

The use of a continuously variable electrical current to represent information. *See* Digital.

Alternative Common Access Method

Allows several SCSI host adapters to be controlled from a single driver. *See* Chapter 10.

Application

Short for software application. A program applying the computer's hardware and operating system to a specific task. The most common application in use today is a word processor.

Arithmetic Logic Unit (ALU)

This is the number-crunching part of your CPU. It does all the numeric manipulations handled by the CPU. Some microprocessors and computers have a floating-point unit (FPU) to handle numbers involving decimal places or fractions. The ALU performs operations on the data as directed by the control unit.

ASCII

American Standard Code for Information Interchange. The name of the organization that standardized the numbers used to define the most common computer character set; also refers to the character set itself.

ASPI

Advanced SCSI Programming Interface. The most popular universal driver for SCSI devices.

AT

Advanced Technology. Applied to the first machine using the 286. It offered a 16-bit data path, both internal and external.

Attribute command

Allows you to mark a file as read-only, which means that it can't be erased; as hidden, which means that it doesn't show up when a directory is scanned with the DIR command; and to indicate if it's been modified since the last time it was backed up.

AUTOEXEC.BAT

A startup file containing commands or programs that are automatically executed each time the machine comes on.

Backplane

A motherboard.

Basic throughput

Both a hard drive and its controller have a maximum rated throughput, or data transfer rate. If the controller does not match or exceed the rated throughput of the drive, you will not get all the performance your hard disk offers, and it may not even work at all.

Baud rate

The number of times a line changes its electrical state during telecommunications. While it's not exactly interchangeable with bytes per second, they're really fairly equal. This is the standard unit of measure for how fast a modem operates.

Benchmarks

Standardized tests designed to evaluate the performance of a component of your system.

Binary, Bit

Binary numbers have only two possibilities: true or false, 1 or 0, on or off. A bit is a binary digit, the smallest unit of information in a digital computer, and the basis of all its operation. *See* Byte.

BIOS

Stands for Basic Input/Output System. Firmware, or a program burned into a chip on your motherboard. It tells the computer how to boot, how to run the Power-On-Self-Test and to look for an operating system, etc. Some cards, like most current graphics adapters, also have ROMs and their own BIOSes that link to the one in the PC. Flash BIOSes can be changed by software.

Bitmap font

One whose characters are defined in terms of dots placed in a square grid.

Boot cycle / dual boot

The term "booting a PC" is based on the phrase "pulling oneself up by one's own bootstraps." Every time you turn your PC off it loses all memory. It doesn't know anything about the outside world or its own components. The boot cycle includes the Power-On-Self-Test and eventual access to the operating system. For DOS, this means a C prompt; for Windows, Program Manager or the Desktop. To dual-boot means to allow the computer to start up under either one of two operating systems.

Bootable

That means that you can actually use that disk to boot your system. Under MS-DOS this means that the two hidden system files and Command.com have been copied to the disk.

Buffer

An area in memory used for the orderly storage of data, until it is retrieved for processing.

Bulletin board system (BBS) software

Communications software which can handle electronic mail, automatic file transfer, electronic messaging, and even electronic shopping.

Bus board

A few computers have been produced with one circuit board containing the bus and its connectors, and a separate board containing the processor and other chips.

Bus connector

The sockets on the motherboard that expansion cards are plugged into. There are a number of different bus connectors, depending on the type of bus built into the computer. These include the original 8-bit bus on the XT; the Industry Standard Architecture (ISA) bus found on the AT and many modern computers; The Extended Industry Standard Architecture (EISA) and Micro Channel Architecture (MCA) 32-bit bus; VESA local bus; and PCI.

Bus master

The sub-system, on the motherboard or a SCSI host adapter, that controls the work of the bus. In ISA computers the microprocessor normally does this job. EISA computers and MCA computers allow multiple bus masters with the CPU as arbitrator.

Bus mouse

A mouse which comes with its own expansion card and does not use a serial port.

Bus

The circuitry connecting the CPU and the other components of the system such as the disk controller, graphics adapter, etc. The type of bus and its width (the size of the unit of data it can handle) determines what devices can be added and the speed at which they will function.

Byte

The smallest unit of data moved around in a computer; usually contains eight bits. *See* Bit.

Cache

A special type of memory used to speed up operations in a computer. Because many of the sub-systems of a computer, such as the hard disk, are not as fast as the microprocessor (CPU), the cache controller stores (in special fast RAM chips) information "expected" to be required by the CPU. Because the cache can feed the data to the CPU faster than the hard disk can, this will improve the speed of operations. The information stored is whatever was last used. Performance of the cache, and therefore the amount the cache can speed up operations, is a function of the size of the cache and, more importantly, the intelligence of the cache controller.

Capacitive switches

Keyboards operated by detecting a change in the electrical impulse at the switch points.

Carpal Tunnel Syndrome

One of several types of repetitive stress injury (RSI).

Case

The metal (or metal and plastic) box that the primary components of a PC are mounted inside.

CCITT

International Consultative Committee for Telephony and Telegraphy: This is a French group organized under the United Nations, and responsible for most of the communication standards for modems.

CD-R

Compact Disc-Recordable. A device capable of recording CD-ROM discs.

CD-ROM

Compact Disc-Read Only Memory. CD-ROMs are organized in a single track that spirals from the center of the disk to its outside. The data is recorded as a series of pits burned into the underside surface of the platter. A laser beam is used to detect whether specific points on a disk are pitted or not and that information is translated into data that your computer can read. CD-ROM drives are grouped by transfer speed, with 150Kb/second called single-speed, 300Kb/sec. called double-speed (2x), etc. Quad-speed (600Kb/sec., 4x) is now entry-level, with 6x and 8x coming on.

CHKDSK

A program which verifies the integrity of your disks and their filing system.

Characters per second (CPS)

The measure of the speed of a dot-matrix printer.

Chip

A silicon wafer etched with layers of circuitry; also called an integrated circuit (IC).

CISC

Complex Instruction Set Computer. The most common types used in PCs today. These are very complex designs because they can be operated using very complex instructions that offer a great deal of flexibility in programming. Compare RISC.

Clock / clock cycle

See Speed.

Clusters

Several sectors on a disk grouped together.

CMOS

Complimentary Metal Oxide Semi-conductor. Chip which identifies which components are on the system and allows us to not only modify the date and time in the computer's internal clock, and lets us tell it when we add new components to the system. *See* CMOS chip and Setup.

CMOS chip

These chips have very low electrical demand and are used to store the firmware programs the computer will need to function. CMOS chips are provided with batteries so that they will remain functional without outside power.

Com port

A serial Communications port, also called an RS-232 connection. *See* Serial port.

CONFIG.SYS

A startup file which contains commands that can generally only be run by invoking this file during the boot process. It allows you to set certain parameters that DOS will observe while the machine is operating, and allows you to load device drivers for things such as network cards, scanners, or fancy video adapters.

Common page description language (PDL)

Method of sending information to a printer.

Compression

A method of saving some of the space taken up on disk by data and programs. A special type of program (algorithm) condenses and expands the files as needed.

Conducted noise

This is interference in the system's operation caused by erratic fluctuations in the electrical power. Also called "dirty" power.

Conductive keyboards

Keyboards that have a rubber sheath with raised dots for each key, sometimes referred to as "rubber dome" or "sheath" keyboards. Each of the raised rubber spots contains carbon. When you depress the key the carbon is pressed down to complete a circuit located underneath.

Configuration

The selected components used in a computer; also, their hardware and software settings.

Control Unit

This part of the CPU chip exercises direct control over everything that goes on inside the processor and might be considered the hub of the entire computer.

Co-processor

A chip which performs operating functions of the system to reduce the load placed on the microprocessor, and so speed up operations. For example, a math co-processor handles complex math for the system.

CP/M

Control Program for Microprocessors. The early PC operating system.

CPU

Central Processing Unit. The large chip in a computer that manipulates the data and executes instructions. It is also called the processor or the microprocessor.

Crash

To lock up, stop running (with possible damage). Used with both hardware and software.

CRT

Cathode Ray Tube. Sometimes used to refer to a computer's monitor.

Cursor pad

Key group used to navigate the active location of the pointer on the screen. The cursor keys, usually indicated by arrows, let us move the cursor position as desired.

Cursor

A flashing bar or block used to indicate the current active position on the screen. This is the point at which any typing performed will be entered on the display.

Cylinder

All of the tracks located at the same distance from the center of the spindle on each platter of a hard disk or a similar storage device.

DAC

Digital-to-Analog Converter. The operating system sends a stream of data in the form of binary numbers to the graphics adapter. The card processes these signals through a DAC circuit, which then forwards an analog signal to the monitor.

Data

Information stored or used by a computer, usually consisting of bits and bytes stored in files.

Data bus

A bundle of wires used to transfer the data to and from the CPU. The wider the data bus, the more information can be moved at a time and (if the software is capable) the more complex the information can be.

Data compression

Methods used in modem communications and data storage that can cut the size of the transfer in half. It uses fancy algorithms that encode the data, and a reverse procedure is used at the other end to expand it. There are both hardware and software implementations.

Data separation circuit

This is a part of the hard disk controller which insures that data may be read consistently from the disk.

Daughter cards

Expansion cards that attach directly to other cards to add additional functionality, such as memory, that would not be able to fit inside a normal full-slot dimension, or for an accessory module which is purchased as an option but not included with the basic card.

Defragmenter

A routine that goes through your disk and reorganizes the files for efficiency and speed.

Default

The standard or automatic setting of a feature in hardware or software.

Device driver

Software which allows the CPU to access expansion hardware. Drivers are subroutines that DOS or other operating systems trigger and run to operate hardware, such as a mouse, since the information needed is not built into the operating system.

DIN

A round cable connector used to attach many common devices to a PC, like a keyboard, as well as mice, hand-scanners, and the like.

Digital Audio Tape (DAT)

A backup medium which uses a helical-scan device similar to that found in VCRs.

DIP switches

Dual In-line Package. A series of small switches, usually built into a small plastic block and mounted on the surface of a circuit board. These work much like a row of light switches. When the circuit is closed (on), electricity can flow through the position, enabling a feature or setting a value. When the circuit is open (off), no current flows through and the feature is disabled or a different value is set.

Digital

The use of standardized electrical pulses to represent information. PCs use binary digits.

Directory

Divisions similar in function to the separate drawers in a filing cabinet, allowing you to organize the files on your hard drive.

Discardable memory

An area in global memory that can be released by an application for use by Windows or another application.

Disk drives

Devices which store large amounts of information permanently, and which can be used to bring data into the system and to remove data from the system and take it to another machine. In effect, disk drives are both input and output devices. They require an expansion card and cables so that they can communicate with your machine. The whole assembly is referred to as the storage sub-system. *See* Floppy disk; Hard disk.

DMA

Direct Memory Access. Allows direct access to the system's RAM buffer without having to go through the system's CPU. This has two benefits. One is that the device can address memory faster than would otherwise be possible; and the other is that the CPU is freed from that task so that it can do other things. DMA is provided through different channels known as (of course) DMA channels, and managed by a special chip or circuit called the DMA controller.

DOS

Disk Operating System. DOS is the predominant operating system for PCs at this time. It comes in two flavors: IBM (PC) DOS and MS- DOS or Microsoft DOS.

Dot Matrix

These printers work using a ribbon similar to that found in typewriters, and use a series of needles that are fired from a head through the ribbon to force ink onto the page. Dot matrix printers can be broken down into two groups: 9-pin and 24-pin models.

dpi

Dots per inch, a measure of the relative number of ink or toner dots on a page. A higher dpi means greater resolution and a sharper printed image.

DPMI

DOS Protected Mode Interface. A sophisticated memory-management method.

DRAM

Dynamic Random Access Memory. A common type of memory chip.

Driver

See Device Driver.

DSND

Dark and Stormy Night Disk. A floppy disk you create that contains all the files needed to get a computer back on line if the primary copies on the unit's hard drive become corrupted.

DSP

Digital Signal Processor. A sophisticated chip adaptable to uses in communications, sound, etc.

Edutainment

Multimedia programs aiming at a high integration of interactivity, intellectual content, and fun.

EEMS

Enhanced Extended Memory Specification. This type of memory management allows you to run more than one program at the same time. LIM 4.0 and later compliant programs can use up to 32Mb of expanded memory, compared to the 8Mb allowed under earlier versions of the standard.

E-IDE

Enhanced IDE, supporting four devices, and hard drives larger than 750 Mb. *See* IDE.

EISA

Extended Industry Standard Architecture. This a 32-bit bus architecture allowing 32 bits of information to be passed simultaneously and is designed to operate at 8Mhz per second. The EISA bus has several design characteristics that allow it to transfer data at up to 32Mb per second. This bus allows multiple processors in the machine, any of which can take over the bus.

Emulation

The imitation or mock-up of a computer process in software, to bypass patents or to avoid the cost of additional hardware. Example: some printer drivers emulate Hewlett-Packard plotters.

EMS

Expanded Memory Specification, also known as LIM (Lotus/Intel/ Microsoft, the developers) and bank-switched memory. A memory-management method which utilizes the portions of the first 1Mb of RAM above the 640K level. This protocol switches banks of memory into and out of a 16K window and gives access to as much as 8Mb of additional memory. A DOS strategy now obsolete.

Encoding scheme

Data is processed from "raw data" inside the computer before it's stored on disk, tape or other medium. Encoding is used to implement error detection and, in some cases, compression of the data.

Error correction algorithms

A method used in modems to check and make sure that the information received is the same as the information sent. In some cases these are embedded in software known as exchange protocols.

ESDI

Enhanced Small Device Interface. An improvement of MFM technology designed to provide higher capacity and better performance in hard drive storage. These units require a special controller and are usually formatted with 34 sectors per track. Most have access speeds of 15 to 18 milliseconds, with data transfer rates of over 10 megabytes per second.

Ethernet

The most common set of network hardware and software protocols (technical standards).

Expanded memory

A method allowing storage of data in RAM by programs as a sort of swap area, allowing them to manipulate larger files than would be possible in the conventional 640K environment. It's commonly referred to as LIM extended memory, based on the initials of the firms (Lotus, Intel, and Microsoft) that designed the standard.

Expansion cards

These are circuit boards which allow the addition of extras or power to expand the function of the computer. Expansion cards are automatically connected to the motherboard. There are a host of different kinds of cards, including those which attach external devices such as scanners or CD-ROM drives, and sizes from full-size to half-size. Daughter cards connect to expansion cards.

Expansion slot

Connects an expansion (or adapter) card to your system's data bus (the pathway used to transfer data to and from the CPU and your system's memory).

Extended memory

Memory used by 80286 and higher computers to allow programs to use memory above 1Mb. Operating environments such as Microsoft Windows make use of this ability.

External Cache

Newer CPUs can address external cache. This is an area of memory that can be used to hold frequently-used instructions to speed up operations. Today it is common to find from 64Kb to 512Kb of external memory on most motherboards.

External data path

This is the number of bits that can be moved between the CPU and other components of the computer, such as RAM and expansion cards.

Facsimile (Fax)

A method of transmitting documents over telephone wires. Fax-modems can handle both fax and normal serial communications.

Fast SCSI

A SCSI standard twice as fast as the original specification, offering a maximum transfer of up to 10Mb per second over either an 8- or 16-bit data path.

Fast-Wide SCSI

A SCSI standard which provides for up to 40Mb per second over a 32-bit path.

File Allocation Table (FAT)

This is a list used by the operating system to determine what disk space is actually in use.

Firmware

ROM instructions made an integral part of certain chips in a computer. This contains the basic instructions for running the system or subsystem in question.

Fixed-function accelerator

Specialized graphics chips (sometimes referred to as engines), that are programmed to take over certain parts of the work of performing display functions.

Floating point notation

This kind of manipulation involves decimal-point computation and is more intensive than just handling the numbers directly. Early PCs could be equipped with an auxiliary microprocessor called "math" or "numeric" co-processors. Most 486 chips and all Pentium processors are equipped with these built-in floating-point capabilities and have no use for a math co-processor.

Floppy disk(ette)

> Made from a flexible plastic which is coated on each side with a thin layer of magnetic-sensitive material. By changing the magnetic properties of small portions of the material, it is possible to represent data. Floppies are usually 5.25-inch or 3.5-inch, and vary in storage capacity.

Format (high-level)

> The process of preparing a disk so the operating system can use it to store data. Formatting checks the disk physically for bad portions, and sets up a table (the FAT), allowing DOS to store and find information.

Format (low-level)

> A more basic preparation of a disk for the operating system which will be storing information on it.

Free memory

> The area of global memory that is still available for use by Windows.

Function keys

> Keys which invoke a specific action and can be used by programs as short-cut keys, allowing the user to issue commands with a single push of a button.

Gigabyte (Gb)

> A thousand Megabytes; a billion. *See also*, Byte.

Global memory

> The total amount of memory used by Windows.

Graphical environment (Graphical User Interface, or GUI)

> Instead of issuing cryptic commands, the user can manipulate program windows and icons on the screen and move files around without having to issue any typed commands.

Graphics tablets or digitizers

Input devices which use either a pen-shaped stylus or a puck over a special pad to move the cursor on the screen.

Hard boot

Occurs when the on/off switch or the reset switch is used. In a hard boot, the computer goes through its hardware-testing sequence (the Power-On-Self-Test), as well as loading its operating system and following the directions in the CONFIG.SYS and AUTOEXEC.BAT files.

Hard-copy

Printed on paper.

Hard disk

A thin metal platter coated with magnetic material used to store data. The primary storage components of most PCs, hard disks are relatively efficient and inexpensive, but need care.

Hardware

The metal, Fiberglass, silicon, etc. parts of a computer including the CPU, memory, drives, keyboard, video, printer, etc. *See* Software.

Hertz (Hz)

The frequency of an event, measured in cycles per second. Compare kilohertz (KHz) and megahertz (MHz).

Hexadecimal notation

A numbering system using 16 digits, 0 through F.

High-color displays

Allow either 15 or 16 bits per pixel producing roughly 32,000 or 65,000 possible colors.

High Memory Area (HMA)

The first 64K block of extended DOS memory, running from 10000 to 11000 Hex.

I/O, Input/Output

The process by which the microprocessor communicates with the outside world. Input comes from the keyboard, mouse, scanner, modem, etc. Output goes to the video monitor, printer, modem, etc. Input/Output may also be used to refer to transfer of information between programs.

I/O module

This module in the CPU acts much like a traffic cop, routing commands in and out of the CPU and queuing instructions for execution.

IAPx86

Intel Advanced Processor x86 (the "x" is the specific number like 3 or 4). Used for the Intel family of processors which includes those known as the 286, 386 and 486.

IBM clone (IBM-compatible)

A PC or computer which can run all the software developed for the IBM-PC.

Icon

A small picture, used to represent a program, operation, file type, etc. A key feature of a GUI.

IDE

Integrated Drive Electronics. Much of the electronics used to control the unit (formerly found on the hard disk controller board) are housed inside the drive. The actual mechanics are integrated into the drive itself. A simple card called a "paddle board" connects the drive to the system.

Image or mirror backup

This method involves making the total backup of an entire disk or storage system. It is usually done using a tape drive or a second hard disk. Every file on the disk is saved.

Incremental and archival backup

If you already have a mirror of your entire disk or your data sub-directory, incremental backups can be used to add changed versions of existing files and files created since the last (mirror) backup.

Ink-jet printers

Uses print-head technology, but instead of pins striking a ribbon, the ink jet actually squirts ink directly onto the paper.

Interface

The appearance and operation of the screen a user sees. Graphical user interfaces (GUIs) like MS Windows are considered much easier to use than character-based interfaces like DOS.

Interlacing

Interlaced displays draw only half of the lines across the monitor with each pass. Then they come back and repeat their travels, drawing the other lines. Interlaced displays were designed to get higher resolution with less memory on the card, as they only have to manage half the pixels at one time. They tend to flicker and cause eyestrain.

Interleave

A method of storing information on a hard disk. Information is stored on a disk in sectors that aren't necessarily contiguous. Interleaving can use every other sector (interleave of two) or can skip 2 or more sectors between. Each CPU type will have an interleave number which provides optimum speed of data access.

Internal Cache

Intel 486 and later CPUs have a built-in cache. This is special memory that is set aside sort of like a scratch pad. Using this memory is faster than going into the processor's hardware to find an instruction, and so it will speed up certain operations of your computer. *See* Cache.

Internal data path

The circuits along which data move within the CPU itself.

Internet

A world-wide "network of networks" used for business, government, education, and fun. Called "the Net" for short, it is growing phenomenally. Exploring it is called "Surfing the Net."

Interrupt request (IRQ)

Sometimes referred to as Interrupt vectors, Interrupts are a method used in your computer to allow a device to signal the CPU that it needs attention. The device must be assigned a unique IRQ number to avoid a conflict. These are traditionally set by use of switches found on the surface of expansion cards, but more and more are settable by software. *See* Plug and Play.

Interrupt Vector Table

A table of 256 software Interrupts located in the first kilobyte of memory. Each Interrupt number is assigned to a specific subroutine or event.

Interrupt

The method by which peripherals request attention by the CPU. There are three types of Interrupts: Nonmaskable Interrupts (NMI) demand attention instantly. Maskable Interrupts, used by most hardware, are queued by the Interrupt-controller chip and passed on to the CPU in order of priority. Software Interrupts are jumps to one of the subroutines stored in the Interrupt Vector Table.

IPO model

Input, Process, and Output. These three functions are the core of all computer operations. Data has to go into the machine, be manipulated by it, and a result obtained.

ISA

Industry Standard Architecture. A bus which allows only the CPU to have control of the system, with all other processors in the machine slaved (subordinated) to it.

Jumper

A very simple form of switch. The pins coming out of the board are the poles and the small conducting sleeve, called a jumper, is used to close the circuit. If there is no jumper, the circuit is open or off. When you put the jumper on the pins, it's closed, completing the circuit.

K

While outside of the computer world, this stands for 1,000, in computers, K means 1,024.

Kodak Photo-CD format

This allows you to read disks produced with the Kodak film-to-digital imaging equipment, and display photographs on your monitor, transfer them, and edit them.

LADDR

Layered Device Driver Architecture. One method of providing SCSI device modules.

LAN

See Local Area Network. Two or more computers, usually within a building, connected together.

Laser printers

Devices which work by passing a laser beam over a photo-sensitive drum. This changes the electrical charge of sections of the drum, based on light and dark portions of the final image. As the drum moves it picks up very fine pieces of black plastic called toner which are than transferred to the paper passing through the machine. A heated roller melts the plastic into the page, making it permanent.

LIM Memory

Lotus/Intel/Microsoft (for the vendors who developed the standard). This is a technique allowing the computer to expand the amount of memory available for operations above the DOS 640K conventional memory limit.

Line printers

Includes most simple dot-matrix printers; accept data from the computer as a series of binary numbers and match those numbers to the ASCII character set.

Local Area Network (LAN)

Computers connected together so they can share files and resources. It requires the use of special network cards and software.

Local bus architecture

Provides a special bus access that hooks directly to your system's central processing unit. This allows (at least in theory) for faster operations. Exact performance will vary with the type of card and how well it is designed.

Magneto-Optical

M-O. A type of drive using a combination of both magnetic and optical technology to position and write data.

Mainframe

Large (expensive) computers which can handle hundreds of users at once.

Maximum data transfer rate

A measurement of how fast the hard drive can move data into the system.

MB or Mb

Megabyte. 1,048,576 bytes—usually thought of as a million bytes.

MCA

Micro-Channel Architecture. The bus used in the IBM PS/2 Model 50 and up. The MCA design allows a computer to have more than one microprocessor and allows any of the processors in a machine to have control.

Mean-Time-Between-Failure (MTBF)

An average value, usually in hours of use, for how long a device should last under normal use.

Media

The name for the object data is stored on. Hard and floppy disks are magnetic media, as the information is stored in magnetic coding on the disks. CD-ROMs are one of several types of optical media wherein the information is stored by a method readable by optical devices.

Mega

1,048,576 when applied to computers. Outside of computers, it's one million. MegaHertz (MHz) refers to the internal clock speed of a computer (how quickly it can execute instructions).

Megabyte (Mb)

1,048,576 bytes—usually thought of as a million bytes.

Membrane Switches

A type of keyboard switch which has a membrane underneath the key. When the key is touched, pressure is exerted against the membrane, closing the switch.

Memory chips

Microscopic banks of switches. By holding an electrical charge they store a value of "on." If they have no current they are turned "off."

Memory map

Describes how RAM is organized and where specific instructions or data are loaded into RAM. This map can be divided up into regions. Memory is traditionally broken up into segments of 64K each. Conventional memory occupies the first ten segments, yielding 640K. The remaining six segments, making up the first Mb of RAM on the system, are referred to as the DOS High Memory Area.

Memory modules

Combination-style memory chips holding various combinations of (usually) DRAM. *See* DRAM, SIMM, and SIPP.

Memory refresh

DRAM memory must constantly be refreshed or the chips will "forget" the information. DMA channel 0 is dedicated to this task.

Memory

The parts of the computer that remember things. Types of memory include read-only memory (ROM), random access memory (RAM), extended memory, and expanded memory. In early PCs, conventional memory was the number up to 640K that was installed on the motherboard. In 286 and up computers, memory usually refers to the total number of Mbs installed, including the first Mb.

MFM

Modified Frequency Modulation. This technique of storing information on a hard drive generally divides tracks into 17 sectors with 512 bytes in each sector, and has transfer rates of about 5 megabytes per second. MFM technology is also sometimes referred to as the ST506 interface.

Microcomputer

Smaller than a minicomputer (which is smaller than a mainframe). PCs are microcomputers, and are essentially computers on a chip.

Microcontroller

A microprocessor used to control a specific operation. They may be found in your keyboard, microwave ovens, and cars. They are also called "embedded controllers."

Microprocessor

The CPU (Central Processing Unit) in a microcomputer. This is the chip that actually executes commands and processes information.

Minicomputer

A computer which is smaller (and less expensive) than a mainframe. They support under a hundred users.

MNP

Microcom Networking Protocol. MNP 4 provides advanced error correction, while MNP 5 provides compression. In fact, MNP 5 can compress files to almost half their original size, which saves considerable time in transferring data over cables or telephone lines.

MOV

Metal Oxide Varistor. The most common type of surge protector. These short out the excess voltage (usually referred to as clamping).

Modem

Modulator/Demodulator. A device which converts outgoing numbers from a binary computer into tones that can be carried over a telephone line. Modems also convert incoming analog sounds into their digital equivalents so that the computer can absorb them.

Monitor

A display tube and its controls that receive output from your computer.

Motherboard (mainboard)

The main collection of chips on the computer. It holds all the chips, and therefore provides all the functions, that are considered standard for that class of PC.

Mouse

A pointing device used to provide input to a computer by moving the cursor and sending signals equivalent to Enter.

ms

Millisecond, one-thousandth of a second. Nanosecond (ns) is one billionth of a second.

Multimedia, MPC

PCs and programs using high-quality and high-speed video, high-fidelity sound, and significant interactivity to produce life-like and compelling effects. *See* Chapter 11.

Multi-tasking

An operating system that is able to do more than one job at a time. Compare single-tasking.

Multi-user

An operating system that allows many users, each doing a separate task, to use a single computer. UNIX/XENIX is a multi-user operating system.

Network

A computer hardware/software system which allows you to connect a number of PCs including those of different design, such as mainframes, minis, PCs, and Macintoshes. The networked computers can share devices such as printers, CD-ROMs and modems—depending on the type of network you have. Networks can be divided into two types, dedicated and peer-to-peer.

Noise interference

Electrical, magnetic, or radio interference which disturbs the workings of a computer.

Non-interlaced display

A system which draws every line on the screen with each pass.

Null modem cable

A device that reverses certain wires in the cable structure so that the device can imitate two modems working over a telephone line.

Numeric co-processor

A special chip which does floating-point calculations, logarithms, and trigonometry.

Numeric keypad

A calculator-style block of keys which is often included on modern keyboards. This allows the rapid entry of strings of numbers, as well as standard arithmetic symbols (+, -, =, ÷).

OCR

Optical Character Recognition. Software enabling a computer to recognize the letters in a scanned document and turn them into editable text files.

OEM

Original Equipment Manufacturer.

On-line

Connection to another computer, usually an interactive, real-time remote connection over phone lines to a BBS, the Internet, or a service provider (CompuServe, America Online, etc.).

Operating environment

A program which mediates between the operating system and the application. Microsoft Windows 3.x is an example of an operating environment. It operates to communicate with DOS for the advanced applications written for it, and modifies the DOS screen interface by providing a graphical display.

Operating system

A program which enables the computer to perform work. The operating system provides basic services like opening and closing files, managing their location on the disk, reporting information to the monitor, and routing output to your printer.

OS/2

Operating System 2, by IBM/Microsoft (Operating System 1 is DOS). An operating system for PCs that allows multi-tasking and other advanced features.

Parallel port

This connection is like highways several lanes wide. Data can move at a faster rate. They are also commonly known as printer ports, as they are commonly used to connect printers to a PC.

Parity

A system used to check each byte of data for errors. Even parity means that the ones in the byte, plus the parity bit, must add up to an even number. If they don't the computer knows that there is an error. For odd parity, the sum must be an odd number.

PC Card / PCMCIA Card

A credit-card-size expansion circuit board used in portable / laptop / notebook computers.

PCI

Peripheral Component Interconnect. A local bus standard tying the expansion bus directly to the CPU. Unlike VL-Bus, which peaks out at 40Mhz, PCI can handle up to 133Mb per second.

PCL

Printer Control Language. One of several PDLs (Page Description Languages) developed by Hewlett-Packard to control their LaserJet laser printers. As a de facto standard, often emulated.

Pentium

A true 64-bit processor. It includes a number of advanced design features, including separate caches for code and data, that, along with its wider bus, will offer enhanced performance.

Personal Information Manager (PIM)

These software products serve as a combination Rolodex and personal secretary. You can keep track of schedules, appointments, to-do lists, and manage telephone logs.

Phase change

(P-C). Read/writable drive units which use a powerful beam and can write data in one pass.

Pixels (pixel/picture elements)

The tiny dots making up the picture on the monitor's screen, or stored in memory or on disk. The more pixels there are stored for each location (pixel depth), the more colors possible. *See* High-color and True-color.

Planar board

A motherboard.

Plotter

A specialized device using ink pens to create scale drawings, blueprints, diagrams, etc.

Plug and Play (PnP)

The ability of a system to correctly identify a device automatically, and integrate it with other components on the system so that all work, harmoniously. Windows 95 goes a good ways towards PnP, the given of Macintosh systems but the dream of DOS users for over a decade.

Port

As a noun, either (A) a physical receptacle or jack, enabling a cable connection to be made; or (B) a location (address) in RAM used by hardware or software. *See also* Parallel port; Serial Port; Com port. As a verb, port means to adapt a software program written for one operating system so that it runs on another.

POST

Power-On-Self-Test. The hardware tests, contained in the ROMBIOS, which the computer goes through in a hard boot.

PostScript Page Description Language

PostScript is a very sophisticated programming language designed to produce sophisticated graphics and scalable fonts on laser printers.

PostScript fonts

> Those in which characters are defined mathematically, rather than as individual dots.

Power supply

> A device which converts electrical Alternating Current from the wall socket into Direct Current at the proper voltage for your machine.

Print-Screen

> In many cases you can use the printer's line-print mode to send the current screen displayed on the monitor directly to the printer. Try either pressing the Print-Screen button on your keyboard, or the Shift/Print Screen combination.

Processor

> The part of the computer that executes commands and manipulates data. It is also called the microprocessor and the CPU (Central Processing Unit). In PCs this is a single chip.

Protected Mode Operation

> Used by 286 computers operated at Mhz.

Protected mode

> The methodology which made the 286 and up line of processors compatible with earlier PC processors. In real mode, the processor is limited to the 8086 family of abilities or instruction set. In protected mode an extended set of instructions is available. They can directly address up to 16Mb of RAM. It offers a 16-bit data path, both internal and external. The 386 and above chips can also operate in virtual mode, which allows them to function as if multiple 8086 or 8088 chips were present.

PS/2

> Personal System 2. A family of IBM microcomputers using a patented bus called MCA. *See* MCA.

Queue

An ordered, sequential row or stack. Used with instructions, documents sent to the printer, etc.

RAID storage system

Redundant Array of Independent Disks. Several hard drives are chained together to look like one large disk. It is designed so if one of the drives fails, no data is lost and the system continues operating.

RAM

Random Access Memory. Any part of this memory (hence "random access") may be used by the CPU. Each storage site (or location) in RAM has a unique address and the CPU can read from or write to these addresses. System memory, extended memory and expanded memory are all part of RAM. Unlike ROM (Read Only Memory) it is volatile, not permanent: when you turn off your computer, all information stored in RAM is lost.

Raster line

A single horizontal line of dots across the monitor screen.

Read/write heads

These devices can read the value of the information stored on magnetic media (most floppy and hard drives) by detecting the magnetic polarity of the particles on the platter. A device called a head actuator is used to move the arm across the platter to position the head quickly to any location on the disk.

Real mode

286 and above processors can operate in real mode, which means that they can pretend to be very fast 8086 or 8088 computers. 286s and above can also operate in protected mode, which has an extended set of instructions. 386s and above add virtual mode, in which they can function as if they were a number of 8086 or 8088 machines.

Reflective scanners

Those which scan material such as paper or photographs.

Refresh rate

The speed in which the the monitor screen is re-energized. This is expressed in hertz (Hz), and is the number of times per second that the beam passes over the screen.

Refresh

DRAM memory must constantly be refreshed or the chips will "forget" the information. DMA channel 0 is dedicated to this task.

Registers

The width of the high-speed data storage area inside the CPU. The earliest PCs had 16-bit data registers while the more recent Pentium microprocessors have a 64-bit register. The width and number of its registers determines the number of bits the CPU can work on at one time.

Repetitive Stress Injury (RSI)

If you are continually executing the same motions over and over again, you are at risk of RSI.

Reset Button

This switch provides a function similar to that of the Control/ Alternate/Delete combination in DOS. Pressing and releasing it will cause your system to reboot without switching the power off and on.

Resolution

The number of pixels displayed in an image. For example, the basic VGA resolution is 640 pixels horizontally by 480 pixels vertically.

Resources /resource conflict

See System Resources.

RFI

Radio Frequency Interference. Radio waves which interfere with another electrical signal.

RISC chip

Reduced Instruction Set Computer. A chip with streamlined command set, which can speed up performance and optimize the CPU's design.

RLL

Run Length Limited. A method of encoding data on hard disks. It is similar to MFM but can record more data in the same space. It is as reliable as MFM only if the hard drive is RLL-certified by the manufacturer.

RMA number

Return Merchandise Authorization number. A permission code you may need if you must return a purchase for repair, replacement, or credit.

ROM address

Base I/O address. The place in memory where the address of ROM chips of peripherals are located. When the computer is booted, it searches for ROM chips attached to the system and reads the information from them. This information is stored in the memory space above the ROM address. No two ROMs may have the same memory address, nor can the information of one overlap that of another. Many expansion cards, such as graphics adapters, hard drive controllers, and SCSI host adapters, must have memory addresses. The floppy controller, parallel and serial ports and game port do not have memory addresses, as the instructions for these devices are built into the ROM BIOS on the motherboard.

ROM

Read-Only Memory. What is used to boot your computer. This kind of memory never changes. It is usually burned into a chip with set values. An example of ROM is the instructions for performing your computer's Power-On-Self-Test (POST). Your system's ROM contains the options that are used by the operating system to manage its resources. Many of the add-in cards that are placed in your computer also contain their own ROMs. Newer flash ROM can be changed via software to update.

Root Directory

The basic directory (such as C:\) at the top of the directory structure of each hard disk or partition of one.

Run Length Limited (RLL)

A technique of entering information on a hard drive. This uses a special controller which formats up to 26 cylinders per track, allowing up to twice the data to be stored on the same-size MFM drive; to be reliable it must be RLL-certified by the manufacturer.

SCSI

Small Computer Systems Interface. An intelligent interface for connecting peripherals to a computer. It comes in several versions (*See* Chapter 10) and allows drive manufacturers to use any encoding scheme they choose for hard drives. A SCSI host adapter card allows connection of up to 8 devices using just one expansion slot. SCSI support is not built into the BIOS of most current PCs, making installation a careful job. Chapter 10 has a discussion of Fast, Wide and Fast-Wide SCSI.

SCSI bus

A special high-speed data-tranfer connection. Each device on the SCSI chain is intelligent, having its own internal controller which can send, receive, and execute SCSI commands through the host adapter. A SCSI device can handle data internally almost any way it wants to—as long as it can communicate with the host adapter using standard SCSI commands and formats. This gives SCSI incredible flexibility.

SCSI host adapter

What a SCSI controller is called.

SCSI IDs

Everything on the SCSI chain, including the adapter, has a unique ID number, ranging from zero to seven. This number works much like a mail stop address, allowing data to be moved to an addressee independent of the host PC's bus.

SCSI-2

An improvement of the basic SCSI standard that leaves less room for proprietary host adapters, and includes new commands that provide for specific support for new devices in the future.

Scanner

A device which converts an analog image on paper into digital form, for use inside a computer.

Scanning frequency

In a monitor, the speed in which it can scan from one corner to another. There are usually two numbers provided: one is the horizontal scan rate, which is measured in kilohertz (Khz). This is the time it takes the monitor to scan from the leftmost edge of the screen to the right edge.

Sector

The basic storage unit on a disk.

Seek time

The amount of time a hard disk head takes to find a track. It's expressed in milliseconds (ms). Seek time, combined with transfer rate, is used to rate the speed of a hard disk.

Selective backup

With this method you just back up the specific files that you feel are so important that you can't afford to lose them.

Serial mouse

A mouse attached to one of your computer's serial or Com ports.

Serial port

These connections carry data in a steady stream, much like a one-lane highway. These are also commonly referred to as Com or communications ports. *See* Port, Com port, Parallel port.

Server

A computer used as the central, controlling heart of a network; usually, tower systems with fast CPUs, big, fast hard disks, and extensive security, back-up, and communications capabilities.

Settle time

The length of time it takes the heads on a hard disk to come to rest after finding a track.

Setup

A program used to store information in the CMOS chip of the 286 and up computers. Also, a software routine which installs an application on a computer.

Shareware

Software distributed on the honor system. Anyone may copy and try it. Pay if you use it.

Shrink-wrapped

Commercial software sold in plastic-wrapped packages.

SIMM

Single In-line Memory Module. An eight or nine-chip memory module which installs in a single socket on the motherboard.

SIPP

A variation of the SIMM module. Instead of edge connectors like those found on SIMMs, SIPPs use pins.

Single-user

An operating system which allows only one person to perform work on a computer at a time.

Single-user, multitasking

An operating system or environment which allows a single user to do multiple tasks simultaneously. Windows 3.1, OS/2 and VM/386 are examples.

Single-user, single-task

An operating system, such as DOS, which allows only one person to do only one task at a time.

Soft boot

Occurs when you use the Control-Alt-Del key sequence on the keyboard. The hardware checks are omitted and only the operating system and system files are loaded.

Software

The programs which put computer hardware to work. A program is a long list of instructions to a computer's CPU and/or other subsystems.

Sound card

An expansion circuit board which gives a PC the ability to record and play hi-fi sound.

Speed, CPU speed, clock speed

Registers and bus width determine the potential of a CPU's performance. The clock speed determines how fast it can go. This is measured in megahertz (Mhz) or millionths of a second. Inside your microprocessor is a timing device that is used to synchronize its operation. One spin of the clock is known as a clock cycle. Generally speaking, a microprocessor can execute one set of instructions with each clock cycle. Some clock-doubled CPU chips run at twice their original speed internally to increase performance; some are even clock-tripled.

Spikes or power spikes or voltage spikes

These are very short-lived jumps in the power supply, sometimes lasting only for about a billionth of a second. These can cause difficulties with your computer's RAM, producing erratic program behavior or may, if you are writing to disk, cause a problem with the file being written.

SRAM

Static Random Access Memory. These are memory chips which do not require regular refreshing and are usually used for cache memory.

ST412/ST506

The original hard drive in microcomputers. The interface developed for these drives by Seagate Technologies, a hard-disk manufacturer, is still in use, although the original drives themselves are not.

Stack

Essentially this is the CPU's scratch pad. If the CPU is interrupted during a task for something more urgent, it saves a note to itself about what it was doing so it can resume the task as soon as the urgent task is completed.

Startup files

Special files that you can create to fine-tune your system's operation, set desired preferences and configure options that aren't covered either in the BIOS or the system Setup. There are two of them in DOS, CONFIG.SYS and AUTOEXEC.BAT.

State

The particular way in which various sub-systems, such as memory locations, registers and logic gates, are set. These conditions may be referred to as On-Off, High-Low, and Zero-One.

Storage memory

Storage memory is memory that's stored outside of the RAM area that can be read and written to. One example is the data stored on hard disks. This is sort of semi-permanent memory; it's there as long as you want it to be.

Sub-system

A major operational component of a PC system besides the mother-board, usually consisting of circuitry and one or more devices. Hard/floppy disks and power supplies are all sub-systems.

Surges, power surges, voltage surges

Longer-lived (sometimes several milliseconds) increases of voltage coming into the computer; contrast with spikes.

Surge protector

Device which filters electrical power received from the wall plug and prevents over-voltage from reaching the computer.

System board

See motherboard.

System memory

The memory in the computer that the operating system can directly access. Under DOS this is usually 640K, although in DOS 5.0 and above and DR DOS 6.0 another 64K (high memory) can also be utilized.

System parameters

FILES=40 is an example of a system parameter, or instruction within predefined limits. Most system parameters are setup in CONFIG.SYS.

System requirements

The specific kind of hardware needed to run a particular software application effectively.

System Resources

Either (A) the available DMA Channels, IRQ assignments, memory port addresses, and Com ports available for use on a system by the operating system or devices; or, (B) the allocation of memory by Windows.

Task

The job (usually an application program) that the computer is doing.

TCP/IP

A set of technical communications protocols (standards) for accessing the Internet.

Terminator

An electrical resistor that insures reliable communication by preventing excess signal noise on the line. If you mount only the internal or external devices to a SCSI host adapter, then the last device on the chain and the host adapter itself are terminated. If you mount both internal and external devices, then the host adapter is unterminated and the farthest devices, both internal and external, are terminated.

Track

A band running in a circle around the disk. These tracks are divided into short arcs called sectors.

Trackball

Basically a mechanical mouse twisted around, so that the buttons are still on the top, but the ball that is normally on the bottom is now where it can be operated by the thumb or by the palm of the hand.

Track-to-track access time

The length of time the heads of a disk drive take to move from one track to another. This number is indicative of the speed at which the disk can read information.

Transparency or slide scanners

Used to bring in images from slide material, i.e. color transparencies.

True-color images

Produced by 24-bit adapters which can render up to 16.7 million colors per pixel.

TrueType fonts

First used in Windows 3.1, these character sets are defined as mathematical descriptions rather than as individual dots, and are more efficient than bit-mapped fonts.

TSR

Terminate-and-Stay-Resident. This is a program which responds to a signal from the user (usually what is known as a Hot-Key sequence) and pops up ready for use. TSRs are loaded before application software and remain in RAM, available for use. TSRs sometimes present conflicts which masquerade as hardware problems.

TTL

Transistor-to-Transistor Logic. A type of video signal output which is based on digital technology found in some older monitors; newer monitors use Analog signal output.

Turbo switch

This connects to the motherboard and allows you to slow down the speed of the machine in the event that some piece of software can't support the high-speed setting of the CPU.

UART

Universal Asynchronous Receiver/Transmitter. A standard design used for communications chips.

UNIX

An operating system developed by AT&T in the early 1970's to run phone switching. It is a true multiuser, multitasking operating system with low overhead and easy connection of different tasks.

Uninterruptable Power Supply (UPS)

A device which offers surge protection as well as on-line battery back-up. In the event of an under-voltage or a complete failure of power, the UPS provides back-up power based on batteries. When the power fails, the UPS switches over to battery power, thus keeping your PC on-line. In the past UPSes included a hefty measure of line-conditioning circuitry to protect equipment.

Utilities

Programs which extend the reach of the operating system or environment. Some provide easier ways to manage your files, some offer security enhancements, while some show you exactly what's going on inside the system.

V-DOT (Department of Transportation) standards

These are standards set by the CCITT for error correction and advanced handshaking protocols that allow for very fast modem communications over telephone lines between computers.

VCPI

Virtual Control Program Interface. A sophisticated memory-management method.

VESA Local Bus

The Video Equipment Standards Association has specified a standard, a uniform local bus design (Abbreviated as VL-Bus). This couples a standard 16-bit expansion slot with part of an MCA expansion connector, placed in front of it. The standard allows local bus transfer rates of up to 40Mhz, and local bus cards can easily perform 50% faster than their ISA counterparts.

VGA

A video standard which allows for 256 colors at 640x480 resolution. VGA cards are also known as 8-bit color cards, because two to the eighth power equals 256. While not part of the standard, Super VGA (SVGA) offers more colors and up to 1024x768 resolution.

Virtual

Synthesized, using computer programs and/or memory.

Virtual mode

386 and above machines can use this mode to pretend to be multiple 8086 or 8088 processors. Microsoft Windows 3.1 uses this mode. *See* Protected mode and Real mode.

Virus

Invasive program embedded within another program, which does annoying or even damaging things to a computer's operation and/or your software programs.

Voltage spike

An electrical attack on the system, consisting of a single high-voltage burst.

Voltage surge

An electrical attack on the system, consisting of a long wave of higher voltage.

Wide SCSI

A SCSI standard which provides for a data path of either 16 or 32 bits. It provides for a throughput of up to 10Mb per second.

Wizard

Microsoft's term for an interactive program that leads the user step-by-step through a process.

Word

The smallest unit of data a processor can manipulate. For the 8088, a word is 1 byte (8 bits). The 8086 and the 186, 286, 386/SX and 486/SX processors use a word length of two bytes (16 bits). The 386, 486 and 586 (i.e., the Pentium) use a 4 byte (32-bit) word. When upgrading RAM, you must add as many chips as there are bits in the processor's word length.

WORM

Write Once, Read Many. One type of optical drive.

Write Precompensation

Timing changes used by a hard disk to protect the integrity of data recorded on the inner (smaller) tracks of a hard disk.

Xenix

A version of UNIX developed for microcomputers. It is currently being replaced by UNIX in the more powerful microcomputers of today.

XMS

Extended Memory Management. A sophisticated memory management method.

ZIF Socket

A Zero Insertion Force chip socket with either a little lever on one side or the other of the CPU, or a square bracket-shaped handle going around three sides of the CPU. A ZIF socket makes inserting and removing delicate, expensive CPU chips much easier.

APPENDIX I

CD-ROM PROGRAMS

GETTING STARTED

Please read the last page of the book, "CD-ROM Disk Instructions" first. It contains an overview of using the many fine programs on the CD-ROM disk at the back of the book.

TESTING AND REGISTERING THE PROGRAMS

Most of the programs on the CD-ROM are shareware (try-before-buy), and some are freeware (no charge).

Terms of trial for shareware are set by the individual authors; in general, if you find yourself using some software after a trial run and are actually relying on it, the shareware honor system dictates that you pay for it by registering it according to its individual requirements; these are contained in a file along with the program. While we all love a bargain, many of these authors derive their livelihood from their work, and deserve to be paid for it just as you do for yours. Shareware prices are typically less than for commercial programs, and authors will often show their appreciation for registration by sending you other programs, free updates or upgrades, full manuals, etc. Do the right thing.

FINDING AND USING PROGRAMS ON THE CD-ROM

Consult the following material for an overview of the programs. In this Appendix, we have printed their Readme files (or excerpts from them) to give you an idea of what the programs do. The individual programs, along with their Readme and installation files, reside in separate Folders (Directories) on the CD-ROM. These Folders are named after the program (or in some cases, a collective name). Insert the CD-ROM disk into your drive, and access it under Windows (or DOS, if that's what you're running). Open the appropriate Folder/Directory and then look at the Readme, Manual or similar file. Files with extensions like .doc, .txt, and .1st will be likely to tell you whether you wish to try a program if the Readme file does not. While the Readme file should give you specific directions on how to copy or install a specific program, *you should follow the directions we give in this Appendix for best results.* The program authors did not assume their programs would be on a CD-ROM, and their installation instructions typically assume that you are beginning from a floppy disk. So, *please follow our directions in this Appendix*, under "How to Install the Programs onto your Hard Disk."

Some of these programs run under DOS, some under Windows 3.x, and some under Windows 95. Check the Readme file for the particular program. In general, most programs, whether DOS or Windows, should run under Windows 95 even if not specifically written for it, though no one can guarantee that any particular one will run, or run as intended. The safest course is to run it as the author says to.

How to Install the Programs onto your Hard Disk

Most of these programs were supplied to us on floppy disk and were not originally designed to be installed from our CD-ROM. Therefore, the usual procedure to install a given program will be:

1. Choose the program from the introductory notes we provide here. You might well also browse the Readme and similar files on the CD-ROM itself.

2. Note what type of program it is, DOS or Windows.

3. If you are a DOS user, you'll only be able to run DOS programs. If you're running Windows, you should be able to run all the programs.

Windows users *might* be able to skip Steps 4 and 5; it will depend on the individual program's installation process.

NOTE

---

4. For DOS programs: Observe your program's Folder/Directory name on the CD-ROM and create an identical Folder/Directory on your hard disk. (Consult your operating system manual if you need help to do this).

5. Copy all the files in your program's CD-ROM Folder/Directory into the one you made in Step 4.

    Use the DOS Copy or XCopy commands to do this, or do it with File Manager in Windows 3.x or My Computer in Windows 95. See your respective manual.

6. In the program's new directory on your hard drive, open its Readme or similar file. You can use most word processors, or a text editor, Windows Write, Notepad, Wordpad, etc. Files with extensions like .doc, .txt, and .1st will be likely to have last-minute notes and installation instructions from the program's author. You may wish to print them out as well, using your text editor or word processor.

7. Follow, carefully, the installation instructions for that particular program. In general:

DOS Programs: In some cases, you can run a DOS program by typing its name (or, in Windows, selecting it and double-clicking); in most cases, it will have been provided in a compressed form to save space on the disc. Follow the directions to expand the program on your hard disk. Next run its Install or other program as directed, then the program itself.

Windows Programs: In Windows 3.x, use the Program Manager's File...Run... dialog boxes to run your program's Setup or Install program. In Windows 95, use the Run command from the Start button menu. Or use Explorer, My Computer, etc. to select the file, then double-click it.

INDIVIDUAL PROGRAM NOTES AND DIRECTIONS

These notes contain brief descriptions of the individual programs on the CD-ROM (or in a few cases, notes about programs collected under one heading or Directory/Folder). You can use these notes to select the programs you are interested in installing and trying out. In many cases we provide specific instructions to supplement those given above. If your CD-ROM drive is something other than drive D:, substitute the drive letter for your CD-ROM drive in all the following examples. Then simply follow on-screen instructions.

ASQ, CD-ROM Directory \ ASQ

This program, as covered in the text of the book, especially Chapter 4, is a free program from Qualitas, the makers of 386 to the Max. ASQ is a DOS program that will provide details of how your system uses its resources. The compressed file is named ASQC.EXE. Create an ASQ Directory on your hard drive and copy this compressed file into it. When in this new ASQ Directory, type **ASQC** and press **Return**. Two new files will be created, ASQ.EXE and ASQ.HLP. Type **ASQ**, then press **Return** to run the program. After this you may delete the

ASQC.EXE file to save space on your hard drive; don't erase the other two files by mistake.

S-PROT, CD-ROM Directory: \ S-PROT

A free program from Command Software, this program will test your system for viruses, but it will not remove them or repair their damage. The company sells another program called F-PROT, that handles that part of the operation. S-PROT is covered in Chapter 3. Install it as in the previous section: create an S-PROT Directory; copy the file SProt into it; type **SPROT** and push **Return**. The file will-decompress automatically, and you may then run it.

Winsleuth Gold, CD-ROM Directory: \ WINSLTH

This is a major diagnostic program that can tell you almost all about your system's configuration. It requires Windows 3.1, and runs basically well under Windows 95. You can upgrade it to a more powerful version, Winsleuth Gold Plus, or a Windows 95 version. To use it, create a WINSLTH Directory on your hard disk, and copy the file WINS into it. Then type **WINS** and press **Return**. The file will decompress automatically and you may then install it under Windows.

Integrity Master, CD-ROM Directory: \ IMASTER

This is the evaluation version of Integrity Master(tm) (Version 2.51). Integrity Master is a high-performance, award-winning program offering virus scanning, data integrity, security, CMOS protection, and change management in one easy-to-use program. We recommend that you make and keep your files in a directory called \IM_HOME. Copy into it all four files from the CD-ROM. To install under DOS, just type **SETUPIM** and hit **RETURN**. To install IM under Windows, use the File Manager to execute the file IMSETUP.BAT in the \IM_HOME Directory (or select **Run** under Program Manager and type **C:\IM_HOME\IMWIN**) *Please read the notes on using IM under Windows near the end of its Readme.doc file.*

Snooper, CD-ROM Directory: \ SNOOPER

Snooper is a system information utility. It "snoops around" your computer to report its configuration and operating characteristics. You can use Snooper to keep an eye on your memory and disk usage.

Snooper can help you when you are installing new peripherals or software by showing you what resources are already in use. Also, when you talk to technical support personnel, Snooper can help you answer many of their questions about your computer, and can let you edit your CONFIG.SYS and AUTOEXEC.BAT files. Create a SNOOPER Directory on your hard disk, and copy all the files from the CD-ROM Directory into it. Read or print out the Read.me file for further directions. Snooper runs best under DOS.

FPLAN-KWIK Retirement Planner, CD-ROM Directory: \ FPLANRP

A Windows 3.1 easy-to-use retirement planning tool, focusing on strategies needed to achieve retirement income goals. Click the **File** menu of Windows Program Manager, select **RUN**, type **D:\FPLANRP\ SETUP** and press **OK**.

FPLAN-KWIK Estate Planner, CD-ROM Directory: \ FPLANEP

A Windows 3.1 easy-to-use estate-preservation and tax-planning tool, focusing on strategies needed to meet estate income needs. Click the **File** menu of Windows Program Manager, select **RUN**, type **D:\FPLANEP\SETUP** and press **OK**.

FPLAN-KWIK Life Insurance Planner, CD-ROM Directory: \ FPLANLI

A Windows 3.1 easy-to-use life insurance planning tool, focusing on strategies needed to meet family income needs. Click the **File** menu of Windows Program Manager, select **RUN**, type **D:\FPLANLI\ SETUP** and press **OK**.

Plan-KWIK Income Protection Planner, CD-ROM Directory: \ FPLANIP

A Windows 3.1 easy-to-use income protection planning tool, focusing on strategies needed to meet family income needs in the event of disability. Click the **File** menu of Windows Program Manager, select **RUN**, type **D:|FPLANIP\SETUP** and press **OK**.

Paint Shop Pro For Windows, CD-ROM Directory: \ PSP

An award-winning Windows graphics program, combining photo retouching, painting, image format conversion, and screen capture. Click the **File** menu of Windows Program Manager, select **RUN**, type **D:|PSP\SETUP** and press **OK**.

CommEx, CD-ROM Directory: \ COMMEX

CommEx 1.10: Common Dialog Extensions for Windows 3.1/3.11. Adds file Find, Copy, Delete, Rename, and MakeDir functions to most Open and Save dialogs.(Also adds 3-D look.) Fully functional evaluation copy. By Cottonwood Software. Click the **File** menu of Windows Program Manager, select **RUN**, type **D:|COMMEX\SETUP** and press **OK**.

SuperDIR, CD-ROM Directory: \ SDIR

A DOS power-user's Directory-sorting and listing utility. SuperDIR v1.11. Formats for database import or DOS piping, multiple /exclude file and directory masks, can sort ALL files in a tree (not just within subdirectory). Many sorting and output options, attribute filters, etc., comma/quote/tab/space delimited output, more! Create SUPERDIR Directory (Example: Type **MD C:\SDIR** and then press **Return**).

Copy all the files in the CD-ROM Directory SDIR into it. To run the program, type **SDIR** and then press **Return**.

Open Windows, CD-ROM Directory: \OW

A collection of interesting Windows utility programs, some of them award-winners. BailOut v2.0 is a flexible "Quick Exit" program, allowing you to save open files. Freeware. WinFlash v3.1 lets you create your own decks of custom flashcard decks to memorize facts. WinJottr v1.0 is an ever-ready desktop note-taker; sits anywhere, holds a month's worth of random data. WinKillr v1.00 is a program to automate the closing of Windows and DOS programs. It will Save open files. WinPrice v1.0 selects the best pricing between two alternatives. WinUpD8R v4.1 can keep your files up to date on multiple machines while providing backups. To install any of these programs, click the **File** menu of Windows Program Manager, select **RUN**, type **D:\OW\OWSETUP.EXE** and press **OK**.

Peeper, CD-ROM Directory: \PEEPER

Multiple-format Windows file viewer; can handle over 21 different file formats, including spreadsheets, databases, documents, and graphics files. Has Drag and Drop features. Honored by Windows Magazine and ZiffNet. To install, click the **File** menu of Windows Program Manager, select **RUN**, type: **D:\PEEPER\SETUP** and press **OK**.

Space Hound, CD-ROM Directory: \SPACEH

This multi-purpose Windows utility program finds duplicate files, "sniffs out" wasted disk space, and creates printable Directory maps, other functions. Honored by Windows Magazine and ZiffNet. To install, click the **File** menu of Windows Program Manager, select **RUN**, type: **D:\SPACEH\SETUP** and press **OK**.

Smilershell/95, CD-ROM Directory: \SMILE95

Windows 95 and NT control center. Quick-launches and switches programs, finds files, etc. Offers the "ultimate" Windows command line.

"A Must Have" (Windows Magazine). To install, click the **File** menu of Windows Program Manager, select **RUN**, type: **D:\SMILE95\INSTALL** and press **OK**.

Smilershell 3.1, CD-ROM Directory: \ SMILE31

Similar to SMILERSHELL 95, above. To install, click the **File** menu of Windows Program Manager, select **RUN**, type: **D:\SMILE31\INSTALL** and press **OK**.

WinU, CD-ROM Directory: \ WINU

Windows 95 menu system with timeout and security access features. Ideal for parents wishing to limiting children's access to the family PC, in-store demos, etc. Very customizable. To install, click the **File** menu of Windows Program Manager, select **RUN**, type: **D:\WINU\INSTALL** and press **OK**.

Rev. Lowell's Treasury of Humor
CD-ROM Directory: \ LOWELL

Windows 3.1 hyper-indexed collection of great anecdotes, funny stories, zingy one-liners, etc. Searchable. Illustrated. Print or copy chosen items. Chosen over Rev. Lowell's 30-year career. To install, click the **File** menu of Windows Program Manager, select **RUN**, type: **D:\LOWELL\INSTALL** and press **OK**.

Steenburgh's Stuff, CD-ROM Directory: \ SSTUFF35

A set of 22 separate batch-file programming utilities, which together comprise a complete batch file programming system. You can create complete miniature applications and handy utility files normally within the reach only of professional programmers. Advanced video, music, environment, string manipulation, and interactive features are all within your grasp. Highly praised. To install: create SSTUFF on your hard disk. Copy the self-extracting file SSTUFF.EXE from the CD-ROM into it. Then type: **SSTUFF** and press **Return**. This will expand the files. The type **Install** and press **Return**.

Mouspeed, CD-ROM Directory: \MOUSPEED

A DOS program to configure your mouse's horizontal and vertical speeds and the acceleration rate. To install it, create a directory MOUSPEED on your hard disk and copy the files from the CD-ROM into it. Then type **MOUSPEED** and then press **Return** to extract the files. Then type **INSTALL** and press **Return** and follow the directions.

Notetaker, CD-ROM Directory: \NTAKER

A small memory-resident DOS program (TSR) for note-taking, viewing, and printing aid. Pops up a Notetaker screen from within a DOS program. You write a note, and return to work. Can be loaded into upper memory blocks. To install it, create a directory NTAKER on your hard disk and copy the files from the CD-ROM into it. Then type **NTAKER** and then press **Return** to extract the files. Then type **INSTALL** press **Return** and follow the directions.

Spooler, CD-ROM Directory: \SPOOLER

A DOS program for sending files to a buffer while they await the printer. You then return to work in your program. To install it, create a directory SPOOLER on your hard disk and copy the files from the CD-ROM into it. Then type **SPOOLER** and then press **Return** to extract the files. Then type **INSTALL** and press **Return** and follow the directions.

Ssaver, CD-ROM Directory: \SSAVER

A DOS TSR (Terminate and Stay Resident program) which blanks your screen after a 3-minute delay or after pressing a hot-key. Can be loaded into upper memory blocks. To install it, create a directory

SSAVER on your hard disk and copy the files from the CD-ROM into it. Then type SSAVER and then press **Return** to extract the files. Then type **INSTALL** and press **Return** and follow the directions.

Print Commander, CD-ROM Directory: \PRINTCOM

A DOS program allowing you to change various functions of your printer from your keyboard. To install it, create a directory PRINT-COM on your hard disk and copy the files from the CD-ROM into it. Then type **PRINTCOM** and then press **Return** to extract the files. Then type **INSTALL** and press **Return** and follow the directions.

Above and Beyond, CD-ROM Directory: \ABOVE

An award-winning, powerful Windows 3.1 Personal Information Manager (PIM) for planning, managing, and tracking one's active business and personal life. Innovative *dynamic* schedules manage workflow effectively; enter them once. Print them out to take with you. Also includes a pop-up calendar, alarms, timers, contact data base, etc. High praise from PC Magazine. To install, click the File menu of Windows Program Manager, select **RUN**, type: **D:\ABOVE\INSTALL** and press **OK**.

Baseball Statistics, CD-ROM Directory: \BASEBALL

Microfox Baseball Statistics for Windows. Keeps track of years, leagues, teams, players and schedules, games, fields, and umpires. To install: Make a Directory BASEBALL on your hard disk. Copy the files from the CD-ROM to your new directory. Read the documentation files.

EZ-Tree, CD-ROM Directory: \EZTREE

EZ-Tree Genealogy System for DOS. A genealogy program for keeping track of and reporting on people in multiple family trees. To install: Make a Directory EZTREE on you hard disk. Copy the files from the CD-ROM to your new directory. Read the documentation files.

Hard Disk Menu IV, CD-ROM Directory: \ HDM

A hard disk Menu and Security system for DOS and LANs. Contains many advanced menu features. To install: Make a Directory HDM on you hard disk. Copy the files from the CD-ROM to your new directory. Read the documentation files.

Shareware Database, CD-ROM Directory: \ PR

MicroExcel's Shareware Database. A comprehensive (over 1300) programs!) database of shareware products. The database also serves as a demonstration of Perfect Recall, a comprehensive information tracking and management system for personal and business use. Another example of Perfect Recall is an Internet Resources database. Runs under DOS or Windows. To use: review the Readme.1st file in the \PR Directory of the CD-ROM. Near the end of this file are instructions to (A) run the program from the CD-ROM or (B) install the programs and files to your hard disk.

INDEX

CD-ROM Disk Instructions

For Upgrade & Maintain Your PC, 2nd Edition

On the CD-ROM at the back of this book you will find dozens of programs. Some are mentioned in the text (ASQ; Winsleuth Gold; S-Prot; Integrity Master; Snooper); most are not. You will find many useful utilities, as well as some interesting and entertaining programs covering a wide spectrum. Here we can just give you instructions on where to find the programs; in Appendix I, we tell you a little about the programs, and show you how to access and install them. We hope that you will find at least some of them useful and/or entertaining.

A Cautionary Note About the Programs

We have tested only those programs specifically mentioned in the text of the book. All the others are provided by the courtesy of their authors, and we cannot make any warranty about their specific usefulness to you. If you have questions or problems about a particular program, please contact its company or author at the address provided in its Readme or Registration file on the disk. Neither the author nor MIS:Press is able to provide support for any of the programs. If you have a defective CD-ROM, contact MIS:Press for a replacement.

Testing, and Registering the Programs

Most of the programs on the CD-ROM are shareware (try-before-buy), and some are freeware (no charge).

Terms of trial for shareware are set by the individual authors; in general, if you find yourself using some software after a trial run and are actually relying on it, the shareware honor system dictates that you pay for it by registering it according to its individual requirements; these are contained in a file along with the program. While we all love a bargain, many of these authors derive their livelihood from their work, and deserve to be paid for it just as you do for yours. Shareware prices are typically less than for commercial programs, and authors will often show their appreciation for registration by sending you other programs, free updates or upgrades, full manuals, etc. Do the right thing. Enjoy!